Nāṭyacūḍāmaṇi of Somanārya

The Nāṭyacūḍāmaṇi of Somanārya is an unpublished musicological work written in Sanskrit and is accompanied by a Telugu commentary. The author of this work is Aṣṭāvadāna Somanārya who is said to have lived during the reign of King Acyutarya of the Vijayanagar Empire (1540 AD). The Telugu commentary seems to belong to a later period. The present edition is brought out with the help of fifteen manuscripts. Though the title reads Nāṭyacūḍāmaṇi, the available text mainly consists of chapters on Gīta and Vidya and only a few verses relate to Nāṭya. Somanārya's work presents some of the traditional musicological views in a tangential manner and it has made a strong influence on many later works of South India.

Dr. V. Premalatha is an Assistant Professor of Music in the Department of Performing Arts, Sri Venkateswara University,Tirupati, Andhra Pradesh,India. A Post-graduate in Music from the Madurai Kamar University and Ph.D. from the University of Madras, under the guidance of Dr. N. Ramanathin. Study of music manuscripts has been her area of study and she has compiled a comprehensive Catalogue of music manuscripts from all over the world. She has completed an UGC Major Resejrch Project on the music manuscript collection of the Oriental Research Institute, S.V. University, Tirupati. She is also a recipient of the National Culture Fellowship in Arts for Music (Junior) awarded by the Sangeet Natak Akademi, New Delhi. She has presented research papers at National and Intematinal Seminars held all over India and has published research articles in the Joumals of Music and research reference materials and music lessons in www.musicresearch.in and www. musicacademymadras.in

Prakāṣikā Series
No. 15

General Editor
DIPTI S. TRIPATHI

सोमनार्यविरचितः नाट्यचूडामणिः

[तेलेगुटिप्पणीसहितः]

आङ्गलभाषानुवादेन संवलितं मूलम्

सम्पादक

वे. प्रेमलता

राष्ट्रीय पाण्डुलिपि मिशन

नई दिल्ली

तथा

देव पब्लिशर्स एण्ड डिस्ट्रीब्यूटर्स

प्रकाशक :

राष्ट्रीय पाण्डुलिपि मिशन

11, मानसिंह रोड,
नई दिल्ली–110 001

दूरभाष: 2338 3894; फैक्स: 2307 3387

E-mail: directornamami@nic.in
Website: www.namami.nic.in

सह–प्रकाशक :

देव पब्लिशर्स एण्ड डिस्ट्रीब्यूटर्स

द्वितीय तल, प्रकाशदीप बिल्डिंग,
22, दिल्ली मैडिकल एसोसिएशन रोड
नई दिल्ली–110002

दूरभाष: 43572647

e-mail: devbooks@hotmail.com
website: www.devbooks.co.in

ISBN 978-93-80829-02-9 (Series)
ISBN 978-93-80829-25-8
प्रथम संस्करण: 2014

मूल्य: ₹ 480.00

Nāṭyacūḍāmaṇi of Somanārya

[with a Telugu Commentary]

A Critical edition and Translation

Editor

V. Premalatha

National Mission for Manuscripts

Dev Publishers & Distributors

Published by:
National Mission for Manuscripts
Indira Gandhi National Centre for the Arts
11 Man Singh Road
New Delhi 110 001
Phone: 91 11 2307 3387
E-mail: directornamami@nic.in
Website: www.namami.nic.in

and Co-published by:
Dev Publishers & Distributors
2nd Floor, Prakash Deep,
22, Delhi Medical Association Road,
Darya Ganj,
New Delhi-110002
Phone : 011-43572647
e-mail: devbooks@hotmail.com
website: www.devbooks.co.in

ISBN 978-93-80829-02-9 (Series)
ISBN 978-93-80829-25-8
First published 2014

Contents

Foreword xiii
Preface xvi
Acknowledgement xix
Abbreviations xxi
Key to Transeiteration xxiii
Note on Diacritical marks

1
Introduction

1. Manuscripts of the work 1
1.1 Manuscripts consulted for the Edition 1
1.2 Description of Mansucripts 3
1.2.1 G98 3
1.2.2 G17 4
1.2.3 B13 5
1.2.4 T65 6
1.2.5 G86 7
1.2.6 G89 8
1.2.7 G07 9
1.2.8 G91 9
1.2.9 G24 10
1.2.10 Sp 10
1.2.11 G38 11
1.2.12 V41 12
1.2.13 G18 13
1.2.14 V08 14

1.2.15	M	17
2.	Title of the Work(s)	19
2.1.	Nāyacūḍāmaṇi(NC) -Svararāgasudhārasa (SRS)	20
2.1.1	Views of the scholars on the title NC/SRS	20
2.1.2	References to NC and SRS in Musicological works	21
2.1.3	Conclusions drawn from the readings in the Mnuscripts	21
2.2.	Saṅgītaratnākara (SR)	23
2.2.1	References made by Scholars	24
2.2.2	References to SR in Musicological works	24
2.2.3	'SR' in the text of the Manuscripts	24
2.3	Svarārṇava (SA)	25
2.3.1	Views of the Scholars on SA and Somanārya	26
2.3.2	Inferences	27
2.4	Tāladaśaprāṇaprakaraṇam (TDPP)	28
2.5	Tālakalābdhi (TK)	29
2.5.1	Other Scholars who speak of TK	30
2.5.2	The TK Manuscript	30
3.	Name of the Author	31
3.1	Somanārya and Somanātha	32
4.	Date of Somanārya	33
4.1.	Views of Scholars on the date of Somanārya	33
4.2.	References in Musicological Works	34
4.3.	References from the Manuscript readings	35
5.	Collation and Edition	36
5.1	Scribal Peculiarities	36
5.2	Scribal Errors	38
5.3	Relationship between the Manuscripts (Stemma Codicum)	39
5.4	Archetype	42
5.5	Methodology Adopted for Collation and Edition	43
5.6	Emendations	46

5.7	Interpolations in the Manuscripts	49
5.7.1	G98 and its transcripts (G17 & B13)	49
5.7.2	G91	50
5.7.3	G38, Sp	51
6.	Analysis of the Work	52
6.1	Extent of the work	52
6.2	Summary of contents	54
6.2.1	Nāya (NC-1)	54
6.2.2	Gītādhyāya (NC-2)	54
6.2.2.1	Nāda	54
6.2.2.2	The greatness of gīta	54
6.2.2.3	Svara	55
6.2.2.4	The production of nāda	55
6.2.2.5	Sthāna - Śruti	55
6.2.2.6	Grāma, Mūrcchanā	55
6.2.2.7	Śruti	56
6.2.2.8	Ten kinds of svara-s	56
6.2.2.9	Ten embellishments and defects of svara-s	56
6.2.2.10	Eighteen śruti-s	56
6.2.2.11	Grāma (again)	57
6.2.2.12	Śruti-jāti-s	57
6.2.2.13	Vādī, Samvādī, Vivādī and Anuvādī svara-s	57
6.2.2.14	Rāga	57
6.2.2.15	Classification of rāga-s	57
6.2.2.16	Varieties of singers and their blemishes	58
6.2.2.17	Musical Forms	58
6.2.3	Vādyādhyāya	58
6.3	Organisation of the Work	59
6.4	Analysis of the Contents	61
6.4.1	Readings from Earlier Sources	61
6.4.2	Different Interpretations	62
6.4.2.1	Definition of the term Nāda	62
6.4.2.2	Five stages of production of svara-s	62

6.4.2.3	Vādī, Samvādī, Anuvādī and Vivādī svara-s	62
6.4.2.4	Ālipti	63
6.4.2.5	Aṅga-s of a Prabandha	63
6.4.3	New Concepts	64
6.4.4	Ambiguous passages	68
6.4.4.1	Characteristics of Maurī	69
6.4.4.2	Vādya lakṣaṇa	70
6.5	Commentary of the Work	70
6.5.1	Contents of the Commentary	71
6.5.2	Date of the Commentary	76
7.	Somanārya in other musicological works	77
7.1	Mahābharatacūḍāmaṇi (MBC)	78
7.1.1	Contents of the Chapter on music	78
7.1.2	Sources referred to in MBC	79
7.1.3	"Somanārya" in MBC	79
7.1.4	Observations	80
7.2	Bharatakalpalatāmañjarī (BKM)	82
7.2.1	Contents of the work	82
7.3	Rasikajanamanollāsini sārasaṅgraha-bharataśāstra (RJM)	83
7.3.1	Contents of the work	84
7.3.2	Observations	84
7.4	Sārasaṅgrahabharata (SSB)	86
7.4.1	The SSB manuscript	87
7.4.2	Contents of SSB	87
7.4.3	Observation	88
7.5	Gānavidyārahasyaprakāśini (GVRP)	88
7.5.1	Contents	89
7.6	Saṅgītamakaranda (SM)	89
7.6.1	NC and SM	90
7.7	Abhinavabharatasārasaṅgraha (ABSS)	92
7.8	Other Works	92

2

Edited Text of NC with Commentary in Devanagari and Telugu scripts with variant readings and notes followed by ANUBANDHA 94

3

Roman Transliteration of NC with Commentary 281

4

English Translation of NC with Commentary 355

APPENDICES

1. Attributes of svara-s 414
2. Atributes of rāga-s 424
3. Lakshana-s of 32 rāga-s in NC 428
4. List of 32 rāga-s in various works 430

Bibliography 432

Index of half-line verses 437

Foreword

The origin of texts in performing arts in India can be traced to Nāṭyaśāstra. It is a magnum opus that inspired later scholars and experts to write on different art forms like drama, music, dance, painting etc. Its influence on later writings on art all over India, from Kashmir to Kanyakumari and from Gujarat to Assam is indisputable.

Sixteenth century in Indian history has been a period of extreme intellectual activity. Literary works in all forms, be it creative literature or theoretical works on criticism, artistic genres etc. were written during this period in different languages. Nāṭyacuḍāmaṇi is one such work of sixteenth century which is attributed to Somanārya. The extant manuscripts of this work contain three chapters dealing with Nātya, gīta and vādya. The editor of this text feels that the original name of the work must have been Nāṭyacuḍāmaṇi and the chapter on Gīta or probably the commentary of this chapter was called Svararāgasudhārasa. She also feels that Saṅgītaratnākara was a additional title given to this work and that the text originally must have been called Nāṭyacuḍāmaṇi. This is a work in Sanskrit with Telugu commentary but the commentary might have been composed at a later date and might not have been a part of the original text.

The present critical edition has been done on the basis of fifteen manuscripts some of them on palm leaf and others on paper. Three scripts, Devanagari, Ṭelugu and Grantha haven been found which are a proof of the popularity of this text as well as the wide geographical area in which it must have been read. This text has been extensively quoted in later works of music.

Dr. V. Premlatha is suitably equipped to edit such text, with her training in music as also the knowledge of Sanskrit language. She has done this work with due diligence and used a large number of manuscripts to critically edit the work of Somanārya.

The National Mission for Manuscripts is happy to present to the scholarly world this text on music which will be useful in studying the development of Indian classical music as also the development of style of texts written on the same. This is second work on music that the Mission is publishing, the first one being a critical edition of Rāgārṇava. I do hope musicians and scholars alike will find this text of interest to them.

M/s Dev Publishers have done a good job of printing this text which contains text not only to Devanagari script but also Telugu and Roman script. Printing of critical edition of such a text requires accuracy. There may be errors in spite of all care that has been taken to avoid the same. The Mission would welcome comments on improvement of the presentation.

DIPITI S. TRIPATHI
Director

New Delhi
Makar Sankranti, 14 January, 2014

Preface

Study of music manuscripts had been my area of research and as part of my Ph.D., I prepared a catalogue of manuscripts on music containing information from various sources. During my field visit to the Saurāṣṭra Sabhā, Madurai, which is famous for the Vālājāpet collection of music manuscripts, I came across a palm-leaf and a paper manuscript titled Saṅgītaratnākara of Somanātha(nārya). On studying the contents, it was found that this work was different from the Saṅgītaratnākara of Śārṅgadēva and it contained a few peculiar concepts, noticed in many later works. This led me to make a detailed study of this unpublished work.

The name Somanārya occurs in Music literature from the 16th century onwards. He is known to be the author of Nāṭyacūḍāmaṇi, an unpublished work available in the form of palm-leaf and paper manuscripts in different libraries. Only three chapters of his work are extant, namely, those dealing with nāṭya, gīta and vādya. The work is accompanied by a Telugu commentary.

The present study has revealed that Somanārya's work has three different titles, namely Nāṭyacūḍāmaṇi, Saṅgītaratnākara and Svararāgasudhārasa. Though the manuscripts are differently titled as mentioned above, Nāṭyacūḍāmaṇi must have been the title of the original work, and the chapter on gīta or the commentary to the chapter on gīta was called Svararāgasudhārasa. Saṅgītaratnākara appears to be only an additional name given to Somanārya's work in order to get credence. Further the Telugu commentary seems to have been composed at a later period, as concluded by a study of its contents and the literary style.

Search for the manuscripts containing the text of Somanārya, finally left me up with fifteen manuscripts, available in the libraries of Chennai, Tanjavur, Madurai, Tirupati and Mysore. Some were palm-leaf manuscripts and the others were paper transcripts, written in Devanagari, Telugu and Grantha scripts.

Copies of all the fifteen manuscripts were obtained, collated and edited according to the general rules prescribed for Textual Criticism (by scholars like S. M. Khatre). The edited text includes the suggestions or emendations of the editor noted within '[]'. The variant readings from all the sources have been given in the footnotes. In the course of collation, it was discovered that this work spoke of certain new concepts and presented certain old concepts in a form that deviated widely from the traditional understanding, presented by some of the popular works. Hence, though the manuscripts were highly corrupt with grammatically defective readings, it is attempted to make a critical edition with translation, in order to assess the contribution of this work in the background of the Indian Musicological tradition. The readings in some of the transcripts show that there had already been attempts to correct the text.

Some extracts presented in the Abhinavabharatasāra-saṅgraha of Mummaḍi Cikkabhūpāla correspond to Somanārya's work. Many later works like Mahābharatacūḍāmaṇi Bharatakalpalatāmañjarī, Rasika-janamanollāsini-Sārasaṅgrahabharata etc. show close resemblance to the work of Somanārya. It is also found that a few verses in the Saṅgītamakaranda of Nārada exist verbatim in Somanārya's work. All the works seem to be aware of both the mūla and the commentary, as evident from the readings found in them. It is also interesting to see that all these works had extracted mainly those concepts spoken in the chapter on gīta. These works were of immense use for the edition of Nāṭyacūḍamaṇi as secondary testimonia.

This multi-faceted task has yielded a tentative text and an English translation. Efforts have been taken to remove the discrepancies and to strengthen the text as a whole. Finally the study of those musicological traditions that preceded Somanārya in time and those that were contemporaneous with his work, were useful in portraying the musicological stand-point of Somanārya as a trend setter.

There are some shortcomings in Nāṭyacūḍāmaṇi from the musicological point of view. For example, there occurs no table of contents or proper colophon statements indicating the scope of the work. The topics are not arranged in the usual order as seen in works belonging to other musicological traditions. Though many terms have come from earlier sources, the delineation of their concept reveals a tangential approach and great deviations from accepted interpretations. Finally the whole style of musicological presentation in this work is of the `Listing' and `Classifying' kind rather than descriptive. No attempt to present a homogeneous picture of a musical system is evident in this work.

The present edition begins with a critical Introduction which includes a detailed discussion of the manuscripts of the work, title, author and date of the work, various aspects of Lower and Higher Textual criticism and the influence of Somanārya's work on later works. The second chapter consists of the edited text of Nāṭyacūḍāmaṇi in Devanāgari script and the Telugu commentary in Telugu script with the variant readings from the source manuscripts in their respective scripts given in footnotes. Notes on the readings, emendations etc. are also given in the footnotes. A small portion of the text was considered ambiguous and hence has been placed towards the end of the work titled, "anubandha".

The third chapter gives a Roman transliteration of the mūla and the Commentary and the fourth chapter is a rough English translation of the whole work. Attempt has been made to present only a verbatim translation, in order to get the real picture of the work.

I express my sincere gratitude to Dr. N. Ramanathan, retired Head, Department of Indian Music, Universty of Madras for his scholarly guidance throughout this research work. I am grateful to Prof. R. Sathyanarayana of Mysore for his valuable guldelines on textual criticism and for lending me the copies of rare works. I thank the librarians and other staff of the Government Oriental Manuscripts Library, Chennai, Taryavur Maharja Seifoji's Sarasvati Mahal Library, Taryavur, Saurashtra Sabha, Madurai and Oriental Research lnstitute, S.V. University, Tirupati for getting me the copies of manuscrlpts for this edition. My sincere thanks to the Late Y.R. Swami, Professor Chinni Krishnayya, Mrs. Hema Ramanathan and Dr. Rajalakshmi for asslstlng me in the edition and translation of the work. My heartfelt thanks to Prof. P.V. Ramachandran, Miss. V. Sireesha, Dr. V. Sathyavati, Mr. J. Udaya Bhaskar for their kind assistance.

I thank the University Grants Commission, New Delhi for awarding me the Junior Research Fellowship (1995-2001) to carry out research and the University of Madras for granting me permission to publlsh my Ph.D. dissertation. I wish to convey my sincere gratitude to the National Manuscripts Mission, New Delhi for taking up the publication of this work.

V. PREMALATHA

Abbreviations

ABSS	Abhinavabharatasārasaṅgraha
BB	Bharatabhāṣya
BKM	Bharatakalpalatāmañjarī
BS	Bharatasāttiram
BSe	Bharatasēnāpatiyam
CDP	Caturdaṇḍīprakāśikā
Datt.	Dattilam
GVRP	Gānavidyārahasyaprakāśini
MBC	Mahābharatacuḍāmaṇi
N.Sik	Nāradīyāśikṣā
NC	Nāṭyacuḍāmaṇi
NN	Nartananirṇaya
NS	Nāṭyaśāstra
RJM	Rasikajanamanollāsini-sārasaṅgrahabharataśāstra
RS	Rāgasāgara (manuscript)
RTC	Rāgatālacintāmaṇi
SA	Svarārṇava
SAd	Saṅgītādhyāya
SC	Saṅgrahacūḍāmaṇi
SCand	Saṅgītacandrikai of Mānikka Mudaliyār
SCud	Saṅgītacūḍāmaṇi
SM	Saṅgītamakaranda
SMK	Svaramelakalānidhi
SN	Saṅgītanārāyaṇa
SP	Saṅgītapārijāta

SR	Saṅgītaratnākara
SRaj	Saṅgītarāja
SRS	Svararāgasudhārasa
SSB	Sārasaṅgrahabharata
SSP	Saṅgīta sampradāya pradaśinī
SSPS	Saṅgītasvaraprastārasāgaram
SSS	Saṅgītasamayasāra
SSSS	Saṅgītasarvārthasārasaṅgrahamu
SSud	Saṅgītasudhā
STR	Śivatattvaratnākara
SSur	Saṅgītasūryodaya
TDPP	Tāladaśaprāṇaprakaraṇa
TK	Tālakalābdhi

Libraries

GOML -	Government Oriental Manuscript Library, Chennai
TMSML -	Tanjavur Maharaja Serfoji's Sarasvati Mahal Library, Tanjavur

Key to Transliteration

VOWELS

अ a	आ ā	इ i	ई ī = ī	उ u	ऊ ū
(but)	(palm)	(it)	(beet)	(put)	(pool)
ऋ ṛ	ए e	ऐ ai	ओ o	औ au	
(rhythm)	(play)	(air)	(toe)	(loud)	

CONSONANTS

Guttural	क ka	ख* kha	ग ga	घ gha	ङ ṅa
	(skate)	(blockhead)	(gate)	(ghost)	(sing)
Palatal	च ca	छ cha	ज ja	झ jha	ञ ña
	(chunk)	(catchhim)	(john)	(hedgehog)	(bunch)
Cerebral	ट ṭa	ठ* ṭha	ड/ड़ ḍa	ढ*/ढ़ ḍha	ण* ṇa
	(start)	(anthill)	(dart)	(godhead)	(under)
Dental	त ta	थ tha	द da	ध dha	न na
	(path)	(thunder)	(that)	(breathe)	(numb)
Labial	प pa	फ* pha	ब ba	भ bha	म ma
	(spin)	(philosophy)	(bin)	(abhor)	(much)
Semi-vowels	य ya	र ra	ल la	व va	
	(young)	(drama)	(luck)	(vile)	
Sibilants	श śa	ष ṣa	स sa	ह ha	
	(shove)	(bushel)	(so)	(hum)	
Others	क्ष kṣa	त्र tra	ज्ञ jña	ळ* l	ॠ* ṝ
	(*kṣātriya*)	(*triśūla*)	(*jñānī*)	(play)	

अं (—) ṁ or ṃ *amusūra* (nasalisation of preceding vowel) like *saṁskṛti/or soṃskṛti*

अः *visarga* = ḥ (aspiration of preceding vowel like (*prātaḥ*)

ऽ *Avagraha* consonant #' consonant (like-*imé vasthitā*)

Anusvāra at the end of a line is presented by m (म्) and not ṁ

*No exact English equivalents for these letters.

Note on Diacritical Marks

Standard diacritical marks for Devanagari script have been used throughout. However long and short syllables for "e" and "o" as "ē" and "ō" are distinguished only for the words in Telugu and Tamil languages.

1

Introduction

1. Manuscripts of the work

Nāṭyacūḍāmaṇi of Somanārya is edited with the help of fifteen manuscripts obtained from various libraries in India. This edition has been carried out using the various aspects of higher and lower textual criticism.

1.1 Manuscripts consulted for the Edition

The Manuscripts containing the work of Somanārya exist under different titles like,

a. Nāyacūḍāmaṇi (NC)
b. Svararāgasudhārasa (SRS)
c. Saṅgītaratnākara (SR)
d. Tāladaśaprāṇaprakaraṇa (TDPP) and
e. Saṅgītādhyāya (SAd)

The manuscripts are assigned code numbers (siglum), denoted by three characters. The first character, a Roman alphabet, indicates the place of deposit of the manuscript. Thus, G stands for GOML, Chennai, T for TMSSML, Tanjavur, V for Sri Venkatesvara University, (ORI) Tirupati, B for Baroda (Oriental Institute, Baroda), S for Saurashtra Sabha, Madurai and M for Mysore (Sri Varalakshmi Academy of Fine Arts). The next two characters in figures represent the last two digits of the Manuscript number or the respective iibrary accession number. In case a manuscript is not assigned any number (as in the case of private collections), it is left blank. e.g. "M" The following table lists the manuscripts along with their titles, manuscript numbers, places of deposit and sigla (code).

	Title	Msno	Source	Sigla
1.	NC	D12998[1]	GOML, Chennai	G98
2.	NC	R11917 (T of G98)	GOML, Chennai Baroda[2]	G17
3.	NC	26213 (T of G98)	Oriental Institute, Baroda	B13
4.	NC/ SRS	Green no:65	TMSSML	T65
5.	SR	R8186a	GOML, Chennai	G86
6.	SR	D13024	GOML, Chennai	G24
7.	SR	R16607	GOML, Chennai	G07
8.	SR	- (T of 7)	Saurashtra Sabha, Madurai	Sp[3]
9.	SR	R1538 (T of 7)	GOML, Chennai	G38
10.	SRS	R8189	GOML, Chennai	G89
11.	SRS	D2591	GOML, Chennai	G91
12.	SRS	7508	ORISVU, Tirupati	V08
13.	SRS	R641	ORISVU, Tirupati	V41
14.	SRS	-	Sri Varalakshmi Academy of Fine Arts, Mysore	M
15.	SAd	R11918 (T of R366e)	GOML, Chennai	G18

1. T refers to the Transcript.
2. A photocopy of this Manuscript was consulted from Brown's collection deposited at the Department of Indian Music, University of Madras.
3. Sp and G38 are the transcipts of a palm-leaf manuscript of the Saurashtra Sabha numbered "7". This original was not accessible and hence its paper transcript which wasnot assigned any number has been consulted for the edition. To avoid confusion, this manuscript is assigned "Sp", meaning the paper transcript from Saurashtra Sabha.

Besides the above, the following transcripts of NC available in different places have been referred to by scholars. However these have not been consulted for the present edition, since they are only copies of the already consulted mss.

a. Raghavan's collection (at Adyar Library),
b. Department of Musicology, BHU, Varanasi,
c. International Institute for Comparative Music and Studies and Documentation, Berlin (now Venice) -Mukund Lath in the introduction to the edition of Dattilam,
d. French Institute of Indology, Pondicherry - Alain Danielou in the introduction to the edition of Le Gītālaṅkāra.

1.2 Description of Mansucripts

The details of the fifteen mss consulted for the present edition are furnished below.

1.2.1 G98

This is a Paper manuscript written in Telugu script and consists of 17 pages. The contents in this manuscript are jumbled and not continuous and hence the arrangement of topics also does not follow a proper order. The beginning verse of NC, "nityānandakaram..." (NC 1, 1) is found on p.14 of the manuscript. At two places, the text is duplicated and a few verses occur more than twice at different places. The repeated portions corresponding to NC 1, 10cd-18 and NC 2, 2-12 are given below. In both places, the (repeated) texts in p.8-9 and p.9-10 are accompanied by a commentary.

NC verses	G98
1, 10cd -18	from p.14, line:15 to p.15, line:5
	from p. 8, line:2 to p. 9, line:8 (with comm.)
2, 2-12	from p.15, line 6 to p.15, line:19
	from p. 9, line:8 to p.10, line 6 (with comm.)

It is interesting to note that the readings slightly vary at the two places. In the present edition, the repeated text is marked G98a, (G17a and B13a in the case of the transcripts). Some portions of the text in this manuscript are interpolations from different works (See 5.7 below). Even in the interpolated part, there are repetitions. Besides, many verses are missing in this manuscript.

On the reverse of the last page of this manuscript, the following two verses are in a different handwriting.

"ṣaḍjagrāmo
nandyāvartotha jīmūtassubhadro grāmakāstrayaḥ |
ṣaḍjamadhyamagāndhārāstrayāṇāṃ janmahētavaḥ ||
kramātsvarāṇāṃ saptanāṃ ārohaścāvarohaṇam |
mūrcchanētyucyatē grāmastā ētāssapta sapta ca ||"

This passage, which talks about the origin of ṣaḍja, madhyama, gāndhāra svara-s respectively from the three grāma-s, nandyāvarta and the like, does not appear to belong to NC. In the restored copy, G17, this passage is written beneath the text separated by a dotted line. But it is skipped in the Baroda transcript, B13.

1.2.2 G17

G17 is a Paper manuscript written in Devanagari and Telugu scripts consisting of 23 pages. It is a restored copy (transcript) of G98 made in the year 1952-53. There is a note in the front page of the manuscript that reads as follows: "The leaves are put in disorder in the original manuscript D12998. This copy also copied according to the original. But the beginning is found on 9(b)/page 18". The Saṃskṛta verses are copied in Devanagari script and the Telugu commentary in Telugu script. In between the text, the page numbers of the original manuscript are noted in the margin. The copyist of this manuscript has made some errors, most of which have been corrected with red ink. Some portions of Telugu passages are skipped while copying, which have been inserted in a smaller writing, probably by a different person. This manuscript suggests some better readings which are written within [ ] or ( ) or just written nearby, without any indication. At a few places where a verse lacks meaning or the reading is corrupt, a "?" is placed. Some basic grammatical errors (like the inclusion or deletion of the visarga etc.) have been corrected without acknowledgement. Some of the repeated portions found in the manuscript, are marked in the margin, with a long line.

1.2.3 B13

B13 is also a paper transcript of G98 written in Devanagari and Telugu scripts and consists of 27 pages. This is found in the collections of the Oriental Institute, Baroda, listed under the manuscript number, 26213. According to the details furnished in the front page, this has been transcribed in the year 1960 from D12998 of GOML, Chennai. Against the column, source, it is mentioned "Pandya Rasiklal Maniklal, Linawada", and in the column, cost, "gift". Probably, this manuscript might have been transcribed and donated/gifted to the Baroda Library by Pandya Rasiklal Maniklal of Linawada. A print out of this manuscript made from the microfilm of Robert Brown, deposited at the Department of Indian Music, University of Madras, was consulted for the present investigation.

As pointed out above, in G98, the text begins on p.14. In this transcript, however, the commencing verses of NC have been brought to the beginning. Corrections of some minor grammatical errors of the original manuscript have been directly carried out in this transcript without suggesting them in '[ ]'. However the repeated portions of the original are retained as such. Like G17, in this manuscript too, the Saṃskṛta verses are copied in Devanagari script and the Telugu commentary in Telugu script. It is interesting to note that when the exemplar, G98 contains an erroneous reading, then a better reading is suggested in G17, whereas it is corrected and incorporated without suggestion in B13. For instance in NC 2,51cd, G98 reads "śuddhaḍjānu", G17 suggests "śuddha[ṣa]ḍjānu" whereas B13 reads directly, "śuddhaṣaḍjānu". These kinds of variations in readings are noted at many places.

1.2.4 T65

T65 is a palmleaf manuscript written in Grantha script. This is titled, "Saṅgīta-Nāṭyacūḍāmaṇi", noted under the collections of P Subrahmanya Sastri in the Stock Register. The top leaf of this manuscript reads the title as Nāṭyacūḍāmaṇi as well as Svararāgasudhārasam-Gītādhyāyam. In the margin of the first leaf, it is written "Bharatalakṣaṇam". The top leaf also reads the names, "Pazamārneri Subrahmaṇya Sāstri" and "Kuppusvāmi" (probably denote the owner(s) or the scribe of the manuscript). This manuscript has comparatively lesser number of gaps (lacunae), which usually arise due to injury and damage to the leaves.

The text relating to NC is found from fol.1a-46a. From fol.46b, the codex contains another work, in a different handwriting, the title of which is not mentioned in the flyleaf. This work deals with the description of mela-s and janya-s, which closely resemble the mela-s mentioned in the Svaramelakalānidhi of Rāmāmātya.[1]

The work begins with the verse, "nityānandakaram..." (NC 1,1) and after Nāṭyotpatti, switches over to Gītādhyāya (as in the case of G98), which is almost complete. The prose passage found before the section on Nāṭyotpatti (NC 1, comm. 8) is exclusively seen in this manuscript. It reads thus:

> *"lōkamandu bharatagranthakartalu bahumandi kalugu ganaka. vārla yokka śāstraṃ ellanuṇḍi saṅgrahiñci saṅkṣēpaṅgānu nāyacūḍāmaṇi anēi granthaṃ lōkōpakāraṅgānu aṣā **[va]dhāna prasiddhuṇḍaina Somanāryu**[ni] cāta lē[la]kṣaṇa lakṣiyaṃ[kṣyaṃ] ceppaprascunnadi."*

1. In ff. 46b-47a, the names of the following mēla-s are found: mukhāri, mālavagauḷa, śrīrāgam, sāraṅganāṭa, hindoḷam, śuddharāmakriyā, dēśakṣi *****, kannaḍagauḷa, suddhanāa, nādarāmakriyā, śuddhavarāḷikā, lalinoppuriti??, vasantabhairavī, kēdāragauḷa, hiñjujjikā, sāmavarāḷikā, rēghupti, sāmanta and kāmbhoja. These resemble the mēla-s of Svaramēlakalānidhi.

(Even though in this world, there are many writers on dramaturgy, all their writings from here have been collected and for the benefit of humanity, the practice and theory, have been presented by Somanārya, well-known as Aṣāvadhāni, in his work called Nāṭyacūḍāmaṇi). This is a significant passage in the work, since this is the only place in the commentary, where Somanārya is specifically mentioned as the author of NC.

A small portion of the text is seen repeated in folio.2. Therefore the subsequent leaf is marked, "2 repeat", which was probably written by the library staff. In the prose section dealing with the attributes of the svara-s, the description of the svara, pañcama, originally seems to have been missing. This portion should have been written in leaf-10, which was not found in between leaves 9 and 11. In the margin of leaf 11, there is a note, "10 missing". But on reading through the whole manuscript, it was found that, towards the end of the codex, a piece of leaf was found inserted, of which one-third portion was cut and missing. This had the missing portion relating to the description of the svara, pañcama, in the same handwriting. Thus it is clear that this fragmentary leaf was not noticed, while numbering the folios. The manuscript ends with the colophon statement,

> *"śrī kāmākṣī ambā sahāyaṃ. kara kṛtamaparādhaṃ kṣatu***santaḥ. sāmaiyya lāvi[likhi?]taṃ śrī rāmārpaṇamastu. śrī kāmākṣīdētyā[vyā]rpaṇamastu|| "*

1.2.5 G86

G86 is a palm-leaf written in Telugu script. This codex contains Bharatārṇava in ff.1-82 and the portion relating to NC in ff. 83a-118a. This manuscript was presented in the year 1948-49 to GOML, Madras by His Holiness Arulnandi Tambiran of Kasi mutt, Tiruppanandal, Tanjavur district.

G86 contains the whole of Gītādhyāya and a part of the Vādyādhyāya. The manuscript is injured and has been eaten away by insects at many places. The corners are highly damaged that the first and the last lines of some leaves could not be read. At many places, there are inter-linear insertions, marked by a "+"[1] sign. The manuscript ends with,

> *"śrī rāmānujātīnnamaḥ. śrī gurucaraṇāravindābhyān-namaḥ. śrī gurubhyonnamaḥ. śrī paramaguruvenamaḥ. śrī paripūrna[ṇa]guruvaina***[maḥ]. śrī cā[śā]radhā [dā]mbāya namaḥ. śrī bālāmbike namaḥ. śrī śrī śrī śrī"*

1.2.6 G89

G89 is a Palmleaf manuscript written in Telugu script. This was presented in the year 1948-49 by His Holiness Arulnandi Tambiran of Kasi Mutt, Tiruppanandal, Tanjavur district. This palm-leaf manuscript is also very much damaged and the leaves are not in order. Since the corners of the leaves are broken and injured, the original pagination made by the scribes is not visible. There are two numberings (one made by the staff of GOML and the other by IGNCA, New Delhi (for the purpose of microfilming), which do not coincide at some places. Folios 84(b), 96b, 97, 98, 99, 100b, 101, 106b, 107, 108b, 109 and 110 are blank.

The text pertaining to Somanārya begins from fol.45a. The other work in the codex is Vināyakatālam (from fol.4a). This contains the text of some dance compositions such as kavuttuvam-s, śabda-s (of which some are by Meraṭṭūr Kāsināthа), some jati passages /sollukaṭṭu-s (resembling that of an Alārippu of the South Indian dance repertoire), daru-s etc. The leaves are jumbled that some containing daru-s, compositions comprising of the sollukaṭṭu-s (pāhākṣara-s) and a few leaves containing a note on the gestures of hands also figure in between NC and the succeeding leaves. There is also a portion on the seven tāla-s and their classification based on the five jāti-s. It is not known to which (main) text, this belongs. It is probably because of this section on the tāla-s, that the editors of the Catalogue have mentioned that the work (R8189) "runs upto saptatāla prakaraṇam".

1. Sometimes there are two or three "+" signs at the place of insertion.

Two different scribes seem to have written the text of Somanārya's work, which is apparent from two different handwritings - one from fol.45a and the other from fol.55 onwards. The leaves containing dance compositions (vināyakatālam?) are in a different handwriting. The leaves pertaining to NC contain the whole of Gītādhyāya and a section of Vādyādhyāya. The extent of the work and the readings are very much similar to those of G86, but G89 gives better readings (particularly in the vādya section). The inter-linear insertions seen in G86 (inserted with a '+' mark) are missing in G89. In the front leaf the following passage is seen:

> *"piṅgaḷanāma saṃvatsaram tainēla iruvaināluguи tēdi vināyakatāla no[po]stakālu vrāsinadi. ī postakāluku ṣaṇṭe velāyutuḍu tāla postakālu"*

[The book vināyaka tāla was written on 24th of the month of Tai in the year Piṅgala. This is the tāla book of ṣaṇṭe velāyuda]. It is not known whether this statement applies to NC also, that is seen in the same codex.

1.2.7 G07

G07 is a palm-leaf written in Telugu script and titled Saṅgītaratnākara in the Acquisition Register. The flyleaf reads Svararāgasudhārasa and the heading found in the margin of the first leaf mentions Saṅgītaratnākara. The manuscript is in a very good condition. The text begins with the Gītādhyāya on fol.121a and ends incompletely in the middle of the description of 'Eighteen śruti-s' (NC 2, 79ab) on fol.137b. This manuscript resembles G86 in most of its omissions and variants.

1.2.8 G91

G91 is a paper manuscript written in Telugu in 35 pages. This is in a very bad condition and the pages are too brittle. The text is written on both the sides and in a few pages the writing on one side is visible on the other, causing confusion. Hence it becomes difficult tc decipher the readings. However the writing is very neat and tiny and there are only a few scribal errors when compared to other manuscripts. Only the first page (upto the penultimate line) and the last few lines of the last page (p.35) of this manuscript, contain NC. The text in the remaining 33 pages is an interpolation. (details given in 5.7 below).

1.2.9 G24

G24 is a palm-leaf manuscript written in Telugu script, in 73 pages. The Descriptive Catalogue remarks that this is "same as the above", thus giving an impression that this too contains the Saṅgītaratnākara of Śārṅgadeva (the manuscript described previous to this in the Catalogue, that is D13023, is the Saṅgītaratnākara of Śārṅgadeva). But on going through the manuscript, it becomes clear that it contains the Gītādhyāya of NC and another work along with it, which could not be identified. However a cursory study shows that it deals with the origin of the svara-s and their attributes. It is interesting to note that gamaka is also one among the various attributes of the svara-s.

The leaves are very much mixed up and jumbled. The readings near the margins could not be read due to injuries to the leaves. Hence the page numbers could not be identified. The available text from this manuscript is almost continuous but skips the commentary dealing with the individual description of the svara-s. This manuscript is full of scribal errors (spelling mistakes). However in some contexts, this manuscript has helped in restoring the text, when the readings in other manuscripts are not satisfactory.

1.2.10 Sp

In the collections of the Saurashtra Sabha, Madurai (Walajapet manuscripts), there exist two palm-leaf manuscripts and a paper manuscript, titled Saṅgītaratnākara. The paper manuscript is the transcript of one of the palm-leaf manuscripts, which bears the number '7'. As stated earlier, this was not accessible and has not been consulted. This palm-leaf manuscript and its paper transcript (made in 1943) ascribe the work to Somanāthasvāmi. The other palm-leaf manuscript was not available for sudy. For the present edition, the paper transcript of the palm-leaf numbered 7 has been consulted and noted as Sp. It is written in both Telugu and Tamiz scripts and consists of 105 pages.

On the front page, the author's name is given as "Somanāthan (āryan) ezudiyadu", which means, 'written by Somanāryan'. Then there is a table of contents based on the sub-headings or the topics dealt with. Appropriate indications are found in the manuscript in between the text, regarding the leaf number, line number and the side (front or reverse) of the original manuscript.[1] This manuscript contains the original and the commentary in both Telugu and Tamiz characters alternatively. Accordingly, in the Tamiz version, the letters kha, ga, and gha are marked with ka suffixed with the numerals 2, 3, and 4 respectively as subscripts. The visarga is marked with the letter "ha". It is observed that there are slight variations between the Telugu and the Tamiz versions at a few places.

The manuscript begins on p.3, with the heading, "'Saṅgītaratnākaram. 22 śrutulaku lakṣaṇam" and the text upto p.11, is an interpolation.[2] The text then switches over to NC with the heading, "Śubhamastu. vādi anuvādi". From here onwards, the readings match with NC and ends with the Gītādhyāya. There is a colophon statement at the end reading, "vyayanāma samvatsara tainela 26 tēdīna dvādaśi guruvāramu ī Saṅgītaratnākaramu sampurṇamu. Bhānukoṭi Vīrāsāmi Naṭṭu**[vanār pusta?]kam||" Goddess Śāradāmbā is saluted often in this manuscript.

1.2.11 G38

This is another copy of the same palm-leaf manuscript discussed above

1 For instance, "patram 8, mudal vari, munpakkam" meaning leaf 8, first line, front side

2 Detailed discussion of this is made under 'Interpolations' (See 5.7 below) The interpolated portion pertains to fol. 1- 4a of the original palm-leaf. The text in fol. 4a breaks off and fol. 4b is blank. Somanārya's text begins from fol. 5a - this was observed when the manuscript was browsed, while cataloguing the music Mss of Saurashtra Sabha, Madurai.

(from the Saurashtra Sabha, Madurai) which was transcribed in 1953-54 for GOML, Chennai. It is indexed in the Telugu section under the name, 'Saṅgītaratnākaramu'. The name of the author is mentioned as Somanāthasvāmi. Although the source of this transcript ("transcribed from a manuscript from Saurashtra Sabha, Madurai") is mentioned in the front page, other details are not given. But in the last page it is marked "7" in a square, which probably indicates the manuscript number of the original palm-leaf manuscript. Though G38 and Sp are transcripts of the same original, the readings differ (see 5.5 below). Both of them seem to give identical variant readings at many places, which in a few cases, might probably have existed in the original, introduced by a knowledgeable scribe. The manuscript runs to 43 pages and the extent of the work is identical to Sp.

1.2.12 V41

V41 is a paper manuscript originally found in the GOML, Chennai and now transferred to the Oriental Research Institute, Tirupati. A note found in the last page of the manuscript indicates that this has been transcribed from a manuscript of Kodaṇḍarāma Aiyangar of Ramnad, for the year 1920-21. The manuscript is written in Telugu script and runs to 92 pages. The text pertaining to Somanārya is found on pp.1-2 and pp.70-81; pp.3-69 and pp.86-92 contain the work Saṅgītasārasaṅgrahamu of Tiruvenkaṭakavi. From p.82 to p.85, there occur some verses with Telugu meaning ("artham") which deal with bāndhava hasta-s and nṛtya-hasta-s. The former includes, dampati-hasta, mātṛ-hasta, pitṛ-hasta, śṛśrū-hasta, nanānda-hasta, jyēṣṭa-kaniṣṭa-bhātṛ-hasta, putrī-hasta, snuṣātnī-hasta and sapatnī-hasta. It is not clear to which main work this portion belongs. There are many gaps in between, which is learnt from the remark, "granthapāta" made by the copyist.

The first two pages contain portions of the Vādyādhyāya (NC 3, 10-25). From p.70 to p.81, a part of the Gītādhyāya is found, which begins with the heading, "Saṅgīta Svararāgasudhārasamanu granthamandu gītādhyāyamu. atha gītādhyāyē vakṣyatē" on p.70. The available text corresponds to NC

1,1 to NC 2,19, which lists the rasa-s for the svara-s. The rest of the attributes are missing. Then the text switches over to the description of the attributes of the individual svara-s. After this description, there is a gap and then follows the rāga section. Here again a few verses are missing in between. Mānavalli Rāmakṛṣṇa Kavi has had access to this manuscript, and the readings from this, are noted and sometimes suggested as variants in V08 (See 1.2.14 below).

1.2.13 G18

G18 is a paper transcript written in Devanagari script. It is a restored copy of the palm-leaf manuscript, R366e. The codex of R366e contains only two and a half folios devoted to NC. This palm-leaf manuscript was purchased in the year 1911-12 from K Ramasvami Ayyangar of Magadi, Mysore province. The Catalogue titles it as "Sangītādhyāyah' and does not mention the name of the author. In the remarks column it is stated, 'similar to the above' (the previous entry being Svaramelakalānidhi - R366d). A verse from the text of the manuscript, reading "svarāṇām lakṣaṇam samyak Somanāryeṇa kīrtitaḥ" is also quoted in the catalogue, which suggests that the editor of the Catalogue did not want to link this reference to Somanārya, with the author of the manuscript. However Raghavan (Raghavan, 1933:101) and Krishnamachariar (Krishnamachariar, 1974:860) have taken Somanārya to be the author of this work, found in R366e.

The text begins in the middle of the second line of fol.55a. The previous line ends with the colophon statement indicating the end of the rāga chapter of Svaramelakalānidhi of Rāmāmātya. The leaves are broken to a length of two to three inches towards the sides and hence the text belonging to that portion of the manuscript could not be transcribed in the restored copy. It begins abruptly with the verse, "saptasvaraissamastamyo jagadētaccarāca-ram" and then enumerates the various attributes of svara-s. Though these attributes resemble those found in other manuscripts of NC, the construction and the language differ totally. Further R366e contains only the main text (verses) and no commentary. So this manuscript may not have been the original Somanārya's NC or a copy of it, but a work based on Somanārya's, somewhat on the lines of Bharatakalpalatāmañjarī and Rasikajanamanollāsini, to be described in 7.2 & 7.3 below. So attributing the authorship of this manuscript to Somanārya as done by Raghavan and Krishnamachariar may not be totally valid. However that the GOML regarded R366e as related to Somanārya, is apparent from the fact that the manuscripts, D12998 and R366e have been restored as successive transcripts numbering R11917 and R11918, in one notebook.

Some of the significant features observed in the readings of this manuscript are:

a. The order of many verses differs when compared to other manuscripts.
b. It gives some verses that are not found in other manuscripts, as for instance, those listing the names of 18 śruti-s and 21 mūrcchanā-s.[1]
c. After the 38th verse (NC 2, 38), the following colophon is seen: "iti gītādhyāyē prathamāśvāsaḥ". This kind of division of the sections within a chapter (into āśvāsaḥ) is not noticed in any other manuscripts of NC.

Due to the bad condition of R366e, its transcript G18 has been consulted through out. Although the verses relating to the attributes of svara-s are different from other manuscripts, G18 has a few verses resembling NC (NC 2, 40cd-58ab, 63cd-77, 78cd-80). However for correcting the grammatical errors in the manuscripts of NC, the readings in G18 had been of great help.

1.2.14 V08

V08 is a paper manuscript written in Telugu script, transcribed by M R Kavi. It actually starts from the back-side of the notebook, numbered 7508. This work is listed in the front page as, "svararāgasudhākara (imperfect copy)". This manuscript seems to be a copy made from a paper manuscript

1. These verses have been placed in the footnotes in the edited text.

from Tirunelvely, which is evident from a note given on p.1, thus: "From another manuscript. (Tinnevelly P), manuscript parts copied on loose sheets". Again on p.1a, it is written, "compd. [compared?] with S/5-2-34.[1] The introductory portion of the text (NC 1,1) begins from p.1 and is continued on p.1b.[2]

In p.1a, begins the Gītādhyāya, with the verse, "nṛttam vādyam..."(cf. NC 2,1). The text in p.1 and p.1b are portions pertaining to the Introduction and nāṭyotpatti. The statement, "From another manuscript" raises a doubt, if this portion of the manuscript is related to the rest of the portion, namely the Gītādhyāya.

Some of the significant aspects observed in this manuscript are given below.

a. In the beginning of the manuscript, on p.1a, it is written "notes". This probably means that the entire manuscript is not a true copy (transcript) of its original.
b. Although it was an attempt to copy the entire manuscript, at a few places, the text in the Saṃskṛta portion has not been completely copied. For example, in the middle of Gītādhyāya, the verses dealing with śruti-jāti-s, vādī, samvādī etc. are not given. Instead there is a gap of two short dotted lines and it is stated, "(saṃ.ratnāka. ślōkālu - dīptāyatādi) vādī samvādī etc."
c. The commentary has not been copied completely. At a few places, the commentary is copied in the form of short hints. "tel. comm: ubhaya saṃyōgamu - jantramandu" (NC 2, comm.6). Sometimes they are given within brackets, like, "toluta mandramādigā nettina svaramulu

1. It was discovered that the number, S/5-2-34, denoted the 'shelf number 'of GOML, that is the number of the shelf in which the Telugu paper manuscript R641, titled Saṅgītasārasaṅgrahamu was usually kept. This manuscript has since been transferred to ORISVU, Tirupati.
2. The pagination is made thus: 1, 1a, 1b and then 2, 3, 4, etc.

sthāyi anabaḍu" (NC 2, comm.64ab). Sometimes it is stated, "comm. has not been copied here" and "comm. combined for all the above items" (at the commencement of the description of the attributes of the svara-s) ".

d. In the first three pages, variant readings have been suggested at some places. It is not known whether these are Kavi's suggestions or the variant readings from some other source. Some of them seem to be the parallel readings noted from V41, which is supported by the remark made in the first page: "compd [compared?] with S/5-2-34", that corresponds to V41. For instance, V08 gives "kamalam" as a variant for "analam" in NC 2,3ab which is actually the reading found in V41.

e. At some places, a syllable or a word is scored off and a different reading is given. Here again, it is difficult to say whether these corrections were a result of a comparison of the manuscript copy with the original manuscript, or they represent Kavi's suggestions. Most of them seem to be an attempt by Kavi to emend the readings.

f. Against some verses, cross-references from other works are given, in the right margin of the page, as for instance, "saṃ.ratnā" [SR of Śārṅgadeva], "cf. bharatakalpalatā-p.87" etc.

g. After the verse, "ātmamadhyagataḥ prāṇaḥ..." (NC,2,81) there appears a colophon, "ityēvam Somanāryeṇa svanā[rā]rṇavamudīritam(?)". This is not seen in any of the other manuscripts.

Kavi's approach to the Manuscript

This manuscript appears to be different from others, that they incorporate some scholarly markings of Kavi. The following readings are in support of this.

a. With respect to the verses quoted from the earlier works, the traditional readings are suggested. For example, the names of the mūrcchanā-s as found in Nāṭyaśāstra have been suggested in the place of readings of

Somanārya. However it is curious to note that at some places, readings from SR of Śārṅgadeva have not been suggested, in the places where NC seems to have borrowed from it. Instead, different readings are seen. For example, in the context of the origin of nāṭya, the manuscripts give the reading, "prayogamudyatam dṛṣṭvā". SR 7,5ab reads "prayogamuddhatam smṛtvā", for which Kavi has suggested "prayogamadbhutam dṛṣṭvā".

b. At some places, he seems to have modified the verse to suit the commentary. e.g., "nābhihṛtkaṇṭha-vadanamūrdhāsu dhvanirucyatē" NC 2,40. Here although readings of the original verses in all the manuscripts coincide with SR 1,3,4cd, the commentary is seen to alter the order of the parts of the body. The order in the original verses is - navel, chest, throat, head and the mouth. In the commentary the order is - navel, chest, throat, face and then the head. Kavi suggests a reading, which accords with the latter one.

c. The texts of some of the verses have been totally re-phrased or/and re organised For example, verses 19, 30 & 34 of the Gītādhyāya.

For the reasons stated above, though V08 has helped in restoring the text at many places, it could not be considered as "a manuscript" but a copy, scrutinised by a scholar.

1.2.15 M

M is a paper transcript copy of the "Bengeri manuscript", containing fragments of Somanārya's NC in pp.148-152. About this manuscript, Sathyanarayana writes in the Introduction to the ABSS (p.lxix) thus:

"The Bengeri Manuscript is a remarkable palm-leaf codex containing fragments of Bharatārṇava (chapters I, II, III, IV, VII), Nāṭyaśāstra, Abhinayadarpaṇam (or Saṅgītaratnākara), Svararāgasudhārasa of Aṣṭāvadhāna Somanārya (chapters on gīta and vādya) and a very late work called Svaradīpikā composed under the joint authorship of Bharata

and Nārada(!). It contains a Telugu commentary throughout and, on one occasion a few lines of comment in Kannada. A very important feature of this work is the presentation of well over a hundred songs, datable at 16th century onwards; these include gīta-s, prabandha-s and ślokavarṇa-s, everyone of them being given in solfa-notation, along with the name of the rāga, tāla and tāla-graha to which it is set. The collection contains rare songs from Bhaṇḍāru Lakṣmīnārāyaṇa Kavi, author of 'Saṅgīta Sūryodaya and court-musician of Kṛṣṇadevarāya of Vijayanagar and from Vyāsarāya, the great saint of Karnataka. The manuscript contains several features of interest and I hope to describe it fully at a later date and publish it in the Varalakshmi Academy Publication Series in the future. An exact copy of the manuscript was sent to our Board of Research for opinion, and later the manuscript itself was generously donated to the Academy's library by Sri H G Bengeri, musicologist, educationist and research scholar from Haveri. The manuscript is about 200 years old and is very damaged."

At a different place he (Sathyanarayana, 1970:96) writes,

"Analysing a paper manuscript copy of the palm leaf codex on music and dance received by his Board of Research from Sri Bengeri of Haveri, the speaker described it as of Saṃskṛta language, Telugu script and containing a Telugu commentary. The name of the scribe or date of copy were not available in the manuscript which was about 150-200 years old."

On the portion relating to Somanārya's work, he says (ibid, p.97),

"Analysing the text of the Svararāgasudhārasa from which only parts of the Gītādhyāya, the Vādyādhyāya and the Nṛttādhyāya were extracted in the above manuscript, Sri Sathyanarayana said that a little corrupt as the text was, it has several interesting descriptions and terminology; it could offer good collative material for the edition of the work."

The manuscript includes a small portion on Nāṭyotpatti, a few verses and commentary from the beginning and the end of the Gītādhyāya and the section on Vādya. This section of the text is of greater importance to the present work, since apart from G86 and G89, this is the only manuscript, which contains Vādyādhyāya. There seems to be more lacunae in between. At many places, the present owner of the manuscript, (Sathyanarayana) has suggested some readings. He has also given cross-references from other related works like SR of Śārṅgadeva, BKM, RJM, ABSS, Abhinayadarpaṇa, Bharatakośa and so on. This paper transcript is copied in Telugu script[1] and the cross-references and quotations made by Sathyanarayana are in the Kannada and Devanagari scripts.

2. Title of the Work(s)

As stated earlier, manuscripts containing the work of Somanārya are titled differently, though the contents are almost similar. The various titles of the works that are ascribed to Somanārya as seen in catalogues and other writings of scholars are:

a. Nāṭyacūḍāmaṇi (NC),
b. Svararāgasudhārasa (SRS),
c. Saṅgītaratnākara (SR),
d. Tāladaśaprāṇaprakaraṇam (TDPP),
e. Svarārṇava (SA) and
f. Tālakalābdhi (TK)

Among these, the contents of the manuscripts titled SRS and SR are identical. They consist of Saṃskṛta verses with a commentary in Telugu. There are two manuscripts titled NC (T65 and G98), which is again similar

1. The Telugu script of this manuscript is different from other Mss written in Telugu. This seems to have been written by a person who knew Kannada as well, which is seen from the way a few letters like "ha", "ka", "ta" "ṣa" etc. are written. Most of them resemble Kannada characters.

to the manuscripts titled SR and SRS. Of these, T65 has a commentary and is also called SRS. The other manuscript (G98) contains some other texts interpolated within. A small portion of the text gets repeated and the repeated portion is accompanied by a commentary. Hence from the titles, the relation between NC, SRS and SR manuscripts could not be determined. TDPP, is being attributed to Somanārya only on the basis of a note written on the top margin of the manuscript. There do not exist any manuscripts titled SA and TK ascribed to Somanārya.

Each of the titles is being analysed below and the observations are based on the views expressed by scholars, references found in the musicological works and the readings of the manuscripts.

2.1. Nāṭyacūḍāmaṇi (NC) - Svararāgasudhārasa (SRS)

With regard to NC and SRS, it is difficult to conclude whether the two are independent works or, as stated above, identical. This issue has been discussed or referred to by many scholars in their writings.

2.1.1 Views of the scholars on the title NC/SRS

a. Vasudeva Sastri mentions that SRS is a part of NC and the rāgalakshaṇa-s dealt in it resemble today's rāga-s (Vasudeva Sastri, 1948:180).
b. Raghavan states that SRS is the same as NC; it is later than Rāgavibodha, since its author, Somanātha is cited in it (Raghavan, 1933:79-80).
c. Desai quoting Raghavan states that SRS is the other name for NC (Desai, 1979:431).
d. Kavi mentions that Somanārya is the author of SRS and NC (Kavi, 1951:xxii).
e. Krishnamachariar (Krishnamachariar, 1974:860) and Suresh Chandra Banerji (Banerji, 1990:53,110) probably following him, state that Somanārya is the author of SRS or NC and it has seven chapters.

f. Sathyanarayana mentions that SRS is also called NC (Sathyanarayana, 1994:264).

In the above statements, we find that the two works under discussion are being related as "NC and SRS" and as "NC or SRS". "NC and SRS" would mean that these two are different works; "NC or SRS" would imply that these are the same works.

2.1.2 References to NC and SRS in Musicological works

Somanārya's work seems to have had a strong influence on many musicological works written in the later period (15th century onwards). The Tamiz works Bharatasēnāpatiyam (BSe, p.49), Mahabharatacūḍāmaṇi (MBC) and Bharatasāttiram (BS) mention that "Sōmarāyan" (Somanārya) wrote a work called Bharatacūḍāmaṇi (see 2.2 below). This Bharatacūḍāmaṇi could probably mean Nāṭyacūḍāmaṇi (for the usage of the terms Bharata and Nāṭya, see Sathyanarayana, 1969:67-68).

While the mention of the name Bharatacūḍāmaṇi could imply the work is Nāṭyacūḍāmaṇi, the name SRS is not found to be mentioned in any of the later works.

2.1.3 Conclusions drawn from the readings in the manuscripts

Verses 1-18 of the first chapter of NC (comprising the introductory verses and 'nāṭyotpatti'- the origin of nāṭya) are exclusively seen in the manuscripts titled NC (G98, T65) and V08 and are missing in the manuscripts titled SR/SRS. V08, titled SRS is a manuscript copied by M R Kavi. From the note made by him on the top margin of the page, it can be seen that the text pertaining to 'Nāṭyotpatti' has been copied from a different manuscript (see 1.2.14 above). Hence it is inferred that NC and SRS do not represent two names of a single work (as in the case of Nānyadeva's Bharatabhāṣya and Sarasvatihṛdayālaṅkārahāra) and the text pertaining to the origin of nāṭya, in all probability, forms part of NC and not SRS.

There is a chapter on gīta in manuscripts bearing both the titles. As per the list in 1.1 above, there are three manuscripts titled NC, bearing the numbers, G98, G17 and B13 of which G17 and B13 are only transcripts of G98. There are five manuscripts of SRS, namely, G89, G91, V08, V41 and M. V08 is a copy more in the form of notes made by M R Kavi. T65 bears both the titles NC and SRS on the flyleaf. Incidentally, T65 although bearing the titles, NC and SRS, contains in its text the third name of the work, SR. The text pertaining to the gīta chapter is found to be identical in both the groups of manuscripts, except for the following omissions in G98, G17 and B13.

a. The verse containing the name SRS.
b. Verses that deal with the lakṣaṇa-s of a set of 32 rāga-s.
c. Verses that delineate the attributes of the 32 rāga-s.
d. Verses describing the twenty-five blemishes of a singer (gāyaka doṣa) individually.

In the edited text it could be seen that the name NC occurs only at one place in the introductory verses before 'nāṭyotpatti', thus:

aṣṭāvadhānavikhyāta Somanāryeṇa vakṣyate||
nāṭyacūḍāmaṇirnāma grantho vibudhasammataḥ || (NC 1,5)

This verse is found in G98, G17, B13, T65 and V08. The name SRS occurs as part of the original text at one place, namely, in the beginning of the gīta chapter,[1] thus:

"saṅgītaśāstraṃ saṅgṛhya svararāgasudhārasam|
aṣṭāvadhānavikhyātaṃ Somanāryeṇa vakṣyate ||"

(NC 2,1)

1. Originally a similar verse, but wrongly constructed, was found at the beginning of the gīta chapter. Hence this verse which was found at the beginning of the section on rāga-s has been shifted to the beginning of the gīta chapter.

This verse is missing in G98, G17 and B13, thereby suggesting that, this verse does not form part of NC. A colophon statement found at the end of the chapter on gīta reads, "iti svararāgasudhārasākhyo gītādhyāyaḥ samāptaḥ" (Thus ends the chapter on gīta named Svararāgasudhārasa.)

Among the manuscripts having the title SRS, only G89 contains the above colophon. This is because in the other manuscripts namely, G91, V08, V41 and M the gīta portion has many missing passages. However this colophon is also seen in manuscripts titled SR and this will be discussed in 2.2 below.

The above observations suggest the following.

1. Probably, each of the chapters in the work of Somanārya could have been titled differently, that is,

   a. NC might have been the title of the (first) chapter on nāṭya.
   b. SRS might have been the title of the next chapter, gīta (svara and rāga).
   c. TDPP might have been the chapter on tāla.
   d. There is also a chapter on vādya, but the title is not known.

2. It has been mentioned already that the work of Somanārya contains a Telugu commentary. Perhaps this commentary to the gītādhyāya was called SRS, since there are some contradictions in the accounts presented by the original and the commentary (see 6.5.1 below).

2.2. Saṅgītaratnākara (SR)

There already exist two printed works by the name, Saṅgītaratnākara. One is written by Śārṅgadeva (13th century) and the other is a much later work containing descriptions of rāga-s based on the kanakāṅgī-ratnāṅgī nomenclature of the Seventy-two mela-s.[1] Further five manuscripts namely,

1. A work in Kannada based on a manuscript at GOML; edited by Mariappa Bhatt.

G86, G07, G24, G38 and Sp attributed to Somanārya, are also titled Saṅgītaratnākara.

2.2.1 References made by Scholars - Sambamurthi

Sambamurthi (Sambamurthi, 1970:appendix.5) ascribes the work, SR to Somanāthasvāmi noticed in the collections of the Saurashtra Sabha, Madurai. In his article 'The Walajapet Manuscripts', in the Journal of the Madras Music Academy (JMA), 1943 (Sambamurthi, 1943:87), the name of the author of this SR is given as Hēmanāthasvāmi, which probably is an error.

2.2.2 References to SR in Musicological works

There is a quotation in verse 63 of BSe, also seen in BS and MBC, which states, 'Śārṅgadeva wrote a work on Bharata consisting of one lakh verses in Saṃskṛta and preached it to Somarāya (Somanārya?); he in turn composed Bharatacūḍāmaṇi in an abridged form consisting of 4,000 verses'.

In the commentary to verse 55 of the first section of the music chapter of MBC, Somanārya's work is referred to as 'ratnākaram' ("Somanāthīyam ennum ratnākaram"), which probably suggests the title, SR.

2.2.3 'SR' in the text of the manuscripts

The name SR is seen in the manuscripts as the title of the work noted either in the flyleaf or in the margin of the first page. With respect to the text proper, the name SR does not occur anywhere in the mūla but is seen only in the commentary. It occurs as a colophon statement towards the end of the chapter on gītā, in the manuscripts titled SR and SRS, thus:

"saṅgītaratnākaramandu saṅgrahiñci saṅkṣēpamugānu jantra-gātrāniki sammandamgānu aṣṭāvadhāna sōmappā jēsina saṅgītaratnākaram gītādhyāyam samāptaḥ." (NC 2, comm.364)

(Thus concludes the chapter on gīta of Saṅgītaratnākara, composed by

Aṣṭāvadhāna Sōmappā, having collected from Saṅgītaratnākara, in a concise way, on the instrument and vocal music.)

This idea is identical with the statement made in the Tamiz works - MBC, BS and BSe. From the above colophon, it becomes clear that

a. It is only the commentator who ascribes the name SR to the work of Somanārya, since it does not occur in the mūla.
b. Somanārya's work is based on SR (however Śārṅgadeva's name has not been mentioned in this context.)

Hence it could be inferred that SR does not seem to represent a separate work of Somanārya. It is found that in the manuscripts titled SR, the name NC does not occur and only the name SRS figures. The manuscripts commence only with the gīta chapter and the initial portions containing 'nāṭyotpatti' and other details are completely absent. So in the SR manuscripts, wherever the introductory verse and colophon are present the name SRS occurs.

SR might be an additional title assigned to the work, in order to give due recognition, since SR of Śārṅgadeva is regarded as a monumental work greatly acclaimed. Secondly, since the text draws many portions from the SR of Śārṅgadeva (although the views deviate at many places), it could have been titled SR.

2.3 Svarārṇava (SA)

It is said that Tyāgarāja, the composer, was influenced by a divine text named "Svarārṇava", a fact mentioned by him in one of his compositions, commencing with the words, 'Svararāgasudhārasa' in the rāga, Śaṅkarābharaṇa[1]

"rajatagirīśūḍu nagajaku delpu svarārṇava marmamulu

1. Scholars like Raghavan (Raghavan, 1932:101) Sambamurthi (Sambamurthi, 1970:appendix.5) state thus.

vijayamugala tyāgarājuḍerukē viśvasiñci telusukō manasā"

(Oh mind, please know these from the victory of Tyāgarāja, who absorbed the secrets of Svarārṇava that was preached by Śiva to Pārvati.)

2.3.1 Views of the Scholars on SA and Somanārya

Scholars have tried to associate Somanārya with Svarārṇava as shown below.

* Alain Danielou (Danielou, 1949:148) mentions SA as a work attributed to Somanārya available at 'Tanjore' (probably the Sarasvatai Mahal Library).
* Raghavan (Raghavan, 1932:101) states in his article in the JMA, that 'SA may be part of NC or may be another separate work' and adds, 'according to Sundaram Iyer of Tanjore, a section on rāga-s of SA by Somanārya was found in the family of the descendants of Śyāmā Śāstri and a copy is deposited in the Sarasvati Mahal Library, Thanjavur'. Again he (Raghavan, 1933:79) states that 'a fragment of this work [NC?] was secured from private possession by P S Sundaram Ayyar and produced as the SA connected with Śrī Tyāgayya's life'.
* Later, Raghavan presented an edited text of SA, titled "The So Called Svarārṇava" in the appendix to the JMA, 1953. Unfortunately, the source for this text is not mentioned. From the critical notes in the footnotes, it is learnt that he had consulted SR of Śārṅgadeva and the NC manuscript D12998 (G98) from GOML.
* Sambamurthi notices SA in the collections of the Saurashtra Sabha, Madurai[1] (Sambamurthi, 1970:appndx-p.5). According to him, SA was written on a broad palm-leaf in Grantha characters. He states that

1. There exists a paper manuscript titled "Svarārṇavam", in the collections of the Saurashtra Sabha, Madurai, which was noted while cataloguing the Mss stock of the Sabha. But the manuscript is very brittle and the pages have got stuck to each other along the written lines. Hence it is very difficult to decipher the readings.

'the clue for some rāga-s was got from SA, and Singarācārya got some of the verses of SA from the disciples of Tyāgarāja and published them in the Gāyakalocanam'. Then he has briefly listed the topics dealt with in SA.

Further he says that the verse,

ātmamadhyagatoprāṇaḥ prāṇamadhyagatodhvaniḥ |
dhvanimadhyagato nādaḥ nādamadhyē sadāśivaḥ ||

is found exclusively in SA. Then he states that a section in the work (SA) is titled SRS.

In V08, the manuscript titled Svararāgasudhārasa, copied by M R Kavi and consulted for the present edition, there occurs a colophon statement, which is not seen in any other manuscripts attributed to Somanārya. The colophon reads,

"ityevam Somanāryeṇa svanā[rā]rṇavamudīritam (?)".

This sentence occurs just after the Śloka, ""ātmamadhyagatoprāṇaḥ...".

2.3.2 Inferences

On analysing the statements mentioned above, it is observed that:

a. The manuscript of SA is not available presently to comprehend its contents and that of the author. The short note given by Sambamurthi, in his book, Great Composers, is the only available reference with regard to the contents of the work. Enough details are not available from the fragmentary/incomplete edited text of SA in the JMA, 1953 by Raghavan.
b. Sambamurthi's reference is an important evidence to claim that there

really existed a work under the title, SA, in the codex of which also existed the work SRS. This should have probably led to the attribution of SA to Somanārya.

c. Again, this might have probably misled scholars like P S Sundaram Iyer, (and based on him, Raghavan) and Alain Danielou to attribute SA to Somanārya.

d. With respect to the verse, "ātmamadhyagatoprāṇaḥ", since it is seen in all the manuscripts of Somanārya, and also in some printed texts like, MBC, SSB, RJM, it might be stated that the original source for this verse could have been Somanārya's work (NC) or all these works should have borrowed from some "subhāṣita"?.

e. The existence of this verse in the manuscript of SA (both Sambamurthi's SA and Raghavan's SA) could also suggest that the portion of the text probably belonged to Somanārya's work in that codex and not to the portion that contained SA.

f. The colophon statement found in the manuscript copied by Kavi (V08), could be an adscript,[1] made by Kavi himself, influenced by the connection between the verse "ātmamadhyagatoprāṇaḥ.., the work Svarārṇava and the author Somanārya.

2.4 Tāladaśaprāṇaprakaraṇam (TDPP)

A paper manuscript numbered D12990 titled Tāladaśaprāṇaprakaraṇam is ascribed to Somanārya.[2] A transcript of this manuscript is found in the Library of the Department of Musicology, Banaras Hindu University, Varanasi. It is small but incomplete work containing verses in Saṃskṛta and a Telugu Commentary and deals with the Tāladaśaprāṇa-s followed by the illustration of the sapta tāla-s. There in no colophon or any other indication regarding the name of the main work and the author, anywhere in the

1. An adscript is an insertion of interlinear or marginal gloss or note within the text. (Khatre, 1954:90)
2. This manuscript is not presently found in the shelves of the library.

manuscript, except for the heading found in the beginning which reads,

"svararāgasudhārasamaniyēḍu[?]granthamanunandali tāladaśaprāṇaprakaraṇamu"

(This is the Tāladaśaprāṇaprakaraṇa in the work called Svararāga-sudhārasa.)

Manuscripts dealing with Tāladaśaprāṇa-s are noted in the manuscript libraries like GOML and TMSSMḶ. There already exists a Telugu work called Tāladaśaprāṇapradīpikā by Polūri Govindakavi, who is also the author of the work, 'Rāgatālacintāmaṇi'.

Meanwhile Somanārya is also associated with Tālakalābdhi, as its author or at least of the commentary, with the authorship of the original being attributed to Acyutarāya (Kavi, 1951:xxii). It is to be pointed out here that, Tālakalābdhi is regarded as the first technical work to treat the tāladaśaprāṇa-s in an exhaustive and extensive manner (Sathyanarayana, 1994:264, Kavi, 1951:xxii).

2.5 Tālakalābdhi (TK)

Kavi speaks of a rare tāla text, Tālakalābdhi, also called as Tālakalāvārdhi and attributes it to Acyutarāya, the successor of Kṛṣṇadevarāya of the Vijayanagara Empire (Kavi, 1951:xxii). Extracts from this tāla work are given in Bharatakośa, under the authority, "Acyuta" and "Acyutarāya", which have been the sole reference material in this regard. But he does not give the details of the manuscript sources for these extracts.

While commenting on the text, Kavi states that Somanārya could have written this tāla text or at least its commentary, citing the colophon, "sītārāmagurum natvā somabhaṭṭanyatē granthē tālakalāvārdhau"

(Kavi, 1951:248)

Whether this Somabhaṭṭa and Somanārya were two names of a single person, is not known, although Somanārya's teacher was also one Sītarāma (see section 3 below)

2.5.1 Other Scholars who speak of TK

According to Sathyanarayana (Sathyanarayana, 1994:264), Acyutarāya was the first to make a detailed treatment of tāladaśaprāṇa-s, and could have probably been influenced by Somanārya. T V Mahalingam (Mahalingam, 1975:270) and C Panduranga Bhatta (Bhatta, 1998:121) quoting Mahalingam, also mention that Somanātha, a contemporary of Acyutarāya has commented on the tāla work of Acyutarāya, called "Tālamahodadhi".

2.5.2 The TK Manuscript

A palm-leaf manuscript titled 'Tālalakshaṇam' numbered D12992 of GOML is attributed to Kohala.[1] This is a Saṃskṛta work with a Telugu commentary. Most of the extracts given in Bharatakośa under the name 'Acyuta' and 'Acyutarāya' and the paraphrases/quotations from a few rare texts can be traced to this manuscript. In folio 36a, the following reference is found.

"grahālu mūḍu anēṭi māṭa saṅgītaratnākara nṛttacūḍāmaṇi tālakalāvilāsaṃ saṅgītavidyāvinodaṃ saṅgītamaṇidarpaṇaṃ caturasabhāvilāsaṃ kātyāyanamataṃ, jayana āñjanēyamataṃ modalaina matamvārki yēka sammatamanē telusukonēdi."

(That the 'graha-s' are three, is known to be accepted together in the works like saṅgītaratnākara, nṛttacūḍāmaṇi, tālakalāvilāsa, saṅgītavidyāvinoda, saṅgīta-maṇidarpaṇa, caturasabhāvilāsa, kātyāyanamataṃ, jayana āñjanēyamataṃ and others.)

This sentence from the manuscript accords with the words of Kavi in Bharatakośa. Hence this work perhaps could be the Tālakalābdhi referred to by Kavi (Premalatha, 2009: 94-102).

Hence it could be conjectured that the subject requires lot of research to evaluate the contribution of Somanārya to tāla. It becomes essential to

1. This manuscript is restored under R7979

examine all the works mentioned above on tāla-s and the tāladaśaprāṇa-s, in particular. Otherwise, it becomes difficult to assess Somanārya's contribution to tāla-s, based on the single available manuscript, with an ambiguous heading on the first page. With regard to TK, though the discovery of the manuscript might indicate the work as TK, it is still not certain about Somanārya's role in it, since his name is not found anywhere in the available mss. Therefore, this has to be dealt with separately and has not been attmped here.

With regard to other titles discussed above, the name Svararāgasudhārasa covers only the gītādhyāya. Hence it could be conjectured that the mūla of gītādhyāya along with the Telugu ṭīkā came to be assigned the name SRS. And, perhaps the mūla alone of the entire text, without the ṭīkā, represented NC. For the present purpose, this work is being called by the name NC only.

3. Name of the Author

Somanārya, the author of NC is recognised as an Aṣṭāvadhāni (a person who can concentrate on eight different things at the same time) in all the manuscripts. The title "Aṣṭāvadhāna" is very famous in the Andhra region.[1] It is the title conferred on poets, who are skilled in attending and answering eight different scholars, who are well versed in their subjects.

P K Rajagopala Iyer, (Rajagopala Iyer, 1982:64) describes 'aṣṭāvadhāna' thus:

bhāvaśca rāgatālau ca śrutirlayasamanvitā |
sabhā sakhā tathātmā cāvadhēyaṃhyaśakaṃ smṛtam||

(The concentration on the eight elements namely, emotion (bhāva), melody (rāga), time measure (tāla), tonic (śruti), time duration (laya), audience (sabhā), friend (sakhā) and the mind (ātmā) [is known to be aṣāvadhānam.])

1. Information given by Prof. Chinni Krishnayya, Retd. Professor of Telugu, Presidency College, Chennai and Sri Swami, whose expert advice was sought by the researcher while translating the Telugu Commentary.

It is also said that Somanārya is the student of one Sītarāma. (Kavi, 1951:xxii).[1] Probably it should be this Sītarāma, who is being saluted, in the beginning verse of NC.

nityānandakaram śāntam nirmalāṅgam suśobhanam |
nīrajapatranayanam sītārāmamaham bhajē || (NC 1,1)

Sathyanarayana also opines that Somanārya, the student of Sītarāma could be the teacher of Acyutarāya.[2]

The study of the manuscripts of NC reveals that the name of the author also occurs as "Somanātha" at many places. Besides, he is called "Somappa" (NC, 2, comm.180) and "Somasūri" too (NC 2, 189).

3.1 Somanārya and Somanātha

In the palm-leaf manuscript found in the Saurashtra Sabha, Madurai, the name of the author is mentioned as "Somanātha".[3] Some scholars (Raghavan, 1933:79-80, Danielou, 1949:32, Desai, 1979:431) appear to have confused this name, with that of the author of Rāgavibodha.

There were quite a few writers with their names beginning with "Soma". Mudikondan Venkatrama Ayyar (in the introduction to the music chapter of the MBC, p.xx) speaks of three writers on music, commencing with the name, 'Soma'- Somanātha, the author of Rāgavibodha, Somēśvara, the author of Saṅgītaratnāvali and Somēśvara III, the author of Mānasollāsa. He makes it clear that the name 'Somanāthan quite often cited in the music chapter of the MBC, should be Somanārya, the author of NC only and not the author of Rāgavibodha'.

If it is a fact that Somanārya was also called by the name 'Somanātha,' then in the statement of T V Mahalingam that 'Somanātha commented on

1. Scholars like Sathyanarayana (Sathyanarayana, 1994:264) and Acharya Brhaspati (Brhaspati, 1966:37) also give this information.
2. ibid
3. But in the front page of the paper transcript, it is written, " Somanāthan (āryar)"

the tāla work of Acyutarāya', the reference could be to Somanārya. Further there is a reference to a scholar by the name, 'Somanātha kavi', noticed in the period of Kṛṣṇadevarāya and Acyutarāya, who wrote "Vyāsayogicarita", the biography of the Madhva saint Shri Vyāsarāyatīrtha in the campū form[1] (Sharma, 1961:252). Perhaps this Somanātha who also lived during the same period in the same region, could have been the Somanārya, the author of NC.

Hence it could be that Somanārya was also called by the name, Somanātha.

4. Date of Somanārya

A few scholars have discussed the period to which Somanārya belonged. The following is an assessment, from various sources, of the probable date of Somanārya.

4.1. Views of Scholars on the date of Somanārya

Among the various scholars who have expressed their views on the date of Somanārya, only Krishnamachariar, Kavi and Raghavan present original findings. Others base their views on one of these three scholars. The different views are summarized below.

a. Krishnamachariar and probably following him, Suresh Chandra Banerji, are of the opinion that Somanārya could be Nacana Somana, the author of Uttara Harivamsa, who lived in the reign of King Bukka, which can be inferred from the reference of the grant dated 1344 A.D. (Krishnamachariar, 1974:860, Banerji, 1990:53 & 110)
b. Kavi assigns the date 1540 A.D (Kavi, 1951:318, 741).
c. Raghavan states that the work is later than that of Rāgavibodha of Somanātha (1609), who is quoted in the section called Caturaṅgaprastāra in the rāga chapter of SRS (Raghavan, 1933:79-80).
d. Desai too assigns the date as later than that of Rāgavibodha (1609),

1. The period of this Somanātha kavi is given as 1480-1540 A.D.

quoting Raghavan (Desai, 1979:431).

e. Alain Danielou gives two dates at two places in his book- in p.32 it is said, "after 1609" and in p.144, it is "c.1650". The former date reflects the influence of Raghavan's views.

f. Sathyanarayana refutes the opinion of Alain Danielou and fixes the date 1540 A.D., agreeing with Kavi's views (Sathyanarayana, 1960:xiii).

g. Mudikondan Venkatarama Ayyar in the introduction to the MBC (p.xx) states that it can be assumed that Somanārya lived within 300 years. Since this has been written in 1955 (the date of edition of MBC), the actual date could refer to 300 years before 1955 i.e., 1655 A.D.

4.2. References in Musicological Works

a. 'Somanārya' is saluted and his name enumerated along with those of poets and scholars, by Polūri Govindakavi, in the commencing passages of the Telugu Work, Rāgatālacintāmaṇi (RTC 1,6). Hence Somanārya could be placed before Polūri Govindakavi.

b. A few passages cited in ABSS under the source 'matāntara', are found to exist in Somanārya's work. The date of this (saṅgraha) work is tentatively placed between 1600 and 1670 AD by Sathyanarayana (Sathyanarayana, 1960:xxxii). Therefore Somanārya should have composed his work before 1600 A.D.

c. In the beginning of the work, BKM, the author after offering salutations to Goddess Sarasvati, 'Ambā' and the vidvat (the scholars), states that the present work (BKM) is being compiled from many earlier works on music,

pūrvoktairbharatācāryairyaduktaṃ granthakoṭiṣu |
tatsāraṃ tu samuddhṛtya saṅkṣepeṇa viracyate ||

(BKM,p.4)

Following this, the names of works that were mentioned by Bharata and others are listed

> bharatādulacē jēppabaḍina garanthambula yokka nāmambulu........ Kohalīya, Arjunīya, Somanāthīya, Svararatnāvalī, Kāḷātataraṇamu, Sāhityadarpaṇa, Haripālīyasāhiti, Śṛṅgāratilakaṃ, Rasaratnapradīpikā, Śṛṅgāradarpaṇamu, Mātaṅgaḥ, Kāśyapa, Śṛṅgāradīpikā, Rasamañjarī, Saṅgītasarvasva, Rasakaḷikā, Bārhaspatyaṃ, Mārutīyaṃ, Mātṛguptīya, Saṅgītaratnākara, Nāradīyaṃ, Sāhityacandrodaya, Nandikēśa, Saṅgītacūḍāmaṇi, Śārṅgadeva, Saṅgītasūryodaya and Dattilaṃ.
>
> (BKM,p.5)

"Somanāthīya" in the above quotation, probably refers to Somanārya's work. Moreover, though BKM was compiled in the 19th century[1] (since it speaks of 72 melakartā-s and janya-rāga-s), the source works listed above seem to belong to a very early period. The prominent works of the sixteenth and the seventeenth centuries, namely those of Rāmāmātya, PundarīkaViṭala and Vēṅkaṭamakhi expounding the mela system, are conspicuous by their absence.

4.3. References from the Manuscript readings

The names of early writers on music like Dattila, Kohala, Hanumān, Arjuna and Nandikēśvara are mentioned in the introductory verses of NC. Besides, verses from Dattilam are quoted at a few places (NC 2,45-46 = Datt. 8,9; NC 2,100 = Datt. 38cd -39 ab). In the context of prabandha, one, King Pratāpa (King Jagadekamalla?) is acknowledged (NC 2,182). Above all, there are passages in the commentary of this work, which acknowledge that SR (of Śārṅgadeva) as the source for the compilation of this work. Many verses from the SR of Śārṅgadeva are found verbatim in the gītādhyāya (NC 2,163 = SR 3,22cd-23; NC 2,163-176 = SR 3,25-38; NC 2,182-183 =

1. This work was edited with a Telugu paraphrase by B Ankaji Sastri and P Subba Rao in 1887 A.D.

SR 4,12cd-14ab and so on). So it could be firmly said that the work belongs to the post-ratnākara period.

From the observations above, following conclusions can be arrived at:

a. If Somanārya had lived during the reign of Acyutarāya, the successor of Kṛṣṇadevarāya of the Vijayanagara Empire, his period could be mid 16th century.
b. As Somanārya was also called by the name 'Somanātha', he need not be placed after Rāgavibodha (a work of another Somanātha assigned to 1609 AD), since both are different.
c. Based on the citations found in ABSS, Somanārya's date can be fixed sometime earlier than 1600 A.D.

The discussion here only relates to the date of Somanārya, the author of NC, i.e., the mūla and not to the date of the commentary. The commentary probably belongs to a later period, which is discussed in detail in 6.5.2 below.

5. Collation and Edition

Fifteen manuscripts were consulted for the edition of the NC of Somanārya. As mentioned earlier, some of them are palm-leaf manuscripts and the others paper transcripts. They are written in different scripts like Devanāgari, Telugu and Grantha. Each manuscript possesses a peculiar kind of writing and some are in more than one handwriting (written by more than one scribe). A study of the writings of each manuscript reveals a lot of peculiarities and after considering them, a collated text has been arrived at. Taking into account the various characteristics of the manuscripts, the methodology adopted in editing the text, is described in this section.

5.1 Scribal Peculiarities

The following are some of the scribal peculiarities observed in different manuscripts.

* Nowhere in the manuscripts, are the verses numbered.
* In most of the manuscripts, the mūla is marked by the words "śloka" or "ślo". At some places, such markings are not found. The commencement of the mūla in such cases, is inferred by the occurrence of a double stoke "||", found towards the end of the commentary preceding the main text. The commentary is indicated by, "ṭīkā" (e.g., G86, G89, G38, Sp), or through the syllables "ṭkī" (G07) or "ṭī" (G38). In M it is written as "artham".
* In G86 and G89, at the end of each topic, there is a peculiar symbol, which looks like the syllable, "śrī", surrounded by some circular design.
* An additional syllable is added to the conjunct consonants in G86, G89, G07

  e.g. mandu as manddu, saṅgīta as saṅggīta
* Unnecessary vertical strokes (punctuation marks) and absence of full stops at the required places, are noticed in G86, G89 and G07. Probably, the copyist might have placed these strokes, after each word or words, depending on the manner in which it was dictated to him.
* G86, G89 do not seem to be copied from another manuscript by sight, but taken down as dictation; this is evident from the nature of mistakes found in them. (See "Scribal errors" below)
* T65 reads some of the Telugu words in a 'Sanskritised' form, as for instance, caturbhuja for nālugubhuja, nētrālu for kannulu and so on.
* G86, G07 show transposition of words like "vedapuruṣuḍu gotrarṣi" for "gotrarṣi vedapuruṣuḍu"
* The syllable 'ṛ' in words like 'ṛṣi' is seen written either as 'ri' or 'ru' (riṣi/ ruṣi) in G86, G89, G24 and G07 at many places.
* The letter, 'śru' occurring in words like 'śruti' is written as "śṛ" in most of the manuscripts (For e.g., G86, G89).
* In almost all the palm-leaf manuscripts written in Telugu script, the vowel 'i' and 'u' are written as 'yi' and 'vu'; hence words like 'yiti', 'yityevam' and 'vubhaya' instead of 'iti', 'ityevam' and 'ubhaya' are seen.

* At some places, the consonants are split; like, 'rū' is written as 'ra' and 'u' (e.g., T65).
* G86, G89 seem to have been influenced by Tamiz language. For instance, there are some readings thus: vātyam and vāttiyam for vādyam, vyavakāra for vyavahāra etc.
* The avagraha sign is seen only in the recently transcribed manuscripts such as B13, G17 and V08 and not in the earlier ones.
* Some words in G86, G89 and M particularly in the vādya chapter end with the vowel, "ē" like 'vīṇē' for 'vīṇā', which is common in the Kannada language.
* Page headings or marginal headings are not seen in most of the manuscripts. However M has page headings. G38 and Sp incorporate the page headings of the exemplar as part of the text. (These are noted in footnotes in the edited text.)

5.2 Scribal Errors

A plenty of scribal errors are observed in the manuscripts and some of them are found transmitted to others also. A few seem to be visual errors, like transposition of letters and words, omission of a part or the whole of a verse or passage. Some are caused due to phonetic misinterpretation. Most of the errors in G86 and G89 support this. The errors found in G24 and G07 suggest a lack of knowledge of the subject on part of the scribes, since even the names of the svara-s are wrongly spelt. Surprisingly, these manuscripts provide some useful readings in a few places.

The following are some of the errors noticed in general:

a. Confusion of letters that look similar like, tha (ഥ) / dha (ധ) / ya (യ) in Grantha script; and the following in Telugu script : tha (థ) /dha (ధ), kau (కౌ) /rau (రౌ), ḷa (ళ) /śa (శ), te ( ) / tai (తై) any consonant with ā (kā - NS) / au (kau - కౌ), ā (rā - రా) / aṃ (raṃ- రం)[1]

1. The Telugu characters illustrated here are those available in the software, However in the Mss, they look slightly different.

b. The vowel 'ē' or consonants ending with ē are written as short syllables in G86, G89, G98, G24, G07 etc. (All are palm-leaf manuscripts)

c. Spelling errors due to improper pronunciation: (mostly met with in G86, G89)

   * 'dha' for 'tha', 'da' for 'ta' (at many places in most of the manuscripts.)
   * Words ending with "halant" into words ending with the vowel "u". e.g. gāyettu for gāyet, kārayettu for kārayet (G86- folio-111b, line-6)
   * 'ścā' or 'sya' for 'syāt' (G38- p15, line-22; G86-folio.99a, line-6).
   * īśvara for ī svara (G86- fol.96a, line-3)
   * Transposition of letters: vyararīcat for vyarīracat (G98,p.15, line-2), sarva for svara (G89- folio.82a, line-3)etc.

d. Confusion in the use of letters of the same varga/group. nāśikayā for nāsikayā (NC 2, 359), pāda for pāṭa (NC 2, 370) etc.

e. Absence of visarga ":", at many places

f. The syllable 'ddha' is written as 'dha' only in G38

A few words or half verses are missing in some manuscripts. Sometimes they break with a word in the middle of a verse and they again continue with the same word in the commentary.

5.3 Relationship between the Manuscripts (Stemma Codicum)

"Assembling and arranging the entire material consisting of manuscripts and testimonia in the form of a genealogical tree is called 'stemma codicum' or pedigree' in Textual Criticism (Khatre, 1954:31). Thus by careful analysis of the readings of different manuscripts, the inter-relationships between the manuscripts and the earliest among them (the one which could have been nearer to the original text) could be determined.

To draw a geneological tree, all manuscripts were first placed in a chronological order. In the present case, the date of transcription of a few manuscripts is available. These are found as colophon statements or marked in the beginning or end of the manuscripts, probably made by the copyists. G89 reads "piṅgala - tai - 24th" (See 1.2.6 above). But since other details such as star and tithi are not given, the exact date could not be deduced. However" piṅgala- tai" could relate to the years 1678 / 1738 / 1798 / 1858.[1]

The date of transcription of S07, the exemplar of G38 and Sp (See 1.2.10, 1.2.11 above) is "vyaya- tai- 26th- dvādaśī, guruvāram". This colophon is copied in both the transcripts. Though all the details such as the name of the year, month, day, date and tithi are mentioned, this could not be matched to an exact date in the English Calendar. Probably it could be related to the 8th February, 1827.[2] The dates of copying of the transcripts are:

Manuscript	*Year of Transcription*
V41	1921
Sp	1943
G17	1952-53
G38	1953-54
B13	1960

Since all the manuscripts could not be dated from colophons alone, an attempt is being made to analyse the relationship among the manuscripts from the nature of their readings. The following observations are made.

1. The Hindu Calendar (South Indian) consists of a cycle of sixty years each of which carries a name. Thus a year with a particular name recurs every sixtieth year.
2. As stated earlier, any particular year in the Hindu Calendar comes once in sixty years. Hence in order to find out the exact English date from the details, one has to equate it with the corresponding years of the English calendar. Thus the 26th day of the month tai, corresponds to the following English dates: Friday, 24th January, 1707 (dvitiya); Thursday, 5th February, 1767 (saptami); Tuesday, 6th February, 1827 (Dasami) and Monday, 7th February, 1887 (caturdasi). The next vyaya year corresponds to 1947, which is obviously not possible, since the paper transcript, "Sp" was made in 1943. Among the other four dates, only in the year 1827, the tithi Dvadasi falls on a Thursday in the second half of the month, Tai. (since the date is 26th Tai). But 26th tai is Tuesday Dasami in 1827, in other words, Thurday Dvadasi would be 28th tai. If the date 26th is treated as an error for 28th, then this ms could probably be dated as February 8th 1827.

a. G17 and B13 are the transcripts of G98; G38 and Sp are the transcripts of S07. Hence they are later than G98 and S07 respectively.

b. In the course of collating the manuscripts, it was found that the readings of G86, G89 and G07 were similar to each other in their acceptances, variations and omissions.

c. As stated in 1.2.1, G98 does not have the commentary portion of the text (except for a few repeated portions). T65 and G98 have identical readings at many places, in the original verses.

d. T65 deviates from the mūla of G86 and G89 in some places, but reads closer to them (and not G38 and Sp) in the commentary.

e. Though there are many spelling mistakes in G24, the major variants resemble those seen in T65. (NC 2, comm.38)

f. The readings in V08 are different from those in other manuscripts; it also incorporates the readings of V41 as variants at some places. The rāga section of V08 is almost the same as that of V41 (except for some omissions in both of them). It is in this section that V08 and V41 differ more from other manuscripts.

g. Some readings of G38 and Sp differ from T65, G86 and G89. Some of the readings in these suggest that they have been corrected. Moreover they contain some additional words and certain phrases of colloquial usage, which are absent in other manuscripts. (For example, G38 and Sp add "svara naḍavaḍika" before listing the svara passages for rāga-s)

h. As pointed out in 1.2.14, the text in V08 is not a perfect copy of its original but a partly attempted editorial work. Much cannot be commented upon M and G18 because only a few portions from these are available for collation.

Based on the above observations, the following tree is drawn.

a. T65 and G98 agree at many places and therefore could have come from a common source (A). Among these two, T65 (or atleast the parent of T65) seems to be an earlier one, since it is free from Interpolations and gives better readings. G24 reads closer to T65.

b. G86, G89 and G07 might have come from a common source (B), of which G86 and G89 (both purchased from Tanjore) are very close. Among them, G89 could be the earlier one since a few omissions in G89 are seen written inserted in between the text with a "+" sign in G86. In addition to this, G86 carries a few more scribal errors, which indicates that it belonged to the next stage of transmission. G07 has restored the inserted portions of G86 as part of the text and this too has many scribal errors. Some elementary errors found in G86, have been actually copied in G07.

c. The source for S07, in turn, G38 and Sp (C) is very much different from (A) and (B).

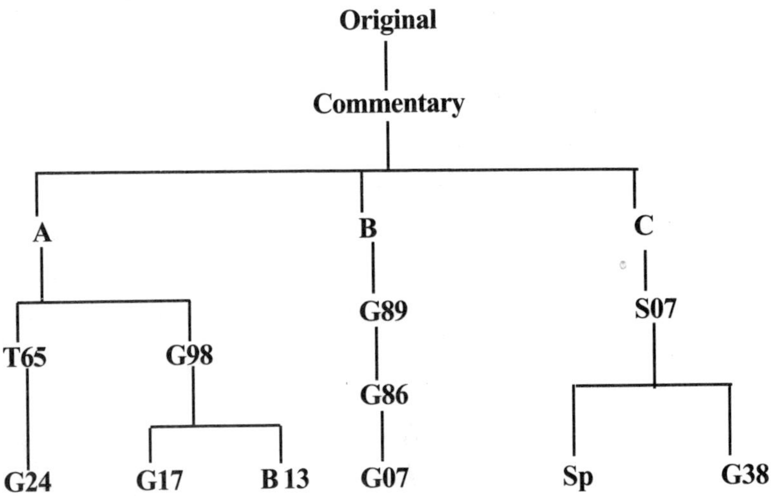

5.4 Archetype

Three manuscripts, namely, T65, G98 and V08 contain the introductory verses and Nāṭyotpatti and among them, the text in G98 is jumbled and V08 is not a true copy of the original manuscript. Hence T65 is chosen as the basic text. Further T65 consists of the first two chapters, with the Gītādhyāya being complete. G86 and G89 contain a complete Gītādhyāya and an incomplete Vādyādhyāya. All other manuscripts are incomplete in one or more chapters/sections. Hence among all manuscripts, T65, G86 and G89 have long sections of the text. Owing to the bad condition of the manuscript, scribal errors and omissions in G86 and G89, T65 is preferred which provides a good continuous text.

With regard to the Vādyādhyāya, four manuscripts, namely, G86, G89, M and V41 (a few verses alone) are available. All are incomplete and have many gaps. But except for a few places, the gap in one manuscript is filled in by the readings of the other. Thus this section is presented as a consolidated version of all the three manuscripts.

5.5 Methodology Adopted for Collation and Edition

* To start with, each half verse found in T65 was treated as a single sentence and serially numbered. Later according to the meaning and context, the verses were numbered. Although most of them are made of four quarters of anuṣṭup, there are some instances with two or six quarters too.
* Since in G98 and G24 the text is jumbled at many places, the corresponding verses were taken from different pages of the manuscript according to the readings of T65 and other manuscripts. The arrangement of verses in T65 coincides with other manuscripts such as G86, G89, G07, G38, Sp and V08, except for a few differences in between due to scribal errors and omissions.
* With respect to the repeated text in G98 and its transcripts, the readings following the Nāṭyotpatti section are treated as the running matter and are noted under the codes, G98, G17 and B13. The repeated portions in each of them (with commentary) are noted as G98a, G17a and B13a respectively. In some cases, where one or two verses are seen twice or thrice in the manuscript at different places, as for instance, the verses in the section on śruti-s, the differences are given with a stroke in between

the two variant readings.

* The physical condition of G89 is very poor and brittle. Many leaves are broken and almost one-third portion of some leaves is not seen. The margins and corners of the manuscript are injured a lot. In between the leaves too, there are more lacunae due to the damage caused by insects. The beginning section upto the Svara-prastāra is worn out while the rāga and the vādya sections are relatively undamaged. Therefore only the rāga and the vādya sections of this manuscript have been consulted.
* Those readings, which could not be read in a manuscript due to damage/ injury and due to lack of clarity, are treated as "lacunae" and marked as "***".
* In a few cases, where the text is missing in T65, the readings of G86 have been taken as the base.
* At some places, the verses are split into quarters and the corresponding commentary is given in between. In these cases, the idea in the original ends with the quarter verse and hence the commentary follows it. While collating, both quarters are taken together and the respective commentary passages combined. A mention regarding this is made in the footnotes.
* Among the 15 manuscripts, the transcripts (G17, B13, V08, M and G18) provide grammatically good readings at a few places. Hence these readings are preferred for the sake of grammar.
* Each verse is numbered serially and the numbering starts afresh in the three chapters. The commentary following a verse is marked "īkā" in the text and "comm. x" in the translation, where x is the verse number that preceded it. The readings in the main text, within [ ] represent the suggestions made by the editor, to restore the text. Some transcripts contain additional readings and these have been duly incorporated.
* The arrangement of the topics in the Gītādhyāya does not follow a logical sequence. Some of the works that were written based on

Somanārya's work, made partial attempts to re-organise the verses. But the order of the main topics follows that of Somanārya's. Hence in the absence of an uddeśa or a table of contents, the text is presented in the same way as found in the original manuscripts.

The following variant readings have been ignored while editing.

a. In the palm-leaf manuscripts like G86, G89, G07 and G24, written in Telugu script, the syllable, "tha" is more often written as "dha."[1] These have been accepted as 'tha' or 'dha' depending on the context.

b. In most of the manuscripts written in Telugu script, (except for the recent transcripts), the syllables "ē" and "ō" are represented as short letters only even in the commentary. That is why, "vēda" reads "veda". These variants have been ignored.

c. Whenever a number is to be indicated, it is noted either in words or in figures. This difference has not been taken into account and the readings in words are preferred.

d. The manuscripts G38 and V41 (transcripts) read all the nouns in Telugu with a suffix, "mu". For instance, 'svaram' or 'svara' as 'svaramu'. Actually, the ausvara "ṃ" is replaced with the letter "mu". Accordingly, the plural forms are read mukhamulu, nētramulu for mukhālu, nētrālu etc. Since the earlier manuscripts are devoid of the syllable "mu", the later readings are not taken. Moreover it is observed continuously in the whole manuscript and hence this reading has not been noted down at each place as a variant reading.

e. In the commentary, whenever the word 'cāta' occurs, G38 and B13 at a few places read 'cēta'. Since 'cāta' is considered to be a colloquial usage, the word 'cēta' has been adopted throughout and has not been

1 The scholars of GOML and TMSSML when questioned about this feature explained that placing dots would damage the leaves. Hence, some palm-leaf Mss are devoid of this syllable. It is said that the "meyyezuttu" (consonants) in Tamiz script, which have a dot on their top, are also written without dots. Similarly when the dot is not placed while writing the letter "ṭha" (hRi) in Telugu script, it would look like "ra"(LRi).

noted as a variant.

f. The word 'jēśi / jēsi' and 'cēsi' have not been properly used in the commentary portion. Hence the appropriate word has been used according to context. The variants in this case has also not been indicated.

g. Single and double strokes are more commonly used in the manuscripts as punctuation marks. Some manuscripts (especially G86, G07) have extra strokes (full stops) after each quarter of a verse (eight syllables) and sometimes even after one-eighth of a verse, that is four syllables. These were not noted down, but only considered for the splitting of the verses.

h. In the commentary, there are many strokes within a sentence. Probably these seem to mean other punctuation marks such as a comma and semicolon. These were retained or rejected, according to context.

5.6 Emendations

Since the manuscripts are highly corrupt and full of scribal errors, the text had to be edited by using methods of both lower and higher textual criticism. Verses conveying parallel ideas are found in a few earlier treatises and some later texts follow Somanārya to a great extent. Besides, the present text is accompanied by a Telugu commentary. Hence the help of the earlier sources, the external testimonia and the commentary, have been used for the purpose of correcting the readings. Whenever a reading is suggested from such sources, it is indicated in the footnotes. The following methods are adopted to edit the text by means of the technique of higher textual criticism:

* Some verses from earlier treatises such as Nāyaśāstra, Dattilam and Nāradīyāśikṣā, are found present verbatim in the NC, although the sources for these verses have not been acknowledged. In such cases, when the manuscripts are corrupt, the parallel readings from the above works have been suggested. For instance, the reading of NC 2,51-52 is based on NS 28,27ab-28ab and 31.

* Though NC resembles SR of Śārṅgadeva at some places, whenever it agrees with the ideas conveyed by SR, the readings of the latter have been suggested. (e.g. NC 2,86-91) But at some places, though the same terms occur, the interpretation is different, thus deviating from the traditional idea. Hence in these cases, the readings from SR were not allowed to replace the manuscript readings (e.g. NC 2, 41, 43).
* A few works written in Saṃskṛta (secondary testimonia) contain extracts and paraphrases of Somanārya's work. The readings from these have been borrowed to fill in the lacunae in the manuscripts (e.g. NC 2,47 based on BKM) and to give grammatically better readings (e.g. NC 2,15 based on BKM).
* Suggestions have also been based on the readings in several later works, which follow the same kind of treatment and speak of similar concepts, as those of Somanārya's. For example, the names of rāga-s were edited on the basis of the readings in ABSS, BKM, RJM, STR, RS etc.
* Readings from SM were also incorporated, since many verses seen in NC are found verbatim in SM. For instance NC 3, 4 is based on SM 1,4, 8ab.
* With regard to the chapter on Vādya-s, many corrupt passages and missing portions have been restored on the basis of ABSS, found as 'extracts' noted under "matāntara" (NC 3, 94-96).
* At a few places, the original text has been reconstructed based on the commentary. In some cases some words of the original text (in Saṃskṛta) were found mixed with the commentary. This was helpful in restoring the original text (e.g. NC 2,75).
* Some passages of the commentary have been restored on the basis of the original text (NC 2, comm.41) and the testimonia (NC 2,comm.76). However, when the commentary differed widely from the original, the readings of the latter have not been forcibly imposed on the commentary. This has been the approach adopted when dealing with the names of thirty-two rāga-s (NC 2,154), defects of singers (NC

2,176) and so on.

* Conjectures have been made at a few places (NC 2,93), where parallel readings did not exist in the earlier works as well as later works like BKM and RJM. Suggestions have also been made to correct readings, where the original verses did not conform to metrical rules (NC 2,79ab).
* Some peculiar usage of technical terms is observed in the commentary. Although it does not agree with the accepted musicological understanding, the terms have been retained uncorrected. For example, the usage of the terms, svara for śruti (NC 2,comm.49), madhyama for madhya (register) (NC 2,comm.44).
* The text is on the whole grammatically defective. There is total confusion in the description of the rāga-s, which are mainly classified according to gender. Neither the names of the rāga-s nor their descriptions are made in accordance with proper gender, as normally followed in Saṃskṛta texts. Since an attempt to restore this, would result in the total re-organisation and reconstruction of the verses, the same has not been done. However in the place of the nouns in feminine gender, found with short vowel endings, long ones have been suggested.
* At a few places, the verses have been shifted or moved in order to get continuity in meaning. Firstly, the commencing verse of the Gītādhyāya was defective in its construction and incomplete in meaning. A similar verse with a slightly different construction was found again at the commencement of the section on rāga-s and it was moved to the beginning of Gītādhyāya. Secondly, verse 46 and the corresponding commentary were originally found after verse 85. Since they should logically come in continuation to verse 45 (both being the citations from Dattilam, 8 and 9) they were shifted thus. Thirdly, in the Vādya section, verse 38 along with the commentary, which should be found at the beginning, was found at the end of the description. They have been shifted in order to get continuity.

5.7 Interpolations in the Manuscripts

The insertion of a word, a line, or a passage within the text of a manuscript, is termed as "Interpolation" (Khatre, 1954:94). In some of the manuscripts presently consulted, a few portions occur in between the text, but are out of context. This includes insertion of one or two words, verses in some cases, and bigger sections in a few others. The occurrence of bigger passages or sections, alone is being discussed here. Other smaller portions, like a word, a verse and a few sentences are given in footnotes and discussed in the textual notes. Interpolated passages occur in the manuscripts G98 (and its transcripts), G91 and G38 & Sp (Saurashtra Sabha manuscripts).

5.7.1 G98 and its transcripts (G17 & B13)

As stated earlier, G98 contains some verses, which are not part of NC and they are not found in other NC manuscripts. Such suspicious sections include

a. some verses resembling SR of Śārṅgadeva,
b. a few verses from some unknown text(s).
c. verses delineating the names of 72 melakartā-s.

The verses resembling SR deal with alaṅkāra, tāna etc. and are found from the line 6 of p.6 to line 2 of p.8. The section containing the names of the 72 melakartā-s, are found from the 8th line of p.11, to the 8th line of p.12. These names resemble those found in works like Saṅgrahacūḍāmaṇi, Saṅgītasārasaṅgrahamu, Rāgalakṣaṇa[1] and Mahābharatacūḍāmaṇi. The list of melakartā-s in the manuscript ends with,

"rasikapriyamelaśca iti rāgadhikārakāḥ ||"

which is followed by the phrase, "melotpatti rāganāmāni ucyante". The word "melotpattirāga", here, probably denotes melakartā. N S Ramachandran has noticed the occurrence of the names of the melakartā-s, in this manuscript.

1. Edited by D K Joshi, Poona, 1914.

(Ramachandran, 1938:41).

5.7.2 G91

This manuscript contains 35 pages. The text found from the penultimate line of the first page to the end of p.34, is an interpolation. This section, which is entirely in Telugu language and script, is found inserted abruptly in the text corresponding to NC 2, 22 and NC 2, 23. In the first page, it reads thus:

> *"śabdolabdasu saṅgītaḥ. yedante yasca jī ****** vikṛta madhyamaṃ. prati madhyamaṃ. cyuta *** "*

Then in p.35, it reads,
"*** ṅgaṃ pluta mēruvaku caturthaṃ varjaṃ varjaṃ kindi lekka gūrci vrāśēdi. ikanu jāti prastārālaku vivaraṃ. * *[vanamandu]nanndu kanuvu tini nīḷḷutāgiyuṇḍē mṛgavaśyādulu. panalagā pirigānam cini ** ndoṣamaiyyuṇḍunu.. ślokaṃ|| kṛṣṇasarpāpitaṃ nādaṃ"

From "vanamandu kanuvu tini", quoted above, the text corresponds to NC (NC comm.11). In fact the text continues from where it broke off in the penultimate line of p.1 of the manuscript. The interpolated text speaks of different varieties of svara-s based on twenty-four śruti-s and seems to present a scheme of 264 (?) mela-s. Then it deals with seven śuddha svara-s, nine vikṛta svara-s, sixteen svara-s being placed on twelve houses, thirty-six śuddha-madhyama mela-s and thirty-six prati-madhyama mela-s and tāla-prastāra. Somanārya's work does not deal with the mela system; the portions on tāla and tāla-prastāra are also not found to have any resemblance to the work, "Tāladaśaprāṇaprakaraṇam" (which is stated to be a portion taken from SRS). The contents of this interpolated passage are not found in any other manuscripts and are extraneous to Somanārya's scheme of topics on music. As for instance, mela-s and tāla-prastāra do not come within the scope of his work.

Hence this entire section should have probably formed a part of another work. Since the interpolated section begins from the middle of a page in this manuscript and terminates in the middle of another page, it is quite likely that the interpolation was present in the exemplar from which this copy was made.

5.7.3 G38, Sp

As pointed out earlier (in 1.2.10 & 1.2.11), G38 and Sp are two paper transcripts of a palm-leaf manuscript (S07) from Saurashtra Sabha, Madurai. In both, the text of Somanārya begins after a few pages. The pages preceding the text contain the following topics-

Prakṛti- vikṛti svara-s,
Names of the 72 melakartā-s
List of janya rāga-s born from the mela-s
Lakṣaṇa-s of a few melakartā-rāga-s and janyarāga-s.

As mentioned in the case of the previous manuscript, these topics do not fall within the scheme of Somanārya's work. The actual text of NC begins with the topic of vādī and samvādī in G38 and Sp. It is curious to see that at the beginning (i.e., at the commencement of the interpolated passage), as well as at the beginning of the text of Somanārya, the invocatory phrase, "śubhamastu", which usually marks the beginning of a work, is seen. This feature also occurs in the exemplar palm-leaf manuscript (S07). However, in S07, the first (interpolated) section ends incompletely on the front side of the fourth folio and the reverse side of fol.4 is left blank. The section from vādī-samvādī, begins afresh from the next folio, with the marginal heading, "śubhamastu". Thus it can be inferred that the melakartā-janyarāga section, probably exists as a different incomplete work in the codex and the copyists of G38 and Sp must have copied both the portions together.

Towards the end of the Gītādhyāya, after the colophon statement, there are a few verses and prose passages in these transcripts. These deal with svaramaṇḍala and svara-s. These verses too are not found in the NC manuscripts and are regarded as interpolations.

6. Analysis of the Work

The NC of Somanarya is composed of Saṃskṛta verses and this has been commented upon in Telugu. Most of the verses are in anuṣup metre (8 syllables in a quarter) while very few are in different metres like indravajrā (11 syllables), vasantatilakā (14 syllables) and śārdūlavikrīḍitā (19 syllables).

6.1 Extent of the work

The work is spread over three main chapters. They are:

a. A fragmentary chapter on nāṭya
b. A complete chapter on Gīta
c. An almost complete (?) chapter on vādya

a. A fragmentary chapter on nāṭya consists of 18 verses.

The work begins with an invocation to Sitārāma, the preceptor of the author, Somanārya and lists many authorities on music. The author states that the work is being written in a condensed form by gathering the concepts from many treatises. This is followed by a note on the origin of nāṭya.

b. A complete chapter on Gīta consisting of 189 verses.

The Gītādhyāya deals with the elements of music, such as, nāda, svara, śruti, grama, mūrcchanā, rāga, gāyaka and the prabandha.

c. An almost complete (?) chapter on vādya consisting of 111 verses

Instruments are classified into five types; structural details and their playing methods are mentioned.

The following table gives the details of the portions of the work that are available from each of the manuscripts towards the edition of NC. NC-1 in this table represents the first chapter on Nāṭya, NC-2, the chapter on Gīta and NC-3, the chapter on Vādya. When a manuscript does not contain a particular chapter it is marked "-".

ms.	NC-1	NC-2	NC-3
G98	1-18	2-32, 34, 36-38ab, 39, 40cd-41, 43, 46-48ab, 51-54, 56-58ab, 59-60, 62, 64-69, 71-95, 98-101cd, 102, 103cd-106, 109-113, 132, 155-158ab, 159-160, 161cd 166, 178-189ab, 180-184ab, 185cd-186	-
G17	1-18	As in G98	
B13	1-18	As in G98	
T65	1-18	1-106, 109-114, 116-118, 119cd-126, 127cd-178, 180-184ab, 185-189	
G86	-	1-68cd, 69-95, 97-106, 108-114, 116-120ab, 121cd-154, 161-168, 169cd-189	1-48, 55ef-89comm
G89	-	1,97-106, 108-114, 116-120ab, 121cd-126, 127cd-154, 161-168, 169cd-171comm., 172ab comm. - 175, 176cd-189	1-39ab, 40cd- 48 55ef- 89 comm
G07	-	1-13, 15-68comm.	-
G91	-	1-13	-
G24	-	5-19, 22-34, 36, 40-54comm.	-
Sp	-	1, 89cd-121ab, 123-127ab, 129cd-189	-
G38	-	1, 89cd-121ab, 123-127ab, 129cd-189	-
V41	-	1-8, 9cd-13ab, 14-19, 104-112, 131-148	10-18ab, 20-25
G18	-	(13-38ab), 40cd-58ab, 63cd-77, 78-80	-
V08	1-18	1ab, 2-34, 40ab-57, 59-64cd, 65-74 78-81, 97-101cd, 102ab, 107-114ab, 117-118, 127cd-128ab, 129-132, 155-156cd,	

		157-158ab, 159-160	-
M	9-18	1-2ab, 3-7 68, 79-8 2ab, 84- 85ab, 86cd-110	2cd-25, 29-

6.2 Summary of contents

The following is only a brief summary of the contents of the work, NC. Detailed discussion of the various concepts is given in 6.4 below

6.2.1 Nāya (NC-1)

Gāndharva is distinguished into three types, namely, Gīta, Vādya and Nartana and Nartana is said to be of three kinds, namely, nāṭya, nṛtta and nṛtya. The origin of Nāṭyavēda and its greatness are then mentioned in the same way as seen in the beginning of the seventh chapter of the SR of Śārṅgadeva. With this, the text proceeds to the Gītādhyāya.

6.2.2 Gītādhyāya (NC-2)

6.2.2.1 Nāda

The Gītādhyāya begins with the definition of the term, nāda, as the combination of nṛtta, gīta and vādya. It is two fold- āhata and anāhata; āhata is produced by the union of two (prāṇa and agni) and anāhata is said to originate from the sky. They are related to ārohiṇi and avarohiṇi respectively. Nāda is said to be manifest or known through the seven svara-s, ṣaḍja, ṛṣabha, gāndhāra, madhyama, pañcama, dhaivata and niṣāda.

6.2.2.2 The greatness of gīta

Saṅgīta is defined as the music produced by the voice, through the svara-s which are placed on instruments like vīṇā, Next the greatness of Gīta is expounded, which closely resembles SR.

6.2.2.3 Svara

Svara-s are associated with many extra-musical attributes (See Appendix-1); the prastāra of the svara-s are said to be born through condensing and expanding (vyasta and samasta). A few svara passages are illustrated under prastāra, the meanings of which are however not clear.

6.2.2.4 The production of nāda

The subject goes back to nāda. Svara-s are said to be produced from the navel, chest, throat, head and mouth regions of man.[1] In these five regions they are atisūkṣma, sūkṣma, puṣṭa, atipuṣṭa and tāra. The svara-s are said to be located in the navel, chest, throat, mouth, base of the tongue, head and cheeks of human beings.

6.2.2.5 Sthāna - Śruti

The nāda[2] is said to be three fold- mandra, madhya and tāra respectively when produced from the chest, throat and head. Further, the svara-s, sa and ri are mandra, ga and ma are madhya, pa, dha and ni are tāra. The mandra sound becomes twenty-two distinguishable pitches and the same becomes sixty-six in madhya and tāra regions. The twenty-two sound positions (śruti-s) are distributed among the svara-s thus: sa-4, ri-3, ga-2, ma-4, pa-4, dha-3, ni-2.

6.2.2.6 Grāma, Mūrcchanā

The names of twenty-one mūrcchanā-s pertaining to three grāma-s are listed (as seen in works like NS etc.). Grāma is defined as the collection of svara-s; the ascent and the descent of the svara-s are called mūrcchanā. It is said that ṣaḍja should be sung as the first and the last svara in each sthāna. Seven svara-s, three grama-s, twenty-one mūrcchanā-s and forty-nine tāna-s are said to constitute the Svaramaṇḍalam. Grāma-s are said to be three in number, namely ṣaḍja-grāma, madhyama-grāma and gāndhāra-grāma and

1. However in the commentary it is navel, chest, throat mouth and head.
2. The commentator interprets nāda as svara.

seven mūrcchanā-s are based on each of them thus:

[1]s r g m p d n - ṣaḍja grāma
m g n s r d p - madhyama grāma
g d r p s m n - gāndhāra grāma

6.2.2.7 Śruti

Śruti is defined as the small pitch, which is just discernible by the ear. It is the gradual rise in the pitch from the mandra to the tāra region.

6.2.2.8 Ten kinds of svara-s

Ten kinds of (movements of?) svara-s, namely sthāyī, svara, sañcārī, āyataṃ, pratyāyataṃ, kampitaṃ, yeḍupu, ḍālu, ugraṃ and muktā are defined. However there are slight variations between the definitions found in the mūla and in the commentary (See 6.4.3 below).

6.2.2.9 Ten embellishments and defects of svara-s

Ten embellishments of svara-s (of Gīta according to works like SR), namely, vyaktaṃ, pūrṇaṃ, prasannaṃ, sukumāraṃ, alaṅkṛtaṃ, samaṃ, suraktaṃ, ślakṣṇṭaṃ, niṣkṛṣaṃ and madhuraṃ and the ten defects such as lokaduṣaṃ, śāstraduṣaṃ, śrutivirodhaṃ, kālavirodhaṃ, punaruktaṃ, gītabāhyaṃ, gatakramaṃ, apārthaṃ, grāmyaṃ and sandigdhaṃ are explained.

6.2.2.10 Eighteen śruti-s

NC speaks of a new concept of eighteen śruti-s, distributed over the seven svara-s. The names of the śruti-s are, nābhikā, atharvaṇī, dastā, aurvī, aticadhā, kambalī, śrīvikā, saralī, nālī, rasanī, rañjanī, ghrāṇinī, pavanī, mandā, maurddhvā, viḍambinī, bhīṣaṇī and sphurantī. Accordingly, sa rests on 3 śruti-s, ri on 2 śruti-s, ga on 4 śruti-s, ma on 2 śruti-s, pa on 3 śruti-

1. This interpretation is found only in the commentary.

s, dha on 2 śruti-s and ni on 2 śruti-s.

6.2.2.11 Grāma (again)

The presiding deities, habitat and the seasons ascribed to the singing of the grāma-s are given.

6.2.2.12 Śruti-jāti-s

Five jāti-s of śruti-s and the jāti-s constituting each of the seven svara-s are mentioned following SR, but the names like tīvrā, kumudvatī are not found.

6.2.2.13 Vādī, Samvādī, Vivādī and Anuvādī svara-s

The four kinds of svara-s, namely vādī, samvādī, vivādī and anuvādī are then spoken of. Vādī is defined as the king and stands for the svara-s in the ascent, (srgmpdns,[1] rgmpdns, gmpdns, mpdns, pdns, dns, ns). The Samvādī svara is called the minister and stands for the svara-s in the descent ([2]sndpmgrs, ndpmgrs, dpmgrs, pmgrs, mgrs, grs, rs). The Vivādī svara is called an enemy and stands for the svara phrases like, smgr-srgm, rpmg-rgmp, gdpm-gmpd, mndp-mpdn, psnd-pdns. The Anuvādī svara is called a friend and stands for the svara-s occuring in the following manner - srg, rgm, gmp, mpd, pdn, dns, snd, ndp, dpm, pmg, mgr, grs.[3]

6.2.2.14 Rāga

Rāga is defined as the collection of the svara-s. Two kinds of ālipti, rāgālipti and rūpālipti, kūatāna, apūrṅa and pūrṅa are defined.

6.2.2.15 Classification of rāga-s

Rāga-s are classified into three kinds, namely śuddha, mitra and saṅkīrṇa. Śuddha rāga-s are thirty-two in number, mitra rāga-s are sixty-four and the

1. Obviously the last svara should be that of the upper octave.
2. Obviously the first svara should be that of the upper octave
3. This kind of an interpretation in terms of svara-s is found only in the commentary.

saṅkīrṇa rāga-s are said to be innumerable. Thirty-two śuddha rāga-s are constituted by eight masculine rāga-s and twenty-four feminine rāga-s. These thirty-two rāga-s are classified into ṣāḍava, auḍava and sampūrṇa, based on the number of svara-s occurring in each of them.

The characteristics of the rāga-s are defined in terms of their ādi-svara (the note on which the musical piece set in a rāga commences, same as graha svara) and the varjya svara (the note to be omitted). Rāga-s are also classified, based on their names (same suffices). Like the seven svara-s, the eight masculine rāga-s too are associated with many extra musical attributes (See Appendix-2). Rāga-s are further classified according to the time suitable for rendering. Thus some rāga-s are to be sung during sunrise, some in the evenings and so on.

6.2.2.16 Varieties of singers and their blemishes

Singers are classified in to three categories, ekala, yamala and bṛnda. Singers with twenty-five kinds of defects are specified.

6.2.2.17 Musical Forms

Definitions for the terms (musical forms?) like, gīta, prabandha, sūlādi, nāmāvalī, cūrṇikā and nāṭakam are then given.

6.2.3 Vādyādhyāya

Instruments are classified into five types, namely, those born of nails, wind, skin, metal and the human body (voice). Names of instruments found in NC are:

stringed	vīṇā, kinnarī, daṇḍī, tumbura, rajābu, kāmākṣī, rāvaṇahasta
wind	muralī, mukhavīṇā, nāgasara, devasara, śaṅkha, kāhala, upāṅga, caṅgu
skin	mṛdaṅga, ḍhakkā, ḍholu, bhērī, ḍamāmī, gaḍibiḍi, tamukku
metallic	kāṃsyatāla, jākaṭa (?)

Structure and playing methods are briefly given for some of the instruments. The text then ends abruptly.

6.3 Organisation of the Work

Generally most of the technical treatises contain "uddēśa" or the table of contents, at the beginning, wherein the different chapters and the topics to be covered in each of them are listed. For example, Bharatabhāṣya lists the contents of all the chapters in verses 11-66 of the first chapter. Similar information is also noted in works like Saṅgītaratnākara (SR 1,1,31-49ab) Saṅgītasūryodaya (SSur 1,19-44cd), Svaramelakalānidhi (SMK 1,37-47) and Caturdaṇḍīprakāśikā (CDP 1,3cd-6ab). There are also a few works, which are devoid of this kind of information like Saṅgītamakaranda of Nārada.

The colophon statements found at the end of the chapters or sections of chapters sometimes describe the number and name of the chapter, as for instance at the end of each paricchēda in the Saṅgītanārāyaṇa of Gajapatinārāyaṇa. But NC lacks all such information. Neither the 'uddēśa' nor any colophon statements indicating the end of chapters are found in it. At the end of the available chapter on Nātya, after nātyotpatti, the text abruptly ends and moves to Gītādhyāya with the statement, "atha gītādhyāyam vakṣyatē". The sections on rāga and vādya begin with the phrases, "atha rāgaḥ" and "atha vādyaḥ" respectively. Except for the colophon, mentioning the end of the Gītādhyāya in the commentary, there is no other proper indication regarding the commencement or the ending of the chapters. Hence it is very difficult to establish the number and the name of the chapters.

NC also lacks a logical sequence in dealing with topics. Since only very little portion is available in the nāṭya chapter, much could not be commented upon. But the arrangement of the topics in the Gītādhyāya does not seem to follow a logical sequence. At some places, there is no continuity in the text and it is characterised by interference from earlier works. It is also noted that a particular subject, which has been dealt with earlier, occurs again at a later place. e.g., Grāma (NC 2,56-58 and again NC 2,82-85).

The order of topics varies at some places from works like SR of Śārṅgadeva. For instance, śruti is taken up first and is then followed by svara in SR, but here svara comes first. While dealing with the svara too, the description relating to the four kinds of svara-s namely, vādī, samvādī, anuvādī and vivādī is given first and the attributes are listed later in SR. But NC reads the attributes in the beginning and the concepts of śrutijāti, vādī etc., almost at the end of the section on svara.

The NC reading (NC 2,86-87) resembling SR,1,3,25cd-31ab appears to be out of place in this context. In SR these verses occur after the definition of the term, svara, (svara-s are said to be caused by śruti-s) and is followed by the discussion on the cause of the svara-s. NC does not speak of the svara-s being caused by the śruti-s. Hence in the absence of the verse,

> *śrutyantarabhāvī yaḥ snigdho'nuraṇanātmakaḥ |*
> *svato rañjayati śrotṛcittaṃ sa svara ucyatē ||*
>
> (SR 1.3.24cd-25ab)

the occurrence of verses dealing with the discussion on the śruti-s being the cause of svara-s, appears to be meaningless. Probably these verses might have existed in the original NC but were missing in the exemplar that was available to the commentator. Hence the verse cited above from SR cannot be suggested. But the available verses following them had to be corrected based on SR readings.

When the later works influenced by Somanārya are observed, it is seen that BKM and RJM had made an attempt to overcome a few displacements in the order of the text. These works read vādī, samvādī etc., soon after the attributes of the svara-s. But MBC is more precise in retaining the format of NC, for the description of vādī, samvādī etc. is seen only at the end of the section on svara. The arrangement of other topics is almost identical in all the works and they follow NC. In order to present the text of NC in its original form as seen in the manuscripts (as intended by the author/commentator), reorganisation of topics has not been attempted.

The chapter on vādya is slightly better in this respect. In the beginning verses, the instruments are classified into five types and the commentary following them lists the various instruments under each category. The description of the individual instruments follows this order to a great extent.

6.4 Analysis of the Contents

A brief summary of the contents of the edited text, NC is already given in 6.2 above. The following is an assessment of the musicological contents of the mūla, which can be grouped under four categories.

a. Readings from earlier sources
b. Different Interpretations of the traditional concepts
c. New Concepts or Information
d. Ambiguous passages

Each of them is being discussed below.

6.4.1 Readings from Earlier Sources

At the commencement, Somanārya states that the work (NC) is compiled by gathering the concepts from the earlier authorities (bharatakartāraḥ). Citations from works like Dattilam, Nāradīyāśikṣā and Saṅgītaratnākara are seen in NC without acknowledgement. While some of the cited verses are identical to those found in the earlier works, there are some changes in others. The musicological concepts that have been adopted from the earlier sources are:

a. Three grāma-s
b. Twenty-two śruti-s
c. Five śruti jāti-s
d. Excellences (guṇa) and blemishes (doṣa) of gīta (but here mentioned for svara-s)
e. Types of singers

f. Defects of singers

6.4.2 Different Interpretations

NC speaks of some well-known concepts found in the Saṅgītaśāstra-s, but interprets them in a different manner. Some of them are discussed below.

6.4.2.1 Definition of the term Nāda

In most of the works, gīta, vādya and nṛtta are collectively termed, 'saṅgīta'. But NC refers to the combination of these three as 'nāda' (NC 2,2ab). The usage of the term 'nāṭda' in the mūla probably denotes an art form but the commentator regards it as a musical sound obtained by the combination of the three elements. Kavi's suggestion of 'nāya' for nāda in his manuscript copy (V08) appears to be pertinent. Since in the Saṅgītaratnākara of Śārṅgadeva, the term saṅgīta especially when classified as mārga and deśī, is synonymous with nāta. At a different place (NC 2,8) however 'Saṅgīta' is defined thus: "Saṅgīta is created through the sound produced by the nāda, when the svara-s are drawn and placed on the instruments like vīṇā."

6.4.2.2 Five stages of production of svara-s

Normally, five stages are identified in the process of the production of nāda, from its conception to its external manifestation as sound. The terms used in the musicological texts for referring to these five stages are atisūkṣma, sūkṣma, puṣṭa, atipuṭa and kṛtrima. But NC substitutes the term, tāra for kṛtrima (NC 2, 41). Again, these five stages of sound production have not been considered for nāda but for svara. This usage can also be seen in SM 1,4,17. It is curious that SM also refers to the five stages of sound production of nāda with kṛtrima (SM 1,4,16).

6.4.2.3 Vādī, samvādī, anuvādī and vivādī svara-s

The four kinds of svara-s namely, vādī, samvādī, anuvādī and vivādī are found in many works. The roles that these svara-s play in a melody are equated with the functioning or behaviour of a king, minister, friend and enemy respectively and are usually described in terms of the intervals of śruti-s between svara-s. In NC, though analogy between the svara-s and the king, minister and so on is given, the characteristics of these types of svara-s are presented differently (NC 2,94-95). Vādī is defined as the svara-s in ascent; samvādī as the svara-s in descent; anuvādī as the succeeding svara-s (in a sequence) and vivādī as the svara-s striking each other. Illustrations to these are found only in the commentary thus:

vādī:	'srgmpdn', 'rgmpdns' and so on upto 'dns', 'ns'
samvādī:	'sndpmgrs', 'ndpmgrs' and so on upto 'grs', 'rs' anuvādī:
	'srg', 'rgm', 'gmp' etc., upto 'mgr,' 'grs'.
vivādī:	'smgr-srgm','rpmg-rgmp' etc., upto 'psnd-pdns'.

This kind of interpreting vādī, samvādī etc., is totally novel and untraditional, but surprisingly, this has been faithfully adopted in many works written in Saṃskṛta, Telugu and Tamiz in the South, even till the twentieth century (See Section 7 below).

6.4.2.4 Ālipti

Ālipti is a term that consistently occurs in NC and adopted by later works like BKM, RJM and SSB. Two varieties of ālipti, namely rāgālipti and rūpālipti are mentioned (NC 2,98). These terms obviously suggest that they are distortions or modifications of the terms that occur in earlier works, namely, ālapti, rāgālapti and rūpālapti. It is not clear why the earlier terms underwent such a transformation.

6.4.2.5 Aṅga-s of a Prabandha

In the Saṃskṛta textual tradition, prabandha is said to consist of six aṅga-s namely, svara, biruda, pada, tēnaka, pāṭa and tāla. NC too speaks of prabandha, but mentions vākya as an aṅga, instead of tāla (NC 2,183), which again is an unusual substitution. It is to be noted that even BKM, RJM and SSB adopt this in the same manner.

6.4.3 New Concepts

NC introduces some new concepts, which are not noticed in the textual tradition that is commonly followed. In fact most of these terms belong to the common textual tradition but the concepts they represent in NC are different. It is surprising to note that many of these have been followed by works like BKM, RJM, SSB and MBC. Some of the new concepts are explained below:

(a) Āhatanāda is related to ascent (āroha) and Anāhatanāda to descent (avaroha). (NC 2,6cd)

(b) Svara-s and rāga-s are associated with many extra musical attributes. (NC 2,13-37 & NC 2,133-154) In earlier works svara-s are found to be associated with attributes like lineage, caste, colour, continent, sage, deity, metre and rasa (SR 1,3,52-59). But in NC, one finds as many as twenty-eight attributes for the svara-s and twenty-four for the rāga-s[1] Apart from the ones mentioned above (lineage, caste, etc.) NC and other works specify the number of faces, eyes, ears, arms, nostrils, feet for the svara-s; further they are associated with food, garment, tree, flower, ornament, star, zodiac, day and the like. (Sathyanarayana, 1984:107-23)

(c) The seven svara-s (ṣaḍja, ṛṣabha etc.) are related to mandra, madhya and tāra (sthāna-s) (NC 2,44). Thus the svara-s 'sa' and 'ri' are referred to as mandra, 'ga' and 'ma' as madhya and 'pa', 'dha' and 'ni' as tāra. Except for the relationship of pitch levels, the significance of the underlying connection is not clear.

(d) The svara 'sa' is said to be uttered in the beginning and at the end during ascent and descent (NC 2,54) This probably reflects the development

1 .See Appendix:-2 for the various attributes found in the Mss of NC, BKM, RJM and MBC

in the performing tradition, where singing scales in ascent and descent, commencing and ending with 'sa', had come into practice.

(e) *Svarālaṅkāra:* The repeated occurrence of the svara-s (mūrcchanā-s) in a particular order is called svarālaṅkāra (NC 2,59). This suggests that the earlier concept of alaṅkāra reflected in works like SR had changed by the time of NC. The commentary gives the following illustration: srgmgr-srgr-srgm, which is specified for the dhruvatāla alaṅkāra in CDP (CDP 3,91)

(f) *Ten varieties of svara-s*: The text speaks of ten varieties of svara-s (NC 2,63-67). They are sthāyī, svara, sañcārī, āyataṃ, pratyāyataṃ, kampitaṃ, yeḍupu, ḍālu, ugraṃ and muktā. They are defined thus:

sthāyī	Commencing the sound from a mandra svara
svara	Commencing the sound from a tāra svara
sañcārī	When a svara moves in the mandra, madhya and tāra regions
āyataṃ, pratyāyataṃ	Svara-s that manifest separately and frequently in the mandra and other regions, in the ascent and in the descent.
kampitaṃ	Quick movement of the svara-s in the three registers (as per mūla)/ the svara-s are rendered with gamaka in the mandra, madhya and tāra regions (as per ṭīkā).
yeḍupu	When a svara stays for a long duration in the three registers
ḍālu	If the svara-s pervade the three (registers), for a short and a long duration (as per mūla) / That which makes the svara-s to shine and move fast in three places (sthāna-s) (as per ṭīkā).
ugraṃ	Commencing from a svara in the madhyama (region)
muktaṃ	The conclusion of the svara-s present (as per mūla)/ making the svara-s, shine as the concluding ones (as per ṭīkā).

Some of these terms occur in treatises in other contexts, but here the concepts they represent are quite new. The definitions of the svara varieties are not very clear and they suggest the characteristics of a svara, in terms of

i. the region, where a svara commences (sthāyī, svara, ugraṃ)
ii. the region(s) where a svara manifests or shines (sañcārī, muktā, yeḍupu, ḍālu)
iii. movement of a svara (kampitaṃ)
iv. duration of a svara (āyataṃ, pratyāyataṃ yeḍupu, ḍālu)

(g) Eighteen śruti-s: Another concept exclusively found in NC and followed in the later works influenced by Somanārya is 'Eighteen śruti-s' (NC 2,78-80). The mūla and the commentary first speak of the twenty-two śruti-s, their distribution among the seven svara-s (4 - 3 - 2 - 4 - 4 - 3 - 2) and becoming sixty-six varieties in three registers. Later 'Eighteen śruti-s' are prescribed for the seven svara-s. Names have been given for twenty-two śruti-s and can be seen in works like Saṅgītarājā (SRaj 2,1,1,70-73) and Saṅgītasudhā (SSud 1,119-140). However the names given for the eighteen śruti-s (see table below) are totally different. So it is not clear whether these Eighteen śruti-s also denoted tonal measures or something else.

The names of Eighteen śruti-s are found in BKM, RJM and MBC. According to Bharatakośa, 'Hanuman mata' speaks of this concept (Brhaspati, 1966:32). Kavi has furnished the names of these eighteen śruti-s in Bharatakośa in different pages, according to the alphabetical order. The following table lists the names of the eighteen śruti-s as mentioned in various works.

NC	**MBC**	**BKM**	**RJM**	**Hanuman mata**
nābhikā	nābikā	nābhikā	nābhikā	nābhikā
atharvaṇī	atarvani	atharvaṇī	atharva	atharviṇī
dastā	dastā	dastā	dastā	dhasā
aurvī	mauravi	caurī/ cavurī	??(caja urya)	cautī

aticadhā	avati	ati	ati	aticaudhī
kambalī	kambili	kambalī	kambalī	kambalī
śrivikā	śrivikā	śravikā	śrivikā	śravikā
saralī	sarali	saralī	saralī	saraṇī
nālī	nāli	nālī	nālī	nālī
rasanī	rasani	rasanī	rasanī	rasanī
rañjanī	rañjani	rañjanī	rañjanī	rañjanī
ghrāṇinī	kuruni	ghrāṇanī	ghrāṇanī	dhrāṇinī
pavanī	pa(pa)ni	padhanī	padhanī	pathanī
mandā	mandā	mandā	mandā	mandrā
maurddhvā	maurtta maurddhavī	[maurttavi?]	maurdhāvī	maurdhā
viḍambinī	vigati[gati?]		kambī	kambī
vikalpinī				
bhīṣaṇī	pakṣaṇī	bhāṣiṇī	bhāṣiṇī	bhāṣiṇī
sphurantī	sphurantī	svarantī	svaranti	svaritī

h) *Classification of Rāga-s:* Rāga-s are classified into three types namely, Śuddha, Mitra and Saṅkīrṇa, the definitions of which are not very clear (NC 2,101-103). These definitions are also found in SM (SM 1,4,52-53). The śuddha rāga-s are 32 in number; mitra rāga-s 64 and the saṅkīrṇa rāga-s infinite. The thirty-two śuddha-rāga-s include eight masculine rāga-s and twenty-four feminine rāga-s. The author relates these three varieties, namely, śuddha, mitra and saṅkīrṇa rāga-s to śuddha, sālaga and saṅkara varieties. Incidentally, the śuddha, sālaga and saṅkīrṇa classification of rāga-s is seen in Aumāpatam and later works.

(i) *Musical Forms:* Definitions are given for some musical forms like Gīta, Sūlādi, Nāmāvali, Cūrnīkā and Nāṭakam; the same are also found in BKM, RJM and SSB. They are defined thus:

a. *Gīta:* singing using the svara-s and rāga-s, with the text based on eight languages and incorporating the "jhaṅkāra" sound (NC 2,181).

b. *Sūlādi*: singing of the svara-s and rāga-s, with the seven tāla-s, dhruva and others and the text based on all languages (NC 2,187).
c. *Nāmāvali*: singing of words from the vēda-s (NC 2,188ab)
d. *Cūrnīka*: singing saṃskṛta in the form of sentences (NC 2,188cd)
e. *Nāṭakaṃ:* use of cūrnīka, prose and verse and rendering of a song relating to a story (NC 2,189ab).

NC is probably the first work in defining these terms in this manner.

(j) Instruments: Description of stringed instruments such as Daṇḍī, (two-stringed) (NC 3,10-19) and Tumbura with seven strings (NC 3,21-25) and wind instruments such as Nāgasara and Devasara (NC 3,38-57) are found in this work. Although the text is not very clear, this work is probably the first one in describing these instruments. Saṅgītapārijāta mentions a stringed instrument by the name Daṇḍī, (SP 2,65-66) but this does not resemble the one mentioned in NC.

Saṅgītapārijāta (SP 2, 47-51) also speaks of a stringed instrument, "Tamburam" and two kinds of it, 'nibadha' and 'anibaddha' and again the descriptions do not coincide with NC. There is an extract from "Nārāyaṇa" on Tumbarī, seen in Bharatakośa, (Kavi, 1951:242-243), which is however not found in the printed text of Saṅgītanārāyaṇa. The description found in this extract too, is different from NC. Regarding Nāgasara, reference is made in Saṅgītapārijāta (SP 2,148-149), but is very brief and seems to be different from what is given in NC.

6.4.4 Ambiguous passages

Some verses found in the Vādya chapter, seem to be out of context, but cannot be treated as Interpolations. One deals with the characteristics of the instrument Maurī and another deals with 'vādyalakṣaṇa'. It is not very clear which instrument is being referred to here. The former is seen in all the three manuscripts, namely G86, G89 and M and the latter in G86 and G89. These two passages are being placed at the end of the edited text of NC as anubandha and the reasons are given below.

6.4.4.1 Characteristics of Maurī

NC speaks of eighteen kinds of instruments, namely, vīṇā, kinnarī, daṇḍī, tumbura, muralī, mukhavīṇā, maurī, nāgasara, devasara, śaṅkha, kāhala, upāṅga, mṛdaṅga, ḍhakkā, ḍholu, bhērī, ḍamāmī and kāṃsyatāla. Of these eighteen, vīṇā and kinnarī have not been elaborately discussed. The treatment of the other sixteen instruments includes the description of their structure, presiding-deities of various parts, playing methods, positions of the hands and invocatory verses for a few. The entire section is commented upon in Telugu. At the end of the description, the name Somanārya or Somanātha occurs, thereby establishing the authenticity of the passage. But four instruments are ascribed to authors other than Somanārya.[1] They are:

Daṇḍī	:	Dattila
Mukhavīṇā	:	Yājñavalkya
Maurī	:	Mataṅga
Upāṅga	:	Śārṅgadeva

Among the above, the verses dealing with Maurī, seem to be ambiguous. The reasons are:

1. Except Maurī, the names of the other three instruments have been listed in the īkā at the beginning (NC 3, 2 comm.).
2. Except for Maurī, all the three have commentary.
3. Except Maurī, all the three contain invocatory verses, i.e., the verses titled 'prārthanā' (e.g., NC 3,20)
4. The style of presentation of the verses describing Maurī differs from that of others. In almost all the cases, the structure of the instrument is

1. However none of them could be traced to the respective printed texts.

described first, and is then followed by the names of the presiding deities of the different parts. Then the method of playing (or holding) the instrument with different hand positions is mentioned which then ends with an invocatory verse and the ṭīkā. With regard to Maurī, the text is too corrupt that it is difficult to comprehend its structure. Further, while listing the presiding deities, the names of the different parts of the instrument (nābhi, patrikā, kumbha and jīvāla) resemble those of a stringed instrument and not of a wind instrument. The actual method of playing is not clearly given but the gain, that accrues to one playing the instrument with single or both hands, is mentioned.

For these reasons this portion of the text is placed outside the mūla, i.e., as anubandha. Incidentally a similar passage is seen in ABSS under "mataṅgamatē" (ABSS 1, 325-333), but is worded differently. Probabaly this passage in the NC manuscripts is an extract from such a source.

6.4.4.2 Vādya lakṣaṇa

This portion is seen in between the description of Nāgasara and Devasara in the manuscripts G86 and G89. The term 'vādya' is defined first and is followed by some verses dealing with a 'performance' that includes instruments also. There are some verses relating the seven svara-s to mandra, madhya and tāra, a unique feature noted in this work (See 6.2.2.5).

Probably, this could be a fragment portion, dealing with skin instruments, but does not appropriately fit anywhere, and hence has not been incorporated in the present edited text. Therefore this portion has also been placed outside, at the end of the edited text (See anubandha of NC).

6.5 Commentary of the Work

The Telugu īkā accompanying NC of Somanārya raises many questions regarding its form and relation to the mūla. There is no internal evidence, by way of introduction or colophon, that establishes the Telugu passage accompanying the Saṃskṛta mūla as a ṭīkā. However it is only from the markings in the manuscripts, such as "ṭīkā", "ṭkī" or "ṭī" etc., that we have to infer that the Telugu passages are ṭīkā. Commentaries to texts are of different kinds.

> *"Rājaśēkhara lists vṛtti, paddhati, bhāṣyaṃ, samīkṣā, ṭīkā, pañjikā, kārikā, vārttikā as the means by which śāstra, which is first introduced in sūtra-s, is then elaborated (Kavyamīmāṃsā, p.5, lines 4-8)"*
> (Ramanathan, 1998:26)

Probably the Telugu passages in NC falls under the category, ṭīkā. "Ṭīkā is defined by Rājaśēkhara as yathāsambhavamarthasya ṭīkanam", which probably means giving the meaning of the mūla verses" (Ramanathan, 1998:29).

Ironically, there are quite a few places where the mūla and the ṭīkā speak differently (See 6.5.1 below).

There is practically no manuscript, which contains only the mūla as we come across in the case of NS and SR. None of the later books like BKM, RJM seem to suggest the existence of Somanārya's work exclusive of the ṭīkā. The style of the ṭīkā is also peculiar. It does not take terms or phrases from the mūla (pratīka) and give explanations (but for a very few exceptions). The ṭīkā does not cite passages from any contemporary or earlier works in agreement or in disagreement with the mūla. The Telugu passages are more in the form of a gloss and sometimes in the form of a summary. As already stated, sometimes the views expressed in the mūla and the ṭīkā are different.

6.5.1 Contents of the Commentary

The contents of the ṭīkā are being examined and observations are furnished below.

* At many places, there is a confusion in the usage of technical terms like

svara, śruti etc. For example, the ṭīkā to verse 49 states that the svara-s are of twenty-two varieties in the chest, throat and the head regions. It is to be noted here that the term 'svara' is being used instead of 'śruti'. At another instance, in the ṭīkā to verse 53, after listing the names of the twenty-one mūrcchanā-s, the passage reads, "svarālaku pērlu". Here again there seems to be a confusion.

* At some places, the ṭīkā gives information in addition to that found in the mūla. These sometimes appear like an extension of what is said in the main text. A few examples:

a The mūla lists the seven svara-s, for which the ṭīkā adds the names of the animals, which are generally related to the origin of the svara-s. (NC 2, comm.7)

b. The mūla mentions that there are three grāma-s and seven mūrcchanā-s (NC 2,58). But interpreting and listing seven mūrcchanā-s for each of the three grāma-s, as sndpmgr (for ṣaḍja), mgnsrdp (for madhyama), gdrpsmn (for gāndhāra) is an information found only in the ṭīkā and reproduced by many texts of the later period.

c. The svara illustration 'srgmgr-srgr-srgm' for svaralaṅkāra is not found in the mūla. (NC 2, comm.59)

d. It is said in the mūla (NC 2,60) that the svara-s should be sung in ascent and descent in the morning, noon and afternoon, by those who seek prosperity. In the ṭīkā, this phenomenon is called "sarali", the term, which does not occur, in the mūla.

e. While defining the term, "suraktam" (one of the svara guṇa-s), the mūla reads it as the synchronisation of vīṇā, vaṃśa and the throat (voice); whereas the ṭīkā adds nāgasara too. (NC 2, comm.71)

f. The svara illustrations for vādī, samvādī, anuvādī and vivādī svara-s given in the ṭīkā do not appear to be a representation of what the mūla describes (NC 2, comm.95) but only an extension.

g. With regard to the lakṣaṇa-s of the rāga-s, the mūla specifies the commencing svara-s and the svara-s to be omitted in a rāga (NC 2,114-130). But the commentator seems to supplement some svara passages for each of them, which resemble the format given in the context of vādī and samvādī svara-s. Probably, this could be an attempt to include vādī and samvādī also as the lakṣaṇa-s of rāga. (NC 2,comm.154)

h. In continuation of the description of the lakṣaṇa-s of the rāga-s, those with similar ādi (graha) svara-s are grouped together in the ṭīkā. Further, rāga-s with same set of svara-s (noted in ascent) are said to belong to the same mela. This approach of grouping rāga-s on the basis of graha svara-s and the mention of mela are not seen in the mūla.

* At some places, the ṭīkā seems to interpret the mūla verses in a different manner. For example,

a. The order of the places in the human body from where the sound emanates is slightly altered in the ṭīkā. Thus the mūla reads navel, chest, throat, head and mouth, whereas the ṭīkā mentions navel, chest, throat, mouth and head. (NC 2, comm.41)

b. Śuddharāga of the mūla is being equated to ghanarāga in the ṭīkā. (NC 2, comm. 176)

c. One of the blemishes of singers, "anavadhāna" is interpreted differently by the ṭīkā (NC 2,177ab). According to the mūla, one who lacks concentration in the singing of sthāya-s is termed "anavadhānaka". But the ṭīkā interprets 'anavadhāna' as singing without the knowledge of sthāyī, svara (the ten types of svaras) etc. Perhaps the commentator took liberty in interpreting the reading "sthāyādiṣu" in the mūla as " sthāyī + ādi" and enumerated the ten varieties of svara.

* There are some passages in the ṭīkā, which seem to reveal a lack of understanding of musicological ideas on the part of the commentator.
  a. NC 2,4ab contains a half-verse, which is the same as the SR 1,3,2ab. Since the whole verse from SR is not taken, a complete meaning is not obtained. Strangely, the commentator tries to present a meaning based on the half-verse alone, which seems to go against the basic philosophy of Śārṅgadeva's work.
  b. Again in NC 2,91, we find the śrutijāti-s being presented in the words of SR 1,3,27cd-31ab. The ṭīkā totally misses the concept of śrutijāti and gives an almost irrelevant interpretation.

  The above two instances suggest some inadequacy in the musicological understanding on the part of the commentator.
* With regard to the Vādya chapter, the ṭīkā is complete only with respect to Nāgasara and Devasara (and Mṛdaṅga, to some extent) but is very brief in most of the cases.
* The sections on the Rāgalakṣaṇa-s in the mūla and the ṭīkā are totally inconsistent. Though both speak of 32 śuddha rāga-s, classified under eight masculine and twenty-four feminine rāga-s (NC 2, 107, 109-112), there seem to be many problems with respect to both the names of the rāga-s and their lakṣaṇa-s. The eight masculine rāga-s in the mūla and the ṭīkā are as follows:

Mūla	Ṭīkā
bhairava	bhairavi
bhūpāla	bhūpāḷa
śrīrāga	śrīrāga
paḍamañjara	paḍamañjari
vasanta	vasanta
mālava	māḷava
baṅgāla	baṅgāḷa
nāṭa	nāṭa

It is seen that the names bhairava and paḍamañjara in the mūla are read as bhairavi and paḍamañjari in the ṭīkā.

The names of the feminine rāga-s are given thus:

	Mūla	Ṭīkā
bhairava	devakriyā	dēvakriya
	megharañjī	mēgharañji
	kurañjī	kurañji
bhūpāla	velāhurī	vēḷāhuri
	malaharī	malahari
	baulī	bauḷi
śrīrāga	hindola	hindōḷam
	balahamsa	balahamsa
	sāverī	sāvēri
paḍamañjara	deśī	dēśi
	lalitā	lalita
	toḍī	tōḍi
vasanta	rāmakrīyā	rāmakrīya
	varālī	varāḷi
	kauśikā	kauśika
māḷava	nārāyaṇī	nārāyaṇi
	guṇḍakriyā	guṇḍakriya
	ghūrjarī	ghūrjari
baṅgāḷa	dhanyāsī	dhanyāśi
	kāmbōdī	kāmbōdi
	nīlāmbarī	nīlāmbari
nāṭa	deśākṣarī	dēvagāndhāri
	āharī	āhari
	sāraṅgā	śaṅkarābharaṇa

It is observed from the above table that dēśākṣarī and sāraṅga are mentioned as the feminine rāga-s in the mūla, whereas the ṭīkā gives devagāndhāri and śaṅkarābharaṇa. The names of 32 rāga-s also occur in the mūla at another context, i.e., while describing the lakṣaṇa-s of the rāga-s (NC 2,114-130). With respect to the masculine rāga-s, seven rāga-s, except mālava are described here. The twenty-four feminine rāga-s that figure in this context are, devagāndhārī, ghūrjarī, nīlāmbarī, varālī, megharañjī, velāhurī, deśī, malaharī, deśakārī, rāmakriyā, toḍī, devakriyā, kurañjī, guṇḍakriyā, sāraṅgā, dhanyāśī, lalītā, āharī, kāmbodī, baulī, balahamsā, nārāyaṇī, śaṅkarābharaṇa and hindola. It is found that devagāndhāri and śaṅkarābharaṇa, which were not listed in the mūla earlier are described here. At the same time, dēśakārī (dēśākṣarī?) and sāraṅgā also figure here. However the descriptions of kauśikā and sāveri are missing. Thus one can observe a kind of inconsistency in the text. The lakṣaṇa-s of the 32 rāga-s found in the mūla and the ṭīkā are given in Appendix-3.

6.5.2 Date of the Commentary

From the above discussion, it is clear that the ṭīkā was not written by the author (of the main text) himself, namely, Somanārya. The period of the author of the mūla (Somanārya) was discussed and tentatively placed before 1600 AD in Section 4 above. The probable date of the commentary is being analysed now.

From the following observations, the commentary of NC could be placed in a later period

* The ṭīkā exclusively uses certain technical terms like, ghanarāga, kalpitam (NC 2, comm.176), raktigāna etc. The terms ghana, naya and dēśī, in the sphere of rāga-s, are found to be used for the first time in the Rāgalakṣaṇamu of Śāhaji (1684-1712 AD.) (Seetha, 1990:xv); and the term, naya is said to be a synonym for rakti (ibid, p.xvi, xix).

However, it is possible that the term, "ghana" was in use even before the period of Śāhaji.

* Some features seen in works like SSud, CDP and SP and SSud are observed in the commentary of NC. For example, the svara phrase "srgmgr - srgr - srgm" is illustrated for the svarālaṅkāra NC 2, comm.59 (CDP 3,91, SP 1,282). Hence it could be inferred that the commentary might have been influenced by these works.

The above statements also seem to suggest a possible influence of the Tanjore musiclogical works on the commentary.

According to Chinni Krishnayya,[1] the commentator of this work probably belonged to the Tanjavur area, since the language used in the commentary is slightly different from that of the Andhra region. This is evident from some readings found in the manuscripts like, "nelli" (āmalaka or 'usiri' in Telugu) (NC 3, comm.78) and "maṭṭatara dēham", (sama dēham) (NC 2, comm.38). In view of the strong literary evidence, it is quite likely that the commentary on NC, was a later creation and by a different author.

7. Somanārya in other musicological works

Some works written in Saṃskṛta and Tamiz appear to have been influenced by Somanārya's NC. Some are in the form of paraphrases of Somanārya's ideas and a few contain short extracts of the text. Works belonging to the nineteenth and the twentieth centuries, written in Telugu and Tamiz also incorporate certain peculiar concepts that are exclusively seen in NC and its commentary.

Among the three chapters available in NC, the contents of the Gītādhyāya (svara and rāga) seem to have been noticed by or referred to a greater extent, in the later works. Extracts of a few verses from the Vādyādhyāya are found in ABSS. The works that show close similarities to the contents of NC are:

1. Based on my personal Interview on 09/05/2001

1. Mahābharatacūḍāmaṇi (MBC)
2. Bharatakalpalatāmañjarī (BKM)
3. Rasikajanamanollāsini-sārasaṅgrahabharataśāstra (RJM)
4. Sārasaṅgrahabharata (SSB)
5. Gānavidyārahasyaprakāśini (GVRP)
6. Saṅgītamakaranda (SM)
7. Abhinavabharatasārasaṅgraha (ABSS)

A note on these works follows:

7.1 Mahābharatacūḍāmaṇi (MBC)

This Tamiz work is edited from a single manuscript in possession of the U V Saminathayyar Library, Chennai. It is published in two volumes. This consists of five chapters, namely,

1. nāṭyōpayōka avayavapēda viniyōka lacaṇaṃ
2. mukūrttāti ēzuvakaitō̲r̲raapinaya lacaṇaṃ
3. capānāyakāti carva vāttiya pāttira lacaṇaṃ
4. saṅkītāti rāka mēḷa lacaṇaṃ
5. tāḷāti mātira kaṇita lacaṇaṃ

The first three chapters deal with nāṭya and the fourth chapter with the musical aspects. The fifth chapter on tāla is however yet to be traced. The contents of the fourth chapter resemble those of NC to a great extent. This work consists of both verses and commentary in Tamiz.

7.1.1 Contents of the Chapter on music

The fourth chapter that deals with music consists of three prakaraṇa-s. The first prakaraṇa deals with the following topics: Saṅgīta - definition, nāda- nādopāsanā, production of nāda, svara-s and their attributes, 22 nāḍi-s (22 śruti-s), śruti-jāti-s, sixteen svarasthāna-s, ten gamaka-s, eighteen śruti-s, ten types of gamaka-s(?) of the svara-s (some names are different from the names given under ten gamaka-s earlier), guṇa and doṣa of daśavidha gamaka svara-s, svaramaṇḍala, twenty-one mūrcchanā-s, alaṅkārasvara, svaraprastāra, vādī, saṃvādī, anuvādī and vivādī svara-s and the benefits of listening to music.

The Second prakaraṇa deals with rāga-s. The names of eight masculine rāga-s are first enumerated and are associated with many attributes. Then the names of twenty-four feminine rāga-s are listed, followed by a list of dūti rāga-s and putra rāga-s (seen in prose form only).

The third prakaraṇa deals with the names of the seventy-two melakartā-s and the lakṣaṇa-s of the janyarāga-s derived from the melakartā-s.[1]

7.1.2 Sources referred to in MBC

Many verses in MBC are constructed in such a way that they reproduce the contents from an earlier work. e.g.

verse 19: "cārru nūlē"

verse 20: "ena nūlirrulaṅkumpārē"

verse 85: "kūrinar nūlvallōrē" and so on. These phrases inform that they are being expounded from some other source (work). Some of the verses are attributed to authorities like Agastiya, "Agastiyar matam" (verses 40 and 60), Śārṅgadeva, "Cārṅkatēvamuni mataṃ" (verse 43) and Somanārya, "Somanātīya matam" (verse 46). Although a majority of the first and the second prakaraṇa-s of MBC are identical with NC, the name Somanārya or Somanātha is acknowledged, only at a few places. e.g. Soṃanāryan (verses 83, 98), Somanātan (verses 73, 100, 104), Somanātiya matam (verse 46), Somanātīyam ennum ratnākaram (55 comm.)

7.1.3 "Somanārya" in MBC

In verse 104, it is said that 'As said by Śiva to Pārvati, Nāradā told Śārṅgadeva, who preached (it) to Somanātha'. In the commentary to verse

1. This resembles the description made in the Telugu work, Saṅgitasarasaṅgrahamu of Truvenkaṭakavi.

98, it is found thus: '(it is) the svaraprakaraṇaṃ in the fourth adhyāya said by Śārṅgadevamuni to Somanātha Mahārājā'. This idea, Somanārya drawing out from Saṅgītaratnākara [of Śārṅgadeva?] is found in the manuscripts of Somanārya, towards the end of the Gītādhyāya. (NC 2, 180 comm.)

The commentary to verse 55 in MBC refers Somanātīyam (Somanārya's work) as ratnākara. (SR?). It is to be noted that manuscripts of NC also exist under the title SR and the commentary (NC 2, 180 comm.) supports this.

7.1.4 Observations

A comparative study of NC and the first and the second prakaraṇa-s of the fourth chapter of MBC, reveals the following:

a. The first prakaraṇa contains 104 verses. Out of these, except for verses 1, 2, 5, 34, 36, 37, 39, 40, 42, 44, 45, 49-52, 57-65 and 99, the rest reflect the same idea as seen in NC. Of the above mentioned verses 1, 2, 5, 49-52 reproduce the concepts of earlier Saṃskṛta treatises like SR of Śārṅgadeva (Chapter-1). Verses 40, 42, 44 and 45 speak of the terms found in Tamiz music. Thus about 80 verses of MBC echo the same concepts, (almost in the same order) as found in NC. The contents of the second prakaraṇa (verses 105-139) dealing with the attributes of the eight masculine rāga-s, resemble NC, except for some variations in the names of the feminine rāga-s.
b. Some concepts unique to NC are seen in MBC, like
   * A number of extra musical attributes to the seven svara-s
   * Relating the svara-s sa and ri to mandra, ga and ma to madhya and pa, dha, and ni to tāra regions.
   * 18 śruti-s
   * 10 types of gamaka-s of svara
   * Interpretation of vādī, saṃvādī, anuvādī and vivādī svara-s

c. Some of the concepts mentioned in the commentary alone of NC are seen in the main verses of MBC (definition of "sarali", illustrative svara-s for vādī, saṃvādī etc.)

d. A few portions of NC are found to be just transliterated into Tamiz in MBC, without a proper understanding of the work. For example, the definition of a few technical terms like the ten gamaka-s, guṇa and doṣa of svara-s and the sruti distinction between the ṣaḍja and madhyama grama-s. A careful study reveals that MBC must have been influenced by the manuscript G86, which is evident from some of the identical errors seen in them. G86 reads "yīsvara" for "ī svara" (NC 2, comm.85) which reading is also found in MBC (97-comm).

e. It is curious to note that references to Somanārya are found in the first two prakaraṇa-s and not seen in the third prakaraṇa. Meanwhile the text of the music chapter appears corrupt. From the introduction, we come to know that the present edition of MBC is based on a single manuscript from the U V Swaminathayyar Library, Chennai. There are two colophons in the manuscript. The first one indicates that it has been copied from the (note)book of Sārantā Nāyakkar, the samasthāna vidvān of the Ramnad court, in the Cittirai month of the year Śrīmukha. The second one states that the melakarta - janya-s have been copied from Cavuḍārpṭṭi Gopālayyar's notebook, in the cittirai month of the year īsvara. From these colophons it is clear that the two sections of this chapter were copied from different sources. Therefore, there is also a possibility that these two represented two different works. In other words, the present edition could be a combination of two different sources, where the former is the one influenced by NC of Somanārya.

The first three chapters of MBC deal with all aspects of dance in detail. Here also references are made to many authorities like Hanumān, Bṛhaspati, Nārada, Arjuṇa, Vināyaka and so on. In the first chapter, (MBC 1, pp.121,194) the commentary mentions "Somanātan matam". It is not clear if these sections are based on Somanārya's work, because the existing portion of NC on nāṭya consists only details of nāṭyotpatti and practically nothing on nāṭya as dance.

7.2 Bharatakalpalatāmañjarī (BKM)

This work consists of Saṃskṛta verses with a Telugu meaning (commentary), both printed in Telugu script. A brief note on this work is as follows:

"The author/s is/are unknown. The work is edited from a single manuscript. by B Ankaji Sastri and P Subba Rao with short Telugu paraphrases, which reveal a clear understanding of the text. Both editors were smārtha brāhmaṇa-s who knew Telugu well and were probably Telugu brāhmaṇa-s. The book was published in Bangalore in 1887 A.D. This became popular as an authoritative textual source with traditional musicians, dancers and litterateurs connected with these arts. (Telugu was a common medium for these arts till about 1940 in Bangalore) The work compiles from many diverse sources without acknowledgement. Even though saṅgīta and sāhitya are dealt with in extenso, they subserve the subject of dancing which is the focus of the book. Such a work fulfilled the needs of the educated (not in the sense of english education!), professional danseuses who were widespread in Karnataka of the 19th century A.D." (R Sathyanarayana, in one of his letters to the present editor, dated 06-03-2000)

7.2.1 Contents of the work

The printed book consists of five prakaraṇa-s. They are Bhāvaprakaraṇa, Svaraprakaraṇa, Rāgaprakaraṇa, Tālaprakaraṇa and Pūrvaraṅgaprakaraṇa. Of these, the content of the verses in the second and the third prakaraṇa-s correspond to NC.

Svaraprakaraṇa

This section deals with the following aspects. Nāda - production, types; Svara-s origin, time of birth and other attributes; Lakṣaṇa of each svara with all attributes (consolidated) svara-prastāra, vādī, saṃvādī, anuvādī and vivādī svara-s, three registers, twenty-two śruti-s, grāma, mūrcchanā, eighteen śruti-s, alaṅkāra, three and nine types of śruti-s, ten varieties of svara-s, guṇa and doṣa of svara-s, definition of the terms, gīta, prabandha, sūlādī, nāmāvalī, cūrṇikā and nāṭaka.

Rāgaprakaraṇa

This deals with the classification and characteristics of rāga-s. The following topics are dealt herewith: śuddha, miśra and saṅkīrṇa rāga-s; ṣāḍava, auḍava and sampūrṇa rāga-s; Eight masculine and twenty-four feminine rāga-s; Various attributes of the masculine rāga-s; Lakṣaṇa-s of the rāga-s in terms of the svara-s occurring in the ascent and the descent (ārohaṇa and avarohaṇa), list of 64 mitra-rāga-s with ārohaṇa and avarohaṇa; alaṅkāra-s, varieties of singers, the qualities and blemishes of singers. This ends with a long list of 1032 rāga-s based on the 72 melakartā-janya scheme.

Observations on the treatment of the subject in BKM, would be taken up along with those on RJM, since the contents of the two works closely resemble each other.

7.3 Rasikajanamanollāsini sārasaṅgrahabharataśāstra (RJM)

This is a Saṃskṛta work, printed in Kannada script. About the book, Dr Sathyanarayana in his letter dated 06-03-2000 says,

"The author is Veṅkaṭasundarasāni, daughter of Mariyāsāni of Halasūru, now a suburb of Bangalore. Both were traditional devadāsi-s, attached to the ancient temple of Somanathesvara of Halasūru and made it a great centre of dance learning. Both mother and daughter were deeply learned in Sanskrit and the arts and had developed a large and precious library of manuscripts of rare Sanskrit works on sāhitya (esp.alaṅkāraśāstra) saṅgīta and nāṭya. They refer to many of these works, in their introduction and compile their work from these authentic sources. It is unfortunate that the collection cannot now be traced, but I have verified the extractions to be

correct from whatever sources I could lay my hands. As always, learned brāhmaṇa-s were their sources of learning and inspiration; in this instance they were encouraged by a 'sthala purohita', Narasimhayya, probably in compilation and editing. The work was published by B Veṅkaṭarāmayya, another brāhmaṇa in 1908 from CTA Press in Mysore. (This Press was a stone's throw from my house on my way to primary school and I knew it well. It specialised in publishing scholarly works of critical editions of great, unpublished Kannada poetical works)."

7.3.1 Contents of the work

The book is divided into four parts (bhāga-s), namely, Kavitvalakṣaṇam, Nāṭakasamvidhānaṃ, Saṅgītaśāstraṃ and Nāṭyābhinayaśāstraṃ. In between, there are some verses extracted from other works (noted under "matāntara").

Saṅgītaśāstraṃ

This part deals with the various aspects of music. It begins with a few verses, describing the greatness of music. The other topics covered in this part are:- nāda - production, types; Svara-s - origin, time of birth and other attributes; Lakṣaṇa of each svara with all attributes (consolidated) svara-prastāra, vādī, saṃvādī, anuvādī and vivādī svara-s, three registers, twenty-two śruti-s, grāma, mūrcchanā, eighteen śruti-s, alaṅkāra, three and nine types of śruti-s, śruti-jāti-s, ten varieties of svara-s, guṇa and doṣa of svara; definition of the terms- gīta, prabandha, sūlādī, nāmāvalī, cūrṇikā and nāṭaka; rāgālipti, rūpālipti, śuddha, miśra and saṅkīrṇa rāga-s, kūatāna, ṣāḍava, auḍava and sampūrṇa rāga-s, eight masculine and twenty four feminine rāga-s, various attributes of the eight masculine rāga-s, varieties of miśra rāga-s, alaṅkāra-s, varieties of singers, the qualities and blemishes of singers.

7.3.2 Observations

The music sections of BKM and RJM reveal a strong influence of

Somanārya's work. However BKM and RJM (some under "matāntara") have incorporated a few verses from SR of Śārṅgadeva that are not seen in NC. With regard to the portions of NC found in these two works, the following points are observed.

(a) The arrangement of topics in BKM and RJM agree with that in NC, except for a change in the occurrence of vādī, saṃvādī svara-s etc. The manuscripts read this at the end of the section on svara (NC 2, 93-95), whereas BKM and RJM read it after svaraprastāra itself.

(b) Both the works give grammatically better readings in many cases.[1] Though both read alike, at some places, there are slight variations between the two, which suggests that both of them had a common corrupt exemplar (manuscript source), which has been corrected by the authors/editors, using their knowledge. This could also perhaps be the reason why a few corrupt readings are found corrected in BKM but copied as such in RJM. For example, the verse commencing "nādopāsanayā devāḥ" in NC 2,4ab is probably a partial reproduction of a verse in SR of Śārṅgadeva. While RJM retains it as such, BKM restores it to the form met with in the SR of Śārṅgadeva.

(c) Many concepts of NC that deviate from the traditional views have been faithfully followed in these works. e.g.

   i. Relating āhata and anāhata nāda to the ascent (ārohaṇa) and descent (avarohaṇa).
   ii. Associating the svara and rāga with many extra musical attributes.
   iii. Equating the svara-s, sa and ri, to mandra, ga and ma to madhya and pa, dha and ni to tāra.
   iv. Expanding the three sthāna-s to nine varieties (mandra-mandra, mandra-madhya etc.).
   v. Definition and illustration for vādī and samvādī svara-s.

1. Maya of the redings have therefore been made use of for editing NC.

vi. The guṇa and doṣa of gīta, being referred to as guṇa and doṣa of svara.
vii. Ālaptī being referred to as ālipta/ālipti.
viii. Vākya being recognised as one of the limbs of prabandha.
ix. Different understanding of kūṭatāna, pūrṇa and apūrṇa

(d) Some new concepts and interpretations, hitherto not seen earlier in any technical treatises, but found in NC are noticed in these works too.

a. Eighteen śruti-s
b. Ten types of svara
c. Definition for gīta, sūlādī, nāmāvalī, cūrṇikā and nāṭaka

(e) A few corrupt readings found in the manuscripts of NC, have been carried down in BKM and RJM. While describing the various limbs of prabandha, some manuscripts of NC read "svayaca" and "svayaśca", the correct reading being "svaraśca", which is found in G38 and Sp (NC 2, 183ab). But BKM, RJM and SSB present the reading "svayaccha". At another instance, in the context of gāyaka doṣa-s, while listing the twenty-five types of defects/defective singers, both the manuscripts of NC and the books BKM and RJM follow the reading given by SR (with a slight variation). The phrase, "miśrako' navadhānaśca" is interpreted by BKM and RJM as miśraka and ekona, instead of miśraka and anavadhāna. These terms occur even in the definitions for the individual doṣa-s.

7.4 Sārasaṅgrahabharata (SSB)

M B Vedavalli mentions a few works written during the period of the last four Voḍeyars (Vedavalli, 1992:119). They are:

a. Svaracūḍāmaṇi, Śrītatvanidhi and Sārasaṅgrahabharata (SSB) of Mummaḍi Kṛṣṇarāja Voḍeyar.

b. Gānavidyārahasyaprakāśini (GVRP) of Karigiri Rao
c. Saṅgītasamayasāra of Subrahmaṇya Ayyar
d. Śrutisiddhānta and Karṇāṭaka Saṅgītaśāstra Vimarśē of Hulugur Kṛṣṇācārya
e. Saṅgītakalpadruma of Muttayyā Bhāgavatar

It is observed that most of the peculiar concepts found in NC are also seen in SSB and GVRP. The following is a note on these works.

7.4.1 The SSB manuscript

About this work Vedavalli says,

> *"The Sarasangrahabharata is an unpublished paper manuscript in the possession of the descendants of Vina Sesanna. The text is in Sanskrit with comments in Telugu on each sloka. The script is that of Kannada. As the title itself [suggests?] it is a work on dance in which music as a limb of dance has been dealt with"* (Vedavalli, 1992:121)

The author of the original text is said to be Kṛṣṇarāja Voḍeyar, the son of Cāmarāja Voḍeyar and the author of the commentary is Pāpanāmātya, probably a court poet (Vedavalli, 1992:122).

7.4.2 Contents of SSB

From the brief summary found in "Mysore as a Seat of Music", SSB consists of three chapters dealing with dance,[1] tāla-s and music (under the heading, "rāga lakṣaṇa") respectively. The section on tāla commences with the ten prāṇa-s of tāla, followed by the 110 tāla-s, sapta tāla-s, varieties of maṭya tāla-s, gana tāla-s, simhanandana tāla and uruvu tāla-s.

Rāga lakṣaṇa (section on music?)

The various topics dealt with in this chapter are nāda, characteristics of svara-s svara-prastāra, vādī, saṃvādī, anuvādī and vivādī svara-s, three

1. The description of the dance chjapter is not furnished in this book.

registers, sixty-six nāḍi-s, grāma, mūrcchanā, eighteen śruti-s, alaṅkāra, three and nine types of śruti-s, śruti-jāti-s, ten ways of uttering the svara, guṇa and doṣa of svara, definition of the terms, gīta, prabandha, sūlādī, nāmāvalī, cūrṇikā and nāṭaka; rāgālipta, rūpālipta, śuddha, miśra and saṅkīrṇa rāga-s, ṣāḍava, auḍava and sampūrṇa rāga-s, eight masculine and twenty four feminine rāga-s, various attributes of the eight masculine rāga-s, seven alaṅkāra-s and varieties of singers. This section ends with the varieties of rāga-s with the same suffices.

7.4.3 Observation

From the topics presented in this book, it is evident that SSB too follows BKM and RJM and in turn NC. Since the original manuscript or its transcript is not presently available, further analysis could not be undertaken. The same is the case with GVRP, discussed below.

7.5 Gānavidyārahasyaprakāśini (GVRP)

"Gāna Vidyārahasya Prakāśinā is a work dealing with the theoretical aspects of music written by Karigiri Rao, a musician in the court of Chamaraja Wodeyar. This work is in Sanskrit with a commentary in Kannada. A copy of this work was made from a paper manuscript in the possession of the family of the author. This is an exhaustive work on the theory of music. In the treatment of a few topics, this work follows Sritatvanidhi and Sarasangrahabharata. But more often the author, quotes extensively from Sangitaratnakara of Sarangadeva, adding elaborate comments based on Kallinatha's commentary. The author carefully points out the differences in views and tradition between Sarasangrahabharata and Sangitaratnakara in the description of several concepts. Wherever there is a discrepancy between the lakṣaṇa and the prevailing practice, he brings it out to our notice. His own comments in such contexts are very useful and informative and show that he had a clear perspective of the history of music."

(Vedavalli, 1992:139-140)

7.5.1 Contents

The first part consists of the following topics. Nāda- production and etymology, sixteen types of svara-s, twenty-two śruti-s from twenty-two nāḍi-s, association of the seven svara-s with the three sthāna-s, twenty-two śruti-s - (dhruvavīṇā- calavīṇā), śruti-jāti-s, vādī, saṃvādī, anuvādī and vivādī svara-s, eighteen śruti-s, three and nine types of śruti-s, śuddha-vikṛta svara-s (based on SR), characteristics of svara-s and ends with svaraprastāra.

The second part commences with the description of grāma (nandyāvarta, jīmūta, śubhadra) mūrcchanā, alaṅkāra, varṇa, ten varieties of svara-s, gamaka-s (as per SR) guṇa and doṣa of gīta, definition of the terms, gīta, prabandha, sūlādī and ālipta. With regard to the section on rāga-s, the text speaks of śuddha, miśra and saṅkīrṇa rāga-s, eight masculine and twenty four feminine rāga-s, lakṣaṇa-s of the rāga-s (kanakāṅgī etc.) varieties of singers, blemishes of singers and ends with āroha and avaroha of the seventy-two melakartā rāga-s and janya-s.

The third part is devoted to Tāla.

7.6 Saṅgītamakaranda (SM)

Saṅgītamakaranda of Nārada is edited from a single manuscript preserved at the Gaekwad Oriental Institute, Baroda. The manuscript is said to have been discovered from Gadwal, which was a part of Vijayanagar Empire.[1] The work consists of two main chapters, the Saṅgītādhyāya and the Nṛtyādhyāya and each one is further divided into four pāda-s. Though the contents are not found in a logical sequence, at many places, the work speaks of the various aspects of gīta, vādya, nṛtya and tāla. It is opined that the work belongs to the pre-ratnākara period.[2] Although it is spaopined thus by the editor of the work, some modern scholars have ascribed a much later date to this work.[3]

1. SM, introduction, p.xi
2. ibid, p.x
3. Ramanathan N, in his lecture delivered on "Śāstra and Śāstra Sampradāya", at the Refresher Course on Music organised by the Faculty of Performing Arts, Banaras Hindu University, Varanasi, July 2009

7.6.1 NC and SM

Some verses in NC are found to be identical with those in SM. They are tabulated below.

Half-line (from NC)	NC	SM
tannādaṃ saptadhā kṛtvā	2,7	1,1,11-12ab
evaṃ svarān samākṛṣya	2,8	1,1,15
kṛṣṇasarpo'pi tannādaṃ	2,12	1,1,23
brāhmaṇau tu samau jñeyau	2,14	1,1,29
atisūkṣmaśca sūkṣmaśca	2,41	1,4,17
catuścatuścatuścaiva	2,50	1,1,85
ṣaḍjādi svarasammiśraṃ	2,97	1,4,49cd
āliptirdvividhā jñeyā	2,98	1,4,50
rāgālipti tannanādi	2,99	1,4,51
yathādyupakrameṇaiva	2,102-103	1,4,52-53
ekasvaravihīnaśca	2,105	1,4,54cd-55
bhairavaścāpi bhūpālo	2,107	1,3,68
evaṃ pradhānarāgāsyuḥ	2,131	1,3,50cd-51ab
evaṃ nirīkṣyātha	2,162	1,4,56
nakhavāyuja carmaja	3,1-2	1,1,7cd-9ab
kacchapi kubjikā	3,3-4	1,4,6-8ab

It is to be pointed out here that most of the verses mentioned above are very significant that, they convey the concepts, which are unique to NC. The following are a few examples, wherein the readings of SM and NC are almost identical with very little variations.

NC	SM
evaṃ svarān samākṛṣya vīṇādiṣu nidhāya ca |	evaṃ svarān samākṛṣya vīṇādiṣu nidhāya ca |
tena phutena nādena saṅgītamakarot	tena cāhata nādena

tathā |	saṅgītamakarottadā ||
athādyupakrameṇaiva rāgaśuddha- mudāhṛtam| upakramya yadā rāgo melanaṃ samamitrakaiḥ ||	yathādyupakrameṇaiva rāgaḥ śuddha udāhṛtaḥ| upakramya yathā rāgo melanaṃ samamiśrakam ||
punastanmārgagamanaṃ sālagaṃ parikīrtitam | saṅkīrṇarāgamitrāṇāṃ gānaṃ saṅkīrṇamucyate ||	punastanmārgagamakaṃ rāgaraṅgaḥ prakīrtitaḥ| saṅkīrṇarāgamiśrāṇāṃ rāgaḥ saṅkīrṇa ucyate ||
ṣaḍjādi svarasammiśraṃ rāgaṃ ca parikīrtitam | āliptirdvividhā jñeyā svarasaṃyojane tathā ||	ṣaḍjādi svarasammiśraṃ gānaṃ ca parikīrtitam | ālāpā dvividhā jñeyāḥ svarasaṃyojane tathā ||
rāgālipti rūpālipti dvayaṃ ca parikīrtitam | rāgālipti tannādi rūpako gītamucyate ||	rāgālapti rūpalapti dvayaṃ ca parikīrtitam | rāgālaptistannādi rūpako gītamucyate ||
evaṃ nirīkṣyātha samastarāgān gāyeta dhīmānadhika prayatnaḥ| jantreṇa vā kaṇha bhavasvareṇa dvayena vā doṣavivarjitā syuḥ||	evaṃ vivakṣyāmi samastarāgān gāyeta dhīmānadhika prayatnaḥ| jantreṇa vākam rabhasā svareṇa dvayena vā doṣavivarjitaḥ syuḥ||

It is observed that only NC and SM read mārdalī as one of the mūrcchanā-s of the madhyama grāma, instead of mārgī, a name traditionally accepted. Further the style of describing the lakṣaṇa-s of rāga-s is identical in SM and

NC. Some of the names of vīṇā-s mentioned in SM are noted only in NC, like for instance Vaiṣṇavī, Saurandrī/Sairandrī etc. Some are found to be referred to in NC and a few works from the Orissa region.[1] e.g., kubjikā. This shows that there should have been some strong relation between these two works, since both belonged to the same geographical area. The only available manuscript of SM is said to have been discovered from Gadwal, which was a part of Vijayanagar Empire (as stated above). Somanārya is also associated with the Vijayanagar Empire - as discussed in Sections 3 & 4 above.

7.7 Abhinavabharatasārasaṅgraha (ABSS)

This is a compilation made by Mummaḍi Cikkabhūpāla from various sources like Nāṭyaśāstra of Bharata, Saṅgītaratnākara of Śārṅgadeva, Saṅgītasudhākara of Haripāla, Svaramelakalānidhi of Rāmāmātyā and Saṅgītopaniśadsāra of Sudhākalaśa. Some are extracted from works attributed to authorities like Dattila, Kohala, Mataṅga and Nārada. A few portions are seen to be cited under "matāntara", "granthāntara" and "sakalamatasaṅgraha" (Sathyanarayana, 1960:appendix-p.1). A few extracts under "matāntara" are attributed to Somanārya and can be located in the Bengeri Manuscript (Sathyanarayana, 1960:introduction-lxiii). The ABSS text is based on a manuscript procured from the Oriental Research Institute, Mysore. The text consists of two chapters- Vādya and Gīta.

The following portions of NC are seen in ABSS.

ABSS	*NC*	*Subject*
1,433	3,69	Mṛdaṅga lakṣaṇaṃ
1,438cd-440;	3,72-73	"
1,441cd-443ab	3,77-78	"
1,638-641ab	3,94-96	Ḍholu lakṣaṇaṃ
2,50	2,61	Definition of śruti

1. Texts like Saṅgītadāmodhara and Saṅgītanārāyaṇa.

Besides, an extract on the instrument, "mauri" attributed to Mataṅga seen in ABSS (p.45-46), also figures in manuscripts G86, G89 and M, though not verbatim. However this portion of the text has not been included in the main body of NC but placed as anubandha (See 6.4.4. above).

7.8 Other Works

A few unique concepts found in NC have been followed by some later works written in Telugu and Tamiz till the early twentieth century. For example, Bharatasāttiram, Bharatasenāpatiyam, Saṅgītasarvārtha-sārasaṅgrahamu, Saṅgītacandrikai, Saṅgītasvaraprastāra-sāgaram follow NC in associating svara-s with a number of attributes and interpreting vādī, samvādī, anuvādī and vivādī svara-s following the lines of NC.

Apart from NC, a few musicological works speak of the 32 rāga-s (eight masculine and twenty-four feminine rāga-s). A table containing the names of the 32 rāga-s as mentioned in various works is given as Appendix-4.

Thus we see that Somanārya's NC had a great influence on many musicologival works written in the South. An analytical study of MBC, BKM, RJM and SSB reveals that these were written with an intention of echoing the ideas of Somanārya. Except for a very few, all unique concepts of NC have been faithfully reproduced in these works. It is also surprising to note that SM too (which is considered to be a pre-ratnākara work) has verses, which are parallel to those found in NC. Thus this peculiar tradition which had probably originated in the Vijayanagar area, was followed in Mysore and Tamil Nadu (Tanjore) areas. And strangely, this tradition did not survive in the Andhra region itself.

2

नाट्यचूडामणिः

[१. नाट्य]

नित्यानन्दकरं शान्तं निर्मलाङ्गं सुशोभनम्।
नीरे[र]जपत्रनयनं सीताराममहं भजे।।१।।
शंभुर्गौरी[१] तथा ब्रह्मा माधवो नन्दिकेश्वरः।
दत्तिलः[२] कोहलश्चैव याज्ञवल्क्यश्च[३] नारदः।।२।।
हनुमान् विघ्नराजश्च षण्मुखोऽपि[४] बृहस्पतिः।
अर्जुनो रावणश्चैव कन्या बाणासुरस्य[५] च।।३।।
एते भरतकर्तारः तत्तत्कर्मप्रयोगतः।
मतानामपि[६] सर्वेषां समाश्रित्यार्थचातुरीम् [?]।।४।।

---

१. T65-शंभुगौरी

२. G98, T65- तत्तिलः; G17- त(द)त्तिलः

३. G98, V08, T65- याज्ञवल्कच, G17-याज्ञवल्कझ्ल्क्यटच

४. The avagraha sign "ऽ" is not seen in the Mss of the earlier period but it is found in the recent transcripts like B13, V08 etc.

५. G98, B13- बाणसुतस्य, G17- बाणसुत(णासुर)स्य

६. G98-आस्सीषामपि, G17- आन्सी(न्ये)षामपि, B13-अन्येषामपि, T65-मातानामपि, The reading in T65 could be a scribal error. G98 originally reads मातानामपि; but the syllables 'मातानां' are seen cut and substituted by आस्सी(?). The rest of the word, मपि, is however retained. This corrected reading could not be read clearly and probably hence the two transcripts, G17 and B13, read different.

अष्टावधानविख्यात[१] सोमनार्येण वक्ष्यते।
नाट्यचूडामणिर्नाम[२] ग्रन्थो विबुधसम्मतः ।। ५।।
लोकेषु बहवस्सन्ति भरतार्थविशारदाः[३] ।
तेषां मतेभ्यः सङ्गृह्य कुर्यान्नाट्यप्रयोगिनीम्[४] [?] **।**
पूर्वशास्त्रानुसारेण ग्रन्थं शास्त्रशिरोमणिम्[५][?] **।। ६।।**
लक्ष्यस्वरूपं प्राकट्यसिद्धये लक्षणत्रयम् ।
लक्षणद्वयमेकं वा लक्ष्यलक्षो प्रदर्शयेत्[६] ।। ७।।
एकलक्षणमन्यस्य व्याख्यानं[७] लक्षणस्य यत्[८] ।
लक्ष्येत्व[९] पेक्ष[क्ष्य]मन्यस्यादत्रैव च[१०] निरूप्यते ।। ८।।

[११]టీకా:- లోకమందు భరతగ్రంథకర్తలు బహుమంది కలుగు(లరు) గనక. వార్ల యొక్క శాస్త్రం ఎల్లనుండి సంగ్రహించి సంక్షేపంగాను నాట్యచూడామణి అనేటి గ్రంథం లోకోపకారంగాను అష్టా*(వ)ధాన ప్రసిద్ధుండైన సోమనార్యు*(ని) చేత లే(ల)క్షణ లక్షియం(క్ష్యం) చెప్పప్రస్సున్నది (చెప్పనున్నది).

अथ नाट्योत्पत्तिः[१२]

गान्धर्वं त्रिविधं गीतवाद्यनर्तनभेदतः।

---

१. T65- विख्यातं, G17- विख्याता, V08- विख्यातः
२. G98- णीर्नाम
३. T65-भरतार्यविषारदः, this could be a scribal error due to the misinterpretation of letters that look more or less similar, because in grantha script, the syllable य and थ closely resemble each other.
४. T65- करान् नाट प्रयोगिनीम्, V08- करं नाटोपयोगिनम्
५. T65- शिरोमणि V08- ग्रन्थो नाट्यशिरोमणिः
६. B13- लक्ष्यलक्षौ प्रदर्शयेत्, V08- लक्ष्मलक्ष्येऽपि दर्शयेत्
७. V08- आख्यानं
८. T65- लक्षणस्य येत्, V08 - लक्षणद्वये
९. G98, G17, T65- लक्षेत्व
१०. G17- त्रैवचच, V08- मन्यस्य तु तत्राचं
११. This commentary portion is seen only in T65
१२. G98, G17, B13- this sub-heading is missing

नर्तनं त्रिविधं नाट्यनृत्तनृत्य[१] प्रभेदतः।।९।।
[२]नाट्यवेदं ददौ पूर्वं भरताय चतुर्मुखः।
ततस्तु भरतस्सार्धं[३] गन्धर्वाप्सरसां गणैः[४]।।१०।।
नाट्यं नृत्तं तथा नृत्यं[५] अग्रे शंभोः[६] प्रयुक्तवान्।
प्रयोगमुद्यतं[मुद्धतं][७]दृष्ट्वा[स्मृत्वा][८]स्वप्रयुक्तंततोहरः[९]।। ११।।
तण्डुना स्वगणाग्रण्य भरताय स्यधिदिशत् [व्यदीदृशत्][१०]।
[११]बुध्वाथ[१२] ताण्डवं तण्डोः[१३] मर्त्येभ्यो[१४] मुनयोऽवदन्।। १२।।

टीकाः:- గాంధర్వవేదం[౧౫] మూడు ప్రకారాలు. గీతవాద్యనృత్తాలు[౧౬]. నృత్తంనర్తనరో మూడు

१. G98- नाट्यं नृत्य नृत्य, G17- नाट्यं [ट्य] नृत्य नृत्त

२. v.10- v.11, cf. SR 7, 3cd - 5cd

३. T65, G98, G98a, G17, G17a - भरतासार्धं, M- भरतास्यार्थं [भरतः सार्धं]

४. M- गन्धर्वाप्सरसां ग [गणैः]

५. G98a, G17a -नाट्यवृत्तं तथा नृत्यं, T65-नाट्यनृत्तं तथा नृत्यं, B13a नाट्यं नृत्यं तथा नृत्तं, M- [नाट्यं] नृत्तं तथा नृत्य

६. V08- शंभु

७. G98a-प्रयोगमुद्यतंद्यतं, V08-प्रयोगमद्भुतं, M-प्रयोगमन्द्रातं[मुद्धतं स्मृत्वा]. This suggested reading is based on SR 7,5ab . उद्यतं could be a scribal error for उद्धतं.

८. All Mss read दृष्ट्वा which does not seem to be appropriate; hence parallel reading from SR has been suggested.

९. M- हः [रः]

१०. T65- तदुना स्वगणाग्रण्यं भरताय न्यदीदिशन्, G98,G17- तुदुना स्वगणाग्राह्यं भरताय न्यदीविशन्, G98a- तदुना श्वगणाग्रह्यं भरताय स्यदीदिशत्, G17a- तदुना श्व (ण्डुना स्व)गणाग्रह्यं भरताय यस्य(न्य)दीदिशत्, B13- तुदुना स्वगुणाग्राह्यं भरताय न्यवीविशन्, B13a-तुदुना स्वगुणग्रह्यं भरताय न्यदीदिशत्, V08- तंडुना स्वगणाग्रण्यं भरताय त्वदीशत्, M- स्यधिदिशत् [व्यदीदृ**]. Since the Mss read erroneously, the reading from SR has been borrowed.

११. cf. SR 7,6cd. SR reads another line after v.12ab (SR 7,6ab), which is missing in all the Mss. This is not noted in V08 but it is suggested in M. However since the idea conveyed in the missing line is not incorporated in the commentary, it has not been suggested here.

१२. B13,B13a- बुद्धाथ, V08- बुध्वातत्

१३. G98, G98a, G17, G17a, B13, B13a, T65- ताण्डमार्ताण्डोः

१४. G98,G17,B13- मन्तेसो, G98a,G17a,B13a - मर्तेसो, T65- मस्र्तेसो, M- मर्तेभ्यो

१५. G98a - గంధేర్వగీతం G17a -గంధర్వే గీతం, T65, B13a- గంధర్వ గీతం

१६. M- గీతవాద్యనృత్యాలు

ప్రోప్రోకారాలు. [1]నాట్య తత్తత్[2]నృత్తా నృత్యాలు[2] ఈ నాట్యవేదం[3] భరతునికి[4] బ్రహ్మ చెప్పెను. ఆ భరతుడు అప్సరసగణాలకు[5] చెప్పి[6] పరమేశ్వరుని[7] ముందర ఆడించెను[8]. ఆ పరమేశ్వరుడు తా కల్పించిన తాండవాలు తండుని చేత భరతునికి చెప్పించెను. ఆ భరతుడు మర్త్యలోకమందు ప్రతిష్ఠితమయ్యేడి[9] కొరకు మునీశ్వరులుకు చెప్పి ఆడించెను.

[१०]पार्वतीत्वनुशासस्मात् लास्यं [पार्वती त्वनुशास्ति स्म
लास्यं][११] बाणात्मजामुषाम्[१२] ।
तया[१३] द्वारवतीगोप्यः[१४] ताभिस्सौराष्ट्रयोषितः[१५] ।। १३ ।।
ताभिस्तु शिक्षिता नार्यः नानाजनपदास्पदाः[१६] ।
एवं परम्पराप्राप्तमेतल्लोके[१७] प्रतिष्ठिम् ।।१४ ।।

---

१. G98a,G17a, B13a - this sentence is missing

२. M- నాట్యనృత్యాలు

३. T65, G98a, G17a, B13a- నాట్యభేదం

४. T65, G98a, G17a- భరతునుకి

५. T65- అప్సర గణాలకు, M- అప్సరోగణాలకు

६. M- జప్పి

७. T65- పరమేశ్వరిని

८. G98a- ఆడించను

९. M- మైయ్యేటి

१०. v.13- v.14, cf. SR 7,7- 8.

११. V08-पार्वतीत्वन्वशासस्मालास्यं, G98,B13,B13a-पार्वतीत्वनुसस्माल्लास्यं, G17- पार्वतीत्वनु सस्मा[त्त]ल्लास्यं, M-पार्वति [ती] त्वनुशालिस्मा [शास्ति स्मा] लास्यां. The reading is suggested from SR 7,7ab

१२. M- प्राणात्मजावु[मु]षा[म्]

१३. T65, G98, G98a, G17, B13, B13a - तयो, G17a- तयो[या]

१४. G98,G98a, G17,G17a, B13,B13a, T65 - गोपाः , M- द्वारावतिगोप्याः

१५. G98,G98a,G17-योषिताः,G17a-योषिता[ः], T65-योषिता, M-स्ता[सौ]राष्ट्रयोषिताम्

१६. G98a,G17a,B13,B13a-पदास्सदा,G98,G17,T65-पदास्सदाः,M-पदास्पदाः[श्रिताः]; (SR reads पदाश्रिताः)

१७. M- पार . . . . [परंपराप्राप्त] मेतल्लोके

టీకా:- పార్వతి కల్పించిన లాస్యం(య)నృత్తం[१] బాణాసురుని[२] కుమార్తి(కుమార్తె)[३] ఉషాకన్యకు[४] చెప్పెను. ఆ ఉషా[५] ద్వారవతి[६] స్త్రీలకు చెప్పెను. వారు చంపన్న[७]దేశాల యున్నది వార్లురూ కడుంవార్లుకుర్లకూ చెప్పగా[८] ఈ తీరున[९] పరంపరయా మర్త్యలోకమందు ప్రతిష్ఠితమాయెను.

[१०]ऋग्यजुस्सामवेदेभ्यो[११] वेदादाथर्वणः[१२] क्रमात्।
पाठानभिनयान् [पाट्यञ्चाभिनयान्][१३][गीतं][१४] रसान्[१५] सङ्गृह्य पद्मभूः[१६]।
व्यरीरचत्[१७] त्रयमिदं धर्मकामार्थमोक्षदम्।। १५।।

---

१. T65, G98a, G17a, B13a- నృత్తం

२. G98a - సురని

३. M- కుమార్త్యకు

४. M- కన్యకకు

५. M- యమా

६. M- ద్వారావతి

७. B13a - ఛప్పన్న, M- ఛంపన్న

८. M- వార్లుకు చెప్పిరి గాగా

९. M- రీతిన

१०. v.15 - v.18, cf. SR 7,9ab-13ab

११. M- रुग्यजुस्सामवेदेभ्यो

१२. T65,G98,G98a,G17,B13,B13a- वेदाद्याथर्वण, G17a- वेदाद्याद्याथर्वण, M- वेदाधा[च्चा]थर्वणः (SR reads वेदाच्चाथर्वणः)

१३. G98,G98a,G17,G17a-पाठानपिसयान्,V08-पाठ्यानभिनय,M-पाठानभि[ठ्यं चाभि] नयान्. The syllable स seems to be a scribal error for the syllable न, which often is confused in the Telugu script. All Mss read this word in the plural form, except V08; since it has been used in the singular form in the earlier texts like NS and SR (NS 1,17 and SR 7, 9), the reading, पाठ्यं has been suggested.

१४. M- गीतान् [गीतं]. For the same reason stated above, गीतं is suggested.

१५. G98, G98a, G17, G17a, B13, B13a, T65- सर्वान्

१६. M- सङ्ग्रंठठ[गृह्य पद्म] भूः

१७. G98,G98a,G17,G17a,B13,B13a,T65- व्यररीच, This reading could be an error caused by anagrammatism (transposition of letters). M- व्यदिरि[व्यरीर]च

कीर्ति[१] प्रागल्भ्यसौभाग्यं[य] वेदाद्यानां [वैदग्ध्यानां][२] विवर्धनम्[३]।

[४]ऐश्वर्यशौर्यधैर्याणां[५] विलासस्य च कारणम्।। १६।।

दुःखार्त[ति]शोकनिर्वेद[६] खेदविच्छेद[७] साधनम्[८]।

अति[९]ब्रह्मपरानन्दमिध[द]मप्यधिकं[१०] फलम्[११] ।। १७।।

जहार नारदादीनां[१२] चित्तानि[१३] कथमन्यथा[१४]।

न किञ्चिद्दृश्यते[१५] लोके दृश्यं[१६] श्राव्यमतः परम्[१७]।। १८।।

టీకా:- నాలుగు వేదాలనుండి క్రమాననే పాఠ్యాలు అభినయం[१८] గీతం రసభావాలు సంగ్రహించి బ్ర్మ(హ్మ) గీతవాద్య[१९] నృత్తాలు[२०] జేసెను[२१]. ఇది(□ ధర్మార్థకామ[२२] మోక్షాలు

---

१. G98, G17- कीर्तिः

२. G17-वेदाद्या[र्था]नां,M-वेदज्ञानां[***], Since the reading in the Mss gives no sense, the parallel reading from SR is suggested.

३. M- विवर्धनम् [प्रवर्धनम्]

४. G98,G17,B13- v.16cd- v.17ab are missing

५. G98a,G17a,B13a-धैर्य शौर्याणां, M- ऐश्व [औदा]र्यशौर्य [***] धैर्याणां. SR reads औदार्य

६. T65,G98a, G17a, B13a - दुःखार्तशोकनिर्वेद, V08- निर्वेदा

७. G17a- भे[खे]दविच्छेद, M- प्रोद[विभेद]विच्छेद, T65, G98- प्रोदविच्छेद

८. M- साधनम् [कारणम्]

९. V08- आदि

१०. M-विप[द]मप्य[भ्य]धिकं, T65,G98,G98a,G17,G17a,B13,B13a- विधमप्यधिकं

११. M- फलम् [धनम्]

१२. M- नारदादि[दी]ना

१३. M- चिंत्तानि[चित्तानि]

१४. M- कदमन्मधा [कथमन्यथा]

१५. M- किंचिद्रु[द्दृ]श्यते

१६. T65, G98, G98a- दृश्य, M- दृस्यं [श्यं]

१७. M- . . . lacunae [श्राव्यमतः परम्] (SR reading- SR 7,13cd is also suggested)

१८. G98a,G17a, B13a- అభినయ

१९. B13a- వాద్యాలు

२०. M- నృత్యాలు

२१. B13a- చేసేను

२२. T65, G98a- కామ్య

యిచ్చేటి□[1] ఐశ్వర్య ధైర్య□సాలకు[2] కారణమైన□ దుఃఖార్త[3] శోక నిర్వేద భే(ఖే)ద□ఛ్చే(ఛే)ద[4] సాద(ధ)కమైన□బ్రహ్మానందముకన్న[5] అధిక ఫల□చ్చేటి□కాబట్టి నారదాది పరమభాగవతులు ఇందున ప్రవర్తిందు(తు)రు. ఇంతకన్నా చూచే[6] శాస్త్రం ఇంతకన్నా □వే శాస్త్రం[7] యితరము లేదు గనుక. ఇది త్రిమూర్త్యాత్మకమైన శాస్త్రమని తెలియు(య)తగినది.

[२.गीताध्यायः]

अथ गीताध्यायं वक्ष्यते[8]

[9]सङ्गीतशास्त्रं[10] सङ्गृह्य[11] स्वररागसुधारसम्।
अष्टावधान[12] विख्यातं[13] सोमनार्येण[14] वक्ष्यते ।। १।।

---

१. T65,G17a- యిచ్చేది□ G98a,B13a- యిచ్చేది

२. M- కా . . . .

३. M- □ఖేద

४. T65- కన్నా, M- బ్రహ్మానందని * * న్న

५. G98a-అధి

६. B13a- చూసే

७. M- ఇంతకంన — తర

८. G98a,G17a,B13a,G86,G07- missing. G98-गीताध्यायं वक्ष्यन्ते, G91-अदा गीताध्या वक्षते, V41-अथ गीताध्याये वक्ष्यते, V08, M- अथ गीताध्यायो वक्ष्यते

९. G98, G17,B13- v.1ab is missing. In other Mss, the following reading is seen.
अष्टावधानविख्यात सोमनार्येण संक्षिपेत्। संगीतशास्त्रसङ्गृह्य वक्ष्ये लोकोपकारकम्।।
అష్టావధాన ప్రసిద్ధుండైన సోమనార్యుడు సంగీత శాస్త్రమందు సంగ్రహించి సంక్షేపంగాను స్వరరాగసుధారసమనే సంగీత లక్షణం లక్షియం లోకోపకారంగా చెప్పుతున్నాడు. Since the construction of this verse is not perfect and complete in meaning, a similar verse, seen at the beginning of the section on rāga-ss, before v.97, (G98,G17,B13- missing), with a better construction has been shifted to this place. The second half of the verse mentioned above is missing in V08.

१०. G86- संगी * * शास्त्रं, G38- संगीतशास्त्र, Sp- सङ्गीतशास्त्र, V08-संगीतशास्त्रे

११. T65, G86, G89 - सङ्ग्रह्य, G38 - संग्रीह्य, Sp- सङ्ग्रहपु

१२. G86, G89- अष्टवधान, G38, Sp - अष्टावदान

१३. G38- विख्यति, Sp- विश्वति

१४. T65- सोमनाख्याण

टीका:- సంగీతశాస్త్రమందు[1] సంగ్రహించి స్వరరాగసుధారసమున్ను (రసము)[2] అష్టావధాన ప్రసిద్ధుండైన[3] సోమనార్యుని చేత చెప్పబడెను[4].

नादं, नादोत्पन्नम्[5]

नृत्तं[6] वाद्यं तथा गीतं मेलनं[7] नादमुच्यते[8]।
[9]रञ्जक [10]स्वरसन्दर्भो गीतमित्यभिधीयते[11]।

---

१. G86- సంగీత శాస్త్రమున్ను, G89- ******, G38- సంగీత శాస్త్రమునందు

२. G38- స్వరరాగసుధారసము, Sp- స్వరరాగసుదారసవచ్చు

३. T65, G86, G89- ప్రసిద్ధుడైన

४. G86, G89- చెప్పబడుచున్నది

५. G98a,G17a,B13a,G86,G07,G91,V08,V41-missing. This sub-heading is seen after the heading, गीताध्यायं वक्ष्यते, It was felt logical in shifting this heading down, i.e., before v.1cd, since the text corresponding to नाद commences here. Probably, these two headings could have been written one below the other, along the margin in the original (PL), which must have been copied together by the scribes.

६. G98, G98a, G17, G17a, B13, B13a - नृत्यं

७. G07- मळनं

८. G86- नाममुच्यते, G07- नापमुच्यते, V08- नाद (नाट्य) मुच्यते. In the popular textual tradition, the union of गीत, वाद्य and नृत्त is called सङ्गीत (SR 1,1,21cd). Most of the Mss here, mention the combination of नृत्त, वाद्य and गीत as नाद. Probably the term नाद, in this case, does not seem to be expressing the fundamental meaning of musical sound but standing for (denoting) a composite art form. In the Nāṭyaśāstra tradition, गानं, वाद्यं and नाट्यं are collectively called नाट्य (NS 28, 7ab) and probably based on this tradition, Kavi, in V08 could have suggested नाट्य for नाद.

९. v.2 is missing in M. They are probably borrowed from SR 4,1ab and SR 1,3,25ab. The existence of this verse here seems to be out of context and probably the reason why M omits them. It is to be noted that there is no commentary for this verse. The author could have perhaps quoted v.2cd, with reference to the term, गीत found in v.1cd. In the same way, v.3ab could have been quoted to define the term स्वर found in v.2cd (स्वरसन्दर्भ).

१०. G98, G98a, G17a, B13a - रञ्जय , V41- रजक

११. G98,G98a,G17-गीतनृत्यदिय्यते, G07-गीतनृर्त्तपिधिय्यते, G17a,B13-गीतनृ[मि]त्यभिदिय्यते, T65-गीत्यनृत्यभिधीयते, G86- गीतनृत्यविधीय्यते

स्वतो[१] रञ्जयति[२] श्रोतृचित्तं[३] स्वरसमुच्यते[४] ।। २।।

టీకా:- నృత్తగీతవాద్యాల[౫] కూడి[౬] పుట్టిన ధ్వని నాదమనబడును[౭].

नकारं प्राणविज्ञेयं[८] दकारमनलं[९] विदुः।

जातः[१०] प्राणाग्निसंयोगात्[११] नाद इत्यभिधीयते[१२] ।। ३।।

టీకా:- నకారం ప్రాణాలని[౧౩] తెలియతగినది[౧౪]. దకారం అగ్నియని తెలియదగినది[౧౫]. ఈ[౧౬] ప్రాణాగ్ని కూటము[౧౭] చేత పుట్టిన ధ్వని నాదమని చెప్పబడును[౧౮].

---

१. G98a,G17a,B13a,T65,G86,G07- स्वरो, G98,G17,B13 -सर्वो This kind of scribal error made due to the wrong placement of the letter व (to form a different conjunct consonant) in Telugu script is noticed in a few more places in this work.

२. G98, G07- रजयति, B13 - रज[ञ्ज]यति

३. G98,G98a,B13,B13a-श्लोकचित्तं, G17a-श्लोक(श्रोतृ)चित्तं, T65,G86- श्लोकंचित्तं, G07- स्लोकं चित्तं, V08- श्रोतृश्चित्तं

४. V08- स स्वर उच्यते, V41- स्वररञ्जितो चित्तं स्वर स्वर समुच्यते

५. G98a,G17a,B13a,T65- నృత్త వాద్యాలు, V41-నృత్య గీత వాద్యములు, M- నృత్యవాద్యగీతాలు

६. G86, G07- చాత , V41- కుడియుండిన

७. G86, G07- పుట్టిన ధ్వని నాదమని చేప్పబడును, M- పుట్టినది ధ్వని నాదమని చేప్పబడును, V41-నాదమని పించును

८. G98,G98a,G17,G17a,B13,B13a,T65,G86,G07,G91,V41-नकारं प्राणविजयं, V08-नकारः प्राणविज्ञेयो

९. G98,G98a,G17,G13,G91- मनिलं, G17a-मलं, V08- दकारो मलनं (कमलं, मनलं), V41- कमलं

१०. G91- जातिः

११. G17- संयोगा, G07- संयोगान, M- संयोगं

१२. T65, G98, G98a, G17, G17a, G86, G07, G91, M - नादमित्यभिधीयते, V41- नादविंदुरितीर्यते

१३. G07,G86- ప్రాణమని, V41- నకారము ప్రాణములని

१४. G86, G07 - తెలియతగ్గది

१५. G86, G07- తెలియతగ్గది

१६. G98a,G17a,B13a- missing

१७. G98a- కూట[illegible], G17a- కూడి[illegible], B13a- కూట[illegible]

१८. G86- చెప్పబడు, T65, G98a, G17a, B13a- పించును, V41- పించబడును

[१]नादोपासनया देवाः[२] ब्रह्मविष्णुमहेश्वराः[३]।

[भवन्त्युपासिता नूनं यस्मादेते तदात्मकाः] ।।४।।

టీకా:-[४]బ్ర[५] ష్ణు మహేశ్వరులు[६] బ్రహ్మోపాసన[७] చేయుచుందురు.

आहतम[ता]नाहत लक्षणम्[८]

आहतोऽनाहतश्चैव[९] स नादो[१०] द्विविधो मतः[११]।

इत्यो[यु]भया[यो]श्च[१२] सम्योगादाहतः परिकीर्तितः।। ५।।

आकाशसम्भवो नादः[१३] अनाहत उदीरितः[१४]।

---

१. This line is the first half of a verse in SR (SR 1,3,2ab.) and the latter half of it is missing in all the Mss. The reading is by itself incomplete in meaning and the commentator interprets it in a different way. RJM (p.121) also reads this incomplete in the same way. Probably the second half could have been missing in the copy that was available to the commentator. Hence the remaining half verse from SR (SR 1,3,2cd) has been suggested here.

२. T65, G86, G07, G91- नादोपासनयोर्देवाः, B13, B13a- नादोपासनया देवा, M- नादोपासनयो देवाः

३. M- प्रह्मविष्णुमहेश्वरः

४. G86, G07- commentary is missing here but found after v.6cd thus: G86- బ్రహ్మ ష్ణు మహేశ్వరులు యీ నాద బ్రహ్మోపాసకులు, G07- బ్రహ్మ ష్ణు మహేశ్వరా ఆహతోనాహతశ్చైవా ఆరోహణ్యవనాహతం. బ్రహ్మ ష్ణు మహేశ్వరులు యీ నాద బ్రహ్మోపాసకులు.

५. G98a, G17a - బ్రహ్మ

६. M- □ —— ల నాద, V41- మహేశ్వరుని

७. T65- న్రు**యిణ్వద బ్రహ్మోపాస్తి, V41- బ్రహ్మోపాస్తిని

८. Missing in all the Mss except M.

९. G07-आहतोनाहतोचैव, G24-आहतोनाहतचैव, V41-missing from here upto आरोहिण्याहतश्चैव, the first half of v.6cd

१०. G98a,G07-ननादो, G17a-ननादो [स], G91- नाद, T65- नादो, M- स नामो [दो]

११. T65,G98,G98a,G17,G86,G07,G91,G24-द्विविधा मतः, M-द्विविधा[धो] मते [तः]

१२. G98,G98a,G17,G17a,B13,B13a-यत्योभयाश्च, G07-यत्यूभयोश्चे, G86-इत्योभायाश्च, G91- ** त्योभयोस्तु, V08- यत्रोभयाश्च, M- यत्योभयोश्चैव [उभयोरपि]

१३. T65, G24-नादः च, M- आकाशसम्भवो . . . हतमुदीरितम् [नादः अनाहत उदीरितः]

१४. T65,G98,G98a,G17,G17a- अनाहतमुदीरितम्, G86- प्रनाहतमुदीरितं, G07- अनागत उदीरितः

आरोहिण्याहतश्चैव[१] अवरोहिण्यावनाहतः[ण्यनाहतः][२] ।।६।।

टीका:-[३]ఆ నాదం[४] ఆ॑తమని[५] అనా॑తమని రెండు ప్రకారాలు[६]. [७](ఆ॑తమనె నాదం శరీరమందు పుట్టెను. అనా॑తమనె నాదం ఆకాశంవల్ల పుట్టెను). [८]ఆరో॑ణీ ఆ॑తమున్ను అవరో॑ణీ అనా॑తమని చెప్పబడును.

---

१. G107-आरोहण्यहतोरचैवा, G86-आरोहिण्यहतश्चैवा, T65- आरोहिण्यहतश्चैवा, G24 - आरोहण्यहतंचैवं

२. G98,G17,B13-वरोहिणवनाहतः, G98a,G17a,B13a-वरोहिण्यावनाहतः, T65-आरोहण्यावनाहतम्, G86-आरोहण्यावनाहतम्, G07-आरोहण्यवनाहतम्, G24-वरोहण्यश्चनाहतं, V08-अवरोहिण्यात्वनाहतः, M-वरोहिणाश्च नाहतम् [अवरोहिण्यानाहतः], V41-ववरोहिण्यवनाहतं. Since the existing reading in the Mss is erroneous with respect to metre and sandhi, this is suggested based on BKM,p. 58.

३. G91-commentary is missing; V08 reads thus: (tel comm: ఉభయ సంయోగము - జంత్రమందు). In G86, this portion of the text is seen inserted in between with a '+' mark. G86 and G07 combine the commentary to v.4cd too.

४. G98a- ఆనందం, T65-అనాదం, G17a, B13a-ఆనందం (నా)

५. G98a- అ॑మని, T65-అ॑తమని, V41- న॑తమని

६. G98a,B13a- ప్రకారాలు, G17a- ద్విప్రకారాలు, G07-2 కలిగెనో, G86- రెండు కలిగెనొ, T65- ప్రకారాలు రెండుప్రకారాలు, M- ******, V41- ఈ ప్రకారాలు

७. G98a, G17a, T65- జాతమందు ఉభయసంయోగం ఆ॑తం. ఆకాశాత సంభవో నాదం అనా॑తం గాత్రమందు, B13a- జాతమందు ఉభయసంయోగం ఆ॑తం. ఆకాశాత సంభవం నాదం. అనా॑తం గాత్రమందు, G86- ఆ॑తమన నాదం ఆకాశంవల్ల పుట్టెను. అనా॑తమనె నాదం శరీరమందు పుట్టెను, G07- ఆ॑తమనె నాదం ఆకాశంవల్ల పుట్టెను. అనా॑తమనె నాదం శరీరమందు పుట్టెను. G24-జంత్రమందు **** అనా॑తం గాత్రమందు, M- **** ఆకాశ సం****** ॑తం ****, V41- జాతమందు భయ సంయోగం ఆకార సంభవ నాదులనా॑తమందు నాదం అనా॑తం గాత్రమందు. In this portion of the commentary in the Mss. the readings of T65, G98a, G17a and B13a are almost similar and they incorporate a few words/phrases from the original text, which are seen in saṃskūta language. G86 and G07 read the words āhata and anāhata transpositioned. Hence a consolidated reading is presented here.

८. G86- ఆరో॑ణీ ఆ॑తము అవరో॑ణీ అనా॑తము. ఈ రీతిన నాదభేదాలు *** డును, G07- ఆరో॑ణి ఆ॑ము అవరో॑ణి అనా॑తము. యీ రీతిన నా నాద భేదాలు చెప్పబడును, G24- ఆరో॑ణీ ॑తమున్ను అవరో॑ణీ అతమున్ను అనరోవాణి అనాతమని చెప్పబడును, M- ఆరో॑ణీ ఆ॑తమున్ను అవరో॑ణి అనా॑తం చెప్పబడును, V41- ఆరో॑ణీ ఆ॑తమున్ను అవరో॑ణి అనా॑తమని చెప్పబడును.

[स्वर लक्षणं][१]

[२]तन्नादं[३] सप्तधा कृत्वा[४] तथा[५] षड्जादिभिः स्वरैः[६]।
षड्जो ऋषभगान्धारौ मध्यमः[७] पञ्चमस्तथा[८]।
धैवतश्च[९] निषादश्च[१०] स्वराः सप्त[११] प्रकीर्तिताः।। ७।।

टीका:- [१२]ఆ నాదం స రి గ మ ప ధ ని[१३] అని సప్త స్వరాలాయను[१४]. ఈ సప్త[१५] స్వరాలు[१६] నెమలి[१७], ఆవు[१८], మేక, క్రౌంచపక్షి, కోకిల, గుర్రం[१९], ఏనుగ[२०]- □ల్లనంటి (□టినుంటి) బుట్టెను[२१].

---

१. G86,G07,V08,G91,M-missing, T65,G98,G98a,G17,G17a-आहतमनाहत स्वर लक्षणं, B13,13a-आहतानाहत स्वर लक्षणं. This seems to be the subject heading to the section on the svara-s. The words आहत and अनाहत were felt unnecessary and hence the heading has been retained thus.

२. cf. SM 1,1,11ab.

३. V08- तन्नादः, G86- lacunae

४. V08- सप्तधाख्यातः, M- सप्त - - - - मध्यमं पञ्च missing in between; breaks off here and reads from the vādya section.

५. G98, G98a, G17, G17a, B13, B13a, T65, G24, G91- तदा

६. T65, G07- षड्जादिस्वरैः

७. All Mss except V08 read मध्यमं

८. G07- पञ्चमं त्तथा, G24- षड्जा रिषम्रं गांधां दा ***चं । पंचमं। मध्यमस्वरं।

९. G98- सैवतैश्च, G98a-यैदैवतैश्च, G17a-यैदै[धै]वतश्च, T65- दैवतश्च, G24- दैवतश्चा

१०. G07,G86- निषादश्चा

११. G98, G98a, G17, G91, T65- स्वरैस्सप्त, G86- स्वरैसप्त, G24- श्वरात्सप्त

१२. G98a,G17a,B13a- this sentence is missing

१३. G86,G07, G24, V41- స రి గ మ ప ధ ని స

१४. T65, G86 - అనేక స్వరాలాయను, G07-□రాలాయను, V41- స్వరములాయేను

१५. G98a, G17a, B13a, G24 - missing

१६. G07, G86 - స్వరాలున్ను

१७. V08 reads the names of the animals alone, by mentioning "Tel. Comm."

१८. V08- వృషభము, G24- వృషభం

१९. G07, G86- సింహ్మం

२०. G98a, G17a, B13a - commentary stops with this

२१. V08- సంభవస్థానములు, G86- దీంట్ల నుంచ్చి పుట్టెను, G07- దీన్ల నుంచి బుట్టెను, G24- □**నుంటి బుట్టేను, T65 -□ * * * * ండి పుట్టెను

[१]एवं स्वरान्[२] समाकृष्य[३] वीणादिषु निधाय च[४]।
तेन फुतेन नादेन[५] सङ्गीतमकरोत् तथा[६] ।। ८।।

टीका:- [७]ఆ సప్త స్వరాలు జంత్రమందు వాయించ్యా (చ ఆ) నాదమందు సంగీతమని పుట్టెను.

शिशुर्वेत्ति पशुर्वेत्ति[८] वेत्ति गानरसं फणिः[९] ।। ९।।

टीका:-ఈ గానరసం శిశువులకు పశువులకు సర్ప్వములకు[१०] తెలుసును.

अजा[ज्ञा]त[११] हृदयस्यन्दो[विषयास्वादो][१२] बालः[१३] पर्यङ्किकातले[१४]।
[१५]रुदन् गीतामृतं[१६] पीत्वा[१७] हर्षोत्कर्षं[१८] प्रपद्यते[१९]।। १०।।

---

१. v.8, cf. SM 1,1,15

२. G24- स्वरा

३. G24- स्वराकृष्य

४. G07- वीणाविदु निदाय चा, G91- वीणाधीश निधाय च, G24- वीणाविषु निधाय चा T65, G86- विनावेषु निधाय चा

५. V08- तेन गात्रेण (फुतेन) नादेन, T65- नेन घातेन नादेन, G07- तेनोदाफुतेन नादेना, G86-तेनोद्फुतेन नादेना, G24- * * * धातेना नादेना

६. G24- तथाः

७. G86- ఆ సప్త స్వరాలున్ను జంత్రమందు వాయంచ్యా నాదమందు సంగ్గీతం పుట్టెను, G07- ఆ సప్త స్వరాలున్ను జింత్రమందు వాయంచగ ఆ నాదమందు సంగీతం పుట్టునూ, V41- missing from here upto v.9ab

८. G86 - शिशुर्वेर्त्ति पशुर्वेर्त्ति, G07-शिशुवेन्ति पशुवेन्ति,

९. G17a, B13, B13a, G91- फणी, G24- फाणि

१०. G07- శిశ్వాలకు పశువులకు సర్వములకు, T65- శిశువులకు సర్పాలకు, G24- శిశు పశు సర్పాలకు, V41- శిశువులకు పశువులకు సర్పాలకు తెలియేను

११. G98, G98a, G17, G17a, B13, B13a - अजाळि, T65, G86- अजाळ, V08-अजा(ज्ञा)त

१२. V08- हृदयस्वंशो, G24- हृदयाश्यादो, V41- ब्रोदयस्यन्दो, Reading based on SR.

१३. G98, G98a, G17, B13, B13a, G91, V41-प्राला, G17a- प्राला[लः], T65, G86, G07- प्राल

१४. G07, G86 - पर्वंन्निकातले

१५. v.10cd- v.11, cf. SR 1,1,28cd-29

१६. T65,G98,G98a,G17,G17a,B13,B13a- मदंसितामृतं, G91- रु * * सिताम्यदं, G24- रुदंगीतामृदौत्व

१७. G98, G17, B13- पीता, G86 - पित्वा, G91- पेत्वा

१८. G24- हरुगोत्करुषं

१९. G24- प्रपध्यते

टीका:- ఏ◻ యెరుగని శిశువు(ని) తొడపైకు పెట్టుకొని[१] గానం చేస్తు రోదన[*]నుండై సంతోషం చేత వుండును[२]

वनेचरस्तृणाहार[३]श्चित्रं[४] मृगशिशः[शुः][५] पशुः।

लब्दो लब्दसु[६]सङ्गीतं[७]मोदन्ते[८] यश्च[९] जीवितम्[१०]

[लुब्धो लुब्धकसंङ्गीते गीते यच्छतिजीवितम्][११]।। ११।।

टीका:- వనమందు కసువుతిని[१२] నీళ్ళుతాగుచు[१३] స్వయం(గా) సంచరిస్తువుండే[१४] మృగపశ్వాదులు[१५] [१६]గానం◻ సంతోషంగా వుండును.

[१७]**कृष्णसर्पोऽपि[१८] तन्नादं श्रुत्वा हर्षं[१९] प्रपद्यते।**

---

१. G24- శిశువును తోడపైకోర్చంట్ట బెట్టుకోని, V41- శిశువును గూర్చుణ్ణనిచ్చి

२. G07- గానంచేస్త సన్తోషముగా వుండు రోదనమ్మాయడు, G86- గానంచేస్తు సన్తోషముగా వుండును*** నంశాయడు, V41- గానము జేసిన రోదనము నిడిచి సన్తోషముగానుండును

३. G98, B13-वनेचरान् तृणाहारान्, G98a, B13a-वनेचरण् त्रिणाहाराण्, G17, G17a-वनेचरण् तृणाहारान्, T65- वनेचरण् त्रिणम्हरण्, G86-वनेचरन् त्रिणम्हरण्, G07- वनेचरण् तृणंहारण्, G24- वनेवरंपरं तृणंहारं, V41- वनेचरंतृणाहारं

४. G86, G07 - चित्र, V08- चितु

५. T65, G98a, G17a, B13a, G86, G91, V08, V41-मृगशिरो, G98,G17, B13,G07- मृगशिलो

६. G98-शब्दो दब्धक, G17,B13- शब्दो दब्धक (लुब्धक), T65,G98a,G17a,G86 - शब्दो लब्धक, B13a,G07- शब्दो लुब्धक V08- श्रुत्वा लुब्धक, G91- शब्दो लब्दसु, G24- लुद्बा लुद्बक

७. G07- सङ्गीतः

८. G86- मोहते, G91- येदंते

९. G98a, G17a, B13a, V08, G24- यच्च, G91- यस्च , V41- यस्स

१०. G86- जीवत्तरः

११. Reading based on SR since the existing reading is not proper;y constructed.

१२. G07- కంవుతిని, G24- కసువృదిని, T65- కసువృగాదిని, V41- గసువుదిని

१३. T65- నీల్లుత్రాభిపుం డే, G24- శ్లోవాగివుం డె, V41- నీల్లుద్రా◻యుండే

१४. G86- స్వయం***సం**రిస్తు****, T65, G24, V41- missing

१५. G86, G07- మృగపశువు, G07- మృగపశ్వ

१६. T65- పసలగా పరిగానంసిని సంతోషపడి వుండును, G24- పసలగా పరిగానంసిని సంతోషచాత వుండును, V41- పరిగానము చేసిన ◻ సన్తోషమునుండును

१७. cf. SMK,2,5cd-6ab, SM 1,1,23.

१८. G07- कृष्णसर्पो श्र, G86- कृष्णसर्प्पा सि, G91- कृष्णसर्पापि, G24- कृष्णोसर्पापि, V41- कृष्णसर्पोर्पि

१९. G24- अरुष

[१]तस्य गीतस्य माहात्म्यं[२] के[३]प्रशंसं[शंसि]तुमीशते[४] ।। १२ ।।

टीका:- [५]కృష్ణసర్పాలు[६] స్వర గీత నాదం □వి సంతోషమైయుండును[७]. కాగా[८] ఆ గీతమహాత్మ్యం[९] యేమని[१०] వర్ణింపశక్యము.

[११]देववंशास्तु[१२] सगमाः [१३] पञ्चमः पितृवंशजः ।

[१४]रिधौ[१५] ऋषिकुले[१६] जातौ निषादोऽसुर[१७]वंशजः ।। १३ ।।

टीका:- స గ మ[१८] దేవవంశం; పా[१९] పితృవంశం; రి ధా[२०] ఋషివంశం[२१]; ని[२२]

---

१. cf. SR 1,1,30ab

२. G07- माहत्मं

३. V08, G07, G86- किं

४. G98-प्रशंसंतुमोस्तं, T65-प्रसन्तुमीरितम्, V08, G07, G86- प्रशंसितुमीरितं, B13,B13a,G91, G24 - प्रशंसन्तुमीरितं, V41-प्रशंसितुमीशृताः

५. This is the only commentary portion available in G91.

६. T65,G86,G07,G24- సర్పాలు, V41- సర్పములు

७. G07, G86- సంతోషింస్తు వుండును, T65, G24- సంతోషం చాత వుండును, V41- సంతోషముగానుండును

८. G07,G86- కాగ, G91- గనక, V41- గానసీ

९. G07- ఆ గీతం యొక్క మాత్వాం, G86- ఆ గీతంయొక్క మహాత్యం, G91, G24 - ఆ యొక్క గీత మహాత్మ్యం, V41- గీత మాహాత్మ్యం

१०. G07- యెవరి చాత, G86- యెవరి చాత వర్ణాంప్పశ్యము, V41- మేమని వర్ణింప శ్యమగును

११. v.13, cf. SR 1,3,52ab-53a. G18 presents the portion dealing with the various attributes of the svara-s in a different manner. Thus here it reads: देवर्षिदेवदेवश्च पित्रर्षि राक्षसः क्रमात्। षड्जादिस्वर प्रृन्दानामिति वंशः समीरितः।।

१२. V08- देववंश्यास्तु, G24- देववंशशस्तु

१३. T65, G98, G17, G86, G07- सगमः , G24- सगम, V41- गमसः

14. V41- this line is missing

15. G86, G07- रिगौ

16. G86, G07 - रिषिकुले

१७. T65- निषादस्सुर, G98, G24- निषादासुर

१८. G24- షడ్జం గాంధార మధ్యమా స్వరాలు, V41- స గ ము

१९. V41- న గ ము, G24- పంచమం

२०. G24- रिषभं दैतालु రిషభం దైతాలు

२१. G86, G07- రిషివంశం

२२. G24- నిషాదం, V41-నిరుద్ధ

రాక్షసవంశం[१]. ఇ[२] స్వరాలకు వంశాలు.[३]

[४]**ब्राह्मणौ तु समौ ज्ञेयौ[५] रिधौ क्षत्रियजातिजौ[६]।**

निगौ वैश्यमिति प्रोक्तौ[७] प इति शूद्रजातिजः[८]।। १४।।

टीका:- స మ[९] బ్రాహ్మణజాతి; రి ధా(ధ)[१०] క్షత్రియజాతి; ని గ వైశ్యజాతి; ప శూద్రజాతి;[११] ఇ[११] స్వరాలకు జాతులు.

[१२]**अशीतिस्सप्ततिष्षष्टिश्चत्वारिंशश्च त्रिंशति[१३]।**

विंशतिः दशमो वर्षः वयः षड्जादिभिस्स्वरैः [षड्जादीनां वयः क्रमात्][१४] ।। १५।।

टीका:- 80, 70, 60, 40[१५], 30[१६], 20, 10 - యెండ్లు ఇది(వి) సప్త స్వరాల వయసు[१७].

---

१. G86, G07- missing

२. T65, G86, G07- ఇది

३. G86, G07- వంశలక్షణం, G24- missing; G91 ends here.

४. G07-v.14 is missing. cf.SM 1,1,29. G18- ब्रह्मक्षत्रियवि ********** काः ।षड्जादिस्वरचाराणामित्येवं जातयः स्मृताः।।

५. T65,G98,G17-ब्राह्मणस्समपाजेयी,B13- ब्राह्मणाःसमपाज्ञेया, G86-ब्राह्मणस्सगमज्ञेयः, G24 -ब्राह्मणस्समपा ज्ञेय, V41- ब्राह्मणा समपा ज्ञेया

६. T65, G98, G17- रिधौ क्षत्रियजातिजा, V41- रिधा क्षत्रियजातिजः

७. T65,G98,G17-नि गा वैश्यमिति प्रोक्तं, G86-नि ग वैश्यमिति प्रोक्ता, G24-निगौ दशमिति प्रोक्तौ, V41- नि गा वैश्य इति प्रोक्तं

८. T65,G98,G17,B13,G86-पाकल्या शूद्रजातयः, G24-पौ यिति शूद्रजातिजौ, V41- पानन्या शूद्रजातयः, V08 suggests (पञ्चमः) probably cited from SM.

९. G86- స గ మ, V41- స మః, G07- missing

१०. G24- ధా

११. T65, G86, G07- ఇది

१२. G18- अशीतिस्सप्ततिः *********** दश। विंशतिर्दश इत्येवं वयोधर्म उदाहृतः।।

१३. T65- अशीतिसप्ततिषष्टिचत्वारिंशश्चत्रिंशत, G98- असीतिसप्ततिषष्टि चत्वारिंशच्चत्रिंशतु, G17- असी(शी)तिसप्ततिषष्ठी चत्वारिंशच्चत्रिंशतु (त्), G86- अशीतिस्सप्ततीष्टषष्टि चत्वारिशश्चत्रिंशत, G07- अशीतिस्सप्ततीषष्टिचत्वारिंशश्चत्रिंशत्, V08- अशीतिसप्त षष्टच (तिः षष्टिः) चत्वारिंशच्चत्रिंशतिः, G24- असतिसप्ततिषष्टि चत्वारिंशश्चत्रिंशति, V41- अष्टतिसप्ततिषष्टिचत्वारिंशच्च विंशतिः

१४. G24-विंशतिर्दशमोर्ष वयो षड्जादिभिश्वरैः, V41-दशमो वर्षदयो षड्जादिभिस्स्वरैः, V08-विंशश्च(दश)तुर्दशवर्षः षड्जादीनाम् वयो मतम्, Since all the Mss except V08, read in the instrumental case, which is not appropriate in the present context, the parallel reading from BKM (p.62) is suggested.

१५. G24 - 50

१६. V41- missing

१७. G86, G07- యీ యెండ్లు సప్తస్వరాలకు వయసు, G24- ఇ(వి)క్రమానసే సప్త స్వరాలకు వయస్సులు, V41- ఇ సప్త స్వరాల వయస్సు

[१]पद्माभि[भः] पिञ्जर[रः][२] स्वर्णवर्ण[र्णः][३] कुन्दप्रभा[ऽ]सितः[४]।
पीतः कर्बुर[५] इत्येते[६] वर्णाः[७] षड्जादिषु स्मृताः[८]।। १६।।

టీకా:- ఇది([९] షడ్జాది[९] సప్త[१०]స్వరాలకు వర్ణాలు[११].

[१२]जम्ब्रूशाककुशक्रौञ्च[१३]शाल्मलीश्वेत[१४]नामसु[१५]।
द्वीपेषु[१६] पुष्करश्चैव स्वराणां देशमीरितम्[१७]।। १७।।

టీకా:- ఇ[ ]స్వరాలకు దేశాలు[१८]

---

१. v.16, cf. SR 1,3,54cd-55ab; G18- पद्मगारूत्मत स्वर्ण कुन्दनीलहरिद्रकाः। धूम्रश्चैषां वर्णमिति स्वराणां वर्ण ****।।

२. V08- पद्माक्षः पिंगळः, V41- पद्माभि पंजरं

३. G24- स्वर्णवर्णं

४. G86, G07- रुद्रप्रभासितं, G24-कुंड्डप्रभाशितः, V41- कुन्दविभागतः

5. T65-पीतकर्बूर, G98,G17,B13-पीतः कर्पूर, G86-पीत कर्ज्जुर, G07-पीत शर्जर, G24-पीतः कर्बूर, V41- पिहितः पिबितः

६. G24- पित्येते

७. G98,G17,B13,T65,G86,G07,G24,V41- वर्णो

८. G86, G07- स्वराणां वर्णलक्षणम्, T65,G98,G17,B13,G24, V41- षड्जादिभिस्वरैः

९. G24-missing

१०. G86-missing

११. V41- ఇట్లు సప్త స్వరములకు వర్ణములు, T65 - స్వరాలకు వర్ణం - seen before the verse (resembles a sub-heading)

१२. v.17, cf. SR 1,3,55cd-56ab; G18- जम्ब्रू *********** क्रौञ्चशशाल्मलि ************* षद्जादिस्वराणांदेश ईरितः।।

१३. G86- जम्बुशाकाकुचक्रौञ्चा, V41- जम्बूशाकाकुशाक्रौञ्च

१४. G24- शाल्मलिद्वेत, G07 - शाल्मलीशेकता

१५. G86- नाम चा, G07 - नाम च, V08- नामकाः (सु), G24- नामनसु

१६. G24- द्वीशेष, V08- द्वीपासु (पेषु)

१७. V08- पुष्करश्चेत (चैव) स्वराणां देशमोरितः, V41- पुष्करै चैव स्वराणां स्थितिरीरितः

१८. G86- యీ షడ్జాది సప్త స్వరాలకు వర్ణాలు, T65- స్వరాలకు దేశాలు- seen before the verse (resembles a sub-heading)

[1]वह्निर्वेदः[2] शशाङ्कंश्च[3] लक्ष्मीनाथस्तथैव च[4]।
नारदस्तुम्बुरुश्चैव षड्जादि ऋषयस्तथा[5]।। १८।।

టీకా:- ఇ[6] స్వరాలకు గోత్రఋషులు[7].

[8]सति धी[वी]रे[9]ऽद्भुते रौद्रे बीभत्से च भयानके।
हास्यशृङ्गारयोश्चैव[10] षड्जादी[11] रसयस्तथा

१. G18- अग्निवेदशशाङ्काश्च विष्णुशङ्कर नारदाः। तुम्प्रुरुश्च स्वराणांतु गो *************।।

२. G98, G07- वन्हिर्वेद, G17, B13, T65 - वह्निर्वेद, G24- वंह्निर्वेदा, V41- वह्निस्वेद. While earlier texts like SR mention vēdhāḥ for vēda, the present text reads erroneous, which has been wrongly followed by the commentary to read vēdapuruṣa and is also followed by MBC. vēda does not seem to fit in this context. However BKM and RJM read different names like āṅgīrasa and bhārghava. Further the commentator treats these as gōtraūṣi-s and not ūṣi-s (seers.)

३. G98, B13- शशांकस्य, V41- श्शशांकश्च

४. G98, B13-लक्ष्मीनाथस्तदैव च, G17-लक्ष्मीनाथस्तदै[थै]व च, G07- लक्ष्मिनादस्तदेव चा, V08- लक्ष्मीनाथ धराहितः, V41- लक्ष्मीनादस्तदैव च. In all, only six names are specified. But the commentary attributes names of seven seers for the seven svara-s. The additional name that does not figure in the original is Śiva, probably why V08 suggests □dharāhitaḥ□ ?

५. G86- रुषयस्तथा, V08- ऋषयः स्मृताः

६. V41- missing

७. G86-□క్కు స్వరాలకు గోత్రరుషులు, G07- □ల్లా స్వరాలకు గోత్రఋషులు, T65- ఇది స్వరాలకు రిషిలు

८. G18- वीराद्भुतौ तथारौद्रप्रीभत्सौ भयहास्यकौ। शृङ्गारश्चेति षड्जादिस्वराणां रस ईरितः,T65- सतिधीरेत्सुते रौद्रे भीभत्से च भयानके, G98, G17- सतिधीरेद्भुते रौद्रे भीभत्से च भयानके, G86- सतिरेभ्यादद्रेपिरौद्रे भीभत्स च भयानके, G07-सतिरेभ्दुधेकाद्री रौद्रे भीभत्स च भयानके, G24 - सति वे *****दृते रौद्रे प्रिभीत्स भयामके, V41-सतिधीरेद्भुतारौद्रे भीभत्से च भयानके, V08 - वीरस्तथाद्भुतो रौद्रो प्रीभत्सश्च भयानकः The Mss (except V08 and G18) have retained the vocative case of SR format, which is suitable for the present description but specifies one rasa for each svara. V08 and G18 seem to have deviated from the SR format, by dropping the first two letters sati and converting all Locatives into Nominatives. The significance of the word sati (read as sari in SR) is not clear.

९. dhīra is used as a synonym to vīra, which is traditionally accepted as the name of a rasa and hence it is suggested here.

१०. G98- हास्यश्रीहरयोश्चैव, G17, B13- हास्यशृङ्गारयोःश्चैव, V08-हास्यश्रृंगारयो, (हास्यः श्रृंगार) इत्येते

११. V08- षड्जादीनां

[षड्जादीनां रसाः स्मृताः][1] ।। १९ ।।

టీకా:- ఇ[2] స్వరాలకు రసాలు[3].

[4]वह्निर्ब्रह्मा[5] गारदा च[6] शर्वः[7] श्रीनाथभास्करः[रौ][8] ।

गणेश्वरादयो देवाः[9] षड्जादीनां च[10] देवताः[11] ।। २० ।।

టీకా:- [12]ఏరు షడ్జాది[13] స్వరాలకు దేవతలు.

[14]श्वेतः पीतो[15] रक्तः नीलः[16] हरिद्रावर्णवत् तथा[17] ।

चित्रवस्त्रक्षौमवस्त्रौ[18] षड्जादीनामलङ्कृताः[19] ।। २१ ।।

---

१. T65,G98,G17,B13- सप्तयस्तथा, G07- रिषयस्तथा, V08- रसा मताः The word rasayaḥ is incorrect and hence parallel reading from BKM has been suggested.

२. T65, G86, G07, V41- ఇది

३. V41- stops here and continues to read from the consolidated attributes of each svara.

४. G24- v.20 is missing; G18- अग्निर्ब्रह्माच वाग्देवी ईश्वरो विष्णु ************* ।।

५. G98- वन्हिब्रह्मा, T65, G86, G07- वह्निब्रह्मा, V08- पद्मा ब्रह्मा

६. G86- श्यारदाचा

७. T65- सर्व, G86-शर, V08- शर्व

८. T65,G98,B13,G86-श्रीनाथभास्करः, G17-श्रीनाथभास्कराः, V08-रीनाथभास्करौ, G07-the rest is missing.

९. G86 - गणैश्वरादेया देवाः, V08- गणेश्वरः क्रमादेवं (रादयोदेवाः)

१०. G86- तु

११. T65- धैवतः

१२. G07, G24 - commentary missing

१३. G86- missing

१४. G24 - v.21 is missing; G18- श्वेतंचहरितं रक्तं नील *********** स्त्रंच षड्जादि स्वराणां वसनंभचेत् ।।

१५. G98,G17, B13- श्वेतपीतो

१६. G98,G17, B13- रक्तनीलं, V08- रक्तनील

१७. G86- हरिद्रावर्णावस्तधा, G07- हरिद्रावर्नाचस्तधा, V08- हरिद्रावर्ण भास्वरः (कास्तथा)

१८. T65-चित्रवस्त्रे क्षौमवस्त्रे, G98,G17,B13-चित्रवस्त्रक्षौमवस्त्रे, G86- चित्रवस्त्रक्षौमवस्त्र, G07- चित्रवस्त्रक्षामवस्त्रा

१९. T65- लङ्कृताम् , G98, G17, B13- लंकृतम्, G86- लङ्कृता, V08- लङ्कृतिः (ताः)

టీకా:- ఇది(□ స్వరాలకు వస్త్రాలు.

[१]दध्यन्नं[२] पायसं भक्ष्यं[3] चित्रान्नं पिष्टयुक्पयः[४]।

शुद्धान्नं तण्डुलंश्चैव[५] षड्जादीनां च[६] भोजनम्[७] ।।२२।।

టీకా:- [८]ఇది(□ స్వరాలకు భోజనం.

[९]कुङ्कुमागरुकस्तूरिकर्पूरं रोचनं[१०] तथा।

चन्दनं परिमळद्रव्यं[च परिमलं][११] षड्जादीनां च[१२]लेपनम्।।२३।।

టీకా:- ఇది(□ స్వరాలకు లేపనగంధం[१३].

[१४]जाती[१५]चम्पकपुन्नागमल्लिकाकेतकी तथा[१६]।

करवीरः पद्मपुष्पं[१७] षड्जादीनामलङ्कृताः[१८] ।। २४।।

---

१. G18- दध्यन्नं पायसापूपं चित्रान्नं गुळपिष्टकम्। शाल्यन्नं तण्डुलंचैव स्वराणां भोजनं भवेत्।।

२. G24- दद्यन्नं

3. G98- भक्ष्य, G86,T65- भक्ष्या

४. G07- च पिष्पयुक्वयः, V08- विषयुक्ययः (फ्रिल्वयुक्यः), G24- विष्वयः क्रियः

५. G24- तण्डुलचैव, V08- तण्डुलाश्चैव

६. G86, G07, V08- तु

७. G07- भाजनम्

८. G07 - commentary missing

९. G18- *********** कर्पूरं रोचनं तथा। श्रीगन्धं यक्षपङ्कश्च स्वराणां गन्धमुच्यते।

१०. G07- गोरोचनं, G24- गेचनं

११. V08- चन्दनं स परिमळं (परिमळद्रव्यं) , G24- परिमला * * * गन्द्धं. The reading in the Mss does not seem to be metrically correct and hence has been suggested thus. V08 too suggests this reading.

१२. G86, G07- तु

१३. G86, G24- గంధలేపనం, G07- సుగంధలేపనం

१४. G18- जाजीच चम्पकाचैव वकुलंमल्लिकातथा। केतकी करवीरश्च पद्मंच कुसुमं भवेत्।।

१५. G98, B13, T65, G86,G07,G24- जाजी, G17- जाजि[ती] The text uses a few words in the Telugu form in the original text too and therefore the names in saṃskūta are suggested.

१६. V08 - सुमाः (तथा)

१७. G86- करवीरः पद्मपुष्पाः, G07- करवीरपद्मपुष्पं, G24- करवीरः पद्मपुष्पा, T65, G98, G17, B13- करवीरः पद्मपुष्पः

१८. T65,G98,G17,B13- मलङ्कृतम्, G24- नलङ्कृतम्

టీకా:- ఇ□స్వరాలకు అలంకారములు[१].

[२]मुक्ताफलो नीलवज्र[३]वैडूर्यो मरकतो[४] मणिः।

गोमेध[द]को पुष्यरागः[५] षड्जादीनां च[६] भूषणम्।। २५।।

టీకా:- ఇది(□ స్వరాలకు భూషణాలు.

[७]खड्गकुन्त[८]गधाचक्रं[९] भिण्डिपालस्तथैव च[१०]।

नाराचमङ्कुशं चेति[११] स्वराणामायुधं स्मृतम्[१२]।। २६।।

టీకా:- ఇ□[१३] స్వరాలకు ఆయుధాలు[१४].

[१५]हंसश्च[१६] सिंहभेरूण्ड[१७]हरिणीमकरी तथा[रास्तथा][१८]।

शुकश्च शारिका चैव[१९] षड्जादीनां च[२०] वाहनम्।। २७।।

---

१. T65- ఇతి అలంకృతం, G24- ఇ□స్వరాలకు పుష్పాలు

२. G18- मोक्तिकं नीलवज्राणिवैडूर्यं पद्मरागकम्। गोमेधिकं पुष्यरागं स्वराणां भूषणं भवेत्।।

३. G24- वज्रा

४. G07- मरतशो, V08- मरकतानि च (मरकतो मणिः)

५. G98, G17, B13, T65, G86- गोमेधको पुष्यरागः, V08- गोमेधिकः पुष्यरागः, G24- गोमेधिकपुष्यरागौ

६. G86, G07- तु

७. G18-खड्गकुन्त गदाचक्रभिन्दिपाला *गास्तथा। अङ्कुशंचापि षड्जादि स्वराणामायुधं भवेत्।।

८. V08- खड्गं शंभो (कुंतो)

९. G24- चक्र

१०. G07- पिंडिपालस्तदैव च, G24- फ्रिंडिवालनदैव चा

११. G98 - नाराशीरंकुशंचेति, G17 - नारासीरंकुशंचेति, T65 - नाराचीरंकुशंचेति, G07- नाराचीकंकुशंचेति, G24- नारांविरंकुशंचेति

१२. G07-स्वराणौमायुधं स्मृतम्, V08-स्वराणामायुधा स्मृताः (मायुधं स्मृतम्), G24- स्वराणामायुधं शृता

१३. T65, G86, G07- ఇది

१४. G86, G07- ఆయుధములు

१५. G18- हम्सः सिंहश्च भेरुण्डश्चक्रोनक्रश्शुकस्तथा। पारावतश्च षद्जादिस्वराणां वाहनं भवेत्।।

१६. G98, G17, B13, T65, G86, G07,G24- हंसाश्च

१७. G07- सिंहप्रोरूडौ, G24- सिंहप्रोरूडां, V08- सिंह भेरुण्ड (डा)

१८. V08- हरिणीमकरी तथा (रास्तथा), G24- हरिका *** कलित्तधा

१९. G98,G17,B13,T65- शुककाक क्रमादेवं, G86, G07- शुकशुक क्रमादेवं, G24- शुकशारि क्रमादेवं

२०. G86, G07- त्तु

టీకా:- ఇది(□ స్వరాలకు వా॑నాలు.

[१]चूतखर्जूरकदळी जम्बीरो दाडिमी तथा[२]।

द्राक्षा पुन्नागवृक्षाश्च[३] षड्जादीनां प्रकीर्तिताः[४]।। २८।।

టీకా:- ఇ□ షడ్జాది[६] స్వరాలకు వృక్షాలు.

[७]गान्धर्वि[गन्धर्वी]किन्नरी[८]यक्षी किम्पुर्षी[९] नागकन्यका[१०]।

सुरस्त्रीराक्षसी[११]तासाम्[१२]षड्जादीनां तु पत्रयः[पत्नयः][१३]।।२९।।

టీకా:- □ షడ్జాది[१४] స్వరాలకు పెండ్లాలు.

[१५]क्रमादनुष्टुप् गायत्रि[त्री][१६] त्रिष्टुप् च[१७] बृहती तथा[१८]।

---

१. G18- चूतः खर्जूरकदळी जम्म्रीरोदाडिमस्तथा।द्राक्षा ********** पिक्ष इत्येते स्वराणां फलभूरुहः।।

२. G24- तथौ

३. G98, G17, B13, T65- वृक्षेवं, V08- वृक्षाणां (वृक्षास्तु), G24- वृक्षेषु

४. V08- प्रकीर्तितम्

५. T65, G86, G07- ఇది

६. G86- missing

७. G18- गान्धर्वीकिन्नरी यक्षीकिंपुर्षी पन्नगी तथा। अमरी राक्षसीचैव स्वराणां योषितः स्मृताः।।

८. G98- गांधर्वकिन्नरी, G17- गांधर्वकिन्नर T65- गांधर्प्रकिन्नरी, G07- गांधर्विकोन्नरि, G24- गांधर्विदेन्नरि

९. T65,G07-यक्षकिम्पुरुषी G98-यक्षकिंपुर्षि, G17-यक्षकिंपुरुष, B13-यक्षोकिंपुर्षी, G86-यक्षकिंपुरुषा, G24-यक्षकिंपुरिषि

१०. G24- नागकन्यकौ

११. G98- राक्षसौ, G17- राक्षसा, G24- राक्षशी

१२. G86- प्रोक्ता, G07- प्रोक्तौ, V08- चैव

१३. G98,G17,B13-पतीरिताः, T65,G24-पतिरितः, G86-तु पद्मयः,V08-स्त्रियः स्मृताः This could be an error caused due to phonetic misinterpretation.

१४. G86, G07- □ సప్త

१५. v.30, cf.SR 1,3,58cd-59ab;G18-********* श्चापि गायत्री त्रिष्टुप्च प्रह्रतीतथा।पङ्क्ति**णिक्च जगती स्वराणां छन्द ईरितः।।

१६. G98-क्रमादनुष्टगायत्रि, G86-क्रमादनुष्टुपुद्गायत्रि, G07-क्रमादनुष्टुपुदायत्री, V08- क्रमादनुष्टुप्प्रगायत्री, G24-क्रमादनिष्टुगायत्रि

१७. G86- त्रिष्टुपुद्, G07- त्रिष्टुद्, V08- त्रिष्टुप्प्रच, G24- त्रिष्टुपुः

१८. V08-प्रगुतीस्तथा

पङ्क्त्यष्णजगतीचन्दो[१] [पङ्क्त्युष्णिक्जगतीच्छन्दो][२]

षड्जादीनामुदाहृतम्[३] ।। ३० ।।

టీకా:- [४]ఇ□స్వరాలకు ఛందస్సులు.

[५]स्थूलसूक्ष्म[६] स्थूलदीर्घं[७] समपुष्टि[ट]स्तथैव[८] च ।

दीर्घादि[ति][९]स्थूलदेहश्च[१०] षड्जादीनां क्रमाद्वदेत् [भवेत्][११] ।। ३१ ।।

టీకా:- [१२]ఇ□సప్త స్వరాలకు ఆకృతి.

[१३]शततारास्चित्रवसु[१४]मखा[घा] चोत्तर[१५]फल्गुनी[१६] ।

---

१. G98-पङ्तिश्च जगतीछन्दो, G17,B13-पङ्क्तिश्च जगतीछन्दो, G86,G07-पंज्तीश्च जगतीश्चन्दो, V08-पंक्तिः त्रिजगतीच्छन्दः, T65-पंङ्क्तिश्च जगतीश्छन्दो.

२. The commentary reads uṣṇik for dhaivata, which is not seen in the original text of any of the Mss, except G24 (in a corrupt form). Since SR too mentions uṣṇik for dhaivata, the present reading has been suggested.

३. G24- मुदाहृतः, V08- क्रमाद्भवेत्

४. G24- commentary missing

५. G18- *********** स्थूलंदीर्घं मध्यमदीर्घकम्। कुंजंकृशमतिस्थूळं स्वराणां देह ईरितः।।

६. G17- स्थूलंसूक्ष्मं, V08 - स्थूलदीर्घो, G24- स्तूलसूक्ष्म

७. V08-स्थूलसूक्ष्मः, G24- स्तूलदीर्घा

८. T65,G86-समपुष्टितधैव, G17-समपुष्टितथैव, G07-समपुष्टिस्तदैव, V08-समदृष्टिस्तधैव, The reading is suggested on the basis of BKM. The commentary however reads kubja .

९. V08- दीर्घश्च

१०. G98, B13- स्थूलदेहाश्च, G17- स्थूःलदेहाश्च, V08- स्थूलदीर्घश्च

११. T65, G98, G17, B13-क्रमादृते, G86-क्रमाद्विदुः, G07- क्रमं द्विदुः, V08- मुदाहृतम्

१२. T65- commentary missing, G07-సప్త స్వరాలకు ఆకృతి, G24- ఇ□స్వరాలకు దేహలు

१३. G18- शतताराच चित्राच धनिष्टामख उत्तराः। पूर्वाषाढानुराधाच नक्षत्राणि क्रमाद्भवेत्।।

१४. G98-शततताराश्चित्रवसु,G17-शततताराश्चित्रवसु, G86-शतेतारश्चातरनु, G07-शशीतारश्चातमनु, G24-शततंराश्चित्रवसु, V08-शततारा चित्रवसु

१५. G98, G17- मखाश्चोत्तर

१६. G24- फल्गुणि

पूर्वाषाढा मैत्रभश्च[१] स्वराणां जन्मऋषभाः [जन्मर्क्षाः भवेत्][२] ।। ३२।।

టీకా:- ఇ[౩] స్వరాలకు జన్మనక్షత్రాలు[౪].

[५]चतुस्ते[त्री]द्विमुखीश्चैव[खञ्चैव]चतुर्मुखि[ख]चतुर्मुखि[खम्][६] ।

त्रिमुखि[ख]द्विमुखीचैव[खञ्चैव][७] स्वराणामाननं वदेत्[८] ।। ३३।।

టీకా:- ఇ[౯] స్వరాలకు ముఖాలు.

अष्टौ रसचतुर्बाहु[१०]रष्टावष्टारसस्त[रष्टावष्टौ करास्तथा][११] ।**

ऋतुश्चतुकराश्चैव[१२] स्वराणां बाहुरीरितः[१३] ।। ३४।।

---

१. T65-पूवषाडामैत्रभश्च, G86- पूर्वाषाडश्च मेत्तंच्च , G07- पूर्वाषाडम्च मंत्रंच्च, V08 - पूर्वाषाढामैत्रभंच, G24- पूर्वाषाडामैतृलंच्च

२. G98,G17,B13-जन्मऋक्षान् स्वरान् वदेत्, T65-जन्मऋषान् स्वरान् वदेत्, G86,G07- स्वराणां जन्मऋषभाः, G24-जन्मतिक्षों स्वरांवधे, V08- जन्मर्क्षः क्रमतो भवेत् जन्मर्क्षाः seems to be a better word to denote the birth stars than other variants found in the Mss.

३. T65,G86,G07- ఇది

४. T65,G24- నక్షత్రాలు

५. G98,G17,B13-v.33 is missing; G18- चतुस्त्रिद्विमुखंचैव चतुर्मुखचतुर्मुखम्। त्रिमुख ********* ननं भवेत्।।

६. G86-चतुस्त्री द्विमुरोश्चैव चतुर्मुखचतुर्मुख, G07-चतुस्त्री द्विमुखीश्चैवा चतुम्मुखचतुर्मुखी, G24- चतुश्रि द्विमुखंचैव चतुर्मुखचतुर्मुखः, V08- चतु .... द्विमुखश्चैव चतुश्चतुमुखास्तथा

७. G24- श्रिमुखं द्विमुखं चैव, V08- त्रिमुखं द्विमुखं चैव

८. G24- स्वराणामाननं वदं, V08 - स्वराणामाननानिवै

९. T65,G86,G07- ఇది

१०. G86-अष्टादशचतुर्बाहु, G07-अष्टावनचतुर्बाहु, G24-अष्टारसचतुर्बाहु

११. T65,G98,G17- अष्टादष्टोरसस्तथा, B13-अष्टादष्टारसस्तथा, G07- रष्टावः सप्तदा, G24-अष्टावष्टार सप्तधा. According to the commentary, the text seems to list the numbers in the sequence-8,6,4,8,8,6,4. Since the number, "six" is present in the next line (ūtu) in all the Mss, the term rasa to mean six, is redundant. Moreover a word relating to "arm" is also seen in each half of the lines. Hence the reading is suggested thus.

१२. G07- ऋतिचतुरकाश्चैव

१३. G98,G17-बाहुमीरितम्, G86,G07,B13-बाहुरीरितः, G24-बाहुमीरिरिता, V08 reads differently thus: अष्टांसश्चश्चतर्बाहुरष्टांसाष्टांसकौ तथा। ऋत्वंसश्चृतुकरश्चैव स्वराणां बाहुनिर्णयः।।

టీకా:- ఇ□[1] స్వరాలకు బా⁰వులు[2].

[3]**अष्टौ ऋतुचतुश्चैव[4]अष्टावष्टौ तदै[थै]व चा[च]।**

ऋतुवेदाक्ष[क्षि]सङ्ख्या च स्वराणां नेत्रमीरितम् ।।३५।।

టీకా:- [5]ఇది(□ షడ్జాది స్వరాలకు నేత్రాలు[6].

अष्टौ ऋतु[7]चतुश्रोत्राः[8] अष्टावष्टौ श्रुतिस्तथा[9]।

रसवेदा श्रोत्रसङ्ख्या[10] षड्जादीनां श्रुतिर्वदेत्[11]।।३६।।

టీకా:- ఇది(□ షడ్జాది స్వరాలకు శ్రోత్రాలు[12].

[13]**मुखसङ्ख्या[14] नासिकां च स्वराणां पादतिङ्[?] वदेत्[15]।।३७।।**

టీకా:- షడ్జాది స్వరాలకు ముఖసంఖ్యా ప్రకారఅన(రాన)[16] నాసికలు పాదాలు స్వరజ్ఞానములు(నులు) చెప్పినారు[17].

---

१. T65,G86,G07- ఇది

२. G86, G07- భుజాలు

३. G98,G17,B13,G24- v.35 is missing, V08- missing upto v.39

४. G86,G07- अष्टाऋतुचतुश्चैवा

५. G24- commentary missing

६. G86, G07- కన్నులు

७. G98, G17- अष्टौऋतौ, G07- अष्टौरुकृ

८. G98, G17 - चतुश्रोत्रः

९. G86 - कृतिस्तथा

१०. G86- रसवेदाश्चूत्रसंख्या, G07- कसभेदा श्रोत्रसंख्या

११. G24- श्रुतिर्वदे

१२. G24- ఇ□యీూ సంఖ్యా క్రమాన షడ్జాది స్వరాలకు శ్రోత్రాలు, G86, G07- చెవులు

१३. G24- missing from here upto v.39 except for a commentary in between. G18- मुखैः समानसंख्याश्च नासिकाः परिकीर्तिताः। मुखसंख्याद्विगुणिजाश्चक्षुः श्रुतिकरांघ्रयः।।

१४. G07- मुखड्या सेत् [lacunae in between ?]

१५. G98, G17- पादिदिङ् वदेत्, G86- पादविङ् वदेत्

१६. This seems to be a scribal peculiarity. At another place rū is read as 'ra' and 'u'.

१७. G86- షడ్జాది స్వరాలకు ముఖసంఖ్యా ప్రకారాన నాసికలు పాదాలు జాన్నవు చెప్పబడెను, G07- ఇ□సంఖ్యా ప్రకారానా నాసికలు పాదాలు జాన్వ చెప్పబడును

स्वराणां लक्षणं सम्यक्[१] सोमनार्येण कीर्त्तितम्[२] ।

[३]सङ्ग्रह्य विधिवत्तत्र विस्तरेण[४] तथैव च ।। ३८।।

टीका:- షడ్జాది స్వరాలకు □స్తారంగా లక్షణాలు[५] సోమనాచార్యుని చేత[६] చెప్పవ(బ)డుచున్నది[७].

[८]షడ్జ[९] స్వరానికి[१०]-□వవంశం-బ్రాహ్మణజాతి-యేండ్లు 80[११]-పద్మవర్న(ర్ణం)[१२] - జంబూద్వీపం- □రసం-అగ్ని గోత్రఋషిః[१३]- హంసవాహనం[१४]-అగ్నిదేవతా[१५] - నాలుగు[१६] ముఖాలు-ఎని□ది భుజాలు-ఎని□ది శ్రోత్రములు(త్రాలు[१७]-ఎని□ది

---

१. G86, G07 - समण्

२. T65, G98, G86, G07- कीर्तित: G18- reads the following colophon after this, which is not seen in any other Mss: इति गीताध्याये प्रथमाश्वासः ।।

३. G98, G17, B13, T65, G18 - v.38cd is missing.

४. G07- विस्तारेण

५. T65- లక్షణం

६. G86, G07- సంకోచ□సంగ్గ

७. G86, G07- చెప్పుతువున్నాడు. The following is seen only in T65 and G24; T65- స్వరరాగధ్వని వాదిసంవాది అనువాది చ □వాది నాద***శ్చ ఇది మొదలైన సప్తసావరాలకు ఉత్పన్నం. సంక్షేపించి - సముచ్చయంగా సావర రాగాలకు ప్రస్తారమేరువులు సోమనాచార్యుని చాత చెప్పపడేను. G24 - శ్లోకం॥ స్వరరాగాద్యనీ వాదిసంవాది అనువాది చ। నాత గీత స్వరం మొదలైన సప్తస్వరాలకు ఉత్పన్నం। సంక్షేపించి। సముచ్చయంగా స్వరరాగాలకు ప్రస్తార***రువు సోమనాచార్యుని చాత చెప్పంబడేను

८. The readings in V08 are not complete and are noted down in the form of hints and hence the variant readings, if any, are based on the available information.

९. G86, G07- షడ్జమ

10. V41- స్వరానకు

११. T65- ఎండ్లు - 80 ఎండ్లు వయసు, G98, G17, B13-800 వయస్సు, V41- వంయేండ్లు వయస్సు

१२. G86- పీతవర్నం

१३. G86-అగ్నిగోత్రంఋషి అ**, G07- అగ్నిగోత్రంఋషి అగ్ని

१४. G98, G17, B13- add అనుష్టుశ్ఛందస్సు before

१५. G86, G07- దేవతా అగ్నిః

१६. G86- ****, In the Mss, the numbers are sometimes expressed in words and sometimes in figures. The numbers in words have been preferred.

१७. T65,G98,G17,B13,G86,G07- missing

నేత్రాలు[1]-నాలుగు నాసికలు-రెండు పాదాలు[2]-స్థూలదేహం[3]-ఖడ్గాయుధం-శ్వేతవస్త్రం[4] - జాజీపుష్పం - కుంకుమగంధం - దధ్యాన్న[5] భోజనం- మాణిక్యభూషణం -చూతవృక్షం[6] - గంధర్వస్త్రీ[7] - శతభిషానక్షత్రం - కుంభరాశి - శనివారం[8]. యీ తీరున షడ్జమస్వరం[9] అనుష్టుపు ఛందస్సున పుట్టి ప్రకాశిస్తున్నది[10].

ఋషభస్వరానికి [11]-ఋషివంశం-క్షత్రియజాతి-యేండ్లు-70[12]-అళదివర్నం(ర్ణం)[13]-శాకద్వీపం-అద్భుతరసం-వేదపురుషుడు గోత్రం ఋషి[14]-బ్రహ్మఅధిదేవతా - పసురు(పు)కోక[15] - పాయసభోజనం - అగరుగంధం - సంపంగిపువ్వులు[16] - నీలభూషణం - కుంతాయుధం - సింహాసనం -ఖర్జూరఫలవృక్షం[17] - కిన్నరస్త్రీ[18] - చిత్తానక్షత్రం - శుక్రవారం - తులారాశి - మూడు ముఖాలు[19] -ఆరు భుజాలు - ఆరు[20]

---

౧. V41- missing

౨. T65, G98, G17, B13- missing

౩. V41- missing

౪. G07- శ్వేతవర్నం

౫. V41- దధ్యన్న

౬. V08- ధా□డివృక్షం, G86- ధా□***, G07- ధా□డిఫలవృక్షం, V41- మా□డిఫలవృక్షం

౭. G98, G17- గాంధర్వ స్త్రీ, G07- గాంధర్వ శ్రీ

౮. T65, G98, G17, B13, V41- శనివారం కుంభరాశి

౯. G98-స్వరానుకు, G17-స్వరానికి, B13-స్వరానకు; G98,G17,B13- end with this and the rest of the commentary is missing.

౧౦. T65, V41- ప్రకాశిస్తున్నందును

౧౧. G86, G07- అథ ఋషభస్వరః, V41- రిషభ స్వరమునకు

౧౨. T65- 70 యెండ్లు వయసు

౧౩. V41- ఆలదివర్ణం

౧౪. T65- గోత్రేఋషిః, V41- వేదపురుషుడు గోత్రము ఋషిగోత్రము

౧౫. T65- పసురుకోను, G07 పసురుకోళ్ళు, V08- క్షమా వస్త్రం

౧౬. G07, V41- సంపంగిపూలు, V08- వకుళం పుష్పం

౧౭. T65- ఫలవృక్షః

౧౮. G07- కిన్నరశ్రి

౧౯. V41- the order of the organs differs and reads thus: మూడు ముఖాలు, 6 నేత్రాలు, 6 చెవులు, 6 భూజాలు, 2 పాదాలు

౨౦. G07- తొం□డి

నేత్రాలు-ఆరు శ్రోత్రాలు[१] -మూడు నాసలు (నాసికలు)[२] -రెండు పాదాలు- మధ్యమ[३] స్థూలదేహం-గాయత్రిఛందస్సు (న)యందు[४] ఋషభ స్వరం పుట్టి ప్రకాశిస్తున్నది[५]. గాంధర్వ(గాంధార)స్వరానికి[६]-దేవవంశం[७] - వైశ్యజాతి - 60 యేండ్లు[८] - బంగారువర్నం(ర్ణం) - చంద్రుడు గోత్రఋషి[९] - రౌద్రరసం[१०] - సరస్వతి అధిదేవతా - కుశద్వీపం - రక్త వస్త్రం[११] - కజ్జాయం[१२] - కస్తూరిగంధం - పున్నాగపుష్పం - వజ్ర భూషణం - గదాయుధం - భేరుండు(డ)వాహనం[१३] -కదళీవృక్షం - [१४]యక్షస్త్రీ - రెండు ముఖాలు - నాలుగు భుజాలు[१५] - 4 నేత్రాలు - ద్వి నాసికా - 2 పాదాలు- దీర్ఘ దేహం - ధనిష్టానక్షత్రం - తులారాశి[१६] - శనివారం - యీ తీరున గాంధారస్వరం త్రిష్టుపుచ(ఛ)ందస్సు(న)యందు పుట్టి ప్రకాశిస్తువున్నదీ(ది)[१७]

---

१. G07- 9 సూత్రాలు

२. T65, G86- missing

३. G86, G07- మధ్యమం

४. V41- ఛందమూనందు

५. T65- ప్రకాశిస్తున్న వుండును, V41- రిషభము ప్రకాశించును

६. G86, G07- అథ గాంధారస్వరం, V41- గాంధారస్వరమునకు

७. V41- శుర వంశము

८. T65, V41- 60 యెండ్లు వయసు

९. G86, G07- గోత్రఋషి చంద్రుడు

१०. V41- the order of description varies thus: కుశద్వీపం-సరస్వతిఅదిదేవతా-రౌద్రరసం

११. V41- నల్లనివస్త్రం, listed at the end.

१२. T65 - కజ్జాయం, V41- పాలన్నము

१३. V41- గండభేరుండ వాహనం

१४. From here V41 reads very differently thus: బృహతిఛందస్సు- గొప్ప శరీరము- రోహిణి నక్షత్రము- మంగలవారము- కన్యారాశి-రెండు ముఖాలు- రేండు నాసికలు- నాలుగు భుజాలు-నాలుగు నేత్రాలు- నాలుగు చెవులు- బ్రగోత్రర్షి- నల్లనివస్త్రము- ఈ తీరున గాంధార స్వరము ప్రకాశమగును.

१५. T65, G86- చతుర్భుజాలు

१६. G07- రాశి, T65 - missing

१७. T65- త్రిష్టుప్ఛందస్సున ప్రకాశమవును, G86-త్రిష్టుచందస్సుయందు పుట్టి ప్రకాశింస్తున్నది

మధ్యమస్వరానికి[1] - దేవవంశం[2] - బ్రాహ్మణ[3]జాతి - 40 యేండ్లు[4] - మోల్లమోగ్గ[5] వర్ణం - క్రౌంచద్వీపం[6] - కృష్ణుడుగోత్రఋషి[7] - భీభత్సరసం -ఈశ్వరుడు అధిదేవతా[8] - నీలవస్త్రం - కలవంటకం[9] - కర్పూరగంధం - మల్లికాపుష్పం[10] - వైడూర్యభూషణం - చక్రాయుధం - జింకవాహనం[11] - నిమ్బ(మ్మ)ఫలవృక్షం[12] - కింపురుష స్త్రి - నాలుగు ముఖాలు - ఎని□ది భుజాలు[13] - [14]ఎని□ది శ్రోత్రాలు - ఎని□ది నేత్రాలు - నాలుగు నాసికలు - రెండు పాదాలు[15] - మట్టతరదేశం - మఖా(ఘా)నక్షత్రం - [16]సింహరాశి - ఆదివారం - యీ తీరున[17] మధ్యమస్వరం బ్ర(బృ)హతిచ్ఛందస్సు(న)యందు పుట్టి ప్రకాశిస్తున్నది[18]

[19]పంచమస్వరం(స్వరానికి) - పితృవంశం - శూద్రజాతి - 30 యేండ్లు వయస్సు - నీలవర్ణం - శాల్మలిద్వీపం[20] - ఈశ్వరుడు గోత్రరిషి - భయరసం - □ష్ణు అధిదేవతా - అళదివర్ణం- చలి□డి[1] భోజనం-గోరోచనగంధం-మొగిలి[2] పూలు - మాణిక్యభూషణం[3] - భిండివాలాయుధం

౧. G86, G07- అధ మధ్యమ స్వరానికి

౨. V41- దైవవంశం

౩. G86, G07- బ్రహ్మణ జాది

౪. T65, V41- 40 - యొండ్లు వయస

౫. G86- ****, T65- మొల్లమొగ్గలు, V41- వెల్లమొగ్గ

౬. V41- missing

౭. G86 - ******క్రిష్ణుడు, G07- గోత్రరిషి కృష్ణుడు

౮. V08- శివుడు-దేవత, V41- ఈశ్వరుడు దేవత

౯. T65- కలవందకం

౧౦. G86- మ * ** పువ్వులు

౧౧. G86- సింహ్మ వాహనం, G07- జింకర వాహనం

౧౨. T65- निम्बवृक्षं నింబ వృక్షం

౧౩. T65- బాహువులు

౧౪. V41- ఎని□ది నేత్రములు, ఎని□ది చెవులు

౧౫. V41- missing

౧౬. T65- ఆది వారం, సిహ్మ రాశి

౧౭. V41- యీ రీతున

౧౮. T65- బ్రహతిచ్ఛందస్సున ప్రకారసమవును, G07- బ్రహస్పతిస్ఛందస్సుయిందు బుట్టి ప్రకాశిస్తు వున్నదీ, V41- బృహతిచ్ఛం దస్సున ప్రకాశించును

౧౯. G86, G07 - description missing , V41- మధ్యమ స్వరమునకు

౨౦. V41- శాకద్వీపము

- మొసలి[४] వాహనం - దాడిమవృక్షం - నాగకన్యకా - నాలుగు ముఖాలు - ఎనిమిది భుజాలు - ఎనిమిది శ్రోత్రాలు - ఎనిమిది నేత్రాలు[५] - నాలుగు నాసికలు - రెండు పాదాలు - కుబ్జదేహం - ఉత్తరానక్షత్రం - కన్యారాశి[६] - బుధవారం. ఈ తీరున[७] పంచమస్వరం పంక్తిఛందస్సున ప్రకాశించును[८].

దై(ధై)వతస్వరానికి [९]- ఋషివంశం - క్షత్రియజాతి - 20 యేండ్లు[१०] - పీతవర్ణం - శ్వేతద్వీపం[११] - నారదుడు గోత్రఋషి[१२] - హాస్యరసం - సూర్యుడు అధిదేవతా - వర్న(ర్ణ)వస్త్రం[१३] - పాలు భోజనం[१४] - శ్రీగంధం[१५] - గన్నేరు పూవులు[१६] - గోమేధికభూషణం - నారాచాయుధం - చిలుకవాహనం - ద్రాక్షావృక్షం - దేవతాస్త్రీ - మూడు ముఖాలు[१७] - ఆరు[१८] భుజాలు[१९] - ఆరు[२०] నేత్రాలు[२१] - ఆరు శ్రోత్రాలు[२२] - మూడు[२३] నాసికలు - రెండు పాదాలు - పూర్వాషాఢానక్షత్రం - ధనురాశి - గురువారం - దీర్ఘదేహం -

---

१. V08- చలిచి(పి)ండి భోజనం, T65- చలిపిండి
२. V08- మగిలి, V41- మొగలి పువ్వు
३. V41- missing from here upto వాహనం
४. V08- మసలి
५. V41- ఎనిమిది నేత్రములు ఎనిమిది శ్రోత్రములు
६. V41- రాసి
७. V41- రీతున
८. T65- ప్రకాశం ***- leaf broken
९. G86- అథ దైవతస్వరం, G07- అధ దేవస్వరం, V41- దైవత స్వరమునకు
१०. T65, V41- 20 యెండ్లు వయస్సు
११. V41- శాల్మలీద్వీపం
१२. G86- గోత్రం ఋషి నారదుండు, G07- గోత్రం ఋషి నారదులు
१३. G86- వర్నవస్త్రం, V41- స్వర్ణవస్త్రం
१४. T65- పాలభోజనం
१५. G86- స్త్రీ గంధం
१६. T65- గిన్నరుపూలూ, G86- గిన్నెరు పువ్వులు, V41- గన్నేరు పూలు
१७. V41- మూడు భుజాలు
१८. G07- 9
१९. T65, G86, V41- బాహువులు
२०. G07-9
२१. G07- 9
२२. V41- చెవులు
२३. V41- ఏడు

యీా తీరున దేవతా(ధైవత)స్వరం[1] ఉష్ణిచ్ఛ(ఖ్ఛ)ందస్సున ప్రకాశమవును[2].
నిషాధ(ద)స్వరానికి [3]- రాక్షసవంశం - వైశియ(శ్య)జాతి - యేండ్లు 10[4] -
ధూమ్ర వర్ణ[5] - పుష్కర ద్వీపం - శ్రృంగారరసం - తుంబురుడు గోత్రఋషి[6] -
▭ాయకుడు[7] అధిదేవతా - పట్టువస్త్రం - బియ్యం[8] భోజనం - పరిమళగంధం
- తామరపువ్వులు[9] - పుష్పరాగ భూషణం- అంకుశాయుధం - గోరువంక[10]
వా▭నం లవంగవృక్షం[11] - రాక్షసస్త్రీ[12] - రెండు[13] ముఖాలు - నాలుగు[14]
భుజాలు - 4 శ్రోత్రాలు - 4 నేత్రాలు[15] - 2 నాసికలు - 2 పాదాలు -
అతిస్థూలదే▭ం - అనో(ను)రాధా[16] నక్షత్రం - వృశ్చికరాశి - మంగళవారం[17] -
యీా తీరున[18] నిషాధ(ద)స్వరం జగధీ(తీ)శ్ఛందస్సున ప్రకాశమవును[19].

[1]स्वस्वस्थान[2]विपर्यासात्[3] समस्तव्याप्तमेव[4] च।

---

౧. V41- యీా రీతున ధైవతస్వరము

౨. G86- ఉష్ణచ్ఛందస్సుయందు పుట్టి ప్రకాశింస్సున్నది, G07- ఉష్ణశ్చలధ్వస్సు యెందు పుట్టి ప్రకాశిస్తున్నదీ, V41- ప్రకాశించును

౩. G86, G07- అథ నిషాధ స్వరం

౪. T65, V41-10 యెం డ్లు వయస్సు

౫. G07- ధూపు వర్నం, G86- ధూ * * * gap upto శ్రృంగారరసం

౬. G86- గోత్రఋషి తుంబురుడు, G07- గోత్రర్షి తుంబురుడు, V41- తుంబురుడు గోత్రర్షి

౭. T65, G86- ▭ాయకుండు, V41- ▭ాయకుండధిదేవతా

౮. G07- బీయం భోజనం

౯. V41- తామర పూలు

౧౦. T65, G07- గోర్వంక

౧౧. T65, V41- వేలంగ వృక్ష, G86- లవంక వృక్షం

౧౨. G07- రాక్షస శ్రి

13. G07- 5

౧౪. G07- 4 - 4

౧౫. G86, V41 - 4 నేత్రాలు 4 శ్రోత్రాలు

౧౬. T65- అనుషం నక్షత్రం

౧౭. T65, V41-అంగారకవారం

౧౮. V41- రీతున

౧౯. G86- జగధీశ్ఛ్ఛందస్సున పుట్టి ప్రకాశిస్తున్నది, G07- జగతిశ్ఛంధస్సుంధు పుట్టి ప్రకాశిస్తున్నదీ, V41- ప్రకాశించును

क्रमात् स्वराणां सप्तानां प्रस्तारोऽयमितीरितः[५] ।। ३९।।

టీకా:- స్వరాలకు యొక్క[६] తమ తమ స్థానం [illegible]ర్యాసం వల్ల వ్యస్త-సమస్తాలుగ సప్త స్వరాలకు ప్రస్తారం పుట్టును. స్వరాలకు[७] లక్ష్యం చెప్పును.

అథ షడ్జం

స స స స స స స స స స

రి రి రి రి రి రి రి రి రి రి

గ గ గ గ గ గ గ గ గ గ

మ మ మ మ మ మ మ మ మ మ

ప ప ప ప ప ప ప ప ప ప

ధ ధ ధ ధ ధ ధ ధ ధ ధ ధ

ని ని ని ని ని ని ని ని ని ని

స స స స స స స స స స

షడ్జ ప్రస్తారం[९]

రి రి రి రి రి రి రి రి రి రి

---

१. v.39 was initially found before the prose passages delineating the attributes of svara-s, i.e., after v.38. Since these lines speak of svara-prastāra, they have been shifted to this place. Probably the copyists might have copied along with the previous portion, because the passages are arranged in such a way that in all the PL Mss, they are written on one side of a single leaf and the svara passages on the other side. These svara passages which were originally found along with the individual svara attributes, have been moved to the end after v.39.

२. G86- स्वस्वस्थंन, G07- स्वस्वस्थांन

३. G98, G17, T65, G86v, G07- विपर्यास्यात्

४. T65- समस्तौ व्युत्पत्तमेव

५. G98, T65-प्रस्थारोयमितीरितः, G86- प्रस्तारोयमितिरीरितः, G07- प्रसाजायमितीरितः

६. G86, G07- missing

७. G07- ఈ స్వరాలకు

८. G07- missing

९. T65- అథాష్టమ ప్రస్తారః

గ గ గ గ గ గ గ గ గ గ

మ మ మ మ మ మ మ మ మ మ

ప ప ప ప ప ప ప ప ప ప

ధ ధ ధ ధ ధ ధ ధ ధ ధ ధ

ని ని ని ని ని ని ని ని ని ని

స స స స స స స స స స

(ఋషభ ప్రస్తారం)

గ గ గ గ గ గ గ గ గ గ

మ మ మ మ మ మ మ మ మ మ

ప ప ప ప ప ప ప ప ప ప

ధ ధ ధ ధ ధ ధ ధ ధ ధ ధ

ని ని ని ని ని ని ని ని ని ని

స స స స స స స స స స

గాంధార ప్రస్తారం[౧]

మ మ మ మ మ మ మ మ మ మ

ప ప ప ప ప ప ప ప ప ప

ధ ధ ధ ధ ధ ధ ధ ధ ధ ధ

ని ని ని ని ని ని ని ని ని ని

స స స స స స స స స స

రి రి రి రి రి రి రి రి రి రి

గ గ గ గ గ గ గ గ గ గ

మధ్యమ ప్రస్తారం[౨]

ప ప ప ప ప ప ప ప ప ప

---

౧. T65, G07 - missing

౨. T65, G07- this svara passage in missing. one third of the leaf of T65 is broken and missing and hence this portion of the svara passage could not be read.

ధ ధ ధ ధ ధ ధ ధ ధ ధ ధ

ని ని ని ని ని ని ని ని ని ని

స స స స స స స స స స

రి రి రి రి రి రి రి రి రి రి

గ గ గ గ గ గ గ గ గ గ

మ మ మ మ మ మ మ మ మ మ[१]

(పంచమ ప్రస్తారం)

ధ ధ ధ ధ ధ ధ ధ ధ ధ ధ

ని ని ని ని ని ని ని ని ని ని

స స స స స స స స స స

రి రి రి రి రి రి రి రి రి రి

గ గ గ గ గ గ గ గ గ గ

మ మ మ మ మ మ మ మ మ మ

ప ప ప ప ప ప ప ప ప ప

ధైత(వ)త ప్రస్తారం[२]

ని ని ని ని ని ని ని ని ని ని

స స స స స స స స స స

రి రి రి రి రి రి రి రి రి రి

గ గ గ గ గ గ గ గ గ గ

మ మ మ మ మ మ మ మ మ మ

ప ప ప ప ప ప ప ప ప ప

ధ ధ ధ ధ ధ ధ ధ ధ ధ ధ

(నిషాద ప్రస్తారం)

(అధ స్వర ప్రస్తారం)

---

१. This svara passage is seen in G07 only.

२. T65, G07- missing

స రి గ - రి గ మ - గ మ ప

స రి గ మ - రి గ మ ప

స రి గ వం- ప వూ రి గ వూ

ధ ధ ని - మ ప ధ - ప ధ ని ధ

ని స - గ మ [1]ప ధ మ ప ధ ని

ప ధ ని స - ప ధ - గ మ ప ధ ని

మ ప ధ ని స -

[2]స - రి - గ - మ - ప - ధ - ని - స -

స - రి - స - రి - గ - వం - రి - రి -

ధ స గ స రి * * * * * *

స రి స వం వం రి గ వం

వం గ రి ప ప స రి ప

గ వం ధ స రి ధ స ధ

స రి గ వం ప ధ ని స

ధ స గ స రి వం వం గ

స రి గ వం ప ధ ని - స

ని - రి - స - రి- గ - వం - రి - రి -

ధ స గ స రి గ వం గ

ప రి స వం వం రి గ వం

వం గ రి ప ప ప రి ప

గ - మ - ధ - స - రి - ధ - స - ధ -

ని - ని - ని - రి - గ - మ - ని -

స - ని - ధ - ప - మ - గ - రి - స -

1. G86- missing upto స రి గ మ ప ధ ని స   స ని ధ ప మ గ రి స

2. T65- this and the following svara passages are missing

రి గ మ ప ధ ని స
గ మ ప ధ ని స
మ ప ధ ని స
ప ధ ని స
ధ ని స
ని స
స

ని ధ ప మ గ రి స
ధ ప వం గ రి స
ప వం గ రి స
వం గ రి స
గ రి స
రి స
స

స రి గ మ ప ధ ని స
స స గ మ ప ధ ని స
స స మ ప ధ ని స[1]
స స ప ధ ని స[2]
స స ధ ని స
స స ని స
స స స స
మ ని ధ ప[3]
మ ప ధ స
గ రి రి స
మ ని[4] ధ ప ధ ని స
స రి గ
స మ ని
స రి రి
స మ మ మ
ప ధ ని స

१. G07- this line is missing

२. G86- this line is missing

३. G86- ప missing, G07- ప ని ధ స

४. G07- రి

రి రి గ గ[౧]

ని గ[౨]

ని ప స రి

గ మ మ మ ని ధ ని[౩]

ని ప రి ధ ప ధ

గ[౪] రి ధ ధ ప ని

స గ రి మ ని

రి గ స మ ప ని[౫]

ని స స మ మ ధ ని[౬]

స మ ని ధ ప[౭]

స స స రి గ గ[౮]

ని ధ ని స స

గ రి రి స ని

ధ ని గ ప ని స

ప మ గ రి స

స రి గ మ స మ ప ధ

రి ధ వం ప వం గ రి స

స రి గ మ స[౧] మ ప ధ

---

౧. T65- గ missing

౨. T65 - this line is missing

౩. G07- గ మ ప ని ధ ని

౪. G86, G07 - ని

౫. G86- రి గ స మ ***

౬. G86- ని గ స మ ప ధ ని, G07- స రి మ ప ధ ని

౭. G86- స మ ని ధ ప మ, G07- స మ ని ధ ప మ ప

౮. T65 - reads one more గ

రి ధ మ ప మ గ రి స[२]
ప[३] మ గ రి స ని
ధ ప మ గ రి స
మ స ధ ని స ని
గ మ ప ధ ని స
ని ధ ప మ మ గ రి
స రి గ మ ప ధ

స రి గ మ ప ధ ని స   స
రి గ మ ప ధ స స ని   రి రి
గ మ ప ధ ని స ప ధ   గ గ స
మ ప ధ ని స గ మ ప   మ మ మ మ
ప ధ ని స స రి గ మ   ప మ గ ప ప[४]
ధ ని స స రి స రి[५] గ   ప ధ రి ధ మ ప
ని స మ ప మ గ రి స   రి ని స స స[६]

टीका:- మంద్ర[७] మధ్యమ తారకాలు భూలోకమందు[८] స్వరం వ్యాపకం[९].

[१०]षड्जस्वरादि भूलोके[११] प्रकाशार्थं[१२] नृणामथ[१३] ।
[१]नाभिहृत्कण्ठमूर्धास्येष्वाविर्भावयति ध्वनिम्[२] ।। ४० ।।

---

१. G86, G07- omit స
२. T65 stops with this; the rest of the prastāra portion is not seen.
3. G07- స
4. G07 – ప మ గ గ ప
५. G86- reads one more స రి
६. G07- రి స స స స
७. G86- మందర, G07- ముందర, G24- మద్ర
८. T65,G86- భూలోకములందు, G24- స్వరాలు భూ[illegible]యందు
९. G24- స్వర వ్యాపకం, G86, G07- read ।।१।। after this.
१०. G98,G17,B13 - v.40ab is missing
११. V08- षड्जादयः स्वरा लोके, G86- षड्ज ****
१२. V08, G86, G07, G24 - प्रकाशार्धं
१३. V08- नृणां मताः, G86, G07- नृणांसदा, T65- नूणां मथ, G24- नृणामधा

[3]अतिसूक्ष्मश्च[4] सूक्ष्मश्च पुष्टश्चैवातिपुष्टकः[5]।
तारश्चेति तथा[6] ज्ञेयः[7] पञ्चधा देहजः स्वरः[8] ।।४१।।

టీకా:- షడ్జాది స్వరాలు భూలోకమందు ప్రకాశార్థం[9] కొరకు మనుష్యుల యొక్క [10]నాభి హృదయ కంప్పం (కంఠం) అశ్య(ఆస్య) శిరసులయందు[11] అతిసూక్ష్మముగాను[12] (సూక్ష్మముగాను పుష్టముగాను) అతిపుష్టి (ష్టముగాను) తారకంగాను ఐదు ప్రకారాలుగ మనుష్యుల దేహమందు స్వరాలు పుట్టును.

[13]नाभ्यां हृदि च कण्ठे च जिह्वामूले च नासयोः[14]।
कपा [पो]ले मूर्ध्निदेशे च क्रमात् षड्जादयो भवेत्[1]।।४२।।

---

१. cf. SR 1,3,4cd

२. G98a, G17a, B13a - नाभिहृत्कण्ठमूर्धास्येष्वाविर्भावयते ध्वनिम्, G86 - नाभिहृत्कंठ मूर्धादिस्वेस्वेष्वादिर्विभावयो ध्वनिः, G07-नाभिहृत्कंठमूर्धादिस्वेस्वेष्वादिर्विचालवय स्वनिः, T65-नाभिहृत्कंठमूर्धादियेस्वेष्वादिर्विभावयते ध्वनिः, G24- नालिहृत्कंठमूर्ध्नाश्वेष्वाविभाविये‍ते ध्वनिः, V08- नाभिहृत्कंठवदनमूर्धासु ध्वनि रुच्यते, G18- नाभिहृत्करमूर्धास्येष्वपि भावयता ध्वनि.

३. v.41, cf. SM 1,4,17

४. T65- अतिसूक्ष्मं च, G86, G07- अतिसूक्षंच, G98, G17, B13- नादोऽतिसूक्ष्म, G24- अतिसूक्ष्मं च

५. G98, G17-पुष्टोपुष्टिश्चक्रित्रिमः, G98a, G17a-पुष्टोपुष्टिश्चकृत्रिमः, B13, B13a-पुष्टोऽपुष्टश्चकृत्रिमः, T65, G86-पुष्टौ चैवातिपुष्पकौ, G07-पुष्टौ चैलातिपुष्पकौ, G18-पुष्टिश्चैवातिपुष्टिकः, G24- पुष्टौद्वारेतिपुष्टकौ

६. T65, G86, G07, G24- ताराश्चेति च, G18- तारश्चैव

७. G86- विज्ञेयाः, T65, G07- विज्ञेयं, G24-विजयः, G18- विज्ञयाः

८. G98,G17,B13-इति पञ्चाभिधाधत्ते पञ्चस्थानस्थित/तः क्रमात्, T65-पंचधादेहज स्वराः, G86- पंचधादेहिजा स्वराः, G07, G24 - पंचदादेहजा स्वराः, G18- पञ्चधादेहजाः स्वराः The readings from v.41cd - v.50 are slightly different in G98 and its transcripts. They seem to follow SR as is clearly evident from the readings. It is also noted that those verses which are not seen in SR, but found in the present text are missing in G98 also. Probably this portion of G98 looks more like an interpolation from SR, and therefore the variant readings are placed in the footntoes. It is to be pointed out here that G98 contains many such interpolations, (including SR) in between.

९. G86, G07, G24- ప్రకాషార్థం

१०. G24- adds నాభి యొక్క before

११. T65- కంఠ హృదయం నాభి ఆస్య శిరస్యులబందు, G86, G07- నాభిహృదయం శిరస్సు దీష్లయందు

१२. G86- సూక్ష్ంగ పుష్టి, G07- సూక్షం పుష్టి, G24- అతిసూక్ష్మ శూక్ష్మ పుష్టి

१३. G98,G17,B13 - v.42 is missing

१४. T65- नाभिहृदयकण्ठश्च जिह्वमूले तु नासिका, G86- नाभिहृदयकण्ठश्च जिन्ह्वमुले तु नासिका, G07- नाभिहृदयकण्ठं च जिन्ह्वमूले तु नासिकांग, G24- नाभिहृदयकण्ठश्च शिह्वं मूले तु नाशिका, V08- नाभिहृदयकण्ठाश्च जिह्वामूलं च नासिका

टीका:- [२]నాభి హృదయం నద (కంఠ) జిహ్వామూల నాసికా కపోల మూర్ధ్ని యందు షడ్జాది స్వరాలు వుండును.

[३]व्यवहारे त्वसौ त्रेधा[४] हृदि मन्द्रोऽभिधीयते[५] ।

कण्ठे मध्यो[६] मूर्ध्नि[७] तारः[८] त्रिधा तु परिकीर्तितः[९] ।। ४३।।

टीका:- షడ్జాది స్వరాలు వ్యవహారమందు[१०] హృదయ మందర(ంద్ర)మనిన్ని కంఠ మధ్యమనిన్ని శిరస్సు[११] తారకమనిన్ని, హృదయం కంఠం మూర్ధ్ని[१२] - యీా మూటియందు[१३] (మూడింటియందు), మందర(ంద్ర) మధ్యమ తారకాలని[१४] మూడు ప్రకారాలాయను.

[१]सरि[री] मन्द्रौ[२] गमौ मध्ये[यौ][३] पधनी तारकाः स्मृताः[४] ।। ४४।।

---

१. T65-कपोले मूर्ध्नि देशस्ताः क्रमात् षड्जादयस्वराः, G86-कपोले मूर्ध्नि देशस्ताः क्रमं षड्जादयस्वराः, G07- कपाले मार्दि देशस्ताः क्रमं षड्जादयस्वराः, G24- कपोले मूर्ध्नि देशधमा क्रमात् षड्जादयस्वराः, V08-कपालं मूर्धदेशस्तु स्वरस्थानानिवै नृणाम्. G18 gives a grammatically better reading than other Mss and hence v.41 is taken from it. However the word कपाल is not supported by other Mss both in the original and in the commentary. Hence कपोल has been suggested.

२. T65- నాభి హృదయం కంఠ జిహ్వామూలం నాసికా కపోల మూర్ధ్ని శిరస్సుయందు షడ్జాది స్వరాయు వుండును, G86- బొట్టుమొదలు హృదయం కంఠ జింహ్మ మూలం నాలిగ అడుగు నాసికా మూలం కపోలం మూర్ధ్ని శిశిరస్సుయందు షడ్జాది స్వరాలు వుండును, G07- మెడమొదలు హృదయం కంఠ జింహ్మ మూలం నాలికె అడుగు నాసికా మొదలు కపోలమ శిశిరస్సుయందు షడ్జాది స్వరాలు వుండును. The readings in G86 and G07 seem to mention the word in saṃskūta and then its Telugu equivalent.

३. cf. SR 1,3,7ab

४. G86,G07-त्रिधा, G24-त्र्येधा

५. V08,G18-हृदिमन्द्रोविधीयते, T65,G86,G07-हृदिमन्दोर्विधीयते, G24-हृदिमन्दोर्विधीयते

६. T65, G86, G07- कण्ठ मध्ये, G24-करमध्ये

७. G98, G86-मूध्नि, G07- मूर्धि, G24- मूर्धि

८. T65, G07, G24- तारा, G86-तारु, G18- ताराः

९. G98, G17, B13- द्विगुणश्चोत्तरोत्तरः (SR too reads the same), V08-स्वरस्तु परिकीर्तितः, G86-त्रिदास्तु परिकीर्तितः, G07- त्रेदारस्तु परिकीर्तितः, T65- त्रैदास्तु परिकीर्तितः, G24- त्रैदास्तु परिकीर्तिताः

१०. G86- వ్యవకార మందు, T65- వ్యవహారాలయందు, G24- వ్యవహారాలయందు మూడు ప్రకారాలాయను- the rest of the commentary is missing.

११. G86, G07- శిరొ

१२. G86- హృదయకంఠ మూధ్వి, G07- హృదయకంఠ మూర్ధి

१३. G86 - యీా మూటయందు, G07- యీా మూడియందు

१४. T65- తారకాలనునిను

टीका:- షడ్జరి(ఋ)షభాలు[५] మన్దర(ంద్ర)మందున్ను, గాంధారమధ్యమాలు, మధ్యమమందున్ను[६] పంచమ దై(ధై)వత[७] నిషాదాలు తారకమందున్ను[८] ఆశ్రయించియుండును[९].

[१०]**नृणामुरसिमन्द्रस्तु**[११] **द्वाविंशतिगतोध्वनिः**[१२] **।**

स एव कण्ठे[१३] **मध्यस्यात्**[१४] **तारः**[१५] **शिरसि गीयते**[१६] **।। ४५।।**

टीका:- మనుష్యుల[१७] హృదయమనే మంద్రమందు[१८] షడ్జాది[१९] స్వరాలు ధ్వనిభేదాలుగ ఇరు(ర)వైరెండు ప్రకారాలాయను. ఆ తీరుననే కంఠ మధ్యమమందు[२०] ఇరు(ర)వైరెండు ప్రకారాలు[२१]. శిరస్సా(స్తా)రకమందు[२२] 22 ప్రకారాలాయను[२३].

[१]**उत्तरोत्तरतारासु[तारस्तु] वीणायामधरोत्तरः**[२] **।**

---

१. G98,G17,B13- v.44cd and v.45 are missing; V08 reads lines v.44cd and v.45 after v.53.

२. T65,G86, G07- सरिमन्द्र, G18- सरिर्मन्द्रे, G24- सरिमध्ये

३. G86, G07- गमौमध्य, V08- रिगी मध्यौ, G24- गमो मध्ये

४. T65- तारकाशृतः, G86- तारकाशृता, G07- तारका **ताः, G24- तारकाश्रिताः

५. T65- షడ్జఋషభాలుకు, G86- షడ్జఋషభములు, G07- షద్జరుధభంలు

६. G24- మమధ్యమందున్ను

७. G86, G07- ద్రైవతమని

८. T65- తారకమందుకన్ను, G86- మ **దున్ను, G24- తారకమందు

९. G86, G07- వుండును

१०. v.45- v.46, cf. Datt. 8,9

११. T65-नृणां मुखशिरार्थस्तु, G86- नृणा मन्द्रस्तु, G07- नृणामु-क मि मन्द्रस्तु, G24- नृणौ मुरशिमद्रस्तु

१२. G07- द्वाविंशतगतोध्वनि , G18- द्वाविंशतिगलो ध्वनिः. Datt. reads द्वाविंशतिविधो ध्वनिः

१३. G86- स विंश कंठ, G07- षिस विंश कंठे, T65- स एव कंठ

१४. G18- मध्यश्च, G24-मध्यस्य तु

१५. T65,G86, G07- तार, G24- तारकर

१६. G86-शिरसिगियेत्, G07-शिरसिगय्यते, G24- करशिगिय्यते, T65- शिरसिनिर्यते

१७. T65- మనుష్యులు

१८. T65, G86, G07- మందిరమందు

१९. G86, G07- షడ్జాద్లు

२०. G86, G07- commentary missing from స్వరాలు, G24- కంఠమందు

२१. G24- ప్రకారాలాయను

२२. T65- శిర్థానమందు. The three regions of the human body, namely the chest, throat and head are being related to the three regions/registers, mandra, madhya and tāra. Hence it is suggested thus,

२३. G24- ప్రకారాలాయలు

इति ध्वनिविशेषास्ति[ते][३] श्रीवीण[४] श्रुतिरञ्जितः[५] [श्रवणाच्छ्रुतिसंज्ञिताः][६] ।। ४६ ।।

[७] [मन्द्रादिषूक्ताश्श्रुतयश्शुद्धतन्त्र्यो नव स्मृताः] ।।४७।।

టీకా:- [८]మన్ద్రా(ంద్రా)దిషు శ్రుతయః। మందా(ంద్రా)ది శ్రుతులు మంద్ర ము(మ)ంద్రం - మంద్ర మధ్యమం - మంద్ర తారకం - మధ్య మంద్రం[९] - మధ్యమ మధ్యమం - మధ్యమ తారకం[१०] - తారక మంద్రం - తారక మధ్యమం - తారక తారకం. యీ ప్రకారాన[११] శ్రుతి భేదాలు 66 అని తెలుసుట[१२].

[१३]हृद्यूर्ध्वा[र्ध्वे][१४] नाडीसंलग्ना[१५] नाड्यो द्वाविंशतिः क्रमात्[१६] ।

[१][तिरश्च्यस्तासु तावत्यः श्रुतयो मारुताहतेः][२] । ४८

१. v.46- v.47 and the corresponding commentary were originally found after v.85. Since it is the continuation of what is said in v.45, they have been moved to this place. This verse appears again in NC, 3, 6.

२. G86- विणया मंद्द * * * * * * * *

३. G17- विशेषास्त, B13- विशेषोऽस्ति, G86- विशोषोस्ति

४. G98, G17, B13- श्रीवीणा, G86- श्रिविण

५. G98, B13- रञ्जिता, G17-रञ्जिताः

६. Suggested reading is based on Datt. The reading of the latter half in the Mss is different from the original Datt. reading and is seen in RJM (p.134) too in the same way. However this verse is not found in BKM.

७. This is missing in all the Mss, but is found in BKM(p.89) and RJM(p.134), and is seen before the Comm to v.47. This has been suggested here, based on BKM and RJM, with the support of two saṃskūta words मन्दादिषु श्रुतयः, occurring in the commentary. The idea of nine varieties is also seen highlighted here.

८. G98,G17,B13 read the commentary thus: శ్రుతి భేదాలు 66

९. T65- మధ్య మంధ్యమం

१०. G86- మ * * మ తారకం

११. G86- రీతిన

१२. T65 - missing

१३. v.48- v.49, cf. SR 1,3,8cd-10ab

१४. G18-हृदूर्ध्व, G07-हृद्वोध्व, T65,G86-हृद्योर्द्वा, G24- हृद्योद्वा, V08- हृद्योर्ध्वे

१५. G86, G07- नाडि सलज्ञात् T65- नाडि संलज्जात्, G24- नादि सुलज्ञात्

१६. G98,B13-द्वाविम्शतिर्मता, G17,G18-द्वाविंशतिर्मताः, T65- द्वाविम्शति क्रमात्, G86- द्वोध्वाविंशति क्रमात्, G07- ड्योधाविंशति क्रमात्, G24- नाज्योर्धविंशति क्रमात्. T65,G86,G07 read the following commentary, which is missing in G24. अनेटदिग (G07- अनेलतिगा)। स्वराल ध्वनि भेदालु। २२। प्रकारालुग आयनु। आ तीरुनोने - कं मध्यम मंदु। This seems to be the incomplete version of the commentary to v.45. G86 and G07 read the second half of v.48ab after this commentary.

उच्चोच्चतरतायुक्ताः[३] प्रभवन्त्युत्तरोत्तरम्[४]।

एवं कण्ठे तथा[५] शीर्षे[६] श्रुतिर्द्वाविंशतिः[७] क्रमात्। ४९

టీకా:- హృదయ మంద్రమాదిగా[८] కంఠ మధ్య[९] పర్యంతం 22 నాడి భేదాలు గలవు[१०]. [११]ఆ నాడులయందు[१२] తగిలి(తగిన) వాయువు[१३] చేత కొట్టు(ట్ట)బడి[१४] [१५]ఉత్తరోత్తరంగ[१६] స్వరాలు ఇరు(ర)వైరెండు భేదాలాయను. యీ ప్రకారాననే కంఠ మధ్యమందు[१७] ఇరు(ర)వైరెండు[१८] ప్రకారాలు. శిరస్థానమందు[१९] ఇరు(ర)వైరెండు ప్రకారాలాయను[२०]. స్వరాలు భేదాలైన క్రమం[२१]

[१]चतुश्चतुश्चतुश्चैव[२] षड्जमध्यमपञ्चमाः।

---

१. G98,G17,B13- v.48cd - v.50 missing.

२. T65-तिरश्चसस्तुतापत्वात् चुतयो मारुताहुतः, G86-तिरश्चासास्तुतापत्वाच्चुतयो मारुताहुते, G07-तिरश्चासास्तुतोपत्वाश्चुतयो मारुताहुते, V08-तिरश्चस्तासुतावत्यः श्रुतयो मारुताम(ह)ते, G18-मस्तके तास्तु तावन्त्यो ध्वनयो मारुताहताः, G24-शिरश्चसास्तुतापत्या श्रुशिंयो मारुताहता Since the reading in the Mss is erroneous, parallel reading from SR 1,3,9ab has been suggested.

३. T65, G07- उच्चोच्चारुरतायुक्ता, G86- उच्चोच्चररंतायुक्ता, G18- उच्चैरुच्चारणैर्युक्ताः, G24-यिच्छेचाच्चारुरतायुत्ना

४. G86- प्रभवंत्सुत्तरोत्तरं, G07- प्रभवंत्वुत्तरोत्तरं, G18- प्रभवन्तुत्तरोत्तरम्

५. V08- एवं कंठे तु सा

६. G86,G07- शिर्षे, V08- शीर्षं

७. G86-शृतद्वाविंशति, G07-शिर्षे श्रुतत्वात्रिंशति, G18-ध्वनिर्द्वाविंशतिः, T65-शृतिर्द्वाविंशतिक, G24-शृतिर्द्वाविंशति

८. G86- హృదయ మందర * * *, G07- హృదయ మందరమాదిగ, T65- మన్ద్రామాదికా

९. G86-* * * మధ్య, T65- కంఠ

१०. T65- గలవు

११. T65, G86, G07, G24- read యీ స్వరాలు before.

१२. T65, G86, G07- నాడి యందు

१३. G24- వాయువుల

१४. G86, G07- కట్టబడి

१५. T65,G86,G07,G24-add thus: T65,G86- ఉచ్చైరుచ్చారణంగా, G07- ఉచ్చైకుచ్చారణంగా, G24-వుచ్చారుచ్చరంగా- this is not being included in the main text, as it is redundant.

१६. T65- ఉరోత్తరంగ, G24- ఉత్తరోత్తరంగా- the rest of the commentary is missing

१७. T65- మధ్యమమందు

१८. G86- missing

१९. Probably this should read శిరస్తారకమందు

२०. T65- ప్రకారాలు

२१. G86- స్వరాల భేదాలు యతెక్రమం, G07- రాల భేదాలు యదెక్రమం

द्वौ द्वौ निषादगान्धारौ[३] त्रिस्त्रिः ऋषभधैवतौ[४] ।। ५०।।

टीका:- షడ్జమధ్యమపంచమాలు[५] నాలుగేశి ప్రకారాలును[६]. ఋషభ[७] దై(ధై)వతాలు మూడేశి ప్రకారాలును[८]. నిషాద[९]గాంధారాలు రెండు ప్రకారాలాయను[१०]. ఇది గూడ 22[११]. (ఈ) తీరుననే మధ్యమ తారకాలయందు[१२] భేదాలాయా(య)ను[१३]. □లకు పేళ్ళు (□కి పేర్లు)[१४].

[१५]आद्या चोत्तरमन्द्रा स्याद्रजनी चोत्तरायता[१६] ।
चतुर्थी[१७] शुद्धषड्जा तु[१८] पञ्चमी मत्सरीकृता[१९] ।
अश्वक्रान्ता तु[१] षष्ठी स्यात्[२] सप्तमी चाभिरुद्गता[३] ।। ५१।।

---

१. v.50, cf. SSS 3,4cd-5ab, SMK 2,29cd-30ab, CDP 3,2ab-3cd, SM 1,1,85; STR 6,7,23cd-24ab
२. G07- चतुश्च चतु चतुश्चैवा , G24- श्चेतुश्चेतुश्चतुश्चैवा
३. G86- द्वौ द्वौ निषादगान्धार, G07 -द्वौ निषादगान्धार, G24- द्वौ द्वौ निषादगान्धारं
४. T65-त्रित्रिऋषभदैवताः, G86-त्रित्रिरुषभदेवताः, G07-त्रित्रिऋषदेनताः, V08- त्रित्रिर्षभधैवतौ, G24- त्रि त्रि रिषभादैवता
५. G07- యీా □ం మధ్యమ పంశ్చమాలు
६. G86- ప్రకారాలాయను, G07- ప్రాకారాలా లాయను, G24- నాలుగే ప్రకారాలాయను
७. G07- ఋష, G24- నిషభ
८. G86, G07, G24 - ప్రకారాలాయను
९. G07- నికాద, G24- రిషవం
१०. G07- తారకాగాతాయను - 2
११. T65, G86- యిది కూడ, G24- యిది కూడా ఇ□2 యో
१२. G24- తారాకాలాయదు
१३. G24- భేధాలును
१४. G86, G07- దీనుల పేళ్ళు, G24- □ పేళ్ళో
१५. v.51- v.52, cf. NS 28,27ab-28ab,31
१६. T65-आद्यां उत्तरमंद्रस्यात् वज्रनीरोक्तरायथा, G86-अंध्यं मन्द इति प्रोक्तं रजनिचोत्तरायतः, G07-आध्यं मन्द इति प्रोक्तं तर्जनीप्रोत्तरायतः, G18-आद्यामुद्राद्वितीयाच व्रजनीचोत्तरोत्तरी, G24- आद्यां उत्तरमंद्र स्यात् व्रजनिरोत्तयस्तथा
१७. G86-चतुर्द्धि, G07-चतुर्धि
१८. G98-शुद्धड्जानु, G17-शुद्ध[ष]ड्जानु, B13-शुद्धषड्जानु, T65-शुद्धषड्जात्, G86-शुद्धषड्जस्यात, G07-शुद्धषड्जास्यात्, G18- शुद्धषड्जा च, G24- शंतषष्टा तु
१९. G98,B13-पत्सरीकृताः, G17-वत्सरीकृताः, G24-वत्सरीकृतः, G86,G07-सत्वरीकृता, G18-चत्वरी तथा

सौवीरी[४] हरिणाश्वा च[५] स्यात्[६] कलोपनता[७] तथा।
शुद्धमध्या[८] तथा चैव[९] मार्दवी पारवी[१०] [मार्गी च पौरवी[११]] तथा।
हृष्यका चेति विज्ञेया[१२] मध्यमग्राममूर्च्छनाः[१३] ।। ५२।।
[१४]नन्दा विशाला[१५] सुमुखी[१६] चित्रा चित्रवती सुखा[१७]।
आलापा चेति[१] गान्धारग्रामा[मे][२] स्युः[३]सप्तमूर्च्छनाः[४] ।। ५३।।

---

१. G98, G17, B13- अश्वक्रान्ता च, G18- अश्वक्रान्ती च

२. G17- पषीस्यात् , G86, G07- षष्टिस्यात्

३. G98,G17,B13,T65,G86-सप्तमी चाभिरुद्धता, G07-सप्तमी नाभिरुद्घता, G18- सप्तभिश्चाभिरुद्गता. G18 reads the following verses after this, which is missing in all other Mss. अष्टमी साविदीचैव नवमी हरिणी तथा। दशमी च तथा कल्कापनयेति च संज्ञिता। एकादशी शुद्धमध्या द्वादशी मार्धवी तथा। त्रयोदशी पारवीति हृष्यका चे चतुर्दशी। नन्दा पञ्चदशी प्रोक्ता विशाखा षोडशी स्मृता। संमुखी सप्तदशमी चित्रात्वष्टादशी मता। एकोनविंशतिश्चित्रावर्तिनी परिकीर्तिता। सुखा तु विंशतिः प्रोक्ता आलापास्त्वेकविंशतिः। प्राचामतेनाभिहिता एकविंशति मूर्छनाः। मन्द्राव्रजन्युत्तरा च शुद्धषड्जा च गत्वरी। अश्वक्रान्त्युद्गताचैव षड्जग्रामस्य मूर्छना।

४. T65- साविरु, G98-साविरी, G17-साविठी, B13- साविरि, G86- सावेरि, G07- सावीधि, G18- साविती, G24- सावेरि

५. G98,G17,B13,G07-हरिणीद्या च, T65-हरिणिद्वौ च, G86-हरिणादौ चा, G18-हरिणीचैव, G24- हरिणा द्वौ च

६. T65, G98, B13- सात् G17- स्तात्, G24- शात्, G18 - missing

७. T65-नल्कोपयनं, G98,G17,B13-नल्कोवनयं, G86,G07-कल्लोपयनं, G18-कल्कोपनया, G24-नल्कोपनयं

८. T65, G86, G07- शुद्धमध्य, G24- शुद्यमध्य

९. T65, G86, G07- चैवा

१०. T65-मार्दळिपारवि, G86,G07-मूर्द्धळी पारळी, V08-मार्दवी(र्ग) पौरवी SM reads two ways: मादली पौरकी' (1,1,60) Uमार्द्दली पौरली' (1,1,93).

११. reading based on NS 28,31

१२. G07- विज्ञेयं , G24- धिग्गेयं

१३. G98, G17,B13- मूर्छना, G07- मूर्चना, T65,G86- मूर्च्छना, G24- मध्यमंग्राम मूर्च्छनं

१४. v.53, cf. SR 1,4,25cd-26ab

१५. V08- नन्दा विशाखा, G24-नन्द्रा दिशाल

१६. G86- समुखा, G07-सुमुखा

१७. T65, G86, G07- सुखी, G24- सुख

टीका:- [५]మంద(ఉత్తరమంద్ర)[६], రజని, ఉత్తర(ఉత్తరాయతా), శుద్ధా(శుద్ధషడ్జా), సత్వరీ(మత్సరీకృతా)[७], అశ్వక్రాంతా[८], ఆభిరుద్ధ(గ)తా[९], సా□(సౌ□)[१०], ౕరిణి(ణాశ్వా)[११], కల్లోపనా(కలోపనతా)[१२], శుద్ధమధ్యా[१३], మార్ద□(మూర్గి)[१४], పారళీ(పౌర□)[१५], ౕృష్యకి(కా)[१६], నందా, □ాల(లా)[१७], సుముఖీ[१८], చిత్ర(త్రా), చిత్రవతి(తీ), సుఖా, ఆలాపా[१९] - ఇ□[२०] షడ్జమ(షడ్జ)[२१] మధ్యమ గాంధార గ్రామములు చేత మూడు (21) పేళ్ళు(పేర్లు)[२२]. స్వరాలకు పేళ్ళు(పేర్లు). ఇదే ఆరోణి[२३] అవరోణి అ(ఆ)యితే మూర్చ్ఛనాదులనబడును.

आद्यन्तौ[१] षड्जमाश्रित्य[२] मन्द्रमध्यमतारकाः[३]।

---

१. G98, G17, B13- आलापेति च, T65, G86, G07, V08-आलापश्चेति

२. reading based on SR 1,4,26ab

३. G86-ग्रमास्सु, G07-ग्रामस्सु, V08-ग्रमेस्यात्, G18- गान्धारीग्रामाः स्युः, G24- ग्रामास्तु

४. G17- मूर्चनाः, B13- मूर्छना, G98, T65, G86- मूर्च्छना, G07- मूर्चना

५. The names in the following prose passage have been suggested based on the original text and NS 28,28 & 31. Some of them are written in an abbreviated form.

६. G24 - మంద్ర

७. G24- సత్సరీ

८. T65, G24 - అశ్వక్రాంత్తం

९. G24- ఆభిరుద్ధతి

१०. G86- *******, G07- సు□ు, G24- సావేరి

११. G24- షరిణి

१२. T65- కల్కోపనయి, G24- కల్కోపన ఇ

१३. G86- శుద్ధమాధ్యా

१४. G86- మూర్న్ ధ్ధలి, G07- మూర్ధ్వీ, G24- మార్ధారి

१५. G24- పార□

१६. G86- ౕృష్యని, G24- ౕృౕృష్యకి

१७. G24- □ారి

१८. G86- సముఖీ

१९. G86, G07- ఆలాప, G24- ఆతాప

२०. G24- reads commentary thus: ఇటు షడ్జమ గాంధార గ్రామాలచాత మైయ్యేటు యిరవైయొక్క స్వరాలు పేల్లు. యి□ఆరోణ అవరోణి యి□తే మూర్చ్ఛనాదులనబడును.

२१. G07- షడ్జను

२२. G86- మూడెండు 2, G07- మూడెండ్లు 21,

२३. G86- హారోణి

आरोहिण्यवरोहिण्यौ[४] षड्जाद्यन्तौ[५] स्वरान् वदेत्[६] ।। ५४।।

టీకా:- మంద్రమధ్యమతారకాలు[७] ఆధ్య(ద్య)ంతాలయందు[८] షడ్జస్వరాన్ని[९] ఆశ్రయించివుండును. ఆరోహణియందు[१०] అవరోహణియందు[११] షడ్జాద్యంతాలుగా స్వరాలు పలుకవలెను.

[१२]ध्वनिभेदाः क्रमादेवं[१३] भवन्ति षष्टिषड्डुत्तरा[१४] ।। ५५।।

టీకా:- కాగా ఈ ప్రక్రారణ(రవే)[१५] షడ్జాది స్వరాలు వుందర(మంద్ర) మధ్యమతారకాలయందు ధ్వనిభేదాలు అరు(ర)వై ఆరు ప్రకారాలు కలిగను[१६].

ग्राम स्वरसमूहः स्यात्[१७] स्वरारोह्यवरोहिणी[१८] ।

मूर्च्छनेति स्वरा ज्ञेया[१] तयोर्भेदं[२] क्रमाद्भवेत्[३] ।। ५६।।

---

१. G86- आध्यांत्तौ, G07- आध्यांत्ता, V08- आद्यतं, G18- आद्यंद्वौ

२. G86- षड्जमाशृत्य, G07- षड्जमाशृत्वा, G24- षड्जमाश्रित्या

३. G98- मध्यमतारका, B13- मध्यमतारकौ, V08- मध्यगतारगाः

४. G98,G17-आरोहिण्यवरोहिश्च, B13-आरोहण्यवरोहश्च, G86-आरोहिणि अवरोहश्च, G07-आरोण्यवरोहश्च, V08-आरोहिण्यवरोहश्च, T65-आरोहिणिअवरोहश्च, G24-आरोहंण्यवरोहाश्य

५. G86-षड्जांद्यंतु,G07-षड्प्राद्यंतु,V08-षड्जांद्यांतान्,G18-षड्जादन्तान्,G24- षड्जाद्यांत्तो

६. T65- स्वरान् स्वदेत्, G98- स्वरान्यदेत्, G17- स्वरान्य (न् व) देत्, G24- स्वरावदेत्

७. G07- తారాలు

८. G24- ఆధ్యంత్తాలయేందు

९. G86- షడ్జమ స్వరాన్ని, G24- సడ్జ స్వరం, T65- షడ్జమ స్వరం

१०. G24- ఆరోహణియెందూ

११. G24- అవరోహణియెందూ

१२. G98, G17, B13- this verse is missing

१३. T65- प्रमादेवं, G24- ध्यभेदा क्रमंदेवं

१४. T65- भवेत्षष्ठि षठ्नरः,G86- भेवे***षष्टिरुत्तरः, G07- भवेष्ट षष्टिरुत्तरः,G18- भवेत् षष्टिः षड्डुत्तराः,G24- च्चिवत् सष्टि षड्डुतरा

१५. G86- యీా క్రమాన ****, G07- యంద్రమాను***, G24- యీా ప్రకారేను

१६. G86- ప్రకారం కలిగను, T65- ప్రకారాలు ఆయను

१७. T65, G98, G17- समोहस्यात्, G86- समूहस्यात् , G07, V08- समूहस्य

१८. T65-स्वरोह्यवरोहिणि, G86-स्वरांगुह्य ***, G07- ाट्की।।स्वयंग्गोह्यो।वरोहिणी।, G18-स्वरारोहावरोहणे, V08- स्वरारोह्यवरोहिणौ

टीका:- స్వర సమూహం గ్రామమనిన్ని స్వరారోహణి(ణి అవరోహణి)[४] మూర్ఛనా అనిన్ని తెలియతగినది. □కి[५] భేదాలు క్రమంగా చెప్పుచున్నాడు[६].

[७]सप्तस्वरास्त्रयोग्रामाः[८] एकविंशति मूर्च्छनाः[९] ।
ताना एकोन[१०]पञ्चाशदित्येते[११] स्वरमण्डलम् ।। ५७।।

टीका:- సప్తస్వరాలకు గ్రామాలు మూడు[१२], మూర్ఛనా[१३] ఇరు(ర)వైయొక, తానానాలు(తానాలు)[१४] నలువైతొ□మ్మది - ఇట్లని[१५] స్వరమండలమందు చెప్పుచున్నది.

[१६]षड्जमध्यमगान्धार[१७]ग्रामाश्च परिकीर्त्तिताः[१८] ।

टीका:- షడ్జగ్రామమనిన్ని[१९] గాంధారగ్రామమనిన్ని[२०] మధ్యమ గ్రామమనిన్ని[२१] 3[२२] ప్రకారాలు.

[१]षड्जग्रामाश्रितां हे[ह्ये]ते[२] विज्ञेयस्सप्तमूर्च्छना[नाः] ।।५८।।

---

१. G07- मुंचनेति स्वयज्ञेयं, G18- मूर्छनेति स्वरोज्ञेयः
२. G07- तयो भद्रं, G86- तया भेदं, T65- तयोरभेदं
३. V08- क्रमाद्वदे, T65, G98,G17, B13, G86,G07- क्रमाद्वदेत्
४. G07- స్వకారోహ
५. G86, G07- దీంల
६. G86- * *మంగా చెప్పుచున్నాడు, T65- క్రమాన చెప్పమా
७. v.57, cf. N.Sik. 2,4. This verse seems to be a citation made by this author, which has also been commented upon.
८. G86- सप्तस्वरास्त्रयोग्रामं, G07- सप्तस्वरं स्त्रयोग्रामे
९. G07- मुंचना, T65,G86- मूर्च्छना, G98,B13- मूर्छना
१०. T65, G86, G07- तानेकोन
११. B13- येतत् , G86- इत्यते, G07- इत्यैते, G18- पञ्चाश * * * * * *
१२. G07- missing
१३. G07- మూర్ఛ
१४. G86- స్తానాలు, G07- స్థానాలు
१५. T65- ఇష్టని, G07- యిదిని
१६. V08- this half verse missing (after this, it reads: ग्रामाः, मूर्छनाः)
१७. G17- गान्धारा
१८. G18 - breaks off here and reads from v.63ab
१९. T65- గ్రామాని
२०. T65- గ్రామాని
२१. T65- గ్రామాని
२२. T65- ఈ, G07- missing

టీకా:- స ని ధ ప మ గ రి[3] అని[4] రెండు[5] (ఏడు) మూర్ఛ్ఛనలు షడ్జగ్రామమును ఆశ్రయించి వుండును. మధ్యమగ్రామ మూర్ఛ్ఛనా[6]. మ గ ని స రి ధ ప[7] అని ఏడు మూర్ఛ్ఛనలు[8] మధ్యమగ్రామమును ఆశ్రయించి వుండును. గాంధారగ్రామ మూర్ఛ్ఛనా. గ ధ రి ప స మ ని అని ఏడు మూర్ఛ్ఛ(న)లు[9] గాంధార గ్రామమునే[10] ఆశ్రయించి వుండును.

> **क्रमात् सरिगमादीनां मूर्च्छनाश्च पुनः पुनः[11]।**
> **स्वरालङ्कार इत्येवं[12] कथितो गानवेदिभिः ।। ५९।।**

టీకా:- క్రమంగ షడ్జాది స్వరాలు మాటికీ మాటికీ[13] మధ్యే మధ్యే ఆరోణి[14] అవరోణిగ పలికితెను. అ☐స్వరాలంకారం. స రి గ మ గ రి - స రి గ రి - స రి గ మ. ఇట్లా(లు) పలికే స్వరం[15] అలంకారమని చెప్పబడును.

> **पूर्वाह्णकाले[16] मध्याह्ने[17]ऽपराह्णेऽभ्युदयार्थिभिः[18]।**
> **सप्तस्वराणामारोह्यवरोहिणि[1] क्रमाद्वदेत्[2] ।।६०।।**

---

१. G98, G17,B13, V08- this half-verse is missing

२. G86, G07- हेति

३. G86- స ని ధ ప మ రి స, G07- స ని ధ ప మ గ రి స

४. G86, G07- అనె

५. G07- missing

६. T65- మధ్యమ మూర్ఛ్ఛనా, G07- మధ్య గ్రామ మూర్ఛనా

७. G86, G07- మ గ ని రి ధ ప

८. G86- అనే – మూర్ఛ్ఛనాలు, G07- అనే 2 మూర్ఛనాలు

९. G86- మూర్ఛ్ఛనా, G07- అనే – మూర్ఛ్ఛనా

१०. T65, G86- ग्राममने గ్రామమనే

११. G86- मूर्च्छना * * * नः प्पुनः

१२. T65, G98, G17, B13, G86, G07- स्वरालंकारमित्येवं

१३. T65- మూటికీ మూటికీ, G07- మాట్కి మాట్కి

१४. T65 - అవరోణి

१५. G86, G07- యిందులో పలికిన స్వరాలు

१६. G98- पूर्वान्हकाल, G86- पूर्वाण्हाकाल , B13,T65- पूर्वाह्नकाल

१७. T65- मध्याह्नकाल, G98- मध्यान्हे, G86- मध्याण्हाकाल

१८. G98,G17-पराह्णेभ्युदयादिभिः, B13-पराह्णेऽभ्युदयादिभिः, T65-पराह्नभ्युदयादिभिः, G86-पराण्हात्सुदयादिभिः, G07- पूर्वं। ण्हात्सदयादिषः।

टीका:- శ్రేయస్సు కోరేటివారు ప్రాతఃకాలమందు[3] మధ్యాన్నః(న్హః)కాలమందు సాయంత్రకాలమందు[4] సప్తస్వరాల యొక్క ఆరోణి అవరోణి అనవచ్చును[5]. ఇతరకాలమందు[6] అనరాదు. దీని పేరు సరళి.

[7]प्रथमश्रवणाच्छब्द:[8] श्रूयते[9] ह्रस्वमात्रकः[10] ।

सा श्रुतिस्तु[11] परिज्ञेया[12] स्वरावयवलक्षणम् ।। ६१ ।।

टीका:- తొలుత అనుమంద్రమున[13] స్వరం తెలియుట[14] తారకమంటి[15] మెల్లనే లిన్నస్వరం[16] శ్రుతి అనబడును.

सूक्ष्मस्स्वरोहि[17] सूक्ष्मत्वान्नतु श्रवणगोचरः[18] ।

तारश्श्रुति[19] कडोरत्वात् त्याज्य[20] एव न संशयः[21] ।। ६२ ।।

टीका:- మెల్ల(గా)నే[1] అంతస్వరం[2] ☐రంజితమైయుండ[3], బిగ్గలాన్న(బిగ్గర అన్న) స్వరం[4]

---

१. B13-सप्तस्वराणामारोहावरोहिणि, V08-सप्तस्वराणामारोहामवरोहां, G86-सप्तस्वराणामरोह्वा अवरोहिणि, G07-सप्तस्वरानां म्हरोह्र अवरोहिणी
२. G98- क्रमाद्भवेत् B13, V08 - क्रमाद्व्रजेत्
३. T65- రేపొన్తలా
४. T65- మాపటన్తలోను, G07- lacunae upto 'అనరాదు'
५. G86- అ****ను
६. T65- ఇతరకాలాలమందు
७. G98,G17,B13 - v.61 is missing. cf. ABSS,2,50; STR,6,7,21cd-22ab
८. T65- प्रथमश्रवणाश्च शप्रद्घा, G86- प्रथमश्रवणशप्रद्घा, G07- प्रथमश्चवरो शप्रद्घा
९. G86, G07- श्रोयते, V08- श्रुतते
१०. T65- ह्रस्वमंद्रकः, G86- ह्वस्वरमंद्रकः, G07- ह्रस्वमंद्रकः
११. T65- सस्सुतिसतु, G07- सा श्रुति स
१२. G07- परिज्ञेयं
१३. T65- అనుమందరాన, G86,G07- మందరానా
१४. T65- స్వరమన, V08- స్వరమనే
१५. T65- తారకమాంట, G86- తారకమాంట్టెను, G07- తారకమాడెను
१६. T65- అంతస్వరం, G07- అన్నస్వరం, V08- అనుస్వరం
१७. G86,G07-सूक्ष्मस्सरोहि, V08-सूक्ष्मस्वरोहि(ऽति)
१८. G07- श्रवेणगोचरः
१९. G98, B13- तारश्रुति, G17- तारः श्रुति, V08- तार श्रुतिः, G86- टीक।। तारको श्रुति, G07- तारको शृति
२०. G86- कांत्योवातीज्या, G07- कंतत्वाज्य
२१. G98,B13- त्याज्य न संशयः, G17- (त्याज्य ?) न संशयः, T65- योरव न संशयः, G86- विव न संशयः, G07-एव सश्शयः

ఁతుం[5] కఠోరమైయుండును గనక[6]. కాగా ఆ రెండు కారాదు[7]. శ్రుతి మధ్యమంగా[8] పలుకవలెను.

[9]स्थायिस्वरोऽथ सञ्चारी[10] तथाहतमनाहतौ

[तथायतप्रत्यायतौ][11] ।

कम्पितं[12] येडुपु डु[डा]लु[13] उग्र[ग्रं]मुक्ता[14] दशास्मृताः[15] ।।६३।।

టీకా:- స్థాయి, స్వరం, సంచారి, ఆయి(య)తం[16], ప్రత్యాయతం, కంపితం, యెడుపు[17], డాలు, ఉగ్రం[18], ముక్తాయి- ఈ షడ్జాది స్వరాలు పది భేదాలుగా వుండును[19].

आदौ मन्द[1]स्वरानु[दु]क्तं[2] स्थायि[यी] इत्यभिधीयते[3] ।

---

१. T65- text repeats from మెల్లనే seen in the previous commentary upto this.

२. G86, G07- యెత్తినస్వరం

३. G86, G07- యుండును

४. G86, G07- కించిన్నిక్కిలి పల్కిన స్వరం

५. G86, G07- ఁతుక

६. G86 - missing

७. G86- ఆ రెండు వర్జించవలెను, G07- ఆ రెండున్న వజించ వలెను

८. G07- మధ్యముగా

९. G98, G17,B13 - v.63 is missing

१०. T65- स्वरोथसञ्चारि

११. G86- तयाहतमनाहतो, T65, G07- तयाहतमनाहतौ, G18- तथाहतमनाहतम्. āyata and pratyāyata are the technical terms to be enumerated here but are represented through the terms āhata and anāhata (which actually define the terms under issue); hence this reading is suggested.

१२. G86, G07- कंपित

१३. V08- येडुपुनोच्चि, G86- यीडपुड्डाल (डाला/ डालु/ डालं - not clear), G07- यीडपु डालं, G18- य * * * * र्थाल

१४. V08- उग्रमुग्र, T65- उश्रंमुक्ता, G18- रुग्रमुक्ता

१५. V08-वशात् स्मृताः,G86-दशाफलास्मृतं, G07-रशाफलंस्मृतं, T65-दशाफलास्मृताः

१६. G86- ఆయత్రం, G07- ఆయుతం

१७. G86, G07- యిడుపు

१८. T65 - missing

१९. G86- పల్కును, G07- పలుకునూ. V08 reads commentary thus: (స్థాయీ, స్వరం, సఞ్చారి, ఆయతం, ప్రత్యాయతం, కంపితం, యెడుపు, డాలు, ముక్తా -యీ షడ్జాది స్వరాలు 10 భేదాలుగా బలుకును)

टीకా:- తొలుత మంద్రమాదికా యెత్తె(త్తే) స్వరాలు స్థాయి అనబడును[४].

तारकादौ[५] स्वरानु[दु]क्तं[६] स्वरेति[७] परिकीर्तितः।

టీకా:- [८]తొలుత తారకమాదికా యెత్తె(త్తే) స్వరాలు స్థాయీస్వర[९]మనబడును.

[१०]मन्द्रमध्यमतारेषु[११] सञ्चारिकचर[श्चर]स्वरः[१२] ।।६४।।

టీకా:- మంద్రమధ్యమతారకాలయందు[१३] స్వర ప్రకాశంగా పలికినది సంచారి అనబడును.

स्वरान्[राः] मन्द्रादिषु[१४] स्थाने[१५] पृथग्व्याप्तं पुनः पुनः।

आहतं चायतंचापि[१६] प्रत्यायतमनाहतम्[१७] ।।६५।।

టీకా:- స్వరాలు మందర మధ్యమ తారకాలయందు ప్రత్యేకాలుగా ప్రకాశింపుచున్న(ప్రకాశించును)[१८]. తిరుగ తిరుగ ఆరోణి స్వరాలు ఆయితమనబడును[१९]. అవరోణి[१] ప్రత్యాయతమనబడును[२].

---

१. V08- आदौ मान्द्रात्, G86- अधौ मान्द्रौ, G07- आदौ मान्द्रौ, G18- अथ मन्द्र

२. G98, G17, B13- स्वरानोक्तं, V08- स्वरान् मुक्ता, G18- स्वरादुक्ताः

३. G98, G17, B13- मित्यभिधिय्यते, G07- इ तृभिदिय्यते, V08-मित्यभिधीयते

४. V08 reads commentary thus: (తొలుత మంద్రమాదిగానెత్తిన స్వరములు స్థాయి అనబడు). In G86, G07 the commentary is seen after the following half verse.

५. T65, G86, G07- तारकादि, G18- आ तारक

६. G07- स्वयनुक्तं, V08- स्वरान्मुक्तं, G18- स्वरादुक्तौ

७. G18- सस्वरः

८. V08 reads commentary thus: (तारकादिगानेत्तिन स्वरलु - स्वरमनप्रड्नु)

९. T65- స్థాయీ, G07 probably omits in between and reads together thus: తొలుత మంద్రమాదిగయెత్తి స్వరాలు స్థాయి స్వరమనబడును.

१०. V08- v.64cd and the following commentary are missing.

११. G86- **रेषुस्तु, G07- मध्यमरेष

१२. G98,G17,B13-संचारकचरस्वरः, G86-संचारिरीचरस्वरः, G07-नंचारिरचरस्वरः, G18-संचारि कंपवान् स्वरः

१३. G07- తారకాలమందు

१४. V08- मन्द मध्यम तारादि, G07- स्वरान्नं द्रादिक्षु, G18- स्वरामन्द्रादि

१५. G18- संस्थाने

१६. V08- चैवमाहतं, T65,G98,G17,B13,G86,G07- चैवमायातं

१७. G98,G17,B13-प्रत्याहतमनाहतं, G86,G07-प्रत्यायतमनायतं, V08-प्रत्याहतमनाहतौ ? G18 - साहतमनाहतम्

१८. G86- చునుండును, G07- చుండును

१९. G07 the rest of the commentary is missing.

त्रिस्थानेषु स्वरान् वेग[३] गमनं कम्पितं विदुः [४] ।

टीका:- మంద్ర మధ్యమ తారకాలయందు[५] స్వరాల[६] గమకం చేత పలికినది కంపితమనబడును[७].

स्वरदीर्घ[र्घं]त्रियस्थाने[त्रिस्थाने][८] व्याप्तं यु[ये]डुपुरुच्यते[९] ।

टीका:- స్వరం నిలుకడుగ త్రిస్థానాలయందు ప్రకాశింపు జేసేది[१०] యెడుపు[११] అనబడును[१२].

ह्रस्वदीर्घ त्रिषु[१३] व्याप्तं[१४] स्वरान्[१५] डालु[१६] प्रकीर्तितः[१७] ।।६६।।

टीका:- వేగ నిలుకడలుగాను[१८] స్వరాలు త్రిస్థానాలయందు ప్రకాశింప జేశేది[१९] డాలు అనబడును.

मध्यमादौ[१] स्वरानु[दु]क्तं[२] उग्रं[३] च परिकीर्तितः[तम्][४] ।

---

१. T65 adds అయింది

२. T65- ప్రత్యాయమనబడును

३. G86, G07- स्वरान्वेगः, G18- स्वरावेग

४. G17- कंवि(पि)तं विःदुः, T65- कम्पितं विधुः

५. G07- తారాలయెందు

६. G86, G07- స్వరం

७. G07- కలపితమనబడును

८. G98,G17,B13-स्वरादीर्घायतस्थाने, T65-स्वरदीर्घयतस्थाने, G07-स्वरदिर्घ त्रियस्थाने, V08- स्वरदीर्घं त्रयोस्थाने, G18- स्वरदैर्ध्य त्रयस्थाने; suggested reading based on BKM

९. V08- सा येडुपुरुच्यते, G86, G07- यिडपुरुच्यते, G18- यडपुरुच्येत

१०. G86- జేశేది, G07- చేశేది

११. G07- యెడపు

१२. V08 reads the commentary thus: (స్వరాలునిలుకరగా త్రిస్థాయులయందు ప్రకాశింప చేసేది యెడుపు); G86, G07- commentary is found continuous alongwith the previous one.

१३. G07- ह्रस्व दीधृ त्रेषु, V08- ह्रस्व दीर्घ त्रिषु, G18- ह्रस्व दीर्घस्त्रिषु

१४. T65, G18 - व्याप्तः

१५. V08- स्वरा, G18- स्वरो

१६. V08- डालुः, B13- ढालुः, G18- दालुः

१७. B13- प्रकीर्तिताः

१८. G86, G07- కడగాను

१९. G07- ప్రకాశింపు చేశేది

టీకా:- [५]మధ్యమాదియందు స్వరమెత్తి ప్రకాశింప జేశేది[६] ఉగ్రమనబడును.

स्वराणां मोचनं[७] व्याप्तं मुक्तमित्यभिधीयते[८] ।। ६७ ।।

టీకా:- [९]స్వరాలు ఠీకల్లా(ఠీకల్ల)[१०] ముక్తాయిగ ప్రకాశింప జేసినది[११] ముక్తమనబడును.

[१२]**व्यक्तं पूर्णं प्रसन्नं च सुकुमारमलङ्कृतम्[१३] ।**
समं सुरक्तं श्लक्ष्णञ्च[१४] निकृष्टं[१५] मधुरं[१६] तथा[१७] ।
[१८]**दशैते स्युर्गुणा गीतं[ते][१९] शाङ्र्गदेवेन कीर्तिताः [तत्र व्यक्तं स्फुटैः स्वरैः][१] ।। ६८ ।।**

---

१. G86- मध्यमादा, G07- मध्यमानु, G18- मध्यमादि

२. G98,B13,T65- स्वरासक्तं, G17-स्वरासक्तिम् , G07- स्वरानुत्तं, V08- स्वरामुक्तं

३. G98,G17,B13-अग्रं, T65-मग्रं, G07-उग्रौ, G18- मुग्रं

४. G07- चे परितर्तितं, G18-तत् परिकीर्तितम्

५. V08- reads commentary thus: (మధ్యమాది యందు స్వరాలు పలికినదే పలికి ప్రకాశింప జేయుట ఉగ్రము).

६. G07- ప్రకాశింపు జేశి

७. G86- मुचनं, G07- मुंचनं , T65, G98, G17, B13- मोदनं

८. V08- स्वरेति परिकीर्तितम्, T65, G98, G17, B13-मुक्तेति परिकीर्तितम्, G86-मुक्तेति परिकीर्तितः

९. V08 reads commentary thus: (ముక్తాయిగా ప్రకాశింప జేశేది ముక్తము)

१०. G86- స్వ * ** టికల్లా, G07- స్వరాలు ఠీకల్ల

११. G86- జేశెది

१२. v.68- v.73ab, cf. SR 4,374-379ab. This whole section on the qualities of gīta resembles SR and hence at places where the Mss give grammatically defective readings, parallel readings from SR have been suggested accordingly.

१३. G86- सुकुमारनुलंकृतं, G07- सुकुमारानलंकृतं

१४. G86- समनुरतंशक्षंच्च, G07- समंसुरत्नंशिक्षंच, V08- समं स रत्नं शुक्लंच

१५. V08- निष्कृष्टं, SR reads विकृष्टं

१६. G98- मधुरा, T65- मधुर

१७. T65- तदा

१८. G86, G07 - v.68ef is missing

१९. T65- दशैवेस्युर्न्नुणागीत, G98-दशैते स्युर्नुणागीतं, B13-दशैते स्युर्गुणांगीते, V08-दशैतेऽस्य गुणातीताः. Since गीतं would be grammatically incorrect, the reading from SR has been taken.

टीका:- [२]వ్య క్తం, పూర్ణం, ప్రసన్నం, సుకుమారం, అలంకృతం, సమం, సురక్తం, శ్లక్ష్ణం, నికృష్టం, మధురం - ఈ పదిన్ని గీత స్వర గుణాలు.

प्रकृति प्रत्ययंयोच्यं[प्रत्ययैश्चोक्तं][३] छन्दोरागपदस्वरैः[४] ।

टीका:- స్ఫుట స్వరాల[५] చేత పదముల యొక్క ప్రకృతి ప్రత్యయాల[६] చేత అన్నది వ్య క్తమనబడును[७].

अंगेस्वरान् पूर्णगमकं[पूर्णं पूर्णाङ्गगमकं[८]] प्रसन्नं

प्रकटीकृतम्[९] ।। ६९ ।।

टीका:- గానమందు స్వరాలు పూర్ణంగా వుండేది[१०] పూర్ణం ((2)) స్వర ప్రకటనం[११] ప్రసన్నం[१२]. (3)

[१]सम्यक् शारीरकृतं[ञ्च][२] सकुमारं विदुर्बुधाः[३] ।

---

१. T65-शार्ङ्गदेवेना कीर्तिताः, V08-शाङ्र्गदेवेन कीर्तितः; All the Mss acknowledge Śārṅgadēva in the second quarter of this line, which is different from SR 4,375b. SR contains partially the definition for vyaktam, which is seen in the commentary to v.69ab. Hence in order to have a complete definition for the term, vyaktam, the parallel reading from SR is suggested.

२. G86,G07 - list missing

३. G98, G17, B13- प्रत्ययंवोच्यं, G86- प्रत्यश्चोच्या, G07- प्रत्ययश्चोस्य, V08- प्रत्ययाच्चोक्तं.

४. G86- छंदानागधर स्वरः, G07- चंदनागव स्वरैः, V08- at the end ।। व्यक्तं।।.

५. G07- స్ఫుట స్వీరాలు

६. G86- ప్రత్యాల, G07- ప్రతియాల

७. T65- వ్యక్తం

८. T65, G98, B13- अंगेस्वरान् पूर्णगमकं, G17- अंगेस्वरान् पूर्णगम, G86- अंगेन् स्वरान् पूर्णगमरः, G07- आंगेस्वरान् पूर्नगवरः, V08- अंगेस्वरान् पूर्णगमकान्, The reading is suggested from SR 4,376a. The readings in the Mss are erroneous and have one syllable more than that allowed by the anuṣṭup metre. The commentator seems to have had a different reading for this half (indicating in the gāna), which tally with the readings in BKM,p.93, RJM,p.136 and MBC,4,75. However in the reading provided in the Mss, it is seen that the main technical term under issue, namely, pūrṇaṃ does not figure.

९. G86- प्रसन्न कटीकृतं

१०. T65- adds అనేది

११. T65- ప్రకటినం, G07- ప్రకీటినం

१२. G86- ప్రసంస్తం

टीका:- లెస్సగా శారీరం[४] కలిగినది సుకుమారం[५] (4).

त्रिस्थानेषु प्रकाशं च अलङ्कृतमुदाहृतम्[६] ।। ७० ।।

टीका:- మంద్ర[७]మధ్యమ తారకాలయందు వ్యాప్తి కలిగినది అలంకృతం (5[८]).

समाक्षरैर्लयस्थाने[९] व्याप्तं सममितीरितम्[१०] ।

टीका:- సమాక్షరాల చేత[११] లయస్థానం కలిగినది సమం[१२] ((6)).

सुरक्तं[१३] वल्लकीवंश[१४]कण्ठध्वन्येकतां गता[१५] ।। ७१ ।।

टीका:- □త్(□హా)[१६] పిల్లాంగో□(పిల్లంగ్రో□)[१७], నాగస్వరం తన[१८] గాత్రానికి[१९] శ్రుతి ప్రమాణ(ణం)[२०] ఏక[२१] స్వరమైతే[२२] సురక్తం[२३] (7).

नीचोच्चद्रु[ध्रु]तमध्यादौ[१] श्लक्षणत्य[वे] श्लक्षणमुच्यते[२] ।

---

१. G98,G17,B13- v.70 is missing; differ from SR reading.

२. G86- सम्यश्चौरिरयिरतः, G07- स्वंमृक्षौरीरयिरतः, T65- संत्यत्स्यानिरकूरितः

३. G86- इतिर्विमेः, G07- इतिर्विमेदि, T65-इतिर्विदाः

४. G86- ***** రీరం

५. G86- సకుమారం

६. V08- प्रकाशंचेदलंकृतं

७. T65, G07- మందర

८. G86, G07- ।१।।

९. T65, G86, G07- समाक्षरैलयस्थाने SR reads समवर्णलयस्थानं.

१०. G98- व्याप्तिस्सममितीरतः, G17, B13-व्याप्तिस्सममितीरितः, G07-व्याप्तस्सममीरितः, T65, G86-व्याप्तंसममुदीरितः

११. G07- చాల □ల్లంగో□

१२. G86, G07- □ము

१३. V08- स्वर रत्नं (?)

१४. G86, G07- वंशं

१५. G98,G17,B13-कुलध्वनिगतांदतम्, G86,G07-कंध्वनि नितांडतं, T65- कंध्वनि गतांदत्तम्

१६. G86- □ు, G07- □ు

१७. T65,G86- □ల్లంగ్గో□

१८. T65- తను, G86- త **

१९. G86, G07- గాత్రాన్ని

२०. G86- ప్రమాణానన, G07- ప్రమాణాన□

२१. G07- missing

२२. G86- స్వర ** తె

२३. G86- సు ******, G07- సురకం॥ 7 ॥

టీకా:- యెక్కుడు తక్కుడు[3] ధృతమధ్య[4] □ంబాలయందు నూతనమైయు[5] □ం[6] శ్లక్ష్ణం[7] ((8)).

उच्चैरुच्चारणादुक्तं[8] निकृष्टं[9] भरतादिभिः ।। ७२ ।।

టీకా:- శారీరం[10] బిగ్గిన[11] పలిగిన్నది(పలికిన)[12] నిష్కృష్టం (నికృష్టం)[13] (9[14]).

मध्यमं[मधुरं][15] धुर्यलावण्य[16]पूर्णं जीव[जन]मनोहरम् ।

టీకా:- [17]శారీరం[18] చక్కతనం గలిగి[19] జీవాళంగ పాడిన స్వరాలు మధురం (10)[20].

संक्षिप्य[21] सोमनार्येण[22] स्वराणां गुणमीरितम् ।। ७३ ।।

టీకా:- సంక్షేపంగాను[1] స్వరాల గుణాలు సోమనార్యుని[2] చేత చెప్పబడెను[3].

---

१. G98, G17, B13- नीचोच्यधृतिमध्यादौ, G86- *****मध्यादौ, G07- निभोद्यद्य त्तमाध्यादौ, T65- नीचैच्यद्धृतिमध्यादौ

२. G98- श्लक्षत्यश्लक्ष्ममद्यते, G17- श्लक्षत्यश्लक्ष्ममद्यते, B13- श्लक्ष्णत्यश्लक्ष्णमुद्यते, G07- श्लक्ष्णत्य श्लक्णमुच्यते, V08- श्लक्ष्णतेश्चक्ष्ण मुच्यते

३. G86, G07 - తక్కువై

४. G86- ధృతమధ్యమ, G07- దృతమధ్య

५. G07- తమైయుండుట

६. G86- ******, G07- missing

७. G86 -శస్ణమనబడును, G07- శ్లక్షమనబడును

८. G98, G17, B13- उच्चैरुच्चारणादत्तं, G07- उच्चैउच्चारुणामक्तं

९. T65, G86, G07, V08- निष्कृष्टं

१०. G86- శిరిరం

११. G07- బిగన

१२. G86- పలిగిన□ G07- పల్కిన□

१३. G07- పృష్టం

१४. T65, G07 - missing.

१५. B13- मध्यमं [मा], G86- मध्यम, V08- मधु मा.

१६. All Mss except V08 read लावण्यं

१७. V08- (శారీరం సందనం గలిగి జీవాళంగానూదిన స్వరాలు మధురం -)

१८. G07- missing

१९. G07- కలిగితె

२०. T65, G86 - missing

२१. G98, G17, B13- संजप्य

२२. G86- सौमनार्येण, G07- सेमशार्वेण, V08- सौमनार्येण

दृ[दु]ष्टं लोकेन[४] शास्त्रेण श्रुतिकालविरोधि च।

पुनरुक्तं गीतबाह्यं[५] गतक्रममपार्थकम्[६]।

ग्राम्यं[७] संद्धि[दि]ग्ध[८]मित्येवं दशधा गीतदुष्टदा[ता][९] ।। ७४।।

టీకా:- దృష్టం[१०], లోకం[११], శాస్త్రం (లోకదుష్టం, శాస్త్రదుష్టం,) శ్రుతివిరోధం, కాలవిరోధం, పునరుక్తం, బాహ్యం, గతక్రమం, అపార్థం, (గ్రామ్యం,) సందిగ్ధం[१२] ఈ పదిన్ని[१३] స్వర గీతాలకు[१४] దోషాలు.

[१५]अपस्वरेण दुष्टं[१६] च शास्त्रहीन[१७]मशास्त्रकम्।

టీకా:- అపస్వరాలన్నది దృ(దు)ష్టం[१८]; శాస్త్ర వ్యతిరిక్తంగ[१९] అన్నది అశాస్త్రం.

[१]श्रुतिश्रुति[काल][२]विरोधं च [एकैकश्च विरोधतः] ।। ७५।।

---

१. G07- సంక్షిపంగాను సంక్షిపంగాను (repetition)

२. G07- సోమశార్యని

३. G86- చెప్పబడునున్నది, G07- చెప్పబడుచున్నదీ

४. V08- पृष्टलोकेन, G07- दृष्टं ** केन

५. G98,G17- पुनरुत्वांगितं वाह्यं B13- पुनरुत्वांगितं वाह्वं, V08- पुनरुक्तांकितं प्राह्यं. The commentary, BKM, RJM, MBC read only प्राह्यं. SR reads कलाप्राह्यं. The reading in V08 seems to be based on BKM (p.95).

६. G86- गतक्रममपार्दिकं, G07- गतक्रममपार्धितम्, T65- गतक्रममपार्त्तिकं

७. G98,G17,B13- ग्राम्य, V08- ग्राह्य, G07- ग्रामम्

८. V08- संधिग

९. T65, G86- दुक्कधा, G17- दुष्टदा(ता), V08- विरोधिता, G07- दुष्टधा

१०. G07- missing

११. T65- missing

१२. G07- సందిక్షం

१३. T65- పది గీత

१४. G86- □తాలకు, G07- గోత్రాలకు

१५. V08- v.75 - v.77 are missing

१६. G98- वृष्टं, T65,G86,G07- दृष्टं

१७. G07- शास्त्रयीन

१८. T65,G86- దృష్టం

१९. G07- శాస్త్రర్యతిరిక్తంగ

టీకా:- ఒక్కొక్క శ్రుతికి[३] □ోధంగ అన్నది శ్రుతి□ోధం[४]. లయ□ోధంగా అన్నది కాల□ోధం.

आरोहिण्यवरोयु[ह्यु]क्तं अन्योन्यं पुनरुक्ती [रुक्तं] च[५] ।

టీకా:- ఆరోహణియందు అవరోహణి[६] అన్నది[७] పునరుక్తి.

असंबान्द[ध][८] स्वराद्बाह्यं[९] हीनस्वरगतक्रमाः ।। ७६ ।।

టీకా:- ఇతి (అసంబంధముగా స్వరాలన్నది బాహ్యం[१०]) అనబడును. స్వరాలు రీడ్చి (□చి) అనేది గతక్రమం.

अर्थहीनमपार्थं च ग्राम्यं च कठिनस्वरैः[११] ।

టీకా:- ఇతి అర్థహీనంగ(గా) పల్కినది[१२] అపార్థం; పింగేలా(?)[१३] శ్రుతి పలికినది[१४] కఠిన(గ్రామ్య)మనబడును[१५].

सन्दिग्धं पदसन्दिग्धं[१६] दशदा[धा]गीतदुष्टधा[ता][१७] ।। ७७ ।।

టీకా:- స్వరోకోదుకు(?)[१] సందిగ్ధం. ఈ పది(న్ని) స్వరాలకు దోషాలు.

---

१. In the main text, the explanations relating to श्रुतिविरोध and कालविरोध are missing. The commentary incorporates some saṃskūta words (श्रुतिश्रुतिविरोधं च- see the following foot note), which might have formed part of the main text. BKM(p.95) and RJM(p.126) give a complete half-verse. Present reading is being suggested from RJM.

२. G86- शृतिशृधि, G07- शृतिशृति

३. G86- శృధి, G07- శృతి

४. G07- adds పునరుక్తం- which is probably part of the following sentence.

५. G07- पुनर्युक्तिचा

६. G86- ఆరోహణి

७. G86, G07- missing

८. G07- अनम्प्राध

९. G98, G17, B13- स्वराद्वाह्य, G07- स्वराप्रद्राह्यम

१०. This portion is missing in the Mss and hence supplemented from BKM(p.96)

११. T65- कदिनस्वरैः

१२. G07- పల్కి□

१३. G86- యిడిబంగ్గి, G07- ఇతిబంగి

१४. G86, G07- పల్కినది

१५. G86, G07- కఠినపడును

१६. G07- पदंनंदिग्धं

१७. B13, G07- दुष्टदा, G17- दुष्टधा(ता)

[2]అష్టాదశ శ్రుతులకు[3] లక్షణం.

[4]**नाभिकाथर्वणि[णी][5] धस्ता[6] षड्जस्वरसमाश्रिताः[7]।**

టీకా:- నాభికా[8] అథర్వణి[9] ద(ధ)స్తా ఈ మూడున్ను[10] షడ్జమును ఆశ్రయించి వుండును.

धैवीरचेतितधा[औवी चातिचधा] चैव[11] ऋषभ[12]

स्वरमाश्रितौ[ते][13] ।। ७८।।

టీకా:- ఔర్వి[14] అతి(చధా)[15] ఈ రెండు ఋషభ స్వరాన్ని[16] ఆశ్రయించి వుండును.

कांबवि[कम्बली][17] श्रिविका[18] सरली[सर्ली][19] नालि[ली][20]

गान्धारमाश्रिताः[1]।

---

१. G86- స్వరోరోదంకడ, G07- స్వరోకోదంకుడ

२. G98, G17, B13, V08 - this sub- heading is missing

३. T65- స్వరాలకు

४. G18- v.78ab is missing; reads the following which is not found in any of the Mss. नाभिशतर्वणी धाता चर्विका चार्चतीति च। शाम्भवि स्रविकाथैव सरळी चाथनाळिका। रसनी रञ्जनी चैव प्राणिनी पन्द(च)नी तथा। मन्दा मौदाळि कम्प्री च भीषणी च स्फुरन्तिका। सप्तस्वराः श्रुतास्त्वेताः श्रुतयोऽष्टादश स्मृताः।

५. G07- नाभिकार्ध्वशि

६. G98,G17, B13- धस्तात्, T65- दस्तात्, G86- रस्तत्, G07- रस्तात्

७. G98,G17,B13, V08-समाश्रिता, T65- समाश्रितः

८. G86, G07- నాభిః

९. G07- అధర్ని ణి

१०. G86, G07- ఈ ముడు

११. G98, G17- धैर्वीरचेतिधाचैव, B13-दैर्वीरचेतिधाचैव, G86-औविचेतितधाचैवा, G07-औविचेतिदाचैव, V08-अधर्वी अतिचधा (?) चैव, G18- चार्विकाचार्चतीचैव

१२. G07- वृषभ

१३. T65, G98, G17, B13-स्वरमाश्रुतः, G86,G07- स्वरमाश्रताः, G18- स्वरमाश्रिताः

१४. G86- జౌం (?), G07- జౌ

१५. G86 - అచెతి, T65- అదతి

१६. T65- ఋషభస్వరమున్ను, G07- ఋషభస్వరమున్ను

१७. G86, G07 - कांप्रम्रव, G18- शाम्भवी

१८. G98, G17, B13- श्रविका, T65, G86, G07- श्रिविका, V08- स्त्रिविका, G18- स्वविका.

१९. In order to conform to metrical rules, this reading is suggested.

२०. V08- गौळी, G86- नां, G07- ना

టీకా:- కంబలి[२] శ్రీ[illegible]ా[३] సరళి నాళీ[४] ఈ నాలుగు గాంధారమున్ను(మును)[५] ఆశ్రయించి వుండును.

रसनी[६] रञ्जनी चैवा[व] मध्यमस्वरमाश्रिताः[ते][७] ।।७९।।

టీకా:- [८]రసని రంజని ఈ 2 మధ్యమ స్వరమున్ను ఆశ్రయించి వుండును.

घ्राणिनी[९] पवनि[नी][१०] मन्दा पञ्चमस्वरमाश्रिताः[११] ।

టీకా:- ధ్రాణిని[१२] పవని మంద ఈ మూడున్ను[१३] పంచమస్వరమును[१४] ఆశ్రయించి వుండును.

मौर्द्धवा[१५] विडम्बिनश्चैव[विडम्बिनीचैव][१६] धैवतस्वर[१७]माश्रितौ[ते][१८] ।

టీకా:- మూర్ధా(మౌర్న్ ధ్వ)[१९] [illegible](డ)ంబి ఈ రెండు దై(ధై)వత స్వరమున్ను ఆశ్రయించి వుండును[२०].

भीषणी[१] च स्फुरन्ती च निषाध[द]स्वर माश्रितौ[ते][२] ।। ८०।।

---

१. G98,G17,B13,G18-गान्धारमाश्रिता, G86- गांधारमाश्रतः, G07- गांदारमाश्रताः
२. G86- కంబ, G07- కంబ□
३. G86- ౖహ్రి[illegible]ా
४. G07 - ends here
५. T65- గాంధారాను
६. G98, G17, B13, G86 - रजनि, V08- सरसी T65-ररनी
७. G86- स्वरमंकृतौ
८. T65 - commentary missing.
९. G86- * णादि, V08- घ्राणनी, G18- प्राणिनी
१०. G18- पचनी
११. G86- माश्रताः, G98,G17,B13-माश्रिता
१२. G86- * * ణిని
१३. T65- మూడు
१४. G86- పంచమస్వరము
१५. G86- मौध्वा, V08- मौद्धा
१६. G98-विदिम्भ्रिनश्चैव, G17-विडम्भ्रिनश्चैव,B13-विदम्भ्रिनश्चैव, G86-दिकंभ्रिधश्चैव, V08-रीकम्भ्रिनीचैव, G18- मन्दामोदाविकंभ्रीच
१७. T65, G86- दैवतस्वर
१८. G98, G17, B13, G18- माश्रिताः, V08- माश्रिता, T65- माश्रुतः
१९. G86- మూర్ధాది
२०. G86 - ।९८।।

टीका:- భేషని(భీషణీ) స్ఫురంతి(స్ఫురంతీ)[३] ఈ[४] రెండు నిషాధ(ద)స్వరాను(స్వరమును)[५] ఆశ్రయించి వుండును. కూడా శ్రృతులు[६]. -18. ఈ సప్తస్వరాలకు[७] ఆధారదేవతలు.

आत्ममध्य गतः[८] प्राणः[९] प्राणमध्यगतो[१०] ध्वनिः।

ध्वनि[११]मध्यगतो नादः नादमध्ये[१२] सदाशिवः[१३] ।। ८१।।

टीका:- [१४]ఆత్మ[१५] మధ్యమందు[१६] ప్రాణవాయువు[१७] వుండును. ప్రాణ మధ్యమందు స్వరధ్వనులుండును. ఆ[१८] స్వరధ్వని[१९] మధ్యమమందు[२०] నాదముండును. ఆ[२१]

---

१. G98, G17- प्रैषणी, B13- भैषणी, T65- प्रैषनी, G86- भेषनि, V08- भैषिणी

२. G98, G17, B13, G18- माश्रिताः, V08- माश्रिता, T65- माश्रुतः G18 breaks off here and reads ten types of svara-s.

३. G86- భేషస్ఫరం

४. G86 - missing

५. G86- * * * ముంన్ను

६. G86- * **శ్రుత్లు,V08 reads commentary thus: అని శ్రుతులు 18

७. T65 - adds శ్రుతులకు

८. G98, B13- आत्ममध्य गत, T65- आत्ममध्यगता, V08-आत्ममध्ये गतः

९. G86-प्राणा

१०. T65- प्राणमाध्यगतो, V08-प्राणमध्ये गतो

११. G86- ध्रुव, V08- नाद (ध्वनि)

१२. V08- चोर्ध्व मध्ये, G86- नाधमध्य

१३. G86- गतो हरिः

१४. V08- ఇత్యేవం సోమనార్యేణ స్వనార్ణవముదీరితం(?) - this colophon is seen only in V08; breaks off with this; there are 2 short dotted lines followed by the statement:(సం రత్నాక. శ్లోకాలు - దీప్తాయతాది) వాది సంవాది etc. Then begins the section on rāga-s, thus: అథ రాగః

१५. T65- అంత

१६. T65- మధ్యమమందు

१७. G86- ప్రాణవాయు

१८. G86- missing

१९. G86- స్వరమధ్యమంద్దు

२०. G86- missing

२१. G86- missing

నాదమధ్యమందు జగత్కర్త యైన ఈశ్వరుడుండును[1]. [2]కాబట్టి స్వరగీత ధ్వనిలుకు(ధ్వనులకు) ఆదా(ధా)రదేవతా జె(జ)గదీశ్వరుండు ఇట్టే(ట్లే) చెప్పబడు(డె)ను. శ్రుతి అన్నందుకు[3] లక్షణం.

[४]षड्जग्रामः पञ्चम[मे]श्च[स्व]चतुर्थश्रुति[५]संस्थिते[६]।
स्वापान्त[स्वोपान्त्य]कृ[श्रु]तिसंस्त[संस्थे][७]ऽस्मिन्[८] मध्यमग्राम इष्यते[९]।। ८२।।

[यद्वा धस्त्रिश्रुतिः][१०] षड्ज[जे] मध्यमे तु चतु[तुः]श्रुतिः।
[रिमयोः[११] श्रुतिमेकैकां[१२]] गान्धारश्चेत्समाश्रुताः[श्रितः][१३]।
[पश्रुतिं धो निषादस्तु धश्रुतिं सश्रुतिं श्रितः][१४] ।। ८३।।
गान्धारग्राम माचष्ट[१५] तदा तं नारदोमुनिः।
[प्रवर्तत[ते]][१६] स्वर्गलोके[१७] क्रमेते[१८] न महीतले[१९] ।। ८४।।

---

१. G86- జెగశ్వేరుడు వుండును
२. G86- కాగా దీనులకు ఆదారదేవతా జెగదీశ్వరుడు
३. G17- అంతం(నే)ందుకు, G98, B13- అంతందుకు
४. v.80cd- v.83cd, cf. SR 1,4,2cd-5cd. The suggested readings are based on SR.
५. G86- चतुर्ध** तिसां
६. G86- ****तः, B13- संस्थितौ
७. T65, G98, G17, B13- सोपान्तेश्रुतिसंस्ति
८. T65, G98, G17, B13- स्मि
९. G98- ईर्ष्यते, T65- ईक्ष्यते, G86- मीक्षत्
१०. T65, G98, G17, B13, G86 - यद्वादशश्रुति
११. G98, B13- रिषयो, G17- रि(ऋ)षभो, T65, G86-ऋषयो
१२. G86- मे * *नां, T65, श्रुतिमेखेनां
१३. G98,G17,B13-गान्धारत्से समाश्रितः, T65-गान्धारःसेमाश्रितः
१४. T65, G98, G17, B13- प्रस्तृतिंदो निषादस्तु ग श्रुति प्र श्रुति स्मृता, G86- पश्रुति *** निषादस्तु ग श्रुति प्र कृति श्रुताः
१५. T65, G98-मावष्ट, G17- माव(च)ष्ट, G86- माष्डाच्च
१६. T65- प्रवर्थत, B13- प्रावर्तत, G86- प्रवर्धत
१७. G86- स्वरंलोके
१८. G98, B17-क्रमेतो, B13- क्रमेशो, G86- क्रमेण
१९. G86- स महंतले

[१]क्रमात् ग्रामाः[२]त्रयो [ग्रामत्रये] देवाः ब्रह्मविष्णुमहेश्वराः[३]।
हेमन्त[४]ग्रीष्मवर्षासु गातव्यास्ते[५] यथाक्रमम् ।। ८५।।

टीका:- [६]ఈ తీరున నారదుండు[७] భూలోకమందు సంగీత[८] ప్రవర్తితమైయేది[९] కొరకు షడ్జ గాంధార మధ్యమ గ్రామాలని జేశే(సె)ను[१०]. షడ్జమగ్రామానికి[११] బ్రహ్మ అధిదేవతా. భూలోక దేశం. మధ్యమగ్రామానికి [ష్ణు] అధిదేవతా. భువర్లోకదేశం. గాంధార గ్రామానికి ఈశ్వరుడు అధిదేవతా. స్వర్గిదేశం[१२]. [illegible]మంత, గ్రీష్మ, వర్షా ఋతు[१३]యందు షడ్జమధ్యమగాంధరాలు (గాంధారగ్రామాలు) పాద(డ)వలెను[१४]. ఈ స్వర నాదం[१५] చతుర్దశభువనాలు[१६] వ్యాప్తమైయుండును[१७]

---

१. v.83cd - v.84ab, cf.SR 1,4,7cd-8ab
२. G98, B13, T65- क्रमा ग्रामा, G86- क्रमा क्रमाद्ग्राव
३. G86- त्र ** ** ब्र ** ** *श्वरः
४. G86- हेमंद
५. T65- खातव्यास्ते, G86- खोरवस्तु
६. The Mss read the following, prior to this part of the commentary: స్వరాలకు శ్రుతులు వచ్చిన క్రమం షడ్జానికి నాలుగో స్వరం, శ్రుతిమధ్యమానికి ఐదోస్వరం సోపాంత్యాలు శ్రుతులు. షడ్జ గ్రామానికి మూడు శ్రుతులు; మధ్యమ గ్రామానికి నాలుగు శ్రుతులు; గాంధార గ్రామానికి ఓకోక్క శ్రుతి; పంచమానికి దైవత నిషాదాలు శ్రుతులు. దైవతానికి పంచమ శ్రుతి. నిషాద ఋషభాలకు సోపాన్య శ్రుతులు This seems to be an attempt at explaining v.80cd - v.83ab, though not clearly worded. A similar idea is conveyed in MBC,4,1,94-95.
७. T65- నారదుడు
८. T65 - missing
९. G86 - ప్రవర్న్ తింప్పు జెశ
१०. G86- చేశను
११. G86- * * డ్జ * *మానికి
१२. G86- సువర్లోక దెశం
१३. G86- గ్రీ * * * త్యుల
१४. G86- పాతవలను
१५. G86- యీశ్వర నారదాదులు
१६. G86- చతుర్దశభువనాల
१७. G86- వ్యాపకం జెశి వుందురు

[१][ननु श्रुतिश्चतुर्यादिरस्त्वेवं][२] स्वरकारणम्।
[त्र्यादिनां तत्र पूर्वासां श्रुतिनां हेतुता][३] कथम् ।। ८६।।
ब्रूमस्तुर्य[र्या][४] तृतीया[ऽऽ]दि[५] श्रुति[तिः] पूर्वा[ऽ]भिकाङ्क्षया।
ना[नि]र्धार्यते[ऽ]तश्श्रुतयः[६] पूर्वा[७] अत्य[प्य]त्र[८] हेतवः।। ८७।।
दीप्ता[ऽऽ]यता[९] च[१०] करुणा[११] मृदुम[र्म]ध्य[१२] जातयः[१३]।
श्रुति[ती]नां[१४] पञ्च[१५] [तासां][१६] च सर्वे[स्वरे]ष्वेवं[१७] व्यवस्थितम्
[स्थितिः][१८] ।। ८८।।

दीप्ता[ऽऽ]यता मृदृर्मध्य षड्जेस्वे[स्यात्][१९] ऋषभे पुनः[२०]।

---

१. v.86- v.91, cf.SR 1,3,25cd-31ab. The suggested readings are based on SR. It is to be noted that in SR, the context is after the definition of svara. The occurrence of these verses here does not seem to be logical.

२. G98,T65-समश्चतुश्चतुर्यादि तस्येवं, G17,B13-समश्चतुश्चतुर्यादि तस्यैवं, G86- समश्रातिश्चतुर्यादितस्त्येवं

३. G98,G17, B13- त्र्यादिना तत्र पूर्वासौ श्रृणां हेतु ततः, T65- त्र्यादिना तत्र पूर्वासौ श्रृणां हेतु तत्, G86- श्र्यादिना तत्र पू****श्चृतिनां हेतवः

४. T65- ब्रमस्तुर्य, G86- भ्रूमतुर्य

५. T65- त्रितिर्यादि, G86- त्रितियादि

६. G98, G17, B13, G86 - त श्रुतयः

७. G98, G17, B13 - पूर्व

८. G86- अत्सत्रि

९. G86- दिप्तायर्त्ता

१०. G98- चा

११. G98, T65- करणा, B13- करुणी, G86- करण

१२. T65, G86- मृदुमध्यम

१३. G98, G17,B13- अजायतम्, T65-जातयम्

१४. T65, G98, G17, B13- श्रुतिना

१५. T65, G86- पंचम

१६. G98, G17, B13- सातं, T65-साता, G86-स्धां

१७. T65, G17, B13, T65- सर्वेष्वेवं, G86- सर्वेष्येवंवं

१८. G86- द्रवस्तितः

१९. G86- षड्जस्ये

२०. G98- रिषभे पुनः, G17- रि(ऋ)षभे पुनः, G86- ऋषभस्यसः

संस्थिता[१] करुणा[२] मध्या[३] मृदुर्गान्धार[४] ते[के][५] पुनः।। ८९।।
दीप्ता[ऽऽ]यते[६] मध्यमे[७] ते म्य[मृ] दुमध्ये च[८] संस्थिते[९] ।
मृदुर्मध्या [ऽऽ]यताख्या[१०] च करुणा[११] पञ्चमे स्थिता[१२]।। ९०।।
करुणा[१३] चायता मध्या[१४] धैवते[१५] सप्तते[मे][१६] पुनः।
दीप्ता मध्येति[१७] तासां[१८] च जातिनां[१९] ब्रूमहेऽधुना[२०] ।।९१।।

---

१. G98, G17, T65 - सस्थिता, G86- संद्धिता, G38, Sp-सम्स्तेजा

२. G86- रगुणा

३. T65, G98, G17, B13- मध्य

४. G38, Sp - मृदुगान्धार

५. G38- ति

६. Sp- दीपायते

७. G38, Sp-मध्यमे

८. T65 - तत् मृदुर्मध्येव, G98, G17- तस्मृदुर्मध्ये च, B13- तन्मृदुर्मध्ये च, G38- ति मृदुर्मथे च, Sp- ति मृदुर्म देशे

९. G86- *****, G38-सन्विते, Sp- संस्विते

१०. T65- मृदुमध्यायदाख्या, G86- * *दुमध्यायदाख्या, G38, Sp- मृदुमध्यासुताख्या

११. Sp - करुणो

१२. T65, G86- पञ्चमस्तथा, G38- प *** मस्तथा, Sp- परिमस्तथा

१३. Sp- करुणी

१४. G98, B13- मध्य, G86- मध्ये

१५. G86, G38, Sp- दैवते

१६. G86- omits

१७. G38,Sp- दीप्तारुमध्य

१८. G98, G17,T65- तानां

१९. G86- जातिना

२०. G98- ब्रमहीधुना, G17- ब्रूमही(हे)त्धुना, T65- ब्रमहीदिना, G38, Sp-प्रमृदाधुना. SR reads ब्रूमहे भिदाः\ and lists the names tīvrā, etc. after this. The present text does not read these names. RJM(p.135) too reads ब्रूमहेधुना and skips the names. This section is not seen in BKM but MBC lists the names following SR.

టీకా:- [१]దీప్త(తా) (ఆయతా, మృదు) మధ్యా కరుణాయనే[२] స్వరాలకు[३] నామధేయాలు[४]. షడ్జాతి(ది) సప్త స్వరాలు[५] ఒకటికన్న ఒకటి[६] మృదువు గనుక[७], ఒకటికన్న ఒకటి[८] దీప్తము[९] గనక[१०]. ఒకటికన్నా ఒకటి మధ్యమం గనక[११]. షడ్జ[१२] స్వరమాదిగాను ఋషభ[१३] గాంధార మధ్యమ పంచమ దైవతా(ధైవత) నిషాదములుగా యెక్కుడు తక్కుడు శ్రుతులు[१४] మందర(ద్ర)మధ్యమతారకాల[१५]యందు సప్తస్వరాలని[१६] పించుకొనెను[१७].

श्रुत्युत्पत्ति[त्तिः][१८] स्वराणां च सोमनार्येण कीर्तितः[१९] ।।९२।।

టీకా:- సప్త స్వరాలకు[२०] శ్రుత్యుత్పన్నాలు[२१] సోమనార్య(ర్యు)ని చేత చెప్పప(బ)డుచున్నది[२२].

---

१. The commentary following this could not be organised to give a meaningful idea. However, this commentary must have formed part of this work, since the □characteristic usage□ of the term svara for śruti is seen.

२. G86- కరణ***, G38- కరుణాయని, Sp- కరుణీయనే

३. G38- సర్వాలకు

४. G86- ***మధేయాలు, G38- నామధేయములు

५. G38- స్వరములు

६. T65, G86- ।1। గా

७. G38- మృదువు గనుక ఒకటికన్న ఒకటి, Sp- మృదువు గనత ఒకటికన్న ఒకటి probably a repetition.

८. Sp- గనత

९. G38, Sp- దీప్తం

१०. G38, Sp- గనుక గనత

११. G38, Sp- గనుక గనత

१२. G86- షడ్జాది

१३. G86- రుషభ, G38, Sp- రిషభ

१४. T65, G86- దైవతానికి తమ తమ

१५. G38- తారకముల

१६. G38- స్వరములని

१७. T65, G86- పిచ్చుకొనును

१८. G17- श्रुत्युत्पत्तिः, G86- तृच्युत्प

१९. T65, G86- उच्यते

२०. G38- స్వరములకు

२१. T65- లు *********, G86- శృతులయొక్క స్వరాలయొక్క * * * పుట్టుకలు

२२. G86- సో ****** చాత చెప్పపడును, G38, Sp- సోమనార్యుని చేత చెప్పబడేను

चतुर्विधं स्वरं वादि[दी] संवादि[दी] च विवाद्यपि[१]।

[२]अनुवादी च तत् प्रोक्ता [तेषां लक्षणं चोच्यते][३]।। १३।।

టీకా:- [४]స్వరాలకు[५] నాలుగు ప్రమాణాలు[६]. అది[७] వాది, సంవాది[८] [illegible]ాది[९] అనువాది[१०] అని చెప్పబడెను[११].

वादि[दी]स्वरश्च[१२] राजास्यात्[१३] मन्त्री[१४] संवादिरिष्यते[१५]।

---

१. G38- चतुर्विधा स्वरा वादि संवादि च वि **** न्दिपि, Sp- चतुर्विधा स्वरा वादि संवादि च विवादिपि, G86- चतुर्विधं स्वराणां तु वादि संवादिरेव च। resembles SR 1,3,47cd-48ab.

२. T65-अनुवादी च तत् वोक्ता, G86- विवादि अनुवादी च प्रमाणं स्वरवेदिभिः, G38- अनुवाणा चत् तत् प्रोक्ता प्रयोगो ** हास्वतः, Sp- अनुवादी चत् तत् प्रोक्ता प्रयागो प्राहुतस्युतः T65, G98, G17, B13 - the rest of the verse is missing. In B13, a dotted line is seen after प्रोक्ता, probably to indicate the incompleteness of the verse.

३. This quarter verse is missing in most of the Mss. In SR, this is the commencement of the explanation for the term, vādī. Since the present text takes a different interpretation for the terms vādī etc., the reading from SR is obviously out of place, probably the reason why it has been dropped by most of the Mss. G86 has composed a totally new verse, which does not appear to be grammatically correct. Support to this reading is seen in the commentary in T65 (ప్రమాణాలు), although G86 uses the term ప్రాణాలు (which might be a scribal error). But the entire exercise seems to have been directed towards omitting the definition for vādī. G38 and Sp seem to have filled up the quarter with the words of SR (प्रयोगे प्राहुलः स्वरः), which again gives no meaning. BKM reads उच्यते गानवेदिभिः and RJM- प्रथिता गानसूरिभिः, which do not seem to be a proper reading and hence this reading has been suggested.

४. G38- adds ఇట్లు, Sp- adds ఇలాగున

५. T65, G38, Sp- స్వరాలు

६. G86- ప్రాణాలు, G38- ప్రాకారములు, Sp- ప్రాకారాలు

७. Sp- ఎట్లాగాంటె, G38- అది ఎట్లాగనగా

८. G86- సంవా * *, G38- సంప్వాది

९. G86- [illegible]ా ******

१०. G38- నాలుగు స్వర ప్రాకారములు, Sp- నాలుగు స్వర ప్రాకారాలు

११. G86- చెప్పపడును, G38, Sp- చెప్పబడును

१२. T65, G98, G17, G86, G38, Sp- वादिस्वराश्च

१३. G98,G17,B13-राजश्च, T65-राजस्चात्, G86-राजास्यां, Sp- राजास्यान्ते

१४. T65, G98, G17- मंत्रे, G86- नन्त्रि

१५. G98, G17- रीक्ष्यते

विवादिस्वर[१] वैरि[री]स्यात् अनुवादी च भृत्यवैः[कः][२] ।। १४ ।।
प्रोक्ता[क्तो] राजस्वरारोहे [राजास्वरारोहो][३] वरेन्नम्त्र्यवरोहिणि
[वदेन्मन्त्र्यवरोहिणी][४] ।
स्वरसंघट[ट्ट]नं वैरि[री] भृत्सः[यः][५] पार्श्वस्वराद्वदेत्
[रो भवेत्][६] ।। १५ ।।

टीका:- వాదిస్వరం రాజు; సంవాదిస్వరం[७] మంత్రి[८]; □వాదిస్వరం[९] వైరి; అనువాదిస్వరం[१०] భృత్యుండు[११]. సప్త స్వరాలకు[१२] ఆరోహణి[१३] వాది, రాజని[१४] చెప్పబడును. [१५]స్వరములయొక[१६] అవరోహణి సంవాది అనబడును. సప్త స్వరాలున్ను[१७] తమలోతాము ఒకటికి ఒకటి[१८] కొట్టుబడుట □వాది వైరి అనబడును. [१९]స్వరములు[२०] తమలోతమకు

१. T65, G17- विवादस्वर, G86- विवादी च स्य

२. G86- ****** अनुवादिच भृत्यकृते, G38, Sp -वैरिवि च प्रमृत्युर्वहित् समन्तिः

३. T65-रजस्वरारोहे, G86- राज्जास्य आरोहि G38-रजस्वराणाहि, Sp-रजस्वराणोहि

४. T65- वदेन्म**** the rest of the verse is missing, G98, G17, B13- वदेत् the rest of the verse is missing. G38- वदेन्यन्तपवरोहिणि, Sp- वदेन्यत्पवरोहिणि. suggested readings based on BKM(p.79)

५. T65, G98, G17, B13 - missing upto this, G38, Sp- घातम्वदेत्विविप्रमृत्वः

६. T65, G98, B13- पार्श्व स्वराद्यचेत्, G17-स्वराद्यंचेत्, G38, Sp- पार्श्व सराद्वदेतू

७. T65 - commentary missing upto this.

८. T65- మంత్రం

९. G86- missing

१०. G86- missing

११. G38, Sp- బృత్యుండు

१२. G38- స్వరములు, Sp- స్వరాలు

१३. G86- ఆరోణి

१४. T65, G86- అ□రాజ అని

१५. T65 reads only స్వడును for the rest of the sentence. Probably there is a gap here. the first syllable స్వ could be from the word స్వరముల and డును could be the last two syllables of the word అనబడును. G86- అ స్వరాల అవరోహణి * * * **వాది మంత్రియ□చెప్పబడును.

१६. Sp- స్వరాలయొక్క

१७. G38- స్వరములు, □స్వరాలు

१८. G38, Sp - missing

१९. T65, G86 - this sentence is missing.

२०. Sp- స్వరాలు

పార్శులు(పార్శ్వ)వల్ల[१] సంబంధము[२] అనువాది భృత్యుండనబడును. ఇందుకు స్వరాలయందు లక్ష్యం[३]. స రి గ మ ప ధ ని స। రి[४] గ మ ప ధ ని స । గ మ ప ధ ని స[५] । మ ప ధ ని స। ప ధ ని స[६] । ధ ని స[७]। ని స। స। దీని[८] పేరు వాది. రాజస్వరమనబడును[९]. స ని ధ ప మ గ రి స[१०]। ని ధ ప మ గ రి స। ధ ప మ గ రి స। ప మ గ రి స। మ గ రి స। గ రి స। రి స। స। దీని పేరు సంవాది. మంత్రియనబడును[११]. [१२]సమ్మ[१३] గ రి స రి గ మ। రిప్ప[१४] మ గ రి గ మ ప। గ ధ ప మ గ మ ప ధ। మన్ని[१५] ధ ప మ ప ధ ని। పస్స[१६] ని ధ ప ధ ని స। ఈ తీరున అలంకారాదులయందు[१७] వచ్చు స్వరములు □వాది వైరి అనబడును[१८]. స రి గ। రి గ మ। గ మ ప। మ ప ధ। ప ధ ని। ధ ని స[१९] । స ని ధ[२०]। ని ధ ప। ధ ప మ।

---

१. Sp- పార్శ్వాలవల్ల

२. Sp- సంబంధం

३. G38, Sp- ఇందులకు లక్ష్యం□□వాది స్వర వైరిత్యా అనువాధీ చ బృత్యవత । ఇందులకు లక్ష్యము ।టీ । స్వర లక్షణము చెప్పదను - The underlined portion seems to be part of the previous verse found in between the commentary. ఇందులకు లక్ష్యం seen twice could be a repetition

४. T65- ని, G86- రి గ * * ప ధ ని స

५. T65- గ మ ప ధ ని స is missing

६. G38- ద ప ని స

७. G38- ప ని స

८. G38, Sp- దీనికి

९. G38- రాజ స్వరములు అని చెప్పబడును, Sp- రాజు స్వరాలు అని చెప్పబడును

१०. T65, G86- స ని ధ ప మ గ రి స is missing

११. G38- మంత్రి అని చెప్పబడును

१२. G38, Sp- adds స రి మ, రి ప, గ ప మన్ని, ప స, ధ రి, ని గ before.

१३. G38 - స మ

१४. G38, Sp - రి ప

१५. G38, Sp- మ ని

१६. G38, Sp- ప స

१७. G86- అలంకారాలయందు

१८. T65,G86- this sentence is missing, G38, Sp -The text gets repeated and the word లయం is seen added before in the repeated portion.

१९. T65 - the last svara of each phrase in the ascent is long, like స రి గా etc.

२०. G38, Sp - missing

ప మ గ। మ గ రి। గ రి స. ఈ తీరున[१] స్వరాలు పార్శ్వాల[२] [३]అనువాది భృత్యస్వరమనబడును[४]. గీత, ప్రబంధ, అలంకార, రాగగానాదులయందు[५] ఈ నాలుగు ప్రకారాలుగ సప్త స్వరాలు కలసి వచ్చును.

[६]धर्मार्थकाममोक्षाणामिदमेकै[वै]क[७] साधनम् ।। १६ ।।

టీకా:- ధర్మార్థకామ్యమోక్షాలు యీ 4 సాధనములు ప్రత్యేకంగ **వు**(?)నుల స్వరూపం జ్ఞానుల చేత[८] ఎవరు గానం చేస్తున్నారో వార్లకున్ను[९] ☐న్నవార్లకున్ను[१०] చతుర్విధఫల పురుషార్థములల(లు) కలుగునని[११] శాస్త్రములు చెప్పుచున్నది గనక తెలిశి(సి)☐తగ్గది[१२]

---

१. T65, G38 - తీరు

२. G38- పార్శ్యాలవల్ల, Sp- పార్శ్వలవల్ల, G86- సంబంధించ్చుకోని వుండుట భృత***డు

३. G38- adds ఆరోణి అవరోణియందు తాకునది, Sp - adds ఆరోణి అవరోణియందు తాకేది. This kind of adscripts are seen at many places in G38 and Sp.

४. T65, Sp - భృత్యస్వరాలనబడును, G38- బృత్యు స్వరములనబడును

५. G86- నాధులయ *****

६. G98,G17,B13,G86 - this line is missing

७. G38, Sp- मोक्षाणमिदमैकैक

८. T65-this whole sentence is read thus: ఇట్లా స్వర ఉపజ్ఞానం చాత, G38- ఇట్లు స్వరూపము గానము చేత , Sp-ఇట్ల స్వరూపం గానము చేత

९. T65, Sp- వార్లకు, G38 - వారికి

१०. T65- ☐న్న, G38, Sp- ☐న్నవారికి

११. G86- పురుషార్థము గలుగుని, G38- పుషార్థములు కలదని, Sp- పురుషార్థములు గలదని

१२. T65- శాస్త్రమందు చెప్పినది, G38- సామవేదమునందు చెసి వాయున్నది, Sp- సామవేదమునందు చెప్పియున్నది

अथ रागः[१]

[२]षड्जादि[३]स्वरसम्मिश्रं[४] रागं च परिकीर्तितम्[५] ।। ९७ ।।

టీకా:- షడ్జాది[६] స్వరసం[మి]శంగ[మి]శం)[७] రాగమని చెప్పబడును[८].

आलिप्तिर्द्विविधा[९] ज्ञेया[१०] स्वरसंयोजने तथा।

रागाल[लि]प्ति रूप[पा]लिप्ति[११] द्वयं च परिकीर्तितम्[१२] ।। ९८ ।।

---

१. G98,G17,B13-missing, G86-अथा रागलक्षणं, G89-अथ रागलक्षणं, G38-अथा रागाः,Sp-अदा रागाः,V08-अथ रागाः

२. v.97 - v. 99, cf. SM 1,4,49cd-51cd.

३. Sp-षड्जाति

४. G38-स्वरसम्हिश्रं, Sp-स्वररसंमित्रं

५. G98,G17,B13- रागपंजर कीर्तितः, T65- रागं च परिकीर्तितः

६. Sp- షడ్జాతి

७. Sp-స్వరంరసం[మి]శ, G38- స్వర సం[మి]శ

८. T65- చెప్పబడేను

९. G86- अदिप्त द्विविधा, G89-अविप्त द्विविधा , T65- आलिप्त द्विविधा, G98, G17, B13- अवलिप्त द्विदा

१०. T65, G98, G17, B13- ज्ञेयं

११. G98,G17,B13,G86,G89- रागलिप्ते रूपलिप्ते, T65-रागलिप्ते रापलिप्त, G38-रागलिप्तरूपलिप्तिं, Sp-रागलिप्त रूपलिप्त. Since the present text uses the term ālipti and not ālapti (as found in many texts), this reading is suggested. However V08 has used ālapti and ālipti at two different places. (see footnote below)

१२. T65,G98,G17-परिकीर्तिताः, B13-परिकीर्तित, G86,G89, G38,Sp- परिकीर्तितः

టీకా:- స్వరరాగ సంబంధమున[१] రాగ(గా)లిప్తి రూప(పా)లిప్తి[२] అని రెండు ప్రకారాలు[३].

राग[गा]लिप्ति तन्नामाद्यैः[तन्ननादि][४] रूपको[५] गीतमुच्यते।

स्वरैः रागाः[६] प्रगायन्ते[७] स्वरस्थानविपर्यया[८] ।। ९९ ।।

టీకా:- తన్నునాదము[९] రాగ[१०]మనబడును. ఆ తన్నా(తన్నునా)దాలు[११] స్వరాల[१२] చేత[१३] ప్రకాశింప[१४] జేసి పాడినది[१५] గీతమనబడును.

---

१. T65- స్వరరాగ సంబంధమైన, G38- స్వరరాగ పద్ధతి రెండు ప్రాకారములు, Sp-స్వరరాగ పద్ధతి రెండు ప్రాకారాలు

२. G86- రాగ * * * * ** పలిప్తితా, G89- రాగలిప్తి రూపలిప్తా

३. Sp- ప్రాకారాలు

४. G 98-रागलिप्तै तन्ननाद्यैः, G17-रागलिप्तै तनन्माद्यैः, B13- रागलिप्ते तन्मनाद्यैः, G86-रागलिप्तं तु तन्नादैः, G89- रागलिप्तं तु तन्ना the rest is missing. G38-रागलिप्ति तननाड्वैः, Sp-रागलिप्तितननाट्यैः V08-रागालप्तिस्तन्ननादेन. The reading तन्ननादि is suggested here on the basis of SM.

५. Sp- रूपरो (The syllables रो and को often get confused in the Mss written in Telugu script)

६. T65,G17,B13,V08- स्वरै रागाः, G86, G89- स्वरे रागाः, G38, Sp-स्वरै राग

७. G86- प्रकायंते, G38-प्रगायन्तै

८. T65, G98, G17, B13- स्वरस्थानविपर्ययम्, G38, Sp- स्वस्वस्ताविपर्यय, V08-द्यष्ट (स्वर) स्थान रूप्यय (विपर्ययाः) (?)

९. G86, G89- తన్నాదము, G38,Sp- తన్నునాదుల చేత కూడినది

१०. T65, G86, G89- రూపక

११. G38, Sp- ఆ తన్నునాదులు

१२. G89- ******, G38- స్వరముల

१३. G86- చె **** శింప్ప, G89- *****

१४. G89 - ***** , G38, Sp- ప్రకాసింప

१५. G86- ****నది

[१]अपूर्णश्चैव[२] पूर्णश्च[३] कूटतानास्तथैव च[४]।

టీకా:- ఆ రాగగానం[५] అపూర్ణమునిన్ని పూర్ణమునిన్ని రెండు ప్రకారాలు[६]. [७]కూటతానసం□శ్రం అపూర్ణం.

---

१ v.100 resembles Datt.38cd and 39ab. However, the present work differs widely. Dattilam talks about kūṭatāna-s and the description of which actually commences from 38ab. On the otherhand, NC ignores 38ab. With regard to 38cd, the reading is slightly different and does not give the meaning,when the strings are struck ignoring the order, the complete and the incomplete mūrcchanā-s are kūṭatāna-s. Here the emphasis is on the two terms apūrṇa and pūrṇa; the term kūṭatāna and its concept are left undiscussed in the commentary. The relevance of bringing in the verses from Dattilam is not very clear. Only the commentary portion to v.100ab in G38 and Sp have two words आ रागगानं, which could link the subject of kūṭatāna to the treatment of rāga, which preceeded it. The commentary to v.100ab ends with the phrase, कूटतानसंमिश्रं अपूर्णं, which is treated by G38 and Sp as part of the main text (noted as श्लोक) and not as part of commentary. However these words have been incorporated in the main verses of BKM and RJM, The reading in BKM कूटतानं च संमिश्रमपूर्णं पूर्णमेव च। (p.102) varies from the Mss. Because of the inclusion of this information on kūṭatāna, pūrṇa and apūrṇa in BKM and RJM in this context, there is a hesitation to drop these verses or shift them to a location near the treatment of grāma and mūrcchanā.

२. G89- अपूर्णाश्चैव, G38, Sp- अपूर्णश्च

३. G86, G89- पूर्णाश्चा, G38, Sp- वपूर्णश्च

४. T65- कूटेतानास्तथैव च, G38- कूटतानस्मृति स्नुताः, Sp- कूटतानस्मृते स्मृताः, V08- कूटतानास्तुते स्मृताः

५. T65, G86, G89 - missing, G38- ఆ రాగగానము

६. G38- ప్రాకారములు రెండు, Sp- ప్రాకారాలు రెండు

७. G98, G17, B13 this portion is missing. G38- చ అంపూర్ణం, Sp- చ అపూర్ణం

पूर्णं[१] पञ्चसहस्रानि[णि][२] त्रयस्त्रिंशस्तु[३] सङ्ख्यया[४] ।।१००।।

టీకా:- (5033)[५] భేదాలుగా జేశినది[६] పూర్ణమనబడును.

शुद्धमिश्र[त्र]श्च[७]सङ्कीर्णा[र्णाः][८] रागास्तु त्रिविधाः स्मृताः[९]।

द्वात्रिंशत् शुद्धमित्याहुः[१०] मित्रत्यौषष्मिव च [चतुष्षष्टिस्तथा मित्रम्[११]]।

---

१. T65, G98, G17, G86, G38- पूर्ण, Sp- पूरण

२. G86, G89 - पंचसहिस्त्रा, G38- पंचस अस्त्राणि, Sp- वञ्चस अस्त्राणि, V08- पञ्चादश (पूर्णपञ्च) सहस्राणि

३. B13- त्रयस्त्रिंशत्तु, G38- त्रयत्रिदशस्तु, Sp- त्रयत्रिदशस्तु, V08- त्रयत्रिंशस्तु

४. G86, G89, G38, Sp- संख्यय The splitting differs in G38 and Sp.

५. T65- 5000 వేల భేదాలు, G86,G89- భేదాలు 1000 ముప్పైమూడు, G38,Sp -5 పలు

६. G38- 33 తానవరసలుచేత గానం చేసినది, Sp- 33 తానవరశలుచేత గానం చేసినది

७. G98, G17, B13- शुद्धमिश्राश्च, G38 -शुध मित्राश्च, Sp- शुभ मित्राश्च, V08-शुद्ध मित्राश्च

८. T65- संकीर्व , G86, G89-सङ्कीर्णं , G38- सङ्खर्णा

९. G98- रागास्युस्तिविधा स्मृताः, G17- रागास्युस्त्रिविधा स्मृताः, रागाः स्युस्त्रिविधाः स्मृताः T65- रागास्यु त्रिविधा स्मृताः, G86- राग ****** विधा स्मृताः, G89-रागस्तु त्रिविधा स्मृताः, G38- रागश्यु त्रिविधा श्वतः, Sp- रागस्यु त्रिविधा श्वतः

१०. G98 - द्वात्रिंशश्शुद्धमित्याहुः, G17 - द्वात्रिंशशुद्धमित्याहुः, T65- द्वात्रिंशंचुदमित्राहु, G86,G89-द्वात्रिंशश्शुद्धमित्राश्च, G38- द्वात्रिंश शुधमित्राहु, Sp- द्वात्रिंश शुद्धमित्राहु, V08- द्वात्रिंशच्छुद्धमित्याहुः

११. B13-मित्र[श्र]त्यौ षष्ठिमेव च ,T65-मित्रतुवौषष्ठिमेव च , G86-मित्र *****मेवच, G89- मित्रत्सौ षष्ठिमेव च, G38- मित्रत्सौ सष्ठिदोवचः, Sp- वित्रत्सौ सष्ठिदोवचः, V08-मित्रास्युः षष्ठिवेव च; According to the commentary, the number of mitra rāga-s should be 64, which is not spelt correctly in any of the Mss. BKM and RJM have overcome this by using the term चौषष्ठि instead of चतुष्षष्ठि. Hence this reading is suggested.

अनन्तानन्तसङ्कीर्ण[र्णं] शुद्धसालगसङ्कराः[१] ।। १०१।।

टीका:- రాగాలు[२] మూడు ప్రకారాలు[३]. శుద్ధాలని □త్రాలని[४] సంకీర్ణాలని చెప్పప(బ)డును.[५] [६]శుద్ధరాగాలు 32; □త్రరాగాలు 64; సంకీర్ణం అనంతం.

[७]अधाद्युपक्रमेणैव[८] राग[गं] शुद्धमुदाहृतम्[९]।

उपक्रम्य[१०] यदा रागो[११] मेलनं[१२] सममित्रकैः[१३]।। १०२।।

---

१. G98, G17, B13 - v.101ef is missing. T65, G86, G89 seem to be incomplete. T65- अनन्त राग संकाराः, G86- अनन्त राग संक्करा, G89- अनन्त राग स*****, G38-अनन्तसन्ति सकीशुध पाळग संकरः, Sp- अनन्तसन्ति संकीर्ण शुद्ध साळग सङ्करः The commentary does not recognise the words sālaga and saṅkara.

२. G38, Sp- రాగములు

३. G38- ప్రాకారములు

४. G38- □త్రలని

५. G86, G89- వుండును, G38, Sp- మూడు ప్రాకారములు

६. T65- 32 శుద్ధ రాగాలు। 64 □త్ర అనంతం సంకీర్ణం, G38- 32 శుధ రాగములు। అరవై నాలుగు అనన్తాలు సంకీర్నాలు, Sp-32 రాగాలు అరవైనాలుగు □త్రలు అనన్తాలు సంకీర్నాలు, V08- (32 శుద్ధ రాగాలు, 64 □శ□త్రాలు, అనంతాలు సంకీర్ణములు)

७. v.102 - v.103, cf. SM 1,4,52-53.

८. G98,G17,B13 - अनाद्युपक्रमेणैव, G86- अधाद्युप**मेणैव, G38-यदाद्युवक्रमेणैव, Sp- यदाद्युवक्रमेणैव, V08- यधाद्युपक्रमेणैव Though there are different readings in the Mss and SM, none of them seem to give a proper meaning

९. G38- शुधमदांप्रतं, Sp- शुद्धमुदांव्रतं. With this half-verse, V08 stops and continues to read from v.107ab. The following reference is given: ... (भरतकल्पलता p.102)

१०. G86, G89- उपक्रंया

११. T65- यदा लाभो, G86- यधारकं, G89- यधारगं, G38, Sp- यदा रोग

१२. T65- मैळनं

१३. B13-सममित्र[श्र]कैः

पुनस्तन्मार्गगमनं नाळंग[सालगं] परिकीर्तितः[तम्][१]।

सङ्कीर्णरागमित्राणां गानं[२] सङ्कीर्णमुच्यते[३]।। १०३।।

टीका:- ఇట్లు(ఎట్లా)[४] రాగముపక్ర□స్తున్నదో[५] ఆ తీరుననే 32 రాగాలు[६] [७]గానం చేసేది (శుద్ధరాగం). శుద్ధరాగముపక్ర□ంచి, □త్రరాగాలు చేత గానం చేసి,

---

१. T65-पुनस्तन्मार्गिमेवे च, G86-पुनस्तन्नार्गमेव च, G89-पुनस्तन्मार्गमेव च- these three seem to be Incomplete,Sp-नादं च दरिकीर्तितः Having prescribed śuddha in v.102ab, v.102cd & v.103ab dont give the definition of mitra as such. The reading comes close to sālaga.

२. T65- मित्राणा गान, Sp- मित्राण्यं

३. G38- संकीर्णमुचरत्

४. G86, G89- ఇట్లగా, T65, Sp- ఇట్లా

५. T65- రాగవంపక్రవంస్తునాడో, G86- రాగవుంపక్ర□స్తు**, G38- రాగముపక్ర□ంస్తున్నాడో, Sp- రాగము ఉపక్ర□స్తున్నాడో

६. G38- రాగము, T65 omits the passage from this ३२ రాగాలు and reads from, the next ३२ రాగాలు thus: సాళగమని పించుకొనును. □త్రరాగాలు సంకీర్ణరాగాలు చాత గానం చేశి. This could be a visual error.

७. G38 and Sp read slightly different; G38- గానము చేసేది శుధం దీని పేరు ఘనం. శుధం రాగము ఉపక్ర□ంచి □త్ర రాగములను గానము చేసి తిరిగి శుధాన తిరునది 32 రాగముల సాళగముని పించుకోనును. దీని పేరు పన్దరాయతు □త్రరాగములు సంకీర్ణ రాగములు చేత గానము చేసే, Sp- గానము చేశేది శుద్ధం. దీని పేరు ఘనం. శుద్ధం రాగము ఉపక్ర□ంచి □త్రరాగాల గానం చేసి తిరుగ శుధాన తీరేది తిరునది 32 రాగాలు సాళగమని పించుకోనును. దీని పేరు వందరాయతు □త్రరాగాలు సంకీర్ణరాగాలు చేత గానం చేసి - It is curious to note that G38 and Sp equate the term śuddha rāga with ghanam. Towards the end of this prose passage, it is mentioned that these 32 rāga-s are called rakti in dēśī [?] The same concept of relating śuddha rāga to ghana is again noticed in the context of the miśra (gāyaka dōṣa-s - v.176)

తిరుగ(తిరిగి) శుద్ధాన తిరిగేది[१] సారళగ(సాలగ)మని పించుకొనును[२]. □త్రరాగాలు చేత గానం చేశి శుద్ధాన ముక్తాయి[३] చేసేది[४] దేశ్యకు వాడ(వాటి దండే)[५] రక్తిగానమని[६]పించును[७]. ఈ ముప్పై రెండు రాగాలు[८] ఈ తీరుననే[९] భేదాలాయను[१०]

षाडवौडवसम्पूर्ण[११]स्वरै रागाः[१२] प्रकीर्तिताः[१३] ।

स्वस्वस्थान[१४]विपर्यासात्[१५] स्वराणां[१६] सम्भवन्त्यमी[१७] ।। १०४ ।।

టీకా:- స్వరాలయొక్క తవంతవ □ర్యాసం వల్ల స్వరకూట□గా[१८]

---

१. G86, G89- add ३२ రాగాలు after this.

२. G89- పించుకొనేను

३. G89- శుద్ధానము స్తా (ప్తో)యి, G38- శుధానము ****, Sp- శుధానముక్తాయి

४. G86- జేశేది G38, Sp- చేసినది

५. G86- దేశ్యకర వాడదండి, G89-దేశియకర వాడదం దండి, G38-దేశీయమునక వాడిదండి, Sp- దేశీయానకు వాడి దండి

६. G86- గానళుసం, G89- గానళుని, T65- గానమన

७. G38, Sp- పించుకొనేను

८. G38- రాగములు

९. G38, Sp- ఏ తీరున

१०. Sp- భేదాలాయిన

११. G98, G17, B13 - षाडवौडवसंकीर्ण, G38, Sp - षाडवौडवसम्पूर्ण, T65- षाडवौडविसेम्पूर्ण

१२. T65- स्वरै राग, G86, G89- स्वरे राग, G38- स्वरैराग, Sp- स्वके राग

१३. G38, Sp- प्रकीर्तितः

१४. G38, Sp- स्वस्वस्तान

१५. G98- विपर्यासा, G17- विपर्यासाः, T65, G86, G89, G38, Sp-विपर्यास

१६. Sp- स्वराणो

१७. G98, G17- संभवत्यमा, G86, G89 - सम्भवत्यमि , T65- सम्भवंत्यतः, G38- सम्भयत्यपिः, Sp- संभयत्यजन्

१८. G38- సరకూట□గ

షాడవౌడవసంపూర్ణ[१]రాగాలు[२] పుట్టేనని చెప్పబడును[३].

[४]एकस्वरविहीनश्च[५] षाडवः[६] परिकीर्तितः।

पञ्चस्वरसमायुक्तः औडवः[७] परिकीर्तितः[८]।

सप्तस्वर[९]समायुक्तः[१०] सम्पूर्ण इति[११] कथ्यते[१२]।। १०५।।

टीका:- ఆరు స్వరాలది షాడవం[१३]. ఐదు స్వరాలది[१४] ఔడవం[१५]. ఏడు స్వరాలది[१६] సంపూర్ణం. ఈ తీరున[१७] షాడవౌడవసంపూర్ణాలని[१८] రాగాలకు భేదాలు[१९] చెప్పబడును[२०].

---

१. G86- షాడవౌడ * * * ** పూర్ణ, G89- షాడవౌడవ సంపూర్ణా, G38- షాడవ అఉడవ సంపూర్ణాం, Sp- షాడవ అవుడవ సంపూర్ణ

२. G38- రాగములు

३. G89- జెప్పబడును, T65,Sp- చెప్పబడేను

४. v.105, cf. SM,1,4,54cd-55cd

५. G86, G89- विहीनस्या, T65, G98, G17-विहीनस्य, V41- विभागश्च

६. G86- षाडवप्परि, G38, Sp- षाडवौ

७. T65, G98- समायूक्तं औडवं, G17- समायुक्तामौडवं, B13- समायुक्त औडवं, G38, Sp - समायुक्तावौडव

८. G17- परिकीर्तितम्

९. G38- सप्तसर

१०. G98, G17, G38, Sp- समायुक्तं

११. G98, G17, G38- संपूर्णमिति, Sp- संपूर्णं यिति

१२. G38, Sp- खद्येति

१३. G86- 6 *******, G38-6 స్వరములది□షాడవం, V41- ఆరు స్వరములు షాడవం

१४. G86- స్వరా **** , G38- స్వరములది, Sp- స్వరాలు అది

१५. T65- ఔడవం, G38- అఉడవం, Sp- అవుడవం

१६. G38- స్వరములది, Sp- స్వరాలు అది , V41- సప్త స్వరాలు

१७. V41- ఈ రీతున, G38, Sp- missing

१८. T65- షాడకాడవసంపూర్ణాలని , G38- షాడవవౌడవసంపూర్ణాలని

१९. G86, G89- రాగ భెదాలని, G38- రాగములకు భేదములని, Sp- రాగాలకు భేదాలని

२०. T65- చెప్పబడేను

क्रमादेवं[१] स्वराणां च नामोद्देशं[२] कृतस्वराः[?][३]।

टीका:- క్రమాననే[४] షాడవౌడవసంపూర్ణాలనే[५] 3[६] స్వరాలకు[७] దేవతలు[८] 32 రాగాలని పేర్లు పెట్టినారు(?)[९].

स्त्रीपुंरागसमाख्यातः[१०] द्वात्रिंशद्गीतपारगैः[११] ।। १०६ ।।

टीका:- ఆ 32 రాగాలకు[१२] గానవేత్తలైన[१३] దేవతలు[१४] పురుషరాగాలని[१५] శ్రీ(స్త్రీ)రాగాలని[१६] 2 ప్రకారాలు[१७] చెప్పినారు[१८]. అది ఏదంటే[१९] ప్రత్యేకంగా[२०] లక్షణం[२१] చెప్పెదను[२२].

---

१. G86, G89- क्रममादेवं
२. V41- नामोदेश
३. G98, G17, B13- कृतस्वरा, G86, G89- कृतस्सरः Probably could be कृतं पुरा
४. T65, G89- క్రమానని, G86- క్రమా ***ని, G38- క్రమమునసే, V41- క్రమముగా
५. G86- ***డ***సంపూర్ణాలన్నే, G38- షాడవౌడవసమ్పూర్ణములను, V41- సంపూర్ణములనె
६. T65, G38, Sp- ४
७. G38- స్వరములకు
८. V41- missing
९. T65, G86, G89, Sp-పెళ్ళు బెట్టినారు, V41- adds అది యేవన్ననను
१०. G98,G17,B13-स्त्रीपुंरागसमायुक्तः,T65-श्रीपुंरागसमात्युत्तः,G86- श्रीपुंरागसमाख्यातः, G89- स्त्रिपुंरागसमाख्यातः, G38- स्त्रीपुंरागसमाख्यतः, V41- आ पुंराग समाख्यात
११. G38- द्वांत्रिंशगीतपारंगेः, Sp- द्वाम्त्रिंशगीतपारगैः This is again found in v. 112ef.
१२. G38- రాగములు, Sp- రాగాలు, V41- రాగాలలో
१३. G86,G89- గానవేదులైన, G38- గానవేత్తలైన, Sp- గానవేత్తుడ యిన
१४. T65, G86, G89- దేవతులు
१५. G86, G89- పురుషరాగాలు, G38- పురుష పురుష రాగములని
१६. G38- శ్రీరాగములని, Sp- శ్రీరగాలని
१७. G86,G89- ప్రకారాలని, G38- ప్రాకారములని, Sp- ప్రాకారాలు
१८. Sp- అ□చెప్పినారు
१९. T65-అది యంటె, G38- అ□ఏవనగా, Sp- అ□యేవంటె
२०. G38- ప్రత్యేకముగా
२१. Sp- missing
२२. T65- చెప్పుము, G86, G89- చెప్పుమా, Sp- చెప్పెను, V41 reads slightly different thus: ఆ ముప్పదిరేండు రాగాలలో స్త్రీరాగములని పురుషరాగములనియు దేవతలు గల్పించినారు. ప్రత్యేక లక్షణములు జేప్పేము.

[१]भैरवै[व]श्चापि भूपालो श्रीरागो पडमञ्जरः।

वसन्तो मालवश्चैव[२] बङ्गालो नाटकस्तथा ।

[३]एतेऽष्टरागाः पुंरागाः अन्यास्त्रीरागसंज्ञिकाः[४] ।। १०७ ।।

టీకా:- [५]భైర□[६] భూపాళం[७], శ్రీరాగం[८], పడమంజరి[९], వసంతం[१०], మాళ□ బంగాళ, నాట[११], ఈ ఎని□దిన్న(న్ని)[१२] [१३]పురుషరాగాలనిన్ని[१४], కడమ 24[१५] శ్రీ(స్త్రీ)రాగాలని[१६]

१. T65, G86,G89, G98, G17, B13- v.107 is missing, V41- भूपालो भैरवश्चैव श्रीरागो रागपंजरः, this verse is seen after the following commentary. v.107ab, v.107cd, cf. ABSS 2,1014, SM 1,3,68, STR 6,8,29ab-30ab, SN 1,124

२. G38, Sp- वंसन्तोमाळवश्चैव

३. V41- अष्टरागा इमेधियाँ पुरुषा इति स्मृतिः।।

४. G38- रन्यस्त्रीरागसंजिकः, Sp- रन्ये स्त्रीरागसंजिनः

५. V08- 8x3 స్త్రియః, G98,G17,B13 add పురుషరాగం before, which probably is the sub-heading given by the scribe.

६. T65, G86, G89, G38, Sp-

७. G98- భూతాళం

८. G86,G89- స్త్రిరాగం

९. G98- పటమంజరీ, G17- పడ(ద)మంజరీ, B13- పదమంజరీ, V41- రాగపంజరి. Though these are masculine rāga-s, the commentary does not read them in masculine gender as seen in other texts like Sadrāgacandrōdaya, Saṅgītadarpaṇa, Śivatattvaratnākara etc., which speak of this concept. The same is also noticed in the feminine rāga-s, where the names of the rāga-s do not end with a long vowel. Hence the long vowels are suggested at appropriate places in the original alone but are not treated seriously with respect to the commenatary, since Telugu language allows short vowel endings for nouns in feminine gender.

१०. G38- వంసంతము, Sp- వంసంత

११. V41- the series changes slightly thus: బంగాళ నాట వసంత మాళ□

१२. G98, G17, B13, G86, G89 - 8

१३. T65,G98,G17,B13- this sentence is missing; V41- ఈ యేని□దియు బురుష రాగాము। దీనికి శ్లోకము (then follow v.107)

१४. G38- రాగములనియు, Sp- రాగాలు అనిన్ని

१५. G38, Sp- 24 ను

१६. G38- శ్రీ రాగములనియు, Sp- శ్రీ రాగాలు అని

చెప్పినారు.

[१]अष्टा[टौ]राग[गा]स्त्रयस [यस्स]ङ्ख्या[२] भार्यारूपं कृतस्वरः[?][३] ।। १०८ ।।

టీకా:- ఈ[४] ఎని□ది పురుషరాగాలకు[५] ముగ్గురు ముగ్గురు[६] స్త్రీలుగా[७] ఆ[८] 24 స్త్రీరాగాలును[९] దేవతలు[१०] జేసినారు[११]. [१२]ఆ క్రమం చెప్పె(ద)ను[१३]. వా□ల్ల(ర్ల) యొక్క నామోదే(ద్దే)శం[१४] చెప్పె(ద)ను[१५].

देवक्रिया मेघरञ्जी[१६] कुरञ्जी[१७] भैरवस्त्रियः[१८] ।

वेलाहुरि[री][१९] मलहरी च[२०] बौली चैव[२१] नृपस्त्रियः[२२] ।। १०९ ।।

---

१. T65, G98, G17, B13- v.108 is missing
२. G86, G89- अष्टारागत्रयसङ्ख्या, V41- अष्ट रागात्रयस्संख्या
३. V41- कृतः सुरः
४. G86,G89,G38,Sp- missing
५. G38- రాగములకు, Sp- రాగాలకు
६. V41- రాగమొక్కంటి ముగురు, G38, Sp- omit one ముగ్గురు
७. G38- శ్రీలుగా, Sp- స్త్రిలుగా, V41- స్త్రీ రాగాలనియు
८. G38, Sp- missing
९. G38- శ్రీరాగములను, Sp- శ్రీరాగాలను
१०. G89- దేవతులు
११. G38- ఏర్పరచినారు, Sp- ఏర్పరచినా, V41- జెప్పినారు
१२. G38- (Incomplete). ఆ క్రమము చెప్పదను the rest missing
१३. G86- చెప్పు **** , T65, G89- చెప్పుము, V41- జెప్పేదము
१४. G86, G89- నామోద్వేశం, Sp- నామదేశం
१५. Sp- చెప్పెను
१६. T65, G86, G89, G98- मेखरञ्जी
१७. G38- शुरंजि, V08- कुरुंजी
१८. G98,G17,B13- भैरवप्रिया, T65, G86- भैरवि स्त्रियाः, G89- *****, G38- भैरवश्रीयः, Sp- भैरवश्रियः
१९. G86- वेळापुरि, G89- ***पुरि, G38, Sp- वेळाहुळि
२०. T65-मल्लरिश्च,G98,G17-मल्लरीश्च, G89-मलहरिच्छ, G38, Sp- मल्वरी च, V08-मल्लारिश्च,V41-मल्लरिश्च
२१. T65-प्रौळिश्चैव, G98,G17-भैळीचैव, G86-प्रौळिश्चैव, G89- प्रौळिश्च**, G38-भौळिश्चव, Sp-भौळिश्चैव
२२- G86, Sp- नृपश्रियः, G38- नृपश्रीयः

श्रीरागपत्नो[त्न्यो][१] हिन्तो[दो]ली[२] बलहंसपुरी[सावेरी][३] तथा।

देशी च ललिता तोडी[४] पडमञ्जरी[र][५]योषिता[६] ।। ११० ।।

रामक्रिया[७] वराली च कौशिका[८] मधुयोषिता[९] ।

नारायणी गुण्डक्रिया[१०] घूर्जरी[११] मालवस्त्रियः[१२] ।। १११ ।।

---

१. G98,G17,B13,V08,V41-श्रीरागपंतु, G86,G89-स्त्रीरागंप्पंतु, T65-स्त्रीरागंवंतु. the suggested reading is noticed in BKM and RJM.

२. G98,G17,B13-हिंदोळं, T65-हिंत्तोळं, V41,V08- हिन्दोळ, G38, Sp- हिन्धोळं

३. T65,G89-बहुसंसाहुरि, G86- **हः**सा**रि, G98, G7, B13 - बहुसंमाहुरी, V41,V08-बलहंसाहरी. There is an inconsistency in reading the names of 32 rāga-s, both in the original text and the commentary. Balahamsa is being suggested here based on the reference made in v.128cd and the commentary. With respect to the third rāga, G98, G17 and B13 read māhuri, but the commentary reads sāhuri and sāveri at two different places. However none of these three have been described in the next section, which deals with the characteristics of rāga-s. Hence sāveri is being suggested here based on the commentary. V08 and V41 read it as āharī, but in the present work, it is mentioned as one of the feminine rāga-s under nāṭa.

४. G38, Sp- ललितां तोडि

५. G86- पडमांजरि, Sp- वडमञ्जरि, V08, V41- पलमंजरि

६. G86, G89, G38, Sp, V08, V41- योषितः

७. G86,G89, G38, Sp- रामक्रिय

८. G86, G89- कौशिक, T65- काशिक, V08, V41- नासिका

९. G86,G89, G38, Sp- मधुयोषितः, V08, V41- मधुयोगतः

१०. T65, G89, G38, Sp- गुण्डक्रिय, G86- कुण्ड्डक्रिय, V08- गुण्डकरी

११. T65, G86, Sp- घुर्ज्जरि, G38- घर्जरि, V08, V41- गुज्जरी

१२. G98- माळस्त्रिया, G17- माळवी स्त्रिया, B13- माळ[व] स्त्रिया, G86, G89, T65?- माळावस्त्रियः, G38- माळविक्रियः, Sp- माळाविश्रियः

[१]धन्याशी चैव काम्बोदि[दी] बौली[नीला][२] बङ्गालयोषिता।

देशाक्षरी[३] वराली[आहरी][४] च सारङ्गा[५] नाटयोषिता[६]।

स्त्रीपुंरागाः[७] समाख्याता[८] द्वात्रिंशद्गीतपारगैः[९]।। ११२।।

---

१. T65- धन्यासी चैव काम्बोदि भौळि बाङ्गाळयोषिता, G86- धन्यशि चैव काम्बोदि भौळि **गा **योषितः, G89- धन्यशि चैव काम्बोदि भौळि बंगाळयोषितः, G17, B13- धन्यासी चैव काम्बोदि बौळी बङ्गाळयोषिता, G38-धन्याशी चैव काम्बोदि भौळि भंगायोषितः, Sp- धन्यशि चैव काम्बोदि भौळि भंगायोषितः, V08- धन्यासी चैव कांभोजी छाया बंगाळयोगतः, V41- धन्यासी चैव कांभोदी छाया बंगाळयोगत

२. Baulī has already been mentioned as a feminine rāga of bhūpāla. Hence nīlā (nīlāmbari) is suggested, since it is described in v.116ab. The commentary also refers to nīlāmbari as a feminine rāga of Baṅgāla. Reference to this rāga is found in the commentary too.

३. V08, V41- देशाक्षि

४. G98, G17, B13- वराटा, V08, V41- रीतिगौलश्च. The original text reads varālī and the commentary āharī. Since varālī is already mentioned as one of the feminine rāga-s under vasanta (which is noticed in ABSS, STR, BKM, RJM, RS, BS and MBC) the rāga āharī is being suggested here instead of varālī. V08 and V41 read rītigaula, which is not found anywhere in the Mss presently consulted.

५. T65-सारंगो, G86-सारंग, G89- सारंगं, G38,Sp- साळाङ्गो, V08, V41- साहिरी; In some texts like BKM, RJM etc. sāraṅga is considered as a masculine rāga.

६. B13,G86,V08,V41- नाटयोषितः, G38- नाटयोस्त्रीतः, Sp- नाटयोस्त्रितः

७. T65- स्त्रीपुंरागा, G98- स्त्रिपुंराग, G86, G89, G38, Sp,स्त्रीपुंराग, V08- स्त्रीरागाः, V41- स्त्रीरागोस्समाराध्या

८. T65- समाख्यातं, G98, G86, G89- समाख्यातः, G17- समाख्याताः, G38, Sp- समाख्यात, V41- v.113- v.130 are missing; reads the following prose section found exclusively in this Ms thus: దేవక్రియా మేఘరంజి కురంజి- ఈ మూడును భైర[illegible] స్త్రీలు. వేళాఁరి మలఁరి బౌళి - ఈ మూడును భూపాల యొక్క స్త్రీలు ******* గముకు స్త్రీలు ఁందోళము మాఁరీ బిలాఁరి - ఈ మూడును శ్రీరాగా *** బలఁంస ఆఁరి దేశి ఈ మూడును రాగపంజరి స్త్రీలు. దేవక్రియ గుజ్జరి గౌళ - ఈ మూడును మాళవ స్త్రీలు. ధన్యాసి కాంభోది కన్నడగౌలి ఈ మూడును బంగాళ స్త్రీలు. ** శాక్షి ఆఁరి రీతిగౌల ఈ మూడును నాటరాగానకు స్త్రీలు

९. T65- द्वात्रिंशं गीतपारगैः, V08- द्वात्रिंशद्गीतपारनैः

టీకా:- ఈ[1] చెప్పిన క్రమాన[2] ఆ స్త్రీరాగాలు[3] 24న్ను, 8[4] పురుషరాగాలకు[5] ఎని[illegible]దింటికి[6] సతులు. [illegible]దికి నామధేయాలు[7] వచ్చిన క్రమం[8] చెప్పెను[9].

षाडवौडवसम्पूर्ण[10]स्वरैर्गायन्ति देवताः[11]।

स्वस्वनाम्ना[12] रागमिति[13] वदेद्द्वात्रिंशद्भेदतः[वदेत् रागं इति द्वात्रिंशभेदतः][14] ।। ११३ ।।

టీకా:- షాడవౌడవసంపూర్ణాలనేటి స్వరాల చేత దేవతలు[15] గానం చేసి తమతమ[16] నామధేయాల[17] చేత 32 రాగాలకు[18] నామాంకితాలు[19] జేసినారు[20]. ఈ రాగాలకు[21] షాడవౌడవసంపూర్ణ[22] భేధా(దా)లు[23] చెప్పెదను [24].

---

१. G38, Sp- ఇపుడు
२. G38- క్రమమున
३. G89- *******, G38- శ్రీరాగములు, Sp- శ్రీరాగాలు
४. T65, Sp - missing
५. G38- రాగములకు, Sp- రాగాలు
६. G86, G89 - missing, G38- [illegible]ం, Sp- 8 న్ను [illegible]
७. G38- నామధేయములు, Sp- నామధేయులు
८. Sp- క్రమ
९. G86- చెప్పుము, T65- చెప్పుమా , G38- చెప్పెదను
१०. G89- षाडवौडसंपूर्ण, G38, Sp- षाडवौडवसम्पूर्ण
११. G86- दैताः, G89- *****
१२. G86, G89- स्वस्वन्नमा, G38, Sp- स्वस्वनामा
१३. G86, G89- रागमित्
१४. G98,G17-वरेत्यदशभेदतः, B13-पठेत्यदशभेदतः, T65-वरेत्यादशभेदतः, G86-वदेद्वादशभेदतः, G89- वदेद्यादशभेदतः, Since the present construction does not conform to metrical rules, it is suggested thus.
१५. G86- దేవత * *,T65, G38, Sp- దేవతులు
१६. T65- missing
१७. G38- నామదేయ, Sp- నామధేయ
१८. G38- రాగములకు
१९. G86, G89- నామంకితముగా, G38- నామంకితములు, Sp-నామగీతాలు
२०. G38- చేసినారు, Sp- చేశినారు
२१. G38- రాగములకు
२२. Sp- సంపూర్ణా
२३. T65- రాగభేదాలు, G38- అనేటి భేదములు, Sp- అనేటి భేదాలు
२४. T65, G86, G89- చెప్పుమా Sp- చెప్పెను

[१]षाडवौ[वो] देवगान्धारि[री][२] गादि वर्जो[वर्ज्यो][३] निषादकः।
भैरवि पूर्णरागस्यात्[४] पञ्चमादि प्रकीर्तितः[५] ।। ११४ ।।
[६]वौ[औ]डवो[७] घुर्जरि[री] प्रोक्तो गादि वर्जो[वर्ज्यौ] रिगौ तथा।
श्रीरागो [षा]डवश्चैव[८] दा[धा]दि रि[ऋ]षभवर्जकः[९] ।। ११५ ।।
नीलाम्बरि[री] षाडवस्यातु[स्यात्] मादि[१०] वर्जो[वर्ज्यो] रि च स्वरः ।
वराली षाडवो रागो[११] गादिर्मध्य [गादि मध्यम] वर्जितः[१२] ।। ११६ ।।
मेघरञ्जि[ञ्जी][१३] मध्यमादि धनि[नी] वर्ज[वर्ज्यौ][१४] तदौडवः[१५] ।

---

१. G98, G17, B13 - missing till v.131. V08- missing upto v.116. Though the description is about the rāga-s based on gender classification, the construction does not seem to strictly follow the grammatical rules pertaining to sanskrit. The text is presented in the same manner as found in the Mss.

२. G38- षाडवू देवगान्धारि, Sp- षाडवौडवगान्धारि

३. The word 'varjya' is uniformly read as 'varja' in the Mss. Hence 'varjya' is being suggested in the following verses.

४. G38- पूर्णरागस्या, Sp- पूर्णरागास्यु

५. T65, G89- न्नादि वर्ज्जो रि च स्वरः, G86- न्नादि वर्ज्जो नि च स्वरः

६. T65, G86,G89- v.115 is missing.

७. G38- देडवो

८. Sp- श्रीरागो पडवश्चैव

९. Sp- वर्जरः

१०. Sp- सादि

११. G38- वराषाडवौ राग, Sp- वराळि षाडवौ राग

१२. G86-पा आ***मध्य, G89-पा आदिर्मध्य, T65-पादिर्मध्य विवर्जितः, G38- गादिर्मध्य *** र्जतः

१३. T65, G86- मेखरंजि, G89- मेखुरंजि

१४. G86, G89- वर्जल

१५. T65-तथा धवः, G86,G89- तथा वधः, V08-देवक्रिया मेघरंजी ध नि वर्ज तथौडवः

वेलाहुरि[री][1] औडवश्च[2] गादि वर्जो [वर्ज्यौ][3] सरी[4] स्वरौ[5] ।। ११७ ।।

देशिकारी च[6] सम्पूर्णो[7] मध्यमादौ प्रकीर्तितः[8] ।

मलहरि[री][9] षाडवो रागः[10] गादि[11] रु[ऋ]षभ वर्जितः[12] ।। ११८ ।।

[13]देशकारि[देशीरागो][14] षाडवस्या[स्स्यात्][15] दाधि [धादि][16]

वर्जो[वर्ज्यौ] निषादकः ।

रामक्रिया[17] औडवस्या[स्स्यात्][18] गादि[19] वर्जो[वर्ज्यौ] रिसौ स्वरौ[20] ।। ११९ ।।

---

१. G38- वेळायुरी

२. G89- ******** , G38, Sp- वौडवश्च, V08- औडवस्या

३. Sp- वर्जा

४. V08- स म

५. T65- स्वका, G86, V08- स्वरा, G38- स्वशा

६. G38, Sp- देशकारिश

७. V08- संपूर्णो, G38, Sp- संपूर्ण

८. G86,G89-मध्यमावि प्रकीर्तितः, T65-मध्यमाविष्प्रकीर्तितः, V08- मध्यमादि प्रकीर्तितः. This rāga has does not figure anyhwere in this work.

९. V08- मल्हरिः

१०. G38, Sp- षाडवौ राग

११. V08- missing

१२. V08- निषादस्वरवर्जितः

१३. T65- missing, V08 missing upto v.126

१४. G38, Sp- देशकार. A rāga of this name is not seen in this work. On the other hand, the description given here agrees with the rāga deśī. Hence it is suggeseted thus.

१५. G89- षावस्या, G89- ****, G38, Sp- षाडवश्च This kind of error (misinterpretation of the last one or two syllables) could be probably due to the text being written, on listening to some dictation.

१६. G86, G89- ददि

१७. G38, Sp- रामक्रिय

१८. G86- औडव **, G38, Sp- वौडवस्य

१९. G86, G89 ददि

२०. G86, G89- रिसंस्वरौ, G38- रिसौ स्वका, T65- रिसौसका

तोडि[डी] सम्पूर्णरागस्यात्[स्स्यात्] गान्धारादि प्रकीर्तितः।

[१]देवक्रिया[२]औडवस्यात्[स्स्यात्][३] ना[न्या]दि[४] वर्जो[वर्ज्यौ]

रिसौ स्वरौ[५]।। १२०।।

पडमञ्जरि[र][६]रागस्यात्[स्स्यात्][७] षाडवः[८] परिकीर्तितः।

[९]निषादादिस्तथा वर्जं[१०] रि[ऋ]षभस्वरमेव च[११]।। १२१।।

औडवस्या[स्स्यात्][१२] घूर्ज्जरागा [कुरञ्जिका][१३] मादिर्न्रिस [मादि

निसाऽ]पि[१४] वर्जितः।

गुण्डक्रिया महारागः षाडवः परिकीर्तितः।। १२२।।

गान्धारादिस्तथा[१५] वर्जो[वर्ज्यौ][१६] मध्यम[१७]स्वरमेव च।

---

१. G86, G89- v.120cd - v.121ab are missing

२. G38- देवक्रिय, Sp- दैवक्रिय

३. G38, Sp- वौडवस्यात्

४. G38- न्मादि, Sp- सादि

५. G38- रिसौस्वर, T65- सौसका

६. G38- पडमंजिरि

७. T65, Sp- रागस्य

८. G38, Sp- षाडव

९. G38, Sp- v.121cd - v. 122 are missing

१०. G86,G89- निषादोधि तधा **ज्जं

११. G86-मेवचा

१२. G86- औडवर्ज्जा, G89-****स्या

१३. ghurjari is already described in v.115ab above. Since the characteristics described in this verse match with the rāga kurañji, found in the commentary, it has been suggested. Moreover description of this rāga is not found in this section.

१४. G86, G89- गोमादिर्न्रिसदि

१५. G86,G89- गान्धारादि सदा

१६. Sp- वर्जा

१७. G38, Sp- मध्यमे

सारङ्गरागः[१] सम्पूर्णः[२] पञ्चमादिस्तथैव च[३]।। १२३।।

वसन्तः[४] षाडवो रागः[५] न्यादि[६] वर्जश्च पञ्चमः।

धन्याशि[शी] षाडवो[७] रागः गादि वर्जो[वर्ज्यो][८] निषादकः।। १२४।।

ललिता[९] षाडवो[१०] रागः ना[न्या]दि[११] वर्जो[वर्ज्यो][१२] ग स[च]स्वरः[१३]।

नाटरागश्च सम्पूर्णः[१४] स षड्जादिरुदाहृतम्[१५] ।। १२५।।

आहरि[री][१६] पूर्णरागस्यात्[स्स्यात्][१७] मध्यमादि प्रकीर्तितः[१८]।

काम्बोदि[दी][१९] पूर्णरागश्च स्वरैः सर्वे[वैः] समर्पितैः[२०]।। १२६।।

---

१. G89- ********, G38, Sp -सळंगराग

२. T65, G86- संपूर्ण, G89- संपूर्णा

३. G38, Sp- पंचमादिस्तदेवतः

४. G38, Sp- वन्सन्तरि

५. G38, Sp- षाडवो राग

६. G86, G89- न्यातिदि, G38- न्म्यादि, G38- ह्यादि

७. G38, Sp- षाडवौ

८. T65- वर्ज

९. G89, G38, Sp- ललित

१०. G38, Sp- षाडवौ

११. G89- ******, G38- न्म्यादि, Sp- ह्यादि

१२. G86- वर्जं, G89- ******

१३. T65- भज स्वरः, G38- रि सः स्वरः, Sp- रस स्वरः

१४. T65- संपूर्णाः, G38, Sp -सम्पूर्ण

१५. G86, G38- सषड्जदिरुदाहृतं, SP- सषड्जातिरुदाहृतं

१६. T65- आहरीश्च, G86, G89- आहिरिश्च

१७. T65- पूर्णरागास्यात्, G86- पूर्णारागस्यात्

१८. T65, G96, G89- प्रकीर्तिताः

१९. G38, Sp- कांभोज

२०. G86- स्वरैस्सर्वेः स्समर्भिधेः, G89-स्वरैः सर्वैः स्समर्भिधेः, G38- स्वरै स्वरै समुज्जतैः, Sp- स्वरै स्वरै समुद्भितैः

[१]वौडवो[बङ्गालो] षाडवौ[वो] राग[गो]

न्यादि वर्जो[वर्ज्यो] म स[च] स्वरः।

[२]गौ[बौ]ली षाडवरागश्च न्यादि वर्जो[वर्ज्यौ]

वसस्वराः [गमौ स्वरौ][३] ।। १२७ ।।

भूपाल[लः] षाड्वो[४] रागो गादि

षड्जादिवर्जितः [षड्जविवर्जितः][५]।

[६]बलहंसे श्र संपूर्ण[बलहम्सा च सम्पूर्णा][७]

गान्धारादि प्रकीर्तिताः[ता] ।। १२८ ।।

नारायणी निषादादि औडवः परिकीर्तितः।

धैवतो[८] पञ्चमश्चैव[९] स्वरौ वर्जो[वर्ज्यौ][१०] यथा क्रमम्।। १२९ ।।

शङ्कराभरणो[११] रागः[१२] सम्पूर्णो[१३] गादिरुच्यते।

---

१. T65, G89,V08 - v.127ab is missing. In G86, v.127ab is seen after v.129ab. Since v.129 defines the rāga nārāyaṇī, this has been shifted here.

२. G38, Sp- v.127cd - v.129ab are missing.

३. G86-व्यादिवर्जो वस्स्वराः, G89-व्यादि वर्जा वसस्वराः, V08-प्रौळिष्षाडव रागस्यादिवर्जो समस्वरा The suggestions made here are based on the description given in the commentary.

४. V08- औडवो

५. G86,G89- वर्जिताः, V08- मध्यमादि प्रकीर्तितः

६. V08- v.128cd is missing

७. G89- *********** पूर्ण, T65- बहलंसस्च ससंपूर्णः

८. G38, Sp- दैवत

९. G86, G89- पंच्चलोचैव

१०. G86, G89- स्वरावर्जं, G38, Sp- स्वरवद्य, T65- स्वरावर्जा

११. G86, G89- शंकराभरणा, G38- शंकरःबरणो

१२. G86- राग **, Sp- राग

१३. G86- ****, G89-संपूर्ण, G38- सम्पूर्ना

हिन्दोलः[१] षाडवश्चैव[२] रि वर्जो[वर्ज्यो][३] मध्यमादिकः[४] ।। १३० ।।

[५]एवं प्रधानरागास्युः[स्स्युः][६] लक्षणोक्तं[७] यथा[८] क्रमम्।

अनन्तास्युति[सन्ति][९] सन्दर्भ[र्भाः][१०] रागासङ्कीर्णरूपिणः[११] ।। १३१ ।।

టీకా:- ఈ తీరున[१२] దేవతలు[१३] తమ నామధేయాల[१४] చేత 32[१५] రాగాలని[१६] చెప్పి □ికి □త్రా(త్రు)లు[१७] 64 అని చెప్పి ఈ రాగభేదాలు[१८] చేత అనంత రాగాలని[१९] చెప్పినారు. అది ఏ తీరునంటె(టే)ను[२०].

---

१. G86,G89-इन्द्वोळ, T65- वान्दोळ, G38-****, Sp- हिन्दोळ

२. G38, Sp- षाडवौश्चैव, V08- षाडवश्चैवं

३. G86- रि वर्जि, G89- रि वर्ज, T65- रु वर्जा, V08- रिवर्जा

४. Sp- मध्यमादितः

५. cf. SM 1,3,50cd-51ab, 51c

६. G38, Sp- रागस्यु, V41- रागाश्च

७. G38- लक्षमोक्तं, Sp- अक्षरोक्तं

८. V41- यधा

९. G86-अनंत्तानन्ति, G89-******, G38-अतान्सति, Sp-अनन्तंसति, V08- अनंतास्संति, V41- अनंताति

१०. G86, Sp, V41 - सन्दर्भा, G38- सन्दभां

११. G86-रागसंकीर्ण ****, G38-रागसंकीनरूपिणिः, Sp-रागसंकीर्णरूपिणि, V08- रागाः संकीर्णरूपिणः , V41- रागास्संकीर्णरूपकाः

१२. V41- రీతున

१३. T65, G86, G89, Sp- దేవతులు

१४. G38, V41-నామధేయముల, Sp- నామధేయాల

१५. T65- missing, V41- షాడవౌడవ సమ్పూర్ణరాగములు రాగభేధాలు

१६. G38- రాగములను

१७. G38- వాటికి □త్రలు, Sp- □ికి □త్రలు, V41- missing

१८. G86- రాగాలు భేదాల, G89- missing from అని, G38- రాగభేదముల

१९. G38- రాగములని

२०. G38- అ□తీరునయనగా

काम्बोदि[दी][१] पञ्चधा प्रोक्ता[२] नाटः[३] पञ्चविध स्मृतः[४]।

[५]वरालि[ली] सप्तधा चैव अष्टौ[६] गौलमिति स्मृतः[७]।

धन्याशी[८] द्विविधा चैव[९] रागभेदाः[१०] प्रकीर्तिताः[११] ।। १३२।।

టీకా:- కాంబోది 5[१२], నాట 5[१३], వరాళి 7, గౌళ 8, ధన్యాశి 2[१४], ఇట్లు[१५] రాగాలు[१६] ప్రకాశార్థం[१७] కొరకు భేదాలాయను గనకే[१८], సు(శు)ద్ధ[ ]త్రసంకీర్ణాల[१९] చేత అనంతరాగాలని[२०] చెప్పబడును[२१]. ఈ రాగాలు[२२] స్వరూపకథనం చెప్పెను[२३].

१. G38-कांभोन्धि, Sp-काम्भोदि, G17-काम्भोदी, V08,V41- कांभोजी, G86- **बोदि
२. V08- विप्रा
३. T65, G38, Sp- नाट, V08, V41- नाटा
४. G89-पञ्चविधास्मृतः, G38,Sp-पञ्चविधा श्रुतः, V08-पञ्चविधा स्मृताः, B13-पञ्चविधः स्मृतः
५. V08- वराळीचाष्टधाचैव सप्त गौळमिति स्मृतम्
६. Sp- अष्ट
७. G86- गवुलमिति स्मृताः, G89- गौ********, G38, Sp- श्रुतः, B13- श्रुताः
८. G89- **** शि, V08- धन्यास, G17, V41- धन्यासी, B13- धनायासी
९. T65, G98, G17, B13,G86, G38, Sp- द्विविधाश्चैव तु
१०. T65, G38, Sp- रागभेदा
११. G38, Sp- प्रकीर्तितः
१२. G38- కాంభోది 2, Sp- కాంభోది 7
१३. T65- missing
१४. G86- 3
१५. G86- ****,T65, G89, Sp - ఇట్ల
१६. G38- రాగములు
१७. G86- ప్రకారమ, G89- ప్రకారం, Sp- ప్రకాసార్థ, V41- ప్రకాశము
१८. G89- భేదాలా *****, G38, Sp- భేదాలాయా గనుక
१९. G86- సుద్ధ[ ]త్రసంకీర్ణల, G89-****[ ]త్రసంకీర్ణాల, G38- సుధ[ ]త్రసంకీర్ణరాగముల, Sp- సుద్ధ[ ]త్రసంకీర్నరాగాల
२०. G38- రాగములని
२१. G38, Sp, V41- చెప్పబడెను
२२. G38- రాగములకు, V41- గములకు
२३. T65, G86, G89-చెప్పుమా, G38- చెప్పెదను, V41- చేప్పము

[1]विप्रा[2] भैरवि[व]भूपाल[लौ][3] क्षत्रिया[त्रौ][4] श्रि[श्री]रागपञ्चरि[ञ्जरौ][5] ।**

वैश्या[यौ][6] वसन्तमालव्यो[यौ][7] शूद्रौ[8] बङ्गालनाटकौ[9] ।। १३३ ।।

టీకా:- [10]ఇ☐[11] రాగాలకు జాతులు.

श्वेतौ[12]भैरवि[व]भूपालौ[13] रक्तो[क्तौ][14] श्रि[श्री]रागपञ्जरौ[15] ।

पीतौ वसन्तमालव्यौ[16] कृष्णौ[17] बङ्गालनाटकौ[18] ।। १३४ ।।

టీకా:- ఇ☐రాగాలకు వర్ణములు[19].

शंभुर्विष्णुश्शारदा[20] च[21] [विष्णुश्च शारदा][22] लक्ष्मीभास्करनारदाः[23] ।

---

१. G98, G17, B13 - v.133 - v.154 are missing
२. G38, Sp- विप्र
३. T65,G38,Sp,V41-भैरविभूपाळं
४. G38, Sp- क्षत्रियो, G89- ******, V41-क्षत्रिये
५. G38, Sp- रागमञ्जरि, V41- रागपंजरः
६. G38, Sp- वश्या
७. G86, G89- वसन्तमाळस्या, Sp- वसन्थमाळव्यो, V41- मालक्यौ
८. G38, Sp- शूद्र, V41-शूद्रा
९. G86, G38, Sp- बगाळनाटक
१०. T65 reads this after v.133ab
११. G38, Sp- missing, T65, G86, G89- ఇది
१२. G38, Sp - श्वेतो
१३. G86- भैरविभूपालो
१४. G38, Sp - रक्त
१५. G89, Sp - स्त्रीरागपंजरि, G38- स्त्रीरागवंजरि, G86, T65- श्रिरागपंजरि
१६. G89- ******, G38, Sp- पीत वसन्तमाळ, V41- मालक्यौ
१७. G38, Sp- कृष्टौ, T65,G86, G89-कृष्णा
१८. G89- बंगाळनाटका, Sp - रिङ्गाळनाटकः G38, T65, G86- बङ्गाळनाटकः
१९. G86, G89, T65- రాగాలకు వర్ణం, G38- రాగములు కర్ణము రాగములకు దేవతులు, Sp- రాగాల వర్ణం రాగాలకు దేవతులు
२०. G86- शंभुर्विष्णुश्चारदा, T65-शंप्रुर्विष्णुशारदा , G38, Sp- शंभोर्विष्णुशारदा
२१. G86, G89, T65- चा
२२. The reading in the Mss does not conform to metrical rules and hence it is being suggested thus.
२३. T65 - लक्ष्मिप्रास्करनारदा, G86, G89 - लक्ष्मिप्रास्करनारदः, G38, Sp- लक्ष्मीभास्करनारदः

गणेशस्तुम्बुरूर्देवाः[१] रागाणां[२] परिकीर्तिताः[३] ।। १३५ ।।

టీకా:- ఇ□[४] రాగాలకు దేవతలు[५].

मोदकं ब[भ]क्ष्य [६]शुद्धान्नं[७] दध्यन्नं[८] पायसं फलम् ।

चित्रान्नं[९]च पयोन्नं[१०] च रागानां[णां]भोजनं स्मृतम्[११] ।। १३६ ।।

టీకా:- (ఇ□) రాగాలకు భోజనం[१२].

श्वेतश्चित्रो[१३] रक्तनीलौ[१४] हरिद्रापीतवासना[कम्][१५] ।

नववस्त्र[स्त्रं] पट्टवस्त्रं[१६] रागाणां वस्त्रमीरितम्[१७] ।। १३७ ।।

టీకా:-(ఇ□) రాగాలకు వస్త్రం[१८].

---

१. T65-गनेशस्तुंबुरोदेवः, G86,G89-गनेशस्तुंबुरो देवाः, G38-गनेशस्तुंबुणादेवा, Sp-गनेशस्तुम्बुरोदेवा

२. G38,Sp- रागानां

३. G38, Sp- परिकीर्तितः

४. T65, G86, G89, G38, Sp- missing

५. T65- దే□లు, G89- *****, G86, G38- దేవతులు

६. G38, Sp - मोदुकंभक्ष्य, V41-मोदकं शुद्ध

७. T65- सिद्धान्न, G86-शुद्धान्न, G38- शुधानां, Sp- शुद्धानां, V41-भक्ष्यान्नं

८. T65, G86, G89- दध्यन्न, G38, Sp- दध्यानां

९. T65-तित्रान्नं, G38-चित्रानां

१०. G86,G89-षयोन्नं, G38-प्रवयोन्नं

११. G38- भोजनस्कृतः, Sp- भोजनसृतं

१२. V41- ఇ□రాగాలకు భోజనములు

१३. G86- श्वेतश्चोत्रो

१४. T65, G86, G89- रक्तनील, G38, Sp- रक्तनीला

१५. T65- वाससा, G89-********, G38- पितवासस, Sp- पितवासन, V41-पितवाससः

१६. G86 - नववस्त्रः पट्टौवस्त्रः, G89 - *******वस्त्रः, G38 - नववस्त्रापटुवस्त्र, Sp-नववस्त्रावटुवस्त्र

१७. G38- वस्त्रमीरितः

१८. G86, G89- ఇది రాగానికి వస్త్రం, G38- రాగములకు వస్త్రములు, Sp- రాగాలకు వస్త్రాలు, V41- ఇ□రాగాలకు వస్త్రములు

कर्पूररोचनं[१]गन्धं कस्तूर्यगरुकुङ्कुमम्।

कदम्बं[२] च सुगन्धं[३] च रागाणां लेपनं वदेत्[४] ।। १३८ ।।

టీకా:- ఇ□[५] రాగాలకు గంధం.

वज्रमुक्ताफलो नील[६]माणिक्यपुष्य[ष्य]राग च[७]।

गोमेधि[द]कश्च[८] वैडूर्यं[९] पद्मरागश्च[१०] भूषणम् ।। १३९ ।।

టీకా:- ఇ□[११] రాగాలకు భూషణాలు.

गदाखड्गौ[१२] शार्ङ[ङ्र्ग]कुन्तौ[१३] शरचापहलायुधम्[१४]।

परशुर्भिण्डिवालश्च[१५] रागाणां आयुधं वदेत् ।। १४० ।।

టీకా:- ఇ□[१६] రాగాలకు ఆయుధాలు.

---

१. G86,G89- गोरोचनं, T65- कांचनं

२. G38, Sp- कन्दंप्र

३. T65- अनुगन्दं, G38, Sp- सुगन्धम्स्य, G86, G89 - सुनन्दं

४. G38- देवकम्वदेत्, Sp- लेपनंवदत्

५. T65, G86, G89- ఇది, G38, Sp- missing

६. G38, Sp- नीला

७. V41- वज्रमुक्तोत्पलो नील माणिक्यं पुष्यरागकं

८. G86- गोमेधि **च्च, Sp- गोमेधकश्च

९. G38, Sp- वैडूर्य

१०. G86- ***** षणं, G38, Sp- पद्मरागस्य, V41- पद्मरागाश्च

११. G86, G89- ఇది, T65, G38, Sp-missing

१२. T65- गदाखड्गा, G38- गजषड्ग, Sp- गजकड्ग

१३. T65- शार्ङकुन्दा, G38- शाञ्निकुन्त, Sp- शार्ङ्गिकुन्त

१४. G86,G89-चरचापहलायन्धः, G38- शरगावललायुधा, Sp- शरडापहलायुध, V41- शरचापहलायुधः

१५. G38- परशुर्भिडिवालश्च, Sp- परशुर्प्रिडिवालश्च

१६. T65, G86, G89- ఇది, G38,Sp- missing

मल्लिका जाजि[ति][१] वकुल[२] कुन्दश्चम्पककेतकी[३]।

द्रोणश्च पारिजातश्च रागाणां कुसुमां[मं] वदेत्[४] ।। १४१ ।।

టీకా:-ఇ□[५] రాగాలకు పువ్వులు[६].

हंसो बर्हिशारिका च[७] भेरुण्डो[८] कोकिलश्शुकः[९]।

चक्रवाहश्चकोरश्च[१०] रागाणां[११] वाहनं वदेत्[१२] ।। १४२ ।।

టీకా:- ఇ□[१३] రాగాలకు వాహనాలు.

द्राक्षकण्टक[१४]खर्जूर[१५]कपित्थश्चूतदाडिमाः[१६]।

कदली नारीकेलश्च[१७] रागाणां[१८] फलवृक्षकाः[१९] ।। १४३ ।।

---

१. G38- प्राजि
२. T65- वकुळा, G86, G89- ****, V41- मुकुल
३. T65-कुन्दचम्पककेतकैः, G86-***द्दंशचम्पककेतकः, G89-*****चम्पककेतकि, G38- कुन्दश्चम्पकखि***, Sp- कुन्दश्चम्पकखेतकि
४. G89-न्वदेत् , G38- स्वदेत्
५. T65, G86, G89- ఇది, G38, Sp- missing
६. G86,G89- పూలు, Sp- పూవులు, V41- రాగముకు బూలు
७. T65, G86, G89-शारिकं च, G38- चारिक च, Sp- चारिकश्च
८. G38, Sp- भरुन्डो
९. T65, G38- कोकिलशुकः, G86- कोकिलश्चुकः
१०. G89- ****** , T65, G86- चक्रवाकचकोरच, Sp - चक्रवारश्चकोरश्च, V41- चक्रवाकश्चकोरश्च
११. G86-रा ** णां, G38, Sp- रागानां
१२. Sp- वदत्
१३. G86, G89- ఇది, T65, G38, Sp- missing
१४. T65- द्राक्षाखण्डकि, G86, G89- द्राक्षाखंटळि, G38- द्राक्षकंठकी, Sp- द्राक्षकंठकि
१५. G86, G89- खर्जूरा
१६. T65 - कपित्थश्चूतदाडिमा, G86, G89-कपिद्दश्चूतंचदाळिमा, G38, Sp - कप्पिधाश्चुतदाडिम्म
१७. G86, G89, G38, Sp - नारीकेलश्च कदलि, V41- नारीकेळश्च कदळी, Though according to commentary, नारीकेल should precede कदलि, (in the order in which it is specified for the rāga), the present reading seems to be better with respect to metre.
१८. G38, Sp- रागानां
१९. T65, G86, Sp-फलवृक्ष च, G89- *******, G38-फलवृक्ष चा

టీకా:- ఇ□[१] రాగాలకు ఫలవృక్షాలు[२].

जम्बूशाककुशा[श][३]क्रौञ्च[४]पुष्करश्वेतशाल्मली[५] ।

द्वीपाश्चनवखण्डाश्च[६] रागाणां[७] देशमीरितम्[८] ।। १४४ ।।

టీకా:- ఇ□[९] రాగాలకు దేశాలు[१०].

करुण[११]वीरश्रृङ्गार[१२]प्रीब[भ]त्स[१३]भयमद्भुतम्[१४] ।

हास्यशान्तरसाश्चैव[१५] रागाणां[१६] रसमीरितम्[१७] ।। १४५ ।।

టీకా:- ఇ□[१८] రాగాలకు రసాలు.

जलोदको[कौ]त्तराभाद्र[१९] उत्तरारोहिणीमखा[घा] [२०] ।

---

१. T65, G86, G89- ఇది, G38, Sp- missing

२. T65- పువ్వుల వృక్షాలు

३. G86- ******* क कुच, G89- जन्बू शाक कुच, G38,Sp- जेम्भो शाख कुशः, V41- जम्बोशाककुशा

४. G38, Sp- क्रंच

५. G86,G89-पुष्कश्वेतश्च शाल्मलि, G38-षुष्करः श्वेतशाल्मदि, Sp-पुष्करश्वेतसाल्मदि

६. T65- द्वीपाश्चनप्रखण्डाश्च, G38- दीपाश्चनदखण्डाश्च, Sp- दीपाश्चनवखण्डाश्च

७. Sp- रागानाम्

८. G86- दशमीरितः, G89- दे*****तः

९. G86, G89- ఇది, T65, G38, Sp- missing

१०. G38, Sp- ద్వీపాంత్ర దేశాలు

११. T65, G86, G89- करुणा

१२. G38- श्रुंगारौ, Sp- श्रुङ्गारा

१३. G86, G89- भीबत्सा, G38- भीबत्सौ, Sp- भीभत्सौ

१४. G86- भयवद्भुता, G89- भयवद्वता, G38, Sp- भयमद्भुता

१५. G86- हास्यंशान्तंरसाश्चैव, G89- हास्यंशान्तरसाश्चैव, G38- आस्यशान्तारसाश्चैव, Sp- आश्यसान्तरसाश्चैव

१६. G86, G89- रा *****, G38, Sp- रागानां

१७. G86, G89- रसमीरितः

१८. T65, G86, G89- ఇది, G38, Sp- missing

१९. T65,G86-जलोडकोत्तराभात्रा, G89-जलोडकोत्तराभाद्र G38- जललोदकोतराभाद्रा, Sp- जललोदकोत्तराभाद्रा It is interesting to note that some of the stars are indicated here through their respective dēvatā-s, like jala and udaka (water) for pūrvāṣāḍhā, mitra (Sun) for anurādhā. The days and lagna specified in the following verses are also in accordance with the stars.

२०- T65- रोहिणोमखा, G86- रोहिणिमखा, G38, Sp- रोहिणिमख

मूला[१] मैत्रा जन्मतारा[२] रागाणां[३] च क्रमाद्वदेत्[४] ।। १४६ ।।

టీకా:- ఇ□[५] రాగాలకు జన్మనక్షత్రాలు.

गुरुवारं सौम्यवारं[६] भृगुवारं[७] रविस्तथा ।

गुरुभौमा[८] जन्मवारा[रं][९] रागाणां[१०] च क्रमाद्वदेत्[११] ।। १४७ ।।

టీకా:- ఇ□[१२] రాగాలకు జన్మవారాలు[१३].

धनुषीमीन[१४]कन्या च वृषभो[१५] सिंह्म[सिंह]राशि च[१६] ।

चापवृचि[श्चि]कराशौ[१७] च रागाणां[१८] लग्नमीरितम् ।। १४८ ।।

టీకా:- ఇది[□][१९] రాగాలకు లగ్నాలు[२०].

---

१. G86-मूल

२. G38, Sp- मैत्रजन्मतार, V41- मैत्रौ जन्मतारा

३. G38, Sp- रागानां

४. G38- क्रद्वेदेत्

५. G86, G89- ఇది, T65, G38, Sp- missing

६. G86- गुरुवारं *******, G89- ****सौम्यवारं, G38, Sp- गुरुवारसौम्यवारं , V41- गुरुवारस्सौम्यवारः

७. T65, G86, G38, Sp- भ्रृगु वारं, V41- भृगुवारो

८. T65, G86, G89 -गुरुवारं, Sp- गुरुधौमा

९. G86, G89- जेन्मवार G38, Sp- जन्मवार

१०. G38, Sp- रागानां

११. G86,G89-क्रमोद्वदेत्, G38-क्रमाध्यते, Sp-क्रमाध्यत, V41 reads differently thus: भौमवारो जन्मवारः चन्द्रवारः क्रमाद्वदेत्।।

१२. G86, G89- ఇది, T65, G38, Sp- missing

१३. G86,G89- జెన్మవారాలు

१४. T65, G86- धनुषिमीन, G38- धनुर्गमीं, Sp- धनुर्लमीनं

१५. Sp- रिषभो

१६. G89- सिं *****, G38, Sp- सिम्हहार च

१७. G86-चापवृश्चिकराशै, T65-चापवृच्चिकरासौ, G38-छापवृश्चिकराळौ, Sp-चारुवृश्चिकराळौ, V41-breaks off here.

१८. T65,G86,G38,Sp- रागानां

१९. G86- ****, T65,G38,Sp- missing

२०. T65,G38,Sp- రాసులు

द्विचतुष्पञ्च[1] सङ्ख्या च[2] रागाणां[3] आननं वदेत् ।
चतुरष्टौदशा[4] सङ्ख्या[5] रागाणां[6] बाहुरीरितः[7] ।। १४९ ।।

టీకా:- (ఇ□)రాగాలకు బాహువులు[8].

चतुर्वसुदशश्रोत्रा[त्रं][9] रागाणां[10] नेत्रमीरितम् ।। १५० ।।
रु[ऋ]ग्वेद भैरविभूप यजु[जुः] श्रीरागपंतिकौ[पञ्जरौ][11] ।
सामवशन्तु[सन्त][12] मालव्यौ[13] खिल बङ्गालनाटकः[कौ][14] ।। १५१ ।।
किन्नरो[15] यक्षकिंपुरुष[पुर्ष]गन्धर्वस्सिद्धतुबु[म्बु]राः[16] ।
देवता नागवंशेषु[17] रागसञ्जातयस्मृ[स्मृ]ताः[18] ।। १५२ ।।
विश्वामित्रवसिष्ट च[श्च][19] गौतमोत्रिभृगुश्शुकः[20] ।

---

१. G86, G89- द्विचतुष्या च, G38- **चतुपंच, Sp- वचतुपंच

२. G38, Sp- सङ्ख्याश्च

३. G38- गाणां, Sp- गानम्

४. T65- चतुरष्टादशा, G38, Sp- चतुरष्टौदशः

५. G38, Sp- संख्य

६. G38, Sp- रागानां

७. G86- बाहुदीरित, G89- बहु ***** , G38, Sp- बाहुमीरितं

८. G38, Sp - బాహులు

९. T65- चतुर्वसुदशश्रोत्रं, G89- चतुर्वसुदशश्रोत्र, G38- चतुर्वसुदेशश्रोत्रः, Sp- चेतुरर्सदेशश्रोत्रः

१०. T65, G86, G38, Sp- रागानां

११. G86-वंतिकौ, T65- भंजिका, G38- मेळज स्त्रीरागपंचक, Sp- यजस्त्रीरागपञ्चक

१२. T65, G86, G89- सामवंशातु, Sp- नामवशन्तु

१३. G86- माळव्ये, G89- मा***, G38, Sp- मानव्यो

१४. G86- नीलबगाळनाटक, G89- *** बगाळनाटका, T65- बिलबगाळनाटक

१५. G38-किन्नेरो

१६. G38-गन्थर्वसिथत्तुम्म्रुरः, Sp- गन्धर्वसिद्धतुम्म्रुरः

१७. T65-वंशेष, Sp- वंसेषु

१८. G86- रागसंजातयस्मृतः, G38- रागासजातयस्मृतः, Sp- रागासंज्ञातयस्रुतः

१९. G38, Sp- वशिष्टा च

२०. T65- गौतमेत्रिभ्रृगुश्शुकः, G86- **तमोत्रि भ्युकश्चकः, G89 -******* शुकः, G38- गौतमोत्रिभ्रृगुश्नुकः

जमदग्नि[1] भरद्वाज रागाणां[2] गोत्रमौनिवत्[मीरितम्][3] ।। १५३ ।।

स्तू[थू]लौ[4] भैरवी[व]भूपालौ[5] समौ[6] श्रीरागपञ्जरौ।

कुंजा[कुबजौ][7] वसन्तमालव्यौ[8] दीर्घ[र्घौ][9] बङ्गालनाटकौ[10] ।। १५४ ।।

टीकाः:- (ఇ□రాగాలకు ఆకారః(రాలు)[11].

[12]భైర□[13] రాగానికి[14] కిన్నరవంశం[15]- బ్రా(బ్రా)హ్మణజాతి- తెల్ల[16] వర్ణం- స్థూలదేహం- 2 ముఖాలు- 4 హస్తాలు[17]- 4 శ్రోత్రాలు -4 నేత్రాలు - □త్స్య□త్రగోత్రం - కుశద్వీప[18]దేశం-

---

१. G86- जेमदग्नि

२. T65- गोत्रमौनिवित्, G89- गोत्रमौनिवात्, G38- गोत्रवनानिवत्, Sp- गोत्रमौनिवद्

३. T65, G86, G38, Sp- रागानां

४. G86, G89- शीता, T65- सीतौ, Sp- स्तूता

५. G86- भैरविभूपाळो, T65, G38, Sp- भैरविभूपाळौ, G89- this verse is repeated.

६. G38- सव, Sp- सपरौ

७. G38- कुम्खा, Sp- कुम्भा

८. G86- माळ **** ,G89- माळव्यो, G38- माळव्य, Sp- माळख्य

९. G89- दीर्सु

१०. T65- भंगाळ नाटकः, G86- भंगाळ नाटका, G38, Sp- भङ्गाळनाटकौ

११. T65- రాగాలంకారః, Sp- యీ రాగాలకు ఆకారం, G38 and Sp read the following colophon, which is not seen in T65, G86 and G89 : G38- మంగళ మహా శ్రీ శ్రీ శ్రీ జేయును. శ్రీ శారదాంబ దే□నమస్తుభ్యం. సంగీతరత్నాకరమందు క్రమ□యం లక్షణగ్రన్థము శ్రీ శ్రీ శ్రీ జేయును. Sp- మంగళ మహా శ్రీ శ్రీ శ్రీ జాయను॥ శ్రీ శారదాంబ దే□నమస్తుభ్యం. శ్రీ జాయను సంగీతరత్నాకరంమందు క్రమ□యం లక్షణగ్రన్థం శ్రీ శ్రీ శ్రీః జాయను

१२. G38, Sp- read the following sentence which is probably the heading seen in the original భైర□రాగం ఛందస్సులు, గోత్రాలు శుభమస్తు. అథా రాగప్రస్తారం. భైర□

१३. The commentary reads the rāga bhairava as bhairavi only.

१४. G38- రాగమునకు

१५. G38- అంశము, Sp- ఆశం

१६. G86,G89, Sp- తెల్లని, G38- తెల్లటి

१७. G86, G89-అస్తాలు

१८. G86- *** శద్వీప

ఈశ్వరుడు దేవత(అధిదేవతా)[१] -ఉడుములు[२] భోజనం- తెల్ల[३]వస్త్రం- కర్పూరగంధం- వజ్రభూషనం(ణం)- గధా(దా)యుధం- మల్లెపూలు[४]- ొసవాొనం[५] - ద్రాక్షావృక్షం[६]-కరుణ రసం[७]- పూర్వాషాడానక్షత్రం[८] - గురువారం[९] - ధనుర్లగ్నం[१०] - ఋగ్వేదఛందస్సు - దేవక్రియ, మేఘరంజి[११], కురంజి[१२] సతులు[१३].

దేవక్రియ 5 స్వరాల[१४] చేత ఔడవ[१५]మని పించుకొనును. నిషాదాది. రి(ఋ)షభ షడ్జమ(షడ్జ)వర్జం[१६]. నినిని - గగగ- మమమ- ధధధ - పపప[१७] -నిగమధప[१८]

మేఘరంజి[१९] 5 స్వరాల చేత ఔడవం[२०] -మధ్యమాది- ధై(ధై)వత[२१]నిషాదవర్జం[२२]

---

१. Sp- దేవతా; The word adhidēvatā is read as atidēvata or dēvata or dēvatā at different places. In order to have consistency, adhidēvatā has been used in the description of all the rāga-s that follows.

२. G89- కుడుముల, G86- *** డుముల, G38, Sp- కుడుములు

३. G86, G89, Sp- తెల్లని, G38- తెల్లటి

४. G38, Sp- మల్ల పుష్పం

५. G89- ొంవాొనం

६. G86, G89- ద్రాక్షవృక్షం, G38,Sp- ద్రాక్షఫలవృక్షం

७. G86- పరుణా ***

८. G38, Sp- పూర్వాషాడ

९. G38, Sp- గురువారం జన్మవారం

१०. G38, Sp- ధనుర్రాసి లగ్నం, G86- *****

११. T65,G86, G89- మేఖరంజి

१२. G86- ****

१३. G38, Sp- add - ఈ ముగ్గురు

१४. G38- స్వరముల 5 స్వరముల, Sp- స్వరాల (5 స్వరాల)

१५. G86- దెవ, G89- దవ

१६. G86- ***

१७. T65- ప

१८. G38, Sp- ని గ మ ప ద ప

१९. T65,G86, G89- మేఖరంజి

२०. G38, Sp - వౌడవ

२१. T65, G86, G38- దేవత

२२. G86- నిషా ***ర్జం

- మమమ- ససస- రిరిరి- గగగ- పపప- మసరిగప.

కురంజి 5 స్వరాలు చేత ఔడవమని[1] పించుకొనును[2] -మధ్యమాది - నిషాదషడ్జ[3]వర్జం-[4]మమమ- రిరిరి- గగగ- ధధధ- పపప- మరిగధప - □రు భైర□స్త్రీలు[5].

భర□ సంపూర్ణరాగం పంచమాది[7]- సప్తస్వరాలు - పపప- ధధధ[8]- నినిని- సస స- రిరిరి- గగగ- మమమ- పధనిసరిగమ. ఈ తీరున శంఖచక్రగదా[9]ఖడ్గధారయై[10] ప్రకాశింపుచుంనుడు (చుండు)ను[11].

భూపాళ రాగానికి[12]- యక్షవంశం- బ్రాహ్మణజాతి[13]- తెల్లనివర్నం(ర్ణం)[14] - □అధిదేవతా[15]-తెల్లవస్త్రం[16]-అపూపభక్ష్యం[17]- గోరోచనగంధం[18]- ముక్తా[19]భూషణం-

१. G38, Sp- వౌడవమని

२. T65, పించు, Sp- పించుకోను

३. T65, G86, G89- omit

४. G86, G89 మమమ నినిని ససస రిరిరి గగగ। -these additional phrases are seen before this line.

५. G38- ఈ 3 మూ శ్రీలు, భైర□ భార్యలు, Sp- యీ 3 శ్రీలు। భైర□ భార్యలు

६. G86- సం * * * * చ్చమాది

७. G38- శ్రీ భైర□

८. T65, G86, G89- మ మ మ

९. G38- గధా

१०. T65, G89- ఖడ్గధారియై, G86- ఖడ్గధారియైర

११. G38,Sp- ప్రకాశింపుచూ యీ భైర□రాగం ముగ్గురు భార్యలతోను, దేవక్రియ, మేఘరంజి, కురంజి □ సతులతో ప్రకాశింపుచు వుండును. భైర□పురుష రాగము – శ్రీ శ్రీ శ్రీ శ్రీ శ్రీ –

१२. G38- రాగమునకు

१३. G38, Sp- బ్రాహ్మణజాతి

१४. G86- తెల్లని వర్నం, G38- తెల్లటి వర్ణము

१५. G89- అధిదేవత

१६. G86, G89- తెల్లని వస్త్రం, G38, Sp- తెల్లటికోక

१७. G38,Sp- కజాయభోజనం

१८. G38,Sp- గోరోజనం గంధం

१९. G38- ముత్యములు, Sp- ముత్యాలు

ఖడ్గాయుధం- జాజిపుష్పం[१]- నెమలివా□నం- పనసవృక్షం[२]- జంబూద్వీప[३]దేశం -□రసం- పూర్వాషాడానక్షత్రం[४]- గురువారం[५]- ధనుర్లగ్నం[६]- నాలుగు ముఖాలు- ఎని□ది భుజాలు- ఎని□ది నేత్రాలు- ఎని□ది శ్రోత్రాలు- వశిష్ఠ[७]గోత్రం- ఋగ్వేద[८]ఛంధస్సు[९]- స్థూల[१०]దే□ం- (వేళా□రి మల□రి బౌళి □ సతులు)[११]

[१२]వేళా□రి[१३]- ఔడవం 5 స్వరాలు[१४]- గాంధారాది- షడ్జ[१५]రి(ఋ)షభవర్జం. గగగ- మమమ- పపప- ధధధ- నినిని[१६]- గమపధని[१७]- మపధని- పధని- ధని- నిధపమగ.

మల□రి[१८] షాడవం- ఆరు స్వరాలు[१९]- దై(ధై)వతాది[२०]- నిషాదవర్జం. ధధధ-

---

१. G86- ****
२. G38, Sp- ఫలవృక్షం
३. G86,G38,Sp- జంభూ ద్వీపదేశం
४. G38, Sp- పూర్వాషాడ జన్మనక్షత్రం
५. G38, Sp- జన్మ వారం గురువారం
६. G38- ధనురాశిలఘ్నము, Sp- ధనుర్రాశిలగ్నం
७. G89- వసిష్ఠ, G86, G38- వశిష్ఠు
८. G38, Sp- రుగ్వేద
९. T65, G86, G89 - చందస్సు
१०. Sp- స్తూల
११. Towards the end of description of each masculine rāga, the names of the three feminine rāga-s are listed at each place. Since it is missing here, the same has been suggested.
१२. G38- వేళావురి, మల□రి, భవుళి, 3 భార్యలు, Sp-వేళావురి మల□రి భవుళి ముగ్గురు భార్యలు (probably the page heading in the original Ms)
१३. G38, Sp- వేళా□రి నడవడిక షడ్జ ****
१४. G38- పౌర * * * * రాలు, Sp- వౌడవం * * * స్వరాలు
१५. G86,G89- షడ్జమ, G38, Sp- షడ్జ***
१६. G38- న న న
१७. G38, Sp - the remaining svara passage is missing.
१८. G38, Sp- మల□రి నడవడిక
१९. G86- షాడ * * * * * స్వరాలు, G38- స్వరములు
२०. G86, G89- దెవజాతి, T65, G38- దేవతాది

ససస- రిరిరి- గగగ- మమమ- పపప- దసరిగమప- సరిగమప- రిగమప- గమప- మప- ప- మగరిసధ.

బౌళి ఔడవం[१] -ఐదు స్వరాలు-నిషాదాది మధ్య(మ)గాంధారవర్జ్యం[२]. [३]నినిని- ససస-రిరిరి- (పపప- ధధధ- నిసరిపధ-) సరిపధ- రిపధ- పధ- ధపరిసని[४]- □రు భ ూపాళానికి సతులు[५].

భూపాళరాగం[६] షాడవం- 6 స్వరాలు- గాంధారాది- షడ్జమ(షడ్జ)వర్జం- [७]గగగ[८]- రిరిరి- మమమ- పపప- ధధధ- నినిని[९]- గరిమపధని- రిమపధని- మపధని- పధని- ధని- నిధపమరిగ- [१०]ఈ తీరున భూపాళ రాగం ప్రకాశించును.

శ్రీరాగం[११]- కింపురుష[१२]వంశం- క్షత్రియజాతి[१३]- రక్త[१४]వర్ణం- సమదేం[१५]- శారదా

---

१. G86- వౌడవం
२. T65- మధ్యమ వర్జ్యం, G86- ****వర్జ్యం, G89- మధ్యమ ***, Sp- మధ్య గాంధారి వర్జం
३. G38, Sp- add దాని నడవడిక
४. G38, Sp- ధ। ధ రి స ని
५. G86- సవ్రతులు, G38- □ళ్లు భూపాళ సతులు, Sp- □రులు భూపాళం సతులు
६. G86- భూళం రాగం, G38- భూపాళము రాగమునకు, Sp- భూపాళం రాగానకు
७. G38, Sp- add దాని నడవడిక
८. G86- ***
९. G38, Sp-add ససస
१०. T65 - missing, G38- యీ తీరున భూపాళ రాగమునకు వేళాఁరి మలఁరి జాతి ముగ్గురు భార్యలతో కలసి ప్రకాశించును. యీ తీరున భూపాల రాగం ప్రకాశించును. ఇది పురుషుడు. Sp- యీ తీరున భూపాళ రాగానకు వేళాఁరి మలఁరి భౌళి ముగ్గురు భార్యలతో కలశి ప్రకాశించును. యీ తీరున భూపాల రాగం ప్రకాశించును. యీ రెండు యీ పురుషుడు.
११. G38- స్త్రీరాగమునకు, Sp- స్త్రీ రాగానకు
१२. G38, Sp- పురుషవంశం
१३. G86- వం**త్రియజాతి, G38, Sp- క్ష త్రి జాతి
१४. G38- యుర్రటి, Sp- ఎఱ్ఱని
१५. G89- శారద అధిదేవత, G38- శారదాదే□అధిదేవతా, Sp- సారదాదే□అధిదేవతా. G38 and Sp read the following, which is probably an interpolation of the page heading/marginal marks from the original: G38- స్త్రీరాగము స్త్రీరాగము అనునది పురుషవంశము; భార్యలు ముగ్గురు. ఁందోళము, బలఁంస, సావెరి Sp-(స్త్రీరాగం అనెది పురుషవంశం, భార్యం ముగ్గురు. ఁందోళం, బలఁంస, సావెరి

అధిదేవతా- ఘృతాన్న[౧]భోజనం- రక్త[౨]వస్త్రం- శ్రీగంధం- నీల[౩]భూషణం- శాంఙ్గాయుధం[౪]- గోరువంక[౫] వాహనం-ఖర్జూరవృక్షం[౬]- వకుళ పుష్పం[౭]- శాకద్వీపదేశం[౮]- శృంగారరసం- గౌతమగోత్రం- గురువారం[౯]- ఉత్తరాభాద్రనక్షత్రం[౧౦]- □సలగ్నం[౧౧]- [౧౨]యజుర్వేదఛందస్సు- 5 ముఖాలు- 10 హస్తాలు[౧౩]- పది శ్రోత్రాలు- పది నేత్రాలు- హిందోళం[౧౪], బలహంస, సాహురి(సావేరి) స్త్రీలు[౧౫].

హిందోళం[౧౬]- షాడవం- 6 స్వరాలు[౧౭]- మధ్యమాది- రి(ఋ)షభవర్జం. మమమ- ససస- గగగ- పపప- ధధధ- నినిని- మసగపధని- సగపధని- గపధని- పధని- ధని- నిధపగసమ[౧౮].

---

౧. G38, Sp- నేయివంటక

౨. G38- యెఱ్ఱటికోక, Sp- ఎఱ్ఱనికోక

౩. G38- నీలములరత్న, Sp-నీలాలరత్న

౪. G38- శాంఙ్నిమాయుధము, Sp- శారంగిమాయుధం

౫. G89- *****

౬. G38, Sp- ఫలవృక్షం

౭. G38, Sp- వళపువ్వులు

౮. G86- శాక *** దేశం, G38, Sp- శాఖదీపదేశం

౯. G38, Sp- గురువారం జన్మవారం, G86- **** వాహనం, G89- గరుడవాహనం

౧౦. G38, Sp- జంమనక్షత్రం

౧౧. G38, Sp-□రాశి లఘ్నం

౧౨. G38, Sp - add సమదేహం. a repetition since it is already mentioned after 'varṇaṃ'

౧౩. G86-అస్తాలు, G38, Sp- పన్దిస్తనాలు

౧౪. G86- ఇందోలి

౧౫. T65-****, G38- హిందోళము బలహంస జరి; స్త్రీలు 3 గురు శ్రీరాగమునకు □ల్లు భార్యలు, Sp- హిందోళం భలహం సావేరి స్త్రీలు ముగ్గురు శ్రీరాగానకు □ల్లు భార్యలు. The names of the feminine rāga-s are not consistent; See Introduction for detailed discussion of this.

౧౬. G38, Sp- హిందోళం నడవడిక

౧౭. G86- స్వ***

౧౮. G38- splitting differs thus:- ని, ద ప గ స మ

బలూంస[1]- సంపూర్ణం- ఏడు స్వరాలు[2]- గాంధారాది. గగగ- నినిని- సససమమమ- పపప- ధధధ[3]- రిరిరి- గనిసమపధరి[4]- నిసమపధరి- సమపధరి- మపధరి- పధరి- ధరి- రిధపమసనిగ[5]

[6]సావేరి రాగం- ఔడవం- మధ్యమాది- రి(ఋ)షభనిషాదాలు వర్జం. మమమ- పపప-ధధధ- సస స- గగగ[7]- మపధసగ- పధసగ- ధసగ- సగ- గసధపమ[8]- శ్రీరాగానకు(నికి)[9] [దు] సతులు[10].

శ్రీరాగం- షాడవం- 6 స్వరాలు- దై(ధై)వతాది- రి(ఋ)షభవర్జం. [11]ధధధ- నినిని- సస స- గగగ- మమమ- పపప- ధనిసగమప- నిసగమప- సగమప[12]- గమప- మప[13].

పడమంజరి రాగానికి[14]- గంధర్వవంశం[15]- క్షత్రియజాతి[16]- ఎ(ర)వర్నం(ర్ణం)[17]-

---

१. G86- బలూం, G89- బలూంసం

२. G38- స్వరములది, Sp- స్వారాలది

३. T65- గగ - నిని - సస- మమ- పప- ధధధ missing from here upto the next ధధధ in sāvērī, G86, G89- గగ - నిని - సస- మమ- పప- ధధధ

४. G86, G89- గ ని స మ ప ధ ని

५. G86, G89- రి ధ ప మ స రి గ

६. T65 - missing

७. G38, Sp- ధ ధ ధ

८. T65,G86,G89- సగధపమ

९. G38- శ్రీరాగమునకు, Sp- స్త్రిరాగానకు

१०. G38, Sp- యీ ముగ్గురు సతులు

११. G38, Sp- add దీని నడవడిక స్వరం

१२. T65- గ స మ ప

१३. G38- ఈ ప్రకారం శ్రీరాగం ముగ్గురు భార్యలతో కలసి ప్రకాశించును - శ్రీశ్రీశ్రీశ్రీ - Sp- యీ ప్రకారం శ్రీ రాగం। పడవంజరి ముగ్గురు భార్యలతోడి। ముగ్గురు భార్యలతో కలశి ప్రకాశించును.

१४. G38- పడవంజరి ముగ్గురు భార్యలతోడి (page heading of the original) పడమంజిరి రాగము, Sp- పడవంజరి రాగం

१५. T65, G86, G89- గాంధర్వ వంశం

१६. G89- క్షత్రిజాతి

१७. G86,G89- యర్రని వర్ణం, G38- ఎర్రటివర్ణము; లక్ష్మిదేవత, Sp- ఎఱ్ఱనివర్ణం లక్ష్మీదేవతా- this portion is seen after భుధవారం

లక్ష్మి (అధి)దేవతా[౧]- దధ్యాన్నం భోజనం- కస్తూరిగంధం- మాణిక్య[౨] భూషణం- కుంతాయుధం[౩]- మొల్లపూలు[౪]- గండభేరుండ[౫] వాౕనం- వెలగవృక్షం[౬]- క్రౌంచద్వీపదేశం[౭]- భీ(బీ)భత్సరసం- ఉత్తరానక్షత్రం[౮]- బుధవారం[౯]- కన్యాలగ్నం[౧౦]- రెండు ముఖాలు[౧౧]- 4 భుజాలు- 4 నేత్రాలు- 4 శ్రోత్రాలు- అత్రిగోత్రం[౧౨]- యజుర్వేదఛందస్సు[౧౩]- సమ[౧౪] దేౕం- నల్లని[౧౫]కోక- తోడి, లలిత, దేశి □ల సతులు[౧౬] . దేశి[౧౭]- షాడవం- 6 స్వరాలు- దై(ధై)వతాది[౧౮]- నిషాద[౧౯] వర్జం. ధధధ- ససస- రిరిరి- గగగ- మమమ- పపప- ధసరిగమప- సరిగమప- రిగమప- గమప- మప- పమగరిసధ[౨౦].

---

౧. G89- లక్ష్మిదేవత

౨. Sp- మాణిక్యం

౩. Sp- కుండాయుధం

౪. G38, Sp- మల్య పుష్పం

౫. T65- గేడభేరుండ, G38- ఘండభేరండము, Sp- ఘుండజరండం

౬. G38, Sp- ఫలవృక్షం

౭. T65, G86, G89 - ద్వీపం.

౮. G38, Sp - ఉత్తరజన్మనక్షత్రం

౯. G38, Sp- బుధవారంజన్మవారం

౧౦. G38, Sp- కన్యారాశి లఘ్నం

౧౧. G86, G89- 4 ముఖాలు, Sp- 2 ముఖము

౧౨. T65 - missing

౧౩. G86- యజుర్వె ** చందస్సు

౧౪. G38, Sp- సామ

౧౫. G86- **ల్లని, G38, Sp- నల్లటి

౧౬. T65- తోడి లలిత దేశి □స్సతులు, G86- తో *** లలిత దె*** □ల సతులు, G38- 3 భార్యలు తోడి, దేశి, లలిత □ల సతులు, Sp- ముగ్గురు భార్యలు తోడి దేశి లలిత

౧౭. G89- దే, G38, Sp- దేశి నడవడిక

౧౮. G89- దైతాది

౧౯. T65, G86, G89- రిషభ, G38-నిషాడ

౨౦. T65- సమపమపపమపగరిధప, G38, Sp- సమపమపపమపగరిపధ

లలిత[१] - షాడవం[२]- 6 స్వరాలు[३]- నిషాదాది- గాంధారవర్జం[४]. నినిని- ససస- రిరిరి- మమమ- పపప- ధధధ- నిసరిమపధ- సరిమపధ- రిమపధ- మపధ- పధ- ధపమరిసని.

తోడి- సంపూర్ణం- గాంధారాధి(ది)[५]- గగగ- రిరిరి- ససస- మమమ- పపప- ధధధ- నినిని- [६]గరిసమపధని-[७]రిసమపధని- సమపధని- మపధని- పధని- ధని- (నిధపమసరిగ)[८]

పడమంజరి రాగం[९] - షాడవం[१०]- 6 స్వరాలు- నిషాదాది- రి(ఋ)షభవర్జం- నినిని- ససస- గగగ- మమమ- పపప- ధధధ- నిసగమపధ[११]- సగమపధ- గమపధ[१२]- మపధ- పధ- ధపమగరిసని(ధపమగసని)[१३]

---

१. T65- లలితా, G38, Sp- లలిత నడవడిక

२. T65, G38, Sp- షాడవః

३. G89- స్వరాలకు, G38- స్వరములు

४. G38, Sp- వర్జితం

५. G38, Sp- ఇక తోడి నడవడిక లక్షణం. తోడి సంపూర్ణ రాగం

६. All Mss add the following set of phrases, which is felt redundant T65, G86,G89- రిరి - గగ- మమ- పప- ధధ- నిని, G38, Sp- రిరిరి - గగగ- మమ- పప- ధధ- నిని

७. G86, G89 read once more రిసమపధని -సమపధని T65- రిగసమపధని- సగమపధని- గమధని, G38, Sp- రిసగమపధని- సగమపధని- గమపధని

८. This passage seems to be incomplete, since at all places, it ends with a set of notes in descent and hence this phrase is being suggested.

९. G38, Sp include a sub heading- ఇక పడమంజరి రాగ నడవడిక

१०. T65,G38, Sp - omit

११. G86- * * * గమపధ

१२. T65- గమమధ

१३. ri is an omitted note for this rāga. Since the reading in the Mss include ri in this phrase, this reading has been suggested. G38 and Sp add after this thus:- పండమంజిరి రాగం. యీ రీతిన ప్రకాశించి తోడి దేశి లలిత యీ ముగ్గురు సతులతో కలసి ప్రకాశించివుండురు, Sp- పడవంజరి రాగం యీ రీతి ప్రకాశించి తోడి దేశిక లలిత యీ ముగ్గురు సతులతో కలశి ప్రకాశించు వుదురు.

వసంత[1]రాగానికి-సిద్ధవంశం[2]- వైశ్యజాతి- పీతవర్ణం- భాస్కరదేవత(అధిదేవతా)[3]- ఫలభోజనం- పసురు(పసుపు)కోక- అగరుగంధం[4]- పుష్యరాగభూషణం[5]- ధనుర్భా(ర్బా)ణాయుధం[6]- సంపంగిపూలు[7]- కోకిలవాహనం- మా□డిఫలవృక్షం[8]- పుష్కరద్వీపదేశం[9]- భయరసం[10]- రోహిణినక్షత్రం[11]- శుక్రవారం[12]- వృషభలగ్నం[13]- 4 ముఖాలు- 8 భుజాలు- 8 నేత్రాలు- 8 శ్రోత్రాలు- కుబ్జదేహం[14]- భృగుగోత్రం[15]- సామవేదఛందస్సు[16]- రామక్రియ, వరాళి, కౌశిక - ముగ్గురు సతులు.

[17]రామక్రియ - 5 స్వరాల[18] చేత- ఔడవమని[19] పించుకొనును[20]- గాంధారాది-

---

౧. Sp- వసంతం రాగం, G38- adds the heading from the original thus: వసంతము సతులు

౨. G38- శిదవంశం, Sp- సిధ వంసం

౩. G38, Sp- భాస్కరుడు దేవత

౪. G38-అఘరుగంధము, Sp- అధరుస్త్దం

౫. G86- పుష్యరా ***షాణాలు, G89- పుష్యరాగభూషణాలు

౬. G38- ధనుర్భాణములు ఆయుధము, Sp- ధనుర్భాణలు ఆయుధం

౭. T65- సంపేగిపూలు, G86- సంపంగి***, G38-రుంపంగేవులు, Sp-సంపంగి పువ్వులు, adds the heading from the original thus: వసంతం సతులు రామక్రియ వరాళి

౮. G86- వృక్షం, G89- *****

౯. T65, G86, G89- పుష్కరద్వీపం

౧౦. G86- భయరరసం

౧౧. G38, Sp- add జన్మనక్షత్రం

౧౨. G38, Sp - add జన్మవారం

౧౩. G89- వృభ లగ్నం, G38- వృషభరాశిలఘ్నము, Sp- ఋషభరాశిలగ్నం

౧౪. G86- **** , G89, G38, Sp- కుజ్జ

౧౫. G38- బృగురుషిగోత్రం, Sp- బృగుఋషిగోత్రం

౧౬. G86- సామవేదంచంద్దస్సు

౧౭. G38- రామక్రియ స్వరము నడవడిక, Sp- రామక్రియా స్వరం నడవడిక

౧౮. G86- ఔడవం 5 స్వరాలు, T65- 5 స్వరాలు, G38- 5 స్వరాలు

౧౯. G38, Sp- అవుడవముని

౨౦. T65- పించును

రి(ఋ)షభ[१] వర్జం. [२]గగగ- మమమ- పపప- ధధధ[३]- నినిని- గమపధని- మపధని- పధని- ధని[४]- [५]నిధపమగ.

[६]వరాళి[७]- షాడవం- 6 స్వరాలు- గాంధారాధి(ది)- మధ్యమ[८] వర్జం[९]. [१०]గగగ- ససస- [११]రిరిరి- పపప- ధధధ- నినిని- గసరిపధని- సరిపధని- రిపధని- పధని- ధని- నిధపరిసగ.

కౌశిక పూర్ణరాగం- 7 స్వరాలు[१२]- గగగ- ససస- (రిరిరి-)[१३] మమమ- పపప- ధధధ- నినిని- గసరిగమపధని(గసరిమపధని) [१४] -సరిమపధని[१५]-రిమపధని[१६]-మపధని- పధని-ధని-నిధపమరిసగ[१७]- □ు[१८] వసంత రాగానికి[१९] సతులు.

---

१. G89- వృషభం

२. G38, Sp- add దీని నడవడిక

३. G86- ****ధ

४. Sp- again పధని- ధని (repetition)

५. G86- నిధపమ** , T65- missing

६. T65- missing upto వర్జం - end of this line

७. G38, Sp- ఇక వరాళి

८. G86, G89 - omit

९. G89- ***** , G86- వృభవ

१०. G38,Sp- add 'దీని నడవడిక స్వరం'

११. G86, G89- missing from here upto the next 'ససస', found under kauśika.

१२. G38- ఇక కౌశిక సంపూర్ణ రాగము; సంపూర్ణ 7; Sp- ఇక కౌశిక సంపూర్ణ రాగం సంపూర్ణం G86, G89- missing

१३. Since this is a complete rāga, this svara phrase is being suggested

१४. T65- గరిగమపధని. The Mss read the note 'ga' twice, which could be a scribal error.

१५. T65, G86, G89- స రి గ మ ప ధ ని

१६. G86, G89- రి గ మ ప ధ ని, గ మ ప ధ ని

१७. T65- ని ధ ప మ రి గ స

१८. G38,Sp-□్లు ముగ్గురు

१९. G38- రాగమునకు, Sp- రాగానకు

వసంత రాగానికి- 6 స్వరాలు చేత[१] షాడవం- నిషాదాది- పంచమవర్జం[२]- నినిని- రిరిరి[३]- గగగ- మమమ- ధధధ- ససస- నిరిగమధస[४]- రిగమధస[५]- గమధస- మధస- ధస- నిధమగరిస(సధమగరిని)[६].

మాళ□ రాగానికి[८]- తుంబురువంశం[९]- వైశ్యజాతి- పీతవర్ణం[१०]- నారదుండుదేవత(అధిదేవతా)[११]- పాయసభోజనం- పసుపు[१२]కోక- కుంకుమగంధం- గోమేధి(ద)కభూషణం- ‾లాయుధం[१३]- మొగలిపూలు[१४]- జింక[१५]వా‾నం- దాడిమ[१६]వృక్షం[१७]-

---

१. G86, G89- omit

२. G86- పంచమ వర్జం షాదాది, G89- పంచమ వర్జం నిషాదాది

३. G86, G89- omit

४. G86, G89- రి రి గ మ ధ స

५. G89- reads twice, T65- నిగమదస, Sp- మాళ□పురుషరాగం నారాటి గుండక్రియ ఘుర్జరి సతులు (page heading from the original)

६. G86, G89- ని గ ధ మ గ రి స, T65- రి ధ మ గ రి స, The existing reading in the Mss is not proper; it should probably read the notes in the descending order and hence this reading is suggested. G38, Sp add thus: G38- వసంత రాగం ముగ్గురు సతులతో కూడ ప్రకాశించి వుందురు - శ్రీ శ్రీ శ్రీ శ్రీ శ్రీ - మాళ□పురుష రాగము, నారాణి, గుండక్రియ, ఘుర్జరి, సతులు (page heading from the original), Sp- వసంత రాగం ముగ్గురు సతులతో కూడ ప్రకాశించి వుందురు

७. Sp- ఇఖ మాళ□

८. G38- రాగమునకు

९. G38, Sp- తుంబురవంశం

१०. T65- పీత వర్ణం పీత వర్ణం

११. G86, G89- నారదుడు దేవత

१२. T65, G86, G89- పసరు

१३. G38-అలాయుధము, G86, G89-missing

१४. G38- మోగలి పువ్వులు, G86, G89-missing

१५. G86- శింక్క, G38, Sp- చిలుక

१६. G38- దాడి□

१७. T65, G38, Sp- వృక్షం, G89- ****

శ్వేతద్వీపదేశం[१]- అద్భుతరసం-మఖా(ఘా)నక్షత్రం[२]- ఆదివారం[३]- సింహలగ్నం[४]- ఐదు ముఖాలు- పది భుజాలు- పది నేత్రాలు- పది శ్రోత్రాలు- కుబ్జ దేహం[५]- సామవేదఛందస్సు[६]- శౌనక[७]గోత్రం- నారాయణి, గుండక్రియ[८], ఘుర్జరి[९]- □రు[१०] సతులు.

నారాయణి[११]-ఔడవం[१२]-5 స్వరాలు- నిషాదాది[१३] -దై(ధై)వతపంచమవర్జం[१४]- నిని- సస[१५]- రిరి- గగ- మమ- నిసరిగమ- సరిగమ- రిగమ- గమ- మగరిసని[१६]- గరిసని-రిసని[१७]- సని.

గుండక్రియ[१८] - 6 స్వరాలు[१९] చేత షాడవం[२०]- గాంధారాది[२१] మధ్యమవర్జం- గగగ- ససస- రిరిరి- పపప- ధధధ- నినిని-గసరిపధని[२२]-సరిపధని-రిపధని- పధని-

---

१. T65,G86, G89- ద్వీపం

२. G86- మ **** , G38, Sp- మఖజన్మనక్షత్రం

३. G38, Sp- add జన్మవారం

४. G38- శింహరాశిలగ్నం, Sp- సింహరాశిలగ్నం

५. G86- కుంజ, G89- ******, Sp- కజ్జ

६. G89- ******

७. G38, Sp- శవనకాది

८. Sp- కుండక్రియ

९. G89, G38- ఘుర్జరి

१०. G86, G89 - omit, G38- 3 గురు, Sp- యీ ముగ్గురు

११. G86-** రాయణి

१२. Sp- అవుడవం

१३. G38- నిషాది

१४. G89- ******* , G38, Sp- దెవతపతపంచమ

१५. G86, G89- స స స

१६. T65- మ గ రి స రి ని

१७. T65, G38, Sp- missing

१८. G38- ఇక గుండక్రియ నడవడిక, Sp- ఇఖ కుండక్రియ నడవడిక

१९. G38- 6 స్వరముల, Sp- 6 స్వరాల, G86- 6 స్వరాలు

२०. G89- షావం

२१. G86- గాంధా***** , G89- ********

२२. T65- గ స రి గ ప ధ ని

ధని- నిధపరిసగ[1]- ధపరిసగ[2]-పరిసగ[3]-రిసగ- సగ.

ఘుర్జరి[4]- 5 స్వరాలు[5] చేత ఔడవం[6]- గాంధారాది- రి(ఋ)షభదై(ధై)వత[7]వర్జం[8]- గగగ- ససస- మమమ- పపప- నినిని- గసమపని- సమపని- మపని- పని- నిపమసగ- పమసగ- మసగ- సగ[9]- [10]□తు[11] మాళ□రాగానికి[12] సతులు.

మాళ□సంపూర్ణరాగం[13]- 7 స్వరాలు- గాంధారాది- గగగ- ససస- రిరిరి- మమమ- (పపప-)[14] ధధధ- నినిని[15]- గసరిమపధని[16]- సరిమపధని[17]- రిమపధని[18]- మపధని[19]- పధని[20]- ధని- నిధపమరిసగ[21]- ధపమరిసగ[22] (పమరిసగ- మరిసగ- రిసగ-

१. T65- ని ద రి స గ

२. G86- ప రి స గ

३. T65- స రి స గ

४. G89- ఘుర్జురి, G38- ఘుర్జరి యొక్క నడవడిక, Sp- యిఖ ఘుర్జరి నడవడిక

५. G38- స్వరముల, Sp- స్వరాల

६. Sp- అవుడవం

७. G38,Sp - missing

८. G38- adds సొరము నడవడిక, Sp- స్వరం నడవడిక

९. G38, Sp- missing

१०. T65 - this line missing

११. G38, Sp-□ర్లు

१२. G38- రాగమునకు, Sp- రాగానకు

१३. G38- మాళ□రాగము సంపూర్ణము

१४. Since this is a sampūrṇa rāga, this phrase is suggested.

१५. G89- నిని

१६. G86, G89- గసరిమధని

११७. G86, G89- సరిమధని

१८. T65 - రిపమధని, G86, G89- రిమధని

१९. G86, G89- మధని

२०. G86, G89- missing

२१. T65- నిధసమరిసగ, G38, Sp- నిదపమగరిస, Sp adds బంగాళ భార్యలు ధన్యాశి కాంభోది నీలాంబురి (page heading from the original)

२२. G38, Sp- ప మ గ, ద ప గ

సగ).[१]

బంగాళ రాగానికి[२]- దేవవంశం- శూద్రజాతి[३]- నీలవర్ణం[४]- □ాయకుడుదేవతా(అధిదేవతా)[५]- కలవంటకభోజనం- నూతనవస్త్రం[६]- కదంబగంధం- వైడూర్యభూషణం- పరశు ఆయుధం- ద్రోణపుష్పం[७]- చక్ర(వాక)వాహనం[८]- నారికేళవృక్షం[९]- పుష్కరద్వీపదేశం[१०]- హాస్యరసం- మూలానక్షత్రం[११]- గురువారం[१२]- ధనుర్లగ్నం[१३]- రెండు ముఖాలు- నాలుగు భుజాలు- నాలుగు నేత్రాలు- నాలుగు శ్రోత్రాలు[१४]- ఉన్నతదేహం- జమదగ్నిఋషిగోత్రం (జమదగ్నిగోత్రం)[१५] - ఋగ్వేదఛందస్సు- ధన్యాశి, కాంబోది, నీలాంబరి- సతులు[१६]

ధన్యాశి[१७] - 6 స్వరాలుచేత షాడవం- గాంధారాధి(ది)- నిషాదవర్జం- గగగ-

१. The reading is incomplete and hence these svara passages are suggested based on the sequence of the svara-s, followed in other cases. G38,Sp add thus:G38- మాళ□రాగముతో 3 సతులు కలసి ప్రకాశించు వుందురు - శ్రీ శ్రీ శ్రీ శ్రీ శ్రీ, Sp- మాళ□రాగంతో ముగ్గురు సతులు కలశి ప్రకాశించి వుండురు। శ్రీ శ్రీ శ్రీ శ్రీ శ్రీ -
२. T65- రాగం, G38- బంగాళ, భార్యలు, ధన్యాశి, కాంభోజి, నీలాంబం (page heading from the original), రాగమునకు
३. G86- శూత్రజాతి
४. Sp- వర్నం, T65- Missing from here and joins at the lakṣaṇa of Nāṭa
५. G38, Sp- ఇందుకు □ాయకుండు దేవత
६. Sp- సూత వస్త్రం
७. G38- పువ్వులు, Sp- పూలు
८. G38,Sp- add వాహనం
९. G38,Sp- ఫలవృక్షం
१०. T65,G86,G89- పుష్కర ద్వీపం, G38- దృష్కర ద్వీపదేశం
११. G89- మూల, G38, Sp- add జన్మనక్షత్రం
१२. G38,Sp- add జన్మవారం
१३. G38,Sp- ధనురాశి లఘ్నం
१४. G38, Sp- read శ్రోత్ర first and then నేత్ర
१५. G86, G89- జమతగ్ని
१६. G38, Sp- □ు సతులు
१७. G38, Sp- add ధన్యాశి నడవడిక స్వరం

ససస- రిరిరి- మమమ- పపప- ధధధ- గసరిమపధ[౧]- సరిమపధ- రిమపధ- మపధ- పధ- ధపమరిసగ[౨]- పమరిసగ- మరిసగ- రిసగ[౩]- సగ.

కాంబోది[౪]- 6 స్వరాలచేత షాడవం[౫]- మధ్యమాధి(ది)- రి(ఋ)షభవర్జం- మమ[౬]- సస- గగ- పప- ధధ- నిని- మసగపధని- సగపధని- గపధని- పధని- ధని- నిధపగసమ- ధపగసమ- పగసమ- గసమ- సమ.

నీలాంబరి- 6 స్వరాలచేత షాడవం- మధ్యమాధి(ది)- రి(ఋ)షభవర్జం- మమమ- ససస[౭]- గగగ- పపప- ధధధ- నినిని- నిధపగసమ- ధపగసమ- పగసమ- గసమ- సమ- మసగపధని- సగపధని- గపధని- పధని- ధని- □రు బంగాళానికి శ్రీ(స్త్రీ)లు[౮].

బంగాళం 5 స్వరాలు[౯]- ఔడవం[౧౦]- నిషాదాది గాంధారమధ్యమవర్జం- నినిని- ససస- రిరిరి- పపప- ధధధ- నిసరిపధ- సరిపధ- రిపధ- పధ- ధపరిసని- పరిసని- రిసని- సని[౧౧].

నాట రాగానికి[౧౨] నాగవంశం- శూద్రజాతి- నీలవర్ణం-

---

౧. G89 - పప ******** రిమపద - సరిమపద

౨. G38, Sp- ధపమగసగ

౩. G38 - missing

౪. G38- ఇక కాంబోది, Sp- యిఖ గాంబోది

౫. G89- ****

౬. G38, Sp - add దీని నడవడిక స్వరం

౭. G38, Sp- మ మ, స స

౮. G38- బంగాళ రాగమునకు □ 3గురు సతులు, Sp- బంగాళ రాగాన్కి □ ముగ్గురు సతులు and add: G38- బంగళ రాగ నడవడిక సౌరము, Sp- బంగాళ రాగ నడవడిక స్వరం

౯. G38- స్వరముల, Sp- స్వరాల

౧౦. G38, Sp- అవుడవం

౧౧. G38- బంగాళ రాగము 3 భార్యలతో వెలసి ప్రకాశి ంచు వుందురు, Sp- బంగాళ రాగం। ముగ్గురు భార్యలతో మెలగి ప్రకాశిస్తూ వుందురు

౧౨. G38- adds నాట రాగము సతులు (subject heading?), G38, Sp-నాట రాగము

తుంబురుదేవతా(అధిదేవతా)[१]- పాలు అన్న భోజనం[२]- పట్టుకోక- పరిమళగంధం[३]- పద్మరాగభూషణం[४]- బిండివాలాయుధం[५]- పారిజాతపుష్పం[६]- చకోరవాహనం- కదళీఫలవృక్షం[७]- నవఖండదేశం[८]- శాంతరసం- అనో(ను)రాధానక్షత్రం[९]- మంగళవారం[१०]- వృశ్చికలగ్నం- 4 ముఖాలు- 8 భుజాలు- 8 శ్రోత్రాలు- 8 నేత్రాలు[११]- ఉన్నతదేహం- భారద్వాజగోత్రం- అథర్వణవేద ఛందస్సు[१२]- దేవగాంధారి, శంకరాభరణం, ఆహరి[१३] స్త్రీలు[१४].

దేవగాంధారి[१५] 6 స్వరాలు చేత షాడవం- గాంధారాది- నిషాదవర్జం- గగ- సస- రిరి- మమ- పప- ధధ- గసరిమపధ- సరిమపధ- రిమపధ- మపధ- పధ- ధపమరిసగ[१६]- పమరిసగ- మరిసగ- రిసగ- సగ.

శంకరాభరణానికి[१७] 7 స్వరాలు[१८]- సంపూర్ణరాగం[१९]- దై(ధై)వతాది- ధధ- నిని- సస- రిరి- గగ- మమ- పప- ధనిసరిగమప- నిసరిగమప[२०]- సరిగమప-

१. G38- తాంబురు దేవత, G86, G89- తుంబురుడు దేవతా
२. T65- క్షీరాన్న భోజనం
३. T65, G38, Sp - పరిమేళ గంధం
४. G86- ప * * * గ భూషణం
५. G38- పిండివాల[illegible]యునం, Sp- భిండివాలం ఆయుధం
६. G86, G89- పూలు, G38- పుష్పములు, Sp- పుష్పాలు
७. G86- కదళీవృక్షం
८. G86- నవఖండ్డా దేశం, T65- నవఖండాలు దేశం, Sp- నవకండదేశం
९. G38, Sp- అనోజ గోత్రం
१०. G38, Sp- missing upto వున్నత దేహం
११. G86- 8 నేత్రాలు 8 శ్రోర్త్రాలు, G89- 8 నేత్రాలు 8 శ్రోత్రాలు
१२. G86- చందస్సు
१३. G86- ఆహరి శంక్కరాభరణం, G89- ****** , G38- ఆహిణ, Sp- ఆహరి
१४. T65- [illegible]డు స్త్రీలు, G38, Sp- missing
१५. G38- add దేవగాంధారి సొర నడవడిక, Sp- add దేవగాంధారి స్వరం నడవడిక
१६. Sp- ధపమరిసధ
१७. G38, Sp- శంకరాభరణం
१८. Sp- స్వరాల
१९. G38, Sp- సంపూర్ణం, T65- missing
२०. G86- missing

రిగమప- గమప- మప- పమగరిసనిధ- (మగరిసనిధ)[१] గరిసనిధ- రిసనిధ- సనిధ- నిధ-

ఆ॰రి[२] సంపూర్ణరాగం- 7 స్వరాలు[३]- మధ్యమాది[४]- మమ(మ)[५]- రిరి(రి)- సస(స)- గగగ- ధధధ- పపప- నినిని[६]- మరిసగధపని[७]- రిసగధపని[८]- సగధపని[९]- గధపని[१०]- ధపని[११]- పని[१२]- నిపధగసరిమ[१३]- పధగసరిమ[१४]- ధగసరిమ[१५]- గసరిమ[१६]- సరిమ- రిమ[१७].

నాట రాగం[१८] - 7 స్వరాలు- సంపూర్ణం[१९] - షడ్జాది- సససా- రిరిరి- గగగ-

---

१. This phrase is missing and this is suggested on the basis of the sequence followed in other rāga-s.

२. G89- హ॰గిరి, G86- ఆగిరి, G38- ఆహ॰రి

३. G86- సంపూర * * * * స్వరాలు, G38, Sp add 'దీని నడవడిక'

४. G38, Sp- మాధ్యమాది

५. In order to have uniformity, the phrases with three svara-s are suggested.

६. T65- మమ-రిరి-గగ-ధధ-పప-నిని, G86- మమ-నిని-గగ-ధధ-పప-నిని, G89- మమ-సస-గగ-ధధ-పప-నిని

७. Sp- మరిసగపధని

८. G38- రిసగపధని

९. G38- సగపధని

१०. G38, Sp - గపధని

११. G38, Sp - పధని

१२. G38- ధని

१३. G86- నిధపగసరిమ

१४. G86- ధపగసరిమ

१५. G86- పగసరిమ

१६. G38- adds సరిమ before గసరిమ

१७. G86- రి **

१८. G86- ******, G89- నాట రాగానికి స్త్రీలు. నాటకు, G38- నాటకానికి □దు 3 సతులు. నాట రాగము ససంపూర్ణము. దాని నడవడిక స్వరము; నాట రాగము, Sp- నాట రాగాన్కి □ల్లు ముగ్గురు సతులు. నాట రాగం సంపూర్ణం, దాని నడవడిక స్వరం. నాట రాగం

१९. T65, G38, Sp - missing

మమమ- పపప- ధధధ- నినిని- సరిగమపధని- రిగమపధని- గమపధని[१]- మపధని-
పధని- ధని- నిధపమగరిస- ధపమగరిస- పమగరిస- మగరిస- గరిస- రిస[२]-

[३]देशाक्षरी च गान्धारि[री] सारङ्गाख्या[४] च भैरवी ।

देवक्रिया रक्तहंसि[सी][५] मालवी रागपञ्जरः[६] ।। १५५ ।।

भूपालश्च मुखारी च हिन्दोली[७] घूर्जरी[८] तथा ।

एते[९] सूर्यांशजा[जाः][१०] प्रोक्ताः[११] सायंकालेषु निन्दिताः ।

[१२]प्रभाते[१३] गीयते[१४] येन[१५] स नरस्सुखमेधते[१६] ।। १५६ ।।

---

१. G86, G89- missing

२. G86, G89 read an extra set of svara-s thus: సరి******** రిగమపధనిస- గమపధనిస- మపధనిస- పధనిస- ధనిస- నిస, G89- సరిగమపధనిస- రిగమపధనిస- గమపధనిస- మపధనిస- పధనిస- ధనిస- నిస, G38 and Sp add thus: G38- నాట రాగము 3గురు సతులతో ప్రకాశించి వుందురు। శ్రీ మేల మ~ శ్రీ శ్రీ జేయును, Sp- నాట రాగం ముగ్గురు సతులతో ప్రకాశించి వుందురు। శ్రీమతి మహా శ్రీ శ్రీ జాయను

३. G86, G89- v.155- v.160 are missing; G38, Sp add thus: G38: శుభమస్తు శారదాంబయవేనమః రాగకాలము దానివేళ పాడునది. కాలాకాలము, Sp- శుభమస్తు శారదాంబయవేనమః రాగకాల దానివేళ పాడేది. కాలాకాల.

४. G38,Sp- सारङ्गख्या

५. V08- रक्तहम्स

६. T65, G38, Sp,V08- पञ्जराः

७. G38-हिन्दोळ

८. G38, Sp- गुर्जरी

९. G38- येति

१०. T65,G98, B13, Sp- सूर्याम्शज, G38- सूर्याम्शीज, V08- सूर्यांशाजाः

११. G38, Sp, V08- प्रोक्ता

१२. V08 - missing

१३. G38- प्रभाति

१४. G98, G17, B13- नियुते, T65- नीयते, G38- गीयेति

१५. G38, Sp- यान

१६. G98 - सनरस्सुखमेयुते, B13 - सनरस्सुखमेयु[ध]ते, G38 - सनरासुखमेधति, Sp- सनरासुखमेधत

టీకా:- [१]దేశాక్షరి, దేవగాంధారి, సారంగ, భైరవి, దేవక్రియ, రక్తహంసి, మాళవి, పడమంజరి[२], భూపాళం, ముఖారి, హిందోళం, ఘుర్జరి[३]- ఈ రాగాలు సూర్యాంశ(అంశ)యందు[४] పుట్టినవి ఇవి ప్రాతఃకాలమందు పాడవలెను.

आहरि[५] शङ्कराभूषा[६] सायंकाले प्रगीयते[७] ।। १५७ ।।

టీకా:- [८]ఆహరి శంకరాభరణం, సాయంకాలమందు గానం చేయవలెను[९].

सर्वे रागाः प्रगायन्ते[१०] सायंकाले प्रशस्यते[११] ।

पूर्वापरात्र मध्यात्र[ह्ने][१२] रागान् गायं[रागगानं][१३]प्रशस्यते[१४] ।। १५८ ।।

టీకా:-[१५]పూర్వాహ్న, మధ్యాహ్న[१६], అపరాహ్నమందు కడమ రాగాలు గానం చేయవలెను[१७]. ఇది రాగ కాలం.

[१८]**मुखारिका रेवगुप्ति[१९] घण्टारं[२०] माधवादितः** [?][२१] ।

---

१. T65- missing
२. Sp- పడవంజరి
३. G38- ఘుర్జరి
४. G38- సూర్యాంశయెందు
५. G38, Sp - अहरि
६. G38- शंकराभूपो, Sp-शंकराभूषो
७. G38- प्रगीयति
८. T65 - missing
९. Sp- చాయవలెను
१०. G38- सर्वे राग प्रणम्यति, Sp- सर्वे राग प्रणम्यन्ति
११. G38- प्रशस्यति, V08- प्रशस्यतः
१२. G38,Sp- मध्यात्र
१३. Since the reading in the Mss does not convey proper sense, this reading is suggested.
१४. G38- प्रशस्यति
१५. T65 - missing
१६. G38- మధ్యాన్న
१७. G38- చేయవలెను
१८. G38, Sp- read the sub heading దేశీయరాగాలు
१९. G98, G17, B13- रेवगुप्तिः, G38, Sp, V08- मुखारि कापि रेगुप्ति
२०. T65- गण्टारं, V08- घण्टारव
२१. T65- माभवाभितः, G38-माभवारितः, V08- मभाभितः

देशि[१] सम्भव[२] मित्राश्च[३] रागाणां[४] परिकीर्तिताः[५] ।। १५९ ।।

टीका:- [६]ముఖారి, రేగుప్తి, కాపి[७], ఘంటారాగేణ(ఘంటారవం) మాధ□ ఇ□మొదలైన□ 64 □త్రరాగాలు దేశీయ సంభవాలని[८] చెప్పబడును.

क्रमात् सप्तस्वराणां[९] च स्वस्वस्थानविपर्यया[१०] ।

षाडवौडवसम्पूर्णा[र्णाः] रागा[गाः][११] प्रस्तारसम्भवाः[१२] ।। १६० ।।

टीका:- సప్త స్వరాల యొక్క[१३] తమతమ □ర్యాసం వల్ల, 5 స్వరాల, 6 స్వరాల, 7 స్వరాలు[१४] 32 రాగాలు, 64 □త్రాలు[१५], ప్రస్తార సంభవాలుగా[१६] భేదాలై[१७] చతురంగప్రస్తార రాసులయ్యే[१८].

---

१. V08- देश

२. G38- सम्खाव, Sp- सभाव

३. G38, Sp- मित्राम्श्च, V08- मिश्राम्च

४. G38, Sp- रागानां

५. G98, G17, T65, G38, Sp- परिकीर्तितः

६. T65 missing, V08 reads- ఈ 6 □శములు దేవ సంభవములు

७. G38- పాఫి

८. G38- సంఖావములని

९. G38- सर्वाणां, Sp- सर्वाणी

१०. G98, G17, B13- स्वस्वस्थानविपर्ययः, G38, Sp- स्वस्वस्तानाविपर्यय, V08- स्वस्वस्थानविपर्ययात्

११. V08- सम्पूर्णारागा, G38, Sp- सम्पूर्ण राग

१२. T65, G98- प्रस्थार सम्भवः, G17- प्रस्था(स्ता)र सम्भव(वाः), G38- प्रस्तार सम्खवा, Sp- प्रस्तार सम्भवा

१३. G38- యొక్క

१४. T65- missing

१५. G38, Sp- □తలు

१६. G38- సంఖవములుగ

१७. Sp- భేదాలయి

१८. T65, G38,Sp- రాసులైరి

[१]బై	దె[२]	మే[३]	కు[४]
ప	ని[५]	మ	మ
ధ	గ	స	రి
ని	మ	రి	గ
స	ధ[६]	గ	ధ
రి	ప[७]	ప[८]	ప
గ			
మ			

భూ[९]	వే[१०]	మ[११]	బౌ[१२]
గ	గ	ధ	[१३]ని
రి	మ	స	స
మ	ప	రి	రి
ప	ధ	గ	ప
ధ	ని	మ	ధ
ని[१४]		ప	

---

१. This entire portion (list of svara-s in ascending order) is missing in T65.

२. G38, Sp-వె

३. G38, Sp- వం

४. G38- రి, Sp - సిం, V08-((కురవంజి[?]కాంబోజి)

५. Sp, V08- రి

६. G38,Sp,V08- ప

७. G38,Sp,V08- ధ

८. G38, Sp - మ

९. G38, Sp- భు, V08- (భూపాల)

१०. G86, G89- దే, G38, Sp- ధె, V08- (వేళాౕ౨రి)

११. G86, G89- మే, Sp- దు, V08- (మాళవ)

१२. G86, G89, G38, Sp- భౌ, V08- (బౌళి)

१३. V08- సరిగమపధని

१४. V08- missing

శ్రీ[१]	హిం[२]	[భ][३]	సా[४]
[५]ధ	మ	[६]గ	మ
ని	స	రి	ప
స	గ	స	ధ
గ	ప[७]	మ	స
మ	ధ	ప	గ
ప	ని	ధ	
		ని	

ప[८]	దే[९]	ల[१०]	తో[११]
ని	ధ	ని	గ
స	స	స	రి
గ	రి	రి	స
మ	గ	మ	మ
ప	మ	ప	ప
ధ[१२]	ప	ధ	ధ
			ని

---

१. G86, G89- స్త్రి, V08 - (శ్రీరాగ)

२. V08- (హిందోళ)

३. G86, G89- ల, G38, Sp- భ, V08 - missing ?

४. V08- (సావేరి)

५. V08- నిగగమపరిస

६. In the previous commentary portion balahamsa reads గనిసమపధని

७. V08- missing

८. G86- పా, V08- పా (పా)

९. G86, G89 - ద్రై, G38, Sp- వై, V08- (దేవగాంధారి)

१०. V08- (లలిత)

११. V08- (తోడి)

१२. V08- రిధ

వ[१]	రా[२]	వ[३]	క్రా[४]
ని	గ	గ[५]	గ
రి	మ	స	స
గ	ప	రి	రి
మ	ధ	ప	మ
ధ	ని	ధ	ప
స[६]		ని	ధ
			ని

వరా[వరా][७]	**నా**	**గు**[८]	**ఘు**[९]
[१०]గ	స	గ	గ[११]
స	ని	స	స
రి	రి	రి	మ
మ	గ	ప[१२]	ప
ప	మ	ధ	ని
ధ		ని	
ని			

१. V08- వ (వరాళీ)

२. G86- గా, G89 - ***, V08- (రామక్రియా)

३. G86, G89- మా, V08 - reading not in proper order; probably missing?

४. G38.Sp - శా, V08 - కా (కాంభోజీ)

५. G86, G89- గపధపధని

६. G86- ని, G38, Sp- ధ ని

७. G38- వసా, V08 - reading not in proper order; probably missing?

८. G89 - **many gaps in between,G38- గ

९. G89- description missing upto dhanyāśī, G86, G38- ధ

१०. G86, G89- గపధపధని

११. G86- గసరిమపని, G38- గసరిమపధని, Sp- గసరిమపపధని

१२. G38, Sp- మప

బ	ధ[१]	కా[२]	నీ
ని	గ	మ	మ
స	స	స	స
రి	రి	గ	గ
ప	మ	ప	ప
ధ	ప	ధ	ధ
	ధ	ని	ని

లం[నా][३]	దే[४]	శం[५]	ఆ[६]
స	గ	ధ	మ
రి	స	ని[७]	రి
గ[८]	రి	స	స
మ	మ	రి	గ
ప	ప	గ	ధ[९]
ధ	ధ	మ	ప
ని		ప[१०]	ని

---

१. Sp- ధం, V08- ద

२. G86, G89, G38- రా, Sp- క్రా

३. V08- రామక్రి

४. G86, G89- దో, G38- రెగం, Sp- వేగ

५. G86, G89- శ, Sp- ము

६. Sp- అ

७. Sp- నిం

८. G86, G89 - omit

९. G38, Sp- ప ధ

१०. G38- ప ధ

[1]चतुरंगप्रस्तारम्।

ग[2]	रि[3]	रि[4]	प[5]	ध	नि	स	ध
म	रि	स	म	रि[6]	म	रि	प
प	ध	रि[7]	ग	ध	प	ग	म
म	ग	रि	स	नि	म	स[8]	रि
स	रि	ग	प	ग	स[9]	ध	ग
नि	म	प[10]	ध	म	ध	ग[11]	म
ग	स	ग	नि	रि	ग	ग[12]	प
नि	ध	प	स	स	म	स[13]	नि

१. This table is found only in G38, Sp and V08. G86 reads the first column alone. The readings are mainly taken from G38 and Sp; but in order to agree with the passage, which follows this table, a few readings from V08 are chosen. The significance of the term 'caturaṅgaprastāra' is not clear. However it is observed that the word 'paṭṭi' in the following passage seems to refer to the column of this table and 'illu' (house) to the row; the svara in the specified column and row represents the graha svara of the rāga.

२. V08- स

३. G38- स

४. V08- ग

५. V08- स

६. V08- नि

७. V08- नि

८. V08- प

९. V08- प

१०. V08- म

११. V08- स

१२. G38,Sp - ध

१३. V08- ध

టీకా:- [१]భైర□4 పట్టి[२] 1 ఇల్లు[३] స్వరమాది[४]. మాళ□వరాళి, కౌశిక, గుండక్రియ, ఈ నాలుగింటికి (1)[५] పట్టి 1 ఇల్లు[६]. మేఘరంజికి[७] 1 పట్టి[८] 4 ఇల్లు[९]. [१०]నారాయణి 1 పట్టి 6 ఇల్లు[११]. [१२]బల౯ంస 1 పట్టి 7 ఇల్లు[१३]. [१४]రామక్రియ 2 పట్టి 4 ఇల్లు[१५]. [१६]కురు(ర)ంజి కాంబోది[१७] 2 పట్టి 6 ఇల్లు. భూపాళం తోడికి[१८] 3 పట్టిలు[१९] 5 ఇల్లు[२०]. వేళా౯ురి[२१] 4

---

१. T65- this entire section is missing.G38- ఇది రాగ ప్రస్తారము ప్రస్తార క్రమము, Sp- ఇ□ప్రస్తార క్రమం స్వర ప్రస్తారం

२. G38- భైర□టి। మా□Sp- భైర□పట్టి మాది, V08- భైర□4 పట్టే

३. G86, G89- యింట్టి, V08- యింట

४. V08- స్వరాది, G38,Sp-omit

५. Reading is suggested based on the table.

६. G86, G89- యీా 4 పట్టి ఇల్లు, G38- యి 4 టికి పట్టె 1 ఇల్లు, V08- యీా 4 కి 1 పట్టే ఇల్లు

७. G86, G89- మేకురంజి, V08- మేఘరంజినికి

८. G86, G89- 1 యింట్టి పట్టి, V08- reads పట్టి as పట్టే all through, this section which has not been noted here.

९. G38, Sp- 4 యిండ్లు

१०. G38, Sp- this sentence is missing

११. V08- నారాయణి

१२. G38, Sp- this sentence is missing

१३. G86- బల౯ంస*****, V08- బల౯ంసకు

१४. G38, Sp- this sentence is missing

१५. V08- ఇల్లు ****

१६. G38, Sp- this sentence is missing

१७. V08- రకుజి కాంబోజి

१८. G86, G89- భూపాల తోడికి

१९. G38- 3 పటెలు

२०. G86, G89- 2, G86,G89- read '1' after this.

२१. G38, Sp- వెలావులకి, V08- వెలా౯ురికి

పట్టి 3 ఇల్లు[౧]. నాటకు 4 పట్టి[౨] 4 ఇల్లు[౩]. వసంత రాగానికి[౪] 4 పట్టి[౫] 7 ఇల్లు[౬]. శంకరాభరణానికి[౭] 5 పట్టి[౮] 10(1)[౯] ఇల్లు[౧౦]. శ్రీరాగానికి[౧౧] 5 పట్టి 3 ఇల్లు[౧౨]. దేవక్రియ. పడమంజరి[౧౩] 5 పట్టి[౧౪] 4 ఇల్లు[౧౫]. బౌళి లలిత బంగాళానికి[౧౬] 6 పట్టి[౧౭] 1 ఇల్లు. సావేరి నీలాంబరికి 6 పట్టి[౧౮] 4 ఇల్లు[౧౯]. హిందోళకు[౨౦] 6 పట్టి 8 ఇల్లు[౨౧]. ధన్యాశి

---

౧. G89-****** ఇల్లు, G38- 4 పటెలు 2 యిలు, Sp- నాలుగు పటిలు మూడు యిండ్లు

౨. G38- 4 పటె, Sp- నాలుగు పటి

౩. G38- 4 యిలు, Sp- నాలుగు యిండ్లు

౪. G38- వంసంతమునకు, Sp- వంసతానికి, V08- వసంతకు

౫. G38- 4 పటె

౬. G86- ***ఇల్లు, G38- 6 యిలు, Sp- ఆరు యిండ్లు

౭. G38- శంకరాభరణమునకు

౮. G38- 5 పటే

౯. V08- missing; reading is suggested based on the table

౧౦. G86- 1** ఇల్లు, G38, Sp- యిండ్లు

౧౧. G86-స్త్రీరాగానికి, G38- శ్రీరాగమునకు

౧౨. G38- 5 పటె 2 యిలు, Sp- అయిదు పటి మూడు యిండ్లు

౧౩. G89- ***మంజరి, G38- పడమంజికి, Sp- పడవంజికి, V08- పడమంజరికి

౧౪. G38- 5 పటె, Sp- అయిదు పటి

౧౫. Sp- యిండ్లు

౧౬. G86, G89, Sp- బంగాళికి, G38- బంగాలమునకు

౧౭. G38- 6 పటే, Sp- ఆరు పటి

౧౮. G86- ********, G38- 7 పటెలు, Sp- ఏడు పట్టి

౧౯. G38, Sp- 4 యిండ్లు, V08- యి 4

౨౦. G86- హిందోళికి, G89- హి*****, G38- యిందోలమునకు, Sp- హిందోల

౨౧. G38- 6 పటెలు ******, Sp- ఆరు పట్టిలు

దేవగాంధారికి 8 పట్టి 3 ఇల్లు[१]. [२]ఘుర్జరికి[३] 7 పట్టి 7 ఇల్లు. మలహరికి 8[४] పట్టి 1 ఇల్లు[५]. ఆహరికి[६] 8 పట్టి[७] 3 ఇల్లు[८]. దేశికి[९] 8[१०] పట్టి[११] 1 ఇల్లు[१२].

[१३]మాళ☐, కౌశిక ఏక[१४] మేళం. ధన్యాశి, దేవగాంధారి ఏక మేళం. గుండక్రియ[१६], వరాళి ఏక మేళం[१७]. రామక్రియ[१८], వేళాహురి[१९] ఏక మేళం[२०]. తోడి, బలహంస ఏక

१. G38- దేవగా ****, Sp- దేవగాంధారి, V08- 7 పట్టే ఇల్లు 3
२. G86, G89- this line is found before the description for hindolam. G38, Sp, V08- read దేశికి 7 పట్టి 5 ఇల్లు before. But dēśi is seen at the end again. After this, G38, Sp have many lacunae. G38- *** 7 పటె 7 యిండ్లు*****, Sp- *********
३. G86- **ర్జూరికి, G89- ధర్జూరికి
४. G38 - 8 పటె
५. G38, Sp- 8 యిండ్లు
६. G38- అహరికి, Sp- ఆహరికి
७. G38- 8 పటె
८. G86- ** ఇల్లు, G38,Sp- 3యిండ్లు
९. G86- **శికి, V08-దేశాక్షరికి
१०. G86- missing
११. G38- 8 పటె
१२. G89- ****** ఇల్లు, G38, Sp- 10 యిండ్లు
१३. G86- శ్రీ **** శ్రీ గుచరణార☐భ్యాన్నమః, G38- ఇది చతురంగ ప్రస్తారము క్రమా☐యము సమ్పూర్ణము। శ్రీరామజేయం। శ్రీ శ్రీ శ్రీ జేయును, Sp- యి☐తురంగ ప్రస్తార క్రమా☐యం సమ్పూర్ణం, శ్రీ శ్రీ శ్రీ జాయును.
१४. V08- missing (in the previous page, (p.17 of the Ms) it is written "मालवि", which seems to be out of context there and probably the one that should come here)
१५. G38- యొక్క. G38 reads యొక్క for యేక throughout in this passage and hence the same has not been noted each time.
१६. V08- గుండక్రి
१७. G89- ****** లం
१८. V08- రామక్రి
१९. G89- వేలా***రి
२०. V08 - -do-

మేళం[१]. బౌళి బంగాళం[२] ఏక మేళం[३]. ॅందోళం కాంబోది ఏక మేళం[४]. ఆॅరి నీలాంబరి ఏక మేళం[५]. మలॅరి, దేశి, శంకరాభరణం, శ్రీరాగం[६] స్వర సంబంధం □త్రములు[७]. ఈ చతురంగప్రస్తారం 64[८] ఇండ్లలోని స్వరాలు[९] 64 □త్ర రాగాలకు[१०] సంబంధం[११].

భూపాళం, మాళ□కౌశిక[१२], గుండక్రియ[१३], ధన్యాశి, దేవగాంధారి, వరాళి[१४], తోడి, రామక్రియ, బలॅంస, వేళాॅరి[१५], ఘుర్జరి[१६] - ఇ□[१७] సంబంధ[१८] స్వరాల చేత □త్ర(త్రు)లు[१९]. నీలాంబరి, కాంబోది[२०], ॅందోళం[२१], మేఘరంజి[२२], కురంజి, సావేరి, ఆॅరి[२३]- ఇ□

---

१. V08- -do-

२. G38, Sp- భౌళీ, భంగాళ

३. V08- -do- (this line is found after the following line)

४. G89- యే*******

५. G89- *******నీలాంబరి యేక మేళం, G38- యింధోలి, కాంబోది, ఆॅరి, నీలాంబరి ఈ 4 ను యొక్క మేళము, Sp- ॅందోలి కాంబోది ఆॅరి నీలాంబరి నాలుగు యేక మేళం, V08- ॅందోల కాంభోజి నీలాంబరి ఆॅరి - do-

६. G86- స్త్రిరాగం

७. G86, G89- స్వరసంమంత్త □త్రాలు, G38- స్వరముదం □త్రలు, Sp- స్వరమందం □త్రలు

८. G38- 64 ఇందు 64, Sp- అరబైనాలుగుయును అరబైనాలుగు

९. G89- యిం ********** స్వరాలు, V08- ఇండ్లలో స్వరాలు

१०. G86, G89- □త్రరాగాల

११. Sp - సంమందం

१२. G86- కౌశికా

१३. G86- కుండ్డక్రియం, V08- గుండక్రి

१४. G38, Sp - missing

१५. G89- బ ******** లాॅరి

१६. G86- ఘుర్జురి, G89- ఘుర్జూరి, G38- ఘూర్జరి

१७. G86, G89- missing, V08- ఇ□అ**న

१८. G86, G89, Sp- సంమంద, G38- సమంద

१९. G86, G89- □త్రాలు, V08- స్వరముల చే □త్రములు

२०. G38,Sp- కాంభోది, V08- కాంభోజి

२१. V08 - missing

२२. G38, Sp- ॅందోలి, G86, G89- మేఖరంజి, Sp- మనరంజి

२३. G89- ఆ******, G38, Sp- ఆॅరి

స్వరసంబంధం □త్రా(త్రు)లు[1]. [2]నారాయణి, లలిత, పడమంజరి[3], వసంతం, దేవక్రియ, బౌళి, బంగాళ, స్వరసమంద(బంధ)[4] □తలు. భైర□[5] 32 రాగాలకు స్వర[6] □త్రా(త్రు)లు. నాటకు. . .[7]

[8]वंशजातिवयोवर्ण[9]स्वरूपोत्पन्न[10]मादि च।
सोमनाथ[11]मते प्रोक्तं द्वात्रिंशद्रागलक्षणम्[12] ।। १६१ ।।

टीका:- వంశం[13], జాతి, వర్ణం, స్వరూపోత్పన్నం[14] మొదలైన[15] లక్షణం 32 రాగాలకు[16] సోమనాథియ్యమనే[17] గ్రంథమందు[18] చెప్పబడెను[19].

---

१. G86-*******□త్రాలు, G89- **** సంమందం □త్రాలు, G38- స్వరముంద □తలు, Sp- స్వర సంమందం □తలు
२. V08, G86, G89- this line is missing
३. Sp- పడవంజరి
४. G38- స్వరసంమందు
५. V08- భైర□మొదలైన
६. G38, Sp- missing
७. G38, Sp- missing, Seems to be Incomplete.
८. G98,G17, B13, V08- v.161ab is missing
९. T65- नयोवर्णः, G86, G89- वयोवर्णः
१०. G38,Sp- पोत्पन
११. G86- सोमनदि, G89- ******धि
१२. G98-द्वात्रिंशद्गात्रलक्षणम्, G17- द्वात्रिंशत्गात्र(तृ)लक्षणम्, B13-द्वात्रिंशद्गात्रलक्षणम्, G38, Sp- द्वात्रिंश रागलक्षण्, This half verse is seen after rāgaprastāra. V08- वंश etc. not copied here.)
१३. T65- missing, G38, Sp- వంశ
१४. T65- స్వరూపం ఉత్పన్న, G86- ******, G38, Sp- స్వరూపోత్పనం
१५. Sp- □దలైన
१६. T65- రాగాలకున్ను, G38, Sp- రాగాలున్ను
१७. T65- సోమనాధేయ్యమనే, G38,Sp- సోమనాధయ్యమనే
१८. G86-G89- గ్రంధ్ధమందు , T65- గ్రంధమందు
१९. G86,G89- చెప్పబడును

[१]एवं निरीक्ष्याथ[२] समस्तरागान् गायेत धीमानधिक[३] प्रयत्नः।

जन्त्रेणवा कण्ठ[४] भवस्वरेण[५] द्वयेन वा[६] दोषविवर्जिता स्युः[७] ।। १६२ ।।

టీకా:-[८]ఈ తీరున రాగస్వరూపం[९] తెలిశి(సి)[१०] జంత్రగాత్రాలకు[११] దోషాలు పరిహరించి[१२] బుద్ధిమంతులైనవారు[१३] 32 రాగాలు[१४] 64 □త్రాలు అనంతాలైన[१५] సంకీర్న(ర్ణ)రాగాలు[१६] గానం చేసి[१७] జంత్రమందు వాయించవలెను[१८].

---

१. v.162, cf.SM 1,4,56; set to indravajrā metre.

२. G98-निरीक्ष्याध, G17-निरीक्ष्याध(थ), G38-निरीक्ष्यर, Sp-निरीक्ष्यद, V08-निरीक्षेत

३. G98,G17,B13-एतेन धीमानधिक, T65-येतेतधीमानधीक, G86,G89-गायेत धिमानधीक, G38-गायते निमन, Sp-गायते निमनधिक प्रयत्न

४. T65- जन्त्रेण वाक्कण, G98- जन्त्रेन वा कण, G17- जन्त्रेन वा कण्ट, G86- ज **********, G38- झन्त्रौको वा क, Sp- झन्त्रिको वा कं, V08- यन्त्रेण वा कण

५. G86- भवेस्वरेण

६. G86, G89- द्वयेन हि, Sp- द्वयोन वा

७. G86- दोषलिवर्ज्जिता स्युः, G89- ***** र्जिता स्युः, G38- दो **** श्युः, Sp- दोप **** श्युः, B13, V08- दोषविवर्जिताः स्युः (breaks off here with the statement:- Then gāyakalakṣaṇa, dōṣa:(25))

८. T65- commentary missing

९. G86, G89- రాగస్వరూపకం

१०. G38, Sp- తెలిసి

११. G38- ఝంత్రఘాత్రాలు, Sp- ఝంత్రఝాత్రాలు

१२. G86- పరిహరిన్విం, G89- పరిహరింప

१३. G86- బు***తులైన ***

१४. G86- *****లు, G38- 3 ****

१५. G38- □త్రలు అనంతములు, Sp- □త్రలు అన్నంతాలు

१६. G38, Sp- సంకీర్ణాలు రాగాలు

१७. G38, Sp- చేసి

१८. G86- జంద్రమందు వాయించ్సవలెను, G89- జంద్రమందు వాయింత్సవలెను, Sp- ఝంత్రమందు వాయింత్సవలెను

గాయక భేదాలు[१]

[२]एकलो[३] यमलो[४] बृन्दो[५] गायकास्त्रिविधाः स्मृताः[६]।
एक एव[७] ता[तु] गायत[८] एकलेत्यभिधीयते[९]।
सद्वितीयो[१०] यमलकः[११] सबृन्दो[१२] बृन्दगायकः[१३]।। १६३।।

టీకా:- యెకలుండని[१४] యమకలుండ(లకుండ)ని[१५] బృందకుండని[१६] గాయకులు 3 భేదాలు[१७]. ఒక్కడే[१८] గానం చేసే(చేస్తే)[१९] వాని పేరు యెకలుండు[२०]. ఇద్దరు[२१] గానం చేసే(చేస్తే) వాని పేరు యెమకళుండు (లకుండు)[२२]. బహుమందితో[२३] గానం జేసే(చేస్తే)

१. T65- missing
२. v.163, cf. SR 3,22cd-23
३. T65- यकलो, G86, G89-यिकळो, B13- एकळा
४. T65, G38, Sp- येमलो, G86- येमुलो, G89- येमु****, B13- यमला
५. G98, B13, G86, G38, Sp- बृन्दा, T65- वृंदा, G89- *****
६. G98- गायकाः त्रिविधा स्मृताः, G86- गायकस्त्रीविधा *****, G89-गायकस्त्रिविधा स्मृताः, G38- गायकः स्त्रिविधा शृताः, Sp- गायतः स्त्रिविधा शृताः, T65- गायकस्त्रीविध स्मृताः
७. T65- *******, G86- ********, G89- येक लिव
८. G98, G17, B13-गता येन, T65- *****, G86, G89- गयेत
९. T65- येकल्योत्यभिधिय्यते, G98- एकलेत्यभिधिय्यते, G17- एकलेत्यभिधिय्य(धीय)ते, G86- येकलोत्भिधिय्यते, G89- येकलोत्यभिधिय्यते, G38-येकलोत्यपिदीय्यते, Sp- एकलोत्यपिधीयते
१०. G98- स्वद्वितियो, G17- स्व(स)द्वितीयो, G86, G89- सद्विदियो, G38, Sp- सद्वितीये
११. G38, Sp- येमळगः
१२. G86, G89- संबृंदो, G38, Sp- सद्बृन्दो
१३. T65, G86, G89- बृंदगायकम्
१४. G89- **********, G38-యెకళుండనిన్ని, Sp- యెకళుండు అనిన్ని
१५. G86, G89-యేమండని, G38, Sp- యెమళకుండనిన్ని
१६. G86, G89- బృదకుండని, G38, Sp- బృందకుండనిన్ని
१७. G86- 3 భేదా**, G38, Sp- ఇ□గాయకులు ఈ మూడు భేదాలు
१८. T65- ఒక్క బే, G86- ******, G38, Sp- ఒకండే
१९. G86- **చేసే
२०. G86, G89- వాని పేరు యెకలుండ్డని, G38, Sp- వాడు యెకళుండు
२१. T65- యిందరు, G86- యందు, G38- ఇందుక, Sp- ఇందుకు
२२. G86-యెమళండని పెరు, G89- యెమళం*****, G38, Sp- missing
२३. G86- బహుమందిలో, G89- ***మందిలో, G38, Sp- బహుమండెలో

వాని పేరు[१] బ్రుందకుండు.

గాయక దోషాలు[२]

[३]सन्दष्टो[४]दूप[द्घुष्ट][५]शी[सी]त्कारो[६] भीतकम्पितशङ्कितः [शङ्कितकम्पिताः][७]।

करालि[ली]कपिला[८]काकि[की][९] वितालकरही[१०] तथा [करभोन्मदाः][११]।।१६४।।

साम्बकस्तुब[म्ब]की[१२]वक्री[१३] प्रसारी विनिमीलकः[१४]।

विरसापस्वराव्यक्त[१५]स्थानभ्रष्टं[१६][ऽ]व्यवस्थितः[१७]।। १६५।।

---

१. G86, G89- వారి పేరు, G38, Sp- వాడు

२. G86, G89 - add ఇది, G38, Sp- add ఇక

३. v.164 - v.177, cf. SR 3,25-38. Since the Mss are highly corrupt, parallel readings are being suggested from SR. However, when the present work seems to differ from SR, the readings are suggested accordingly. At some places, parts of a word in a verse had to be based on each of the Mss and in such cases, a consolidated reading is given.

४. T65, G98, G17, B13- संदृष्टो, G86- सदृष्ट**, G89- सदृष्टो

५. Since the reading does not seem to convey any sense, this reading is suggested.

६. T65, G98, G17, B13- नृपशीत्कारे, G86- **** शीत्का***,G38- द्रपळीरौको, Sp- द्रपसीकारो

७. G98-गीतकंपीतशंकिता, G17-गीतकंपी(म्पि)तशंकिता, B13-गीतकम्पितशंकिता, T65-भीतकंपितशंखिताः, G38,Sp- भित्तकंपितशंखिताः, G86- ******** शङ्किताः Reading based on the text following this (description of each defect).

८. G86, G89- काराळि कटिला

९. T65, B13- काटि, G98- काटु, G17- काटु (टी?)

१०. T65- भेताळकवाही, G98, G17, B13- भेताळकवही, G89- विताळ ********

११. SR reads karabha and udbhaṭa, but the present work reads karabha and unmada. (See v.171ab). Hence it is suggested thus.

१२. G98, G17, B13- सांबस्तुतिबकी, G89- ***बकस्तुबकी, G38, Sp- सांबकसुबकी

१३. G86, G89-वक्र, G38- वश्च

१४. G98, G17, B13, T65, G86, G89- विनिमीलिकः

१५. G98,T65-विरसंपन्वराव्यत्कं, G17- विरसंपन्य[च स्व] राव्यत्कं, B13- विरसंपस्वरा व्यत्कं, G38- विरसापस्वराव्यक्तं, Sp- वीरसूपस्वराव्यक्तं

१६. T65, G86- स्थानंभ्रष्टं, G38, Sp- स्तानब्रष्टं

१७. G86, G89- व्यपस्तितः, G38, Sp- व्यवस्तितः

मिश्रकोऽनवधानश्च[१] तथान्या सानुनासिका[२]।

पञ्चविंशतिरित्य[ये]ते[३] गायको निन्दितो मतः[४]।। १६६।।

टीका:-సందష్ట[५], ఉద్ఘ(ఘు)ష్ట[६], సీత్కార[७], భీత[८], కంపిత, శంకిత (శంకిత, కంపిత)[९], కరాళి[१०], కపిలా[११], కాకి, □తాళ[१२], కరళ తథా (కరభ, ఉన్మద)[१३], సాంబక[१४], బకి[१५], వక్రి[१६], ప్రసారి[१७], □వి□లక[१८], □(□)రస[१९], అపస్వరా, అవ్యక్త[२०], స్థానభ్రష్ట,

---

१. G98-मिश्रकोनमधानश्च, G17-मिश्रकोऽनम(व)धानश्च, T65-मिश्रकोनमदानश्च G86, G89-मिश्रकोनमदानश्च, G38- विक्रिकोनवधानश्च

२. G86,G89 तदा स्वानुनासिकः, T65- तदान्नाया सानुनासिका, G38-तथान्या सामनाशिकः, Sp- तधान्या संनाशिकः

३. T65-पञ्चविंशतिरेत्येते, G98-पञ्चविंशतिरेवन्येते, G17-पञ्चविंशतिरेवन्येते (प्रां तैः), B13-पञ्चविंशतिरेवन्येते, G86- पत्र ****** तिरेत्येते, G89- पंचविंशतिरेत्येते, Sp- पंचविंशतिरिस्यते

४. G38, Sp- गायकोन्निन्दिता मतः

५. T65- సంద్రుష్టః

६. G38, Sp- వుద్బుష్ట

७. G38, Sp- శీత్కారః

८. G38, Sp- భితః

९. G38, Sp - శంఖితః

१०. G86, G89- కారాళి

११. G86- కబిలా, G38, Sp- కబల

१२. G38- కితాళ

१३. G86,G89- కరళ, తద్రా, T65- కరళ. The inclusion of the word □tathā□ in this list reveals the degree of corruption in the text.

१४. T65- సాగకః

१५. G86- బ****

१६. G86,G89-*****,T65- వక్తి౭

१७. G86- ****ర, G89- *****

१८. T65, G86- □వి□లికః, G89- *******

१९. T65-సుసా, G86-□ఠ, G89 -□ఠ, G38-□ఠట

२०. T65, G86, G89- అవ్యక్తా

అవ్యవస్తి(స్థి)త[१], □శక[२], ఏకోన(అనవధాన)[३], అన్యః[४] అనునాసిక[५]. ఈ 25 గుణాలున్న[६] గాయకునికి[७] నిందితాలు[८]. □కి[९] ప్రత్యేక[१०] లక్షణాలు.

[११]**सन्दष्टदशना गो[गे]यः[१२] सन्दष्ट[टः] परिकीर्तितः।**

టీకా:- పండ్లు ఈలకరచుకొని[१३] పాడేది[१४] సందష్టమనబడును.

[१५]**उदृ[द्घु]ष्टो[१६] विरसोद्बृष्टः[घोषः][१७]**

---

१. G86, G89- అవ్యసిద్ధః, T65- అవ్యస్థితః

२. G38- □తకః

३. This is a different interpretation made by the commentator/scribe, to read miśraka and anavadhāna as miśraka and ēkōna. But only anavadhāna has been described in the later part of this text (v.177ab) and not ēkōna. It is surprising to note that BKM and RJM too read ēkōna, probably because of the same kind of exemplar available to them.

४. G86, G89- యకోనః అన్యకి

५. T65, G38, Sp- అనునాశికః

६. T65- 25 న్న గుణాలున్న, G38- 24 గుణములున్న, Sp- 25 యిరబై ఐదు గుణాలున్న

७. T65- నాయకునికి, G38, Sp- గాయకుని

८. T65- నిందితాలున్న, G86, G89- నిందితాలుక, G38- నిందితములు

९. G86- ****, G89, G38, Sp- □కి

१०. G86- ****, G89- ప్రత్యేత

११. G98, G17, B13- missing from here upto v.177 (description of each defect)

१२. T65- दशशना गोयः, G38, Sp- दर्शनां गोय

१३. T65- యీలకరుచుక, G38,Sp- యిలకరచుకోని

१४. G86,G89- పాడితె

१५. When one half-verse describes two defects, then in the Mss, it is split into two halves [where the description of each dōṣa ends] and the commentary to the corresponding portion is found in between. Here the verses are retained in the form of two quarters (half -verses) and the corresponding commentary portion is combined accordingly.

१६. G38, Sp- उद्बृष्टो

१७. T65- स्सुहे दृष्टः, G86, G89- विरहो दृष्टः since the reading does not convey proper sense, it is suggested thus.

शी[सी]त्कारि[१] सित्कु[सीत्कृ]तिर्मुहुः[२] ।। १६७ ।।

టీకా:- □ర(□)సంగా అధిక ఘోషంగా[३] పాడేది[४] ఉద్ఘుష్టమనబడును[५] (2[६]). మాటి[७] మాటికి శీ(సీ)త్కారం చేస్తూ(తు) పాడేది[८] సీత్కార[९]మనబడును (3).

भीतो भयास्वि[न्वि]तो गातः[गाता][१०] त्वरया कम्पितो[शङ्कितो][११] मतः[१२] ।

టీకా:- భయంతో గానం[१३] చేసేది[१४] భీతమనబడును[१५] (4). అతివేగంతో పాడేది[१६] కంపిత(శంకిత)[१७]మనబడును. 5.

कम्पितः कप[म्प]नाज्ञे[ज्ञे]यः[१८] स्वभावगात्रशब्दयोः[१९] ।। १६८ ।।

---

१. G86, G89- सीत्क्या

२. T65- सित्कूर्तिर्मुहुः, G38, Sp- शितृतीर्मुहुः

३. G86, G89- missing

४. G38- పాడునది

५. G86- వుద్రుష్ట*****,G38, Sp- ఉద్బ్రుష్టమనబడును

६. Numbering is missing in G38 and Sp and at a few places in T65

७. G38- మాటి మాటి

८. T65- చేస్తున్ను పాడేది□G86, G89- చేస్తునుండే పాడేతి, G38- చేస్తూ పాడునది

९. T65, G38, Sp- శీత్కార

१०. G86- भीमो भयास्वितो गौडः, G89- भी*** ******* गौडः, G38-प्रितो भयनितो घातः, Sp- भितो भयनितो घातः

११. G38, Sp- त्वरयु गंप्रतो "kampita: is described in the following verse as काम्पनाज्ज्ञेयः. Hence "śaṅkhita" is suggested here.

१२. T65- धृतः

१३. G86, Sp- add కూడ, G89- adds కూడా, G38- adds గూడ

१४. G86, G89- చేశేది, T65- జేశేది, G38- చేయునది

१५. G86- భీతము****

१६. G86- అతివేగం**పాడితే, G89-అతివేగం చాత పాడేతి, T65- అతివేగం చాత పాడిది, G38- అతివేగముగా బాడునది

१७. G38, Sp- కంబత

१८. T65- कुपितः कंपनोज्ञेयः, G89- **********, G38-कुप्पितरं प*****ज्ञेयः, Sp- कंपित कंपणश्चया

१९. G86, G89-missing?, G38, Sp- स्वाभारा गात्रशब्दयोः

టీకా:- శరీరమంతవణకుచు[1] పాడేది[2] శంఖిత(కంపిత)[3]మనబడును (6).

[4]करालं कथित[तं] संधि[सद्भिः] करालोत्पादिताननः[5]।

టీకా:-శ(శా)రీర ఎక్కువ తక్కువకా(గా)[6] పాడేది కరాళి అనబడును[7] (7).

[कपिलः स तु यो गायेत् स्वरान्न्यूनाधिकश्रुतीन्][8]।। १६९।।

టీకా:- స్వర చేతకు[9] ఎక్కుడు తక్కుడు[10] శ్రుతి[11] చేత పాడేది కపిల[12]మనబడును (8).

काकक्रूररव[वः][13] काकि[की][14] वितालस्ताल[15] विच्युता[तः][16]।

---

१. T65- శరీరంక్కు మణుగుచు, G86- శరీరమంత్తా మణుగుచు, G89- శరీరమంత్తా మణుకుచు, G38- శరీరమంత యువణకుచు

२. G38- పాడునది

३. T65,G86,G89- శంక్కీత

४. G86, G89- v.169ab and the following commenatary are missing

५. G38- कलाश नंदित *** सप्रिद्ध ककाहत्वादि तानसः, Sp- करास नंदितस्सप्रिद्ध कराहत्वादि तानसः

६. G38, Sp- మకుడు తకుడుగా

७. T65- omits అనబడును

८. T65- कंपितस्सतु गायेत्तु स्वरान् त्वरास्स्यूनाधिकस्तुतिः, G86- कपिलस्वरतो ***यतु *** रास्स्योनाधिकश्रुतिः, G89- कपिलस्वरतो गायतु तरास्योनाधिकश्रुतिः, Sp- कप्रला स तं गायंतु त्वरान्युनाधिकश्रुतिः, G38- कपिला स तु गायत्तु त्वरा न्युनाधिकश्रुतिः A consolidated reading is presented in this case, since no Mss give a complete correct reading.

९. G86- త్వర చాతకు, G89- త్వరచాతను, G38, Sp - omit

१०. G89- *****, T65 - missing

११. G38- కృతి, T65- missing

१२. Sp- కబల

१३. T65- काकःस्य, G86, G89- कारक्रूररवः

१४. G38- रौकि

१५. T65- विताळःस्तार, G86- विताळताळ, G89-वितीलस्ताल, G38- विताळस्***

१६. T65- विद्युतः, G89- विच्यु***,G38- सृमृतः, Sp- पिधृतः

టీకా:- క్రూరరవంగా[१] పాడేది[२] కాకి అనబడును (9); తాళం □డిచి[३] పాడేది □తాళమనబడును (10).

वहनः[४] कम्पितामूर्ध्वं[५] करंबो[भोऽ]भिहिता[तो][६]बुधैः ।। १७० ।।

టీకా:- వణుకుచు పోడవుగానికి(పొడవుగా)[७] పాడేది[८] కరంబ(భ)మనబడును[९] (11).

भा[छा][१०]गवत्वह्नि[हनी]कुर्व[र्वन्] उन्नधोय[न्मदोऽ]धमगायकः[११] ।

शिलाकराश्च[१२] वदनग्रीवं गाता तु[१३] साम्बकः[१४] ।। १७१ ।।

టీకా:- మేఘధ్వనిచేత[१५] ☐నోన్నుకాలుగా[१६] నోరు □గ్గలగా[१७] తెరచి[१८] మెడ పొడవుగా[१९]

---

१. T65- స్వరంగా, G86, G89- క్రూరంగా, G38- క్రూరరకంగా

२. G86- పాడితే, G89- పాడేతి, G38- పాడునవిల, Sp- పాడేదిల

३. T65- □ంబం □డిచి, G86- తాళ□డిచి, G89-*****

४. T65- दहनः, G38, Sp- दहनं

५. T65- कपितामूर्ध्यं, G86, G89- कपितामूध्यं, G38-कम्पितमूर्धं

६. T65- करंभोपिहिता, G86, G89- करंभोपिहिता, G38- करंबोभिहितां

७. T65, G38, Sp- పోడువు

८. G38- పాడునది

९. T65- కరంభసమనబడును, G89- కరంభ ******

१०. The syllables 'cha' and 'bha' look similar in the Mss written in Telugu script, hence they could have been misinterpreted.

११. G86- भोगवंद्यहनि ****उन्नधोधम गायकं, G89- भोगवंद्यप्रनि कुर्वः उन्नधोधम गायकं, G38- प्राग **द्वहनी कंर्षा उन्मदोदम गायकः, Sp- भागद्वहनी कंर्याउन्मंदोदम गायकः

१२. G86- शिताकर च, G89- शिताकर छ, G38, Sp- निताकरा च

१३. G86, G89- ता तु, G38- घाता म, Sp- घाता हु

१४. T65- सांप्राकं

१५. G86, G89-మేఘధ్వనిచ్చాతను, G38- మేఖధ్వని చేతన, Sp- ముఖధ్వని చాతను

१६. G86, G89-☐నోన్నుకల, G38- ☐నూంమతాలు, Sp- ☐నూంమతాలు

१७. G38- బిగి□, Sp- భిగి□

१८. T65- తెరుచి

१९. G89- missing upto the middle of the commentary to v.172ab, which is seen as 'inserted text' in G86, Sp- మెడ పొడువుగా

యెత్తి[१] పాడినది[२] సాంబకమనబడును[३] (12).

तुम्बु[ब]कि[४] तुम्बुकाकारो[५]पु[त्फु]ल्लगल्लस्तु गायकः।

టీకా:- దవడలు గరుచుకొని[६] బకాకారంగా[७] పాడేది[८] బకి[९] అనబడును (13).

वक्रि[क्री]कृतगलो[१०] गायन् धीरैरिति[र्वक्री] उदीरितः[११]।। १७२।।

టీకా:- మెడ వోరగా[१२] జేసుకొని పాడేది వక్రి అనబడును (14).

प्रसारि[री][१३] गि[गी]यते[१४] तज्ञः[ज्ञैः] गात[त्र]गीत[१५] प्रसारिणिः[रणात्][१६]।

టీకా:-[१७]మెడ తిప్పుచు[१८] పాడేది ప్రసారి అనబడును (15).

ने[नि]मीलकस्ततो[१९] गायि[यन्] निमीलक इति स्मृतः।। १७३।।

టీకా:- నేత్రని□లనత్వం[२०] చేత పాడేది[२१] ని□లక[२२]మనబడును (16).

---

१. Sp- ఇతి

२. G86- పాడేది, G38- పాడునది, Sp- పాడిన

३. G86- సాంబమనంబడును

४. T65,G86,G89- मंबाकि, Sp- तुम्बुरि, The commentary reads this as 'baki'

५. G86- तुम्बु****, G38- तुम्बुकारोर, Sp- तुम्बुनाणार

६. G38, Sp- కరచుకొని

७. Sp- బికారంగా, G89-missing upto this.

८. G38- పాడునది, Sp- పాడినది

९. G86- -బకె, G89-బక, G38-బకం, Sp- బికారం

१०. T65- वक्रिकृतकळी, G86, G89- वकृकृदगळो

११. G86, G89- धीरैरतिवुदीरितः, G38- दर*राद यितीरुतः, Sp- दरेरंदयितीरुतः

१२. G86- వోరగా, G38, Sp- వార

१३. T65- प्रसाद

१४. G38,Sp- नियते

१५. G38-त***गात नीत, Sp- तब्रगातनीत

१६. T65- प्रसाराणाः, G89- ********, G38, Sp- प्रसारिणः

१७. T65- missing upto the commenatry to v.173cd

१८. G38-మెడద్రింపుచు, Sp- మెడత్రిపుచు

१९. G86, G89- ని□టికస్తదో

२०. G89- నేత్రనీ□లనత్వం, G38- నేత **□లనత్వ, Sp- నేత్ర□లనత్వం

२१. G89- ******, G38- పాడునది

२२. G86- ని□ల, G89- ***ల

विरस्सो[१] वि[नी]रसो[२] वर्ज्य[३]स्वरगानत[नाद]पस्वरः[४]।

टीका:- [५]రసహీనంగా పాడేది[६] □రస[७]మనిపించుకొనును (17); అపస్వరాల చేత పాడినది[८] అపస్వరమనబడును[९] (18).

गद्गदद्वाचि[ध्वनि]रव्यक्तः[क्तं][१०] वर्णं अव्यक्तमुच्यते[११]।।१७४।।

टीका:- [१२]గద్గద స్వరం చేత[१३] పాడేది[१४] అవ్యక్తమనబడును (19).

स्थानभ्रष्टः[१५] स य [यः][१६] प्राप्तंमशक[प्राप्तुमशक्तः][१७] स्थानकत्रयम्[१८]।

टीका:- మంద్ర[१९]మధ్యమతారకాలయందు[२०] అశక్తుడై[२१] గానం చేసినది[२२] స్థానభ్రష్ట[२३]మనబడును (20).

---

१. T65, G86, G89- वीरसो
२. G86, G89- पिरसो
३. T65- वर्जं
४. T65- स्वरनानदतपस्वरः, G38, Sp- स्व * * * दपसर्वा
५. T65 - this line is missing
६. G38- పాడునది
७. T65, G86, G89- □రసహీన
८. T65- పాడేది, G38- పాడునది
९. T65-అపస్వరహీనమనబడును, G38-అపస్వరములనబడును, Sp-అపస్వరాలనబడును
१०. G86- गद्गदव्याविरयुक्तः, G89- गद्गदव्याविरयुकुः, G38, Sp- गद्गदद्वाविरव्यक्तः
११. G86, G89- फणस्तु व्यक्तमुच्यते, G38- वणस्त्य व्यक्तमुच्येत्, Sp- वणस्तमुक्तमुच्यते
१२. T65- this line is missing
१३. G38, Sp - missing
१४. G86, G89- పాడేనది, G38- పాడునది
१५. G86- स्थानप्रष्टः, G38, Sp- स्थानभ्रुष
१६. T65- स्वयं, G86, G89- श्वय
१७. G86, G89- फलत्वः मळक, G38- प्राप्तिःमसक, Sp- प्राप्तःमशक
१८. G38, Sp- स्तानकत्रियं
१९. G38, Sp- ముద్ర
२०. G86, G89- చాత యందు, G38- యెత
२१. T65, Sp- అశక్తుండ, G38- టీ। అశక్తుండై
२२. G89- *********, G38- గానము చేసిన□Sp- యీ గానం చేసినది
२३. G89- స్తానభ్రష్ట, G38, Sp- స్తానబృష్ఠ

अव्यवस्थित[१] इत्युक्तं[क्त] स्ता[था]नकैर्व्य[रव्य] वस्थितेः[तैः][२] ।। १७५ ।।

टीकाः- తృ(త్రి)స్తా(థా)నాల[३] చేతను నేమకం(నియమ ం) లేక[४] పాడేది[५] అవ్యవస్తి(థి)త[६] మనబడును (21).

शुद्धछायालगौ[७] रागौ[८] मिश्रयं[यन्] मिश्रकस्यतः[स्ततः] ।

इतरेषां[९] तु[१०] रागाणां[११] मिश्रको[१२] भूतिमिश्रणः [भूरिमिश्रणात्][१३] ।। १७६ ।।

टीकाः- ఘనమందు కల్పితాలు[१४] చేసి[१५] పాడినది[१६] ◻శకమనబడును[१७] (22).

स्थायधिष्य[यादिष्व]वधानेन[१८] निर्मुक्तो[१९][ऽ]नवधानकः[२०] ।

---

१. G38, Sp- अव्यवस्तित

२. G86- स्तान कैर*****रितः, G38- स्तानकैरव्यवस्तिति, Sp- स्तानकैरव्यवस्तिते, G89- missing upto the half of v.176ab. This portion is seen as inserted text, in G86.

३. G38, Sp- అ్స్తానాల

४. T65- నేమకు లేక, G86- నెముఖం లా**క

५. T65, G86 - పాడినది, G38-పాడునది

६. T65- అవ్యవస్తితం, G86- అవ్యవృస్తితం

७. G86-शुद्धच्यायालगौ, G38-शुधचायालगो, Sp- शुद्धचायालगो रागौ

८. G86- रकं, T65- प्रागौ

९. G38, Sp- यातरेपो

१०. G86, G89- म, T65- missing

११. G86,G89,G38,Sp- रागानां

१२. G38- मित्रगो, Sp- मिश्रगो

१३. G86,G89- मित्रमश्रणः, T65- प्रुदिमिश्रणः

१४. T65- కపతాలు

१५. G89- ****

१६. G89- ******, G38- పాడునది

१७. G86- ◻శగుడనబడును, G89-***** గుడనబడును, G38,Sp- ◻శకుండనబడును

१८. G86, G89- स्धायिधिष्यरधानेन, G38-स्तायादिष्यवदानेन, Sp- स्तायादिष्ववदानन्न

१९. T65, G86, G89- निर्मुक्ता

२०. G38, Sp- नवधानतः

टीका:- స్థాయీ,[१] స్వరం,[२] ఎడుపు, ఆయత-ప్రత్యాయతం,[३] డాలు, కంపితం[४], ఉగ్రం[५], ముక్తాయి, ఎరుగగ(క) పాడేది[६] అనరధా(అనవధాని)[७]అని పించుకొనును[८] (23).

गेयान्[यं][९] नाशि[सि]कय[या][१०] गायन्[११] गीयते[१२] सानुनासिकः[१३] ।। १७७ ।।

टीका:- ముక్కున[१४] పాడేది[१५] అనునాసికమనబడును[१६] (24[१७]); ఈ తీరున దోషముక్తుండైన[१८] వాడు[१९] గానానకు(నికి)[२०] నిందితుడు[२१].

---

१. G38, Sp- స్తాో

२. G38, Sp- స్వర

३. G38, Sp- ఆయుత ప్రత్యాయుత

४. T65- కంటితః, G86, G89- కంపితః

५. G86, T65- ఉగ్ర, G89- ****

६. G38- ఎరుగక పాడునది

७. G38,Sp- అవధాని

८. T65- అనిపించును, Sp- అనుపించుకొనును

९. G38, Sp- गयन्

१०. T65- नाशिकयि, G86, G89- नाशिकाय

११. T65, G89- गायं, G86- गा**

१२. T65, G86, G89- गिय्यते, G38- गिय्येते

१३. G38, Sp- सानुनाशिकः

१४. G86, G89- ముక్కుతో

१५. G38- పాడునది

१६. G89- అనునా *******డును, G38, Sp-అనుకమనబడును

१७. G38- 24 స్వరము, Sp- 24 సర్వం

१८. T65, G89- ధోక్తుండైన, G86- దోక్తుండైన

१९. G86- వాండు

२०. T65, G86, G89- గానికి, G38- గానమునకు

२१. G86, G89- నిందితుండు, Sp- నిందింతుండు. After this, the following lines are found only in G38 and Sp: G38- సర్వదోషకుండు అని దేవతలు చేసినారు ఈ దోషాలు గానము ☐వారలకు స్వరము ఆప్తలు శిద్ధమ్బును అనేక ఆప్తలు శిద్ధమ్బును Sp- సర్వదోషకుండు అని దేవతులు చేసినారు ఈ దోషాలు గానం ☐వారులకు స్వరం ఆప్తలు శిద్ధించును అనేక ఆప్తలు శిద్ధించును.

[1]वाङ्माधुर्य[र्यं][2] विराजित[3]स्थितमतीः[4] भव्याकृतिर्येकधा[5]
तालज्ञो[6] बहुपाठको[7] विनयवानादिग्रहज्ञानवान्[8] ।
रागाणामखिलार्थवित्[9] प्रणयवान्[10] दोषैर्विहि[ही]नश्शुचिः[11]
चित्तज्ञः[12][13]परनायकस्य[13] स भवेत्[14]भूमण्डले गायकः[15] ।। १७८ ।।
षाडवौडवसम्पूर्ण[16] शुद्धसालगसङ्करः[राः][17] ।
[18]रागैर्गायै[येत्][19] स्वरज्ञानं[स्वरज्ञानी][20] स गायक इतिस्मृतः[21] ।। १७९ ।।

---

१. G38,Sp- ఇక గాయక లక్షణం This verse is different from the verse commonly found in texts like SR. set to śārdūlavikrīḍitā metre.
२. G86- वाङ्मदुर्य, G89- वाङ्मादुर्य, Sp- वाङ्याधुर्या
३. Sp- विराजीत
४. G98,G17,B13-स्थितिमतिः, G86,G89- स्तितमती, G38- स्तितमतिः, Sp- स्तिति
५. G98, G17- भव्याकृतिर्वैकथा, B13- भव्याकृतिर्नैकथा, G86, G89- नव्याकृतिर्येकधा, G38, Sp- भव्याकृतियैकधा
६. G38, Sp- ताळाज्ञ
७. T65, G86, G89- बहुपारको
८. T65- नयवाण् आदिग्रहवाज्ञानवाण्, G86- टि नयवाण् आदि ग्रहवाज्ञानवाण्, G89- टि ****** आदिग्रहवाज्ञानवाण्, G38, Sp- विनयवां आदिग्रक अज्ञानवान्
९. G98-मखिलार्तवि, G17-मखिलार्तवि(र्थवित्), T65-मखिलार्थवि, G86,G89- मखिलार्थ, G38, Sp- मखिलार्त्थवि
१०. G98, G17, G86, G89- प्रणयवाण्, G38, Sp- प्रणवां
११. T65- दोषेर्विनःश्शुचिः, G98- दोषेर्विहिनश्शुचिः, G86- दोषैर्विहि *** शु ** :, G89- दोषैर्विहिनशुचिः, G38, Sp- दोषैविहिनं शुचिः
१२. G98, G17, B13- श्चित्तज्ञा, G86- ***ज्ञः, G89- चित्ताज्ञ, G38, Sp- चितज्ञः
१३. G17- प(न)रनायकस्य
१४. G86- स्वभदे, G89- स्वभवे, G38, Sp- स भव
१५. G38- भूमंडु गायकः, Sp- भूमंडुल गाय
१६. G86- षाडववौडवसम्पूर्न, G89- षाडव *****सम्पूर्न
१७. T65- शुद्धांसाळगसंकरः, G86, G89- सुधासाळवसंकरैः, G38-शुधरालगसन्कराः, Sp- शुद्धरालगसन्कराः
१८. T65, G98, G17, B13 - v.179cd is missing
१९. G86, G89- रागैगायॆ, G38- रागैर्गायै
२०. Reading based on BKM
२१. G38- सगायकैतिसृतः , Sp- सगायकैसृतः

టీకా:- [१]షాడవం, ఔడవ, సంపూర్ణం[२] సుద్ధా(శుద్ధ)[३], సాళగ[४], సంకర, గ్రహ, మూర్చ్ఛనా[५], ఆరోహణి, అవరోహణీ(ణి)[६], త్రిష్థాయీ(స్థాయీ)[७], స్వర[८], సంచారీ, ఆయతప్రత్యాయత[९], ఎడుపు, డాలు, తాయి[१०], ఉగ్రం, ముక్తాయి[११], కంపితం, స్త్రి(స్త్రీ)[१२]పురుషరాగ □త్ర సంకలిత[१३] సంకీర్ణం[१४], ద్వాత్రింశద్రాగలక్షణం[१५], గీత స్వర నాద[१६], వాది అనువాది సంవాది, □ాది[१७] స్వరలక్షణం, తాళకాలం రాగకాలం రాగవేళ[१८] సప్తస్వరలక్షణం, స్వరప్రస్తారం[१९], రాగప్రస్తారం[२०], స్వరరాగగుణదోషం, ధ్వనిభేద, తానోత్పన్న[२१],

---

१. T65, G98, G17, B13- missing upto సంకర
२. G86- షాడవౌడసంపూర్న, G89- షాడ ఔడ సంపూర్న
३. G86- ******, G38, Sp - missing
४. G86, G89- సాళవ
५. B13- మూర్చనః, T65- మూర్ఛనా, G38- మూర్చన, Sp- మూర్ఛన
६. G38, Sp- ఔవరోహణి
७. G86, G89- దృష్థాయి, G38, Sp- త్రిస్తాయి
८. G38, Sp- స్వరం
९. T65- ఆయుతప్రత్యాయుత, G38- ఆయుతాప్రత్యాయుత, Sp- ఆయుతం ప్రత్యాయుతం
१०. Sp- స్తాయి
११. G86, G89, G38- ముక్తాయ
१२. T65, G86, G89, G38, Sp- శ్రీ
१३. G86- రాగ □త ** త్ర సంకిలిత, G89- ***** సంకిలిత, G38, Sp- రాగా □త్రా□త సంకలిత
१४. G98,G17, B13- సకీర్ణం, G38, Sp- సంకీర్ణా
१५. G98, B13- ద్వాత్రింశద్గాత్రలక్షణం, G17- ద్వాత్రింశద్గాత్రలక్షణు, G38, Sp- ద్వాత్రింశంరాగలక్షణం
१६. G98, G17, B13- గీతస్వరాది, G86, G89- గీతస్వరా నాద, G38, Sp- గీతస్వర నాధా
१७. T65- సవాధి □ాధి, G98, G17, B13- □ాది సంవాది
१८. G86, G89- రాగవ్యాళ
१९. T65- స్వరప్రష్థారం, G98, G17, B13- స్వరప్రష్థార
२०. G98, G17, B13- రాగప్రష్థార
२१. T65- తనోత్పన్న, G86, G89- తనోత్పన్న, G38, Sp-తనోత్పన

అలంకార[1], గాయక దోష, గాయక భేదం, యెరిగి[2] వాక్చాతుర్యం కలిగి[3] పరుల[4] చిత్తమెరిగి[5], స్వరరాగాలు జంత్ర గాత్రాల[6] యందు[7] గానం చేసినవాడు[8] గాయకుడు[9].

सोमनाथ[10] मते प्रोक्तं[11] स्वराणां[12] रागलक्षणम्।। १८०।।

టీకా:- ఈ స్వర[13] రాగాల లక్షణ లక్ష్యం[14] సోమనాథ[15]మతమనే[16] లోకోపకార భరత[17] గ్రంథమందు చెప్పబడెను[18]. సంగీతరత్నాకరమునందు[19] సంగ్రహించి సంక్షేపముగాను[20] జంత్రగాత్రానికి[21] సంమందం(బంధం)గాను[22] అష్టావధాన[23] సోమప్పా(ప్ప) జేసిన[24]

१. G38, Sp- అలంకారం
२. G38, Sp - missing
३. G86, G89- వాక్షాతుశ్య గలిగి, G38- వాక్చాతుర్యములు గల్గి, Sp- వాక్చాతుర్యములు గలిగి
४. G98, G17, B13- పరులు
५. G98- చిత్తవేరిగి, G38- చితమెటిగి
६. T65, G86, G89- జంత్రఘాత్రాల, G38- ఝంత్రఘాత్రములు, Sp- ఝంత్రఝాత్రాలు
७. G38, Sp- యుందు
८. G38, Sp- చేసినవాడు
९. T65, G98, G17, B13- గాయకుండు
१०. G38- सोमनाद
११. G38, Sp - *******
१२. Sp- स्वराणं
१३. G89- యీశ్వర
१४. T65- రాగాల లక్షణం లక్షియ్యం, G89- రాగాల లక్షణం లక్షియ, G38, Sp- రాగ లక్షణ లక్ష్యం
१५. G38- సోమనాద
१६. G86- మ ****, G38- మతమునే, Sp- మథమనే
१७. T65- omits
१८. G86,G89- చెప్పబడును, G38, Sp- గ్రంథమందుండెను
१९. G38- మునందు
२०. G38- सक्षिप्तमुगा, Sp- సంక్షేపంగాను
२१. G86, G89- జంద్ర గాత్రానికి, G38- ఝంత్రఘాత్రమునకు, Sp- ఝంత్రఝాత్రానికు
२२. T65- సంమదంగాను
२३. T65, G38, Sp- అష్టావధాని
२४. G38- సో *** న, Sp- స్వర

సంగీతరత్నాకరం గీతాధ్యాయం సమాప్తః[१].

अथा[था] गीता:[तं][२]

[३]अष्टभाषापदैर्युक्तं[४] शब्दझंकार[५]संयुतम्[६] ।

स्वररागैः[७] प्रगायन्ते[८] गीतमित्यभिधीयते[९] ।। १८१ ।।

टीका:- అష్టభాషలయొక్క[१०] పదాలతో[११]గూడి[१२] శబ్దఝంకార[१३] ▯త్రమై[१४] స్వరరాగాల[१५] చేత గానం చేయతగినది[१६] గీతమని చెప్పబడును[१७].

अथा[था] प्रबन्धः

---

१. T65- గీతాధ్యాయస్సమాప్తః V08 ends thus:- ఇది అష్టావధాన ▯ఖ్యాత సోమనార్యుడు చేసి సంగీతరత్నాకరాధ్యాయము (?) G38,Sp- శ్రీ శారదామ్బాయనమః శ్రీ శ్రీ శ్రీ జే/జాయును These (post-colophon) statements are missing in G86, G89 and T65.

२. G38, Sp- अथा गीतः, G98, G17, B13, T65-अथ गीता

३. v.181, cf. SSP part-1, p.47.

४. T65,G86,G89,G98- अष्टभाषावदैर्युक्तं, G17- अष्टभाषाव(प)दैर्युक्त्तं, G38, Sp- अष्टभाषपदैर्युक्तं

५. G98,G17-झंखार, T65-झुंकार, G86, G89-झुक्कार

६. Sp- सैम्युतं

७. G38, Sp- स्वररागा

८. G89- *******

९. G86,G89-गीतमित्यभिधिय्यते,G98-गीतमित्यभिदिय्यते, G38,Sp- गीतमित्याभिधीयते

१०. G38, Sp - missing

११. T65, G89- పాదాలతో, G86- పాదాలుతో

१२. T65- గూడ, G38- గూడిన

१३. T65, G86- ఝుంకార, G89- ఝుక్కార

१४. G38, Sp- ▯శ్రమై

१५. G38- రాగముల

१६. G86, G89- చాయబడినది, G38- చేయబడినది, Sp- చాయబడినది

१७. T65- పించబడును, G89- *********

[१]चतुर्भिः[२] पञ्चभिः[३] षड्भिश्चागैर्यस्ता[ङ्गैर्यस्तु][४] प्रयुज्यते।
तस्मात्[५] प्रबन्धा[धः] कथितैः[तः][६] प्रतापः प्रध्विभुजः[पृथिवीभुजा][७] ।। १८२ ।।
[८]प्रबन्धानि षडङ्गानि[९] स्वरश्च[१०] प्रिरुदं[११] पदं।
त्येनक[तेनकः][१२] पद[पाट][१३] वाक्यं[१४] च प्रबन्धपुरुषा[१५] भवेत्[१६]
[षस्य ते][१७] ।।१८३ ।।

---

१. Texts like SSS 4,2, CDP 9,3 and Jagadēka (ext. in Bharatakōśa,p.389) recognise four dhātu-s and six aṅga-s for a prabandha. According to SR, the aṅga-s for a prabandha could be six, five, four, three or even two. But the present text reads in a different way, thus accepting only four or five or six aṅga-s and does not seem to speak of dhātu-s.

२. G86- चतु**भिः, G38- चतुर्भि

३. G86,G89, T65-पंचभि

४. G86,G89-षध्भिःश्चगैरसां,G98,B13-षड्भिश्चागैर्यस्ता, G17-षड्भिश्चा(रा?)गैर्यस्तु, T65-षड्भिःश्चगैर्यस्ता, G38- षड्जश्चांगैर्यस्मा, Sp- षड्भिःश्चांगैर्यस्मा

५. G89- तसा***त्, G38- तस्त्मा, Sp- तस्मा

६. T65- *****, G38,Sp- खदिता, G98,G17,B13- stop with this quarter verse; however B13 reads कथितैः .... (suggesting that it is incomplete)

७. G89- प्रधापः व्यधिभिवि भुजा, G38- प * * *पृद्वीपि भुजा, Sp- ****पृध्विपि भुजा

८. v.183- v.184, cf. SR 4,12cd-14ab.Suggested readings are based on SR.

९. G89- ***********

१०. G98, G17, B13- स्वयश्च, T65- स्वस्यच, G86- स्वयच, G89- *** यच्च

११. G86, G89- रुदं

१२. G86, G89- तृन्नकं, T65- त्यन्नकः

१३. Since 'pada' has already been listed in the previous line,'pāṭa' is suggested on the basis of SR 4,13a. The commentary reads 'pāṭha'.

१४. Sp- पडवाक्यं; It is strange to note that vākya is being enumerated as one of the limbs, instead of tāla. BKM, RJM, SSB too follow this concept.

१५. G98,G17, B13- प्रबन्धः पुरुषा

१६. G86, G89- भवेतु, G38-भवेतू

१७. Since the following verse commences with 'bhavanti', the word 'bhavēt' here does not seem proper. Hence the reading from SR has been suggested to give a meaningful reading.

भवत्यंग[न्त्यङ्ग]प[व]दाङ्गानि[१] मङ्गलां ते[लार्थ][२] प्रयुज्यते[३]।
[४]यत्र देन्नपदौ नेत्रा[५] तत्वेद बिरुधं करोः[६] [तत्र तेनपदे नेत्रे
स्तः पाटबिरुदे करौ][७]।। १८४।।
स्वरं स्वरं चिर्ध्यांतरं[स्वरं स्वरान्तरं?][८] वाक्यं पदं
कंठस्तथे[थे]ति च[९][?]।
स्वरे तु वर्धनादे[१०] स्यात् बिरुदं[११] वीरवर्धनं[१२][?] ।। १८५।।
पदे करुण पूर्वं[१३] स्यात् गुंभ[फ]नादिषु[१४] तन्यते[१५][?]।
यत्किञ्चिन्नटनं दृष्ट्वा[१६] सर्वपापैः[१७] प्रमुच्यते[१८] ।। १८६।।

---

१. G86- भवेत्यंगपदंगानि, G38, Sp- भव * * * गानि
२. G38- मंगळार्ति, Sp- मंगळार्तिं, this is probably an error caused by improper prouncіation and hence the reading is suggested on the basis of the commentary.
३. T65- प्रयुष्यते. SR reads प्रकाशके
४. T65, G98, G17, B13 - v.184cd - v.85ab are missing
५. G89- **************,G38- यधर्म पधौ नेत्र, Sp- यधार्न पधौ नेत्र
६. G38- तद्वार फ्रिरुदं करौ, Sp- तद्वार बिरुदं नरौ
७. The idea is identical to that which is conveyed in SR 4,14ab. Hence the reading is suggested from SR.
८. G38, Sp- स्वरश्चौध्याम्तरं. The reading of the text and the corresponding commentary from v.185 - v.186ab are not clear.
९. G38, Sp- वाक्यं पद * * * *
१०. T65, G98, G17, B13- स्वरे त वर्धसादे, G38, Sp- स्तदे तु वर्धनोदे
११. G38- शा *******, Sp- श्या तु
१२. G86- पीरवर्धनं, G89- ********
१३. G98, G17, B13 -पूर्वा
१४. G38, Sp- गुम्भनारिषु
१५. G86, G89-तंवत्रे, G38, Sp- त्यंन्यते
१६. T65- यत्किंचि नटनं दृष्ट्वा, G86- यत्किंचि***टनं दृष्टा, G89- यत्किंचि नटनं दृष्टा, G38, Sp- यत्किंचि **********
१७. G86- स्वरपापै, G89- स्व**पापै, G38, Sp- स्वररागै
१८. G98, G17, B13 break here and read commentary on tāna-s.

టీకా:- 4, 5, 6 అంగాల[౧] ఎప్పుడు గూరుస్తున్నారో అప్పుడు ప్రబంధమని భూభుండ్లు[౨] చెప్పెను[౩]. ఆ ప్రబంధం ఆరు అంగాలు[౪]. అది(□ ఏ□యుంటే[౫] స్వరం, బిరుద[౬], పదం, తన్నకారం[౭], పాఠ[౮], వాక్యం. ఈ ఆరు[౯] కూడినది ప్రబంధమని చెప్పబడును[౧౦]. తన్నకారం[౧౧] మంగళార్థం[౧౨] త్ర(ప్ర)యోగింపదగినది[౧౩]. ఎక్కడ తేన్నపా(ప)దాలు[౧౪] ఉన్నదో[౧౫] అక్కడ పాట బిరుదు డాలు(?) చెప్పతగినది[౧౬]. స్వరాంతరం వాక్యం పదంకంఠ వ వర్ధనాదం[౧౭] స్వరం □వర్ధనం[౧౮] బిరుదం(?)- ఈ ప్రబంధ నటనం చూచినవారికి[౧౯]

౧. T65- 5 అంగాలు, G86, G89- 5 6॥ అంగాలు, G38- 4, 5, 6 అంగాలను

౨. G38, Sp- భూభుజుండు, T65- బు□భుడు

౩. G86, G89, T65- చెప్పను

౪. G86- ఆ ప్రబంధమని చే ***లు, G89- ఆ ప్రబంధమని చే 6 అంగాలు, G38, Sp- 6 అంగాలు

౫. G86- అది***ంటి, G89- అది అంటి, T65- అది అంటే, G38- అ□ఏ□యనగా

౬. T65, G86, G89, Sp- బిరుదు

౭. T65- త్యయిన్నకారం, G89 - ***********, G38- జన్యవారము, Sp- జన్యకారం

౮. T65- పాఠా, G38- పాద, Sp- పాఠ

౯. G38- ఈ 6 ను, Sp- యి□6

౧౦. T65- ప్రబంధమనబడును, G38- ప్రబంధమని చెప్పుదురు, Sp- ప్రబంధమని చే ***

౧౧. T65- త్యన్నకారం, G38, Sp- *** రౌరం

౧౨. T65- मंदळार्द, G38- मंगळार्थि

౧౩. T65- దదం త్రయోగిపతగినది missing from here to the next తగినది, G86- త్రయోగింప్పతగిన***, G38,Sp- missing upto వర్ధనాదం in this sentence

౧౪. G86- యెక్కడ **పాదాలు

౧౫. G86- వున్నది

౧౬. G89- ***** చెప్పతగినది

౧౭. G86, G89- పదంకుంఠం వర్ధనాదం, G38- ప్రయు వర్ధనాదము, Sp- ప్రయు వర్ధనారం

౧౮. G38, Sp- స్వరం □ర్ధనం

౧౯. G86- వారి***, G89- ******

సకల పాపాలు పోవును[१]. ☐వారికి సకల శ్రేయస్సు కలవు[२].

ध्रुवादि सप्ततालैश्च[३] स्वर[सर्व][४]भाषापदान्य[दैर]पि।

स्वररागै[गैः][५] प्रगायन्ते[६] सूलादिरिति[७] कथ्यते[८] ।। १८७ ।।

టీకా:- ధ్రువాది[९] సప్తతాళాల[१०] చేతను, సర్వ[११]భాష(షా)లయొక్క పదాలు స్వరరాగాల[१२] గానం జేశినది[१३] సూళాది[१४] అనబడును.

१. G89- ****వును, G38, Sp- పోయి

२. T65- క***, G86- కలుగు, G38, Sp read slightly different: G38-వారికి సకల భోగములు ఐశ్వర్యములు ఆయురాభిర్విభివేది కలిగి వుందురు, Sp- వారలకు సకల భోగాలు ఐశ్వర్యములు, ఆయురాభి☐ద్ధిత్తి కలిగి వుండురు and add further: G38- సంగీతమపి సాహిత్యం సర****ద్వయం ఏక మాపాధురం అన్యధాలోచనామృతం. ఈ ప్రకారము దైవస్వరూపము గనుక గానం శృతులు***డును. రత్నాకర సూర్యోదయము శ్రీ శారదాంబా నీవగరి Sp- సంగీతమపి సాహిత్యం సర**** ద్వయం ఏక☐పాద మధురం అన్యధాలోచనామృతం. ఈ ప్రకారం దైవ స్వరూపం గనుక గానం శృతులు***డును. This line is missing in T65, G86, G89.

३. G86, G89- धृवादि सप्तताळश्चा, G38,Sp- दृवादि सप्तताळश्च

४. The term 'svara' occurs along with rāga in the following line of this verse and the reading 'sarvabhāṣā' was preferred. In the commentary, T65 reads only 'sarva' and hence the same has been suggested here. This kind of error arising due to the confusion between svara and sarva in Telugu script is noted at a few more places in this work.

५. G38, Sp- सर्वरागै

६. G89- प्र******, G38- ********

७. G86- सूळादिरीति, G89- *******रीति

८. G38, Sp- खद्यते

९. G86,G89- ధృవాది, G38, Sp- దృవాది

१०. G38- తాళముల

११. G86,G89- స్వర, G38- వరుస, Sp- పరుష

१२. G86, G89, G38, Sp- రాగాలు

१३. G86, G89- చేశినది, G38- *********, Sp- ******ను

१४. T65- ళాది, G89- సూ *********డును

श्रुत्युक्त[१]पदशब्दानि[२] गेया[यं] नामावलीरितम्[३]।

టీకా:- స్తోత్ర[४] యుక్తమైన పదశబ్దాలు గానం చేశినది[५] నామావళి[६].

गीर्वाणं[ण][७]वाक्यरूपेण[८] गाय[गेया][९] चूर्नीक[र्णिका] कीर्तितः[ता][१०] ।। १८८ ।।

టీకా:- సంస్కృతము[११] వాక్యరూపం[१२] చేత గానం చేశినది[१३] చూర్ణిక అనబడును[१४].

चूर्नी[र्णि]कावाक्यश्लोकैश्च[१५] कथागेयोक्त[क्तं][१६] नाटकम्[१७]।

టీకా:- చూర్ణిక[१८] వాక్య శ్లోకాల[१९] చేత కథాప్రసంగంగా[२०] గానం[२१] చేశినది[२२] నాటకం[२३].

---

१. G86, G89- शृत्यक्त, G38, Sp- स्त्युतुक्त

२. G38- वर्दशब्दानि, Sp- वर्धसब्दानि

३. G86- गेयानिमवलीरितं, G89- गे*****मातलीरितं, G38, Sp- गेयु नामावळिरितं

४. G86- ****త్రి

५. T65- జేశినది (the text gets repeated in G86 and G89 from the previous జేశినది)

६. G38, Sp- నా ****

७. T65- निर्वाणं, G38, Sp- *******

८. T65- वाक्यरउपेणा , G86- वा ***रूपेणा, G89- वाक्यं रूपेणा

९. reading based on BKM,p.99

१०. G89- *************र्तितः

११. G38, Sp- వసంతము

१२. T65- వాక్యర ఉపం

१३. T65- జేశినది, G38, Sp- గానం చేసిన చూర్నీకా వాగానం చేశిన

१४. G38- అది చూర్నీకమనబడును, Sp- అధి చూర్నీక అన *******

१५. G38, Sp- चूर्नीकवाक्यश्लोकश्च

१६. G86- कधागेयोक, G89- **धागेयो**, G38- खदागेयोस्त, Sp- खदागेयोक्त

१७. G89- ********

१८. G86- చ ***ర్ణిక, G89- *********

१९. T65- వాక్యాల స్వరాల

२०. G38, Sp- పేసంగంగా

२१. T65, G86, G89- ను

२२. G38- చేసినది

२३. G38, Sp- అది నాటకం

एतेषाम्[१] लक्षणं सम्यक् वक्ष्यते[२] सोमसूरिणा[३] ।। १८९ ।।

इदि[ति][४] स्वररागसुधारसाख्यो[५] गीताध्याय[यः][६] समाप्तः।

१. Sp- यतसां

२. G86-संयुस्वक्ष्यते, G89-संयिस्वक्ष्यते, G38- सम्यगृ *** सूर्यणं, Sp- संयग ******

३. T65-सोमनारिणः, G89- सोम*****,G38,Sp- सूर्यणं

४. G89- *****

५. G86- స్వరరాగసుధారసాఖ్యా, G89- స్వరరా*****రసాఖ్యా, G38, Sp- స్వరరాగసుధారసాఖ్యారి

६. G38- గీతాధ్యాయం T65- Ends with the following colophon- श्री कामाक्षी अम्म्रा सहायं। करकृतमपराधं क्षतु * * * सन्तः।। सामैय्य। लावि[लिखि?]तं श्री रामार्पणमस्तु। श्री कामाक्षी देत्यार्पणमस्तु।। G38 ends thus:- श्री श्री श्री जेयुनु।, Sp ends thus:- श्री श्री श्री जायनु। శ్రీ కామాక్షీ అమ్మా సహాయం। కర కృతమపరాధం క్షతు * * * సన్తః॥ సామైయ్య లా□(లిఖి?)తం శ్రీ రామార్పణమస్తు. శ్రీ కామాక్షీ దేత్యార్పణమస్తు. G38 ends thus:- శ్రీ శ్రీ శ్రీ జేయును।, Sp ends thus:- శ్రీ శ్రీ శ్రీ జాయను।

३. वाद्याध्यायः

नाधः [अथ वाद्यः][१]।

पञ्चविद[ध][२]वाद्यभेदास्तु लक्षणं वदेत् [वाद्यभेदस्य लक्षणमुच्यते][३]।

[४]नखवायुज चर्मानि[ज][५] लोपा[ह]शारीरजस्व[त]था[६]।

नखाबी[वी]णादयः प्रोक्तं[क्ता]वंशाद्या[द्याः]वायुपूर[रि]ताः।। १।।

चर्माणी[जा] च मृदङ्गाद्याः[द्या][७] लोक[ह]स्तालादयस्तथा[८]।

वि[दे[९]]हनादेन ते युक्ताः वाद्याः पञ्चविधा[धाः][१०] स्मृताः।।२।।

---

१. The word nāda seems to be a scribal error for vādya, which is probably the subject heading. Such headings are noted at relevant places in the present text. It is interesting to note that RJM also reads the word 'vādya' found in v.2cd below, as nāda, suggesting the same kind of error.

Note: This chapter is being edited with only three Mss, namely, G86, G89 and M (V41 reads a few verses only). Since the readings in G86 and G89 are grammatically defective with scribal errors, and plenty of lacunae in all the three Mss, suggestions with respect to grammar is made to make sense. However at many places the text could not be completely edited, as parallel readings in earlier sources or in works like BKM, RJM etc. are not available. Note has not been given for minor corrections with respect to grammar.

२. G89- विदा

३. This kind of expression was felt better and hence is being suggested.

४. v.1 - v.2, cf. SM 1,1,7cd-9ab

५. G89- ***********, carmaja seems to be a better reading for carmāṇi, and hence the reading is suggested thus, the same has also been suggested in v.2ab.

६. G89- सविधा

७. G86- म **दंगाद्याः

८. G89- *************

९. This reading is suggested on the basis of the commentary. A similar reading (dēhanādēna) also occurs in SM.

१०. M- पंच्च***धा

టీకా:- నాధం(దం) వాద్య భేదాలుగా 5 ప్రకారాలు[१]. నఖం(ఖజం)[२], వాయుజం[३], చర్మజం, లోహం(హజం), శారీరం(రజం)[४]. ఈ 5 అనేక భేదాలు ఆయను[५]. వీణ, కిన్నర(రీ), దండే, రజాబు, కామాక్షి - ఇవి మొదలైన తంత్రివాద్యాలు నఖ(జ)మనబడును[६]. మురళి, నాగసరం, దేవసరం, శంఖము[७], ముఖవీణ(ణా)[८], ఉపాంగం[९], ఇవి మొదలైన[१०] ఉపరి వాద్యాల(లు) వాయుజం అనబడును[११]. మృదంగం[१२], భేరి, డ(ఢ)క్కాలు, (ఇవి మొదలైన) చర్మవాద్యాలు- చర్మజం. తాళం, లోహజం అనబడును1[१३]. గాత్రం[१४] శారీరమనబడును[१५]. ఈ వాద్యాలన్ని దేహ నాధ(ద)[१६]యుక్తమైయుండును. ఈ వాద్యాలకు[१७] ప్రత్యేక లక్షణం చెప్పేము (ప్పెదను) [१८].

---

१. Since nakha as such does not denote a class of instruments, the suffix 'ja' has been suggested. The same is the case with all the classes of instruments.

२. M- నాధః ***********

३. M-****యజం

४. G86- చ****లోహం చనీరం, G89- చర్మం లో ********

५. G86- ఈ 5 **** భేదాలు ఆయను, M- ఈ ********

६. M-***** మొదలైన తంత్రివాద్యమనబడును

७. G86- దేవ***శంఖం, G89- వేవసరం *******

८. M - missing

९. M- వుపా*** (ఙ్గము)

१०. M- యువిద్యాద్యం

११. G86, G89- వాయుజం

१२. G86, G89- మృతంగ, M- missing from here upto తాళం

१३. G86, G89- missing

१४. M- గా******

१५. G86- శారీరం, G89-*******

१६. G86- వాద్యాలన్ని****నాధ, G89- వాద్యాలు దేహ నాద

१७. M- వాద్యా***

१८. G86- చెప్పుమా

अधा[थ] वीणः[णा][१]।

[२]कछ[च्छ]पि कछता[कुब्जिका][३] चित्रा महति[ती][४] परिवादिनि[नी]।
जाया हाह[घोषा]वती[५] ज्येष्टा[६] नकुलाद्य[श्चे]ति कीर्त्तिताः[७] ।।३।।
मष[ह]ती[८] वैष्णवी ब्राह्मी रौद्री[९] कार्मुक[कूर्मा च] रावणी[१०]।
सरस्वती किन्नरा[री] च[११] सौरन्द्रि[१२] पोषि[घोष]का[१३] तथा।
दशवीणा[णाः][१४] समाख्यातः[ताः][१५] तन्त्रि विन्यास भाण्डतः [भेदतः] [१६]।।४।।

టీకా:- ఈ పది □లుకుండలు మెట్లు[१७] తంత్రి □యుక్త(మై) [१८]యుండును[१९].

वीणायां च[२०] नृणामिव त्रिस्थानेषु[२१] श्रुत्युत्पत्तिः[२२]।

---

१. G89- अध वीणेः, M- अथ वीण लक्षणम्
२. v.3 - v.4, cf.SM 1,4,6-8ab
३. M- कुफिता[***], It has been attempted to correct the names of the vīṇā-s based on references found in earlier texts, like SM, SN etc.
४. G86- महाती, G89- म ***************
५. M- जा[ज]याहाह [घोषा]वती
६. G86- ज्ये****, M- ज्येष्ट
७. G86- नकुलो **यति कीर्त्तिता, G89- नकुलो ह्यति कीर्त्तिता
८. M- [मह]*** *ती
९. G86, G89- कौत्री
१०. M- रावणि [कूर्मीच रानणी??]
११. G86- किन्नरा ज, G89-किन्नरा च
१२. G86- रारंद्र, G89- सौरन्द्र
१३. G86, G89- पोषके
१४. G86, G89- दशवीणे
१५. M- समाख्यातः [तास्]
१६. G86, G89- तंविन्यासस्य भाण्डकः; Reading based on SM
१७. G86- ఈ*****లు , M- ఈ 10 ని □లు కుణ్డలు మెట్లు
१८. G86, G89- తంద్రి యుక్తమై Reading within the ( ) is seen in the manuscript itself.
१९. M-*****ను
२०. G86, G89- missing
१९. G89- *****नेषु
२२. M- श्रुतोत्पत्तिः

वीणायां च विशेषोस्ती -[१] **।।५।।**

[२]**उत्तरोत्तरतारासु[स्तु]**[३] **वीणायामदुरोत्तरं[मधरोत्तरः]**[४] **।**

इति ध्वनि विशेषोस्ति[षास्ते][५] **श्रुतिः**[६]

श्रवणं[७] **रंजितः [श्रवणाच्छ्रुतिसंज्ञिताः]।।६।।**

టీకా:-మనుష్యులకు[८] ఉత్తరోత్తరంగా మందర(ంద్ర)మధ్యమ తారకాలు పుట్టును. మంద్రాదిషు శ్రుతయః. మంద్రమంద్రం- మంద్రమధ్యమ- మంద్ర[९]తారకం[१०]; మధ్యమమంద్రం[११]- మధ్యమమధ్యమం- మధ్యమతారకం. తారకమంద్రం- తారకమధ్యమం- తారకతారకం.

एवं[१२] **भेदानि षटणष[ट्‌ष]ष्टि**[१३]**सङ्ख्या त्रिस्थानेषु**[१४] **जायते।**

[१५]**त्रिस्थानेषु च एषूक्त्रं[क्तं]**[१६] **द्वाविंशतिविधो ध्वनिः**[१७]**।**

---

१. Seems to be incomplete. This is an important link between v.5 and v.6ab. v.5ab speaks of the point of resemblance between vīṇā and the human body and v.6ab speaks of their difference.

२. v.6, cf.Datt.9. This verse and the following commentary also occur in NC 2,89-90. The suggestions made here are based on Dattilam.

३. M- वुत्तरोत्तरतारसु

४. M- adds मन्दरो[द्रो]मध्यमस्तारा[रः] before वीणायामुदरोत्तरः

५. G86- ***********

६. G86, G89- *****

७. M- श्रुवण [श्रवण]

८. G89- *********, M- **నుష్యులకు

९. G86- *****

१०. M- తార***

११. M- ***మ మంద్రం

१२. G89- ****

१३. G86, G89- षटणषिष्ट,M- षतो [ट्] षष्टि

१४. G86- त्रि ***

१५. v7cd-v.7ef, cf. Datt,42. (Dattilam reads as अथ स्थानानि for त्रिस्थानेषु च) Suggestions are based on Dattilam

१६. G89- येषुक्त्रा, M- यीषा[षि]काः

१७. M- ध्वनि

व्यस्तावि[नि][१] तानि षतंषष्टि[षट्षष्टिं] विद्वान्नं[विद्यात्][२] मन्द्रादिसिद्धये[३]।। ७।।

टीका:- మంద్ర[४] మధ్యమతారకాలయందు 22 ధ్వనిభేదాలు చెప్పబడును[५]. అ□[६] వ్యస్తాలుగా 66 ధ్వని భేదాలు[७] అవును. ఈ 66. మంద్ర[८]మధ్యమతారకాలుగా[९] ధ్వనులు పలుకును[१०].

वीणावाद्यं शारीरमिव रचति [?][११]।

सप्ततन्त्रिमयि[यी] वीणा[१२] सप्तस्वरसमन्विता[१३]।

दर्शणा[ना]त्प[स्प]र्शनाश्चै[च्चै]व[१४] ब्रह्महत्त्यां व्यपोहतु[ति][१५]।।८।।

टीका:- ఈ □ా వాద్యం[१६] □టే ను[१७] శ్రేయస్సు కలుగును[१८].

अथ किन्नरः[री][१९]।

---

१. G86, G89- वुस्तानि

२. M- निषवत् ****द्यान्

३. G86- न्रादि निधये, G89- ********

४. M- మందర

५. G86- భేదా***** , M- భేదాలు చేప్పబడేను

६. M- అది

७. G86, G89- భేదాలుట

८. M- మందర

९. G86, G89- తారకాలు

१०. G86, G89- పలుకు

११. M-वीणावाद्य ******* चति,

१२. G86- सप्त तंत्रि ***, G89- वीणो

१३. G89- वीत

१४. G86- दर्श ****त्पर्शनाचैवा, G89- दर्शनात्वर्शनाचैव

१५. G89- ******, M- व्यपोहतु [ति]

१६. G89- యీ □ వాద్యం, M- □ా వాద్యం

१७. G86,G89- □ట్టి

१८. G86- కలుకు***

१९. M- अथ किन्नर [री] लक्षणम्

[१]आलन्बन[२] प्रचुर[३] कोमल[४]देशनाट्यं[५]
तन्त्रिमुखं[६] नयति ताललयाभिरामा[७][?]।
रागान् शनैरंबिनवान्[८] परिपादमिर्ध्य[९]
ज्ञेयस्तदा[१०] विधिकला खलु[११] किन्नरीती [?]।।९।।

టీకా:- గీతవాద్యనృత్తాలు లయా(య) యుక్తమై[१२] తంత్రిముఖమందు[१३] వాయిస్తే అది కిన్నర అనబడును[१४].

अधा दण्डेः [अथ दण्डि][१५]।

दण्डिका खादिरे जाता[१६] आकृतिर्भानुमूषिका [मुष्टिका [१७]]।
परिणामाङ्गुलिर्द्विस्यात्[१८] द्वयं कास्यं च रूपिणीम्[?][१९]।।१०।।
कांस्यरूपिणी[२०] नाभिश्च चतुरङ्गुलमिश्रिता[२१]।

---

१. v.9 is set to vasantatilakā metre, containing 14 syllables in each quarter.
२. G86- आलंब्बुन, M- आलम्बिन
३. G86- प्रचु
४. G89- रोमल, M- ****
५. G86- **** नाट्य, M- *****ट्यं
६. G86- त**त्रिमुखं, M- तन्त्रिमुखे
७. G86 - ताळलयाभिरावरा, G89- ताळलयाभिरा*****
८. G86- रागाण् शनैरभिनवाण्, G89- ****** शनैरभिनवाण्
९. G86, G89- missing
१०. G86, G89- ज्ञेयस्तधा
११. G86, G89- संखलु
१२. M- గీత వాద్య నృత్తా ******
१३. G86- తంత్రి***ఖమందు , M- **త్రిముఖము**
१४. G89- మందు *************अनप्राडुनु, M- ******అది కిన్న(రం)*******
१५. M- अथ दंड्डे लक्षणम्
१६. G86, G89- जातः
१७. Seems to be a scribal error; otherwise mūṣikā does not convey any sense in this context. The word, 'muṣṭikā', on the other hand relates to a measure.
१८. G86, G89- पलिणाषांगुळद्विस्यात्, M- पलिणाषां[हां ?]गुळद्वि[द्वे]श्यात्
१९. G86- रूपिणीः, G89- रू*****, M- रूपिणिम्
२०. G89- ***स्य रूपिणि, M- कांस्यरू(पि)णि
२१. M- नाभिश्च चतु *********, V41- नाभिस्स्याच्चतुरंगुळमिश्रिता

तुम्बोरग्रे[१] तु शु[सू]चिना चतुरङ्गुलमिश्रितः[२] ।। ११ ।।
पङ्क्ति[त्रि]का[३] या[४] विधातव्या[५] दण्डिका[६] लक्षणं च तत्।
आलम्ब्य[७] पङ्क्ति[त्रि]कामेधा[?][८] नाभि पर्यन्तकादयः[?][९]।
तन्त्रि[त्री]द्वये[१०] विधातव्य[ये][११] निपुणै[णैः][१२] क्षामतंतुना[१३] ।।१२।।
नाभेरधस्तात् कर्तव्यं[१४] तन्त्रि तेनैवतंतुना[१५]।
चतुश्चतुः [१६]प्रकारेण[१७] चतुर्बंधनमेव च[?] ।। १३ ।।
दक्षिणा तन्त्रिका ज्ञेयाः[या][१८] पञ्चमस्वरसंयुता[१९]।

---

१. G86, G89- तंबोरगे

२. G86,G89- मिश्रिता, M -******त (gap- whole line except one syllable) G86,G89 and M read the following which is not clear and seems to be repetitive. कास्यंचिरजिता सोयं आत्म दण्डावलंप्रिनि। तुंप्रुस्य नळिनीपत्रि स्या/सादशावर्तुळाकृतिः। चतुरंगुळा वीस्त्रीर्णं तुप्रुकंठ प्रकीर्त्तितः। षडंगुळ प्रमाणेन किंचित् कांस्यं च रूपिणी। Further read : G86- कांस्यं च ****** कांस्यरूपिणि **** नाभिश्च, G89- कांस्यं च ****वीणाः कांस्यरूपिणि ********, M- ******** च रूपिणि (gap from किंचित्)

३. G86, G89- *******

४. G89- यी

५. G86, G89- तवळं, V41- तस्य

६. G86, G89- दंड्डिगा, M- दण्डिका *****

७. G86, G89, M- अलंब्ब

८. G86, G89- पक्तिकामेदा, M- पङ्क्तिकामेद

९. G86, G89- नाप्रि पर्वतकादयः

१०. V41- तन्त्रिद्वय

११. G86-*******, G89,M-तव्या

१२. G86, V41- निपुणे, G89- नि ****

१३. G86- ** मत ***, G89- *****मतंतुना, M- क्षमतंतुणा

१४. G86- ***भरधनत्तत्तव्यं, G89- नाभेरधनत्त (त्तव्यं?)***व्यं, V41- नाभीरधस्तात्कर्तव्यं

१५. G86- तन्त्रि ले दैवतंतुना, G89- तन्त्रिरे नैवतंतुना, V41- तन्त्रिका नैव तंतुना

१६. G86, G89- चतंश्चतुः, M-चतःश्चतु

१७. G89-प्रारेण, G89- प्रकारिणा

१८. G89- तन्त्रि****याः, M- तंत्रिका ****

१९. G86-पञ्चमस्वर********, M- *****मस्वरसम्युता

वामतन्त्रि समाख्याता[१] षड्जस्वरसमन्विता।। १४।।
एकाङ्गुल प्रमाणेन जीविकौ द्वयकौ भवेत्[२] ।। १५।।
पूर्वतन्त्रिपतिः शंभुः[३] अन्यतन्त्रिप्रिया शिवे[वा]।
दण्डस्या[य] भूमि[४] दैवत्यो [देवता] तुम्बुरम्भोजसम्भ ** [वः][५]।। १६।।**
सरस्वती[६] नाभिदैवं[भेर्देवी][७] ककुंधो[कुभो][८] गरुडध्वजः।
पङ्क्ति[त्रि]का[९]कमल[ला]ज्ञेया[१०]जीविका[११] च सुधाकरः।। १७।।
सर्वदेवमया[य]भूतं[१२] दण्डिकाऽभयदायिनि[१३]।
[१४]गायको दण्डिकामेनां[१५] तर्जनी[न्या] वादयेत् पटु[१६]।। १८।।
[१७]त[द]त्तिलस्य मतेख्यातु[तं] दण्डिकालक्षणं पुरा[१८] ।।१९।।

प्रार्थनं[ना][१९]।

[२०]वाणीं नमामि[२१] वरदां वनजासनस्थाम्[२२]

१. G86-*********ता
२. G89-द्वय******
३. G86, G89- पतिश्शुभुः
४. G86- दंडस्या **मि, M- दंडस्याद्भूमि, V41- दंदस्याद्भूमि
५. G86- तब्बु *** भीजसंभवः, G89- तुम्बुरः भोजसंभवः, V41- तुंबुरंभूजसंभवः
६. M-***स्वती
७. G89- ********** (the whole line)
८. M-कुकुंभो, V41- ककुभौ. This seems to be a better reading in this context.
९. G86- पतिका, G89- **** का
१०. G86,G89-कमलं ग्नेया, M,V41-कमल ज्ञेया
११. G86,G89,M- जिविका
१२. G86- सरस्वदे *****तं, M - सर्वदेवं मयाभूतं
१३. M- भहदायिनि
१४. V41- v.18cd, v.19 are missing.
१५. G86,G89- दंडकामेनां
१६. M- पादयेत् पटा
१७. Though it is attributed to Dattila, it is not found in the available printed text.
१८. M-तन्त्रिलस्य मतेख्यात******डिकालक्षणं
१९. G86- ***र्धन This kind of invocatory verse is given for most of the instruments in this text.
२०. v.20 is set to vasantatilakā metre, containing 14 syllables in each quarter.
२१. G86- *********
२२. G89-स*****, M- वनजासनस्था

वीणाधरां विमललोचन[१]ताण्डवेषु [?][२]।

हराभिरामहृदयां[३] मृदुवाक्य[ख्य][४]सोम्याम्[५]

पारावतीं भगवतीं[६] प्रणमामि देवीम्[७]।।२०।।

टीका:- [८]ఇట్లా[९] లక్షణయుక్తమైన[१०] దండికి[११] నమస్కరించి[१२] ధరించి మంద్ర[१३]మధ్యమతారక స్వరాలు గాయకుడు తర్జని మొదలైన వేళ్ళల(తో)[१४] వాయించవలెను.

अधा[अथ] तुम्बुरः[१५]।

विश्वकर्म[१६]विनिर्माणां[१७] तुम्बुराख्येति[१८] वाद्यतः[?][१९]।

पञ्चतालश्च[२०] विस्तीर्णं[२१] कुर्यात् सम्यक्[२२] सुधारणा[२३]।। २१।।

---

१. G86, G89- विमलोचन, V41- विमलतोदन

२. G89- तां ******

३. G86, G89- हाराभिरामहृदयं, V41- आराम हृदयां

४. V41- मृदुपाश

५. G86, G89- सोम्यिं

६. G86, G89, M- पारावतिं भगवतिं

७. M-प्रणमा*****वीं

८. V41- commentary missing; but reads: ఇతి దండిలక్షణం సమాప్తం

९. G89- missing

१०. G86 - missing

११. M- దండికు

१२. G86- నస్మ్కరించి

१३. M- మందర

१४. M- వేళ్ళ

१५. G86 - तु*****, M- तम्बुर लक्षणम्, V41- तुम्बुरुः

१६. G86- *******, M- [***]विश्वकर्म

१७. M- च[वि]निर्माणां[तु], V41-निर्माणं

१८. G86-तुंब्बु ****ख्येति, M-तब्बुराख्येति

१९. G86,G89-वाद्यताः, M-वाद्यतः [चिकः]

२०. M- पंचताळश्च[***]

२१. G86, G89- विस्तीर्नं, M- विस्तिर्नः[ं]

२२. G86, G89- संम्यिक

२३. M- सुधारणा [********]

द्वितालं प्रथमं[१] कुंभं मध्ये[२] हस्त द्वितालकम्।
द्वारयुग्येकतालाग्रे[३] सिंह्माननयुतश्शिखा [युता शिखा][४]।
द्वारस्योभय[५]पार्श्वे च कीला[६] सप्ता[७] विनिक्षिपेत्[८]।। २२।।
सप्ततन्त्रि[न्त्र्य]श्च[९] तद्वेष्या[ष्ट्या][१०] कुम्भमूले च[११] भ[ब]न्धनम्।
कुम्भमध्ये[१२] तु[१३] [१४]सोपानं न्यस्त[सप्त][१५]तन्त्रि[१६] विनिक्षिपेत्[१७]।। २३।।

प्रार्थना[१८]।

सप्ततन्त्रि[१९] समायुक्तं सप्तस्वरसमन्वितम्।
तुम्बुरुर्देवता[२०] तस्य[तस्मै][२१]नमः[२२] सङ्गीतवेदिकाः[?][२३]।। २४।।

---

१. G86, G89- प्रधम
२. G89-*******
३. G86- द्वारयुग्येताळग्रे, G89- द्वारयु*******, M- द्वारयुग्ने[ये]कताळज्ञे [ग्रे]
४. G86-सिंह्माननयतश्शखा, G89-***हाननयतश्शिखा, M-सिंह्म*****युतः शिखा [हानन युताशिखा]
५. G86- द्वारस्थेर्भय, G89- द्वारस्थूर्भय, M- द्वारस्यो(चो?) भय
६. V41- शिला
७. G86, G89- सप्तौ, M- सह्तौ [सप्त]
८. G86, G89- विनिक्षिप्रित्
९. M- सप्ततंत्रिकश्च [त्रिश्च], V41- सप्ततन्त्रैश्च
१०. M- तद्वेक्ष्य [*****] कुंभमूले
११. M- च [तु]
१२. G86, G89- कुंभमधे
१३. G86- त्, M- च
१४. G89- gap till the end of this line
१५. Since the readings in the Mss are not clear, 'सप्त' is being suggested.
१६. M- न्यस्यां [न्यस्य] तंत्रि [त्रीर्वि], V41-** स्तस्तन्त्री
१७. G86- विनिक्षि**त्
१८. G86, G89-प्रार्थनं
१९. M- सप्त ***** [तंत्रि]
२०. G86, G89- तुंबुरो देवतां, M- तुंबु***वतां
२१. M- तस्या
२२. M- संगीतवेदिका [रु देवं च तन्म्रूरं प्रणमाम्यहम्], V41- संगीतवेदिका
२३. G86, G89, V41- समः

गायको तुम्बुरे सम्यक्[१] वादयेत्[२] तर्जनी[न्या] पट्टु[पट्टु][३]।
सोमनाथमते ख्यातं तम्बुरालक्षणं पुरा[४]।। २५।।

टीका:-లక్షణయుక్తమైన తంబురును గాయకుండు తర్జనాద్యంగులాల[५]చేత వాయించవలెను[६]. రజాబు[७], రావణాస్తం, కామాక్షి[८]తంత్రివాద్యమెల్ల ఇందులోలియ్యం[९].

इति नख वाद्यं।।

अधा[अथ] मुरळि[ली][१०]।

[११]द्वादशाङ्गुलमाकारं सम्यग्वंशेन[१२] कारयेत्[१३]।
आदौ तु रन्ध्रमेखं[कं] च कारयेद्वायुपूरितः।। २६।।
एकैकाङ्गुल तस्याध[धः][१४] सप्तरन्ध्राणि कारयेतु[त्][१५]।
सप्त[र्प]शीर्षं च हस्ते[१६] च धृत्या[त्वा] वादक[कः] वादयेत्[१७]।। २७।।
मूलनाधे[दे][१८]स्थितो विष्णु[णुः] मध्यनाधि[दे]स्थितो विधिः।

---

१. M- तंबुरो संम्यक् V41-तुम्बुरोस्सम्यक्
२. G89- *********** M- ***(द्वा)[वा] दये
३. G86- तज**नि पुट्टु, M- ******* [**बुदुः], V41- तर्जनी पटी पट्टुतर्जनी seems to be a better reading
४. G86- बुरा
५. G89- ******, M- వా ******ంన్యాద్యంగులాల చాత (gap from the beginning of the commentary)
६. M- వా ******
७. G86- రజాబు
८. M- తంత్రివాద్య ******** వాద్య సమాప్తం***
९. G86- లియ్య
१०. M- अधा मु ******
११. M- v.26 - v.28 are missing
१२. G86- संम्यिग्य
१३. G89- वंशे*****
१४. G89- *******
१५. G89- रंद्रंणा *********
१६. G86- हस्तो
१७. G86- **त्या ****ती
१८. The purport of v.28 is not very clear.

अग्रनाधे[दे]स्थितो शंभुः मुरलि[ली] देवतं[ता] हरिः।।२८।।

प्रार्थनं[ना]।[१]

सप्तरन्ध्रसमायुक्तं[२] **सप्तस्वरसमन्वितम् ।**

परब्रह्म[३] **स्वरूपं च मुरली ते नमाम्यहम्**[४] **।। २९।।**

టీకా:-రమ్యమైన వెదురుకోని 12 అంగుల ప్రమాణం జేసి,[౫] మొదట రంద్రం(ంధ్రం)[౬] జేసి, ఆ దిగువ 7 రంద్రా(ధ్రా)లు చేసి[౭], సర్పశిరశ్స్తాలు(ల)[౮] చేత మురళి వాయించవలెను.

सोमनाथमते[९] **प्रोक्तं मुरलि[ली]लक्षणं**[१०] **पुरा**[११] **।। ३०।।**

अथ[१२] **मुखवीणे[णा]**[१३] **।**

उच्यते मुखवीणायां[याः] लक्षणं याज्ञवल्किना[ल्क्येन][१४] **।**

खादिरे[रो] सा च[१५] **दण्डस्य[स्या]द्रक्त**[१६]**चन्दनरूपकैः।।३१।।**

द्वादशाङ्गुलमस्यैवं[१७] **आकारोस्य विधि[धी]य्यते**[१८] **।**

सप्तस्वराणां सङ्ख्यानां[१९] **रंद्राणा[रन्ध्राणि] व**[२०] **समाहरेत्।। ३२।।**

---

१. G89- *****, M- missing

२. M- *************

३. G86- ******

४. M- मुरळि *********

५. G89- అ ******* చేశి, M- అం **** ప్రమాణ ******

६. G89- రద్రం, M- *****

७. G86, G89- జేశి

८. G86, G89- శ్స్తా

९. G86- సోమనాధమత, సోమ*******

१०. G89-********** लक्षणं

११. G86- प्रुरा

१२. G86, G89- अधा

१३. G86-मुखवीणाः, M-मुखवीण लक्षणम्

१४. G86- युज्ञ***ल्किना, G89- युज्ञवल्किना

१५. M- खादिरे ***(णेका) च

१६. M- द्रक्तं

१७. G86-द्वादशांगुळमस्त्येवं, G89- *********

१८. G86, G89- अकोरंस्य विधिय्यते

१९. G86- संरवानां

२०. M- missing

रंद्राध[रन्ध्राधः][१] च निषादस्यात्[२] स्वराश्चैवं वदन्ति च[३]।
ऋग्वेदप्रथमो[मा]मूषा[४] द्वतिये[तीया] च येज[यजु]र्भवेत् ।।३३।।
अथर्वणस्त्रिति[ती]या[५] स्यात् सामवेदस्वरास्थिताः[?][६]।
एकाङ्गुलं च जीवालं मण्डलं दन्त[७]रूपकम् ।। ३४।।
मुखवीणा परेप्राज्ञा[?][८] दन्त[९]रूपेण मण्डलम् [?]।
तद्दारुकमयं चिह्नं[१०] व्याजेन[११] क्रियते तथा [?]।।३५।।

दा[धा]रणश्लोकं।।

[१२]भानुन्नमामि भगवन्तमनन्तभावं[१३]
वीणाधिशु[दिषु][१४] गिरिसुतं तपमण्डलेषु [?]।
मन्दारु[१५] लोकवरदं वनजासनस्थं[१६] वन्देह
शासितमहं विजया वन्दे[१७][?]।। ३६।।

---

१. G86- रंद्र **ध, M- रंद्रेषु
२. M- निषाध[द]स्यात्
३. G86- पर्दंत्ति व, G89-पर्वत्ति**
४. G89- **************, M- ऋग्वेदप्रथमे मुष्टि
५. G86, G89- अधर्वणस्त्रितिय
६. Four elements (parts) are related to the four vēda-s, but their identities are not clear.
७. G86, G89- दण्ड
८. G86-मुखवीणे परेप्राज्ञे, G89-***********
९. G86, G89- दण्ड
१०. G86, G89- दण्डौरुक मया चिन्हं
११. G86, G89- व्यजन
१२. v.36 is set to vasantatilakā metre, containing 14 syllables in each quarter. This verse is so corrupt that a proper sense could not be obtained.
१३. G86- भानुन्न**मि भगवन्तन्तप्रावं, G89- भानून्नमामि भगव************
१४. G86-वीणाविशं, G89- ******शं
१५. G86, G89- वंदारु
१६. G86, G89- वनजाननस्धिं
१७. M- वन्दे शिशोसितमहं विजयायां वन्दे

టీకా:- పూర్వమందు ముఖ☐[१] సూర్యుడు వాయించినాడు. ఇట్లా(ట్లు)[२] లక్షణ[३]యుక్తమైన ముఖ☐[४] ధరించి వాయించవలెను.

[मुखवीणायाः लक्षणं][५] सोमनार्येण कीर्त्तितः[तम्] ।। ३७ ।।

पामू[मु]लनागसरं[६] ।

[७]शिवस्य पञ्चवक्त्रेभं[भ्यः][८] पञ्चस्वरसभुत्भवाः[९] ।

तभृ[च्छृ]त्वा[१०] कुण्डलि[ली][११] गायन्[१२] फणिनागस्वरोच्यते[१३] ।

तद्वात्य[द्य]लक्षणं वक्ष[क्ष्ये] पूर्वोक्त[१४]विधिनामाता [तथा][१५] ।। ३८ ।।

టీకా:- [१६]పూర్వమందు పరమేశ్వరుడు[१७] 5 ముఖాలవల్లనుండి 5 స్వరాలు పుట్టెను.

---

१. G86- పూర్వమందు ముఖ☐**, G89-*****☐

२. G86, G89- యిట్ల

३. G89- లక్ష

४. G86, G89- ముఖ☐

५. This was originally found at the end of the description of maurvi, reading, "मवुरि लक्षणं पूर्वं मतंगमुनि वक्ष्यते। मौर्वि लक्षणं सम्यक् सोमनार्येण कीर्त्तितः।" The whole section dealing with maurvi seems to be ambiguous (see introduction) and hence has been placed towards the end of this text as anubandha. At the end, two consecutive lines in a verse attribute the same section to two different writers. On the other hand, a concluding verse attributing the instrument to Sōmanārya (or Sōmanātha), is missing after the description of mukhavīṇā. Hence it has been edited thus.

६. G86- **मूल ना **

७. v.38 and the following commentary were originally found after the commentary to v.48cd. Since the occurence of this verse here, added more sense to the context, they have been shifted to this place.

८. G86- *********** भं, M- शिवस्य पंच वक्त्रे***

९. M- ***ंचस्वरसभुत्भवः

१०. M- त**त्वा

११. G86, G89- कन्दलि

१२. G89- ******

१३. G89- फणि ना **स्व ** च्यते, M- *****नागस्व *****

१४. G89- तद्वात्यलक्ष******* पूर्वो **, M- ***************कं

१५. G89- विधि *******

१६. M- missing upto శేషుడు

१७. G86- పూ********రమేశ్వరుడు

ఆ 5 స్వరాలు శేషుడు ☐[1] [2]తాను గానం జేసి, ఆ వాద్యం పేరు పాములనాగస్వరమని పలికెను. పూర్వోక్తమైన ఆ వాద్యాల లక్షణం చెప్పును.

अलाबु कोटरं[3] कृत्वा षोडशाङ्गुल मानतः[4]।
मधुवि[पि]ष्टमधो तस्य स्ताव्य[स्थाप्यो][5] जीवाळ नाळदौ[दो]।।३९।।
चतुरङ्गुल[लं] कृत्वाथ[6] वेणुनालौ द्वयोरथा[धः][7]।
प्रमाणं षोडशाङ्गुल्याः[गुलाः][8] सर्वरे[मे]कं[9] च कारयेत्।। ४०।।
अन्ते च कास्य[कांस्य]वलया[यं][10] स्थाप्य वेण्वाग्रतोरधा[धः][11]।
रन्ध्रमेकं च कुर्वीत[12] सप्तरध्राण[न्ध्राणि][13] ततोपरि ।। ४१।।
कुर्यन्[र्यान्] मधुमयस्सर्वे[14] रन्ध्राणां स्थाप्य किञ्चित्[15]।
पञ्चपञ्च[16] स्वरोपेतं[17] आलाबु[18] ब्रह्मदेवता ।। ४२।।
जीवाळ[19] विष्णुवंशेशः[20] रन्ध्राणामष्टमूर्तयः[21]।

---

१. G86, G89- నికి
२. M- తానుగా చే ************వాద్య క్షణం చెప్ప******** missing in between
३. G86- *********रं, M- अलाप्रु कोटिरं
४. G86-षोडशांगुळाः मासतः, G89-षोडशांगुल्याः ******-missing from here upto the first half of v.40cd. The missing portion in G89 is seen inserted with a '+' mark in G86.
५. M- मधुविष्टमधो' स्थाप
६. G86- अचतोरंगुळ कृद्वाता
७. G86- द्वयोरधः
८. G86- प्रमाणां षोडशांगुळयां
९. M- स्वरैरेकं
१०. M- अंते च कार *******
११. G86- साप्य वेण्वग्रत्तोयधा, G89- *************
१२. G86, M- कुर्वित
१३. M- रंध्रा *******
१४. G86- कुर्यन*****र्वे, M- *****धुमयिं सर्वे
१५. G86- रंध्राणां स्तौप्य कंक्किचत्, G89- ***********
१६. G89- ******, M- मुंच पंच
१७. G86, G89- स्वरोपितं
१८. G86, G89-आलाप्रो
१९. M- जीवाळे
२०. G86, G89- विष्णुवंषेषः
२१. G86, G89- रंध्राणामष्टमूर्दयः

कांस्यं च भास्करो भूमि[१] मधुपिष्ट्यादि देवताः[२] ।। ४३ ।।
तद्वाद्यं सर्वनामैश्च[सर्पनामञ्च][३] कथिता[तं] भरतो[ता]दिभिः ।। ४४ ।।
नकारा[रं]नादमित्याहुः[४] गकारं गानमुच्यते।
ताभ्यां[तयोः][५] सम्मेलनं कृत्वा[६] सर्पनागस्वरोच्यते[७] ।। ४५ ।।
शिवस्य[८] पञ्चवक्त्रैच[९][क्त्रेभ्यः][१०] जातः[तं] पञ्चस्वरैर्युतम्[११] ।
तद्वाद्यं[१२] क्षो[श्रो]तुमिच्छामि[न्ति][१३] स[१४] नरः सुखमेधत्[ति][१५] ।। ४६ ।।
वादोक[दको][१६] दक्षिणाङ्गुष्ठमग्ररन्ध्रे स्थितोपरि[१७] ।
मृगशीर्षस्स[स]र्पशीर्ष[१८]करौ[१९] गृह्णाति[२०] च स्वरान्[२१] ।। ४७ ।।
वायुपूरित नादेन[२२] सम्यग्वाद्यं समाचरेत्।
सोमनाथमते प्रोक्तं सर्पवाद्यश्च[स्य] लक्षणम् ।।४८ ।।

---

१. G86- का *********** भूमि , G89-कास्यं च भा*********
२. G86- मधुपिष्टादि देवताः, G89- ******** दि देवताः
३. M- तथा ********** Since the word सर्वनाम does not convey any sense, the reading सर्पनाम is being suggested, which is also supported by the commentary.
४. M- मित्याहु
५. Since the reading is grammatically incorrect, this reading is suggested.
६. G86- ताभ्यां ******त्वा, G89- ********** कृत्वा
७. M- नादस्वरोच्यते
८. G89- **** स्य, M- सिवश्यं
९. G86, G89- पञ्चयक्षेश्च
१०. Since the reading is grammatically imperfect, this reading is suggested.
११. G86- पञ्चस्वरेर्यतं, G89- पञ्चस्वरेर्युतं
१२. M- द्वाद्यं
१३. G86, M- क्षोतुमिच्चामि
१४. G89- **, M- स्व
१५. G86- * रः सुखमेतत्, M- ********
१६. G89- वादो **, M- ******को
१७. G86- दक्षिणांगुष्टामग्ररंध्रारि, G89- ************ तोपरि
१८. G86,G89- मृगशीर्षसर्वशीर्ष
१९. G86, M- ककौ
२०. G86- गृणाति, M- ग्रुंह्णाति
२१. G86, G89- स्वरात्
२२. M- वायूपूरित नादेना

టీకా:- సొరకాయలు(ల) బుర్ర 12 అంగుల ప్రమాణం జేసి[1], [2]అడుగున మైనమెత్తి, నాల్గు అంగుళ ప్రమాణం జీవాళం, కడ్లు(కండ్లు)[3] రెండు ఏకం జేసి[4], వెదురుగో(కో)వులు రెండు 16 అంగుళాల ప్రమాణాన[5] ఏకం జేసి, ఆ సొరకాయ బుర్ర[6] జీవాళకోవులు వెదురుకోవులు[7] కూడా, ఏకం జేసి బంధనంగా మైనంమెత్తి[8], వెదురుకోవుల[9] మొదట ఎడమ పార్శ(ర్శ్వ)మందు[10], అడుగున ఒక[11] రంధ్రం జేసి, పైన 7 రంధ్రాలు జేసి[12], ఆ రంధ్రాలకు సగం పో☐డిచి[13], కడవం[14] అందుకు మైనమెత్తి, [15]వెదురుకోవులు(ల)కొనను[16] కంచకట్టు వేశేది. సొరకాయ[17] బ్రహ్మ, జీవాళాన ☐ష్ణు[18], వెదురుకో(వు) శివుడు[19], 8[20] రంధ్రాలకు అష్టమూర్తులు, కంచుకు ర☐ మైనానికి[21]

---

౧. G86- సొరెకాయలు బు *** 12 అంగుల ప్రమాణంచెశి, M-***** ర 12 అంగులాల ప్రమాణాన

౨. M - missing upto జీవాళం

౩. M- బడ్లు

౪. G86- రంట ***యకం జెశి, G89- రంట***

౫. G86- వెదురుకోవులు అంగుళ ప్రమాణాన, G89- **** అంగుళ ప్రమాణేన

౬. G86- ***** కాయ బుర్రా, M- యే ********

౭. G86, G89- missing

౮. G86- కబందనంగ్గా మైనమెత్తె, G89- బందనంగా మైన*****

౯. G86- వెదురుకోవులు॥16॥, G89- *********

౧౦. M- యడ పార్శ్వంముడ్డు

౧౧. G86- పొగ, M- వక

౧౨. G86- రంధ్ర ***** ధ్రాలు జెశి, M- రంధ్రం చేశి పైన 7 రంధ్రాలు చేశి

౧౩. G86- సఖం పొడి☐డిచి, G89- స** పోడి☐డిచి

౧౪. G89- *****

౧౫. G89- missing upto వేశేది

౧౬. M- వెదురుకోవుల కోనకు

౧౭. M- సొరకాయక

౧౮. M- జీవాళికే ☐ష్ణువు

౧౯. G86- వెదురు***, G89- ఎదురుకో శివుడు

౨౦. G86, G89- missing

౨౧. M- మైనానకు

భూ□ □రు అధిదేవతలు[१]. శివుని 5 ముఖాల[२] పుట్టిన[३] స్వరాలు ఈ వాద్యమందు పలుకును. నకారం నాదం గకారం గానం[४]. ఈ రెంటి[५]యొక్క కూట□ చేత స్వరాలు అన్ని పలుకగా[६] ఈ వాద్యం పేరు[७] పాములనాగసరమని భరతాది ముని(నీ)శ్వరులు చెప్పుదురు[८]. ఈ వాద్యం వాయు పూరిత నాదం చేత[९] వాద్యకో(దకు)డు వెదురకో□ దిగువ రంధ్రం[१०], తన భోట్టన వెలనది□(బొటన వేలునది□)[११] మృగశీర్ష[१२] సర్పశీర్ష □స్తాల చేత సప్త రంధ్రా(లయ)ందు[१३] సప్తస్వరాలు గానం[१४] చేయవలెను[१५]. ఈ వాద్యం[१६] □న్నవారికి అనేక శ్రేయస్సు కలుగును[१७]. లోకోపకారమైన సోమనాథియ్యమనే[१८] భరత(గ్రంథ)మందు ఈ పాములనాగసర లక్షణం[१९] చెప్పిన(యున్న)ది[२०]. [२१]ఈ తీరున[२२] లక్షణయుక్తమైన నాగసరం ధరించి వాయించవలెను[२३].

---

१. G86, G89- దేవతులు
२. G89- *******ల, M- ముఖాలవల్ల
३. G86- బుట్టిన
४. G86- ******నం, G89- నకోర నాదం గకోరు గానం
५. M- రెండు
६. G86- స్వరాలన్ని పలకగ, G89- స్వరాలన్ని ******
७. G89- ******
८. M- మూశ్వరులు చప్పుదురూ
९. G86- ఈ వాద్య ***** రిత నా ***చాత
१०. G86- వాద్యగాండ్లు వెదురుకో□గువ రంధ్రం, G89-**************
११. G86- భోట్ట వెలనధిజ, G89- భోట్న వేలనది□
१२. G86, G89- మృగశిర
१३. G86, G89- రంధ్రాలచాత యెందు
१४. G86- ***********, M- ఎప్త స్వర రాగాలు గానం
१५. G86, G89-**********
१६. G89- యీా వాంద్యం
१७. M- శ్రయస్సు కలుదూ
१८. G86, G89- సోమనాధమనె
१९. G89- ***************, M- పా *********క్షణం
२०. G86, G89- *******
२१. This sentence is found at the commencement of the discription on nāgasara, which has been moved to this place.
२२. G86- ***తీరున, G89- **న
२३. G86- వాయించవలను, M- వాయించ *****

अथ देवसर लक्षणं वक्ष्यते[१]।

[२]*********[**देव] स्वरमितिर्वदेत्।**

టీకా:- శ్రీ కృష్ణుడు వేదనుకో ******* పరు దేవస్వరమని పలికినా ****

***********[चतुर्वि]ंशतिरङ्गुला कु*धः परिकीर्तितः।। ४९।।**

టీకా:- దోషరోతమైన వేదు(వెదు)రుకో□24 అంగుల ***********

*********त्यंगुल्यधो[आदौत्र्यङ्गुल्यधो] भागे रन्ध्रमेकं च कारयेत्।**

***********मधु *********प्त पार्श्वे विमोचनम्।। ५०।।**

तस्योपरिस्ताला[ल]पत्रं वेष्टितं वर्तुलाकृतिः।

तस्याधोष्टाङ्गुलिर्मूलं सप्तरन्ध्राणि कारयेत्।।५१।।

अग्रेत्याङ्गुलि[?] सर्वांगे चतुर्विंशतिरंगुलाः।

मूलाग्रे हेमकौ[रौ]प्यं च कां***[कांस्ये]न वलयं कृतं।। ५२।।**

दप[देव]स्वराधिवो[पो] विष्णु[णुः] रन्ध्राणामष्टमूर्तयः।

देवामधुमयश्वेश[यस्त्वेशः] तालपत्रस्य शारदा।

वलयो[योः] भास्करः[र]श्चन्द्रः एतेषामधिदेवता[ताः]।।५३।।

టీకా:- ఈ దేవసరం మొదట మూడు అంగుల(లం) దిగువ నిడుపోవ(నిడుపున) **(1)రంధ్రం జేసి, ఆ రంధ్రం నడువ మైనమెత్తి పార్శ్వాలు □ిచి, దాని □ద తాడ(డు)ను కట్టి వేసి, ఈ రంధ్రం దిగువ 8 అంగులాలు పో□ిచి, అక్కడ 7 రంధ్రాలు చేసి, దాని దిగువ □శ రంధ్రం ***(ఒ)కటి చేసి, కొనను మూడు రంధ్రాలు పో □ిచి, బంగారు వెండి కంచు చేత నై(పై)నా కట్టు వేయవలెను. దేవసరానికి □ు దేవతా. 8 రంధ్రాలకు అష్టమూర్తులు. మైనానుకు ఈశ్వర***(రుడు). తాలేకుకు(తాటియాకు)** (స)రస్వతీ. వలయాలకు సూర్యచంద్రాడు(దు)లు. □ు అధిదేవతులు.

---

१. G86- अधा देवस्वर वक्ष्यतः (ते। ? not clear), G89- अधा देवस्वर ******* M adds देवसर लक्षणं - probably the page heading.

२. G86,G89 -break off here and read a few verses under the heading vādya lakṣaṇaṃ (which is being placed at the end of this edited text) and read from commentary to v.56cd. There are many lacunae in M; readings are suggested at a few places, based on the available commentary.

अ[आ]दौ भूम्यस्तितो[भूमिस्थिते]वस्त्रे प्रक्षिप्तमूरली[लीं] स्तथा[तथा]।
देवं च प्रार्थनं कृत्वा ग्रुहि[गृही]त्वा वाद[द्य]कोविधा[दः]।।५४।।
मुरलीमूल पीड्यन्ते मृगशि[शी]र्षकरेण च।
सर्पशि[शी]र्षकरेण[णा]ग्रे पीड्यं वाद्यं समाचरेत्।
उभयोः करपीड्यन्ते विष्णुस्ता**** [ण्डवमाचरेत्] ।।५५।।**

[प्रार्थना][१]

अधो[सप्त]रन्ध्रसमायुक्तं सप्तस्वरसमन्वितम्।
*************** **ता तुभ्यं नमाम्यहम् ।। ५६।।**

टीका:- [२]తొలుత[३] భూ□యందు వస్త్రంపరచి[४] ఈ దేవస్వరం, అందు□దవుంచి[५] నమస్కరించి[६], దక్షిణ్హస్తం మృగశీర్ష్హస్తమున్ను[७] వామ్హస్తం సర్పశిర్హస్తమున్ను[८], వాదకుడు[९] ఈ తీరున ధరించి, వాయుపూరిత నాదం చేత[१०] రెండు చ(చే)తులా వాయించవలెను[११]. ఆ నాదానికే □ువు తాండవమాడును.

सोमनाथमते प्रोक्तं देवतास्वरलक्षणम्[१२] ।। ५७।।

---

१. v.56 was originally in between v.54ab and v.54cd above. It is being moved here since this seems to denote the 'Invocatory verse', which is usually found at the end of the description of each instrument, which is then followed by a concluding verse, where the name of the author is found.

२. G86, G89 - read from here

३. G89- ******

४. G86- వస్త్ర పర ***, M- వస్త్ర పరచి

५. G89- అందు □ందవుంచి

६. G86- నమసరించి

७. G86, G89- మృగశీర్షమున్ను

८. G86- సర్ప్పంశిర ****, G89- ****

९. G89- ******

१०. G86- వాయుపూరిత నాద చాత, M- ****** త

११. G86, G89- రెణ్డు చేతుల వాయంత్మవలెను

१२. The instrument (dēvasara) is being called here as dēvatāsvara (synonym?) probably to fill in the syllables required for the metre.

టీకా:- ఈ దేవసర లక్షణం[१] సోమనాదియమున(థియ్యమనే)[२] చెప్పివున్నది[३].

अधा[थ] शङ्खः[४]।

शंखंश्चा[शङ्खञ्च] वर्त्तुलंचैवा[व][५] प्रमाणं तालमात्रकम्[६]।
मूलेभिद्रं[दं] प्रकुर्वि[र्वी]त[७] ओष्टवाद्यं समाचरेत्।
लक्ष्मि[क्ष्मी]शो देवतो[८] तस्य य श्रोतु[ता][९] पुण्यवाण[न्] भवेत्[१०]।। ५८।।

प्रार्थनं[ना]।।

नमोस्तु पञ्चजान्याय[पाञ्चजन्याय][११] नमो जलधिजन्मने[१२]।
नमो नारायणद्यंत्तः[?][१३] नमो वाद्यविशेषणे[१४]।। ५९।।
अर्धचन्द्रकरौ[१५] दृ[धृ]त्वा[१६] वादको[१७] वाद्यमाचरेत्[१८]।
सोमनार्येण[१९] सङ्क्षेप्य वक्ष्यते शङ्खलक्षणम्[२०]।। ६०।।

अधा[थ][२१] काहलः।

---

१. G86, G89 - missing
२. G89- సోమనాదియ్యాముని, M- సోమనాదియ్యన
३. M- చెశి**********
४. G89-अध शंकः, M- शंख लक्षणम्
५. M- शंख च वर्त्तुलंचैवा
६. G86- □ळ मात्रकं, G89- ताल मात्र****
७. M- प्रकुर्विता
८. M- लक्ष्मी तो देवता
९. M- यःश्रोतु
१०. G86- भवे**
११. M-नमो************
१२. G86- नमो जलधिजेन्मने, G89 - न**************
१३. G89 -*********णद्यतः, M- नमो नारायणद्रुत्तः
१४. G89- विशेषणे
१५. G86, G89- अर्धचंद्राका
१६. M-द्रुत्वा
१७. G86, G89- वाचको
१८. M- पा (वा)द्यमाचरेत्
१९. G86- सो ****र्येण
२०. G86- संक्षिप्यि वक्ष्य शंखस्य लक्षणं, G89- संक्षिप्*********************
२१. G89- अध, M- अथा

ताम्रेण[१] कालं[हलं] कुर्यात् रूप[२] षोडशमुष्टिभिः[३] ।।

प्रादेशमात्रमग्रे[४] च वलयं कारयेत[त्त]तः[५] ।

त्रिखण्ड[डो][६]वा[व]चतुःखण्डा[डो][७] एकैकं संयुतं पुनः ।। ६१ ।।

वलयाकृततन्मूले चन्द्रहस्तां[स्त][८] ग्रि[गृ]हीतवान्[९] ।

वादयो गोष्पमह्याभ्यां [वादयेदोष्ठजिह्वाभ्यां][१०] देवता कमलासनः[११] ।। ६२ ।।

प्रार्थनं[ना][१२] ।

नमोस्तु पार्वतीनाथ[१३] नमश्चन्द्रधराय च[१४] ।

नमोस्तु काहळाधिश[१५] नमस्तस्मै वि[पि]नाकिने[१६] ।।६३ ।।

सोमनाथमते ख्यातं[१७] काहलं[१८] लक्षणं पुरा ।। ६४ ।।

टीकाः- [१९]లక్షణయుక్తమైన బో(బూర)రుగకు[२०] నమస్కరించి రెండు[२१] చేతులా ధరించి

१. G86, G89-तांद्रोण
२. M- **************पं
३. G86, G89- शंड्डश मुष्टिभिः
४. G86, G89- माग्रे
५. G86- वलयाकारयूं **** तः, G89- वलयाका **********
६. G89- **खंड, M-अखंडा
७. G86- चतुंख्खंड, M- चतुःखंडं
८. M- छन्द्रहासा
९. G86, G89- ग्रिहीतवाण्
१०. M- वादये ज्येष्ट *****this reading is suggested on the basis of the commentary to v.64, where it is mentioned that the instrument is to be played with the tip of the tongue and lips.
११. G89- ***************, M- ****** कमलाननः
१२. M- omits
१३. G86-नमो **********
१४. G86- *******द्रधराय चा, M- नमः श्चंद्रधराय चा
१५. G86- काहळाधिक, G89- काहलाधीका
१६. G86- नमस्तुस्मिन् विना क *****, G89-नमस्तस्मिन् पिनानिने
१७. G89- ********
१८. G86, G89- कोहळं
१९. G86- ప్రార్థనా, G89 ******, M- ప్రార్థనా
२०. G86- లక్షణయుక్తమై ********, M- లక్షణ *******
२१. G86- *************

పెదవుల నాలికకోన(నాలుకకొన)[1] చేత వాయుపూరిత శబ్దాలు[2] వాయించవలెను. న[బి]రు బాకీలు కాళెలు[3] ఇందులో అంతర్భావం. ఈ కా[ళె][4] లక్షణం సోమనార్యుడు చెప్పినాడు[5].

अथ उपाङ्ग लक्षणम्[6]।

रम्येण[7] रेचकेणै[नै]व रूपं[8] द्वादशमुष्टिभिः[9] ।
रचनिय[नीयं]स्त[त]था चैकं रन्ध्रमस्येव[10] कीर्त्तितः[तम्]।। ६५।।
तर्जनी मध्यमाग्राभ्यां[11] वादनीय[यो]मनीषिभिः[12]।
दण्डस्य[13] लक्ष्मिका दैव[14] रन्ध्रे पवनदेवता ।। ६६।।

प्रार्थनं[ना][15]।।

नमश्चन्द्राय विविधे[16] नमस्सङ्गीतवेदिने[17]।
स्वरत्रययुते[18] तस्मै[तस्तस्मै] [19] नमो जलधिजन्मने[20]।। ६७।।

---

१. M- జింహ్వాగ్రం
२. **G89- ***** లు
३. M- నబిరు బాకిలు భూరు[illegible]
४. G86- అంత్తర్బా[illegible] ********ళ
५. G89- సోమనార్యు********, M- *******ప్పినాడు
६. G86- अवुपाग, G89 अवुपागः
७. G86, G89- रमेण
८. G86- रेचकेनै ******, M- केचकेनेवा रूपं
९. G86, G89- द्वादं न मुष्टिभिः
१२. G86, G89- रंद्रमस्यव
११. G86- तर्जनी मध्य *********, G89- तर्ज***************
१२. G89- *** यीमनि***********, M- वादनिय्यो***मनीशिभिः
१३. G86- दंडनी, M- दंडेस्य
१४. M- लक्षका दैवं
१५. G86- प्रार्धनं।। ~~धार;~~ M- धारण शलोकं, G89- add धार
१६. G86, G89- विधने
१७. G89- नमस्स ************, M- नमः संसि[गी]त वेदिने
१८. G89-**********
१९. G86, G89- तस्मि
२०. G86- ***न्मने

उपाङ्गलक्षणं सम्यक्[१] शाङ्र्गदेवेन[सोमनार्येण][२] कीर्त्तितम्[३] ।।६८।।

టీకా:- ఈ[४] తీరున ఉపాంగ లక్షణయుక్తంగాను[५] వాదకుడు ధరించి[६] వాయుపూరితం(త నాదం) చేత వాయించవలెను[७]. జీనికో[८]☐ చంగు, ఉపరి[९] వాద్యాలు ఇందులో[१०] అంతర్భావం.

[११]आधा[अथ] मृदङ्गः।।

[१२]पुरा मुरासुरं[१३] हत्वा भगवान् देवकीसुतः।
तत्कळेब[व]रमाधाय मर्दलं कृतवान् भुवि[१४] ।। ६९।।
श्रीमत्कञ्च सोद्फतं वुभमयामलकं तथा [?]।
चत्वाकोटिमहाश्रिषौ[?] मृदङ्गश्च यथा क्रमम् ।। ७०।।
जम्बुचन्दनवृक्षे च[क्षेण] मृदङ्गं कारयेद्भुवि।
षड्त्रिंशदङ्गुलं दीर्घं मध[ध्य]मंवर्त्तुला[लं] तथा ।। ७१।।
[१५]अङ्गुष्टौ[ष्ठा]ङ्गुल चू[मा]नेन त्रयः

---

१. M- **म्यक्
२. G86- शाङ्र्तेवेन. Though the name Śārṅgadēva occurs in this context, it is not found in the printed text of SR.
३. M- कीर्त्तितः
४. G86, G89- యే
५. G86- వుపాంగలక్షణం యుక్తగాను, G89- వుపాంగలక్షణం******
६. G86- వాధకుండు దరించి, G89 -************
७. G86- వాయించ***లెను
८. M- జీనుగో☐
९. G86, G89- పూపిరి
१०. G86- యిందో, M- యిందో ***
११. M- missing upto comm. to v.78cd. This portion of the text is very corrupt and hence could not be properly edited.
१२. v.69, cf. ABSS 1, 433
१३. G86-मूरासुरं
१४. G89- मर्धलं ***********
१५. v.72 - v.73, cf. ABSS 1,438cd-440;Readings are suggested from ABSS.

पचाशतङ्गुळः[पञ्चाशदङ्गुलाः]।
दीर्घस्यान्मध्यमस्तू[थू]लं[१] तावत[द]ङ्गुलवर्त्तुलम् ।।७२।।
उभयोरग्रयोश्चैव[२] द्वादशाङ्गुल[३]वर्त्तुलम् ।
तयोश्च मध्यभागेन कर्न्नि[र्णि]का चतुरङ्गुलः[ला]।
कर्न्नि[र्णि]कायां[याः] बहिर्भागे वलयो[ये]न समादृ[वृ]तम्।। ७३।।
विश्वकर्मविनिर्माणं हरिचर्मादयस्तथा [?]।
आहृद्य[त्य] चोकचर्मेण[४] प्रन्धनिय्यं[नीयं] ग्रन्धि[न्थि]युक्तम् ।।७४।।
[५]मकारं विज [बीजं इत्युक्तं] दकारं कुरमेव [अङ्कुरमेव] च।
लंकारं फल सम्योग्यं[६] कुर्वन् मद[द्द]लवाधकः[?]।।७५।।
मृदङ्गं त्रिविधं रूपं चर्मरज्जुश्च पञ्चमं।
प्राणः पञ्च मृदङ्गस्य कीर्त्तितो भरतादिभिः[७]।। ७६।।
[८]देवता[ते] कर्न्नि[र्णि]का[९] द्वद्वौ[द्वन्द्वे] सूर्यचन्द्रमसावुभौ।
वलयद्वितय[१०]स्यापि परिवेषोतदै[षोऽधिदे]वताः ।। ७७।।
ग्रन्थेस्तु विश्वकर्मस्यात् गन्धर्वबन्धदेवताः[११]।
मणिचूडामणौग्रीवे [मणिचूडमणिग्रीवौ]
चरणो[र्मणो]रति[धि]देवताः[ते]।। ७८।।

---

१. G89-**********

२. G86- चैवा

३. G86- द्वादशंगुल

४. G89-*************

५. The original reading in the Mss was thus:'कुर्वन् मदळवाधकः मकारं विज दकारं कुरमेव च। लंकारं फल सम्योग्यं मृदङ्गं त्रिविधं स्मृतम्', but has been rearranged. मृदङ्गं त्रिविधं स्मृतम् seems to be redundant.

६. G89-संयो***********

७. G89- भरता***

८. v.77 - v.78, cf. ABSS 1,441cd - 443ab. Suggested readings based on ABSS

९. G89-**********

१०. G86- वलय***तय

११. G89-**********

టీకా:- పూర్వకాలమందు శ్రి(శ్రీ)రి మురాసురుని గొట్టి వాని కలేబర**(కళేబరం తెచ్చి)[१] మృదంగం జేసి నందికేశ్వరునికి ఇచ్చెను. లోకమందు మారేడు, చంద్ర, జీడి, నెల్లి, నేరేడు, శ్రీగన్ధం[२] ఈ వృక్షమాకులతోను మద్దలం చేయవలెను. ఈ చెప్పిన లక్షణాన మార్దంగి (మృదంగ)[३] లక్షణం.

हृ[हृ]द्याभिजानुदेशे[४] वा जङ्घये[जङ्घायां][५] पादयोस्तथा।
भूम्यादि[६] षड्विधश्चैव[?][७] मृदङ्गं तत्र[८] ता[धा]रयेत्[९] ।। ७९।।
चतुरङ्गुल भूमध्ये[१०] अङ्गुष्टौ[ष्ठौ] श्रे *****योः[११]।
मध्याङ्गुष्ट[ष्ठ]मनामिक्यं निराधारं यथा क्रमम्[१२] ।। ८०।।
अपशब्दमनामिक्यं[१३] कृत विद्याविहीनकम् [?]।
अङ्गुल्यानामिकानां[कया] च मध्यनाटक [ताडन][१४] मेव च[१५] ।। ८१।।
अग्रं च तत्तवाटि[१६] दशधा तत्तधेति च।
[१७]**त धि तो च त धि धि तुलय हधभी** [?]।
तधिकत्तोतट् यस्य मध्यङ्गु[ध्याङ्गु]लवशादिभिः[१८][?]।। ८२।।

---

१. G86- సురుని *************లేబర**
२. G89- *********
३. G86- శాయదల ************** మా *** ంగ్గి
४. G86, G89- ర్వంమాభిజానుదేశే
५. M- च जंघाय (reads this and the following verses after उपाङ्ग लक्षणम् under the heading ढोलु लक्षणं)
६. G86- भूम्योदि, M- भूम्योंवि
७. M- षड्विधं चे*******
८. M-*********
९. G89- तारयेतु, M- ******* त्
१०. G86- चत*****भूमध्ये
११. M- अङ्गुष्ट सिष्ट ********
१२. M- ********* नामिक्यं नि ********
१३. M-*******मनामिक्यं
१४. Since the word नाटक does not seem to be proper in this context, the word ताडन is being suggested, which is seen in the following verses.
१५. G89-*********टकमेव च, M- अङ्गुल्या ************
१६. G86- अग्रं ****** वाटि, M-********** वाटि
१७. M- missing upto the end of v.84ab
१८. G89- मध्यं ************

तोंग्गात[1]धिंग्गणश्चैवा ककुंद्दः कुकुटण् किरः।
जेगतातेय्यतातैता[2] शुद्धताडन[3]मेव च।। ८३।।
अङ्गुष्ठागं[ग्रं] च मूलं च सताळः[तलः] पञ्चभिस्तथा[4]।
एवं च[5] मणिबन्धेत्व तणिप्राह्यं च ततलं[6][?]।
अनामिक[का]तर्जनी च[7] मध्यमं चाथ नाटकं[ताडनं][8]।। ८४।।
अङ्गुष्ठं च कनिष्टं च[9] तर्जनि मध्यमस्तथा[10]।
[11]अनामिकां च संयाति एके च करहस्तयोः ।। ८५।।
शब्दतालविहीनस्या हस्तपूरितनादयो**[?]।
[12]**[अ]क्षरत्रयकं प्राणं यो चनाति
स निन्दितः [जानाति स पण्डितः][13]।। ८६।।
तालं[14] सूचितहस्तं तु शब्दसूचित[15] नादयोः[16]।
तालशब्दादयोर्वाध्यं[द्यं][17] मृदङ्गी मुदितो भवेत्[18] ।। ८७।।
वामहस्तेन ***[दा]रिद्रं[19] दक्षिणहस्तेन[दक्षिणेन च] सम्पदः[20]।

---

१. G89- ******
२. G86- जेगता*****तातैता
३. G86- ताटन
४. G89- च **********, M-***** स्तदा
५. G89- *****, M- सप्तं च
६. M- मणिप्रान्द *****************
७. M-**************
८. G86- मध्य****ध नाटकं, M- मध्यम ********
९. G89- अङ्गुष्टं********, M-***********
१०. G89- ******** मस्तधा, M- मध्यम *****
११. M- missing upto the first half of v.86cd.
१२. G89-*************** स निन्दितः, M-***************** चानाति स नन्दतः
१३. The reading in the Mss seems to convey a sense that is totally contradictory to the context. Hence this reading is suggested.
१४. G86, G89- ताल
१५. M- शप्रद्द**चित
१६. G86, G89- गानयो***
१७. G86, G89- ताळशप्रद्दयोर्वध्यं
१८. G89- मृदंगी *********, M- म्रुदं स म्रुदि** भवेत्
१९. G89-*********रिद्रं, M-*********
२०. G86- दक्षि ******* संपदः, M- *********

वुजा[वृज्या] मृदङ्ग[ङ्गं] ताडौ च ब्रह्मा[ह्म]हत्यां व्यपोहत्[ति][१] ।। ८८।।
नन्दिकेशं हृदिं[२] ध्यात्वा मृदङ्गं ता[धा]रयेत[त्त]तः[३] ।
आदौ[४] स्यादादि[५]तालोयं वादको[६] वाद्यमाचरेत् ।। ८९।।

टीका:- నందికేశ్వరుని ధ్యానం జేసి[౭], సర్వదేవతాకారమైన[౮] మృదంగమును[౯] ధరించి[౧౦], చేత తాళమున్ను పల్కు[౧౧]బడి శబ్దనిర్న(ర్ణ)యమున్ను నందనాద[౧౨] సునాద ఘోషనాదాలు[౧౩] అంగుష్ట తర్జని మధ్యమ అనా☐క కనిష్టక మణిబంద హస్తతల[౧౪] పార్శ్వాంగుళాల చేత[౧౫] దక్షిణ[౧౬] హస్తానను[౧౭] పంచాంగుల మధ్యమ[౧౮] [౧౯]హస్తాల(తల) మణిబంద వామహస్తా**(ల)చేతనున్ను, ఈ చెప్పిన అక్షరపడుఘట్లు (అక్షరం పాడునట్లు) తరగకును[౨౦] నాట్యాదియందు రెండు చేతుల[౨౧] ఉద్గ్రాహం జేసి[౨౨] ఆదితాలా(ళ)లయను వాయించవలెను[౨౩]. [౨౪]గ్రే ***** లోలియ్యం.

१. M- स्नुजा मृदङ्गता ********
२. M- ********** ं
३. G89-**********, M- म्रुदंगं दारयेत्ततः
४. G86- आदो, G89- आतो
५. G86- वादि
६. G86- वा ****, M- नादको
७. M- నందికేశ్వరుని *******
८. G89- సర్వదేవతాకర***, M- ****
९. G89- *******,
१०. M-మ్రుదంగమున్ను ధరించి ***** gap upto నిర్నయమున్ను
११. G86- వలుకు
१२. G86, G89- నందనాధ
१३. G86- ***నాధ ***దాలు
१४. G86, G89- మధ్యమాన☐కనిష్టా మనాబన్ద హస్తతా
१५. M-చాతను
१६. G86, G89- దక్షణ
१७. M- హస్తానున్ను
१८. G89 - Ms ends here.
१९. M- ***** మ హస్తం చాతనున్ను
२०. M- బాట్లు తిరుగను
२१. M- చేతులా
२२. G86- వుగ్రహం జెశి
२३. G86- వలె ***** Ms ends here
२४. The following text is available only in M

ढक्का लक्षणम् ।

ढक्क[क्का]का[खा]दिरकाष॒न दि[दी]र्घयेकादशाङ्गुलम्।

अष्टाङ्गुल प्रमाणेन पार्श्वये[योः] वर्तुलाक्रु[कृ]ति ।। ९० ।।

मध्ये ह्रस्वं प्रकुर्वि[र्वी]त ********** णा।**

वेष्टितंस्चेत सूत्रेण पार्श्वौ संपिड्यते शिवः ।।९१।।

देवता ढक्कवाद्यस्य सूत्रस्य ब्रंह्मदेवता ।

वामहस्तेन ग्रुंह्णियत्[गृह्णियात्] सद्य(व्य) तर्जनि ताडयेत् ।।९२।।

अङ्गुलाग्रं च मूलं च हस्तं प्रधा ****

****[त]र्जन्याद्यङ्गुलैः पार्श्वा सव्य हस्तेन ताडयेत् ।।९३।।**

प्रार्थना।।

****

टीका:- లక్షణయుక్తమైన ఢక్కకు నమస్కరించి వామహస్తం చేత కటకాముఖహస్తేన బట్టి దక్షిణహస్త సూచిహస్త ప్రధానం ********* ల వాయించవలెను. ఈ ఢక్కా లక్షణం సోమనాథియ్యమందు చేప్పినది.

अथा[थ] ढोलु।

[१]कुम्भकर्न[र्ण]स्य बोधार्थं रावणेन विनिर्दितं[मितं]

*********[षोडशाङ्गुलविस्तीर्णं] प्रादेशद्वय संयु***** [मायतम्]**

।।९४।।

**************[डोलावाद्यगतश्चेति] प्रमाणं परिकीर्तितः[तम्]।**

डोकारं दैत्यदेवानां लुकारं रावणेश्वरः ।।९५।।

दौ[द्वौ] द्वौ राक्षसदेवानां डोलावाद्यं प्रचक्षते।

गवश्रिमूर्ति ********[गदमूले ब्रह्मा गदमध्ये हरिस्तथा।]**

[गदाग्रेच भवेद्रुद्रो गदे तिष्ठन्ति देवताः।] ।। ९६ ।।

टीका:- ****లక్షణము********(దక్షిణహస్తం)చేత దక్షిణపార్శ్వమున్ను వామహస్తం చేత వామపార్శ్వమున్ను వాయించవలెను. ఇది రావణ నిర్మితం.

---

१. v.94 - v.96, cf.ABSS 1,638-641ab. Suggestions are based on ABSS, which have been noted by Dr Sathyanarayana in the manuscript, M

भेरि लक्षणम्।

भेरि वाद्य ******* प्रमाणेन ********
महिषिचर्मणाचाद्या[छादि] तश्च[तच्छ]र्मण प्रपीड्यते।।९७।।
आदौ मध्ये तथा चाग्रं[ग्रे] ब्रह्मविष्णुशिवस्थिताम्।
गदेव पार्श्वयोस्तस्या वादको वाद्यमाचरेत्।।९८।।
*********** [सोमनाथमते प्रोक्तं भेरि]वाद्यस्य लक्षणम्।।९९।।**

टीका:- భేరిన్ని గదల చేత వాయించవలేను. ఈ భేరి లక్షణం సోమనాథియ్యమందు చెప్పివున్నది.

डमामि लक्षणम्।।

लोहेन कुम्भौ द्वौ कुर्यः हस्तार्थ वर्तुलाकृतिः।
महिषि चर्म मादः तच्च ****************।१००।।**
******[वा]मदक्षिणहस्ता[तौ] च गदौ[गदे] वाद्यं समाचरेत्।।१०१।।**
कुम्भौ देवौ रविशशि रज्याश्चा[रज्वोश्चा]नन्तर[त]क्षकौ।
गदात्रिमूर्ती दौलाश्च शिवः शक्तिः स्वरूपिणि।।१०२।।
सोमनाथमते प्रोक्तं डमामि लक्षणं पुरा।।१०३।।

टीका:- ఈ **************(తీరున లక్షణ)యుక్తమైన డమా[illegible] రెండు చేతులాగద వాయించవలెను. గడిబిడి, తముకు మొదలైన చర్మవాద్యాలు యిందులో అంతర్భావం.

इति चर्मवाद्यं।

[अथ कांस्यतालं।।]

वर्तुलं कांस्य ************* गुलोमुशै।**
निम्मो[म्नो] मध्यमदेशश्चा अधोर्यङ्गुलमात्रु[त्र]कम् ।।१०४।।
तद्वेको यवमात्रस्य जातं पुष्टिसमाश्रुतिः।
पादोनंगुज[ल] मात्रंतु मध्ये ******।।१०५।।**
******* पट्टु सूत्रं ग्रन्थिस्तस्याग्रतः कुरु ।**
वामतर्भ (र्ज) नितांगुष्ठे वेष्ठितं निश्चलं भवेत्।।१०६।।
अन्ये दक्षिणतर्जन्यां वेष्ठितं प्रभाकरः।

ताण्ड *******************करौ ।। १०७ ।।**

*****[अ]ष्टाविंशत्वलेनैवा[व] कांस्यतालं प्रकल्पयेत्।**

हरनेत्रसमुद्भूता[ताः] ब्रह्माविष्णुमहेश्वरा[राः]।।१०८।।

अश्वमेध फलंचैव प्राप्नुयाद्यो गतस्तथा।

ताल *********** परिकीर्तितः।।१०९।।**

यथा शास्त्रप्रसारेण शुद्धमित्यभिधिय्यते।

मनोविस्तारसहितं नर्तकस्य तु माक्रुतिः।।११०।।

**************** सालग नामकः।**

शुद्ध **********************।।१११।।**

టీకా:- ఇట్ల(ట్లు) లక్షణయుక్తంగా కంచుతాళాలుచేయ (వాయించ)వలెను. జాకట. లో ********[१]

अनुबन्ध

[२]**अधा(थ)मौर्वि**[३]**।**

निर्घोष[४] **विजकौष्टं तु**[५] **मवुरीति**[६] **इति स्मृतः।**
अंगुळैरेकविंशत्याः[७] **त्रयोस्तत्र**[८] **पृथक् पृथक्**[९]**।।**
मवुरी मूलमङ्गुल्याः[१०] **मध्ये च द्वितमङ्गुलम्**[११]**।**

---

१. The text in M ends here. This probably is the concluding portion of this chapter.

२. This passage was originally found after v.37 of NC,3. Since the occurrence of this portion was felt ambiguous, it has been placed here. The text in this section has not been edited.

३. M- अधा मौर्वि लक्षणम्

४. G89- निर्धो**

५. M- प्रिजकोरंत्तु [नंतु], G89-**********

६. G86, G89- मपूरिज

७. G86- अंगुळा***विं***, G89- अंगुलेकविंशत्योः

८. G86- त्रयेस्तुत्र, G89- त्रेयेस्तत्र

९. G86- पृधक्, G89- पृतक् पृधक्

१०. G86, G89- मंदरीमूलमंगुल्कां

११. G86- मद्बे च द्वितयंगुलं, G89- *************

भेदेवा त्रि[१] त्रियंगुळ्यां सर्वांगैरेकविंशति[२]।।
मूलशब्दे स्थितो[३] ब्रंह्मा अग्रे पशुपतिस्तधा[४]।
भेदेवात्रे मध्ये जनार्धनं[५] वक्ष्ये साक्षान्नाममहेश्वरः[६]।।
आध्यतास्यैव[७] संपाद्यं ब्रह्मनाभिसरस्वति।
कमला पत्रिका[८] कुंभा[९] जीवालस्तु[१०] सुधाकराः।।
सप्तरंद्रेण[११] संयुक्तं[१२] सप्तस्वरसमन्वितम्[१३]।
ते मिश्रायेकूणरंद्र मन्र्येकविंशतिः[१४]।।
मवुरि मूलपिड्यन्ते[१५] दक्षिणाग्रकारस्य चा।
उभयोरपि पिड्यः स्य मौर्वि लक्षणमुच्यते।।
दक्षिणेकारपिड्यंते ब्रंह्महत्य घमिष्यते[१६]।
******स्तस्वशप्रद्धस्य[१७] ब्रूणहत्ये[१८] हमिष्यते।।**
उभयोः[१९] करपीड्यंते शंभुस्तांडवमाचरेत्[२०]।

---

१. G89- *******
२. M- भेदेचात्र त्रियंगुळ्याः सर्वांगेरेकविंशति
३. G86,G89- मूलशप्रश्चे स्तितो
४. G86- अग्रे*****तिस्तधा, M- अग्रे पशुपति*****
५. M- ************
६. G86- साक्षान्नाममहेश्वराः, G89- ********महेश्वराः
७. M- आद्यंतास्य च
८. G86, G89- प्रतिकौ
९. G86- ****, G89- कुंभं
१०. G86-*******, M- जीवालेस्तु
११. G89-********, M- सप्तरंद्रिण
१२. G89- ********
१३. M- सप्त *************
१४. M- *********येकरंद्रेण रंद्रमप्येकविंशतिः
१५. G86, G89- मौरि मूषप्रांड्यन्ते. G86, G89 missing from here upto the next दक्षिणे
१६. G86- घमिष***
१७. G89- वाम*********स्य, M- वाम *************
१८. G86- प्रलाणहत्ये, M- **णहत्ये
१९. M- वुभयो
२०. G86, G89- शंभस्तांडवमाचरेत्

मवुरि[१] लक्षणं पूर्व मतंगमुनि[२] वक्ष्यते।
मौर्वि लक्षणं[३] सम्यक् . . . ।।

---

[४]अधा(थ) वाद्य लक्षणं।।

जंद्र[त्र]गात्रहस्तयोश्च मेळनं वाद्यमुच्यते[५]।।

టీకా:- జంత్రానికి[६] మనస్సుకు [७]స్తాలుకు దోక వాద్యం[८] తబంది(?) మంచివాద్యమనబడును.

वाद्यं संघट्टसंकृत्वा वस्त्राभरणभूषितः[९]।
उपाङ्गि गायकोभेतः[१०] सभास्तानं प्रवेश्यते ।।

టీకా:- తన వాద్యం సంఘట్టన చేసుకొని[११] వస్త్రాభరణ భూషితుండై వుపాంగ నాయకుని[१२] కూర్చుక సభాస్తానం ప్రవేశ్యంప్పవలను (ప్రవేశింపవలెను).

नृपते पुरतो तिष्ठण्[१३] पद्मासनकृतां शुचिः।
देवता वन्दनं कृत्वा वादको वाद्यमाचरेत् ।।

టీకా:- పద్మాసనం చేత రాజు ముందర ***కూచ్చుండి[१४] దేవతా వందనం చేశి వాదకుడు వాద్యమాచరించవలెను[१५].

---

१. G86, G89- मौवरि
२. G86, G89- मंगमुनि
३. M- ******** ण [नागसरे]
४. The following text and commentary is missing in M. See Introduction for a discussion on this.
५. G89- जंत्र ************
६. G86- జంద్రానికి
७. G86- స్తాలకు
८. G86- దో **గ వాద్యం
९. G89- **************
१०. G89- उपाङ्गी गायकोपितः
११. G86- *******
१२. G89- వుపాంగినాయకున్ని ******* missing till the end of this sentence
१३. G86- तिष्टण्
१४. G89- రాజు ************
१५. G86- వాద్యంమాచరించవలెను

अधौ मध्ये तदाचाग्रे ब्रंह्मविष्णुशिवस्थिताः।

सर्वदेवमयं[१] हिंध्यं[२] नमामि स्वरपंकजम्।।

టీకా:- సర్వవాదకమైన వాద్యానికి నమస్కరించి భూ□యందు వస్త్రం పరచి అందు□ద ఆ వాద్యముంచి[३] మరి తీసురో(కో)ని వాయించవలెను.

समस्तलोक जननी[४] सर्वसंप्पप्रतायनि।

नमामि त्वां[५] च देवि वाद्यघोषं[६] क्षमस्वमे।।

देही लङ्करणं वस्त्रं[७] लज्जायां रक्षणं परम्।

स्वेतवर्णं शिताहारं लक्षिमदेवं[८] नमाम्यहम्।।

ब्रंह्मे * * * * * * * * भारती लक्ष्मि पार्वती[९]।

दिगीशां सर्वदेवानां वंदे सर्वार्ध सिद्धये।

हस्ताभ्यां वादको[१०] वाद्यं गृहीत्वा वाद्यमाचरेत्।।

టీకా:- భూ********* [११] □ష్ణు, □శ్వ్రశా, భారతీ, రమా దుర్గలుకు[१२] వందనం చేశి వాద్యకాడు రెండు హస్తాల చేత వాద్యం తీసుకోని [१३]మృగశిర సర్పశిర ******(హస్తాల) చేత వాద్యం వాయించవలెను. యీ వాయిద్యం[१४] వాయించే లక్షణం చెప్పెనూ.

स्वरकालस्त्रिधा भेदा मंद्र मध्यम[१५] तारकाः।

---

१. G86- सर्वदेमयं

२. G89- *****

३. G89- **********

४. G86-जेननि

५. G86- द्वां

६. G89- वाद्यभूषं

७. G89- **************

८. G89-*******

९. G89- ब्रंह्मशिवं ******विष्णु ******

१०. G89- वादको वादको

११. G89- ********

१२. G86- దర్గలుకు

१३. G89- ********* upto వాద్యం

१४. G86- వాయాద్యాం

१५. G89- स्त्रिधा *************

एकैकं तन्त्रिदा भेदाः[१] मंद्रमध्यमतारकाः।।
मन्द्र मन्द्रो मन्द्रमध्यमन्द्रस्तारकमुच्यते।
मध्यमंद्रा मध्यमध्य[२]मध्यसा[ता]रक उच्यते।।
तारो मंद्रो तारमध्य तारस्तारकमुच्यते[३]।
षड्जमंद्रमिति प्रोक्तं मध्यमं मध्यमा तथा।।
निषादं तारक प्रोक्तं अंत्या[४] षड्जादि तारकं।
षड्जस्वरं मंद्रमंद्रं रिषभं मंद्र मध्यमं[५]।।
गान्धारं मंद्रतारेति मध्य मध्यममध्यमं।
पञ्चमं मध्यतारेति दैत[व]तं[६] तारकमध्यमं।।
निषादं तारतारेति गसो[७] मंद्रोविजस्वरः ।
सप्तस्वराः[८] क्रमादेवं ताळकावैश्च्य संयुतः।।
ताळकालस्तधा प्रोक्ता[९] धृतमध्यविळंबिता।
येकैक त्रित्रिधा भेधा धृतमध्यविळंबिता।।
———— विष्णु (ता) सांड्वमाचरेत्[१०]।।

---

१. G86- ये *************
२. G89- *************
३. G86- *********
४. G89- निषा***********
५. G86- मंद्र ***मं
६. G89- पंचम ************
७. G86- ग** मंद्रोविजस्वर
८. G86- *****स्वरा**
९. G89- ताल***********
१०. G86- विष्णु*** ंडवमाचरेत्

3

Nāṭyacūḍāmaṇiḥ

1. Nāṭya

nityānandakaraṃ śāntaṃ nirmalāṅgaṃ suśobhanam |
nīre[ra]japatranayanaṃ sītārāmamahaṃ bhaje ||1||
śambhurgaurī tathā brahmā mādhavo nandikeśvaraḥ |
dattilaḥ kohalaścaiva yājñavalkyaśca nāradaḥ ||2||
hanumān vighnarājaśca ṣaṇmukho'pi bṛhaspatiḥ|
arjuno rāvaṇaścaiva kanyā bāṇāsurasya ca ||3||
ete bharatakartāraḥ tattatkarmaprayogataḥ|
matānāmapi sarveṣāṃ samāśrityārthacāturīm [?] ||4||
aṣṭāvadhānavikhyāta somanāryeṇa vakṣyate|
nāṭyacūḍāmaṇirnāma grantho vibudhasammataḥ ||5||
lokeṣu bahavassanti bharatārthaviśāradāḥ |
teṣāṃ matebhyaḥ saṅgṛhya kuryānnāṭyaprayoginīm [?] |
pūrvaśāstrānusāreṇa granthaṃ śāstraśiromaṇim [?]||6 ||
lakṣyasvarūpaṃ prākaṭyasiddhaye lakṣaṇatrayam |
lakṣaṇadvayamekaṃ vā lakṣyalakṣo pradarśayet ||7 ||
ekalakṣaṇamanyasya vyākhyānaṃ lakṣaṇasya yat |
lakṣyetva pekṣa[kṣya]manyasyādatraiva ca nirūpyate|| 8||

ṭīkā:-lōkamandu bharatagranthakartalu bahumandi kalugu[laru] ganaka. vārla yokka śāstraṃ ellanuṇḍi saṅgrahiñci saṅkṣēpaṅgānu nāṭyacūḍāmaṇi anēṭi granthaṃ lōkōpakāraṅgānu aṣṭā*[va]dhāna prasiddhuṇḍaina sōmanāryu*[ni] cēta lē[la]kṣaṇa lakṣiyaṃ[kṣyaṃ] ceppaprascunnadi [ceppanunnadi].

atha nāṭyotpattiḥ

gāndharvaṃ trividhaṃ gītavādyanartanabhedataḥ|
nartanaṃ trividhaṃ nāṭyanṛttanṛtya prabhedataḥ ||9||
nāṭyavedaṃ dadau pūrvaṃ bharatāya caturmukhaḥ|
tatastu bharatassārdhaṃ gandharvāpsarasāṃ gaṇaiḥ || 10||
nāṭyaṃ nṛttaṃ tathā nṛtyaṃ agre śambhoḥ prayuktavān|
prayogamudyataṃ[muddhataṃ] dṛṣṭvā[smṛtvā]
svaprayuktaṃ tato haraḥ ||11||
taṇḍunā svagaṇāgraṇya bharatāya syadhidiśat [vyadīdṛśat] |
budhvātha tāṇḍavaṃ taṇḍoḥ martyebhyo munayo'vadan ||12||

ṭīkā:- gāndharvavēdaṃ mūḍu prakārālu. gītavādyanṛttālu - nṛttaṃ [nartanaṃ] mūḍu prā[pra]kārālu. nāṭya tattat [nṛtta] nṛtyālu. ī nāṭyavēdaṃ bharatuniki brahma ceppenu. ā bharatuḍu apsarasa gaṇālaku ceppi, paramēśvaruni mundara āḍiñcenu. ā paramēśvaruḍu tā kalpiñcina tāṇḍavālu, taṇḍuni cēta bharatuniki ceppiñcenu. ā bharatuḍu martyalōkamandu pratiṣṭhitamayyēḍi koraku munīśvaruluku ceppi āḍiñcenu.

pārvatītvanuśāsasmāt lāsyaṃ [pārvatī
tvanuśāsti sma lāsyaṃ]bāṇātmajāmuṣām|
tayā dvāravatīgopyaḥ tābhissaurāṣṭrayoṣitaḥ ||13||
tābhistu śikṣitā nāryaḥ nānājanapadāspadāḥ |
evaṃ paramparāprāptametalloke pratiṣṭhitam ||14||

ṭīkā:- pārvati kalpiñcina lāsyaṃ[ya]nṛttaṃ bāṇāsuruni kumārtte uṣākanyaku ceppenu. ā uṣā dvāravati strīlaku ceppenu. vāru campanna dēśāla vāriki ceppiri. vārlu [ru] kaḍamavārluku[rlaku] ceppagā ī tīruna paramparayā martyalōkamandu pratiṣṭhitamāya[ye]nu.

ṛgyajussāmavedebhyo vedādātharvaṇaḥ kramāt|
pāṭhānabhinayān[pāṭhyañcābhinayān]
gītān[gītaṃ] rasān saṅgṛhya padmabhūḥ|
vyarīracat trayamidaṃ dharmakāmārthamokṣadam ||15||
kīrti prāgalbhyasaubhāgyaṃ[ya]
vedādyānāṃ [vaidagdhyānāṃ] vivardhanam |
aiśvaryaśauryadhairyāṇāṃ vilāsasya ca kāraṇam ||16||
duḥkhārta[ti]śokanirveda khedaviccheda sādhanam |
ati brahmaparānandamidhamapyadhikaṃ phalam ||17||
jahāra nāradādīnāṃ cittāni kathamanyathā |
na kiñciddṛśyate loke dṛśyaṃ śrāvyamataḥ param ||18||

ṭīkā:- nālugu vēdālanuṇḍi kramānanē pāṭh[ṭhy]ālu abhinayaṃ gītaṃ rasabhāvālu saṅgrahiñci brahma[hmā] gītavādya nṛttālu jēśēnu. idi[vi] dharmārthakāma mōkṣālu yiccēṭivi. aiśvarya dhairyavilāsālaku kāraṇamainavi. duḥkhārta śōka nirvēda bhē[khē]daviccē[chē]da sāda[dha]kamainavi. brahmānandamu- kanna adhika phalamiccēṭivi. kābaṭṭi nāradādi paramabhāgavatulu induna pravartindu[tu]ru. intakannnā cūcē śāstraṃ intakannā vinē śāstraṃ yitaramu lēdu ganuka. idi trimūrtyātmakamaina śāstramani teliyu[ya]taginadi.

2. *Gītādhyāyaḥ*

atha gītādhyāyaṃ vakṣyate|

saṅgītaśāstraṃ saṅgṛhya svararāgasudhārasam|
aṣṭāvadhāna vikhyātaṃ somanāryeṇa vakṣyate|| 1||

ṭīkā:- saṅgītāśāstramandu saṅgrahiñci svararāgasudhā- rasamunnu [rasamu] aṣṭāvadhāna prasiddhuṇḍaina sōmanāryuni cēta ceppabaḍenu.

nādaṃ nādotpannam

nṛttaṃ vādyaṃ tathā gītaṃ melanaṃ nādamucyate |
rañjaya svarasandarbho gītamityabhidhīyate |
svato rañjayati śrotṛcittaṃ svarasamucyate || 2 ||

ṭīkā:- nṛttagītavādyāla kūḍi puṭṭina dhvani nādamanabaḍunu.

nakāraṃ prāṇavijñeyaṃ dakāramanalaṃ viduḥ|
jātaḥ prāṇāgnisaṃyogāt nāda ityabhidhīyate || 3||

*ṭīkā:-*nakāraṃ prāṇālani teliyatagīnadi. dakāraṃ agniyani teliyadagīnadi. ī prāṇāgni kūṭamu cēta puṭṭina dhvani nādamani cēppabaḍunu.

nādopāsanayā devāḥ bahmaviṣṇumaheśvarāḥ |
[bhavantyupāsitā nūnaṃ yasmādete tadātmakāḥ] ||4||

ṭīkā:- brahma viṣṇu mahēśvarulu brahmōpāsana cēyucunduru.

āhatama[tā]nāhata lakṣaṇam|

āhato'nāhataścaiva sa nādo dvividho mataḥ|
ityo[yu]bhayā[yo]śca samyogādāhataḥ parikīrtitaḥ || 5||
ākāśasambhavo nādaḥ anāhatamudīritam [anāhata udīritaḥ] |
ārohiṇyāhataścaiva avarohiṇyāvanāhataḥ[ṇyanāhataḥ]||6||

*ṭīkā:-*ā nādaṃ āhatamani anāhatamani reṇḍu prakārālu. [āhatamane nādaṃ śarīramandu puṭṭenu. anāhatamane nādaṃ ākāśaṃvalla puṭṭenu.] ārōhiṇī anāhatamunnu avaraōhiṇī āhatamani ceppabaḍunu.

[*svara lakṣaṇaṃ*]

tannādaṃ saptadhā kṛtvā tathā ṣaḍjādibhiḥ svaraiḥ |

ṣaḍjo ṛṣabhagāndhārau madhyamaṃ pañcamastathā |
dhaivataśca niṣādaśca svarāḥ sapta prakīrtitāḥ|| 7||

ṭīkā:- ā nādaṃ sa ri ga ma pa dha ni ani sapta svarālāyanu. ī sapta svarālu nemali, āvu, mēka, krauñcapakṣi, kōkila, gurraṃ, yēnugavīrlananṭi [vīṭinunṭi] buṭṭenu.

evaṃ svarān samākṛṣya vīṇādiṣu nidhāya ca |
tena phutena nādena saṅgītamakarot tathā || 8 ||

*ṭīkā:-*ā sapta svarālu jantramandu vāyiñccā [ca ā] nādamandu saṅgītamani puṭṭenu.

śiśurvetti paśurvetti vetti gānarasaṃ phaṇiḥ || 9 ||

ṭīkā:- ī gānarasaṃ śiśuvulaku paśuvulaku sarppamulaku telusunu.

ajā[jñā]ta hṛdayasyando[viṣayāsvādo] bālaḥ paryaṅkikātale |
rudan gītāmṛtaṃ pītvā harṣotkarṣaṃ prapadyate || 10||

ṭīkā:- yemi yerugani śiśuvu [ni] toḍapaiku peṭṭukoni gānaṃ cēstu rōdana hīnunḍai santōṣaṃ cēta vunḍunu.

vanecarastṛṇāhāra ścitraṃ mṛgaśiśaḥ[śuḥ] paśuḥ|
labdolabdasu saṅgītaṃ modante yaśca jīvitaṃ
[lubdho lubdhakasaṅg i te gīte yacchati jīvitam] ||11||

ṭīkā:- vanamandu kasuvutini nīllutāgucu svayaṃ[gā] sañcaristuvunḍē mṛgapaśvādulu gānaṃvini santōṣaṅgā vunḍunu.

kṛṣṇasarpo' pi tannādaṃ śrutvā harṣaṃ prapadyate|

tasya gītasya māhātmyaṃ ke praśaṃsaṃ[śaṃsi] tumīśate||12||

ṭīkā:- kṛṣṇasarpālu svara gīta nādaṃ vini santōṣamaiyuṇḍunu. kāgā ā gītaṃ mahātmyaṃ yēmani varṇimppasakyamu.

devavaṃśāstu sagamāḥ pañcamaḥ pitṛvaṃśajaḥ|
ridhau ṛṣikule jātau niṣādo'sura vaṃśajaḥ|| 13||

ṭīkā:- sa ga ma dēvavaṃśaṃ; pā pitṛvaṃśaṃ; ri dhā ṛṣivaṃśaṃ; ni rākṣasavaṃśaṃ; ivi svarālaku vaṃśālu.

brāhmaṇau tu samau jñeyau ridhau kṣatriyajātijau |
nigau vaiśyamiti proktau pa iti śūdrajātijaḥ ||14||

ṭīkā:- sa ma brāhmaṇajāti; ri dhā[dha] kṣatriyajāti; ni ga vaiśyajāti; pa śūdrajāti; ivi svarālaku jātulu.

aśītissaptatiṣṣaṣṭiścatvāriṃśaśca triṃśati |
viṃśatiḥ daśamo varṣaḥ vayaḥ ṣaḍjādibhissvaraiḥ
[ṣaḍjādīnāṃ vayaḥ kramāt] || 15||

ṭīkā:- 80, 70, 60, 40, 30, 20, 10 yeṇḍlu - idi[vi] sapta svarāla vayasu.

padmābhi[bhaḥ]piñjara[raḥ]
svarṇavarṇa[rṇaḥ] kundaprabhā[,]sitaḥ |
pītaḥ karbura ityete varṇāḥ ṣaḍjādiṣu smṛtāḥ || 16||

ṭīkā:- idi[vi] ṣaḍjādi sapta svarālaku varṇālu.

jambūśākakuśakrauñca śālmalīśveta nāmasu |
dvīpeṣu puṣkaraścaiva svarāṇāṃ deśamīritam || 17||

ṭīkā:- ivi svarālaku dēśālu.

vahnirvedaḥ śaśāṅkaṃśca lakṣmīnāthastathaiva ca |
nāradastumburuścaiva ṣaḍjādi ṛṣayastathā || 18||

ṭīkā:- ivi svarālaku gōtrarṣulu.

satidhī[vī]redbhute raudre bībhatse ca bhayānake |
hāsyaśṛṅgārayoścaiva ṣaḍjādī rasayastathā
[ṣaḍjādīnāṃ rasāḥ smṛtāḥ] || 19||

ṭīkā:- ivi svarālaku rasālu.

vahnirbrahmā śāradā ca śarvaḥ śrīnāthabhāskaraḥ [rau]|
gaṇeśvarādayo devāḥ ṣaḍjādīnāṃ ca devatāḥ ||20||

ṭīkā:- vīru ṣaḍjādi svarālaku dēvatalu.

śvetaḥ pīto raktaḥ nīlaḥ haridrāvarṇavat tathā |
citravastrakṣaumavastrau ṣaḍjādīnāmalaṅkṛtāḥ || 21||

ṭīkā:- idi[vi] svarālaku vastrālu.

dadhyannaṃ pāyasaṃ bhakṣyaṃ citrānnaṃ piṣṭayukpayaḥ|
śuddhānnaṃ taṇḍulaṃścaiva ṣaḍjādīnāṃ ca bhojanam ||22||

ṭīkā:- idi[vi] svarālaku bhōjanam.

kuṅkumāgarukastūrikarpūraṃ rocanaṃ tathā|
candanaṃ parimaḷadravyaṃ [ca parimalaṃ]

ṣaḍjādīnāṃ ca lepanam||23||

ṭīkā:- idi[vi] svarālaku lēpanagandham.

jātī campakapunnāgamallikāketakī tathā |
karavīraḥ padmapuṣpaṃ ṣaḍjādīnāmalaṅkṛtāḥ || 24||

ṭīkā:- ivi svarālaku alaṅkāramulu.

muktāphalo nīlavajraṃ vaiḍūryo marakato maṇiḥ|
gomedha[da]ko puṣparāgaḥ ṣaḍjādīnāṃ ca bhūṣaṇam ||25 ||

ṭīkā:- idi[vi] svarālaku bhūṣaṇālu.

khaḍgakunta gadhācakraṃ bhiṇḍipālastathaiva ca |
nārācamaṅkuśaṃ ceti svarāṇāmāyudhaṃ smṛtam || 26 ||

ṭīkā:- ivi svarālaku āyudhālu.

haṃsaśca siṃhabherūṇḍa hariṇīmakarī tathā [rāstathā]|
śukaśca śārikā caiva ṣaḍjādīnāṃ ca vāhanam|| 27||

ṭīkā:- idi[vi] svarālaku vāhanālu.

cūtakharjūrakadaḷī jambīro dāḍimī tathā |
drākṣā punnāgavṛkṣāśca ṣaḍjādīnāṃ prakīrtitāḥ || 28 ||

ṭīkā:- ivi ṣaḍjādi svarālaku vṛkṣālu.

gāndharvi[gandharvī] kinnarī yakṣī kimpurṣī nāgakanyakā|
surastrī rākṣasī tāsām ṣaḍjādīnāṃ tu patrayaḥ [patnayaḥ] || 29 ||

ṭīkā:- vīru ṣaḍjādi svarālaku peṇḍlālu.

kramādanuṣṭup gāyatri[trī] triṣṭup ca bṛhatī tathā |
paṅtyaṣṇajagatīcando [paṅtyuṣṇikjagatīcchando]
ṣaḍjādīnāmudāhṛtam || 30 ||

ṭīkā:- ivi svarālaku chandassulu.

sthūlasūkṣma sthūladīrghaṃ samapuṣṭi[ṭa]stathaiva ca|
dīrghādi[ti] sthūladehaśca ṣaḍjādīnāṃ kramādvadet [bhavet] || 31||

ṭīkā:- ivi sapta svarālaku ākṛti.

śatatārāscitravasu makhā [ghā] cottara phalgunī |
pūrvāṣāḍhā maitrabhaśca svarāṇāṃ
janmaṛṣabhāḥ [janmarkṣāḥ bhavet] ||32||

ṭīkā:- ivi svarālaku janmanakṣatrālu.

catuste[trī]dvimukhīścaiva [khañcaiva]
caturmukhi[kha] caturmukhi[kham] |
trimukhi[kha]dvimukhīcaiva
[khañcaiva] svarāṇāmānanaṃ vadet || 33|

ṭīkā:- ivi svarālaku mukhālu.

*aṣṭau rasacaturbāhu raṣṭāvaṣṭārasasta***
[raṣṭāvaṣṭau karāstathā]|
ṛtuścatukarāścaiva svarāṇāṃ bāhurīritaḥ ||34||

ṭīkā:- ivi svarālaku bāhuvulu.

aṣṭau ṛtucatuścaiva aṣṭāvaṣṭau tadai[thai]va cā[ca]|
ṛtuvedākṣa[kṣi]saṅkhyā ca svarāṇāṃ netramīritam|| 35||

ṭīkā:- idi[vi] ṣaḍjādi svarālaku nētrālu.

aṣṭau ṛtu catuśrotrāḥ aṣṭāvaṣṭau śrutistathā |
rasavedā śrōtrasaṅkhyā ṣaḍjādīnāṃ śrutirvadet || 36||

ṭīkā:- idi[vi] ṣaḍjādi svarālaku śrōtrālu.

mukhasaṅkhyā nāsikāṃ ca svarāṇāṃ pādatiṅ[?] vadet ||37||

*ṭīkā:-*ṣaḍjādi svarālaku mukhasaṅkhyā prakāraana[rāna] nāsikalu pādālu svara jñānamulu[nulu] ceppināru.

svarāṇāṃ lakṣaṇaṃ samyak somanāryeṇa kīrttitam |
saṅgrahya vidhivattatra vistareṇa tathaiva ca ||38||

ṭīkā:- ṣaḍjādi svarālaku vistāraṅgā lakṣaṇālu sōmanācāryuni cēta ceppava[ba]ḍucunnadi.

ṣaḍja svarāniki - dēvavaṃśaṃ- brāhmaṇajāti- yeṇḍlu - 80 - padmavarna[rṇaṃ] - jambūdvīpaṃ- vīrarasaṃ- agni gōtrarṣiḥ - haṃsavāhanaṃ - agnidēvatā - nālugu mukhālu- enimidi bhujālu- enimidi śrōtramulu[trālu] - enimidi nētrālu - nālugu nāsikalu- reṇḍu pādālu - sthūladēhaṃ - khaḍgāyudhaṃ- śvētavastraṃ - jājīpuṣpaṃ- kuṅkumagandhaṃ- dadhyānna bhōjanaṃ- māṇikyabhūṣaṇaṃ- cūtavṛkṣaṃ - gandharvastrī- śatabhiṣā nakṣatraṃ- kumbharāśi - śanivāraṃ- ī tīruna ṣaḍjamasvaraṃ anuṣṭup- chandassuna puṭṭi prakāśistunnadi.

ṛṣabhasvarāniki- ṛṣivaṃśaṃ- kṣatriyajāti- yeṇḍlu- 70 - aḷadivarnnaṃ[rṇaṃ] - śākadvīpaṃ- adbhutarasaṃ- vēdapuruṣuḍu gōtraṃruṣi - brahma[hmā] adi[dhi]dēvatā- pasuru[pu]kōka - pāyasabhōjanaṃ- agarugandhaṃ- sampaṅgipuvvulu- nīlabhūṣaṇaṃ- kunttāyudhaṃ- siṃha vāhanaṃ- kharjūraphalavṛkṣaṃ - kinnarastrī - cittānakṣatraṃ- śukravāraṃ- tulārāśi- mūḍu mukhālu- āru bhujālu- āru nētrālu- āru śrōtrālu - mūḍu nāsalu [nāsikalu]- reṇḍu pādālu- madhyama sthūladēhaṃ- gāyatrichandassu [na]yandu ṛṣabha svaraṃ puṭṭi prakāśistunnadi.

gāndharva[gāndhāra]svarāniki - dēvavaṃśaṃ - vaiśyajāti- 60 yeṇḍlu - baṅgāruvarnaṃ[rṇaṃ]- candruḍu gōtrarṣi - raudrarasaṃ - sarasvati adhidēvatā- kuśadvīpaṃ- rakta vastraṃ - kajjāyaṃ - kastūrigandhaṃ- punnāgapuṣpaṃ- vajra bhūṣaṇaṃ- gadāyudhaṃ- bhēruṇḍu[ḍa]vāhanaṃ - kadaḷīvṛkṣaṃ- yakṣastrī- reṇḍu mukhālu- nālugu bhujālu - 4 nētrālu- dvi nāsikā- 2 pādālu- dīrgha dēhaṃ- dhaniṣṭānakṣatraṃ- tulārāśi - śanivāraṃ- ī tīruna gāndhāra svaraṃ- triṣṭupuca[cha]ndassu[na]yandu puṭṭi prakāśistu vunnadī[di].

madhyamasvarāniki - dēvavaṃśaṃ - brāhmaṇa jāti- 40 - yeṇḍlu - mōllamōgga varṇaṃ- krauñcadvīpaṃ - kṛṣṇuḍugōtrarṣi - bhībhatsarasaṃ- īśvaruḍu adhidēvatā - nīlavastraṃ- kalavaṇṭakaṃ - karpūragandhaṃ- mallikāpuṣpaṃ - vaiḍūryabhūṣaṇaṃ- cakrāyudhaṃ- jiṅkavāhanaṃ - nimba[mma]phalavṛkṣaṃ - kimpuruṣastri- nālugu mukhālu- enimidi bhujālu - enimidi śrōtrālu- enimidi nētrālu- nālugu nāsikalu- reṇḍu pādālu - maṭṭataradēhaṃ- makhā[ghā]nakṣatraṃ- siṃharāśi- ādivāraṃ- ī tīruna madhyamasvaraṃ- bra[bṛ]haticchandassu [na]yandu puṭṭi prakāśistunnadi.

pañcamasvaraṃ[svarāniki]- pitṛvaṃśaṃ- śūdrajāti- 30 yeṇḍlu vayassu- nīlavarṇaṃ- śālmalidvīpaṃ - īśvaruḍu gōtrariṣi- bhayarasaṃ- viṣṇu adhidēvatā- aḷadivarṇaṃ- calimiḍi bhōjanaṃ- gōrōcanagandhaṃ- mogili pūlū- māṇikyabhūṣaṇaṃ - bhiṇḍivālāyudhaṃ- mosali vāhanaṃ-dāḍimavṛkṣaṃ- nāgakanyakā- nālugu mukhālu- enimidi bhujālu- enimidi śrōtrālu- enimidi nētrālu - nālugu nāsikalu- reṇḍu pādālu- kubjadēhaṃ- uttarānakṣatraṃ- kanyārāśi - budhavāraṃ- ī tīruna pañcamasvaraṃ paṅktichandassuna prakāśiñcunu.

dai[dhai]vatasvarāniki - ṛṣivaṃśaṃ- kṣatriyajāti- 20 yeṇḍlu - pītavarṇaṃ- śvētadvīpaṃ - nāraduḍu gōtrarṣi - hāsyarasaṃ- sūryuḍu athi[dhi]dēvatā- varna[rṇa]vastraṃ - pālu bhōjanaṃ - śrīgandhaṃ - gannēru pūvulu - gōmēdhikabhūṣaṇaṃ- nārācāyudhaṃ- cilukavāhanaṃ- drākṣāvṛkṣaṃ- dēvatāstri- mūḍu mukhālu - āru bhujālu - āru nētrālu- āru śrōtrālu - mūḍu nāsikalu- reṇḍu pādālu- pūrvāṣāḍānakṣatraṃ- dhanurrāśi- guruvāraṃ- dīrgha dēhaṃ- ī tīruna dēvatā[dhaivata] svaraṃ - uṣṇiccha[gcha]ndassuna prakāśamavunu.

niṣādha[da] svarāniki - rākṣasa vaṃśaṃ- vaiśiya [śya] jāti- yeṇḍlu -10 - dhūmra varṇa - puṣkaradvīpaṃ- śṛṅgāra rasaṃ- tumburuḍu gōtrarṣi - vināyakuḍu - adhidēvatā- paṭṭuvastraṃ- biyyaṃ bhōjanaṃ- parimaḷa gandhaṃ- tāmara puvvulu - puṣparāga bhūṣaṇaṃ- aṃkuśāyudhaṃ- gōruvaṅka vāhanaṃ- lavaṅga vṛkṣaṃ - rākṣasa strī - reṇḍu mukhālu- nālugu bhujālu- 4 śrōtrālu- 4 nētrālu - 2 nāsikalu- 2 pādālu- atisthūladēhaṃ- anō[nu]rādhā nakṣatraṃ- vṛścikarāśi- maṅgaḷavāraṃ - ī tīruna niṣādha[da] svaraṃ- jagadhī[tī]śchandassuna- prakāśamavunu.

svasvasthāna viparyāsāt samastavyāptameva ca|
kramāt svarāṇāṃ saptānāṃ prastāro'yamitīritaḥ || 39||

ṭīkā:- svarālaku yokka tama tama sthānaṃ viparyāsaṃvalla vyasta-samastāluga sapta svarālaku prastāraṃ puṭṭunu. svarālaku lakṣyaṃ ceppunu.

atha ṣaḍjaṃ

sa sa sa sa sa sa sa sa sa sa

ri ri ri ri ri ri ri ri ri ri

ga ga ga ga ga ga ga ga ga ga
ma ma ma ma ma ma ma ma ma ma
pa pa pa pa pa pa pa pa pa pa
dha dha dha dha dha dha dha dha dha dha
ni ni ni ni ni ni ni ni ni ni
sa sa sa sa sa sa sa sa sa sa
ṣaḍja prasthā[tā]ram.

ri ri ri ri ri ri ri ri ri ri
ga ga ga ga ga ga ga ga ga ga
ma ma ma ma ma ma ma ma ma ma
pa pa pa pa pa pa pa pa pa pa
dha dha dha dha dha dha dha dha dha dha
ni ni ni ni ni ni ni ni ni ni
sa sa sa sa sa sa sa sa sa sa
[ṛṣabha prastāram]

ga ga ga ga ga ga ga ga ga ga
ma ma ma ma ma ma ma ma ma ma
pa pa pa pa pa pa pa pa pa pa
dha dha dha dha dha dha dha dha dha dha
ni ni ni ni ni ni ni ni ni ni
sa sa sa sa sa sa sa sa sa sa
gāndhāra prasdhā[tā]raṃ

ma ma ma ma ma ma ma ma ma ma
pa pa pa pa pa pa pa pa pa pa
dha dha dha dha dha dha dha dha dha dha
ni ni ni ni ni ni ni ni ni ni
sa sa sa sa sa sa sa sa sa sa
ri ri ri ri ri ri ri ri ri ri

ga ga ga ga ga ga ga ga ga ga
madhyama prastāraḥ

pa pa pa pa pa pa pa pa pa pa
dha dha dha dha dha dha dha dha dha dha
ni ni ni ni ni ni ni ni ni ni
sa sa sa sa sa sa sa sa sa sa
ri ri ri ri ri ri ri ri ri ri
ga ga ga ga ga ga ga ga ga ga
ma ma ma ma ma ma ma ma ma ma
[pañcama prastāram]

dha dha dha dha dha dha dha dha dha dha
ni ni ni ni ni ni ni ni ni ni
sa sa sa sa sa sa sa sa sa sa
ri ri ri ri ri ri ri ri ri ri
ga ga ga ga ga ga ga ga ga ga
ma ma ma ma ma ma ma ma ma ma
pa pa pa pa pa pa pa pa pa pa
dhaita[va]ta prastāraṃ

ni ni ni ni ni ni ni ni ni ni
sa sa sa sa sa sa sa sa sa sa
ri ri ri ri ri ri ri ri ri ri
ga ga ga ga ga ga ga ga ga ga
ma ma ma ma ma ma ma ma ma ma
pa pa pa pa pa pa pa pa pa pa
dha dha dha dha dha dha dha dha dha dha
[niṣāda prastāraṃ]

atha svara prastāram
sa ri ga| ri ga ma| ga ma pa|
sa ri ga ma| ri ga ma pa|

sa ri ga ma| pa mā ri ga mā
dha dha ni| ma pa dha| pa dha ni dha|
ni sa| ga ma pa dha ma pa dha ni |
pa dha ni sa| pa dha| ga ma pa dha ni|
ma pa dha ni sa|

sa| ri| ga| ma| pa| dha| ni| sa|
sa| ri| sa| ri| ga| ma| ri| ri|
da sa ga sa ri * * * * * *
sa ri sa ma ma ri ga ma
ma ga ri pa pa sa ri pa
ga ma dha sa ri dha sa dha
sa ri ga ma pa dha ni sa
dha sa ga sa ri ma ma ga

sa ri ga ma pa dha ni| sa
ni| ri| sa| ri| ga| ma| ri| ri|
dha sa ga sa ri ga ma ga
pa ri sa ma ma ri ga ma
ma ga ri pa pa pa ri pa
ga| ma| dha| sa| ri| dha| sa| dha|
ni| ni| ni| ri| ga| ma| ni|
sa| ni| dha| pa| ma| ga| ri| sa|

sa ri ga ma pa dha ni sa
ri ga ma pa dha ni sa
ga ma pa dha ni sa
ma pa dha ni sa
pa dha ni sa
dha ni sa
ni sa
sa

sa ni dha pa ma ga ri sa
ni dha pa ma ga ri sa
dha pa ma ga ri sa
pa ma ga ri sa
ma ga ri sa
ga ri sa
ri sa
sa

sa ri ga ma pa dha ni sa
sa sa ga ma pa dha ni sa
sa sa ma pa dha ni
sa sa sa pa dha ni
sa sa sa dha ni sa
sa sa ni sa
sa sa sa sa
ma ni dha pa
ma pa dha sa
ga ri ri sa
ma ni dha pa dha ni sa
sa ri ga
sa ma ni
sa ri ri
sa ma ma ma
pa dha ni sa

ri ri ga ga
ni ga
ni pa sa ri
ga ma ma ma ni dha ni
ni pa ri dha pa dha
ga ri dha dha pa ni
sa ga ri ma ni
ri ga sa ma pa ni
ni sa sa ma ma dha ni
sa ma ni dha pa
sa sa sa ri ga ga
ni dha ni sa sa
ga ri ri sa ni
dha ni ga pa ni sa

pa ma ga ri sa

sa ri ga ma sa ma pa dha
ri dha ma pa ma ga ri sa

sa ri ga ma sa ma pa dha
ri dha ma pa ma ga ri sa

pa ma ga ri sa ni
dha pa ma ga ri sa
ma sa dha ni sa ni
ga ma pa dha ni sa
ni dha pa ma ma ga ri
sa ri ga ma pa dha

sa ri ga ma pa dha ni sa	sa
ri ga ma pa dha sa sa ni	ri ri
ga ma pa dha ni sa pa dha	ga ga sa
ma pa dha ni sa ga ma pa	ma ma ma ma
pa dha ni sa sa ri ga ma	pa ma ga pa pa
dha ni sa sa ri sa ri ga	pa dha ri dha ma pa
ni sa ma pa ma ga ri sa	ri ni sa sa sa

ṭīkā:- mandra madhyama tārakālu bhūlokamandu svaraṃ vyāpakaṃ.

ṣaḍjasvarādi bhūloke prakāśārthaṃ nṛṇāmatha |
nābhihtkaṇṭhamūrdhāsyeṣvāvirbhāvayati dhvanim || 40||
atisūkṣmaśca sūkṣmaśca puṣṭaścaivātipuṣṭakaḥ |
tāraśceti tathā jñeyaḥ pañcadhā dehajaḥ svaraḥ || 41||

ṭīkā:- ṣaḍjādi svarālu bhūlōkamandu prakāśārthaṃ koraku

manuṣyula yokka nābhi hṛdaya kamppaṃ [kaṇṭhaṃ] aśya[āsya] śirasulayandu atisūkṣmamugānu [sūkṣmamugānu puṣṭamugānu] atipuṣṭi[ṣṭamugānu] tārakaṅgānu aidu prakārāluga manuṣyula dēhamandu svarālu puṭṭunu.

nābhyāṃ hṛdi ca kaṇṭhe ca jihvāmūle ca nāsayoḥ |
kapāle mūrdhnideśe ca kramāt ṣaḍjādayo bhavet|| 42 ||

ṭīkā:- nābhi hṛdayaṃ nada [kaṇṭha] jihvāmūla nāsikā kapōla mūrdhniyandu ṣaḍjādi svarālu vuṇḍunu.\

vyavahāre tvasau tredhā hṛdi mandro'bhidhīyate|
kaṇṭhe madhyo mūrdhni tāraḥ tridhā tu parikīrtitaḥ || 43||

ṭīkā:- ṣaḍjādi svarālu vyavahāramandu hṛdaya mandara[ndra]maninni kaṇṭha madhyamaninni śirassu tārakamaninni, hṛdayaṃ kaṇṭhaṃ mūrdhvi-yīmūṭiyandu[mūḍiṇṭiyandu], mandara[ndra]madhya-matārakālani mūḍu prakārālāyanu.

sari[rī]mandrau gamau madhye [yau]
padhanī tārakāḥ smṛtāḥ|| 44 ||

*ṭīkā:-*ṣaḍjari[ṛ]ṣabhālu mandara [ndra]mandunnu, gāndhār madhyamālu, madhyamamandunnu pañcamadai [dhai]vata niṣādālu tārakamandunnu āśrayiñci yuṇḍunu.

nṛṇāmurasimandrastu dvāviṃśatigatodhvaniḥ |
sa eva kaṇṭhe madhyasyāt tāraḥ śirasi gīyate || 45 ||

*ṭīkā:-*manuṣyula hṛdayamanē mandramandu ṣaḍjādi svarālu dhvanibhēdāluga iru[ra]vaireṇḍu prakārālāyanu. ā tīrunanē kaṇṭha madhyamamandu iru[ra]vaireṇḍu prakārālu. śiraspā[stā]rakamandu 22 prakārālāyanu.

[mandrādiṣūktāśśrutayaśśuddhatantryo nava smṛtāḥ] ||47||

ṭīkā:- mandā[drā]diṣu śrutayaḥ mandā[ndrā]di śrutulu - mandramu[ma]ndraṃ mandra-madhyamaṃ mandra-tārakaṃ; madhya-mandraṃ madhyama-madhyamaṃ madhyama-tārakaṃ; tāraka-mandraṃ tāraka-madhyamaṃ tāraka-tārakaṃ. yī prakārāna śruti bhēdālu 66 ani telusuṭa.

hṛdyūrdhvā[rdhva] nāḍīsaṃlagnā nāḍyo dvāviṃśati kramāt |
[tiraścyastāsu tāvatyaḥ śrutayo mārutāhateḥ] || 48||
uccoccataratāyuktāḥ prabhavantyuttarottaram |
evaṃ kaṇṭhe tathā śīrṣe śrutirdvāviṃśatiḥ kramāt || 49||

ṭīkā:- hṛdaya mandramādigā kaṇṭha madhya paryantaṃ 22 nāḍi bhēdālu galavu. ā nāḍulayandu tagili [tagina] vāyuvu cēta kōṭṭu[ṭa]baḍi uttarōttaraṅga svarālu iru[ra]vaireṇḍu bhēdālāyanu. yī prakārānanē kaṇṭha madhyamandu iru[ra]vaireṇḍu prakārālu. śirasthānamandu iru[ra]vaireṇḍu prakārālāyanu. svarālu bhēdālaina kramaṃ

catuścatuścatuścaiva ṣaḍjamadhyamapañcamāḥ|
dvau dvau niṣādagāndhārau tristriḥ ṛṣabhadhaivatau || 50||

ṭīkā:- ṣaḍjamadhyamapañcamālu nālugēśi prakārālunu. ṛṣabha dai[dhai]vatālu mūḍēśi prakārālunu. niṣāda gāndhārālu reṇḍu prakārālāyanu. idi gūḍa 22. [ī] tīrunanē madhyama-tārakālayandu bhēdālāyā[ya]nu. vīṇlaku pēḷḷu [vīṭiki pērlu].

ādyā cottaramandrā syādrajanī cottarāyatā |
caturthī śuddhaṣaḍjā tu pañcamī matsarīkṛtā |

aśvakrāntā tu ṣaṣṭhī syāt saptamī cābhirudgatā ||51||
sauvīrī hariṇāśvā ca syāt kalopanatā tathā|
śuddhamadhyā tathā caiva mārdavī
pāravī [mārgī ca pauravī] tathā|
hṛṣyakā ceti vijñeyā madhyamagrāmamūrcchanāḥ || 52 ||
nandā viśālā sumukhī citrā citravatī sukhā |
ālāpā ceti gāndhāragrāmā[me] syuḥ sapta mūrcchanāḥ ||53 ||

ṭīkā:- manda[uttaramandrā], rajani, uttara[uttarāyatā], śuddhā [śuddhaṣaḍjā], satvarī [matsarīkṛtā], aśvakrāntā, ābhirudgha[ga]tā sāviri [sauvīrī] hariṇi[ṇāśvā], kallōpanā [kalōpanatā], śuddhamadhyā, mārdavi[mārgī], pāraḷi[pauravī], hṛṣyaki[kā], nandā, viśāla[lā], sumukhī, citra[trā], citravati[tī], sukhā, ālāpā - ivi ṣaḍjama[ṣaḍja] madhyama gāndhāra grāmamulu cēta mūḍu [21] pēḷḷu [pērlu]. svarālaku pēḷḷu [pērlu]. idē ārōhiṇi avarōhiṇi a[ā]yitē mūrcchanādula-nabaḍunu.

ādyantau ṣaḍjamāśritya mandramadhyamatārakāḥ |
ārohiṇyavarohiṇyau ṣaḍjādyantau svarān vadet || 54||

ṭīkā:- mandramadhyamatārakālu ādhya[dya]ntālayandu ṣaḍjasvarānni āśrayiñcivuṇḍunu. ārōhiṇiyandu avarōhiṇiyandu ṣaḍjādyantālugā svarālu palukavalenu.

dhvanibhedāḥ kramādevaṃ bhavanti ṣaṣṭiṣaḍuttarā ||55||

ṭīkā:- kāgā ī prakāraṇa[mē] ṣaḍjādi svarālu mandara [mandra] madhyamatārakālayandu dhvanibhēdālu aru[ra]vai āru prakārālu kaliganu.

grāma svarasamūhaḥ syāt svarārohyavarohiṇī |
mūrcchaneti svarā jñeyā tayorbhedaṃ kramādbhavet ||56||

ṭīkā:- svara samūhaṃ grāmamaninni svarārōhini[ṇi avarōhiṇi] mūrcchanā aninni teliyataginadi. vīriki bhēdālu kramaṅgā ceppucunnāḍu.

saptasvarāstrayogrāmāḥ ekaviṃśati mūrcchanāḥ |
tānā ekōna pañcāśadityete svaramaṇḍalam || 57 ||

ṭīkā:- saptasvarālaku grāmālu mūḍu; mūrcchanā iru[ra]vaiyoka; tānānālu [tānālu] naluvaitommidi. iṭlani svaramaṇḍalamandu ceppucunnadi.

ṣaḍjamadhyamagāndhāra grāmāśca parikīrttitāḥ |

ṭīkā:- ṣaḍjagrāmamaninni gāndhāragrāmamaninni madhyamagrāmamaninni 3 prakārālu.

ṣaḍjagrāmāśritāṃ he[hye]te vijñeyassapta mūrcchanā[nāḥ] ||58||

ṭīkā:- sa ni dha pa ma ga ri ani reṇḍu [ēḍu] mūrcchanalu ṣaḍjagrāmamunu āśrayiñci vuṇḍunu. madhyamagrāma mūrcchanā ma ga ni sa ri dha pa ani ēḍu mūrcchanalu madhyamagrāmamunu āśrayiñci vuṇḍunu. gāndhāragrāma mūrcchanā ga dha ri pa sa ma ni ani ēḍu mūrccha[na]lu gāndhāra grāmamunē āśrayiñci vuṇḍunu.

kramāt sarigamādīnāṃ mūrcchanāśca punaḥ punaḥ |
svarālaṅkāra ityevaṃ kathito gānavedibhiḥ ||59 ||

ṭīkā:- kramaṅga ṣaḍjādi svarālu māṭikī māṭikī madhyē madhyē ārōhiṇi avarōhiṇiga palikitēnu. avi svarālaṅkāraṃ; sa ri ga ma ga ri| sa ri ga ri| sa ri ga ma| iṭlā[lu] palikē svaraṃ alaṅkāramani ceppabaḍunu.

pūrvāhṇakāle madhyāhne 'parāhṇe'bhyudayārthibhiḥ |

saptasvarāṇāmārohyavarohiṇi kramādvadet || 60 ||

ṭīkā:- śrēyassukōrēṭivāru prātaḥkālamandu madhyānnaḥ[hnaḥ] kālamandu sāyantrakālamandu saptasvarāla yokka ārōhiṇi avarōhiṇi anavaccunu. itarakālamandu anarādu. dīni pēru saraḷi.

prathamaśravaṇācchabdaḥ śrūyate hrasvamātrakaḥ|
sā śrutistu parijñeyā svarāvayavalakṣaṇam || 61||

ṭīkā:- toluta anumandramuna svaraṃ teliyuṭa tārakamaṇṭi mellanē linnasvaraṃ śruti anabaḍunu.

sūkṣmassvaro hi sūkṣmatvānnatu śravaṇagocaraḥ |
tāraśśruti kaṭhoratvāt tyājya eva na saṃśayaḥ || 62 ||

ṭīkā:- mellane antasvaraṃ vinarañjitamaiyuṇḍata, biggalānna[biggara anna] svaraṃ vinu kaṭhōramaiyuṇḍunu ganaka. kāgā ā reṇḍu kārādu. śruti madhyamaṅgā palukavalenu.

sthāyisvaro'tha sañcārī tathāhatamanāhatau
[tathāyatapratyāyatau]|
kampitaṃ yeḍupu ḍu[ḍā]lu ugra[graṃ] muktā daśāsmṛtāḥ || 63||

ṭīkā:- sthāyi, svaraṃ, sañcāri, āyi[ya]taṃ, pratyāyataṃ, kampitaṃ, yeḍupu, ḍālu, ugraṃ, muktāyi- ī ṣaḍjādi svarālu padi bhēdālugā vuṇḍunu.

ādau manda svarānu[du]ktaṃ sthāyi[yī] ityabhidhīyate |

ṭīkā:- toluta mandramādikā yette svarālu sthāyi anabaḍunu.

tārakādau svarānu[du]ktaṃ svareti parikīrtitaḥ|

ṭīkā:- toluta tārakamādikā yette svarālu sthāyīsvaramanabaḍunu

mandramadhyamatāreṣu sañcārikacara[ścara]svaraḥ ||64||

ṭīkā:- mandramadhyamatārakālayandu svara prakāśaṅgā palikinadi sañcāri anabaḍunu.

svarān [rāḥ] mandrādiṣu sthāne pṛthagvyāptaṃ punaḥ punaḥ|
āhataṃ cāyatañcāpi pratyāyatamanāhatam ||65||

ṭīkā:- svarālu mandara madhyama tārakālayandu pratyēkālugā prakāśimpucunnu[prakāśimcunu]. tiruga tiruga ārōhiṇi svarālu āyitamanabaḍunu. avarōhiṇi pratyāyatamanabaḍunu.

tristhāneṣu svarān vega gamanaṃ kampitaṃ viduḥ |

ṭīkā:- mandra madhyama tārakālayandu svarāla gamakaṃ cēta palikinadi kampitamanabaḍunu.

svaradīrgha[rghaṃ]triyasthāne[tristhāne]
vyāptaṃ yu[ye]ḍupurucyate |

ṭīkā:- svaraṃ nilukaḍuga tristhānālayandu prakāśimpu jēsēdi yeḍupu anabaḍunu.

hrasvadīrgha triṣu vyāptaṃ svarān ḍālu prakīrtitaḥ ||66||

ṭīkā:- vēga nilukaḍalugānu svarālu tristhānālayandu prakāśimpa jēśēdi ḍālu anabaḍunu.

madhyamādau svarānu[du]ktaṃ ugraṃ ca parikīrtitaḥ[tam] |

ṭīkā:- madhyamādi yandu svarametti prakāśimpa jēśēdi ugramanabaḍunu.

svarāṇāṃ mocanaṃ vyāptaṃ muktamityabhidhīyate ||67||

ṭīkā:- svarālu viṭikallā [vīṭikallā] muktāyiga prakāśimpa jēsinadi muktamanabaḍunu.

vyaktaṃ pūrṇa prasannaṃ ca sukumāramalaṅkṛtam |
samaṃ suraktaṃ ślakṣṇañca nikūṣṭaṃ madhuraṃ tathā |
daśaite syurguṇā gītaṃ[te] śārṅgadevenakīrtitāḥ
[tatra vyaktaṃ sphuṭaiḥ svaraiḥ] ||68||

ṭīkā:- vyaktaṃ, pūrṇaṃ, prasannaṃ, sukumāraṃ, alaṅkṛtaṃ, samaṃ, suraktaṃ, ślakṣṇaṃ, nikūṣṭaṃ, madhuraṃ, - ī padinni gīta svara guṇālu.

prakūti pratyayaṃyocyaṃ
[pratyayaiścoktaṃ] chandorāgapadasvaraiḥ|

ṭīkā:- sphuṭa svarāla cēta padamula yokka prakūti pratyayāla cēta annadi vyaktamanabaḍunu.

aṃgesvarān pūrṇagamakaṃ[pūrṇaṃ
pūrṇāṅgagamakaṃ] prasannaṃ prakaṭīkṛtam ||69||

ṭīkā:- gānamandu svarālu pūrṇaṅgā vuṇḍēdi pūrṇaṃ [(2)] svara prakaṭanaṃ prasannnaṃ (3)

samyakśārīrakṛtaṃ[ñca] sukumāraṃ vidurbudhāḥ |

ṭīkā:- lessagā śārīraṃ kaliginadi sukumāraṃ (4)

tristhāneṣu prakāśaṃ ca alaṅkṛtamudāhṛtam ||70||

ṭīkā:- mandra madhyama tārakālayandu vyāpti kaliginadi alaṅkṛtaṃ (5)

samākṣarairlayasthāne vyāptaṃ samamitīritam |

ṭīkā:- samākṣarāla cēta layasthānaṃ kaliginadi samaṃ (6)

suraktaṃ vallakīvaṃśa kaṇṭhadhvanyekatāṃ gatā ||71||

ṭīkā:- vinē[vīṇā] pillāmgōvi[pillaṅgrōvi], nāgasvaraṃ tana gātrāniki śrutipramāṇa[ṇaṃ] ēka svaramaitē suraktaṃ (7).

nīcoccadru[dhru]tamadhyādau ślakṣṇatya[ve] ślakṣṇamucyate |

ṭīkā:- yekkuḍu takkuḍu dhūtamadhya viḷambālayandu nūtanamaiyu vidhaṃ ślakṣṇam.

uccairuccāraṇāduktaṃ nikṛṣṭaṃ bharatādibhiḥ|| 72||

ṭīkā:- śārīraṃ biggina paliginna[na]di niṣkṛṣṭaṃ[nikṛṣṭaṃ] (9).

madhyamaṃ[madhuraṃ] dhuryalāvaṇya
pūrṇaṃ jīva[jana]manoharam|

ṭīkā:- śārīraṃ cakkatanaṃ galigi jīvāḷaṅga pāḍina svarālu madhuraṃ (10).

saṅkṣipya somanāryeṇa svarāṇāṃ guṇamīritam ||73||

ṭīkā:- saṅkṣēpaṅgānu svarāla guṇālu sōmanāryuni cēta ceppabaḍenu.

dṛ[du]ṣṭaṃ lokena śāstrēṇa śrutikālavirodhi ca|
punaruktaṃ gītabāhyaṃ gatakramamapārthakam |
grāmyaṃ sanddhi[di]gdha mityevaṃ daśadhā gītaduṣṭadā[tā] ||74||

ṭīkā:- dṛṣṭaṃ, lōkaṃ , śāstraṃ[lōkaduṣṭaṃ, śāstraduṣṭaṃ], śrutivirōdhaṃ, kālavirōdhaṃ, punaruktaṃ, bāhyaṃ, gatakramaṃ, apārthaṃ, [grāmyaṃ,] sandigdhaṃ ī padinni svara gītālaku dōṣālu.

apasvareṇa dṛṣṭaṃ ca śāstrahīna maśāstrakam|

ṭīkā:- apasvarālannadi dṛ[du]ṣṭaṃ; śāstra vyatiriktaṅga annadi aśāstraṃ.

śrutiśruti[kāla] virodhaṃ ca [ekaikasyā virōdhataḥ] || 75||

ṭīkā:- okkokka śrutiki virōdhaṅga annadi śrutivirōdhaṃ; layavirōdhaṅgā annadi kālavirōdhaṃ.

ārōhiṇyavaroyu[hyu]ktaṃ anyonyaṃ punaruktī [ruktaṃ]ca |

ṭīkā:- ārōhiṇiyandu avarōhiṇi annadi punarukti.

asambanda[dha] svarādbāhyaṃ hīnasvara gatakramāḥ|| 76||

ṭīkā:- iti [asambandhamugā svarālannadi bāhyaṃ] anabaḍunu. svarālu rīḍci [viḍici] anēdi gatakramaṃ.

arthahīnamapārthaṃ ca grāmyaṃ ca kaṭhinasvaraiḥ |

ṭīkā:- iti arthahīnaṅga[gā] palkinadi apārthaṃ; piṅgēlā[?]śruti palikinadi kaṭhina[grāmya]manabaḍunu.

sandigdhaṃ padasandigdhaṃ daśadā[dhā] gītaduṣṭadhā[tā] || 77||

ṭīkā:- svarōkōduku[?] sandigdhaṃ; ī padi[nni] svarālaku dōṣālu.

aṣṭādaśa śrutulaku lakṣaṇam| nābhikātharvaṇi
[ṇī] dhastā ṣaḍjasvarasamāśritāḥ |

ṭīkā:- nābhikā atharvaṇi da[dha]stā ī mūḍunnu ṣaḍjamunu āśrayiñci vuṇḍunu.

dhaivīracetitadhā[aurvī cāticadhā]
caiva ṛṣabha svaramāśritau[te] ||78||

ṭīkā:- aurvī ati[cadhā] ī reṇḍu ṛṣabhasvarānni āśrayiñci vuṇḍunu.

kāmbavi[kambalī] śrivikā saralī[sarlī] nāli[lī] gāndhāramāśritāḥ |

ṭīkā:- kambali śrīvikā saraḷi[lī] nāḷī ī nālugu gāndhāramunnu[munu] āśrayiñci vuṇḍunu.

rasanī rañjanī caivā[va] madhyamasvaramāśritāḥ[te] ||79||

ṭīkā:- rasani rañjani ī 2 madhyama svaramunnu āśrayiñci vuṇḍunu.

ghrāṇinī pavani[nī] mandā pañcamasvaramāśritāḥ |

ṭīkā:- dhrāṇini pavani manda ī mūḍunnu pañcamasvaramunu āśrayiñci vuṇḍunu.

maurddhavā viḍambinaścaiva[viḍambinī caiva]
dhaivatasvara māśritau[te] |

ṭīkā:- mūrdhā[maurddhvā] vika[ḍa]mbi ī reṇḍu dai[dhai]vata svaramunnu āśrayiñci vuṇḍunu (18).

bhīṣaṇī ca sphurantī ca niṣādha[da]svara māśritau[te]||80||

ṭīkā:- bhēṣani[bhīṣaṇī] spharanti[sphurantī] ī reṇḍu niṣādha[da]svarānu[svaramunu] āśrayiñci vuṇḍunu. kūḍā śrutulu (18); ī saptasvarālaku ādhāradēvatalu.

ātmamadhya gataḥ prāṇaḥ prāṇamadhye gato dhvaniḥ|
dhvani madhyagato nādaḥ nādamadhye sadāśivaḥ || 81||

ṭīkā:- ātma madhyamandu prāṇavāyuvu vuṇḍunu; prāṇa madhyamandu svaradhvanuluṇḍunu. ā svaradhvani madhyamamandu nādamuṇḍunu. ā nādamadhyamandu jagatkartayaina īśvaruḍuṇḍunu. kābaṭṭi svaragīta dhvaniluku[dhvanulaku] ādā[dhā]radēvatā je[ja]gadīśvaruṇḍu iṭṭē[ṭlē] ceppabaḍu[de]nu.

śruti annanduku lakṣaṇaṃ. ṣaḍjagrāmaḥ pañcama
[me]śca[sva] caturthaśruti saṃsthite|
svāpānta[svopāntya]kṛ[śru]tisaṃsta[the]'
smin madhyamagrāma iṣyate || 82||
[yadvā dhastriśrutiḥ] ṣaḍja[je] madhyame tu catu[tuḥ]śrutiḥ|
[rimayoḥ śrutimekaikāṃ] gāndhāraścet samāśrutāḥ[śritaḥ] |
[paśrutiṃ dho niṣādastu dhaśrutiṃ saśrutiṃ śritaḥ] | | 83 ||
gāndhāragrāma mācaṣṭa tadā taṃ nāradomuniḥ|
pravartata[te] svargaloke kramete na mahītale || 84 ||
kramāt grāmāḥ trayo [grāmatraye]

devāḥ brahmaviṣṇumaheśvarāḥ|
hemanta grīṣmavarṣāsu gātavyāste yathākramam || 85 ||

ṭīkā:- ī tīruna nāraduṇḍu bhūlōkamandu saṅgīta pravarttitamaiyēdi koraku ṣaḍja gāndhāra madhyama grāmālani jēśē[se]nu. ṣaḍjagrāmāniki brahmā adhidēvatā; bhūlōka dēśaṃ; madhyama-grāmāniki viṣṇu-adhidēvatā; bhuvarlōkadēśaṃ; gāndhāra-grāmāniki īśvaruḍu adhidēvatā; svargi dēśaṃ. hēmanta, grīṣma, varṣā ṛtuyandu ṣaḍjamadhyamagāndhārālu [gāndhāra grāmālu] pāda[ḍa]valenu. ī svara nādaṃ caturdaśabhuvanālu vyāptamaiyuṇḍunu.

[nanu śrutiścaturyādirastvevaṃ] svarakāraṇam|
[tryādināṃ tatra pūrvāsāṃ śrutināṃ hetutā] katham || 86||
brūmasturya[ryā] tūtīyā[?]di śruti[tiḥ] pūrvā[?]bhikāṅkṣayā|
nā[ni]rdhāryate[?]taśśrutayaḥ pūrvā atya[pya]tra hetavaḥ ||87||
dīptā[?]yatā ca karuṇā mṛduma[rma]dhya jātayaḥ |
śruti[tī]nāṃ pañca [tāsāṃ] ca sarve[svare]
ṣvevaṃ vyavasthitam [sthitiḥ] || 88 ||
diptā[?]yatā mṛdṛrmadhya ṣaḍjesve[syāt] ṛṣabhe punaḥ |
saṃsthitā karuṇā madhyā mṛdurgāndhāra te[ke] punaḥ|| 89||
dīptā[?]yate madhyame te mya[mṛ]dumadhye ca saṃsthite |
mṛdurmadhyā [?]yatākhyā ca karuṇā pañcame sthitā ||90||
karuṇā cāyatā madhyā dhaivate saptate[me] punaḥ|
dīptā madhyeti tāsāṃ ca jātināṃ brūmahe'dhunā ||91 ||

ṭīkā:- dīpta [āyatā, mṛdu] madhyā kara[ru]ṇāyanē svarālaku nāmadhēyālu. ṣaḍjāti[di] sapta svarālu okaṭikanna okaṭi mṛduvu ganuka, okaṭikanna okaṭi dīptamū ganaka. okaṭikannā okaṭi madhyamaṃ ganaka. ṣaḍja svaramādigānu ṛṣabha gāndhāra madhyama pañcama daivatā[dhaivata] niṣādamulugā yaku[yekku]ḍu, taku[kku]ḍu śrutulu mandara[dra]madhyama tārakālayandu saptasvarālani piñcukonenu.

śṛtyutpatti[ttiḥ] svarāṇāṃ ca somanāryeṇa kīrtitaḥ || 92 ||

ṭīkā:- sapta svarālaku śrutyutpannālu sōmanārya[ryu]ni cēta ceppapa[ba]ḍucunnadi.

caturvidhaṃ svaraṃ vādi[dī] saṃvādi[dī] ca vivādyapi |
anuvādī ca tat proktā [teṣāṃ lakṣaṇaṃ cocyate] || 93 ||

ṭīkā:- svarālaku nālugu pramāṇālu. adi vādi, saṃvādi, vivādi, anuvādi ani ceppabadenu.

vādi[dī]svaraśca rājāsyāt mantrī saṃvādiriṣyate |
vivādisvara vairi[rī]syāt anuvādī ca bhṛtyavaiḥ[kaḥ] ||94||
proktā[kto] rājasvarārohe[rājāsvarāroho]
varennamtryavarohiṇi [vadenmantryavarohiṇī]|
svarasaṅghaṭa[ṭṭa]naṃ vairi[rī] bhṛtsaḥ[yaḥ]
pārśvasvarādvadet [ro bhavet] || 95 ||

ṭīkā:- vādi svaraṃ rāju, saṃvādi svaraṃ mantri, vivādi svaraṃ vairi, anuvādi svaraṃ bhṛtyuṇḍu. sapta svarālaku ārōhiṇi vādi, rājani ceppabaḍunu. svaramula yoka avarōhiṇi samvādi anabaḍunu. sapta svarālunnu tamalōtāmu vokaṭiki vokaṭi koṭṭubaḍuṭa vivādi vairi anabaḍunu. svaramulu tamalōtamaku pārḷala[pārśva]valla sambandhamu anuvādi bhṛtyunḍanabaḍunu. induku svarālayandu lakṣyaṃ. sa ri ga ma pa dha ni sa| ri ga ma pa dha ni sa| ga ma pa dha ni sa | ma pa dha ni sa| pa dha ni sa | dha ni sa | ni sa| sa| dīni pēru vādi; rāja svaramanabaḍunu. sa ni dha pa ma ga ri sa | ni dha pa ma ga ri sa| dha pa ma ga ri sa| pa ma ga ri sa| ma ga ri sa| ga ri sa| ri sa| sa| dīni pēru samvādi; mantriyanabaḍunu. samma ga ri sa| ri ga ma| rippa ma ga ri ga ma pa| ga dha pa ma ga ma pa dha| manni dha pa ma pa dha ni| passa ni dha pa dha ni sa| ī tīruna alaṅkārādulayandu vaccu svaramulu vivādi vairi anabaḍunu. sa ri ga| ri ga ma| ga ma pa| ma pa dha| pa dha ni| dha ni sa | sa ni dha | ni dha pa| dha pa ma | pa ma ga| ma ga ri| ga ri sa| ī tīruna svarālu pārśvāla anuvādi bhṛtyasvaramanabaḍunu. gīta, prabandhaṃ, alaṅkāra, rāgagānādulayandu ī nālugu prakāraluga sapta svarālu kalasi vaccunu.

dharmārthakāmamokṣāṇāmidamekai[vai]ka sādhanam||96||

ṭīkā:- dharmārthakāmyamōkṣālu ī 4 sādhanamulu pratyēkaṅga **vu ** nula[?] svarūpaṃ jñānula cēta evaru gānaṃ cēstunnārō vārllakunnu. vinnavārlakunnu caturvidhaphala puruṣārthamula[lu] kalugunani. śāstramulu ceppucunnadi ganaka teliśi[si]vinataggadi.

atha rāgaḥ|

ṣaḍjādi svarasammiśraṃ rāgaṃ ca parikīrtitam ||97||

ṭīkā:- ṣaḍjādi svarasammiśraṅga[miśraṃ] rāgamani ceppabaḍunu.

āliptirdvividhā jñeyā svarasaṃyojane tathā|
rāgāla[li]pti rūpa[pā]lipti dvayaṃ ca parikīrtitam || 98 ||

ṭīkā:- svararāga sambandhamuna rāga[gā]lipti rūpa[pā]lipti ani reṇḍu prakārālu.

rāga[gā]lipti tannāmādyaiḥ[tannanādi] rūpako gītamucyate|
svaraiḥ rāgāḥ pragāyante svarasthānaviparyayā || 99 ||

ṭīkā:- tannanādamu rāgamanabaḍunu. ā tannā[tannanā]dālu svarāla cēta prakāśimpa jēsi pāḍinadi gītamanabaḍunu.

apūrṇaścaiva pūrṇaśca kūṭatānāstathaiva ca |

ṭīkā:- ā rāgagānaṃ apūrṇamaninni pūrṇamaninni reṇḍu prakārālu.

kūṭatānasammiśraṃ apūrṇaṃ.

pūrṇaṃ pañcasahasrāni[ṇi] trayastriṃśastu saṅkhyayā ||100||

ṭīkā:- [5033] bhēdālugā jēśinadi pūrṇamanabaḍunu.

śuddhamiśra[tra]śca saṅkīrṇā[rṇāḥ] rāgāstu trividhāḥ smṛtāḥ |
dvātriṃśat śuddhamityāhuḥ mitratyauṣaṣṭhimeva
ca [catuṣṣaṣṭistathā mitram]|
anantānantasaṅkīrṇa[rṇaṃ] śuddhasālagasaṅkarāḥ|| 101 ||

ṭīkā:- rāgālu mūḍu prakārālu. śuddhālani, mitrālani, saṅkīrṇālani ceppapa[ba]ḍunu. śuddharāgālu 32 mitrarāgālu 64 saṅkīrṇaṃ anantaṃ.

adhādyupakramēṇaiva rāgaśuddhamudāhṛtam |
upakramya yadā rāgo melanaṃ samamitrakaiḥ || 102 ||
punastanmārgagamanaṃ nāḷaṅga [sālagaṃ] parikīrtitaḥ[tam]|
saṅkīrṇarāgamitrāṇāṃ gānaṃ saṅkīrṇamucyate || 103 ||

ṭīkā:- iṭlu[eṭlā] rāgamupakramistunnadō ā tīrunanē 32 rāgālu gānaṃ cēsēdi [śuddharāgaṃ]. śuddharāgamupakramiñci, mitrarāgālu cēta gānaṃ cēśi, tiruga[tirigi] śuddhāna tirigēdi sāraḷaga[sālaga] manipiñcukonunu. mitrarāgālu cēta gānaṃ cēśi śuddhāna muktāyi cēsēdi dēśyaku vāḍadaṇḍē[vāṭi daṇḍē] raktigānamanipiñcunu. ī muppaireṇḍu rāgālu ī tīrunanē bhēdālāyanu.

ṣāḍavauḍavasampūrṇa svarai rāgāḥ prakīrtitāḥ |
svasvasthāna viparyāsāt svarāṇāṃ sambhavantyamī||104||

ṭīkā:- svarāla yokka tama tama viparyāsamvalla svarakūṭamigā ṣāḍavauḍavasampūrṇa rāgālu puṭṭēnani ceppabaḍunu.

ēkasvaravihīnaśca ṣāḍavaḥ parikīrtitaḥ|
pañcasvarasamāyuktaḥ auḍavaḥ parikīrtitaḥ |
saptasvara samāyuktaḥ sampūrṇa iti kathyate || 105 ||

ṭīkā:- āru svarāladi ṣāḍavaṃ. aidu svarāladi auḍuvaṃ. ēḍu svarāladi sampūrṇaṃ. ī tīruna ṣāḍavauḍava sampūrṇālani rāgālaku bhēdālu ceppabaḍunu.

kramādevaṃ svarāṇāṃ ca nāmoddeśaṃ kṛtasvarāḥ[?] |

ṭīkā:- kramānanē ṣāḍavauḍavasampūrṇālanē 3 svarālaku dēvatalu 32 rāgālani pērlu peṭṭināru[?].

strīpuṃrāgasamākhyātaḥ dvātriṃśadgītapāragaiḥ ||106||

ṭīkā:- ā 32 rāgālaku gānavēttalaina dēvatalu puruṣarāgālani śrī[strī]rāgālani 2 prakārālu ceppināru. adi ēdaṇṭē pratyēkaṅgā lakṣaṇaṃ ceppedanu.

bhairavai[va]ścāpi bhūpālo śrīrāgo paḍamañjaraḥ |
vasanto mālavaścaiva baṅgāḷo nāṭakastathā |
ete'ṣṭharāgāḥ puṃrāgāḥ anyāsstrīrāgasañjñikāḥ || 107 ||

ṭīkā:- bhairavi, bhūpāḷaṃ, śrīrāgaṃ, paḍamañjari, vasantaṃ, māḷavi, baṅgāḷa, nāṭa - ī enimidinna[nni] puruṣa rāgālaninni, kaḍama 24 śrī[strī]rāgālani ceppināru.

aṣṭā[ṭau]rāga[gā]straya sa[yassa]ṅkhyā
bhāryārūpaṃ kṛtasvaraḥ[?] || 108 ||

ṭīkā:- ī enimidi puruṣarāgālaku mugguru mugguru strīlugā ā 24 strīrāgālunu dēvatalu jēśināru. ā kramaṃ ceppenu. vārlla yokka nāmōdē[ddē]śaṃ ceppenu.

devakriyā megharañjī kurañjī bhairavastriyaḥ |
velāhuri[rī] malaharī ca baulī caiva nṛpastriyaḥ || 109 ||
śrīrāgapatno[tnyo] hinto[do]lī balahaṃsapuri[sāverī] tathā|
deśī ca lalitā toḍī paḍamañjarī[ra] yoṣitā || 110 ||
rāmakriyā varālī ca kauśika madhuyoṣitā |
nārāyaṇī guṇḍakriyā ghūrjarī mālavastriyaḥ || 111 ||
dhanyāśī caiva kāmbodi[dī] baulī[nīlā] baṅgālayoṣitā|
deśākṣarī varālī[āharī] ca sāraṅgā nāṭayoṣitā|
strīpuṃrāgāḥ samākhyātā dvātriṃśadgītapāragaiḥ||112||

ṭīkā:- ī ceppina kramāna ā strīrāgālu 24 nnu 8 puruṣarāgālaku enimidiṇṭiki satulu vīriki nāmadhēyālu vaccina kramaṃ ceppenu.

ṣāḍavauḍavasampūrṇa svarairgāyanti devatāḥ |
svasvanāmnā rāgamiti vadedvātriṃśadbhedataḥ[vadet
rāgaṃ iti dvātriṃśabhedataḥ] ||113 ||

ṭīkā:- ṣāḍavauḍavasampūrṇālanēṭi svarāla cēta dēvatalu gānaṃ cēśi tama tama nāmadhēyāla cēta 32 rāgālaku nāmāṅkitālu jēśināru. ī rāgālaku ṣāḍavauḍavasampūrṇa bhēdhā[dā]lu ceppenu.

ṣāḍavau[vo] devagāndhāri[rī] gādi varjo [varjyo] niṣādakaḥ|
bhairavi pūrṇarāgasyāt pañcamādi prakīrtitaḥ || 114 ||
vau[au]ḍavo ghurjari[rī] prokto gādi varjo [varjyau] rigau tathā|
śrīrāgo[ṣā]ḍavaścaiva dā[dhā]di ri[ṛ]ṣabhavarjakaḥ ||115||
nīlāmbari[rī] ṣāḍavasyātu[ssyāt] mādi varjo [varjyo] ri ca svaraḥ
varālī ṣāḍavo rāgo gādirmadhya[gādi madhyama] varjitaḥ||116||
megharañji[ñjī] madhyamādi dhani[nī]

varjaṃ[varjyau] tadauḍavaḥ/
velāhuri[rī] auḍavaśca gādi varjo [varjyau] sarī svarau//117//
deśikārī ca sampūrṇo madhyamādau prakīrtitaḥ /
malahari[rī] ṣāḍavo rāgaḥ gādi ru[ṛ]ṣabhavarjitaḥ //118//
deśakāri[deśīrāgo] ṣāḍavasyā[ssyāt] dādhi [dhādi]
varjo[varjyo] niṣādakaḥ/
rāmakriyā auḍavasyā[ssyāt] gādi varjyo risau svarau //119//
toḍi sampūrṇarāgasyāt[ssyāt] gāndhārādi prakīrtitaḥ/
devakriyā auḍavasyāt[ssyāt] nā[nyā]di
varjo [varjyau] risau svarau //120//
paḍamañjari[ra] rāgasyāt[ssyāt] ṣāḍavaḥ parikīrtitaḥ/
niṣādādistathā varjaṃ ri[ṛ]ṣabhasvarameva ca // 121 //
auḍavasyā[ssyāt] ghūrjjarāgā[kurañjikā]
mādirnnisa [mādi ni sā']pi varjitaḥ/
guṇḍakriyā mahārāgaḥ ṣāḍavaḥ parikīrtitaḥ// 122 //
gāndhārādistathā varjo [varjyo] madhyama svarameva ca/
sāraṅgarāgaḥ sampūrṇaḥ pañcamādistathaiva ca // 123 //
vasantaḥ ṣāḍavo rāgaḥ nyādi varjaśca pañcamaḥ/
dhanyāśi[śī] ṣāḍavo rāgaḥ gādi varjo[varjyo] niṣādakaḥ //124//
lalitā ṣāḍavo rāgaḥ nā[nyā]di varjo [varjyo] ga sa[ca] svaraḥ /
nāṭarāgaśca sampūrṇaḥ sa ṣaḍjādirudāhṛtam // 125 //
āhari[rī] pūrṇarāgasyāt[ssyāt] madhyamādi prakīrtitaḥ /
kāmbodi[dī] pūrṇarāgaśca svaraiḥ
sarve[rvaiḥ] samarpitaiḥ //126 //
vauḍavo[baṅgālo] ṣāḍavau[vo] rāga[go]
nyādi varjo [varjyo]ma sa[ca] svaraḥ/
gau[bau]lī ṣāḍavarāgaśca nyādi varjo
[varjyau] vasasvarāḥ [gamau svarau] // 127 //
bhūpāla[laḥ] ṣāḍvo rāgo gādi ṣaḍjādivarjitaḥ [ṣaḍjavivarjitaḥ] /
balahaṃse śra sampūrṇa[balahamsā ca
sampūrṇā] gāndhārādi prakīrtitāḥ[tā] //128//

nārāyaṇī niṣādādi auḍavaḥ parikīrtitaḥ|
dhaivato pañcamaścaiva svarau varjau [varjyau]
yathā kramam ||129||
śaṅkarābharaṇo rāgaḥ sampūrṇo gādirucyate|
hindolaḥ ṣāḍavaścaiva ri varjo [varjyo] madhyamādikaḥ ||130||
evaṃ pradhānarāgāsyuḥ[ssyuḥ] lakṣaṇoktaṃ yathā kramam|
anantāsyuti[santi] sandarbha[rbhāḥ]
rāgāsaṅkīrṇa rūpiṇaḥ ||131||

ṭīkā:- ī tīruna dēvatalu tama nāmadhēyāla cēta 32 rāgālani ceppi vīriki mitrā[tru]lu 64 ani ceppi ī rāgabhēdālu cēta ananta rāgālani ceppināru. adi ē tīrunaṇṭṭe[tē]nu.

kāmbodi[dī] pañcadhā proktā nāṭaḥ pañcavidha smṛtaḥ|
varāli[lī] saptadhā caiva aṣṭau gaulamiti smṛtaḥ |
dhanyāśī dvividhā caiva rāgabhedāḥ prakīrtitāḥ || 132 ||

ṭīkā:- kāmbōdi 5, nāṭa 5, varāḷi 7, gauḷa 8, dhanyāśi 2, iṭlu rāgālu prakāśārthaṃ koraku bhēdālāyanu ganaka, su[śu]ddha mitra saṅkīrṇāla cēta anantarāgālani ceppabaḍunu. ī rāgālu svarūpakathanaṃ ceppenu.

*viprā bhairavi[va]bhūpāla**[lau] kṣatriyā[trau]*
śri[śrī]rāga pañcari[ñjarau] |
vaiśyā[yau] vasantamālavyo [yau]
śūdrau baṅgālanāṭakau || 133 ||

ṭīkā:- ivi rāgāluku jātulu.

śvetau bhairavi[va]bhūpālau rakto[ktau] śri[śrī]rāgapañjarau|
pītau vasantamālavyau kṛṣṇau baṅgālanāṭakau || 134 ||

ṭīkā:- ivi rāgālaku varṇamulu.

śambhurviṣṇuśśāradā ca [rviṣṇuśca
śāradā] lakṣmībhāskaranāradāḥ|
gaṇeśastumburūrdēvāḥ rāgāṇāṃ parikīrtitāḥ || 135 ||

ṭīkā:- ivi rāgāluku dēvatalu.

modakaṃ ba[bha]kṣya śuddhānnaṃ
dadhyannaṃ pāyasaṃ phalam|
citrānnaṃ ca payonnaṃ ca rāgānāṃ
[ṇāṃ] bhojanaṃ smṛtam || 136 ||

ṭīkā:- [ivi] rāgālaku bhōjanaṃ.

śvetaścitro raktanīlau haridrāpītavāsanā[kam] |
navavastra[straṃ] paṭṭavastraṃ rāgāṇāṃ vastramīritam ||137||

ṭīkā:- [ivi] rāgālaku vastraṃ.

karpūrarocanaṃ gandhaṃ kastūryagarukuṅkumam|
kadambaṃ ca sugandhaṃ ca rāgāṇāṃ lepanaṃ vadet ||138||

ṭīkā:- ivi rāgālaku gandhaṃ.

vajramuktāphalo nīla māṇikyapuṣya[ṣpa]rāga ca |
gomedhi[da]kaśca vaiḍūryaṃ padmarāgaśca bhūṣaṇam ||139||

ṭīkā:- ivi rāgālaku bhūṣaṇālu.

gadākhaḍgau śārṅa[rṅga]kuntau śaracāpahalāyudham |

paraśurbhiṇḍivālaśca rāgāṇāṃ āyudhaṃ vadet || 140 ||

ṭīkā:- ivi rāgālaku āyudhālu.

mallikā jāji[ti] vakula kundaścampakaketakī |
droṇaśca pārijātaśca rāgāṇāṃ kusumāṃ[maṃ] vadet ||141||

ṭīkā:- ivi rāgālaku puvvulu.

haṃso barhiśārikā ca bhēruṇḍo kokilaśśukaḥ |
cakravāhaścakōraśca rāgāṇāṃ vāhanaṃ vadet || 142 ||

ṭīkā:- ivi rāgālaku vāhanālu.

drākṣakaṇṭaka kharjūra kapitthaścūtadāḍimāḥ |
kadalī nārīkelaśca rāgāṇāṃ phalavṛkṣakāḥ || 143 ||

ṭīkā:- ivi rāgālaku phalavṛkṣālu.

jambūśākakuśā[śa] krauñca puṣkaraśvetaśālmalī |
dvīpāścanavakhaṇḍāśca rāgāṇāṃ deśamīritam || 144 ||

ṭīkā:- ivi rāgālaku dēśālu.

karuṇa vīraśṛṅgāra bība[bha]tsa bhayamadbhutam |
hāsyaśāntarasāścaiva rāgāṇāṃ rasamīritam || 145 ||

ṭīkā:- ivi rāgālaku rasālu.

jalodako[kau]ttarābhādra uttarārohiṇīmakhā[ghā] |
mūlā maitrā janmatārā rāgāṇāṃ ca kramādvadet || 146 ||

ṭīkā:- ivi rāgālaku janmanakṣatrālu.

guruvāraṃ saumyavāraṃ bhṛguvāraṃ ravistathā |
gurubhaumā janmavārā[raṃ] rāgāṇāṃ ca kramādvadet ||147 ||

ṭīkā:- ivi rāgālaku janmavārālu.

dhanuṣīmīna kanyā ca vṛṣabho siṃhma[siṃha]rāśi ca |
cāpavṛci[ści]karāśau ca rāgāṇāṃ lagnamīritam || 148 ||

ṭīkā:- idi[vi] rāgālaku lagnālu.

dvicatuṣpañca saṅkhyā ca rāgāṇāṃ ānanaṃ vadet |
caturaṣṭaudaśā saṅkhyā rāgāṇāṃ bāhurīritaḥ || 149 ||

ṭīkā:-[ivi] rāgālaku bāhuvulu.

caturvasudaśaśrotrā[traṃ] rāgāṇāṃ netramīritam ||150 ||
ru[ṛ]gveda bhairavibhūpa yaju[juḥ] śrīrāgapantikau [pañjarau]|
sāma vaśantu[santa] mālavyau khila baṅgāla nāṭakaḥ[kau] ||151||
kinnaro yakṣakimpuruṣa[purṣa] gandharvassiddha tubu[mbu]rāḥ |
devatānāgavaṃśeṣu rāgasañjātayasmṛ[ssmṛ]tāḥ || 152 ||
viśvāmitravasiṣṭa ca[śca] gautamotribhṛguśśukaḥ |
jamadagni bharadvāja rāgāṇāṃ gotramaunivat [mīritam] ||153||
stū[thū]lau bhairavī[va]bhūpālau samau śrīrāgapañjarau|
kuñjā[kubjau] vasantamālavyau dīrgha
[rghau] baṅgālanāṭakau || 154 ||

ṭīkā:- [ivi] rāgālaku ākāraḥ[rālu].

bhairavi rāgāniki - kinnara vaṃśaṃ - bhrā[brā]hmaṇajāti- tella varṇaṃ- sthūladēhaṃ- 2 mukhālu- 4 hastālu- 4 śrōtrālu- 4 nētrālu- viśvāmitra gōtraṃ- kuśadvīpadēśaṃ - īśvaruḍu dēvata[adhidēvatā] - uḍumulu bhōjanaṃ- tella vastraṃ- karpūragandhaṃ- vajrabhūṣanaṃ[ṇaṃ]- gadhā[dā]yudhaṃ- mallēpūlu - haṃsavāhanaṃ - drākṣāvṛkṣaṃ - karuṇarasaṃ - pūrvāṣāḍā nakṣatraṃ- guruvāraṃ - dhanurlagnaṃ - ṛgvēdachandassu- dēvakriya- mēgharañji kurañji satulu.

dēvakriya- 5 svarālacēta auḍavamanipiñcukonunu. niṣādādi-ri[ṛ]ṣabhaṣaḍjama [ṣaḍja] varjaṃ - ni ni ni- ga ga ga- ma ma ma- dha dha dha- pa pa pa - ni ga ma dha pa.

mēgharañji - 5 svarāla cēta auḍavaṃ - madhyamādi dai[dhai]vataniṣādavarjaṃ- ma ma ma- sa sa sa- ri ri ri- ga ga ga- pa pa pa- ma sa ri ga pa.

kurañji- 5 svarālu cēta auḍavamanipiñcukonunu. madhyamādi-niṣādaṣaḍja varjaṃ- ma ma ma- ri ri ri- ga ga ga- dha dha dha- pa pa pa- ma ri ga dha pa- vīru bhairavi strīlu.

bhairavi sampūrṇarāgaṃ pañcamādi - saptasvarālu- pa pa pa-dha dha dha - ni ni ni- sa sa sa- ri ri ri- ga ga ga- ma ma ma- pa dha ni sa ri ga ma- ī tīruna śaṅkhacakragadā khaḍgadhārayai prakāśimpucunnuḍu[cuṇḍu]nu.

bhūpāḷa rāgāniki - yakṣavaṃśaṃ- brāhmaṇajāti - tellanivarnaṃ[rṇaṃ] - viṣṇu adhidēvatā - tellavastraṃ - apūpabhakṣyaṃ - gōrōcanagandhaṃ - muktā bhūṣaṇaṃ- khaḍgāyudhaṃ- jājipuṣpaṃ - nemalivāhanaṃ- panasavṛkṣaṃ - jambūdvīpadēśaṃ - vīrarasaṃ- pūrvāṣāḍānakṣatraṃ - guruvāraṃ - dhanurlagnaṃ - nālugu mukhālu- enmidi bhujālu- enmidi nētrālu- enmidi śrōtrālu- vaśiṣṭa gōtraṃ- ṛgvēda chandassu - sthūla dēhaṃ- [vēḷāhuri malahari bauḷi vīru satulu].

vēḷāhuri - auḍavaṃ 5 svarālu - gāndhārādi- ṣaḍja ri[ṛ]ṣabhavarjaṃ- ga ga ga- ma ma ma- pa pa pa- dha dha dha- ni ni ni - ga ma pa dha ni - ma pa dha ni- pa dha ni - dha ni- ni dha pa ma ga.

malahari ṣāḍavaṃ- āru svarālu - dai[dhai]vatādi - niṣādavarjaṃ- dha dha dha- sa sa sa- ri ri ri- ga ga ga- ma ma ma- pa pa pa- da sa ri ga ma pa- sa ri ga ma pa- ri ga ma pa- ga ma pa- ma pa- pa- ma ga ri sa dha.

bauḷi auḍavaṃ - aidu svarālu- niṣādādi madhya[ma]gāndhāravarjyaṃ - ni ni ni- sa sa sa- ri ri ri- [pa pa pa- dha dha dha- ni sa ri pa dha-] sa ri pa dha- ri pa dha- pa dha- dha pa ri sa ni - vīru bhūpāḷāniki satulu.

bhūpāḷarāgaṃ ṣāḍavaṃ- 6- svarālu- gāndhārādi-ṣaḍjama[ṣaḍja]varjaṃ- ga ga ga - ri ri ri- ma ma ma- pa pa pa- dha dha dha-ni ni ni - ga ri ma pa dha ni- ri ma pa dha ni- ma pa dha ni- pa dha ni- dha ni-ni dha pa ma ri ga- ī tīruna bhūpāḷa rāgaṃ prakāśiñcunu.

śrīrāgaṃ - kimpuruṣa vaṃśaṃ- kṣatriyajāti - rakta varṇaṃ-samadēhaṃ- śāradā adhidēvatā - ghṛtānna bhōjanaṃ- rakta vastraṃ-śrīgandhaṃ- nīla bhūṣaṇaṃ- śārṅgāyudhaṃ - gōruvaṅka vāhanaṃ-kharjūravṛkṣaṃ - vakuḷa puṣpaṃ - śākadvīpadēśaṃ- śṛṅgārarasaṃ-gautamagōtraṃ- guruvāraṃ - uttarābhādranakṣatraṃ - mīnalagnaṃ - yajarvēda- chandassu- 5 mukhālu- 10 hastālu - padi śrōtrālu- padi nētrālu-hindōḷaṃ, balahaṃsa, sāhuri[sāvēri] strīlu.

hindōḷaṃ - ṣāḍavaṃ- 6 svarālu - madhyamādi- ri[ṛ]ṣabhavarjaṃ- ma ma ma- sa sa sa- ga ga ga- pa pa pa- dha dha dha- ni ni ni- ma sa ga pa dha ni-sa ga pa dha ni-ga pa dha ni- pa dha ni- dha ni- ni dha pa ga sa ma.

balahaṃsa - sampūrṇaṃ- ēḍu svarālu - gāndhārādi- ga ga ga- ni ni ni- sa sa sa- ma ma ma- pa pa pa- dha dha dha - ri ri ri- ga ni sa ma pa dha ri - ni sa ma pa dha ri- sa ma pa dha ri- ma pa dha ri- pa dha ri- dha ri- ri dha pa ma sa ni ga.

sāvēri rāgaṃ- auḍavaṃ- madhyamādi- ri[ṛ]ṣabhaniṣādālu varjaṃ-ma ma ma- pa pa pa- dha dha dha- sa sa sa- ga ga ga - ma pa dha sa ga- pa dha sa ga- dha sa ga- sa ga- ga sa dha pa ma - śrīrāgānaku[niki] vīru satulu.

śrīrāgaṃ ṣāḍavaṃ- 6 svarālu- dai[dhai]vatādi ri[ṛ]ṣabhavarjaṃ- dha dha dha- ni ni ni- sa sa sa- ga ga ga- ma ma ma- pa pa pa- dha ni sa ga ma pa-ni sa ga ma pa- sa ga ma pa - ga ma pa- ma pa.

paḍamañjari rāgāniki - gandharvavaṃśaṃ - kṣatriya jāti - erravarnaṃ[rṇaṃ] - lakṣmi [adhi]dēvatā - dadhyānnaṃ bhōjanaṃ-kastūrigandhaṃ- māṇikya bhūṣaṇaṃ- kuntāyudhaṃ - mollapūlu - gaṇḍabhēruṇḍa vāhanaṃ- velaga vṛkṣaṃ - krauñcadvīpadēśaṃ -

bhī[bī]bhatsarasaṃ- uttarānakṣatraṃ - budhavāraṃ - kanyālagnaṃ - reṇḍu mukhālu - 4 bhujālu- 4 nētrālu- 4 śrōtrālu- atrigōtraṃ - yajurvēda-chandassu - sama dēhaṃ- nallani kōka- tōḍi lalita dēśi vīrula satulu

dēśi ṣāḍavaṃ- 6 svarālu- dai[dhai]vatādi - niṣāda varjaṃ- dha dha dha- sa sa sa- ri ri ri- ga ga ga- ma ma ma- pa pa pa- dha sa ri ga ma pa- sa ri ga ma pa- ri ga ma pa- ga ma pa- ma pa- pa ma ga ri sa dha.

lalita ṣāḍavaṃ - 6 svarālu - niṣādādi- gāndhāravarjaṃ - ni ni ni- sa sa sa- ri ri ri- ma ma ma- pa pa pa- dha dha dha- ni sa ri ma pa dha- sa ri ma pa dha- ri ma pa dha- ma pa dha- pa dha- dha pa ma ri sa ni.

tōḍi sampūrṇaṃ gāndhārādhi[di] - ga ga ga- ri ri ri- sa sa sa- ma ma ma- pa pa pa- dha dha dha- ni ni ni- ga ri sa ma pa dha ni- ri sa ma pa dha ni- sa ma pa dha ni- ma pa dha ni- pa dha ni- dha ni [ni dha pa ma sa ri ga]

paḍamañjari rāgaṃ - ṣāḍavaṃ - 6 svarālu- niṣādādi- ri[ṛ]ṣabhavarjaṃ- ni ni ni- sa sa sa- ga ga ga- ma ma ma- pa pa pa- dha dha dha- ni sa ga ma pa dha - sa ga ma pa dha- ga ma pa dha - ma pa dha- pa dha- dha pa ma ga ri sa ni [dha pa ma ga sa ni]

vasanta rāgāniki siddhavaṃśaṃ - vaiśyajāti- pītavarṇaṃ- bhāskaradēvata [adhidēvatā] - phalabhōjanaṃ- pasuru[pasupu] kōka- agarugandhaṃ- puṣyarāgabhūṣaṇaṃ - dhanurbhā[rbā]ṇāyudhaṃ - sampaṅgipūlu -kōkilavāhanaṃ- māmiḍiphalavṛkṣaṃ - puṣkaradvīpadēśaṃ - bhayarasaṃ - rōhiṇinakṣatraṃ- śukravāraṃ - vṛṣabhalagnaṃ - 4 mukhālu- 8 bhujālu- 8 nētrālu- 8 śrōtrālu- kubjadēhaṃ - bhṛgugōtraṃ - sāmavēdachandassu - rāmakriya, varāḷi, kauśika - mugguru satulu.

rāmakriya- 5 svarāla cēta - auḍavamanipiñcukonunu - gāndhārādi- ri[ṛ]ṣabha varjaṃ- ga ga ga- ma ma ma- pa pa pa- dha dha dha - ni ni ni- ga ma pa dha ni- ma pa dha ni- pa dha ni- dha ni - ni dha pa ma ga.

varāḷi - ṣāḍavaṃ- 6 svarālu- gāndhārādhi[di] madhyama varjaṃ - ga ga ga - sa sa sa- ri ri ri- pa pa pa- dha dha dha- ni ni ni- ga sa ri pa dha ni- sa ri pa dha ni- ri pa dha ni- pa dha ni- dha ni- ni dha pa ri sa ga.

kauśika pūrṇarāgaṃ- 7 svarālu - ga ga ga- sa sa sa- [ri ri ri-] ma ma ma- pa pa pa- dha dha dha- ni ni ni- ga sa ri ga ma pa dha ni [ga sa ri ma pa dha ni] - sa ri ma pa dha ni - ri ma pa dha ni - ma pa dha ni- pa dha ni- dha ni- ni dha pa ma ri sa ga - vīru vasanta rāgāniki satulu.

vasanta rāgāniki 6 svarālu cēta ṣāḍavaṃ- niṣādādi pañcamavarjaṃ - ni ni ni- ri ri ri - ga ga ga- ma ma ma- dha dha dha- sa sa sa- ni ri ga ma dha sa - ri ga ma dha sa - ga ma dha sa- ma dha sa- dha sa- ni dha ma ga ri sa [sa dha ma ga ri ni].

māḷavi rāgāniki - tumburuvaṃśaṃ - vaiśyajāti- pītavarṇaṃ - nāraduṇḍudēvata[adhidēvatā] - pāyasabhōjanaṃ- pasupu kōka-kuṅkumagandhaṃ- gōmēdhi[da]kabhūṣaṇaṃ- halāyudhaṃ - mogalipūlū - jiṅka vāhanaṃ- dāḍimavṛkṣaṃ - śvētadvīpadēśaṃ - adbhutarasaṃ-makhā[ghā]nakṣatraṃ - ādivāraṃ - siṃhmalagnaṃ - aidu mukhālu- padi bhujālu- padi nētrālu- padi śrōtrālu- kubja dēhaṃ - sāmavēdachandassu - śaunaka gōtraṃ- nārāyaṇi, guṇḍakriya, ghurjari - vīru satulu.

nārāyaṇi - auḍavaṃ - 5 svarālu- niṣādādi - dai[dhai]vatapañcamavarjaṃ - ni ni- sa sa - ri ri- ga ga- ma ma- ni sa ri ga ma- sa ri ga ma- ri ga ma- ga ma- ma ga ri sa ni - ga ri sa ni- ri sa ni - sa ni.

guṇḍakriya - 6 svarālu cēta - ṣāḍavaṃ - gāndhārādi madhyamavarjaṃ-ga ga ga- sa sa sa- ri ri ri- pa pa pa- dha dha dha- ni ni ni- ga sa ri pa dha ni - sa ri pa dha ni- ri pa dha ni- pa dha ni- dha ni- ni dha pa ri sa ga - dha pa ri sa ga - pa ri sa ga - ri sa ga- sa ga.

ghurjari - 5 svarālu cēta - auḍavaṃ - gāndhārādi-ri[ṛ]ṣabhadai[dhai]vata varjaṃ- ga ga ga- sa sa sa- ma ma ma- pa pa pa- ni ni ni- ga sa ma pa ni- sa ma pa ni- ma pa ni- pa ni- ni pa ma sa ga- pa ma sa ga- ma sa ga- sa ga ' vīru māḷavi rāgāniki satulu.

māḷavi sampūrṇarāgaṃ - 7 svarālu- gāndhārādi- ga ga ga- sa sa sa- ri ri ri- ma ma ma- [pa pa pa-] dha dha dha- ni ni ni - ga sa ri ma pa dha ni - sa ri ma pa dha ni - ri ma pa dha ni - ma pa dha ni - pa dha ni - dha ni- ni dha pa ma ri sa ga - dha pa ma ri sa ga [pa ma ri sa ga- ma ri sa ga- ri sa ga- sa ga]

baṅgāḷa rāgāniki dēvavaṃśaṃ- śūdrajāti - nīlavarṇaṃ - vināyakuḍudēvatā[adhidēvatā] - kalavaṇṭakabhōjanaṃ- nūtanavastraṃ

- kadambagandhaṃ- vaiḍūryabhūṣaṇaṃ- paraśu āyudhaṃ- drōṇapuṣpaṃ - cakra[vāka]vāhanaṃ - nārikēḷavṛkṣaṃ - puṣkaradvīpadēśaṃ - hāsyarasaṃ- mūlānakṣatraṃ - guruvāraṃ - dhanurlagnaṃ - reṇḍu mukhālu- nālugu bhujālu- nālugu nētrālu- nālugu śrōtrālu - unnatadēhaṃ- jamadagniriṣigōtraṃ[jamadagnigōtraṃ] - ṛgvēdachandassu- dhanyāśi, kāmbōdi,'nīlāmbari- satulu.

dhanyāśi - 6 svarālu cēta - ṣāḍavaṃ- gāndhārādhi[di]- niṣādavarjaṃ- ga ga ga- sa sa sa- ri ri ri- ma ma ma- pa pa pa- dha dha dha- ga sa ri ma pa dha - sa ri ma pa dha- ri ma pa dha- ma pa dha- pa dha- dha pa ma ri sa ga - pa ma ri sa ga- ma ri sa ga- ri sa ga - sa ga.

kāmbōdi - 6 svarāla cēta ṣāḍavaṃ - madhyamādhi[di]- ri[ṛ]ṣabhavarjaṃ- ma ma - sa sa- ga ga- pa pa- dha dha- ni ni- ma sa ga pa dha ni- sa ga pa dha ni- ga pa dha ni- pa dha ni- dha ni- ni dha pa ga sa ma- dha pa ga sa ma- pa ga sa ma- ga sa ma- sa ma.

nīlāmbari- 6 svarāla cēta ṣāḍavaṃ- madhyamādhi[di]- ri[ṛ]ṣabhavarjaṃ- ma ma ma- sa sa sa - ga ga ga- pa pa pa- dha dha dha- ni ni ni- ni dha pa ga sa ma- dha pa ga sa ma- pa ga sa ma- ga sa ma- sa ma- ma sa ga pa dha ni- sa ga pa dha ni- ga pa dha ni- pa dha ni- dha ni- vīru baṅgāḷāniki śrī[strī]lu.

baṅgāḷaṃ 5 svarālu - auḍavaṃ - niṣādādi gāndhāramadhyamavarjaṃ- ni ni ni- sa sa sa- ri ri ri- pa pa pa- dha dha dha- ni sa ri pa dha- sa ri pa dha- ri pa dha- pa dha- dha pa ri sa ni- pa ri sa ni- ri sa ni- sa ni.

nāṭa rāgāniki nāgavaṃśaṃ- śūdrajāti- nīlavarṇaṃ- tumburudēvatā[adhidēvatā]- pāluannabhōjanaṃ- paṭṭukōka-parimaḷagandhaṃ - padmarāgabhūṣaṇaṃ - binḍivālāyudhaṃ - pārijātapuṣpaṃ - cakōravāhanaṃ- kadaḷīphalavṛkṣaṃ - navakhanḍadēśaṃ - śāntarasaṃ- ano[nu]rādhānakṣatraṃ - maṅgaḷavāraṃ - vṛścikalagnaṃ- 4 mukhālu- 8 bhujālu- 8 śrōtrālu- 8 nētrālu - unnatadēhaṃ- bhāradvājagōtraṃ- atharvaṇavēda chandassu - dēvagāndhāri, śaṅkarābharaṇaṃ, āhari strīlu.

dēvagāndhāri 6 svarālu cēta ṣāḍavaṃ- gāndhārādi- niṣādavarjaṃga ga- sa sa- ri ri- ma ma- pa pa- dha dha- ga sa ri ma pa dha- sa ri ma pa dha- ri ma pa dha- ma pa dha- pa dha- dha pa ma ri sa ga - pa ma ri sa ga- ma ri sa ga- ri sa ga- sa ga.

śaṅkarābharaṇāniki 7 svarālu - sampūrṇarāgaṃ dai[dhai]vatādi- dha dha- ni ni- sa sa- ri ri- ga ga- ma ma- pa pa - dha ni sa ri ga ma pa- ni sa ri ga ma pa - sa ri ga ma pa- ri ga ma pa- ga ma pa- ma pa- pa ma ga ri sa ni dha- [ma ga ri sa ni dha-] ga ri sa ni dha- ri sa ni dha- sa ni dha- ni dha.

āhari sampūrṇarāgaṃ- 7 svarālu - madhyamādi - ma ma- ri ri- sa sa- ga ga ga [ga ga]- dha dha dha [dha dha]- pa pa pa [pa pa]- ni ni ni [ni ni]- ma ri sa ga dha pa ni - ri sa ga dha pa ni - sa ga dha pa ni - ga dha pa ni - dha pa ni - pa ni - ni pa dha ga sa ri ma - pa dha ga sa ri ma - dha ga sa ri ma - ga sa ri ma - sa ri ma- ri ma.

nāṭa rāgaṃ - 7 svarālu- sampūrṇaṃ - ṣaḍjādi- sa sa sa- ri ri ri- ga ga ga- ma ma ma- pa pa pa- dha dha dha- ni ni ni- sa ri ga ma pa dha ni- ri ga ma pa dha ni - ga ma pa dha ni - ma pa dha ni- pa dha ni- dha ni- ni dha pa ma ga ri sa- dha pa ma ga ri sa- pa ma ga ri sa- ma ga ri sa- ga ri sa- ri sa.

deśākṣarī ca gāndhāri[rī] sāraṅgākhyā ca bhairavī |
devakriyā raktahaṃsi[sī] mālavī rāgapañjaraḥ || 155 ||
bhūpālaśca mukhārī ca hindolī ghūrjarī tathā |
ete sūryāṃśajā[jāḥ] proktāḥ sāyaṅkāleṣu ninditāḥ |
prabhāte gīyate yena sa narassukhamedhate || 156 ||

ṭīkā:- dēśākṣari, dēvagāndhāri, sāraṅga, bhairavi, dēvakriya, raktahaṃsi, māḷavi, paḍamañjari, bhūpāḷaṃ, mukhāri, hindōḷaṃ, ghurjari - ī rāgālu sūryāmsa[mśa]yandu puṭṭinavi. ivi prātaḥkālamandu pāḍavalenu.

āharī śaṅkarābhūṣā sāyaṅkāle pragīyate || 157 ||

ṭīkā:- āhari, śaṅkarābharaṇaṃ, sāyaṅkālamandu gānaṃ cēyavalenu.

sarve rāgāḥ pragāyante sāyaṅkāle praśasyate |
pūrvāparānnamadhyānne[hne] rāgān gāyaṃ
[rāgagānaṃ] praśasyate || 158 ||

ṭīkā:- pūrvānna, madhyāhna, āparāhnamandu kaḍama rāgālu gānaṃ cēyavalenu. idi rāga kālaṃ.

mukhārikā rēvagupti ghaṇṭāraṃ mādhavāditaḥ[?] |
deśi sambhava mitrāśca rāgāṇāṃ parikīrtitāḥ || 159 ||

ṭīkā:- mukhāri, rēgupti, kāpi, ghaṇṭārāgēṇa[ghaṇṭāravaṃ] mādhavi, ivi modalainavi 64 mitrarāgālu dēśīya sambhavālani ceppabaḍunu.

kramāt saptasvarāṇāṃ ca svasvasthānaviparyayā |
ṣāḍavauḍavasampūrṇā[rṇāḥ] rāgā[gāḥ]
prastāra sambhavāḥ || 160 ||

ṭīkā:- sapta svarāla yokka tamatama viparyāsamvalla, 5 svarāla, 6 svarāla, 7 svarālu 32 rāgālu, 64 mitrālu, prastāra sambhavālugā bhēdālai caturaṅgaprastāra rāsulayyē.

bhai	**dē**	**mē**	**ku**
pa	ni	ma	ma
dha	ga	sa	ri
ni	ma	ri	ga
sa	dha	ga	dha
ri	pa	pa	pa
ga			
ma			

bhū	**vē**	**ma**	**bau**
ga	ga	dha	ni

ri	ma	sa	sa
ma	pa	ri	ri
pa	dha	ga	pa
dha	ni	ma	dha
ni		pa	

śrī	**hin**	**ba**	**sā**
dha	ma	ga	ma
ni	sa	ri	pa
sa	ga	s a	dha
ga	pa	ma	sa
ma	dha	pa	ga
pa	ni	dha	
		ni	

pa	**dē**	**la**	**tō**
ni	dha	ni	ga
sa	sa	sa	ri
ga	ri	ri	sa
ma	ga	ma	ma
pa	ma	pa	pa
dha	pa	dha	dha
			ni

va	**rā**	**va**	**kau**
ni	ga	ga	ga
ri	ma	sa	sa
ga	pa	ri	ri
ma	dha	pa	ma
dha	ni	dha	pa
sa		ni	dha
			ni

mā	***nā***	***gu***	***ghu***
ga	sa	ga	ga
sa	ni	sa	sa
ri	ri	ri	ma
ma	ga	pa	pa
pa	ma	dha	ni
dha	ni	ni	

baṅ	**dha**	**kā**	**nī**
ni	ga	ma	ma
sa	sa	sa	sa
ri	ri	ga	ga
pa	ma	pa	pa
dha	pa	dha	dha
dha	ni	ni	

nā	***dē***	***śaṅ***	***ā***
sa	ga	dha	ma
ri	sa	ni	ri
ga	ri	sa	sa
ma	ma	ri	ga
pa	pa	ga	dha
dha	dha	ma	pa
ni	pa	ni	

caturaṅgaprastāram

ga	ri	ri	pa	dha	ni	sa	dha
ma	ri	sa	ma	ri	ma	ri	pa
pa	dha	ri	ga	dha	pa	ga	ma
ma	ga	ri	sa	ni	ma	sa	ri
sa	ri	ga	pa	ga	sa	dha	ga

ni	ma	pa	dha	ma	dha	ga	ma
ga	sa	ga	ni	ri	ga	ga	pa
ni	dha	pa	sa	sa	ma	sa	ni

bhairavi 4 paṭṭi 1 illu svaramādi. māḷavi, varāḷi, kauśika, guṇḍakriya, yi nālugiṇṭki [1] paṭṭi 1 illu. mēgharañjiki 1 paṭṭi 4 illu. nārāyaṇi 1 paṭṭi 6 illu. balahamsa 1 paṭṭi 7 illu rāmakriya 2 paṭṭi 4 illu. kuru[ra]ñji kāmbōdi 2 paṭṭi 6 illu. bhūpāḷaṃ tōḍiki 3 paṭṭilu 5 illu. vēḷāhuri 4 paṭṭi 3 illu. nāṭaku 4 paṭṭi 4 illu. vasanta rāgāniki 4 paṭṭi 7 illu. śaṅkarābharaṇāniki 5 paṭṭi 10[1] illu. śrīrāgāniki 5 paṭṭi 3 illu. dēvakriya paḍamañjari 5 paṭṭi 4 illu. bauḷi lalita baṅgāḷāniki 6 paṭṭi 1 illu. sāvēri nīlāmbariki 6 paṭṭi 4 illu. hindōḷaku 6 paṭṭi 8 illu. dhanyāśi dēvagāndhārikı 8 paṭṭi 3 illu. ghurjariki 7 paṭṭi 7 illu. malahariki 8 paṭṭi 1 illu. āhariki 8 paṭṭi 3 illu. dēśiki 8 paṭṭi 1 illu.

māḷavi, kauśika ēka mēḷaṃ. dhanyāśi, dēvagāndhāri ēka mēḷaṃ. guṇḍakriya, varāḷi ēka mēḷaṃ. rāmakriya, vēḷāhuri ēka mēḷaṃ. tōḍi, balahamsa ēka mēḷaṃ. bauḷi, baṅgāḷaṃ ēka mēḷaṃ. hindōḷaṃ kāmbōdi ēka mēḷaṃ. āhari, nīlāmbari ēka mēḷaṃ. malahari, dēśi, śaṅkarābharaṇa, śrīrāga svara sambandhaṃ mitramulu. ī caturaṅgaprastāraṃ 64 iṇḍlalōni svarālu 64 mitra rāgālaku sambandhaṃ.

bhūpāḷaṃ, māḷavi, kauśika, guṇḍakriya, dhanyāśi, dēvagāndhāri, varāḷi, tōḍi, rāmakriya, balahaṃsa, vēḷāhuri, ghurjari - ivi sambandha svarāla cēta mitrulu. nīlāmbari, kāmbōdi, hindōḷaṃ, mēgharañji, kurañji, sāvēri, āhari - ivi svarasambandhaṃ mitrā[tru]lu. nārāyaṇi, lalita, paḍamañjari, vasantaṃ, dēvakriya, bauḷi, baṅgāḷa, svarasammanda[dha] mitrulu. bhairavi 32 rāgālaku svara mitrā[tru]lu. nāṭaku ....

vaṃśajātivayovarṇa svarūpotpanna mādi ca|
somanātha mate proktaṃ dvātriṃśadrāgalakṣaṇam ||161||

ṭīkā:- vaṃśaṃ, jāti, varṇaṃ, svarūpōtpannaṃ modalaina lakṣaṇaṃ

32 rāgālaku sōmanāthiyyamane granthamandu ceppabaḍu[de]nu.

evaṃ nirīkṣyātha samastarāgān gāyeta dhīmānadhika prayatnaḥ|
jantreṇa vā kaṇṭha bhavasvareṇa dvayena
vā doṣavivarjitā syuḥ ||162||

ṭīkā:- ī tīruna rāgasvarūpaṃ teliśi[si] jantragātrālaku dōṣālu pariharīñci buddhimantulainavāru 32 rāgālu 64 mitrālu anantālaina saṅkirna[rṇa]rāgālu gānaṃ cēsi jantramandu vāyiñcavalenu.

gāyaka bhēdālu.

ekalo yamalo bṛndo gāyakāstrividhāḥ smṛtāḥ |
eka eva ta[tu] gāyata ekaletyabhidhīyate|
sadvitīyō yamalakaḥ sabṛndō bṛndagāyakaḥ ||163||

ṭīkā:- yekaluṇḍani yamakaluṇḍa[lakuṇḍa]ni būndakuṇḍani gāyakulu 3 bhēdālu. okkaḍē gānaṃ cēsē[cēstē] vāni pēru yekaluṇḍu. iddaru gānaṃ cēsē[cēstē] vāni pēru yemakaḷuṇḍu [lakuṇḍu]. bahumanditō gānaṃ jēsē[cēstē] vāni pēru bṛndakuṇḍu.

gāyaka dōṣālu.

sandaṣṭo dṛpa[dghuṣṭa]śī[sī]tkāro
bhītakampitaśaṅkitāḥ [śaṅkitakampitāḥ]|
karāli[lī] kapilā kāki[kī] vitālakarahī
tathā [vitālakarabhonmadāḥ]||164||
sāmbakastuba[mba]kī vakrī prasārī vinimīlakaḥ |
virasāpasvarāvyakta sthānabhraṣṭaṃ[,]vyavasthitaḥ ||165||
miśrako,navadhānaśca tathānyā sānunāsikā |
pañcaviṃśatiritya[ye]te gāyako nindito mataḥ ||166||

ṭīkā:- sandaṣṭaḥ, udṛ[dghu]ṣṭaḥ, sītkāraḥ, bhītaḥ, kampitaḥ, śaṅkitaḥ [śaṅkita, kampitaḥ], karāḷi, kapila, kāki, vitāḷa, karahi, tathā [karabha, unmada], sāmbakaḥ, baki, vakri, prasāri, vinimīlakaḥ, vī[vi]rasa, apasvarā, avyakta, sthānabhraṣṭaḥ, avyavasti[sthi]taḥ, miśrakaḥ, ēkōnaḥ[anavadhāna], anyaḥ anunāsikaḥ. ī 25 guṇālunnu gāyakuniki ninditālu. vīriki pratyēka lakṣaṇālu.

sandaṣṭadaśanā go[ge]yaḥ sandaṣṭa[ṭaḥ] parikīrtitaḥ|

ṭīkā:- paṇḍlu īlakaracukoni pāḍēdi sandaṣṭamanabaḍunu [(1)].

udṛ[dghu]ṣṭo virasodbṛṣṭaḥ[ghōṣaḥ]
śī[si]tkāri sitku [sītkṛ]tirmuhuḥ ||167||

ṭīkā:- virara[vira]saṅgā adhikaghōṣaṅgā pāḍēdi udghuṣṭamanabaḍunu (2). māṭi māṭiki śī[si]tkāraṃ cēstū[tu] pāḍēdi sītkāramanabaḍunu(3).

bhīto bhayāsvi[nvi]to gātaḥ[gātā] tvarayā kampito [śaṅkito] mataḥ|

ṭīkā:- bhayantō gānaṃ cēśēdi bhītamanabaḍunu (4); ativēgantō pāḍēdi kampita[śaṅkita]manabaḍunu (5).

kampitaḥ kapa[mpa]nājñe[jjñe]yaḥ
svabhāva gātraśabdayoḥ ||168||

ṭīkā:- śarīramanta vaṇakucu pāḍēdi śaṅkhita [kampita] manabaḍunu (6).

karālaṃ kathita[ṃ] sandhi[sadbhiḥ] karālotpāditānanaḥ|
ṭīkā:- śa[śā]rīra ekkuva takkuvakā[gā] pāḍēdi karāḷi anabaḍunu (7).
[kapilaḥ sa tu yo gāyet svarānnyūnādhikaśrutīn] ||169||

ṭīka:- svara cētaku ekkuḍu takkuḍu śruti cēta pāḍēdi kapilamanabaḍunu (8).

kākakrūrarava[vaḥ] kāki[kī] vitālastāla vicyutā[taḥ] |

ṭīkā:- krūraravaṅgā pāḍēdi kāki anabaḍunu (9); tāḷaṃ viḍici pāḍēdi vitāḷamanabaḍunu (10).

vahanaḥ kampitāmūrdhvaṃ karambo
[bho,]bhihitā[to] budhaiḥ||170||

ṭīkā:- vaṇukucu pōḍavugāniki[poḍavugā] pāḍedi karamba [bha] manabaḍunu[(11)].

bhā[chā]gavatvahni[hanī] kurva[rvan] unnadhoya
[nmado'] dhamagāyakaḥ|
śilākarāśca vadanagrīvaṃ gātā tu sāmbakaḥ ||171||

ṭīkā:- mēghadhvanicēta hīnōnnukālugā nōru viggalagā teraci meḍa poḍavugā yetti pāḍinadi sāmbakamanabaḍunu(12).

tumbu[ba]ki tumbukākāro pu[tphu]llagallastu gāyakaḥ|

ṭīkā:- davaḍalugarucukoni bakākāraṅgā pāḍēdi bakī anabaḍunu (13).

vakri[krī]kṛtagalo gāyan dhīrairiti[rvakrī]udīritaḥ ||172||

ṭīkā:- meḍa vōragā jēsukoni pāḍedi vakri anabaḍunu (14).

prasāri[rī] gi[gī]yate tajñaḥ[jjñaiḥ]
gāta[tra]gīta prasāriṇiḥ[raṇāt]|

ṭīkā:- meḍa tippucu pāḍēdi prasāri anabaḍunu (15).

ne[ni]mīlakastato gāyi[yan] nimīlaka iti smṛtaḥ||173||

ṭīkā:- nētranimīlanatvaṃ cēta pāḍēdi nimīlakamanabaḍunu (16).

virasso vi[nī]raso varjya svaragānata[nāda]pasvaraḥ|

ṭīkā:- rasahīnaṅgā pāḍēdi virasamanipiñcukonunu (17); apasvarāla cēta pāḍinadi apasvaramanabaḍunu (18).

gadgadadvāci[dhvani]ravyaktaḥ[ktaṃ] varṇaṃ

avyaktamucyate ||174||

ṭīkā:- gadgada svaraṃ cēta pāḍēdi avyaktamanabaḍunu (19).

sthānabhraṣṭaḥ sa ya[yaḥ] prāptammaśaka
[prāptumaśaktaḥ] sthānakatrayam |

ṭīkā:- mandra madhyamatārakālayandu aśaktuḍai gānaṃ cēśinadi sthānabhraṣṭamanabaḍunu (20).

avyavasthita ityuktaṃ [kta] stā[thā]
nakairvya[ravya] vasthiteḥ[taiḥ] ||175||

ṭīkā:- tṛ[tri]stā[thā]nāla cētanu nēmakaṃ [niyamaṃ] lēka pāḍēdi avyavasti[thi]tamanabaḍunu (21).

śuddhachāyālagau rāgau miśrayaṃ[yan] miśrakasyataḥ [stataḥ]|
itareṣāṃ tu rāgāṇāṃ miśrako bhūtimiśraṇaḥ
[bhūrimiśraṇāt] ||176||

ṭīkā:- ghanamandu kalpitālu cēsi pāḍinadi miśrakamanabaḍunu (22).

sthāyadhiṣya[yādiṣva]vadhānena nirmukto[,] navadhānakaḥ|

ṭīkā:- sthāyī, svaraṃ, yēḍupu, āyata-pratyāyataṃ, ḍālu, kampitaṃ, ugraṃ, muktāyi, erugaga[ka] pāḍēdi anaradhā [anavadhāni]anipiñcukonunu (23).

geyān[yaṃ] nāśi[si]kaya[yā] gāyan gīyate sānunāsikaḥ ||177||

ṭīkā:- mukkuna pāḍēdi anunāsikamanabaḍunu (24). ī tīruna dōṣamuktuṇḍainavāḍu gānānaku ninditudu.

vāṅmādhurya[ryaṃ] virājita sthitamatīḥ bhavyākṛtiryekadhā
tālajño bahupāṭhako vinayavānādigrahajñānavān |
rāgāṇāmakhilārthavit praṇayavān doṣairvihi[hī]naśśuciḥ
cittajñaḥ paranāyakasya sa bhavet bhūmaṇḍale gāyakaḥ||178||
ṣāḍavauḍavasampūrṇa śuddhasālagasaṅkaraḥ[rāḥ] |
rāgairgāyai[yet] rsvarajñānaṃ[svarajñānī] sa
gāyaka itismṛtaḥ ||179||

ṭīkā:- ṣāḍavaṃ, auḍava, sampūrṇaṃ suddhā[śuddha], sāḷaga, saṅkara, graha, mūrcchanā, ārōhiṇi, avarōhiṇī[ṇi], tristhāyī, svara, sañcārī, āyatapratyāyata, yeḍupu, ḍālu, ṭhāyi, ugraṃ, muktāyi, kampitaṃ, stri[strī] puruṣarāga mitra saṅkalita saṅkīrṇa, dvātriṃśadrāgalakṣaṇa, gīta svara nāda, vādi anuvādi samvādi, vivādi svaralakṣaṇaṃ, tāḷakāla rāgakāla rāgavēḷa saptasvaralakṣaṇaṃ, svaraprastāraṃ, rāgaprastāraṃ, svararāgaguṇadōṣaṃ, dhvanibhēda, tānōtpanna, alaṅkāra, gāyaka dōṣa, gāyaka bhēdaṃ, yerigi vākcāturyaṃ kaligi parula cittamerigi, svararāgālu jantra gātrālayandu gānaṃ cēśinavāḍu gāyakuḍu.

sōmanātha mate prōktaṃ svarāṇāṃ rāgalakṣaṇam||180||

ṭīkā:- ī svara rāgāla lakṣaṇaṃ lakṣyam sōmanātha matamanē lōkōpakāra bharatagranthamandu ceppabaḍenu. saṅgītaratnākaramunandu saṅgrahiñci saṅkṣēpamugānu jantragātrāniki sammandaṃ[bandhaṃ]gānu aṣṭāvadhāna sōmappa jēśina saṅgītaratnākaraṃ gītādhyāyaṃ samāptaḥ.

athā[tha] gītāḥ[taṃ]|
aṣṭabhāṣāpadairyuktaṃ śabdajhaṅkāra saṃyutam |
svararāgaiḥ pragāyante gītamityabhidhīyate ||181||

ṭīkā:- aṣṭabhāṣalayokka padālatōgūḍi śabda jhaṅkāra mitramai svararāgāla cēta gānaṃ cēyataginadi gītamani ceppabaḍunu.

athā[tha] prabandhaḥ|
caturbhiḥ pañcabhiḥ ṣaḍbhiścāgairyastā[ṅgairyastu] prayujyate|
tasmāt prabandha[dhaḥ] kathitaiḥ[taḥ]
pratāpaḥ pradhvibhujaḥ [pṛthivībhujā] ||182||
prabandhāni ṣaḍaṅgāni svaraśca birudaṃ padaṃ |
tyenaka[tenakaḥ] pada[pāṭa]vākyaṃ ca
prabandhapuruṣā bhavet [ṣasya te] ||183||
bhavatyaṅga[ntyaṅga]pa[va]dāṅgāni
maṅgalāṃ te[lārtha] prayujyate[prakāśake]|
yatra dennapadau netrā tatveda birudhaṃ karoḥ
[tatra tenapade netre staḥ pāṭabirude karau] ||184||
svaraṃ svaraṃ cirdhdhāntaraṃ[svaraṃ svarāntaraṃ?]
vākyaṃ padaṃ kaṇṭhastadhe[the]ti ca [?]||
svare tu vardhanāde syāt birudaṃ vīravardhanaṃ[?]||185||
pade karuṇa pūrvaṃ syāt gumbha[pha]nādiṣu tanyate [?]|

yatkiñcinnaṭanaṃ dṛṣṭvā sarvapāpaiḥ pramucyate ||186||

ṭīkā:- 4, 5, 6 aṅgāla eppuḍu gūrustunnārō appuḍu prabandhamani bhūbhuṇḍlu ceppenu. ā prabandhamu 6 aṅgālu. adi[vi] ēviyaṇṭē svaraṃ, biruda, padaṃ, tannakāraṃ, pāṭha, vākyaṃ. ī āru kūḍinadi prabandhamani ceppabaḍunu. tannakāraṃ maṅgaḷārthaṃ tra[pra]yōgimpadaginadi. ekkaḍa tēnnapā[pa]dālu unnadō akkaḍa pāṭa birudu ḍālu [?] ceppataginadi. svarāntaraṃ vākyaṃ- padaṅ kaṇṭha va vardhanādaṃ. svaraṃ vīravardanaṃ- birudaṃ [?]. ī prabandha naṭanaṃ cūcinavāriki sakala pāpālu pōvunu. vinnavāriki sakala śrēyassu kaluvu .

dhruvādi saptatālaiśca svara[sarva] bhāṣāpadānya [daira]pi|
svararāgai[gaiḥ] pragāyante sūlādiriti kathyate ||187||

ṭīkā:- dhruvādi sapta tāḷālacētanu, sarva bhāṣa[ṣā]la yokka padālu svararāgāla gānaṃ jēśinadi sūḷādi anabaḍunu.

śrutyukta padaśabdāni geyā[yaṃ] nāmāvalīritam |

ṭīkā:- stōtrayuktamaina padaśabdālu gānaṃ cēśinadi nāmāvaḷi.

gīrvāṇaṃ[ṇa] vākyarūpeṇa gāya[geyā]
cūrnīka[rṇikā] kīrtitaḥ[tā] ||188||

ṭīkā:- saṃskṛtamu vākyarūpaṃ cēta gānaṃ cēśinadi cūrnīka anabaḍunu.

cūrnī[rṇi]kāvākyaślōkaiśca kathāgeyōkta[ktaṃ] nāṭakam ||

ṭīkā:- cūrṇika vākya ślōkālacēta kathāprasaṅgaṅgā gānaṃ cēśinadi nāṭakaṃ.

eteṣām lakṣaṇaṃ samyak vakṣyate sōmasūriṇā ||189||

idi[ti] svararāgasudhārasākhyō gītādhyāya[yaḥ] samāptaḥ|

3. Vādyādhyāyaḥ

nādhaḥ [atha vādyaḥ]||

pañcavida[dha] vādyabhedāstu lakṣaṇaṃ
vadet [vādyabhedasya lakṣaṇamucyate] |
nakhavāyuja carmāni[ja] lopā[ha]śārīrajasva[ta]thā |
nakhābī[vī]ṇādayaḥ proktaṃ[ktā]
vaṃśādyā[dyāḥ] vāyupūra[ri]tāḥ||1||
carmāṇī[jā] ca mṛdaṅgādyāḥ[dyā] loka[ha] stālādayastathā|
vi[de]hanādena te yuktāḥ vādyāḥ pañcavidhā[dhāḥ] smṛtāḥ||2||

ṭīkā:- nādhaṃ[daṃ] vādya bhēdālugā 5 prakārālu. nakhaṃ[khajaṃ], vāyujaṃ, carmajaṃ, lōhaṃ[hajaṃ], śārīraṃ[rajaṃ]. ī 5 anēka bhēdālu āyanu. vīṇe, kinnara[rī], daṇḍē, rajābu, kāmākṣi - ivi modalaina tantrivādyālu nakha[ja]manabaḍunu. muraḷi, nāgasaraṃ, dēvasaraṃ, śaṅkhamu, mukhavīṇe[ṇā], upāṅgaṃ, ivi modalaina upari vādyāla[lu] vāyujaṃ anabaḍunu. mṛdaṅgaṃ, bhēri ḍa[ḍha]kkālu, [ivi modalaina] carmavādyālu carmajaṃ. tāḷaṃ, lōhajaṃ anabaḍunu. gātraṃ śārīramanabaḍunu. ī vādyālanni dēha nādha[da]yuktamaiyuṇḍunu. ī vādyālaku pratyēka lakṣaṇaṃ ceppēmu [ppedanu].

adhā[tha] vīṇaḥ[ṇā]|
kacha[ccha]pi kachatā[kubjikā] citrā mahati[tī] parivādini[nī]|
jāyā hāha[ghoṣā]vatī jyeṣṭā nakulāhya[śce]ti kīrttitāḥ ||3||
maṣa[ha]tī vaiṣṇavī brāhmī raudrī kārmuka[kūrmā ca] rāvaṇī|
sarasvatī kinnarā[rī] ca saurandri poṣi[ghoṣa]kā tathā|
daśavīṇā[ṇāḥ] samākhyātaḥ[tāḥ] tantri
vinyāsa bhāṇḍataḥ[bhedataḥ] ||4||

ṭīkā:- ī padi vīṇelukuṇḍalu meṭlu tantri vīṇayukta(mai) yuṇḍunu.

vīṇāyāṃ ca nṛṇāmiva tristhāneṣu śrutyutpattiḥ|
vīṇāyāṃ ca viśeṣostī ||5||
uttarottaratārāsu[stu] vīṇāyāmadurottaraṃ [madharottaraḥ]|
iti dhvani viśeṣosti[ṣāste] śrutiḥ śravaṇaṃ
rañjitaḥ [śravaṇācchrutisañjñitāḥ]||6||

ṭīkā:- manuṣyulaku uttarōttaraṅgā mandara[ndra] madhyamatārakālu puṭṭunu. mandrādiṣu śrutayaḥ| mandramandraṃ mandramadhyama mandra tārakaṃ. madhyamamandraṃ madhyamamadhyamaṃ madhyamatārakaṃ. tārakamandraṃ tārakamadhyamaṃ tārakatārakaṃ.

evaṃ bhedāni ṣaṭaṇṣa[ṭṣa]ṣṭi saṅkhyā tristhāneṣu jāyate|
tristhāneṣu ca eṣūktraṃ[ktaṃ] dvāviṃśatividho dhvaniḥ |
vyastāvi[ni] tāni ṣataṃṣaṣṭi[ṣaṭṣaṣṭiṃ] vidvānnaṃ
[vidyāt] mandrādisiddhaye ||7||

ṭīkā:- mandra madhyama tārakālayandu 22 dhvanibhēdālu ceppabaḍunu. avi vyastālugā 66 dhvani bhēdālu avunu. ī 66 mandra madhyamatārakālugā dhvanulu palukunu.

vīṇāvādyaṃ śārīramiva racati [?] |
saptatantrimayi[yī] vīṇā saptasvarasamanvitā |
darśaṇā[nā]tpa[spa]rśanāścai[ccai]va
brahmahattyāṃ vyepohatu[ti] ||8||

ṭīkā:- ī vīṇā vādyaṃ viṇṭēnu śrēyassu kalugunu.

atha kinnaraḥ[rī] |

ālanbana pracura komala deśanāṭyaṃ tantrimukhaṃ
nayati tālalayābhirāmā [?]|

rāgān śanairambinavān paripādamirdhya
jñeyastadā vidhikalā khalu kinnarīti[?]||9||

ṭīkā:- gītavādyanṛttālu layā[ya]yuktamai tantrimukhamandu vāyistē adi kinnara anabaḍunu.

adhā daṇḍeḥ [atha daṇḍi]|

daṇḍikā khādire jātā ākṛtirbhānumūṣi[muṣṭi]kā|
pariṇāmāṅgulirdvisyāt dvayaṃ kāsyaṃ ca rūpiṇīm[?] ||10||
kāṃsyarūpiṇī nābhiśca caturaṅgulamiśritā |
tumboragre tu śu[sū]cinā caturaṅgulamiśritaḥ ||11||
paṅkti[tri]kā yā vidhātavyā daṇḍikā lakṣaṇaṃ ca tat|
ālambya paṅkti[tri]kāmedhā[?] nābhi paryantakādayaḥ[?]|
tantri[trī]dvaye vidhātavya[ye] nipu ṇai[ṇaiḥ] kṣāmatantunā ||12||
nābheradhastāt kartavyaṃ tantri tenaivatantunā |
catuścatuḥ prakāreṇa caturbandhanameva ca[?]||13||
dakṣiṇā tantrikā jñeyāḥ[yā] pañcamasvarasaṃyutā |
vāmatantri samākhyātā ṣaḍjasvarasamanvitā||14||
ekāṅgula pramāṇena jīvikau dvayakau bhavet ||15||
pūrvatantripatiḥ śambhuḥ anyatantripriyā śive[vā]|
daṇḍasyā[ya] bhūmi daivatyo[devatā]
*tumburambhojasambha**[vaḥ] ||16||*
sarasvatī nābhidaivaṃ[bherdevī]
kakundho[kubho] garuḍadhvajaḥ|
paṅkti[tri]kā kamala[lā] jñeyā jīvikā ca sudhākaraḥ||17||
sarvadevamayā[ya]bhūtaṃ daṇḍikābhayadāyini |
gāyako daṇḍikāmenāṃ tarjanī[nyā] vādayet paṭu ||18||
ta[da]ttilasya matekhyātu[taṃ] daṇḍikālakṣaṇaṃ purā ||19||

prārthanaṃ[nā]|

vāṇīṃ namāmi varadāṃ vanajāsanasthām
| vīṇādharāṃ vimalalocana tāṇḍaveṣu [?] |

harābhirāmahṛdayāṃ mṛduvākya[khya] somyām |
pārāvatīṃ bhagavatīṃ praṇamāmi devīm ||20||

ṭīkā:- iṭlā lakṣaṇayuktamaina daṇḍiki namaskariñci dhariñci mandra madhyama tāraka svarālu gāyakuḍu tarjani modalaina vēḷḷala[tō] vāyiñcavalenu.

adhā[atha] tumburaḥ|
viśvakarma vinirmāṇāṃ tumburākhyeti vādyataḥ[?] |
pañcatālaśca vistīrṇaṃ kuryāt samyak sudhāraṇā ||21||
dvitālaṃ prathamaṃ kumbhaṃ madhye hasta dvitālakam|
dvārayugyekatālāgre siṃhmānanayutaśśikhā [yutā śikhā] |
dvārasyobhaya pārśve ca kīlā saptā vinikṣipet ||22||
saptatantri[ntrya]śca tadveṣyā[ṣṭyā]
kumbhamūle ca bha[ba]ndhanam|
kumbhamadhye tu sopānaṃ nyasta[sapta]tantri vinikṣipet ||23||

prārthanā |

saptatantri samāyuktaṃ saptasvarasamanvitam|
tumbururdevatā tasya[tasmai] namaḥ saṅgīta vedikāḥ[?] ||24||
gāyako tumbure samyak vādayet tarjanī[nyā] paṭṭu[paṭu] |
somanāthamatekhyātaṃ tamburālakṣaṇaṃ purā ||25||

ṭīkā:- lakṣaṇayuktamaina tamburunu gāyakuṇḍu tarjanādyaṅgulāla cēta vāyiñcavalenu. rajābu, rāvaṇahastaṃ, kāmākṣi tantrivādyamella indulōliyyaṃ.

iti nakha vādyaṃ|
adhā[atha] muraḷi[lī] ||

dvādaśāṅgulamākāraṃ samyagvaṃśena kārayet |

ādau tu randhramekhaṃ[kaṃ] ca kārayed vāyupūritaḥ||26||
ekaikāṅgula tasyādha[dhaḥ] saptarandhrāṇi kārayetu[t] |
sapta[rpa]śīrṣaṃ ca haste ca dhṛtyā[tvā] vādaka[kaḥ] vādayet ||27||
mūlanādhe[de]sthito viṣṇu[ṇuḥ] madhyanādhi[de]sthito vidhiḥ|
agranādhe[de]sthito śambhuḥ murali[lī] devataṃ
[tā] hariḥ||28||

prārthanaṃ[nā]|

saptarandhrasamāyuktaṃ saptasvarasamanvitam |
parabrahma svarūpaṃ ca muralī te namāmyaham ||29||

ṭīkā:- ramyamaina vedurukōni 12 aṅgula pramāṇaṃ jēsi, modaṭa randraṃ[ndhraṃ] jēsi, ā diguva 7 randhrālu cēsi, sarpaśirahastālu[la] cēta muraḷi vāyiñcavalenu.

somanāthamate proktaṃ murali[lī]lakṣaṇaṃ purā ||30||

atha mukhavīṇe[ṇā] ||

ucyate mukhavīṇāyāṃ[yāḥ] lakṣaṇaṃ yājñavalkinā[lkyena] |
khādire[ro] sā ca daṇḍasya[syā]drakta candana rūpakaiḥ||31||
dvādaśāṅgulamasyaivaṃ ākārosya vidhi[dhī]yyate |
saptasvarāṇāṃ saṅkhyānāṃ randrāṇāṃ
[randhrāṇi] va samāharet||32||
randrādha[randhrādhaḥ] ca niṣādasyāt
svarāścaivaṃ vadanti ca |
ṛgvedaprathamo[mā] mūṣā dvatiye[tīyā] ca
yeja[yaju]r bhavet ||33||
atharvaṇastriti[tī]yā syāt sāmavedasvarāsthitāḥ[?]|
ekāṅgulaṃ ca jīvālaṃ maṇḍalaṃ danta rūpakam||34||
mukhavīṇā pareprājñā[?] danta rūpeṇa maṇḍalam [?]|
taddāruka mayaṃ cihnaṃ vyājena kriyate tathā [?]||35||

dā[dhā]raṇa ślokaṃ||

bhānunnamāmi bhagavantamanantabhāvaṃ
vīṇādhiśu[diṣu] girisutaṃ tapamaṇḍaleṣu [?]|
mandāru lokavaradaṃ vanajāsanasthaṃ
vandeha śāsitamahaṃ vijayā vande [?]||36||

ṭīkā:- pūrvamandu mukhavīṇa sūryuḍu vāyiñcināḍu. iṭlā[ṭlu] lakṣaṇayuktamaina mukhaviṇa dhariñci vāyiñcavalenu.

[mukhavīṇāyāḥ lakṣaṇaṃ] somanāryeṇa
kīrttitaḥ[tam]||37||

pāmū[mu]lanāgasaraṃ |

śivasya pañcavaktrebhaṃ[bhyaḥ] pañcasvara sabhutbhavāḥ|
tabhṛ[cchṛ]tvā kuṇḍali[lī] gāyan phaṇināgasvarocyate|
tadvātya[dya]lakṣaṇaṃ vakṣa[kṣye] pūrvokta
vidhinā mātā[tathā] ||38||

ṭīkā:- pūrvamandu paramēśvaruḍu 5 mukhālavallanuṇṭi 5 svarālu puṭṭenu. ā 5 svarālu śēṣuḍu vini tānu gānaṃ jēsi, ā vādyaṃ pēru pāmulanāgasvaramani palikenu. pūrvōktamaina ā vādyāla lakṣaṇaṃ ceppunu.

alābu koṭaraṃ kṛtvā ṣoḍaśāṅgula mānataḥ |
madhuvi[pi]ṣṭamadho tasya stāvya[sthāpyo]
jīvāḷa nāḷadau[do] ||39||
caturaṅgula[laṃ] kṛtvātha veṇunālau dvayorathā[dhaḥ] |
pramāṇaṃ ṣoḍaśāṅgulyāḥ[gulāḥ]
sarvare[me]kaṃ ca kārayet ||40||
ante ca kāsya[kāṃsya]valayā[yaṃ]
sthāpya veṇvāgratoradhā[dhaḥ] |

randhramekaṃ ca kurvīta saptaradhrāṇ[ndhrāṇi] tatopari||41||
kuryan[ryān] madhumayassarve randhrāṇāṃ sthāpya kiñcit |
pañcapañca svaropetaṃ ālābu brahmadevatā||42||
jīvāḷa viṣṇuvaṃśeśaḥ randhrāṇāmaṣṭamūrtayaḥ |
kāṃsyaṃ ca bhāskaro bhūmi madhupiṣṭyādi devatāḥ ||43||
tadvādyaṃ sarvanāmaiśca[sarpanāmañca]
kathitā[taṃ] bharato[tā]dibhiḥ||44||
nakārā[raṃ]nādamityāhuḥ gakāraṃ gānamucyate|
tābhyāṃ[tayoḥ] sammelanaṃ kṛtvā sarpa nāgasvarocyate || 45||
śivasya pañcavaktraica [ktrebhyaḥ]
jātaḥ[taṃ] pañcasvarairyutam |
tadvādyaṃ kṣo[śro]tumicchāmi[nti] sa naraḥ
sukhamedhat[ti] ||46||
vādoka[dako] dakṣiṇāṅguṣṭhamagrarandhre sthitopari |
mṛgaśīrṣassa[sa]rpaśīrṣa karau gṛhṇāti ca svarān ||47||
vāyupūrita nādena samyagvādyaṃ samācaret|
somanāthamate proktaṃ sarpavādyaśca[sya] lakṣaṇam||48||

ṭīkā:- sorakāyalu[la] burra 12 aṅgula pramāṇaṃ jēśi, aḍugunamainametti, nālgu aṅguḷa pramāṇaṃ jīvāḷaṃ kaḍlu[kaṇḍlu] reṇḍu ēkaṃ jēśi, vedurugō[kō]vulu reṇḍu 16 aṅguḷāla pramāṇāna ēkaṃ jēśi, ā sōrakāya burra jīvāḷakōvulu vēdurukōvulu kūḍā, ēkaṃ jēśi bandhanaṅgā mainammetti, vedurukōvula mōdaṭa yeḍama pārśa[rśva]mandu, aḍuguna oka randhraṃ jēśi, paina 7 randhrālu jēśi, ā randhrālaku sagaṃ pōviḍici, kaḍama anduku mainametti, vedurukōvulu[la] konanu kañcakaṭṭu vēśēdi. sorakāya brahmā, jīvāḷāna viṣṇu, vedurukō[vu] śivuḍu, 8 randhrālaku aṣṭamūrttulu, kañcuku ravi, maināniki bhūmi. vīru adhidēvatalu. śivuni 5 mukhāla puṭṭina svarālu ī vādyamandu palukunu. nakāraṃ nādaṃ gakāraṃ gānaṃ. ī reṇṭiyokka kūṭamicēta svarālu anni palukagā ī vādyaṃ pēru pāmulanāgasaramani bharatādi muni[nī]śvarulu ceppuduru. ī vādyaṃ vāyupūrita nādaṃ cēta vādyakō[daku]ḍu, vedurakōvi diguva randhraṃ, tana bhōṭṭanavela nadimi[bhoṭṭana vēlunadimi] mṛgaśirṣa sarpaśīrṣa hastāla cēta sapta randhrā[laya]ndu saptasvarālu gānaṃ cēyavalenu. ī vādyaṃ vinnavāriki anēka śrēyassu kalugunu. lōkōpakāramaina sōmanāthiyyamanē bharata[grantha]mandu ī pāmulanāgasaralakṣaṇaṃ ceppina[yunna]di. ī tīruna lakṣaṇayuktamaina nāgasaraṃ dhariñci vāyiñcavalenu.

atha dēvasara lakṣaṇaṃ vakṣyate /

*********[**deva] svaramitirvadet//*

ṭīkā:- śrī kṛṣṇuḍu vēdanukō ******* paru dēvasvaramani palikinā ****

*********[caturvi]ṃśatiraṅgulā ku*dhaḥ parikīrtitaḥ//49//*

ṭīkā:- dōṣarahitamaina vēdu[veda]rukōvi 24 aṅgula ***********

*******tyaṅgulyadho[ādautryaṅgulyadho]*
bhāge randhramekaṃ ca kārayet/
*********madhu *********pta pārśva vimocanam//50//*
tasyoparistālā[la]patraṃ veṣṭitaṃ vartulākṛtiḥ/
tasyādhoṣṭāṅgulirmūlaṃ saptarandhrāṇi kārayet//51//
agretyāṅguli[?] sarvāṅge caturviṃśatiraṅgulāḥ/
*mūlāgre hemakau[rau]pyaṃ ca kāṃ*****
[kāṃsye]na valayaṃ kṛtaṃ//52//
dapa[deva]svarādhivo[po] viṣṇu[ṇuḥ] randhrāṇām aṣṭamūrtayaḥ/
devāmadhumayaśveśa[yastveśaḥ] tālapatrasya śāradā/
valayo[yoḥ] bhāskaraḥ[ra]ścandraḥ eteṣāmadhi devatā[tāḥ]//53//

ṭīkā:- ī dēvasaraṃ modaṭa mūḍu aṅgula[laṃ] diguva niḍupōva[niḍupuna] **[1]randhraṃ jēsi, ā randhraṃ naḍuva mainametti pārśvālu viḍici, dāni mīda tāḍa[ḍu]nu kaṭṭi vēsi, ī randhraṃ diguva 8 aṅgulālu pōviḍici, akkaḍa 7 randhrālu cēsi, dāni diguva miśra randhraṃ ***[o]kaṭi cēsi, konanu mūḍu randhrālu pō viḍici, baṅgāru veṇḍi kañcu cēta nai[pai]nā kaṭṭu vēyavalenu. dēvasarāniki viṣṇu dēvatā. 8 randhrālaku aṣṭamūrtulu; maināṇuku īśvara***[ruḍu]; tālēkuku[tāṭiyāku] **[sa]rasvatī; valayālaku sūryacandrāḍu[du]lu. vīru adhidēvatulu.

a[ā]dau bhūmyastito[bhūmisthite] vastre
prakṣipta mūralī[līṃ]stathā[tathā]|
devaṃ ca prārthanaṃ kṛtvā gruhi[gṛhī]tvā
vāda[dya kovidhā[daḥ]||54||
muralīmūla pīḍyante mṛgaśi[śī]rṣakareṇa ca|
sarpaśi[śī]rṣakareṇa[ṇā]gre pīḍyaṃ vādyaṃ samācaret|
*ubhayoḥ karapīḍyante viṣṇustā **** [ṇḍavamācaret] ||55||*

[prārthanā]

adho[sapta]randhrasamāyuktaṃ saptasvarasamanvitam|
****************** tā tubhyaṃ namāmyaham||56||*

ṭīkā:- toluta bhūmiyandu vastramparaci ī dēvasvaraṃ, andumīdavuñci namaskariñci, dakṣiṇahastaṃ mṛgaśīrṣahastamunnu vāmahastaṃ sarpaśirahastamunnu, vādakuḍu ī tīruna dhariñci, vāyupūrita nādaṃ cēta reṇḍu ca[cē]tulā vāyiñcavalenu. ā nādānikē viṣṇuvu tāṇḍavamāḍunu.

somanāthamate proktaṃ devatāsvaralakṣaṇam||57||

ṭīkā:- ī devasara lakṣaṇaṃ somanādiyamuna[thiyyamane] ceppivunnadi.

adhā[tha] śaṅkhaḥ |

śaṅkhaṃścā[śaṅkhañca] varttulañcaivā[va]
pramāṇaṃ tālamātrakam|
mūlebhidraṃ[daṃ] prakurvi[rvī]ta oṣṭavādyaṃ samācaret|
lakṣmi[kṣmī]śo devato tasya ya śrotu[tā] puṇyavāṇ[n] bhavet ||58||
prārthanaṃ[nā]|
namostu pañcajānyāya[pāñcajanyāya] namo jaladhijanmane |
namo nārāyaṇadyanttaḥ[?] namo vādyaviśeṣaṇe ||59||
ardhacandrakarau dṛ[dhṛ]tvā vādako vādyamācaret |
somanāryeṇa saṅkṣepya vakṣyate śaṅkhalakṣaṇam ||60||

adhā[tha] kāhalaḥ|

tāmreṇa kālaṃ[halaṃ] kuryāt rūpa ṣoḍaśamuṣṭibhiḥ|
prādeśamātramagre ca valayaṃ kārayeta[tta]taḥ |
trikhaṇḍa[ḍo] vā[va] catuḥkhaṇḍā[ḍo]
ekaikaṃ saṃyutaṃ punaḥ||61||
valayākṛtatanmūle candrahastāṃ[staṃ] gri[gṛ]hītavān |
vādayo goṣpamahyābhyāṃ [vādayedoṣṭhajihvābhyāṃ]
devatā kamalāsanaḥ ||62||

prārthanaṃ[nā] |

namostu pārvatīnātha namaścandradharāya ca |
namostu kāhaḷādhiśa namastasmai vi[pi]nākine ||63||
somanāthamate khyātaṃ kāhalaṃ lakṣaṇaṃ purā||64||

ṭīkā:- lakṣaṇayuktamaina bō[būra]rugaku namaskariñci rēṇḍu cētulā dhariñci pedavula nālikekōna[nālukakona] cēta vāyupūrita śabdālu vāyiñcavalenu. navīru bākīlu kāḷelu indulō antarbhāvaṃ. ī kāhala lakṣaṇaṃ sōmanāryuḍu ceppināḍu.

atha upāṅga lakṣaṇam /

ramyeṇa recakeṇai[nai]va rūpaṃ dvādaśamuṣṭibhiḥ /
racaniya[nīyaṃ]sta[ta]thā caikaṃ
randhramasyeva kīrttitaḥ[tam] //65//
tarjanī madhyamāgrābhyāṃ vādanīya[yo]manīṣibhiḥ /
daṇḍasya lakṣmikā daiva randhre pavanadevatā/ /66//

prārthanaṃ[nā] /

namaścandrāya vividhe namassaṅgītavedine /
svaratrayayute tasmai [tastasmai] namo jaladhi janmane //67//
upāṅgalakṣaṇaṃ samyak śārṅgadevena
[somanāryeṇa] kīrttitam //68//

ṭīkā:- ī tīruna upāṅga lakṣaṇayuktaṅgānu vādakuḍu dhariñci vāyupūritaṃ[ta nādaṃ] cēta vāyiñcavalenu. jīnikōvi, caṅgu, upari vādyālu indulō antarbhāvaṃ.

ādhā[atha] mṛdaṅgaḥ /

purā murāsuraṃ hatvā bhagavān devakīsutaḥ/
tatkaḷeba[va]ramādhāya mardalaṃ kṛtavān bhuvi //69//
śrīmatkañca sodphataṃ vubhamayāmalakaṃ tathā [?]/
catvākoṭimahāśriṣau[?] mṛdaṅgaśca yathā kramam //70//
jambucandanavṛkṣe ca[kṣeṇa] mṛdaṅgaṃ kārayedbhuvi/
ṣaḍtriṃśadaṅgulaṃ dīrghaṃ
madha[dhya]maṃ varttulā[laṃ] tathā//71//
aṅguṣṭau[ṣṭhā]ṅgula cū[mā]nena trayaḥ
pacāśataṅguḷaḥ [pañcāśadaṅgulāḥ]/
dīrghasyānmadhyamastū[thū]laṃ
tāvata[da]ṅgula varttulam //72//
ubhayoragrayoścaiva dvādaśāṅgula varttulam /
tayośca madhyabhāgena karnni[rṇi]kā caturaṅgulaḥ[lā]/

karnni[rṇi]kāyāṃ[yāḥ] bahirbhāge
valayo[ye]na samādṛ[vṛ]tam||73||
viśvakarmavinirmāṇaṃ haricarmādayastathā [?]|
āhṛdya[tya] cokacarmeṇa bandhaniyyaṃ
[nīyaṃ] granddhi[nthi]yuktam ||74||
makāraṃ vija [bījaṃ ityuktaṃ]
dakāraṃ kurameva [aṅkurameva] ca|
laṅkāraṃ phala samyogyaṃ
kurvan mada[dda]la vādhakaḥ[?]||75||
mṛdaṅgaṃ trividhaṃ rūpaṃ carmarajjuśca pañcamaṃ|
prāṇaḥ pañca mṛdaṅgasya kīrttito bharatādibhiḥ ||76||
devatā[te] karnni[rṇi]kā
dvadvau[dvandve] sūryacandramasāvubhau|
valayadvitaya syāpi pariveṣotadai[ṣo,dhide]vatāḥ||77||
granthestu viśvakarmasyāt gandharvabandhadevatāḥ |
maṇicūḍāmaṇaugrīve [maṇicūḍamaṇigrīvau]
caraṇo[rmaṇo]rati[dhi] devatāḥ[te]||78||

ṭīkā:- pūrvakālamandu śri[śrī]hari murāsuruni gōṭṭi vāni kalēbara**[kaḷēbaraṃ tecci] mṛdaṅgaṃ jēsi nandikēśvaruniki iccenu. lōkamandu mārēḍu, caṇḍra, jīḍi, nelli, nērēḍu, śrīgandhaṃ ī vṛkṣamākulatōnu maddalaṃ cēyavalenu. ī ceppina lakṣaṇāna mārdaṅgi [mṛdaṅga] lakṣaṇaṃ.

hru[hṛ]dyābhijānudeśe vā jaṅghaye[jaṅghāyāṃ] pādayostathā|
bhūmyādi ṣaḍvidhaścaiva[?] mṛdaṅgaṃ tatra tā[dhā]rayet ||79||
*caturaṅgula bhūmadhye aṅguṣṭau[ṣṭhau] śre *****yoḥ |*
madhyāṅguṣṭa[ṣṭha]manāmikyaṃ
nirādhāraṃ yathā kramam ||80||
apaśabdamanāmikyaṃ kṛta vidyāvihīnakam [?]|
aṅgulyānāmikānāṃ[kayā] ca madhyanāṭaka
[tāḍana]meva ca ||81||

agraṃ ca tattavāṭi daśadhā tattadheti ca/
ta dhi to ca ta dhi dhi tulaya hadhabhī [?]/
ta dhi ka tto taṭ yasya madhyaṅgu[dhyāṅgu]la vaśādibhiḥ [?] //82//
toṅggāta dhiṅggaṇaścaivā kakunddaḥ kukuṭaṇ kiraḥ/
jegatāteyyatātaitā śuddhatāḍana meva ca//83//
aṅguṣṭhāgaṃ[graṃ] ca mūlaṃ ca satāḷaḥ
[talaḥ] pañcabhistathā /
evaṃ ca maṇibandhetva taṇibāhyaṃ ca tatalaṃ [?]/
anāmika[kā] tarjanī ca madhyamaṃ
cātha nāṭakaṃ[tāḍanaṃ] //84//
aṅguṣṭhaṃ ca kaniṣṭaṃ ca tarjani madhyamastathā /
anāmikāṃ ca saṃyāti eke ca karahastayoḥ /85///
*śabdatālavihīnasyā hastapūritanādayo**[?]/*
***[a]kṣaratrayakaṃ prāṇaṃ yo canāti sa*
ninditaḥ[jānāti sa paṇḍitaḥ]//86//
tālaṃ sūcitahastaṃ tu śabdasūcita nādayoḥ /
tālaśabdādayorvādhyaṃ[dyaṃ] mṛdaṅgī mudito bhavet //87//
*vāmahastena ***[dā]ridraṃ dakṣiṇahastena*
[dakṣiṇena ca] sampadaḥ /
vujā[vṛjyā]mṛdaṅga[ṅgaṃ] tāḍau ca
brahmā[hma]hatyāṃ vyapohat[ti] //88//
nandikeśaṃ hṛdiṃ dhyātvā mṛdaṅgaṃ tā[dhā]rayeta[tta]taḥ /
ādau syādādi tāloyaṃ vādako vādyamācaret //89//

ṭīkā:- nandikēśvaruni dhyānaṃ jēsi, sarvadēvatākāramaina mṛdaṅgamunu dhariñci, cēta tāḷamunnu palku baḍi śabdanirna[rṇa]yamunnu nandanāda sunāda ghōṣanādālu aṅguṣṭa tarjani madhyama anāmika kaniṣṭaka maṇibanda hastatala pārśvaṅguḷāla cēta dakṣiṇa hastānanu pañcāṅgula madhyama hastāla[tala] maṇibandha vāmahastā**[la] cētanunnu, ī ceppina akṣarapaḍuphaṭlu taragakunu nāṭyādiyandu reṇḍu cētula udgrāhaṃ jēsi āditālā[la]layanu vāyiñcavalenu. grē ***** lōliyyaṃ.

ḍhakkā lakṣaṇam ||

ḍhakka[kkā]kā[khā]dirakāṣṭhena di[dī]rghayekādaśāṅgulam|
aṣṭāṅgula pramāṇena pārśvaye[yoḥ] vartulākru[kṛ]ti||90||
*madhye hrasvaṃ prakurvi[rvī]ta *********** ṇā|*
veṣṭitaṃsceta sūtreṇa pārśvau sampiḍyate śivaḥ||91||
devatā ḍhakkavādyasya sūtrasya braṃhmadevatā |
vāmahastena gruṃhṇiyat[gṛhṇiyāt]
sadya(vya) tarjani tāḍayet||92||
*aṅgulāgraṃ ca mūlaṃ ca hastaṃ pradhā *****|*
***[ta]rjanyādyaṅgulaiḥ pārśvā savya*
hastena tāḍayet||93||

prārthanā|

******

ṭīkā:- lakṣaṇayuktamaina ḍhakkaku namaskariñci vāmahastaṃ cēta kaṭakāmukhahastēna baṭṭi dakṣiṇahasta sūcihasta pradhānaṃ ********* la vāyiñcavalenu. ī ḍhakkā lakṣaṇaṃ sōmanāthiyyamandu cēppinadi.

athā[tha] ḍholu||
kumbhakarna[rṇa]sya bodhārthaṃ rāvaṇena vinirditaṃ[rmitaṃ]
*******[ṣoḍaśāṅgulavistīrṇaṃ]*
*prādeśadvaya saṃyu*****[māyatam] ||94||*
******* [ḍolāvādyagataśceti] pramāṇaṃ parikīrtitaḥ[tam]|*
ḍokāraṃ daityadevānāṃ lukāraṃ rāvaṇeśvaraḥ||95||
dau[dvau] dvau rākṣasadevānāṃ ḍolāvādyaṃ pracakṣate|
*gavaśrimūrti *********[gadamūle*
brahmā gadamadhye haristathā|]
[gadāgreca bhavedrudro gade tiṣṭhanti devatāḥ] ||96||

ṭīkā:- **** lakṣaṇamu ******** [dakṣiṇahastaṃ] cēta dakṣiṇapārśvamunnu vāmahastaṃ cēta vāmapārśvamunnu vāyiñcavalenu. idi rāvaṇa nirmitaṃ.

bheri lakṣaṇam|
*bheri vādya ********* pramāṇena *******
mahiṣicarmaṇācādyā[chādi] taśca[taccha]rmaṇa prapīḍyate ||97||
ādau madhye tathā cāgraṃ[gre] brahmaviṣṇuśivasthitām|
gadeva pārśvayostasyā vādako vādyamācaret ||98||
******* [somanāthamate proktaṃ bheri]vādyasya lakṣaṇam||99||*

ṭīkā:- bhērinni gadala cēta vāyiñcavalenu. ī bhēri lakṣaṇaṃ sōmanāthiyyamandu ceppivunnadi.

ḍamāmi lakṣaṇam|
lohena kumbhau dvau kuryaḥ hastārthaṃ vartulākrutiḥ|
*mahiṣi carma mā**daḥ tacca ***************||100||*
*****[vā]madakṣiṇahastā[tau] ca gadau[gade]*
vādyaṃ samācaret||101||
kumbhau devau raviśaśi rajyāścā[rajvoścā] nantara[ta]kṣakau|
gadātrimūrtī daulāśca śivaḥ śaktiḥ svarūpiṇi||102||
somanāthamate proktaṃ ḍamāmi lakṣaṇaṃ purā||103||

ṭīkā:- ī **********[tīruna lakṣaṇa]yuktamaina ḍamāmi reṇḍu cētulāgada vāyiñcavalenu. gaḍibiḍi, tamuku modalaina carmavādyālu indulō antarbhāvaṃ.

iti carmavādyaṃ|
[atha kāṃsyatālaṃ||]
*vartulaṃ kāṃsya ************** gulomuśai|*
nimmo[mno] madhyamadeśaścā
adhoryaṅgula mātru[tra]kam||104||

tadveko yavamātrasya jātaṃ puṣṭisamāśrutiḥ/
*pādonaṅguja[la] mātrantu madhye ********//105//*
****** paṭṭu sūtraṃ granthistasyāgrataḥ kuru /*
vāmatarbha (rja) nitāṅguṣṭhe veṣṭhitaṃ niścalaṃ bhavet//106//
anye dakṣiṇatarjanyāṃ veṣṭhitaṃ prabhākaraḥ/
*tāṇḍa ********************karau //107//*
****[a]ṣṭāviṃśatvalenaivā[va] kāṃsyatālaṃ prakalpayet/*
haranetrasamudbhūtā[tāḥ] brahmāviṣṇu maheśvarā[rāḥ]//108//
aśvamedha phalañcaiva prāpnuyādyo gatastathā//
*tāla ************* parikīrtitaḥ//109//*
yathā śāstraprasāreṇa śuddhamityabhidhiyyate/
manovistārasahitaṃ nartakasya tu mākrutiḥ//110//
************** sālaga nāmakaḥ//*
*śuddha ************************//111//*

ṭīkā:- iṭla[ṭlu] lakṣaṇayuktaṅgā kañcutāḷāluceya[vāyiñca] valenu. jākaṭa, lohe ********

4

English Translation of NC with Commentry

1. Nāṭya

I salute Sītārāma, who gives eternal bliss, who is tranquil, who has a blemish-less body, who is beautiful and whose eyes are like the lotus petals. (1[1])

Śambhu, Gaurī, Brahmā, Mādhava, Nandikeśvara, Dattila, Kohala, Yājñavalkya, Nārada, Hanumān, Vighnarāja, Ṣaṇmukha, Bṛhaspati, Arjuṇa, Rāvaṇa and the daughter of Bāṇasura (Uśā), are the creators of bharata (drama), according to the area of their performance (action). Based on the views of all, the treatise named Nāṭyacūḍāmaṇi, as acknowledged by the wise, will be expounded by Somanārya, well known as an Aṣṭāvadhāni. (2-5)

In this world, there are many experts on (the subject of) bharata (drama);
The performance of nāṭya should be framed after considering their opinions;
The treatise (should be written) in conformity with the earlier writings. (6)

For making the practice clear, the scholar <lakṣyalakṣa> should expound the practice of three, two or one lakṣaṇa [?] (7)

One is the definition, the other is the commentary on that, the lakṣaṇa of one with respect to the others is being presented here [?]. (8)

1.The numbers within paranthesis refer to the verse numbers of the edited text of NC.

Even though in this world, there are many writers on dramaturgy, all their writings from here have been studied (lit. collected) and for the benefit of humanity, the practice and theory, have been presented by Somanārya, well known as aṣṭāvadhāni, in his work called Nāṭyacūḍāmaṇi. [comm. 8]

Now nāṭyotpatti

Gāndharva is three fold according to the division into gīta (melodic form-music), vādya (syllabic form of drums) and nartana (kinesthesis)[1]. Nartana (kinesthetic art) is three fold, according to the division into nāṭya (drama), nṛtta (non- representational dance) and nṛtya (representational dance) (9)

To begin with, Brahmā gave the nāṭyaveda to Bharata. Then Bharata, along with a group (an ensemble) of gandharva-s and apsarā-s performed nāṭya, nṛtta and nṛtya in the presence of Śiva. Then Śiva, having remembered his performance of the majestic form of dance <uddhata>, arranged his chief attendant Taṇḍu to make a presentation, fit for bharata. Having learnt the tāṇḍava (dance) from Taṇḍu, the sages communicated it to the mortals. (10-12)

Gāndharvaveda is of three types, namely, gīta, vādya and nṛtta. Nartana is of three kinds; they are nāṭya, nṛtta and nṛtya. Brahmā taught this nāṭyaveda to Bharata. Bharata taught this to the group of Apsarā-s and made them to dance in the presence of Parameśvara. Parameśvara taught the tāṇḍava dance conceived by him to Bharata, through Taṇḍu. Bharata then taught the sages and performed it, in order to establish on this earth. (comm. 12)

Pārvatī taught lāsya to Uṣā, the daughter of Bhaṇāsura. It was taught to the cowherd ladies of Dvārakā by her (and) through them to the women of Saurāṣṭra and through them, the women residing in various regions were taught. Thus this (art), received through in tradition, was established in this world. (13-14)

1. Gāndharva is known as the embodiment of svara, tāla and pada (NS 28,8). Nartana is a common term used to denote the three types- nāṭya, nṛtta and nṛtya in SR (SR 7,2cd,3ab). Here the term nartana seems to be used as a synonym of nṛtya. However the commentator has used the term nṛtta and not nartana (see. comm.12).

Pārvatī taught Uṣā, the daughter of Bhaṇāsura, the lāsya dance conceived by her. That Uṣā taught the ladies of Dvārakā. They taught it to the people of campannadeśa.[1] In this way, with their having transmitted to the remaining people traditionally, (the art) was established in this world. (comm. 14)

Brahmā abstracted the speech <pāṭhya>, gestures <abhinaya>, music <gīta> and sentiments <rasa> from the four veda-s, ṛg, yajur, sāma and atharvaṇa, respectively and created the triad (nāṭya, nṛtta and nṛtya), which bestows dharma (virtuousness), kāma (desire), artha (object) and mokṣa (bliss). (15)

It increases the fame, proficiency, good fortune and cleverness; it is the cause for the manifestation of wealth, valour and courage. It helps destroy the sorrow, despair and distress of those afflicted by grief. This (yields) immense bliss greater than that of realising the absolute (Brahman) (16-17)

Otherwise how could (it) have captured the minds of Nārada and others. There is nothing higher than this to be seen and heard in this world. (18)

From the four veda-s respectively, Brahmā gathered the speech, gestures, music and rasabhāva-s and created the gīta, vādya and nṛtta. These bestow virtuousness, object, desire and bliss. These are the causes for the manifestation of wealth and courage. For those afflicted by grief, (these) are means for removing sorrow, despair and distress. It brings about bliss, greater than that of brahmānanda. Therefore, the ancient sages <Bhāgavata> like Nārada, attached themselves to this. Since there is no other śāstra better than this to be seen and to be listened to, it (has become the greatest of all the śāstra-s) is seen to be a śāstra (art) that is an embodiment of all the three God-s (Brahmā, Viṣṇu and Śiva). (comm.18)

---

1. Saurāṣṭra is interpreted as campannadēśa in the commentary. Reference to a place called campaka dēśa is found in the Sanskrit English Dictionary by Monier Williams (p. 388); a town by the name, campā, in Aṅga (the modern Bhāgalpur or a place in its vicinity; residence of Karṇa) is also mentioned.

2. Gītādhyāya

Now the chapter on gīta will be expounded.

After having compiled the theory of Saṅgīta, the Svararāgasudhārasaṃ will be expounded by Somanārya, known as an Aṣṭāvadhāni. (1)

The Svararāgasudhārasamu, having compiled from Saṅgītaśāstra, is being expounded by Somanārya, famous for aṣṭāvadhāna. (comm.1)

Nāda and the origin of nāda.

The combination of nṛtta, vādya and gīta is called nāda[1]. The arrangement of the svara-s (tones), which pleases is called gīta (music). That which pleases the ears of the listener in its own capacity is called svara. (2)

The dhvani (sound) that emanates from the combination of nṛtta, vādya and gīta is called nāda. (comm. 2)

The syllable 'na' (in the word nāda) stands for (lit. should be known as) prāṇa and the syllable 'da' for fire. It is called nāda, since it is born of the union of prāṇa and agni. (3)

The syllable na is to be understood as prāṇa (the vital air) and the syllable da is to be understood as fire. The sound resulting by the combination of this air <prāṇa> and fire <agni> (nakāra and dakāra) is called nāda. (comm. 3)

Through nādopāsanā, the gods Brahmā, Viṣṇu and Maheśvara .... [become worshipped since they are the embodiment of nāda][2] (4)

1. In the popular textual tradition, gīta, vādya and nṛtta are together termed Saṅgīta. The term nāda here probably has to be understood in the sense of a composite art, consisting of nṛtta, vādya and gīta, and not as a musical sound. However the commentator wants to treat it as a sound and not as a composite art as will be seen in comm.2
2. Although this half verse of SR 1,3,2 is incomplete by itself in meaning, the commentator (comm.4) seems to have extracted meaning from the half verse and interprets it to convey that nāda is worshipped by the three Gods. However the reading in SR conveys a different sense.

Brahmā, Viṣṇu and Maheśvara will be performing nādopāsanā. (comm. 4)

The Characteristics of āhata and anāhata

Nāda is said to be two-fold, āhata and anāhata. Āhata is so called because of (being born of) the union of the two <prāṇa>, the vital air and <agni>, fire. The nāda that originates from the sky is called anāhata. The ascending (sound) <ārohiṇi> is āhata and the descending (sound) <avarohiṇi> is anāhata[1]. (5-6)

That nāda is of two types, namely, āhata and anāhata. Āhata is produced from the body and that which originates from the sky is anāhata. The ascending one is āhata and the descending one is anāhata. (comm. 6)

The Characteristics of Svara

That nāda on being made seven-fold through the svara-s ṣaḍja etc., and is known as seven svara-s, namely, ṣaḍja, ṛṣabha, gāndhāra, madhyama, pañcama, dhaivata and niṣāda. (7)

That nāda becomes seven svara-s, namely, sa, ri, ga, ma, pa, dha and ni. These seven svara-s are born from (the sounds of) peacock, cow, goat, krauñcapakṣī (curlew?), cuckoo, horse and elephant.. (comm.7)

Thus the svara-s are drawn and placed on the instruments like vīṇā, and Saṅgīta is created through the sound produced by that nāda. (8)

These seven svara-s when played as sounds on the instruments (like vīṇā) emerge as Saṅgīta. (comm.8)

Infant understands, animals understand and the snakes (too) understand the joy of music. (9)

The infants, animals and snakes know the joy of music. (comm.9)

The infant laid on the lap, crying, unaware of the enjoyment of objects, on drinking the nectar of gīta, becomes happy. (10)

1. This kind of relating ascent and descent (ārōhiṇi and avarōhiṇi) to āhata and anāhata is unusual in the textual tradition, but is also noticed in SM.

An innocent baby, when placed on the lap, stops crying and becomes happy on listening to music <gāna>. (comm.10)

The deer wandering in the forest, eating the grass, delight in the music played by the hunter and sacrifice their lives (being lured by the music). (11)

The animals while eating the grass, drinking water and wandering in the forest, remain happy listening to the music.[1] (comm.11)

Even the dangerous snake, <kṛṣṇasarpa> becomes happy on hearing the sound (of music). Who are capable of uttering the praise of that gīta (music)? (12)

The dangerous snakes, on hearing svara, gīta and nāda, remain happy. Thus by whom is the greatness of gīta capable of being described? (comm.12)

sa, ga and ma are (born in) the family (lineage) of Gods; pañcama is born in the family of manes; ri and dha are born in the family of sages and niṣāda is born in the family of demons. (13)

sa, ga and ma (born in) the family of Gods; pa in the family of manes, ri and dha in the family of sages, ni in the family of demons. These are the families relating to the svara-s. (comm.13)

sa and ma are known to be (born in) the priestly class, ri and dha are born in the princely class, ni and ga are known to be (born in) the merchant class (and) pañcama is born of the servant class[2] (14)

sa, ma-priestly class; ri, dha- princely class; ni, ga-merchant class; pa-

1. The idea conveyed in the Commentary slightly varies from the mūla
2. Works like SR, SP, STR, SSārāmṛta etc. classify the svara-s, sa, ma and pa under the priestly class; ri and ga under the princely class, ni and ga under the merchant class and kākali and antarā under the servant class. Some Mss of NC too, seem to show this kind of classification in the original. But the reading is corrupt with respect to the servant class. Some read pañcama and some seem to convey kkali and antarā. On the other hand, the commentary does not speak of kākali and antarā svara-s but mentions only pañcama. Since kākali and antarā svara-s are not mentioned in NC, probably the classification underwent change with pañcama being assigned the servant class. This is also noted in works like SM.

servant class. These are the classes relating to the svara-s. (comm.14)

Eighty, Seventy, Sixty, Forty, Thirty, Twenty and Ten years are the age of the svara-s ṣaḍja and others respectively. (15)

Eighty, Seventy, Sixty, Forty, Thirty, Twenty and Ten years - these are the years of the seven svara-s. (comm.15)

lotus-coloured, pale yellow, golden (yellow), jasmine/sparkling white, black, yellow, variegated - these are the colours known in ṣaḍja and others. (16)

These are the colours of the seven svara-s. (comm.16)

jambū, śāka, kuśa, krauñca, śālmalī, śveta, puṣkara are the continents in which, the regions of the svara-s are mentioned(located). (17)

These are the regions (habitats) of the svara-s. (comm.17)

The fire God, Brahmā, Moon, Lord of Lakṣmī (Viṣṇu), Nārada, Tumburu are the seers of ṣaḍja and others. (18)

These are the (family?) seers <gotrarṣi[1]> of the svara-s. (comm. 18)

Heroism, wonder, terror, disgust, fear, mirth and love are the sentiments of ṣaḍja and others[2]. (19)

These are the sentiments of the svara-s. (comm.19)

Fire God, Brahmā, Śāradā (the consort of Brahmā), Śarva (Śiva), Lord of Śrī (Viṣṇu), Bhāskara (Sun God) and Gaṇeśvarā are the presiding deities of ṣaḍja and others. (20)

They are the presiding deities of the svara-s, ṣaḍja and others. (comm.20)

The adornments (garments) of ṣaḍja and others are white, yellow, red,

1. The word "ṛṣi"(seer) has been interpreted by the commentator as gōtrarṣi. It is to be noted that the names specified here do not represent the names of the gōtrarṣi-s as specified in works like BKM (Āṅgīrasa, Bhārgava etc. -BKM,p.69).
2. The mūla and the commentary seem to relate one rasa to each svara. In earlier works like NS and SR, the distribution is different. That is, three rasa-s, namely, vīra, raudra and adbhuta are assigned to ṣaḍja and ṛṣabha. But in NC, by assigning one rasa for one svara, only seven rasa-s are accommodated, and hence, karuṇa, the eight one is missing. BKM brings in karuṇa also, because of which, two svara-s have to be assigned two rasa-s.

dark blue/black, (coloured similiar to) turmeric, variegated and (cloth made of) linen. (21)

These are the garments of the svara-s. (comm.21)

Curd rice, food made of milk and sugar <pāyasaṃ>, eatable <bhakṣyaṃ>, mixed rice, food made of flour and milk <piṣṭayukpayaḥ>, pure rice <śuddhānnaṃ> and raw rice <taṇḍulaṃ> are the food of ṣaḍja and others. (22)

These are the food for the svara-s. (comm.22)

Saffron, aloe, musk, camphor, the yellow pigment <gorocana> and sandal[1] are the perfumes of ṣaḍja and others. (23)

These are the perfumes of the svara-s. (comm.23)

<jātī>, <campaka>, white lotus <punnnāga>, jasmine, <ketakī>, <karavīra> and lotus are the (floral) adornments of ṣaḍja and others. (24)

These are the adornments of the svara-s. (comm.24)

Pearl, sapphire, diamond, lapiz-lazuli, emerald, sardonyx and topaz are the gems ornamenting ṣaḍja and others. (25)

These are the ornaments of the svara-s. (comm.25)

Sword, Spear, Mace, Discus, Short javelin, Iron arrow, Goad are known to be the weapons of the svara-s. (26)

These are the weapons for the svara-s. (comm.26)

Swan, Lion, the Bheruṇḍa bird, Deer, Crocodile, Parrot and Maina are the vehicles of ṣaḍja and others (27)

These are the vehicles of the svara-s. (comm.27)

Mango, Date, Plantain, Lime, Pomegranate, Grape, the Nutmeg tree are the trees for ṣaḍja and others. (28)

These are the trees for the svara-s, ṣaḍja and others. (comm.28)

Gandharvī, Kinnarī, Yakṣī, Kimpuruṣī, Nāgakanyā, woman of the Gods <surastrī> and the woman of the demon <rākṣasī> are the wives of ṣaḍja and others. (29)

1. Parimala is mentioned as the seventh name, which actually does not denote any particular perfume but is a general name for fragrance.

They are the wives of the svara-s ṣaḍja and others. (comm.29)

Anuṣṭup, gāyatrī, triṣṭup, bṛhatī, paṅkti, uṣṇik and jagatī are known to be the metres of ṣaḍja and others. (30)

These are the metres for the svara-s. (comm.30)

Strong, subtle, strong, long, even, long and very strong are the forms (physique) of ṣaḍja and others. (31)

These are the forms of the seven svara-s (comm.31)

Śatabhiṣaj, Citrā, Vasu (Dhaniṣṭā)[1], Maghā, Uttara-Phalgunī, Pūrvāṣāḍhā and mitra (Anurādhā) are the birth stars of the svara-s. (32)

These are the birth stars of the svara-s. (comm.32)

Four, three and two-faced, four-faced and four-faced, three-faced and two-faced are said to be the (number of) faces of the svara-s. (33)

These are the (number of) faces (assigned) for the svara-s. (comm.33)

Eight, taste (six)[2], four arms and eight, eight arms, seaons (six)[3] and four are the (number of) arms (assigned) for the svara-s. (34)

These are the (number of) arms for the svara-s. (comm.34)

Eight, seasons (six) and four, eight, eight, seasons (six), four <veda> are the number of eyes of (assigned to) the svara-s. (35)

These are the (number of) eyes (assigned) for the svara-s ṣaḍja and others. (comm.35)

Eight, seasons (six) and four ears, eight and eight ears; taste (six) and four <veda> are said to be the number of ears of (assigned to) ṣaḍja and others. (36)

These are the (number of) ears for the svara-s, ṣaḍja and others. (comm.36)

The number of faces and nostrils of the svara-s [4]? ? (37)

---

1. Some stars are denoted through the names of their respective deities, viz, vasu for Dhaniṣṭā and mitra (Sun) for Anurādhā.
2. The six original kinds of taste refer to sweet, sour, salt, pungent, bitter and astringent.
3. The six seasons are spring, summer, monsoon, autumn, early winter and winter.
4. From the commentary following verse 38, it is understood that the number of nostrils is equal to the number of faces and all the svara-s are attributed two feet each.

The experts of svara-s (music) said that the number of nostrils and feet of the svara-s are according to the number of faces. (comm.37)

The characteristics of svara-s have been gathered according to rules and elaborately described in a correct manner by Somanārya. (38)

The lakṣaṇa-s for the svara-s ṣaḍja and others have been said by Somanācārya in detail.

For the svara ṣaḍja:- family:Gods, class:priestly, years:eighty, colour:lotus (coloured), habitat:jambū, sentiment:heroism, seer:Fire, vehicle:swan, presiding deity:Fire God, faces:four, arms:eight, ears:eight, eyes:eight, nostrils:four, feet:two, body:stout, weapon:sword, garment:white, flower:jasmine, perfume:saffron, food:curd-rice, ornament:ruby, tree:mango, woman:gandharva(lady), star:śatabhiṣā, zodiac sign:Acquarius, day:Saturday. In this way, the svara ṣaḍja shines having born of anuṣṭup metre.

For the svara ṛṣabha:- family:sages, class:princely, years:seventy, colour:yellow, habitat:śāka, sentiment:wonder, seer:Vedapuruṣa, presiding deity:Brahmā, garment:yellow, food: (food made of milk and sugar) <pāyasaṃ>, perfume:aloe, flower:campaka (a variety of jasmine), ornament:sapphire, weapon:spear, vehicle:lion, tree:date, woman:kinnara (lady), star:cittā, zodiac sign:Libra, day:Friday, faces:three, arms:six, eyes:six, ears:six, nostrils:three, feet:two, body:medium built, the ṛṣabha svara shines being born of the gāyatrī metre.

For the svara gāndhāra: family:Gods, class:merchant, years:sixty, colour:golden, seer:Moon, sentiment:anger, presiding deity:Sarasvatī, habitat:kuśa, garment:red, food:sweet cakes, perfume:musk, flower:tuberose, ornament:diamond, weapon:mace, vehicle:bheruṇḍa, tree:plantain, woman:yakṣa(lady), faces:two, arms:four, eyes:four, nostrils:two, feet:two, body:long, star:dhaniṣṭā, zodiac sign:Libra, day:Saturday. In this way the gāndhāra svara shines being born of triṣṭup metre.

For the svara madhyama: family:Gods, class:priestly, years:forty, colour:jasmine-bud (coloured), habitat:krauñcadvīpa, seer:Kṛṣṇa, sentiment:disgust, presiding deity:Īśvara, garment:dark blue, food:mixed rice, perfume:camphor, flower:jasmine, ornament:cat's eye gem <vaiḍūrya>, weapon:discus, vehicle:deer, tree:lime tree, woman:kimpuruṣa (lady), faces:four, arms:eight, ears:eight, eyes:eight, nostrils:four, feet:two, body:short (limited), star:makhā, zodiac sign:Leo, day:Sunday. In this way, the madhyama svara shines being born of bṛhatī metre.

For the svara pañcama: family:manes, class:servant, years:thirty, colour:blue, habitat:śālmalī, seer:Īśvara, sentiment:terror, presiding deity:Viṣṇu, garment:turmeric(coloured), food:<calimiḍi>, perfume:(yellow pigment) <gorocana>, flower:mangrove, ornament:ruby, weapon:short javelin (or arrow), vehicle:crocodile, tree:pomegranate, woman:nāga (lady), faces:four, arms:eight, ears:eight, eyes:eight, nostrils:four, feet:two, body:short, star:uttarā, zodiac sign:Virgo, day:Wednesday. In this way, the pañcama svara shines being born of paṅkti metre.

For the svara dhaivata: family:sages, class:princely, years:twenty, colour:yellow, habitat:śveta, seer:Nārada, sentiment:mirth, presiding deity:Sun, garment:coloured, food:milk, perfume:sandal, flower:Balsom (oleander), ornament:<gomedaka>, weapon:iron arrow, vehicle:parrot, tree:grape, woman:Celestial lady, faces:three, arms:six, eyes:six, ears:six, nostrils:three, feet:two, star:pūrvāṣāḍā, zodiac sign:Sagittarius, day:Thursday, body:long. In this way the dhaivata svara shines being born of uṣṇik metre.

dFor the svara niṣāda: family:demons, class:merchant, years:ten, colour:grey, habitat:puṣkara, sentiment:love, seer:Tumburu, presiding deity: Vināyaka, garment:silk, food:rice, perfume:??, flower:lotus, ornament:topaz, weapon:hook, vehicle:mynah, presiding tree:clove, woman:demon lady, faces:two, arms:four, eyes:four, nostrils:two, feet:two, body:very stout, star:anūrādhā, zodiac sign:Scorpion, day:Tuesday. In this way niṣādha svara shines, being born of jagatī metre. (comm.38)

The prastāra of the seven svara-s are said (known) respectively through the transposition of their own positions - [NOT CLEAR] (39)

Because of the transposition of their own positions, the svara-s by means of splitting and combination give rise to prastāra. The lakṣya of the svara-s has been said. (comm.39)

mandra, madhyama[1] and tāra svara-s pervade in the world.

For revealing themselves in the world, the svara-s, ṣaḍja and others produce sound in the navel, chest, throat, head and the mouth of men. The five stages in the birth of the svara-s in the human body are atisūkṣma, sūkṣma, puṣṭa, atipuṣṭa and tāra[2]. (40-41)

The svara-s ṣaḍja and others, for the purpose of coming to perception, are produced from the navel, chest, throat, mouth and the head of the human body.[3] The svara-s are born in the human body in five ways as very subtle, subtle, developed, well developed and high forms. (comm.41)

ṣaḍja etc. exist in the region of the navel, chest, throat, root of the tongue, nostrils, cheeks and head in order. (42)

In the navel, chest, throat, root of the tongue, nostrils, cheeks and head the svara-s are located. (comm.42)

In common practice it (svara) is distinguished threefold. (It) is called mandra in the chest, madhya in the throat and tāra in the head. (43)

In common usage, ṣaḍja and other svara-s are mandra in the chest, madhyama in the throat and tāra in the head. In the regions chest, throat and head, they are of three types, namely mandra, madhyama and tāra. (comm.43)

sa and ri are mandra (svara-s), ga and ma are madhya (svara-s), pa, dha and

1. It is to be noted that the commentary calls the madhya region as madhyama (See comm. 43, 44, 45, 47, 50).
2. Texts like SR speak of the five stages of production of nāda as atisūkṣma, sūkṣma, puṣṭa, atipuṣṭa and kṛtrima. But NC uses the tem, tāra for kṛtrima. Similar idea is also conveyed in SM 1,4,17.
3. In the usual way of describing the various stages of production of n ā da, seen in works like SR, the order is navel, chest, throat, head and the mouth. Here, in the commentary, the order is slightly different and the "mouth" precedes the "head". This order is also noticed in one of the songs of Tyāgarāja commencing with the words "śōbillu saptasvara" in the raga Jaganmōhinī, wherein, the phrase, "nābhihṛtkaṇṭha rasana nāsādulalayandu" occurs.

ni are based in the tāra (region)[1]. (44)

ṣaḍja and ṛṣabha are based in mandra, gāndhāra and madhyama in madhyama and pañcama, dhaivata and niṣāda are based in tāra (regions). (comm.44)

In the chest region of men, the mandra sound is of twenty two kinds. In the throat it is madhya, and the same in the head region is tāra. (45)

Because of the variations in the sound, the svara-s, are of twenty two kinds in the mandra, namely the chest region of men; and in the same way, in the throat region or the madhyama, it is of twenty two kinds and in the head region or the tāra also, they are of twenty two types. (comm.45)[2]

We obtain a successively higher pitch as we move up. On the vīṇā, however, the pitch is successively higher as we move down. These specific sounds are known as śruti-s because the ear can distinguish them. (46)

Śruti-s are mentioned in the regions mandra and others and on the Śuddha strings, they are known to be of nine kinds. (47)

The śruti-s (in the region) mandra and others:- mandra-mandra, mandra-madhyama, mandra-tāra, madhyama-mandra, madhyama-madhyama, madhyama-tāra, tāra-mandra, tāra-madhyama and tāra-tāra. In this way, it is (to be) known that, the śruti varieties are sixty-six. (comm. 47)

In the chest, to the vertical upright tube/nerve <nāḍi>, are attached transversely, twenty-two nāḍi-s. On their being struck by air, the same number of śruti-s, which are higher and higher in pitch, are produced successively. In this way, in the throat and in the head, the śruti-s become twenty-two, gradually, one by one. (48-49)

From the mandra, the heart region, upto the throat or madhya, there are 22 varieties of nāḍi-s. The air on appropriately striking the nāḍi-s, the svara-s (tones) break up into twenty-two varieties, one higher (in pitch) than the other. In the same way, (the svara-s) in the throat or madhya, there are twenty-

1. This kind of interpretation does not seem to occur in any other work except the few that follow Sōmanārya

2. The translation to this part of the text is based on Dattilam, ed. Mukund Lath, p.3.

two varieties. In the head region (the svara-s) break up into twenty-two varieties. (comm.49)

The order of the sub-varieties of the svara-s.

ṣaḍja, madhyama and pañcama are of four (varieties) each; niṣāda and gāndhāra are of two each and ṛṣabha and dhaivata are of three each. (50)

ṣaḍja, madhyama and pañcama are of four varieties each; ṛṣabha and dhaivata are of three varieties each and niṣāda and gāndhāra are of two varieties each. In total, (they are) twenty-two. In the same way, the differences are in the madhyama and tāra (regions). Their names: (comm.50)

First one is uttaramandrā, then rajanī and uttarāyatā; śuddhaṣaḍjā is the fourth, matsarīkṛtā is the fifth, aśvakrāntā is the sixth and abhirudgatā is the seventh. (51)

sauvīrī, hariṇāśvā, kalopanatā, śuddhamadhyā, mārgī, pauravī and hṛṣyakā are known to be mūrcchanā-s of the madhyamagrāma. (52)

nandā, viśālā, sumukhī, citrā, citravatī, sukhā and ālāpā are the seven mūrcchanā-s of the gāndhāragrāma. (53)

uttaramandrā, rajanī, uttarāyatā, śuddhaṣaḍjā, matsarīkṛtā, aśvakrāntā, abhirudgatā, sauvīrī, hariṇāśvā, kalopanatā, śuddhamadhyā, mārgī, pauravī, hṛṣyakā, nandā, viśālā, sumukhī, citrā, citravatī, sukhā and ālāpā- these are the names of the (mūrcchanā-s of the) three grāma-s - ṣaḍja, madhyama and gāndhāra. (These are) the names of the svara-s. If they are sung in ascent and descent, it is called mūrcchana. (comm.53)

The mandra, madhya and tāra (are found) with ṣaḍja being the first and the last (svara). ṣaḍja should be spoken as the first and the last in the ascent and descent[1]. (54)

In the mandra, madhyama and the tāra regions, the svara ṣaḍja rests in the beginning and at the end. In the ascent and descent the svara-s should be pronounced, at the beginning and at the ending with ṣaḍja. (comm.54)

The varieties of sounds <dhvanibheda[2]> are sixty-six, in the same way. (55)

1. This seems to explicitly state that the division of mandra, madhya and tāra is based on ṣaḍja (found in the beginning and at the end).
2. This text seems to use the term dhvani for śruti.

In this manner, the svara-s ṣaḍja and others, in the mandra, madhyama and tāra regions, have become sixty-six. (comm.55)

The collection of svara-s is grāma and the ascent and descent (of these svara-s) are known as mūrcchana. Their varieties will be in the following order. (56)

The gathering of svara-s is known as grāma, the ascent and descent of svara-s are known as mūrcchanā. Their varieties are being told by him in order. (comm.56)

The seven svara-s, three grāma-s, twenty-one mūrcchanā-s, fortynine tānā-s-thus (is said) in the realm of svara-s. (These (constitute) the svaramaṇḍalaṃ.). (57)

For the seven svara-s, the grāma-s are three, mūrcchana-s are twenty one and tānā-s are forty nine. Thus it is said in the sphere of svara-s <svaramaṇḍalaṃ>. (comm.57)

ṣaḍjagrāma, madhyamagrāma and gāndhāragrāma have been spoken of (as the three grāma-s). (58ab)

ṣaḍjagrāma, gāndhāragrāma and madhyama grāma - thus there are three varieties. (comm.58ab)

Seven mūrcchanā-s are known to be based on ṣaḍjagrāma. (58cd)

sa ni dha pa ma ga ri are the seven mūrcchana-s based on the ṣaḍjag rāma. The mūrcchanā-s of the madhyamagrāma: ma ga ni sa ri dha pa[1] are the seven mūrcchana-s based on the madhyamagrāma. The mūrcchanā-s of the gāndhāragrāma: ga dha ri pa sa ma ni[2] are the seven mūrcchanā-s based on the gāndhāragrāma. (comm.58cd)

The repeated (occurrence of the) mūrcchanā-s of sa ri ga ma and others in order is called svarālaṅkāra by the experts on music. (59)

When the svara-s ṣaḍja and others are caused to sound again and again in between ascent and descent, they are (called) svarālaṅkāra-s. sa ri ga ma ga ri.

1. This is a view different from the traditional one.
2. This is again a deviation from the traditional view.

sa ri ga ri. sa ri ga ma. The svara-s sung in this manner, are called alaṅkāra[1]. (comm.59)

The ascent and the descent of the seven svara-s are to be sung regularly in the morning, mid-day and afternoon by those who seek prosperity. (60)

People who aim for excellence should sing the ascent and descent of the seven svara-s in the morning, mid-day and evening. It should not be sung in other times. This is called sarali[2]. (comm.60)

The sound of a short duration, that is heard at the moment of first listening is called śruti; being a component of svara. (61)

First, the svara known/recognised in the mandra region, on touching the tāraka (when) heard in a subtle way, is called śruti. (comm.61)

The subtle sound <sūkṣma svara> because of being subtle, is not aurally perceptible; the tāra sound <śruti> should be rejected, on being harsh; there is no doubt in this. (62)

The softly rendered sound <svara> will be devoid of beauty; the loudly sounded (sound) <svara> will be harsh. Therefore these two should not be allowed. The sound <śruti> should be moderately sounded. (comm.62)

sthāyī, svara, sañcārī, āyataṃ, pratyāyataṃ, kampitaṃ, yeḍupu, ḍālu, ugraṃ and muktā- thus they are known to be ten. (63)

sthāyi, svara, sañcāri, āyataṃ, pratyāyataṃ, kampitaṃ, eḍupu, ḍālu, ugraṃ and muktayi - these are the ten varieties of the svara-s ṣaḍja and others. (comm.63)

Commencing the sound from the mandra svara is called as sthāyī. (64ab)

If the svara-s are taken (sounded) from the mandra it is called sthāyi. (comm.64ab)

Commencing the sound from a tāra-svara is called svara. (64cd)

The svara-s that commence from tāra are called sthāyīsvara (comm.64cd)

1. The concept of alaṅkāra seems to have changed from what is seen in earlier works and seems to refer to the sapta tāla alaṅkāra-s, being spoken of in CDP 3,91
2. This seems to be the earliest occurrence of the term saraḷi denoting the singing of svara-s in ascent and descent.

When a svara moves in the mandra, madhya and tāra regions, it is called sañcārī (lit. sañcārika). (64ef)

When a svara is sung brightly, in the mandra, madhya and tāra regions, it is called sañcārī. (comm. 64ef)

Svara-s that manifest separately and frequently in the mandra and other regions, (are called) āyataṃ in the ascent and pratyāyataṃ in the descent. (65)

The svara-s in the mandra, madhya and tāra regions shine individually; these svara-s (occuring) repeatedly, (in) the ascent is called āyitaṃ; (in) the descent is called pratyāyataṃ. (comm.65)

The quick movement of the svara-s in the three registers is known as kampitaṃ. (66ab)

In the mandra, madhya and tāra regions, if the svara-s are rendered with gamaka, it is called kampitaṃ. (comm.66ab)

When a svara stays for a long duration in the three registers <sthāna-s>, it is called eḍupu. (66cd)

That which makes a svara to shine in the three registers with steadiness, is called eḍupu. (comm.66cd)

If the svara-s pervade the three (registers), for a short and a long duration, they are called ḍālu. (66ef)

That which makes the svara-s to shine and move fast in three places (sthāna-s) is called ḍālu. (comm.66ef)

Commencing from a svara in the madhyama (region) is called ugraṃ. (67ab)

Making the svara to shine by commencing with madhyama is called ugraṃ (comm.67ab)

The conclusion of the svara-s present is called muktaṃ. (67cd)

Making the svara-s, shine as the concluding ones <muktāyī> is called muktaṃ. (comm.67cd)

Manifest <vyaktaṃ>, perfect <pūrṇaṃ>, clear <prasannaṃ>, delicate <sukumāraṃ>, embellished <alaṅkṛtaṃ>, equipoised <samaṃ>, deligtful

<suraktaṃ>, smooth <ślakṣṇaṃ>, raised <niṣkṛṣṭaṃ> and sweet <madhuraṃ> are the ten qualities in the gīta. (68)

vyaktaṃ, pūrṇaṃ, prasannaṃ, sukumāraṃ, alaṅkṛtaṃ, samaṃ, suraktaṃ, ślakṣṇaṃ, niṣk ṛṣṭaṃ and madhuraṃ - these ten are the qualities of the svara-s[1] of gīta. (comm.68)

Vyakta is that in which the basic words along with the prefixes and suffixes are pronounced (i.e. sung) with clear and distinct notes. (69ab)

The rendering of tones (syllables?), the words and the suffixes with clarity is called Vyaktam. (comm.69ab)

Pūrṇa is complete with integral parts (aṅga-s of prabandha) and is enriched by shakes (gamaka-s). Prasanna has lucidity of meaning[2]. (69cd)

When the svara-s are sung completely in a song (gāna), it is called Pūrṇam; the revealing (manifestation) of svara-s is called Prasannam. (comm.69cd)

Sukumāra is known by experts to be achieved well through the throat. (70ab)

That which has a sweet tone (in good state) is called Sukumāraṃ. (4) (comm.70ab)

That which shines in the three registers is called Alaṅkṛta (70cd)

That which pervades in mandra, madhyama and tāra regions is Alaṅkṛtaṃ.(5) (comm.70cd)

That which pervades with uniformity of syllables in the regions of gap <layasthāna> is known as Sama. (71ab)

That which obtains the gaps (regions without text?) <layasthāna> incorporated with uniformly placed syllables is Sama. (comm.71ab)

---

1. The mūla follows SR of Śārṅgadēva and calls these ten qualities as those pertaining to gīta. But the commentary uses the term the qualities of the svara-s of gīta. Again towards the end of the portion dealing with the description of the qualities, in verse 73, the original and the commentary read the qualities of svara-s. The same is also noted while defining the defects of gīta. See comm.77. BKM (p.93,95) and RJM (p.126) too mention these as the qualities and the defects of svara-s respectively. MBC (MBC,4,74 &79) mentions them as the qualities and defects of the ten types of gamaka svara-s.
2. The translation to this part (qualities of gīta) is based on the Translation to SR, vol 2, by Premlata Sharma and R K Shringy, pp. 323-324.

The synchronising of the vallakī (vīṇā), flute and throat is called Surakta. (71cd)

If the pitch levels of the vīṇā, flute, nāgasvara[1] and the voice are in a tonal unison, it is Surakta. (comm.71cd)

Ślakṣṇa is indicative of smoothness (of movement) between the low and the high (tones) and the fast and the middle tempo and so on. (72ab)

In the (laya-s) dhruta, madhya and vilamba and in the higher and the lower (regions) making it appear new is Ślakṣṇa (comm.72ab)

Since the pronounciation is high, it is called Niṣkṛṣṭa by Bharata and others. (72cd)

That which is sounded in a high tone (holding the breath) is called Niṣkṛṣṭaṃ (9) (comm.72cd)

Madhura is full of incomparable beauty and is enchanting for people. (73ab)

With a voice endowed with excellence, the svara-s being sung with spirit is Madhura (10). (comm.73ab)

The qualities of svara-s are briefly (concisely) described by Somanārya. (73cd)

In short, the characteristics of svara-s have been said by Somanārya (comm.73cd)

Being defective by the people <lokaduṣṭaṃ>, (and the) rules <śāstraduṣṭaṃ>, incompatibility of pitch levels <śrutivirodhaṃ> and time <kālavirodhaṃ>, repetition <punaruktaṃ>, diverging from the melody <gīta bāhyaṃ>, transgressing proper order <gatakramaṃ>, being devoid of meaning <apārthaṃ>, being indescent or uncultured <grāmyaṃ> and being confused <sandigdhaṃ> - these ten are the defects of melody. (74)

Being defective by the people and the rules, incompatibility of pitch levels and time, repetition, diverging from the melody, transgressing proper order, being devoid of meaning, being indescent or uncultured and being confused-

1. Though the mūla reads only vaṃśa, the commentary includes nāgasvara, which is also noticed in MBC 4,77.

these ten are the defects for the tones and melody. (comm.74)

[1]Defect arising due to the faulty rendering of a note is duṣṭa; not conforming to the laws <śāstra-s> is aśāstra. (75ab)

Duṣṭa (refers to) what is called apasvara (defective note); transgressing the rules is called aśāstra. (comm.75ab)

Śruti(virodha) and kālavirodha are the imcompatibility between each other (75cd)

Imperfection in the use of each śruti is śrutivirodha; imperfection in the use of time <laya> is kālavirodha. (comm.75cd)

Punarukta is sounding the descent in the ascent and vice versa (76ab)

Sounding the descent in the ascent is punaruktam. (comm.76ab)

Bāhya arises out of unconnected (irrelevant) svara; gatakrama refers to the absence of a svara. (76cd)

Singing irrelevant svara-s is bāhya; gatakrama is rendering with omission of svara-s. (comm.76cd)

That which is devoid of meaning is apārtha and grāmya arises (through) the hard (dense) notes. (77ab)

Rendering which is devoid of meaning is apārtha. (comm.77ab)

Arising of doubts in the text of the song is sandigdha; (these are) the ten defects of songs. (77cd)

These ten are the defects of the notes. (comm.77cd)

The characteristics of Eighteen Śruti-s[2]

nābhikā, atharvaṇī and dastā rest on the svara, ṣaḍja. (78ab)

nābhikā, atharvaṇī and dastā - these three embrace the svara ṣaḍja. (comm.78ab)

caurvī and aticadhā rest on the svara, ṛṣabha. (78cd)

caurvī, aticadhā - these two embrace the svara ṛṣabha (comm.78cd)

1. The explanation of the ten defects of melody is not seen in SR.
2. Kavi gives the names of eighteen Śruti-s (with slight variations), according to Hanuman mata in Bharatakōśa

kambalī, śrīvikā, saralī and nālī rest on the svara gāndhāra. (79ab)

kambalī, śrīvikā, saralī and nālī - these four embrace the svara gāndhāra. (comm.79ab)

rasanī and rañjanī rest on the svara madhyama. (79cd)

rasanī, rañjanī - these two embrace the svara madhyama. (comm.79cd)

ghrāṇinī, pavanī and mandā rest on the svara, pañcama. (80ab)

ghrāṇinī, pavanī, mandā - these three embrace the svara, pañcama. (comm.80ab)

maurddhvā and viḍambinī rest on the svara, dhaivata. (80cd)

maurddhvā, viḍambinī - these two rest on the svara, dhaivata. (comm.80cd)

bhīṣanī and sphurantī rest on the svara, niṣāda (80ef)

bhīṣanī, sphurantī - these two rest on the svara niṣāda. In total, the śruti-s are eighteen. (comm.80ef)

The presiding deities of the seven svara-s.

[1]The vital air is situated within the self; sound is situated in the vital air; the musical sound <nāda> is situated in the sound and Lord Sadāśiva is situated in the musical sound. (81)

The vital air is situated in the self. Within the vital air, are situated the sounds of the svara-s. Within the sound of the svara is the musical sound <nāda>. In the centre of that musical sound, exists the Lord, who is the Creator of the world. That is why, it is said that the Lord of the world, (Lord Śiva) is the presiding deity of the sounds of svara and melody <gīta>. (comm.81)

The characteristics of śruti

[2]Pañcama, if located on its fourth śruti makes for the ṣaḍja grāma; but if

---

1. Sambamurthi quotes this verse in his Great Composers- Tyagaraja as the one found exclusively in the work, Svarārṇava.
2. Based on the translation of SR, vol-1, by Premlata Sharma and R K Shringy, pp.163-164.

established on the śruti immediately preceding it, makes for the madhyama grāma. Alternatively, dhaivata of the ṣaḍja grāma is of three śruti-s; while in madhyama grāma, it has four śruti-s. (82)

If gāndhāra takes one śruti each from ṛṣabha and madhyama, dhaivata takes one śruti from pañcama and niṣāda takes one śruti each from dhaivata and ṣaḍja. It becomes gāndhāragrāma as declared by Nārada. This grāma is prevalent in heaven and not in this world (83-84)

The presiding deities in each of the three grāma-s respectively are Brahmā, Viṣṇu and Śiva; they are to be sung in the winter, summer and rainy seasons respectively. (85)

The order of occurence of śruti-s for the svara-s: [not clear] In this way Nārada created the ṣaḍja, gāndhāra and madhyama grāma-s in this world, in order to establish Saṅgīta. For the ṣaḍjagrāma, the presiding deity is Brahma and Earth is the habitat[1]; for the madhyamagrāma, Viṣṇu is the presiding deity and the space between the Earth and the Sun is the habitat. For the gāndhāragrāma, Īṣvara is the presiding deity and heaven is the habitat. The ṣaḍja, madhyama and gāndhāra grāma-s are to be sung in winter, summer and rainy seasons. The (musical) sounds of these svara-s pervade the fourteen worlds. (comm.85)

[2]Well indeed, if such śruti-s as the fourth etc. are admitted to be the cause of the svara-s, how can the their śruti-s such as the third etc., be considered as their cause? We shall presently explain it. Such a śruti, whether fourth or third etc., is determined only with reference to the preceding śruti-s; therefore, they too constitute the cause of the svara-s. (86-87)

There are five classes of śruti-s, viz., dīptā, āyatā, karuṇā, mṛdu and madhyā; their standing among the svara-s is stated to be as under. (88)

dīptā, āyatā and madhyā are found in ṣaḍja; karuṇā and mṛdu find a place in ṛṣabha; dīptā and āyatā are located in gāndhāra and also in madhyama along with mṛdu and madhyā; mūdu, madhyā, āyatā and karuṇā are placed

1. The habitats or (dēśa) are not found in the mūla or SR, but found in N.Sik 1,2,6.
2. Based on the translation of SR, vol-1, by Premlata Sharma and R K Shringy.

in pañcama, and karuṇā, āyatā and madhyā in dhaivata; while dīptā and madhyā are in niṣāda.[1] (89-91)

dīpta, āyatā, mṛdu, madhyā karuṇā are the names of svara-s. (Among) the svara-s ṣaḍja etc., one is mṛdu to the other; one is dīpta to the other and one is madhyama to the other. With ṣaḍja being the first, and for ṛṣabha, gāndhāra, madhyama, pañcama, daivata and niṣāda svara-s, the higher and lower śruti-s in the regions of mandra, madhyama and tāra, are known to be seven svara-s. (Comm.91)

The production of śruti-s of the svara-s is being said by Somanārya. (92)

The production of śruti-s for the seven svara-s is said by Somanārya. (comm.92)

Svara-s are said to be four fold- vādī, samvādī, vivādī and anuvādī.
Their charateristics are being said. (93)

There are four varieties for the svara-s. They are called as vādī, samvādī, vivādī and anuvādī. (comm.93)

vādī svara is the king; saṃvādī is the minister; vivādī svara is the enemy and anuvādī is the servant. (94)

The svara in the ascent is said to be the king; the one in the descent is the minister. The striking of the svara-s with one another is enemy and the succeeding svara is the servant.[2] (95)

vādī svara is called the king; saṃvādī svara is the minister; vivādī svara is the enemy and anuvādī svara is the servant. For the seven svara-s the ascent is vādī, called the king; the descent of the svara-s is called saṃvādī. The clashing of the svara-s is vivādī and is called as the enemy. The association of svara-s, because of their placement in a successive order, is anuvādī and is called servant.

1. The names, tīvrā, kumudvatī etc. found in SR following this verse, are not found in NC.
2. This interpretation of the four kinds of svara-s does not occur in any other work; but largely followed in the works influenced by NC and in many later Tamiz works. This author does not define these in terms of intervals as done by Śārṅgadēva.

For this the illustration, in terms of svara-s (is as follows)

sa ri ga ma pa dha ni sa
ri ga ma pa dha ni sa
ga ma pa dha ni sa
ma pa dha ni sa
pa dha ni sa
dha ni sa
ni sa
sa

Its name is vādī, called the king svara <rājasvara>

sa ni dha pa ma ga ri sa
ni dha pa ma ga ri sa
dha pa ma ga ri sa
pa ma ga ri sa
ma ga ri sa
ga ri sa
ri sa
sa.

Its name is saṃvādi, called the minister.

samma ga ri- sa ri ga ma
rippa ma ga- ri ga ma pa
ga dha pa ma- ga ma pa dha
manni dha pa- ma pa dha ni
passa ni dha- pa dha ni sa.

In this way, the svara-s which occur in the alaṅkāra-s is vivādi, called the enemy.

sa ri ga
ri ga ma
ga ma pa
ma pa dha
pa dha ni

dha ni sa
sa ni dha
ni dha pa
dha pa ma
pa ma ga
ma ga ri
ga ri sa

In this way, the relationship of the svara-s occuring in a successive order is anuvādi called the servant svara. In the singing of the gīta, prabandha, alaṅkāra and rāga-s, these are the four varieties. (comm.95)

This is the only means to achieve the four primary objectives of human life, namely, virtuousness, wealth, desire and bliss. (96)

It is said in the scriptures <śāstra> that one who sings knowing the form of each of these (vādī etc.?) would be endowed with the four primary objectives of human life. (comm.96)

Now rāga

The confluence of the svara-s ṣaḍja and others is called rāga. (97)

The confluence of the svara-s ṣaḍja and others is called rāga. (comm.97)

ālipti[1] is known to be two fold, according to the organisation of svara-s. The two are known as rāgālipti and rūpālipti. (98)

With the association of svara and rāga, they are of two varieties, namely, rāgālipti and rūpalipti (comm.98)

Rāgālipti arises through tannana and rūpaka is called gīta. The rāga-s are sung by the transposition of the svara-s from their (original) positions[2]. (99)

1. Traditional texts use the term 'ālapti', whereas. NC reads it as 'ālipti'. BKM and RJM also follow this.
2. The explanation given for the two terms, rāgālipti = tannana and rūpālipti= gita, is also not clear. Perhaps, the usage of the syllables, 'ta', 'na' etc. in the ālāpa led to the creation of this meaning. SSSS (p.93) mentions a tannakāram, which seems to denote vocal rendering of tānam, incorporating the syllables ta 'na' as different from the tānam of vinā.

The sound tannana is called rāga. Those tannana-s, when made to shine through the svara-s and sung, it is called gīta. (comm.99)

Kūṭatāna is (of two kinds) apūrṇa and pūrṇa. (100ab)

That (melody?) are of two varieites, apūrṇa and pūrṇa. Apūrṇa is the combination of kūṭatāna [?][1] (comm.100ab)

Pūrṇa is of (computed as) five thousand thirty three in number. (100cd)

That which is computed as five thousand thirty three varieties, is called pūrṇa. (comm.100cd)

Rāga-s are known to be of three kinds, namely, śuddha, mitra and saṅkīrṇa. Thirty-two (rāga-s) are called śuddha(rāga-s) and the mitra(rāga-s) are sixty. Infinite are the saṅkīrṇarāga-s. Thus are the śuddha, sālaga and saṅkara (varieties). (101)

Rāga-s are of three kinds. They are called as śuddha, mitra and saṅkīrṇa. The śuddha rāga-s are thirty-two; mitrarāga-s are sixty-four and the saṅkīrṇarāga-s are innumberable. (comm.101)

(if a rāga is sung) only in the manner in which it commenced, it is called śuddharāga. After commencement, if the rāga joins with its allied (rāga-s) and taking that path again, is called śālaga. The singing of all saṅkīrṇarga-s and mitra is called saṅkīrṇa[2] [??]. (102-103)

The rendering of the thirty-two rāga-s in the same way as the rāga commenced, denotes śuddharāga. Commenced with the śuddharāga, and singing on the basis of mitrarāga-s and again coming back to śuddharāga should be taken as sālaga. Singing based on mitrarāga-s, and concluding on

---

1. These terms do not seem to be discussed as in works like Dattilam. The emphasis is more on the two terms apūrṇa and pūrṇa and the term kūṭatāna and its concept have not been discussed.

2. The purport is not very clear, since saṅkīrṇa itself is defined in terms of the coming together of saṅkīrṇa and mitra. The whole description of the rāga-s, from verses 101 103 brings in almost three sets of rāga classes. 1. śuddha, mitra and saṅkīrṇa, 2. śuddha, śālaga and saṅkīrṇa, 3. śuddha (ghanam), rakti and dēśī. These terms seem to resemble the class ghana, naya and dēśī mentioned in the work, Rāgalak ṣaṇamu of Śahajī, wherein the term rakti is used synonymous to naya.

śuddha is a practice, characteristic of deśī and should be taken as raktigāna. In this way, the thirty-two rāga-s have arrived. (comm.103)

The rāga-s are known through the (number of) svara-s being six, five and full complement of svara-s (seven). These are born out of the transposition of the svara-s. (104)

It is said that through the transposition of the svara-s individually, the hextatonic, <ṣāḍava>, pentatonic <auḍava> and complete <sampūrṇa> rāga-s are born as an ensemble (collection) of svara-s. (comm.104)

The one devoid of one svara is called hextatonic; the one consisting of five svara-s is called pentatonic and the one that consists of seven svara-s is called complete. (105)

When there are six svara-s, it is hextatonic; when there are five svara-s, it is pentatonic; of seven svara-s, it is complete. In this way, the different varieties of rāga-s namely, hextatonic, pentatonic and complete are said. (comm.105)

The names of the rāga-s are said in order. (106ab)

The Gods named the thirty-two rāga-s as ṣāḍava, auḍuva and sampūrṇa (for the three types of svara combinations?) (comm.106ab)

The thirty-two (rāga-s) are known to be feminine and masculine rāga-s, by the experts in music. (106cd)

For those thirty-two rāga-s, the Gods, who are well-versed in music, have classified (them) into two, namely masculine rāga-s and feminine rāgā-s. To understand them, I shall tell the characteristics of each. (comm.106cd)

bhairava, bhūpāla, śrīrāga, paḍamañjara, vasanta, mālava, baṅgāla and nāṭa- these eight are masculine rāga-s and the rest are assigned as feminine rāga-s. (107)

bhairavi, bhūpāla, śrīrāga, paḍamañjara, vasanta, mālava, baṅgāla, nāṭa - these eight are said to be masculine rāga-s and the remaining twenty-four were called feminine rāga-s. (comm.107)

The eight rāga-s have three wives (each). (108)

The Gods have created twenty-four feminine rāga-s in the form of three wives of the eight masculine rāga-s. I shall tell that in order. I shall enumerate their names. (comm.108)

Devakriyā, megharañjī and kurañjī are the wives of bhairava. Velāhuri, malaharī and baulī are the wives of the king (bhūpāla). (109)

The wives of śrīrāga are hindolam, balahamsā and sāverī. deśī, lalitā and toḍī are the wives of paḍamañjarī. (110)

Rāmakriyā, varālī and kauśikā are the wives of madhu (vasantā); Nārāyaṇī, guṇḍakriyā and ghūrjarī are the wives of mālava. (111)

Dhanyāsī, kāmbodī and nīlāmbarī are the wives of baṅgāla. Deśākṣarī, āharī and sāraṅga are the wives of nāṭa[1]. The thirty-two (rāga-s) are known to be feminine and masculine rāga-s, by the experts in music. (112)

Thus it is said that twenty-four feminine rāga-s are the wives of the eight masculine rāga-s. Thus I have told the origin of their names (in order). (comm.112)

The Gods sing with the six, five and complete (seven) svara-s. The rāga-s are to be uttered by thier own names and are said to be of thirty-two varieties. (113)

The Gods sang with the six, five and complete (seven) svara-s and they assigned their own names to the rāgas. I shall tell the ṣaḍava, auḍava and sampūrṇa rāga classifications for these rāga-s. (comm.113)

Devagāndhārī[2] is hexatonic; ga is the first (svara) and niṣāda is omitted. Bhairavī is a complete rāga; pañcama is the first (svara). (114)

Ghūrjarī is known to be pentatonic; ga is the first (svara); ri and dha are omitted. Śrīrāga is hexatonic; dha is the first (svara) and ṛṣabha is omitted. (115)

Nīlāmbarī is hexatonic; ma is the first (svara) and ri is the omitted svara.

1. The commentary gives Devagāndhāri, āharī and śaṅkarābharaṇa as the feminine rāga-s of nāṭa.
2. This rāga does not find place in the earlier verses listing the feminine raga-s (v.109 v.112), though it is found in the commentary as a feminine raga of nāṭa.

Varālī is a hexatonic rāga, ga is the first (svara) and madhyama is omitted. (116)

(In) megharañjī, madhyama is the first (svara); dha and ni are omitted[1] and hence (it is) pentatonic. Velāhurī is pentatonic; gāndhāra is the first (svara); sa and ri are the omitted svara-s. (117)

Deśikārī[2] is complete, madhyama is known to be the first (svara). Malaharī is a hexatonic rāga; ga is the first (svara) and ṛṣabha is omitted. (118)

Deśī rāga is hexatonic, dha is the first (svara); niṣāda is omitted. Rāmakriyā is pentatonic; ga is the first (svara); ri and sa are the omitted svara-s. (119)

Toḍī is a complete rāga; gāndhāra is known to be the first (svara). Devakriyā is pentatonic, ni is the first (svara); ri and sa are the omitted svaras. (120)

Paḍamañjarī is said to be a hexatonic rāga; niṣāda is the first (svara) and ṛṣabha is the omitted svara. (121)

Kurañjī is pentatonic; ma is the first (svara); ni and sa are omitted. Guṇḍakriyā is a great rāga, called as heptatonic; gāndhāra is the first (svara) and madhyama is the omitted svara. The rāga sāraṅgā[3] is complete and pañcama is the first (svara). (122-123)

Vasanta is a hexatonic rāga; ni is the first (svara) and pañcama is omitted. Dhanyāśī is a hexatonic rāga; ga is the first (svara) and niṣāda is omitted. (124)

Lalitā is a hexatonic rāga; ni is the first (svara) and ga is the omitted svara. The rāga nāṭa is sampūrṇa; ṣaḍja is described as the first (svara) (125)

Āharī is a complete rāga; madhyama is called the first (svara). Kāmbodī is a complete rāga which is endowed with all the svara-s. (126)

Baṅgāla is a hexatonic rāga; ni is the first (svara) and ma is the omitted svara. Baulī is a hexatonic rāga; ni is the first (svara) and ga and ma are the

1. There seems to be a tendency to omit two successive svara-s as noticed in verse 117, 119, 120, 123 & 129.
2. This rāga does not find place in the earlier verses listing the feminine raga-s (v.109-v.112), nor in the commentary.
3. This rāga is not found in the commentary.

omitted svara-s. (127)

Bhūpāla is a hexatonic rāga; ga is the first (svara); ṣaḍja is omitted. Balahaṃsā is complete; gāndhāra is called the first (svara). (128)

(In) nārāyaṇī, niṣāda is the first (svara) and is called pentatonic; dhaivata and pañcama are the svara-s omitted respectively. (129)

The rāga śaṅkarābharaṇa[1] is complete; gāndhāra is said to be the first (svara). Hindola is heptatonic; ri is omitted; madhyama is the first (svara) (130)

These are the prominent rāga-s and their characteristics are emanated in order. [The mixed forms of rāga-s are of many kinds.] (131)

In this way, the Gods, having said the names of the thirty-two rāga-s and their sixty-four mitra-s, through this rāga classification, explained all other rāga-s. It is (how means) thus: (comm.131)

kāmbodi is known to be five-fold, nāṭa is known to be of five types, varāli is seven-fold and gaula is of eight kinds; dhanyāśī is of two kinds, thus are known the varieties of rāga-s.[2] (132)

kāmbodi - 5, nāṭa - 5, varāli - 7, gaula - 8, dhanyāśi - 2. In this way for the sake of shining, the rāga-s on becoming many fold, are said to be infinite in number, because of the division into śuddha, mitra and saṅkīrṇa. I shall tell the forms of these rāga-s. (comm.132)

bhairavi and bhūpāla belong to the priestly class, śrīrāga and pañjara (paḍamañjara) belong to the princely class, vasanta and mālavi belong to the merchant class, baṅgāla and nāṭa belong to the servant class. (133)

These are the classes of the rāga-s. (comm.133)

bhairavi and bhūpāla are white, śrīrāga and pañjara are red, vasanta and mālavī are yellow and baṅgāla and nāṭa are black. (134)

These are the colours for the rāga-s. (comm.134)

Śambhu, Viṣṇu, Śāradā, Lakṣmī, Bhāskara, Nārada, Gaṇeśa and Tumburu

1. This rāga does not find place in the earlier verses listing the feminine raga-s (v.109-v.112), though it is found in the commentary as a feminine raga of nāṭa.
2. This kind of classification probably refers to the rāga-s having similar suffixes.

are the (presiding) deities of the rāga-s. (135)

These are the presiding deities for the rāga-s. (comm.135)

sweet cake <modakaṃ>, eatable <bakṣya>, pure rice, curd rice, food made out of milk and sugar <pāyasam>, fruits, mixed rice and milk rice are the food of the rāga-s. (136)

They are the food of the rāga-s. (comm.136)

White, variegated, red, dark blue, turmeric (coloured), yellow, new cloth and silk cloth are the garments assigned for the rāga-s. (137)

These are the garments of the rāga-s. (comm.137)

Camphor, gorocana (an yellow pigment), sandal, musk, aloe, saffron, turmeric, fragrance/ perfume <sugandaṃ>[1] are said to be the perfumes of the rāga-s. (138)

These are are the perfumes for the rāga-s. (comm.138)

Diamond, pearl, sapphire, ruby, topaz, sardonyx, lapiz-lazuli <vaiḍūrya> and ruby are the ornaments of the rāga-s. (139)

These are the ornaments for the rāga-s. (comm.139)

Mace, sword, (horny) bow, spear, bow and arrow, plough, axe and short javelin are said to be the weapons of the rāga-s. (140)

These are the weapons for the rāga-s. (comm.140)

Jasmine, Jāti, Vakula, Kunda[2], Campaka, Ketakī, Droṇa and Pārijāta are said to be the flowers of the rāga-s. (141)

These are the flowers for the rāga-s. (comm.141)

Swan, Peacock, Parrot, the Bheruṇḍa bird, Cuckoo, Parrot, Cakravāka bird and the cakora bird are said to be the vehicles for the rāga-s. (142)

These are the vehicles of the rāga-s. (comm.142)

Grape, Jackfruit, Date, Wood-apple, Mango, Pomegranate, Coconut and Plantain are the trees of the rāga-s. (143)

These are the trees for the rāga-s. (comm.143)

Jambū, śāka, kuśa, krauñca, puṣkara, śveta, śālmali and navakhaṇḍa are

1. The term sugandham refers to fragrance in general and not to any particular fragrance.
2. Jāti and kunda are varieties of Jasmine.

the lands (regions) of the rāga-s. (144)

These are the lands (regions) for the rāga-s. (comm.144)

Pathos, heroism, love, disgust, terror, wonder, mirth and tranquil are the sentiments associated with the rāga-s. (145)

These are the sentiments for the rāga-s. (comm.145)

Water (pūrvāṣāḍā), Water (pūrvāṣāḍā)[1], uttarābhādra, uttarā, rohiṇī, maghā, mūlā, and maitrā (anurādhā) are said to be the birth-stars of the rāga-s respectively. (146)

These are the birth-stars of the rāga-s. (comm.146)

Thursday, Wednesday, Friday, Sunday, Thursday and Tuesday are the birth-days of the rāga-s respectively. (147)

These are the birth-days of the rāga-s. (comm.147)

Dhanus, dhanus, mīna, kanyā, vṛṣabha, siṃha, cāpa and vṛccika are the lagna-s[2] of the rāga-s. (148)

These are the lagna-s of the rāga-s. (comm.148)

Two, four and five are said to be the number of faces of the rāga-s; four, eight and ten are the number of arms of the rāga-s. (149)

These are the arms of the rāga-s. (comm.149)

Four, vasu (eight) and ten are said to be the number of eyes and nostrils of the rāga-s (150)

ṛgveda:bhairavi and bhūpāla; yajur(veda):śrīrāga and pañjara (paḍamañjara); sāma(veda) vasanta and mālavi and the remaining (atharvaṇa):baṅgāla and nāṭa. (151)

The rāga-s are known to be (born) in kinnara, yakṣa, kimpuruṣa, gandharva, siddha, tumbura, deva and nāga classes respectively. (152)

Viśvāmitra, Vasiṣṭa, Gautama, Atri, Bhṛgu, Śuka, Jamadagni and Bharadvāja are the Seers of the rāga-s. (153)

---

1. Water is said to be presiding-deity for the star pūrvāṣāḍā and Sun for anurā dh ā hence denoted thus (Information given by Sri Seshadri, Sanskrit Scholar, GOML, Chennai).
2. Probably these should be referred to as rāśi-s.

bhairavī and bhūpāla (are) strong, śrīrāga and pañjara (paḍamañjara) are even, vasanta and mālavi are crooked, baṅgāla and nāṭa are long/tall. (154)

These are the forms for the rāga-s.

For the rāga bhairavi, family:kinnara, class:priestly, colour:white, body:strong, faces:two, hands:four, ears:four, eyes:four, Seer:Viśvāmitra, land:kuśadvīpa, presiding deity:Īśvara, food:small round sweetmeat <modaka>; garment:white, perfume:camphor, ornament:diamond, weapon:mace, flower:jasmine, vehicle:swan, tree:grape, sentiment:pathos, star:pūrvāṣāḍā, day:Thursday, lagna:dhanus, chandas:ṛgveda[1], devakriya, megharañji and kurañji - these three are the wives.

devakriya because of five svara-s (present in it) is called pentatonic. niṣāda is the first (svara); ṛṣabha and ṣaḍja are omitted. ni ni ni- ga ga ga- ma ma ma- dha dha dha- pa pa pa- ni ga ma dha pa

megharañjī because of five svara-s is called pentatonic. madhyama is the first (svara); dhaivata and niṣāda are omitted. ma ma ma- sa sa sa- ri ri ri- ga ga ga- pa pa pa- ma sa ri ga pa

kurañjī because of five svara-s is called pentatonic. madhyama is the first (svara). niṣāda and ṣaḍja are omitted. ma ma ma- ri ri ri- ga ga ga- dha dha dha- pa pa pa- ma ri ga dha pa. These are the wives of bhairavi.

bhairavi is a complete rāga; pañcama is the first (svara) and consists of seven svara-s. pa pa pa- dha dha dha- ni ni ni- sa sa sa- ri ri ri- ga ga ga- ma ma ma- pa dha ni sa ri ga ma . In this way, it shines adorned with conch, discus and mace.

For the rāga bhūpāla, family:yakṣa; class:priestly; colour:white; presiding deity:Viṣṇu; garment:white; food:sweet cake; perfume:gorocana ornament:pearl; weapon:sword; flower:jasmine; vehicle:peacock; tree:jack; land:jambūdvīpa; sentiment:valour; star:pūrvāṣāḍā; day:Thursday; lagna:dhanur; face:four; arms:eight; eyes:eight; ears:eight; Seer:Vaśiṣṭa;

1. The word vēda found in mūla is taken as chandas by the commentator. Probably chandas here refers to vēdic hymns.

chandas:ṛgveda; body:strong. velāhuri, malahari and bauli are the wives.

velāhuri is pentatonic (consists of) five svara-s; gāndhāra is the first (svara); ṣaḍja and ṛṣabha are omitted. ga ga ga- ma ma ma- pa pa pa- dha dha dha- ni ni ni- ga ma pa dha ni- ma pa dha ni- pa dha ni dha ni- ni dha pa ma ga

malahari is heptatonic (consists of) six svara-s; dhaivata is the first (svara); niṣāda is omitted. dha dha dha- sa sa sa- ri ri ri- ga ga ga- ma ma ma- pa pa pa- dha sa ri ga ma pa- sa ri ga ma pa- ri ga ma pa- ga ma pa- ma pa- pa ma ga ri sa dha

bauli is pentatonic (consists of) five svara-s; niṣāda is the first (svara); madhyama and gāndhāra are omitted. ni ni ni- sa sa sa- ri ri ri- pa pa pa- dha dha dha- ni sa ri pa dha- sa ri pa dha- ri pa dha- pa dha- dha pa ri sa ni. These are the wives of bhūpāla

bhūpāla rāga is heptatonic (consists of) six svara-s; gāndhāra is the first (svara); ṣaḍja is omitted. ga ga ga- ri ri ri- ma ma ma- pa pa pa- dha dha dha- ni ni ni- ga ri ma pa dha ni- ri ma pa dha ni- ma pa dha ni- pa dha ni- dha ni- ni dha pa ma ri ga

In this way, the rāga bhūpāla shines.

śrīrāga; family:kimpuruṣa; class:princely; colour:red; body:even; presiding deity:Śāradā; food:ghee rice; garment:red; perfume:sandal; ornament:sapphire; weapon:bow; vehicle:mynah; tree:date; flower:vakula; land:śākadvīpa; sentiment:love; Seer:Gautama; day:Thursday; star:Uttarābhādra;lagna:mīna; chandas:yajurveda; faces:five; hands:ten; ears:ten; eyes:ten, hindolaṃ, balahamsā and sāverī are the wives.

hindola is heptatonic (consists of) six svara-s; madhyama is the first (svara); ṛṣabha is omitted. ma ma ma- sa sa sa- ga ga ga- pa pa pa- dha dha dha- ni ni ni- ma sa ga pa dha ni- sa ga pa dha ni- ga pa dha ni- pa dha ni- dha ni- ni dha pa ga sa ma

balahaṃsa is complete; (consists of) seven svara-s; gāndhāra is the first (svara). ga ga ga- ni ni ni- sa sa sa- ma ma ma- pa pa pa- dha dha dha- ri ri ri- ga ni sa ma pa dha ri- ni sa ma pa dha ri- sa ma pa dha ri- ma pa dha ri- pa dha ri- dha ri- ri dha pa ma sa ni ga sāverī rāga is pentatonic; madhyama is the first (svara); ṛṣabha and niṣāda are omitted. ma ma ma- pa pa pa- dha dha dha- sa sa sa- ga ga ga- ma pa dha sa ga- pa dha sa ga- dha sa ga- sa ga- ga sa dha pa ma. These are the wives of śrīrāga.

śrīrāga is heptatonic; (consists of) six svara-s; dhaivata is the first (svara); ṛṣabha is omitted. dha dha dha- ni ni ni- sa sa sa- ga ga ga- ma ma ma- pa pa pa- dha ni sa ga ma pa- ni sa ga ma pa- sa ga ma pa- ga ma pa- ma pa

For the rāga paḍamañjari, family:gandharva; class:princely; colour:red; presiding deity:Lakṣmī; food:curd rice; perfume:musk; ornament:ruby; weapon:spear; flower:jasmine; vehicle:bheruṇḍa bird; tree:clove; land:krauñcadvīpa; sentiment:disgust; star:uttarā; Day:Wednesday; lagna:kanyā; faces:two; arms:four; eyes:four; ears:four; Seer:Atri; chandas:yajurveda; body: even; garment:red, toḍi, lalita and deśi are its wives.

deśi is heptatonic; (consists of) six svara-s; dhaivata is the first (svara); ṛṣabha is omitted. dha dha dha- sa sa sa- ri ri ri- ga ga ga- ma ma ma- pa pa pa- dha sa ri ga ma pa- sa ri ga ma pa- ri ga ma pa- ga ma pa- ma pa- pa ma ga ri sa dha

lalitā is heptatonic; (consists of) six svara-s; niṣāda is the first (svara); gāndhāra is omitted. ni ni ni- sa sa sa- ri ri ri- ma ma ma- pa pa pa- dha dha dha- ni sa ri ma pa dha- sa ri ma pa dha- ri ma pa dha- ma pa dha- pa dha- dha pa ma ri sa ni

toḍi is complete; gāndhāra is the first (svara). ga ga ga- ri ri ri- sa sa sa- ma ma ma- pa pa pa- dha dha dha- ni ni ni - ga ri sa ma pa dha ni- ri sa ma pa dha ni- sa ma pa dha ni- ma pa dha ni- pa dha ni- dha ni - ni dha pa ma sa ri ga

paḍamañjari rāga is heptatonic; (consists of) six svara-s; niṣāda is the first (svara); ṛṣabha is omitted. ni ni ni- sa sa sa- ga ga ga- ma ma ma- pa pa pa- dha dha dha- ni sa ga ma pa dha- sa ga ma pa dha- ga ma pa dha- ma pa dha- pa dha- dha pa ma ga ri sa ni

For the rāga vasanta, family:siddha; class:merchant; colour:yellow; presiding deity:Sun; food:fruits; garment:yellow; perfume:aloe; ornament:topaz; weapon:bow and arrow; flower:gold flower; vehicle:cuckoo;

tree:mango; land:puṣkaradvīpa; sentiment:terror; star:rohiṇi; day:Friday; lagna:vṛṣabha; faces:four; arms:eight; eyes:eight; ears:eight; body:crooked; Seer:Bhṛgu; metre:sāmaveda; rāmakriya, varāli and kauśika are the three wives.

rāmakriyā because of five svara-s is called pentatonic; gāndhāra is the first (svara); ṛṣabha is omitted. ga ga ga- ma ma ma- pa pa pa- dha dha dha- ni ni ni- ga ma pa dha ni- ma pa dha ni- pa dha ni- dha ni- ni dha pa ma ga

varāli is heptatonic; (consists of) six svara-s; gāndhāra is the first (svara); madhyama is omitted. ga ga ga- sa sa sa- ri ri ri- pa pa pa- dha dha dha- ni ni ni- ga sa ri pa dha ni- sa ri pa dha ni- ri pa dha ni- pa dha ni- dha ni- ni dha pa ri sa ga

kauśika is a complete rāga; (consists of) seven svara-s. ga ga ga- sa sa sa- ri ri ri- ma ma ma- pa pa pa- dha dha dha- ni ni ni- ga sa ri ma pa dha ni- sa ri ma pa dha ni- ri ma pa dha ni- ma pa dha ni- pa dha ni- dha ni- ni dha pa ma ri sa ga. These are the wives of vasanta rāga.

For the rāga vasanta:- because of six svara-s it is heptatonic; niṣāda is the first (svara); pañcama is omitted. ni ni ni- ri ri ri- ga ga ga- ma ma ma- dha dha dha- sa sa sa- ni ri ga ma gha sa- ri ga ma dha sa - ga ma dha sa- ma dha sa- dha sa- sa dha ma ga ri ni.

For the rāga mālavi, family:tumburu; class:merchant; colour:yellow; presiding deity:Nārada; food:dish prepared out of milk and sugar; garment:turmeric coloured; perfume:saffron; ornament:gomedhika; weapon:plough; flower:mangrove; vehicle:deer; tree:pomegranate; land:śvetadvīpa; sentiment:wonder; star:maghā; day:Sunday; lagna:; faces:five; arms:ten; eyes:ten; ears:ten; body:crooked; metre:sāmaveda; Seer:Śaunaka; nārāyaṇi, guṇḍakriya and ghurjari - these are the wives.

nārāyaṇi is pentatonic; (consists of) five svara-s; niṣāda is the first (svara); dhaivata and pañcama are omitted. ni ni- sa sa- ri ri- ga ga- ma ma- ni sa ri ga ma- sa ri ga ma- ri ga ma- ga ma- ma ga ri sa ni- ga ri sa ni- ri sa ni- sa ni

guṇḍakriya because of six svara-s is heptatonic; gāndhāra is the first (svara); madhyama is omitted ga ga ga- sa sa sa- ri ri ri- pa pa pa- dha dha dhani ni ni- ga sa ri pa dha ni- sa ri pa dha ni- ri pa dha ni- pa dha ni- dha ni- ni dha pa ri sa ga- dha pa ri sa ga- pa ri sa ga- ri sa ga- sa ga

ghurjari because of five svara-s is pentatonic; gāndhāra is the first (svara); riṣabha and daivata are omitted ga ga ga- sa sa sa- ma ma ma- pa pa pa- ni ni ni- ga sa ma pa ni- sa ma pa ni- ma pa ni- pa ni- ni pa ma sa ga- pa ma sa ga- ma sa ga- sa ga These are the wives for the rāga mālavi.

mālavi is a complete rāga; (consists of) seven svara-s; gāndhāra is the first (svara). ga ga ga- sa sa sa- ri ri ri- ma ma ma- pa pa pa- dha dha dha- ni ni ni- ga sa ri ma pa dha ni- sa ri ma pa dha ni- ri ma pa dha ni- ma pa dha ni- pa dha ni- dha ni- ni dha pa ma ri sa ga- dha pa ma ri sa ga - pa ma ri sa ga- ma ri sa ga - ri sa ga- sa ga

For the rāga baṅgāla, family:God; class:servant; colour:darkblue; presiding deity;vināyaka; food:mixed rice; garment:new cloth; perfume:turmeric; ornament:lapiz-lazuli; weapon:axe; flower:droṇa; vehicle:cakravāka bird; tree:Coconut; land:puṣkaradvīpa; sentiment:mirth; star:mūlā; day:Thursday; zodiac:Sagittarius; faces:two; arms:four; eyes:four; ears:four; body:tall; Seer:Jamadagni; metre:ṛgveda; dhanyāśi, kāmbodi and nīlāmbari are the wives.

dhanyāśi because of six svara-s is heptatonic; gāndhāra is the first (svara); niṣāda is omitted. ga ga ga- sa sa sa- ri ri ri- ma ma ma- pa pa pa- dha dha dha- ga sa ri ma pa dha- sa ri ma pa dha- ri ma pa dha- ma pa dha- pa dha- dha pa ma ri sa ga- pa ma ri sa ga- ma ri sa ga- ri sa ga- sa ga-

kāmbodi because of six svara-s is heptatonic; madhyama is the first (svara); ṛṣabha is omitted. ma ma- sa sa- ga ga- pa pa- dha dha- ni ni- ma sa ga pa dha ni- sa ga pa dha ni- ga pa dha ni- pa dha ni- dha ni- ni dha pa ga sa ma- dha pa ga sa ma- pa ga sa ma- ga sa ma- sa ma-

nīlāmbari because of six svara-s is heptatonic; madhyama is the first (svara); ṛṣabha is omitted. ma ma ma- sa sa sa- ga ga ga- pa pa pa- dha dha dha- ni ni ni- ni dha pa ga sa ma- dha pa ga sa ma- pa ga sa ma- ga sa ma- sa ma- ma sa ga pa dha ni- sa ga pa dha ni- ga pa dha ni- pa dha ni- dha ni- These are the wives of baṅgāla

baṅgāla is pentatonic because of five svara-s; niṣāda is the first (svara); gāndhāra and madhyama are omitted. ni ni ni- sa sa sa- ri ri ri- pa pa pa- dha dha dha- ni sa ri pa dha- sa ri pa dha- ri pa dha- pa dha- dha pa ri sa ni- pa ri sa ni- ri sa ni- sa ni

For the rāga nāṭa, family:Nāga; class:servant; colour:darkblue; presiding deity:Tumburu; food:milk rice; garment:silk cloth; perfume:sandal; ornament:ruby; weapon:arrow; flower:pārijāta; vehicle:cakora bird; tree:plantain; land:navakhaṇḍa; sentiment:tranquil; star:anurādhā; day:Tuesday; zodiac:Scorpion; faces:four; arms:eight; ears:eight; eyes:eight; body:tall?; Seer:Bhāradvāja; metre:atharvaṇaveda. devagāndhāri, śaṅkarābharaṇaṃ and āhari these are (its) wives.

devagāndhāri because of six svara-s is heptatonic; gāndhāra is the first (svara); niṣāda is omitted. ga ga- sa sa- ri ri- ma ma- pa pa- dha dha- ga sa ri ma pa dha- sa ri ma pa dha- ri ma pa dha- ma pa dha- pa dha- dha pa ma ri sa ga- pa ma ri sa ga- ma ri sa ga- ri sa ga- sa ga

For śaṅkarābharaṇa seven svara-s; (it is a) complete rāga; dhaivata is the first (svara). dha dha- ni ni- sa sa- ri ri- ga ga- ma ma- pa pa- dha ni sa ri ga ma pa- ni sa ri ga ma pa- sa ri ga ma pa- ri ga ma pa- ga ma pa- ma pa- pa ma ga ri sa ni dha- ma ga ri sa ni dha- ga ri sa ni dha- ri sa ni dha- sa ni dha- ni dha

āhari is a complete rāga; (consists of) seven svara-s; madhyama is the first (svara). ma ma- ri ri- sa sa- ga ga- dha dha- pa pa- ni ni- ma ri sa ga dha pa ni- ri sa ga dha pa ni- sa ga dha pa ni- ga dha pa ni- dha pa ni- pa ni- ni pa dha ga sa ri ma- pa dha ga sa ri ma- dha ga sa ri ma- ga sa ri ma- sa ri ma- ri ma.

nāṭa rāga (consists of) seven svara-s; (it is) complete; ṣaḍja is the first (svara). sa sa sa- ri ri ri- ga ga ga- ma ma ma- pa pa pa- dha dha dha- ni ni ni- sa ri ga ma pa dha ni- ri ga ma pa dha ni- ga ma pa dha ni- ma pa dha ni- pa dha ni- dha ni- ni dha pa ma ga ri sa- dha pa ma ga ri sa- pa ma ga ri sa- ma ga ri sa- ga ri sa- ri sa. (comm.154)

deśākṣarī, gāndhāri (devagāndhārī?), sāraṅgā, bhairavī, devakriyā, raktahaṃsi, mālavī, rāgapañjara (paḍamañjari), bhūpāla, mukhārī, hindolī and ghūrjarī are said to be born at the time of sun-rise. In the evenings they are prohibited. A person by whom it is sung in the day, brings pleasure. (155-156)

deśākṣari, devagāndhāri, sāraṅgā, bhairavi, devakriyā, raktahamsi, mālavi, paḍamañjari, bhūpālaṃ, mukhāri, hindolaṃ, ghurjari - these rāga-s were born during sun-rise. These are to be sung in the mornings. (comm.156)

āhari and śaṅkarābhūṣā (śaṅkarābharaṇa) are to be sung in the evenings. (157)

āhari and śaṅkarābharaṇa are to be sung in the evenings. (comm.157)

All other rāga-s shine when sung in the forenoon, afternoon and noon. (158)

The remaining rāga-s are to be sung in the fore-noon, noon and afternoon. Thus is (said) the time for (singing) the rāga-s. (comm.158)

The mitra-s of the rāga-s like mukhārī, revagupti, ghaṇṭāra, mādhava and others are those that are born from the tradition <deśī>. (159)

The sixty-four mitrarāga-s starting with mukhāri, regupti, kāpi, ghaṇṭā mādhavi[?] and others are said to be born of deśī. (comm.159)

heptatonic, pentatonic and complete rāga-s, through the transposition and the permutation of the seven svara-s in order give rise to prastāra-s. (160)

The seven svara-s on changing their own positions, become a five-svara variety, a six-svara variety and a seven-svara variety. On permutations, thirty-two rāga-s become sixty-four mitrarāga-s, by means of the groups of (svara-s) in caturaṅgaprastāra[1].

bhairavi fourth column, first house[2]. the first svara. mālavi, varāli, kauśika, and guṇḍakriya, - for these four, first column, first house. For megharañji, first column, fourth house; nārāyaṇi, first column, sixth house; balahamsa,

1. This is then followed by lists of 32 rāga-s with the svara-s occuring in them arranged in the order in which they have been described in the previous commentary. Later another table is given, which contains the svara-s in a specific format. The following description is based on this table.
2. The svara in the corresponding square seems to denote the beginning svara of the rāga.

first column, seventh house; rāmakriya, second column, fourth house; kurañji and kāmbodi second column, sixth house; for bhūpāla and toḍi, third column, fifth house; velāhuri, fourth column, third house; for nāṭa, fourth column, fourth house; for the rāga vasanta, fourth column, seventh house; for śaṅkarābharaṇa, fifth column, first house; for śrīrāga, fifth column, third house; devakriya and paḍamañjari, fifth column, fourth house; for bauli, lalita and baṅgāla, sixth column, first house; for sāveri and nīlāmbari, sixth column, fourth house; for hindola, sixth column, eighth house; for dhanyāśi and devagāndhāri, eighth column, third house; for ghūrjari, seventh column, seventh house; for malahari, eighth column, first house; for āhiri, eighth column, third house; for deśi, eighth column, first house.

mālavi and kauśika have a same scale <mela>[1]. dhanyāśi and devagāndhāri have a same scale <mela>. guṇḍakriya and varāli have a same scale <mela>. rāmakriya and velāhuri have a same scale <mela>. toḍi and balahamsa have a same scale <mela>. bauli and baṅgāla have a same scale <mela>. hindolaṃ and kāmbodi have a same scale <mela>. āhiri and nīlāmbari have a same scale <mela>. malahari, deśi, śaṅkarābharaṇa, śrīrāga these are mitra-s with relation to the svara-s[2]. The sixty four svara-s in the sixty four houses of this caturaṅgaprastāraṃ is related to the mitra rāga-s. bhūpālaṃ, mālavi, kauśika, guṇḍakriya, dhanyāśi, devagāndhāri, varāli, toḍi, rāmakriya, balahaṃsa, velāhuri and ghūrjari - these are mitra-s through the related svara-s. nīlāmbari, kāmbodi, hindolaṃ, megharañji, kurañji, sāveri and āhiri - these are mitra-s (because of) the relation between the svara-s. nārāyaṇi, lalita, paḍamañjiri, vasanta, devakriya, bauli, baṅgāla - (these are) mitra-s through the related svara-s. bhairavi is related to thirty two rāga-s with svara-s[?]. For nāṭa [incomplete?] (comm.160)

Lineage, class, age, colour, form and origin are the characteristics of thirty-two rāga-s, spoken according to Somanātha. (161)

1. The term mēla is used here in the sense of a scale or an arrangement of svara-s in arāga.
2. The term mitra here probably means those rāga-s having similar commencing notes.

In the treatise called Somanāthiyyaṃ, lineage, class, age, colour, form and origin are the characteristics that have been mentioned for the thirty-two rāga-s. (comm.161)

Having examined various rāga-s, the 'dhīmān' should sing with great effort, with the instruments or the svara-s produced by the voice or through both and should be devoid of any blemish. (162)

In this way, knowing the form (or qualities) of the rāga (-s), by removing the defects of the instruments and voice, the experts, having sung thirty two rāga-s, sixty four mitra-s (rāga-s) and many saṅkīrṇa rāga-s, should play them on the instruments. (comm.162)

Varieties of singers

Singers are known to be of three kinds, namely, ekala, yamala and bṛnda. When only one (person) sings, (he) is called ekala. When he sings alongwith another person, (he) is yamala; when he sings with a group, (he) is a bṛndagāyaka. (163)

Singers are of three varieties:- ekala, yamala and bṛnda. if one sings alone, he is called ekala. If two (people) sing, he (they are?) is called yamala. if he sings with many, he is called bṛnda. (comm.163)

Blemishes of a singer

sandaṣṭa, udghuṣṭa, sītkāra, bhīta, kampita, śaṅkita, karāli, kapila, kāki, vitāla, karabha, unmada, sāmbaka, tumbakī, vakrī, prasārī, vinimīlaka, virasa, apasvara, avyakta, sthānabhraṣṭaṃ, avyavasthita, miśraka, anavadhāna, anunāsikā - these twenty-five (singers) are to be censured. (164-166)

sandaṣṭa, udghuṣṭa, sītkāra, bhīta, kampita, śaṅkita, karāli, kapila, kāki, vitāla, karabha, unmada, sāmbaka, tumbaki, vakri, prasāri, vinimīlaka, virasa, apasvara, avyakta, sthānabhraṣṭa, avyavasthita, miśraka, anavadhāna, anunāsika - these twenty-five blemishes are censured for a singer. The characteristics of each of them. (comm.166)

One who sings with compressed teeth, he is called sandaṣṭa. (167ab)

When it is sung with the teeth and the jaws compressed, it is called sandaṣṭa[1]. (comm.167ab)

(Singing) with a loud spreading voice is udghuṣṭa; sītkāri is (singing) with a shivering voice frequently. (167cd)

Singing in an unpleasant manner, with a loud sound is called udghuṣṭaṃ (2) Singing with a shivering voice repeatedly is called sītkāraṃ (3) (comm.167cd)

The singer who is seized with fear is (called) bhīta; singing in haste is called śaṅkita.[2] (168ab)

Singing with fear is called bhītaṃ (4) singing with high speed is called śaṅkitaṃ (5). (comm.168ab)

Kampita is known by the natural (involuntary) shaking of limbs and voice. (168cd)

Singing by shaking the whole body is called kampitaṃ (6). (comm.168cd)

Karālaṃ is called by the wise as (the music) produced by keeping the mouth wide open. (169ab)

Singing with a low and high tone is called karāli (7) (comm.169ab)

He is called kapila, who sings the svara-s with less or more śruti-s. (169cd)

Singing the svara-s, with the śruti, going up and down is called kapilaṃ (8). (comm.169cd)

Kākī is the one whose voice is as hoarse as that of a crow; vitāla is inept with regard to tāla. (170ab)

Singing in a harsh manner is called kāki (9); singing by ignoring the tāla is called vitālaṃ (10) (comm.170ab)

Karambha is called by the learned as the one who bears a shaking head. (170cd)

Singing with the head (kept) shaking is called karambha (11) (comm.170cd)

---

1. While the mūla reads the blemishes in noun forms the commentary treats them as a quality.
2. Translation to the verses that are identical to those of SR is based on SR Translation (vol-2) by Premlata Sharma and R K Shringy.

One whose voice is shaky like a lamb, while doing vahanī is (called) unmada[1], the inferior singer. Singing with the face and throat kept stiff like a stone, is sāmbaka. (171)

Singing with the throat lifted and kept high is called sāmbaka (12). (comm.171)

The singer who inflates his throat like a gourd is (called) tumbakī. (172ab)

Singing in an unbearable manner, with the cheeks bitten is called bakī (13) (comm.172ab)

One who twists his neck while singing is declared by the wise as vakrī. (172cd)

Keeping the neck aside and singing is called vakri (14). (comm.172cd)

One who stretches his limbs while projecting his song is called prasārī by experts. (173ab)

Rotating the neck and singing is called prasāri (15). (comm.173ab)

One who closes his eyes while singing is known to be a nimīlaka. (173cd)

Singing with closed eyes is called nimīlaka (16). (comm.173cd)

Virasa is the one who is devoid of rasa; apasvara is known by the singing of the svara omitted. (174ab)

Singing devoid of emotions is called virasaṃ (17); singing an irrelevant svara <apasvara> is called apasvara (18). (comm.174ab)

One having a faltering voice and an indistinct pronounciation is said to be avyakta. (174cd)

Singing with fluttering voice is avyaktaṃ (19). (comm.174cd)

Sthānabhraṣṭa is one who is unable to reach the three registers. (175ab)

One who is unable to sing in the mandra, madhyama and tāra (regions) is called sthānabhraṣṭa (20). (comm.175ab)

---

1. The commentary does not seem to interpret unmada at all, though the original text is similar to SR.

Avyavasthita is so called because of disorganised (singing) with reference to the registers. (175cd)

Singing of the three registers, without confining to rules, is avyavasthitaṃ (21). (comm.175cd)

The one who mixes up the śuddha and chāyālaga rāga-s, and also when he intermixes (confuses) other rāga-s he is known to be miśraka. (176)

Singing 'kalpita-s' in 'ghana'[1] is called miśraka (22). (comm.176)

One who lacks concentration in the rendering of sthāyi and others is called anavadhānaka. (177ab)

Singing without the knowledge of sthāyī, svara, yeḍupu, āyata, pratyāyataṃ, ḍālu, kampitaṃ, ugraṃ and muktāyī is called anavadhāna[2] (23). (comm.177ab)

The one who sings the melody through the nose is called anunāsika. (177cd)

Singing with the nose is called anunāsika (24); the one who is endowed with these is unfit to sing. (comm.177cd)

Now the qualities of a singer

In the world, he is the singer, who has a sweet voice (lit. speech), who is eminent, firm-minded, together endowed with a good appearance, (He should be) knowledgeable in the time measure <tāla>, a great scholar, a preceptor, knowledgeable in the ādi and graha[?], knowing the sense of the rāga-s completely, (he is) a leader, who is brilliant, deprived of defects and who knows the mind of other patron [audience?]. (178)

He is known to be a singer, who sings the ṣāḍava, auḍava, sampūrṇa, śuddha, sālaga and saṅkara rāga-s, with the knowledge of svara-s. (179)

He is a singer who is clever in his speech, who knows the minds of the audience, who creates music of svara-s and rāga-s on instruments and voice

1. The commentator interprets śuddha rāga as ghana rāga.
2. Probably sthāya has not been taken in the sense of sthāya as found in SR but in the sense of sthāyi (first among the ten varieties of svara s).

and who is familiar with ṣāḍava, auḍava, sampūrṇa, śuddha, sālaga, saṅkara, graha, mūrchanā, ārohiṇi, avarohiṇī, sthāyi, svara, sañcārī, āyata, pratyāyata, yeḍupu, ḍālu, ṭhāyi, ugraṃ, muktāyi, kampitaṃ, the masculine and feminine rāga-s, mitra alongwith saṅkīrṇa, the characteristics of thirty-two rāga-s, gīta svara nāda, vādi, anuvādi, samvādi, vivādi, the characteristics of svara-s, the time appropriate <tālakāla>, the time specified to sing the rāga-s <rāgakāla>, the characteristics of the seven svara-s, svaraprastāra, rāgaprastāra, the qualities and defects of svara-s and rāga-s, the characteristics of sound <dhvanibheda>, the production of tāna, alaṅkāra, the defects of singer and kinds of singers. (comm.179)

The characteristics of the svara-s and the rāga-s have been spoken by Somanātha. (180)

For the benefit of the world (people), the characterisitcs and practice of svara and rāga have been spoken by Somanātha in this treatise (Bharata, a confluence of dance music and drumming). Thus concludes the chapter on gīta of Saṅgītaratnākara, composed by Aṣṭāvadhāna Somappa, having collected from Saṅgītaratnākara, in a concise way, on the instrument and vocal (music)[1]. (comm.180)

Now gīta

Singing using the svara-s and rāga-s, with the text based on eight languages and incorporating the "jhaṅkāra" sound is called gīta (song) .(181)

Singing based on the text drawn from eight languages, incorporating the "jhaṅkāra" sound and based on svara-s and rāga-s, is called gīta. (comm.181)

Now prabandha

King Pratāpa calls it prabandha, since it is composed of four, five or six aṅga-s. (182)

svara, birudaṃ, padaṃ, tenaka, pāṭha and vākyaṃ are the six aṅga-s of

1. This is a significant portion of the Commentary, where Sōmanārya is said to be the author of Saṅgītaratnākara.

prabandha and are the integral parts of the configuration of prabandha[1]. Of these tena and pāda reflecting auspiciousness and meaning respectively, are its two eyes, pāṭa and biruda are the two hands. (183-184)

[NOT CLEAR] (185)

[NOT CLEAR] On seeing some such dance <naṭanaṃ>, one gets liberated from all the sins. (186)

When four, five or six aṅga-s are assembled together, then the King calls it the prabandha. That prabandha consists of six aṅga-s. They are svara, biruda, pada, tannakāra, pāṭha and vākya. These six are together called prabandha. tannakāra is to be used for auspicious purpose. Where the tenna and pada occur, there pāṭa, biruda and ḍālu[?] are to be said. ??? Those who see the performance of this prabandha dance, are liberated from all the sins. Those who listen, are endowed with all prosperity. (Comm.186)

With the seven tāla-s, dhruva and others and the text based on all languages, the singing of the svara-s and rāga-s, is called sūlādi. (187)

With the seven tāla-s. dhruva and others, singing of the svara-s and rāga -s, based on the text in all languages is called sūlādi. (comm.187)

The singing of words from the veda-s[?] is known as nāmāvalī[2]. 188ab

Singing of the words from stotra-s (hymns in praise of God) is nāmāvali. (comm.188ab)

Singing in saṃskṛta the form of sentences is called cūrṇīka (188cd)

Singing of sentences in saṃskṛta is called cūrṇīka (Comm 188cd)

Use of cūrṇīka, prose and verse and rendering of song relating to a story is nāṭakaṃ [?] (189ab)

With the cūrṇika, (prose) sentences and verses, the description of a story is called nāṭakaṃ (comm.189ab)

The characteristics of these will be expounded by Somasūri. (189cd)

Thus ends the chapter on gīta named Svararāgasudhārasa.

1. In the popular textual tradition, tāla is regarded as one of the limbs of a prabandha, which is substituted in NC by vākya.
2. Nāmāvali is mentioned as a dance form in Nartananirṇaya (NN, 4, 640-641ab) There is an extract from Vēda in Bharatakōśa (p.327) (Saṅgītamakaranda?) which describes Nāmāvali as a variety of dēśinṛtta.

[3. Vādhyādhyāya]

Now Instruments

The characteristics of the five-fold classification of instruments are being said.

(These are the instruments that are) born of nails (chordo-phones) born of air (Aero-phones), born of skin (membrano-phones), born of metal (Idio-phones/Auto-phones) and (the musical sound) born of the human body. Vīṇā and others are called nakha; flute and others are blown with air; those (instruments that are) born of skin are mṛdaṅga and others, those born of metals are cymbals. They (śārīra) are made up of the sound from the human body (voice). Thus instruments are known to be of five kinds. (1-2)

Sound is of five kinds as expressed by the varieties of instruments. (They are) nakhaṃ (born of nails), vāyuja (born of air), carmaja (born of skin), loha (born of metal) and śārīra (born of the human body). These five are of many kinds. The stringed instruments such as vīṇā, kinnarī, daṇḍī rajābu, kāmākṣī are born of nails <nakhaja>. The (air) blowing instruments such as murali, nāgasara, devasara, śaṅkha, mukhavīṇā and upāga are born of air <vāyuja>. The skin instruments like mṛdaṅga, bheri and ḍhakkā, are born of skin <carmaja>. Tāla (the instrument, cymbal) is born of metal <lohaja>. Gātra (human voice) is called śārīra. All these instruments incorporate the musical idea <nāda> of the human body. I shall tell the individual characteristics of these instruments. (comm.2)

Now vīṇā

kacchapi, kubjikā, citrā, mahatī, parivādinī, jāyā, ghoṣāvatī, jyeṣṭā and nakulā are mentioned[?] mahatī, vaiṣṇavī, brāhmī, raudrī, kūrmī, rāvaṇī, sarasvatī, kinnarī, saurandrī and ghoṣakā- (thus vīṇā -s are of ten types based on the (length) of strings. (3-4)

These ten vīṇā-s, consists of the frets, strings ?? NOT CLEAR. (comm.4)

In the vīṇā and men, the śruti-s are produced in the three sthāna-s (registers/

octaves). There is a speciality in the vīṇā...... INCOMPLETE? (5)

We obtain a successively higher pitch as we move up. On the vīṇā, however, the pitch is successively higher as we move down. These specific sounds are known as śruti-s because the ear can distinguish them. (6)

For the human beings, the (sthāna-s) mandra, madhya and tāra are produced one above the other. (The śruti-s in mandra and others?). mandra-mandra, mandra-madhyama, mandra-tāraka, madhyama-mandra, madhyama-madhyama, madhyama-tāraka, tāraka-mandra, tāraka-madhya and tāraka-tāraka. (comm.6)

These variations are sixty-six in number and are born in the three registers <sthāna>. Each of these has been described as containing the twenty-two distinct sounds (namely, the śruti-s that span an octave). When extended to include the mandra and the other (octave, namely, tāra) the range extends to sixty-six śruti-s. (7)

The sound variations are said to be twenty-two in the mandra, madhyama and tāra (regions). They, on compounding, become sixty-six sound varieties. These sixty-six sounds are produced as mandra madhyama and tāra. (comm.7)

The instrument vīṇā is made in the form of the human body.

The seven strings of the seven stringed vīṇā incorporates the seven svara-s. By seeing and touching (the vīṇā), one gets rid of the sin of killing a Brāhmin. (8)

This vīṇā brings about prosperity to the one who listens to it. (comm.8)

Now Kinnarī

[NOT CLEAR] (9)

Music, drumming and dance being based on laya, when played on the strings, then it is called kinnarī. (comm.9)

---

1. SP describes a two stringed instrument by this name (SP 2, 65-66)

Now Daṇḍi[1]

Daṇḍikā is born of (made of) khādira (Acacia catechu) and measures twelve muṣṭi-s[1]. Its circumference is two aṅgula-s[2] and is made of bronze and silver. (10)

The nābhi portion is made of bronze and is of four aṅgula-s. The front portion of the tumba, is pierced with a needle for a length of four aṅgula-s. (11)

[NOT CLEAR. The purport seems to be that two strings should be stretched between the patrikā and nābhi made of earth] (12)

With the same strings, between the nābhi, (it) should be wound four times in four different ways. (13)

The right string incorporates the svara, pañcama; the left string is known to incorporate the svara, ṣaḍja. (14)

There should be two jīvikā-s, of the measure of one aṅgula each. (15)

The presiding deities of the first string is Śiva and (of) the other is Pārvatī; of the daṇḍa is the Earth, the tumbu is Brahmā. Sarasvatī is the (presiding) deity of nābhi and of the kakubha is Viṣṇu. Of the patrikā is Kamalā (Lakṣmī?) and jīvikā is the moon[3] (16-17)

Daṇḍikā is pervaded by all Gods and protects (one) from fear. The singer should dexterously play the daṇḍikā with the index finger. (18)

In conformity of the view of Dattila, the characteristics of daṇḍikā were said. (19)

Invocation[4]

I salute Vāṇī (Sarasvatī), who grants boons, who is seated on the lotus flower, who holds the vīṇā in the tāṇḍava of Vimalalocana (?); I worship Devī, who captures the hearts of' [?] and whose speech is tender and soft. (20)

1. One muṣṭi is the measure of ones fist.
2. Aṅgula is a measure equal to eight barley-corns, a fingers breadth.
3. Similar description is found in works like SR (SR 6,55-56)
4. This kind of invocatory verse is found at many places in this work after the description of the instrument.

The singer should salute the daṇḍī, which possesses all such characteristics, hold and play the mandra, madhyama and tāraka svara-s, with the fingers starting with the index finger. (comm.20)

Now Tumbura[1]

The instrument called Tumbura was created by Viśvakarma (an artisan). It is made to a length of five tāla-s[2], the dharana (stem?) should be made. (21)

First is the kumbha to the width of two tāla-s and at the centre is the stem <hasta> measuring two tāla-s. In the portion ahead, for a length of one tāla (the stem) consists of a hole and the tip portion has the face of a lion. On either side of the hole, seven pegs should be introduced. (22)

Seven strings on having wound (to the pegs) are tied to the bottom of the kumbha. The centre of the kumbha, is elevated and the seven strings are placed on it. (23)

Invocation

I salute Tumbura endowed with seven strings for the seven svara-s. (24)

The singer should play on the Tumbura with perfection by the index finger. The characteristics of Tamburā have been expounded by Somanātha earlier. (25)

The singer should play the Tambura endowed with these characteristics with the index finger and others. Rajābu, Rāvaṇahastaṃ, Kāmākṣī - all these (instruments) are inclusive in this (belong to this category of stringed instruments) (comm.25)

Thus (are said), the (characteristics of) stringed instruments.

1. SP also speaks of a stringed instrument by this name (SR 2, 47-51)
2. One tāla is a measure equivalent to a span, i.e., the distance between the thumb and the middle finger.

Now Muralī

(Muralī) should be made with a bamboo of good quality to a length of twelve aṅgula-s. In the beginning, a hole should be made to blow in the air. (26)

Seven holes should be made beneath that, at a distance of one aṅgula each. The instrumentalist should play (the instrument) by holding (the muralī) with the sarpaśīrṣa hasta[1]. (27)

In the root nada (?) presides Viṣṇu, at the centre is Brahmā, in the front is Śiva. The presiding deity of Muralī is Hari. (28)

Invocation

I salute Muralī, which is in the form of Parabrahmā, consisting of seven svara-s in the seven holes. (29)

Having acquired good bamboo, making it to a length of twelve aṅgula-s, (and then) making a hole in the beginning, seven holes are made underneath. The Muralī is to be played with the sarpaśirṣahasta. (comm.29)

The characteristics of Muralī were spoken by Somanātha earlier. (30)

Now Mukhavīṇā

The characteristics of mukhavīṇā are being expounded by Yājñavalkya. The conical tube/stem (Daṇḍa) is made of khādira, red sandal or silver. (31)

Its body is to a length of twelve aṅgula-s. Seven holes should be made (to) the number of seven svara-s. (32)

Below the hole (From the hole at the bottom?) niṣāda is sounded. The first part is ṛgveda; the second should be yajurveda; on the third is atharvaṇa and the sāmaveda are the svarā-s [?] Jīvāla is of one aṅgula and the ring is made of ivory [or surrounded by ivory? - NOT CLEAR]. (33-34)

[NOT CLEAR] A specimen of the Daṇḍa is made by me through deception [?] (35)

1. sarpaśirṣa hasta: the fingers including the thumb to be close to one another and the palm to be hollowed. (NS , translation, 1967:181)

Invocatory verse

I salute the Sun God, of universal existence, one who is seated on the Lotus, who bestows boons to the people like the mandāru tree, that grants boons to the whole world. I salute NOT CLEAR (36)

In the early days, the Sun God played Mukhavīṇa. The Mukhavīṇa endowed with these characteristics, should be held and played. (comm.36)

The characteristics of mukhavīṇa are expounded by Somanārya. (37)

Nāgasara[1]

From the five faces of Śiva, the five svara-s are born. The snake sings on listening to it and hence is called 'phaṇināgasvara'. I shall speak the qualities of this instrument in accordance to the earlier views. (38)

Long ago, five svara-s were born from the five faces of Parameśvara. Those five svara-s were heard and sung by Śeṣa (snake). That instrument was called 'pāmulanāgasvara'. I shall tell the characteristics of that ancient instrument. (comm.38)

Having made a cavity of the fruit of the bottle-gourd <alābu> to a measure of twelve aṅgula-s and having placed the wax to the lower region of it and having made a tube <jīvāla> of four aṅgula-s, then two bamboo tubes, measuring to a length of sixteen aṅgula-s (should be made and) everything should be made into one (should be combined with each other). (39-40)

At the end of the bamboo, having placed a bronze ring [?], below the bamboo tube, one hole should be made and above that, seven holes should be drilled. [NOT CLEAR']. The presiding deities of the gourd <alābu> is Brahmā; jīvāla is Viṣṇu; bamboo is Īśa; of the holes are the eight mūrti-s[2]; (presiding deities of) the metal (bronze) is the Sun God and wax is the Earth. (41-43)

1. SP mentions a wind instrument by this name (SP 2,148-149).
2. In Tantraśāstra, Śiva is known through the eight forms, called eight murthi-s. They are sarva, bhava, rudra, ugra, bhīma, paśupati, mahādēva and īśāna (Śabda kalpadruma).

This instrument is called sarpanāgasara by Bharata and others. (44)

The syllable 'na' is known to be (denotes) nāda; the syllable 'ga' is called (denotes) gānaṃ. It is called sarpanāgasvara, since it combines both. (45)

He who wishes to listen to this instrument, from which are produced the five svara-s, born from the five faces of Śiva, attains bliss. (46)

The player plays the svara-s by placing the right thumb and holds the svara-s above the hole in the front side, assuming the mṛgaśīrṣa[1] and sarpaśīrṣa hand positions. (47)

With the sound (produced) on blowing in the air, this instrument should be played with perfection. The characteristics of the sarpavādya is spoken according to the views of Somanātha. (48)

Having made the head(?) from the fruit of the gourd measuring twelve aṅgula-s, applying wax to the bottom, a reed <jīvāla> to a length of four aṅgula-s (is taken and) the two eyes are joined together. Two bamboo sticks to a measure of sixteen aṅgula-s are connected. The gourd head, reeds, bamboo sticks are tied together and wax is used for binding them. At the front, back and the sides of the bamboo, having made a hole below, to the top of it, having made seven holes and to those holes, wax is applied partially. To the end of the bamboo, bronze (ring) is fixed. (The presiding deities) of the gourd is Brahmā, of the reeds is Viṣṇu, bamboo is Śiva, for the eight holes, are the eight mūrti-s, for the bronze is the Sun (and) for the wax is the Earth. These are the presiding deities. The svara-s born from the five faces of Śiva, are sounded in this instrument. The syllable na is (denotes) nāda; the syllable ga is (denotes) gānaṃ. Since these two, by their union produce all the svara-s, the name of this instrument is called as pāmulanāgasvara by the sages like Bharata. Through the sound filled (produced by) with air, the player pressing the thumb below, with the mṛgaśīrṣa and sarpaśīrṣa hands, produces music of the seven svara-s in the seven holes. One who listens to this instrument, is bestowed with all fame. For the benefit of the world, the characteristics of

1. Mūgaśīrṣahasta: The sarpaśīra hand with all its fingers pointing downwards, but the thumb and the little finger raised up (NS, translation, 1967:181).

nāgasara were said in the treatise called Somanāthiyyaṃ (comm.48)

Now the characteristics of Devasara

.... it is called devasara. (49ab)

.... (comm.49ab)

A bamboo of good quality is taken to a length of twenty-four aṅgula-s. (49cd)

A bamboo of good quality is taken to a length of twenty-four aṅgula-s, (comm.49cd)

A hole is made below at a distance of three aṅgula-s from the top. Wax is applied to the hole partially, leaving out the either side of it. (50)

Above that, a palm leaf is wrapped around. Below (the hole), after a length of eight aṅgula-s, seven holes are to be made. (51)

(After leaving) ahead of the seven holes thus it measures twenty four aṅgula-s (?) A ring made of gold, silver, bronze is fixed to the bottom portion. (52)

(The presiding deity of) Devasara is Viṣṇu, of the (eight) holes are the eight mūrtī-s, of the wax is Īśa and of the palm-leaf is Śāradā. Of the two rings, are the Sun and the Moon. (These) are the presiding deities for them. (53)

(Of?) this devasaraṃ, after leaving three aṅgula-s below, having made a hole, then wax is applied partially to that hole, leaving out the sides. On that a palm-leaf is wrapped. Below this hole leaving out eight aṅgula-s, seven holes are made. Then [NOT CLEAR]. A ring made of gold, silver and bronze should be bound with wax. The (presiding) deity of Devasara is Viṣṇu. of the eight holes are the eight mūrtī-s. of the wax, is Īśvara, of the palm-leaf is Sarasvatī, of the rings are the Sun and the Moon. They are the presiding deities. (comm.53)

First, with the Murali[1] placed on the cloth, spread on the ground, having offered salutations to the God, the player should take the instrument. (54)

With the mūgaśīrṣahasta, the bottom portion of muralī(?) is played. The instrument should be played by pressing in the front portion with the sarpaśirahasta. When played with both the hands, Viṣṇu performs Tāṇḍava[2]. (55)

Invocation

My salutations to you seven svara-s in the seven holes. (56)

First, a cloth is spread on the ground; this devasvaraṃ is placed on it and after saluting, (the player) assuming the mṛgaśīrṣa hasta in the right hand and sarpaśirahasta in the left hand, should play with both the hands through the sound produced by blowing in the air. To that musical sound, Viṣṇu would perform Tāṇḍava. (comm.56)

The characteristics of Devatāsvara (Devasara) are expounded by Somanātha. (57)

The characterisitcs of this Devasara have been said in Somanāthiyyaṃ (comm.57)

Now Śaṅkha

The Śaṅkha is round (in shape) and measures one tāla (a measure equal to one span). In the lower region, a breaking/splitting (slit) should be made and played as a lip instrument. Lord of Lakṣmī, Viṣṇu is the presiding deity; one who listens to it becomes virtuous. (58)

Invocation

Salutations to Pāñcajanya, salutations to the one born in the ocean; saluations to [NOT CLEAR]. (59)

---

1. There seems to be a confusion at this place. Probably murali is taken here to be synonymous with the instrument dēvasvara, since it is also made of bamboo.
2. This mention of tāṇḍava of being performed by Viṣṇu, seems to be quite strange.

The player should play (this instrument) holding with the Ardhacandrahasta[1]. The characteristics of Śaṅkha will be said (has been said?) in a condensed form by Somanārya. (60)

Now Kāhala

Kāhala should be made with copper; to a measure of sixteen muṣṭi-s. (the measure of ones fist). A ring should be made in the front portion to a measure of one prādeśa[1] (12 aṅgula-s). Then either as a piece of three or four, they are combined together. (61)

Holding the round base portion, (of the instrument), the player should play assuming the candrahasta position with the tongue and the lips. The presiding deity is Kamalāsana (?). (62)

Invocation

Salutations to the Lord of Pārvatī, salutations to the one who bears the moon, salutations to the Lord of Kāhala and others, salutations to Lord Śiva (Pinākini). (63)

The characteristics of Kāhala were expounded by Somanātha. (64)

Saluting the wood (instrument) which is endowed with these characteristics, (it) should be held with both the hands and should be played with the lips and the tip of the tongue through the sound produced by blowing in the air. navīru, bākīlu and kāle (?). - these are inclusive in this. The characteristics of kāhala were said by Somanārya (comm.64)

Now the characteristics of Upāṅga

It (upāṅga) is made to a length of twelve fists and should be created" Only one hole is made to that. (65)

With the index finger and the middle finger, it should be played by people

1. Ardhacandrahasta: the fingers and the thumb so bent as to make a curve like a bow. (NS, translation, 1967:176)

well-versed. The presiding deity of the Daṇḍa is Lakṣmī and that of the hole is the wind God. (66)

Invocation

Salutations to the moon with varied forms, salutations to the experts on music; salutations to the one endowed with three svara-s, salutations to the one born from the ocean. (67)

The characteristics of Upāṅga were well described by Somanārya. (68)

In this way, the player should hold and play the Upāṅga, which is endowed with these characteristics. jīnikovi, caṅgu and vupari vādya-s are inclusive in this. (comm.68)

Now Mṛdaṅga

Long back, the son of Devakī (Lord Kṛṣṇa), after killing the demon, Murāsura took his body and made mardalaṃ, in this world. (69)

[NOT CLEAR] (70)

Mṛdaṅga should be made out of rose apple wood and sandal wood to a length of thirty-six aṅgula-s and a circular ring at the centre? (cylindrical in shape?). (71)

[NOT CLEAR] (72)

On the either side, in the front there is a circular ring (is made) to a measure of 12 aṅgula-s (diameter). At the centre portion of them, there is karṇikā to a measure of four aṅgula-s. At the outer portion of the karṇikā, there is a ring of the same size. (73)

Taking the skin from Hari, (Lord Kṛṣṇa) (the instrument is) made by Viśvakarma; it should be tied with cokacarma (??) having a knot. (74)

The syllable 'ma' is seed; the syllable 'da' stands for the sprout and the syllable 'lam' stands for fruit." [NOT CLEAR] (75)

The form of Mṛdaṅgaṃ is known to be three fold. The skin and the rope make five (parts in all). There are five vital parts of Mṛdaṅgaṃ, expounded by Bharata. (76)

The presiding deities of the two karṇikā-s are the Sun and the moon. Of the two rings are ' (of the) knot is Viśvakarma for Granthi. Gandharva is the presiding deity of the bandha. Maṇicūḍa and Maṇigrīva are the presiding Gods of carma (skin). (77-78)

In early days, Śrihari, killed Murāsura and with his body made the Mṛdaṅgaṃ and gave it to Nandikeśvara. In the world, with the leaves of the trees, (namely) Bael fruit <māreḍu>, khādira <caṇḍra>, cashew nut <jīḍi>, <nelli>, rose-apple <nereḍu>, and sandal, the maddalaṃ should be done. The above mentioned are the characteristics of Mṛdaṅga (comm.78)

Mṛdaṅga should be held in the region between the chest and the knee, in between the foot and the shank, seated on the ground. (79)

At the centre of four angula [??]. The middle and the ring finger should be played without support. (80)

[NOT CLEAR']With the ring finger, the centre portion should be given strokes. (81)

Further the syllables 'tattavāṭi' should be played ten times and then 'tattada.' Playing of 'ta dhi to' and 'ta dhi dhi' [?] With the middle finger should be played. (82)

śuddhatāḍana refers to toṅggāta dhiṅggaṇa kakunddaḥ kukuṭaṇ kiraḥ, jega tā teyya tā tai tā.?? (83)

With the tip of the thumb, base, palm and with the five (fingers) with the ring finger, index finger, middle finger the instrument should be stroked. (84)

In a pair of hands, the thumb, the little-finger, the index finger, the middle finger and the ring finger are used together. (85)

One whose playing is devoid of sound, tāla is to be condemned. (86)

The mṛdaṅga performer is pleased when there is a coordination between the tāla and sound. (87)

Left hand (playing) begets poverty and the right hand (playing) brings prosperity. The mṛdaṅga playing absolves one of killing a Brahmin. (88)

After meditated upon Nandikeśvara in one's heart, starting with the āditāla in the beginning, the Mṛdaṅgaṃ should be played. (89)

Having worshipped Nandikeśvara, the Mṛdaṅga which is the embodiment of all the Gods, should be held, in accordance to the sound of the cymbals (tāla) and in conformity to the sound produced in it, with the thumb, index finger, middle finger, ring finger, little finger, wrist, palm and the sides of the fingers of the right hand and the middle of the five fingers, palm and the wrist of the left hand, with the repetition of the above said syllables, should be played forcefully with both the hands, set to the laya of the āditāla, in nāṭya and other spheres (arts). (comm.89)

The characteristics of Ḍhakkā

Ḍhakkā is made from the wood of Khādira, to a measure of eleven inches. By a measure of eight aṅgula-s, there is a circle/ring to the side. (90)

At the centre it is narrow. It is wrapped by a thread and compressed to the sides. (91)

Śiva is the presiding deity of the instrument Ḍhakkā, Brahmā is the deity of the cord. With the left hand it is held and with the right hand finger it should be struck. (92)

With the tip of the finger, the base and the hand .... The side is struck with the right hand starting from the index finger. (93)

Invocation

Saluting the Ḍhakkā, which is endowed with all these characteristics, it should be played, holding with the left hand assuming the kaṭakāmukhahasta[1] and the right hand assuming the sūcihasta. The characteristics of this Ḍhakkā have been said in Somanāthiyyaṃ. (comm.93)

Now Ḍholu

To awaken Kumbhakarṇa, Ḍholu was constructed by Rāvaṇa. To a length of sixteen aṅgula -s and two prādeśa-s ... known to be the measure of the

1. prādēśa is a measure equal to 12 aṅgula-s.

instrument Ḍhola. (94)

The syllable 'ḍo' symbolises the Gods and Demons and the syllable 'lu' denotes Rāvaṇa. Thus Ḍolu is known to be the combination of demons and Gods. (95)

At the base of the gadā is Brahmā, at the centre is Hari; towards the side is Rudra; in the gadā, reside the Gods. (96)

The right side should be played with the right hand and the left side should be played with the left hand. This was established by Rāvaṇa.

(comm.96)

The characteristics of Bheri

[This instrument seems to be made of the skin of buffalo and beaten up. Brahmā, Viṣṇu and Śiva are supposed to be situated in the front, centre and the side]. The player should play with a stick hitting on the sides.

(97-98)

Thus is said the characteristics of Bheri by Somanātha. (99)

Bheri should be played with the sticks. The characteristics of Bheri are being said in Somanāthiyyaṃ. (comm.99)

The characteristics of Ḍamāmi

Two resonating vessels are made of metal in a circular shape measuring one hasta[1]. With the skin of the buffalo. . . . (100)

The instrument should be played with right and the left hands with two sticks. (101)

The presiding deities of the two vessels are the Sun and the Moon; of the rajya is Ananta and Takṣaka. (of the) gadā are the three mūrti-s and the two daula-s are in the form of Śiva and Śakti. (102)

The characteristics of Ḍamāmi was said by Somanātha. (103)

1. kaṭakāmukhahasta: the ring-finger and the little finger of the kapittha hand to be raised and bent. (NS, translation, 1967, p.178)

2. hasta is the distance between the elbow and the tip of the middle finger.

The Ḍamāmi endowed with these characteristics should be played with two hands and two sticks. The skin instruments such as Gaḍibiḍi, Tamukku and others are inclusive in this. (comm.103)

Thus (ends) skin instruments.

[Kāṃsyatāla

It is made of bronze and circular in shape. The middle portion is depressed by one aṅgula downwards. (104)

[NOT CLEAR] To a three-fourth mātra in the middle, a knot should be made of silken thread (probably) there should be a hole made to a size of one yava and a silken thread should be passed and tied at the end. With the index finger of the left hand, (placed on the) so that it remains firm. The other is held in the right hand index finger. It could also be of twenty-eight aṅgula-s. Being born of the eyes of Śiva, those who play (this instrument) attain a reward of performing the Aśvamedha sacrifice. It is called śuddhā variety when it confirms to the śāstra. (105-111)

The symbol endowed with these characteristics should be played. jāgaṭ (comm.111)

APPENDIX:1

Table showing the attributes of Svara-s

	Source	S	R	G	M	P	D	N
āyudha	BKM	khaḍga	kunta	gadā	cakra	bhiṇḍivāla	nārāca	aṅkuśa
	MBC	katti	kunta	gadai	cakkaram	piṇḍi	nārāca	aṅkusam
	NC-m[1]	khaḍga	kunta	gadā	cakra	bhiṇḍivāla	nārāca	aṅkuśa
	NC-t	khaḍga	kunta	gadā	cakra	bhiṇḍivāla	nārāca	aṅkuśa
	RJM	khaḍga	kunta	gadā	cakra	bhiṇḍivāla	nārāca	aṅkuśa
akṣara	MBC	a, ā	i,i	u, u	e, e	ai	o,o	au, u
	BKM	muktāphala	nīla	vajra	vaiḍūrya	garudam/ paccamaṇi	gōmēdika	puṣyarāga
	MBC	muttu	nīla	vaīram	vaiḍūrya	paccai/ marakata	gōmēdika	puṣparāga
	NC-m	muktāphala	nīla	vajra	vaiḍūrya	marakata maṇi	gōmēdika	puṣparāga
	NC-t	māṇikya	nīla	vajra	vaiḍūrya	māṇikya	gōmēdika	puṣparāga
	RJM	muktā phala	nīla	vajra	vaiḍūrya	garudam/ paccamaṇi	gōmēdika	puṣyarāga
	BKM	dadhyānna	pāyasa	bakṣya	citrānna	payah	śuddhānna	tandulam

MBC	tayir cādam	pāyasac cādam	palakāram	cittira cādam	mā	suttānam	kāpparici
NC-m	dadhyānna	pāyasa	bakṣya	citrānna	piṣṭayukpaya	śuddhānna	tandulam
NC-t	dadhyānna	pāyasa	kajjāyam	kalavanṭaka	calimiḍi	pālu	bhiyyam
RJM	dadhyānna	pāyasa	bakṣya	citrānna	payaḥ	śuddhānna	tandulam
BKM	aṣṭa	ṛtu [6]	catuḥ	aṣṭa	aṣṭa	rasa	catuḥ
MBC	eṭṭu	āru	nāngu	eṭu	eṭu	āru	nāngu
NC-m	aṣṭa	rasa [6]	catuḥ	aṣṭa	aṣṭa	ṛtu	catuḥ
NC-t	enimidi	āru	nālugu	enimidi	enimidi	āru	nālugu
RJM	aṣṭa	ṛtu [6]	catuḥ	aṣṭa	aṣṭa	rasa	catuḥ
BKM	gāyatri	suthala	triṣup	madhu	agni	bṛhati	sarva chandas
MBC	anuṣṭup	gāyatri	triṣṭup	prakiruti	paṅkti	uṣtini	cagati
NC-m	anuṣṭup	gāyatri	triṣṭup	bṛhati	paṅkti	uṣṇik	jagati
NC-t	anuṣṭup	gāyatri	triṣṭup	bṛhati	paṅkti	uṣṇik	jagati
RJM	gāyatri	suthala	triṣṭup	madhu	agni	bṛhati	sarva chandas
MBC	pāl	tēn	kizan	ney	ēlam	kadaḷi	māduḷaṅkani
BKM	sthūla	sūkṣma	sthūla dīrgha	sama	puṣṭa	dīrgha	atisthūla
MBC	tūla	cūkkumam	tūla	uyara	sama	uyara	atitūla

Source	S	R	G	M	P	D	N
NC-m	sthūla	sūkṣma	sthūla dīrgha	sama	puṣṭa	dīrgha	atisthūla
NC-t	sthūla	madhya sthūla	dīrgha	maṭṭatara	kubja	dīrgha	atisthūla
RJM	sthūla	sūkṣma	sthūla dīrgha	sama	saṣṭi	dīrgha	atisthūla
BKM	nārada	sarasvati	anala	divākara	gaṇēśvara	nīlātmaja/ āñjanēya	viduh/ candra
MBC	vanni	piraman	carasvati	ruttiran	mālōn	kaṇapati	cūriyan
NC-m	vahni	brahmā	śāradā	śarva	śrīnātha	bhāskara	gaṇēśvara
NC-t	agni	brahmā	sarasvati	īsvara	viṣṇu	sūrya	vināyaka
RJM	nārada	sarasvati	anala	divākara	gaṇēśvara	māruti	candra
BKM	jambū	śāka	kuśa	krauñca	śālmali	śvēta	puṣkara
MBC	jambū	saka	kuca	krauñca	sālmali	svēta	puṣkara
NC-m	jambū	śāka	kuśa	krauñca	śālmali	śvēta	puṣkara
NC-t	jambū	śāka	kuśa	krauñca	śālmali	śvēta	puṣkara
RJM	śāka	kuśa	krauñca	śālmali	śvēta	puṣkara	plakṣa
BKM	kumkuma	agaru	kastūri	chandra/ paccha- karpūra	gōrōchana	candana	gandha dravyam

MBC	kumkumam	akaru	kastūri	karpūra	gōrōcana	candanam	kadambapoḍi
NC-m	kumkuma	agaru	kastūri	karpūra	gōrōchana	candana	parimala
NC-t	kumkuma	agaru	kastūri	karpūra	gōrōchana	śrīgandha	parimala
RJM	kumkuma	agaru	kastūri	karpūra	gōrōchana	candana	gandhaka drvyam
BKM	āṅgīrasa	bhārgava	kaśyapa	gautama	vasiṣṭha	vātsyāya	kutsa
MBC	agni	vēda puruṣa	candra	kaṇṇan	īsan	nārada	tumburu
NC-m	vahni	vēda	śaṣāṅka	lakṣmināātha	- ?	nārada	tumburu
NC-t	agni	vēda	candra	kṛṣṇa	īśvara	nārada	tumburu
RJM	āngīrasa	bhārgava	kaśyapa	gautama	vasiṣṭha	vātsyāya	kutsa
BKM	brāhmaṇa	kṣatriya	vaiśya	brāhmaṇa	śūdra	kṣatriya	vaiśya
MBC	brāhmaṇa	kṣatriya	vaiśya	brāhmaṇa	brāhmaṇa	kṣatriya	vaiśya
NC-m	brāhmaṇa	kṣatriya	vaiśya	brāhmaṇa	śūdra	kṣatriya	vaiśya
NC-t	brāhmaṇa	kṣatriya	vaiśya	brāhmaṇa	śūdra	kṣatriya	vaiśya
RJM	brāhmaṇa	kṣatriya	vaiśya	brāhmaṇa	śūdra	kṣatriya	vaiśya
BKM	catuḥ	tri	dvimukham	caturmukha	caturmukha	trimukham	dvimukham
MBC	nāngu	mūnru	iru	nāngu	nāngu	mūnru	iru
NC-m	catuḥ	tri	dvimukhi	caturmukhi	caturmukhi	trimukhi	dvimukhi
NC-t	nālugu	mūḍu	reṇḍu	nālugu	nālugu	mūḍu	reṇḍu
RJM	catuḥ	tri	dvimukham	caturmukha	caturmukham	trimukha	dvimukham

Source	S	R	G	M	P	D	N
BKM	vēda	trīṇi	yugma	ambhudhi (4)	yugam (4)	lōka (3)	yamalam (2)
MBC	-	-	-	-	-	-	-
NC-m	?	?	?	?	?	?	?
NC-t	nālugu	mūdu	reṇḍu	nālugu	nālugu	mūdu	reṇḍu
RJM	vēda	trīṇi	yugma	ambhudhi	yugam	lōka	yamalam
BKM	aṣṭṭa	ṛtu	catuḥ	aṣṭa	aṣṭa	ṛtu	vēda
MBC	ṭṭu	āru	nāngu	eṭṭu	eṭṭu	āru	nāngu
NC-m	aṣa	ṛtu	catuḥ	aṣṭa	aṣṭa	ṛtu	vēda
NC-t	enimidi	āru	nālugu	enimidi	enimidi	āru	nālugu
RJM	aṣṭa	ṛtu	catuh	aṣṭa	aṣṭa	ṛtu	vēda
BKM	?	?	?	?	?	?	?
MBC	sadayam	cittirai	aviam	makha	uttiram	purāḍam	anuṣam
NC-m	satatāra	citrā	vasu	makha	uttara phalguni	purvaṣāḍā	maitrabha
NC-t	satabhiṣā	cittā	dhaniṣṭā	makha	uttara	purvaṣāḍā	anurādha
RJM	?	?	?	?	?	?	?
MBC	majnai / mayura	ṛṣapam	madu/ mēṣa	kirauncam	kuyil	pāri/kudirai	yānai
BKM	aṣṭa? (8)	?? (6)	yugam (4)	gajau (2x4=8)	naga (8?)	rasa (6)	vēda
MBC	iraṇḍu	iraṇḍu	iraṇḍu	iraṇḍu	iraṇḍu	iraṇḍu	iraṇḍu

NC-m	?	?	?	?	?	?	?
NC-t	reṇḍu	reṇḍu	reṇḍu	reṇḍu	reṇḍu	reṇḍu	reṇḍu
RJM	vasu	ṣaḍ	yugam	gaja ?	naga ?	rasa	vēda
MBC	vallūru	āndai	kākam	kukkuṭa /kozi	vallūru, āndai	mayūra/ mayil	vallūru/ kākam
MBC	āyul virutti	saupāk kiyam	sāpānam	sorna lāpam	pāvam pōkkum	kārya sitti	santāna sitti
BKM	cūta	kharjūra	kadali	jambīra	dāḍimi	drākṣā	punnāga
MBC	mā	pērindu	vāzai	nāval	māduzai	drākṣai	punnai
NC-m	cūta	kharjūra	kadali	jambīra	dāḍimi	drākṣā	punnāga
NC-t	cūta	kharjūra	kadali	nimba	dāḍima	drākṣā	lavaṅga
RJM	cūta	kharjūra	kadali	jambīra	dāḍimi	drākṣā	punnāga
BKM	jāti	campaka	punnāga	mallikā	kētaki	karavīra	padmapuṣpa
MBC	picci	caṇpaka	punnai	mallikai	tāzai	alari	tāmarai
NC-m	jāji	campaka	punnāga	mallikā	kētaki	karavīra	padmapuṣpa
NC-t	jāji	sampaṅgi	punnāga	mallikā	mogili	gannēru	tāmara
RJM	jāti	campaka	punnāga	mallikā	kētaki	karavīra	padmapuṣpa
BKM	midhuna	kaaka	simha	tulā	dhanus	ghaa	mīna
MBC	kuḍam/	kōl/tulā kumbam	tēn(z?)/ viruccika	singa	kaṇṇi	vil/ dhanusu	tēn(z?) / viruccika

Source	S	R	G	M	P	D	N
NC-m	-	-	-	-	-	-	-
NC-t	kumbha	tulā	tulā	simha	kanyā	dhanus	vṛścika
RJM	nryugma	kaṭaka (midhuna)	simha	tulā	dhanus	ghaṭa	mīna (kumbha)
BKM	karuṇa	vīra	adbhuta	raudra	bhībhatsa	bhayānaka	hāsya, śṛṅgāra
MBC	vīra	arputa	ravutira	pīpatsa	payānaka	āsiyam	ciṅgāram
NC-m	vīra	adbhuta	raudra	bhībhatsa	bhayānaka	hāsya	śṛṅgāra
NC-t	vīra	adbhuta	raudra	bhībhatsa	bhaya	hāsya	śṛṅgāra
RJM	karuṇa?	vīra	raudra	bhībhatsa	bhayāna	hāsya	śṛṅgāra
MBC	yajna puruṣa	ayan/ piraman	mati/ candiran	mayan/ viṣṇu	nārada	tumburu	tumburu
BKM	aṣṭa	ṛtu	catuḥ	aṣṭa	aṣṭa	ṛtu	vēda
MBC	eṭṭu	āru	nāṅgu	eṭu	eṭu	āru	nāṅgu
NC-m	aṣṭa	ṛtu	catuḥ	aṣṭa	aṣṭa	rasa	vēda
NC-t	enimidi	āru	-	enimidi	enimidi	āru	nālugu
RJM	aṣṭa	ṛtu	catuḥ	aṣṭa	aṣṭa	ṛtu?	vēda
BKM	gāndharvī	kinnarī	yakṣī	kimpuruṣī	nāgakanyakā	surastrī	rākṣasī

MBC	kāndaruva peṇ	kinnara peṇ	iyakka peṇ	kimpuruda	nāgappeṇ	surar maḍandai	arakkar kluappen
NC-m	gāndharvī	kinnarī	yakṣī	kimpuruṣī	nāgakanyakā	surastrī	rākṣasī
NC-t	gandharva strī	kinnara strī	yakṣa strī	kimpuruṣa strī	nāgakanyakā	dēvatāstrī	rākṣasa s strī
RJM	gāndharvī	kinnarī	yakṣī	kimpuru (ṣī)	nāgakanyakā	surastrī	rākṣasī
BKM	mayūra	vrṣabha	aja/mēṣa	krauñca	kokila	...?asvam	gaja
BKM	hamsa	simha	bhēruṇḍa	hariṇi	makara	śuka	kāka
MBC	anna	ciṅgam	kanta pēruṇḍa	mān	saluvan	kiḷi	nanavan-tan?
NC-m	hamsa	simha	bhēruṇḍa	hariṇi	makara	śuka	sārika
NC-t	hamsa	simha	bhēruṇḍa	jiṅka	mosali	ciluka	gōruvaṅka
RJM	hamsa	simha	bhēruṇḍa	hariṇi	makari	śuka	kāka
BKM	ravivāra	budhavāra	śanivāra	śukra	sauma	bhauma/ aṅgāraka	bṛhaspati/ guruvāra
MBC	śani	veḷḷi	śani	jnāyiru	putan	viyāzan	cevvāy
NC-m	-	-	-	-	-	-	-
NC-t	śanivāra	śukravāra	śanivāra	ādivāra	budhavāra	guruvāra	maṅgalavāra
RJM	ravi	budha	śani	śukra	sōma	bhauma	bṛhaspati

Source	S	R	G	M	P	D	N
MBC	mavval/ vanamallikai	meellai	kadamba	vañci	neydal	ponnavarai	punnai
BKM	dēva	ṛṣi	dēva	dēva	pitṛ	ṛṣi	asura
MBC	dēva	riṣi	dēva	dēva	pitru	riṣi	rākṣasa
NC-m	dēva	ṛṣi	dēva	dēva	pitṛ	ṛṣi	asura
NC-t	dēva	ṛṣi	dēva	dēva	pitṛ	ṛṣi	rākṣasa
RJM	dēva	ṛṣi	dēva	dēva	pitṛ	ṛṣi	asura
BKM	padmabhah	piñjara	svarṇavarṇa	kunda	asita	pīta	karbūra
MBC	muṇḍaka (red lotus)	paccai	pon	veṇṇiram	karuppu	ūdā	pañcavarṇa
NC-m	padmabhah	piñjara	svarṇavarṇa	kunda prabha	asīta	pīta	karbū (pu)ra
NC-t	padma	aladi	baṅgāru	molla mogga	nīla/aladi	pīta	dhrūma
RJM	padma	piñjara	pīta	haridrā	nīla	raudra?	sanga
(karbu)?							
BKM	śvēta	pīta	rakta	nīla	haridrā	citra	kṣauma
MBC	veḷḷai	pītāmparam	civappu	nīlam	civappu	citra	ūdā
NC-m	śvēta	pīta	rakta	nīla	haridrā	citra	kṣauma
NC-t	śvēta	pasupu	rakta	nīla	aladi?	varṇa	paṭṭu

RJM	śvēta	pīta	rakta	nīla	haritam	citra	kṣauma
BKM	aṣīti	saptati	ṣaṣṭi	pañca	catvāri	trimśat	vimśati
MBC	enpatu	ezupatu	arupatu	nārpatu ?	muppatu	irupatu	pattāṇḍu
NC-m	aṣīti	saptati	ṣaṣṭi	catvārimśat	trimśat	dvāvimśati	daśa
NC-t	80	70	60	40	30	20	10
RJM	aṣīti	saptati	ṣaṣṭ	pañca	catvāri	trimśat	vimśati

APPENDIX-2

Table showing the attributes of Rāga-s

Attribute	Source	bhairavi	bhūpāla	śrirāga	paḍamañjara	vasanta	mālava	baṅgāla	nāṭa
	MBC	katti/ kakāyuda	gadā	caṅgu	kunta	vil/ dhanusu	kalappai/ alāyudha	parasu/ mazuvāyudha	biṇḍi
	NC-m	gadā	khaḍga	śārṅga	kunta	śara cāpa	halāyudha	paraśu	biṇḍivāla
	NC-t	gadā	khaḍga	śārṅga	kunta	dhanur bhāna	hala	paraśu	biṇḍivāla
	MBC	kozuk kaṭṭai	paṇiyāra	citrānna	tayircōru	pāllūṇ	pāyasam	cuddhānnam	pazam
	NC-m	modakam	bhakṣyam	śuddhānna	dadhyānna	pāyasam	phalam	citrānnam	payonnam
	NC-t	uḍumulu	apūpa bhakṣya	ghṛtānna	dadhyānna	phala	pāyasa	kalavanaka	pālanṭna
	MBC	2	8	10	2	8	10	2	8
	NC-m	4	8	10	4	8	10	4	8
	NC-t	nālugu	enimidi	10	4	8	padi	nālugu	8
	MBC	vaira	muttu	nīla	māṇikka	puṣparāga	gōmēdaka	vaiḍūrya	padmarāga
	NC-m	vajra	muktāphala	nīla	māṇikya	puṣyarāga	gomedika	vaiḍūrya	padmarāga
	NC-t	vajra	muktā	nīla	māṇikya	puṣyarāga	gōmēdika	vaiḍūrya	padmarāga
	MBC	sāma	sāma	yajur	yajur	ṛg	ṛg	atharvaṇa	atharvaṇa
	NC-m	ṛg	ṛg	yajur	yajur	sāma	sāma	khila	khila
	NC-t	ṛg	ṛg	yajur	yajur	sāma	sāma	ṛg	atharvaṇa

MBC	sthūla	sthūla	sama	sama	kubja	kubja	dhīrgha	dhīrgha
NC-m	sthūla	sthūla	sama	sama	kubja	kubja	dhīrgha	dhīrgha
NC-t	sthūla	sthūla	sama	sama	kubja	kubja	unnata	unnata
MBC	aran/ īsvara	ari/viṣṇu	sarasvati	lakṣmi	ādittan	nārada	vināyaka	tumburu
NC-m	śambhu	viṣṇu	śāradā	lakṣmi	bhāskara	nārada	vināyaka	tumburu
NC-t	īśvara	viṣṇu	śāradā	lakṣmi	bhāskara	nārada	vināyaka	tumburu
MBC	jambū	kuca	sāka	krauñca	puṣkara	svēta	śālmali	pilaksa
NC-m	jambū	śāka	kuśa	krauñca	puṣkara	śveta	śālmali	navakhaṇḍa
NC-t	kuśa	jambū	śāka	krauñca	puṣkara	śvēta	puṣkara	navakhaṇḍa
MBC	karpūra	gōrōcana	śrīgandha	kastūri	akil	kumkuma	kadamba	suganta
NC-m	karpūra	gorocana	gandha	kastūri	agaru	kumkuma	kadamba	sugandha
NC-t	karpūra	gōrōcana	śrīgandha	kastūri	agaru	kumkuma	kadamba	parimaḷa
MBC	visvāmitra	vasiṣṭa	gautama	atri	brugu	suka	jamadagni	bharadvāja
NC-m	viśvāmitra	vasiṣṭha	gautama	atri	bṛgu	śuka	jamadagni	bharadhvāja
NC-t	viśvāmitra	vasiṣṭha	gautama	atri	bṛgu	śaunaka	jamadagni	bharadhvāja
MBC	brāhmaṇa	brāhmaṇa	kṣatriya	kṣatriya	vaiśya	vaiśya	śūdra	śūdra
NC-m	viprā	viprā	kṣatriya	kṣatriya	vaiśya	vaiśya	śūdra	śūdra
NC-t	brāhmaṇa	brāhmaṇa	kṣatriya	kṣatriya	vaiśya	vaiśya	śūdra	śūdra
MBC	2	4	5	2	4	5	2	4
NC-m	2	4	5	2	4	5	2	4
NC-t	reṇḍu	nālugu	5	reṇḍu	4	aidu	reṇḍu	4
MBC	pūrāḍa	pūrāḍa	uttaraṭṭādi	uttaraṭṭādi	uttiram	maga	mūla	mitra/ anuṣa
NC-m	jala	udaka	uttara bhadra	uttara	rohiṇi	makha	mūla	maitra
NC-t	pūrvāṣāḍa	pūrvāṣāḍa	uttarā bhādra	uttara	rōhiṇi	maga	mūla	anurādha

Attri bute	Source	bhairavi	bhūpāla	śrirāga	paḍamañjara	vasanta	mālava	baṅgāla	nāṭa
	MBC	2	8	10	2	8	10	2	8
	NC-m								
	NC-t	nālugu	enimidi	padi	4	8	padi	nālugu	8
	MBC	pala	drākṣā	pēriṇḍu	vilā	māmaram	mādulai	kadali/ vāzai	kadali/ vāzai
	NC-m	drāksā	khandaki	kharjūra	kapitha	cūta	dāḍima	nārikela	kadali
	NC-t	drāksā	panasa	kharjūra	velaga	māmiḍi	dāḍima	nārikēla	kadali
	MBC	mallikai	picci	mag[illegible]za	mullai	caṅpaka	tāzai	drōna	pārijata
	NC-m	mallikā	jāji	vakula	kunda	campaka	ketaka	drona	pārijata
	NC-t	malle	jāji	vakula	molle	sampangi	mogali	drōna	pārijāta
	MBC	raudra	siruṅgāra	bība[illegible]sa	karuṇa	hāsya	bhaya	adbhuta	vīra
	NC-m	karuṇa	vīra	śrṅgāra	bībhatsa	bhaya	adbhuta	hāsya	śānta
	NC-t	karuṇa	vīra	śrṅgāra	bībhatsa	bhaya	adbhuta	hāsya	śānta
	MBC	cāpa/ danusu	cāpa/ danusu	mīna	kanni	simha/ riṣabha	simha	mēsa	vṛicika
	NC-m	dhanusi	dhanusi	mīna	kanyā	vṛṣabha	simha	cāpa	vṛccika
	NC-t	dhanus	dhanus	mīna	kanyā	vṛṣabha	simha	dhanus	vṛiścika
	MBC	2	8	10	2	8	10	2	8
	NC-m								
	NC-t	nālugu	enimidi	padi	4	8	padi	nālugu	8
	MBC	anna	ciki/ mayura	pakadu/ kada	enkarpul	kōkila	kili	cakravāka	cakōra
	NC-m	hamsa	barhi	sārika	bheruṇḍa	kokila	śuka	cakravāha	cakora
	NC-t	hamsa	nemali	gōru[illegible]aṅka	ganda bhēruṇḍa	kōkila	jiṅka	cakravāka	cakōra

MBC	kinnara	iyakka	kimpuruṣa	gandharva	siddhar	tumburu	dēva	nāga
NC-m	kinnara	yakṣa	kimpuruṣa	gandharva	siddha	tumbura	devata	nāga
NC-t	kinnara	yakṣa	kimpuruṣa	gandharva	siddha	tumburu	dēva	nāga
MBC	pon/ viyāzan	pon/ viyāzan	saumya/ pudan	saumya/ pudan	bhānu/ jnāyiru	sani	tiṅgal	cevvāy
NC-m	guruvāram	guruvāram	guruvāram	budha vāram	śukra vāram	ādi vāram	guruvāram	maṅgala
NC-t	guruvāram	guruvāram	guruvāram	budha vāram	śukra vāram	ādivāram	guruvāram	maṅgala
MBC	veṇmai	veṇmai	civappu	civappu	pon	pon	karuppu	karuppu
NC-m	śveta	śveta	rakta	rakta	pīta	pīta	kṛṣṇa	kṛṣṇa
NC-t								
MBC								
NC-M								
NC-T								

APPFNDIX - 3

LAKṢAṆA -S OF 32 RĀGA-S

Rāga	Category		Graha svara (Ādi svara)		Varjya svara(s)	
	mūla	ṭīkā	mūla	ṭīkā	mūla	ṭīkā
Āharī	Sampūrṇa	Sampūrṇa	m	m	-	-
Baṅgāla	Ṣāḍava	Auḍava	n	n	m	g, m
Balahamsā	Sampūrṇa	Sampūrṇa	g	g	-	-
Baulī	Ṣāḍava	Auḍava	n	n	g, m	g, m
Bhūpāla	Ṣāḍava	Ṣāḍava	g	g	s	s
Bhairava/Bhairavi	Sampūrṇa	Sampūrṇa	p	p	-	-
Deśī	Ṣāḍava	Ṣāḍava	d	d	n	n
Deśikāri	Sampūrṇa		m	-	-	-
Devagāndhārī	Ṣāḍava	Ṣāḍava	g	g	n	n
Devakriyā	Auḍava	Auḍava	n	n	r, s	r, s
Dhanyāśī	Ṣāḍava	Ṣāḍava	g	g	n	n
Ghūrjarī	Auḍava	Auḍava	g	g	r, d .	r,d
Guṇḍakriyā	Ṣāḍava	Ṣāḍava	g	g	m	m
Hindola	Ṣāḍava	Ṣāḍava	m	m	r	r

Kāmbodī	Sampūrṇa	Ṣāḍava	?	m	-	r
Kauśika	-	Sampūrṇa	-	g	-	-
Kurañjī	Auḍava	Auḍava	m	m	n, s	n, s
Lalitā	Ṣāḍava	Ṣāḍava	n	n	g	g
Mālava	-	Sampūrṇa	-	g	-	-
Megharañjī	Auḍava	Auḍava	m	m	d. n	d, n
Malaharī	Ṣāḍava	Ṣāḍava	g	d	r	n
Nāṭa	Sampūrṇa	Sampūrṇa	s	s	-	-
Nārāyaṇī	Auḍava	Auḍava	n	n	p, d	p, d
Nīlāmbari	Ṣāḍava	Ṣāḍava	m	m	r	r
Paḍamañjari	Ṣāḍava	Ṣāḍava	n	n	r	r
Rāmakriyā	Auḍava	Auḍava	g	g	r, s	r, s
Sāraṅga	Sampūrṇa	-	p	-	-	-
Sāverī	-	Auḍava	-	m	-	r, n
Śaṅkarābharaṇa	Sampūrṇa	Sampūrṇa	g	d	-	-
Śrīrāga	Ṣāḍava	Ṣāḍava	d	d	r	r
Toḍī	Sampūrṇa	Sampūrṇa	g	g	-	-
Velāhuri	Auḍava	Auḍava	g	g	s, r	s, r
Varālī	Ṣāḍava	Ṣāḍava	g	g	m	m
Vasanta	Ṣāḍava	Ṣāḍava	n	n	p	p

APPENDIX-4

LIST OF 32 RĀGA-S FOUND IN OTHER WORKS

Source	bhairava	bhūpāla	śrīrāga	paḍa mañjara/ pañcama	vasanta	mālava	baṅgāla	nāṭa/ sāraṅga
ABSS	devakriyā	vēlāvulī	āndhālī	deśī	rāmakriyā	guṇḍakriyā	karṇāṭagaula	deśākṣarī
	megharañjī	malaharī	bhallātī	lalitā	varālī	ghūrjarī	dhanyāsī	āharī
	kurañjī	baulī	māhurī	toḍī	kauśī	gaulī	kāmbhojī	nārāyaṇī
BKM	devakriyā	baulī	āharī	deśī	kauśī	gumḍakriyā	dhanyāśī	deśākṣī
	kurañjī	malaharī	bhallātī	lalitā	rāmakriyā	ghurjari	chāyā	gaula
	megharañjī	velāvali	hindolī	toḍī	varālī	punnāga	karṇāṭagaula	rītigaula
BS	dēvakriyā	vēlāvali	hindōlam	dēsi	rāmakriyā	guṇḍakriyā	dhanyāsi	dēsākṣari
	mēgharañji	malahari	bhallāti	lalitā	varāli	gurjari	kambhōji	gāndhāri
	kuriñji	bauli	sāvēri	tōḍi	kaicika	nārāyaṇi	gauli	sāraṅgā
MBC	dēvakriyā	bilahari	āndhōli	dēsi	gaula	bauli	āhiri	ghaṇṭāravam
	kuriñji	malahari	jujuhuli	lalita	rāmakriya	ghurjari	kalyāṇi	kāmbōji
	mēgharañji	pāḍi	pallāti	mukhāri	varāli	guṇṭakriyā	sāvēri	saṅkarā bharaṇam
RJM	devakriyā	baulī	āharī	deśī	kauśī**/ kauśī	punnāga / - gaulapunnāga	dāyā-	gaula / ritigaula
	kurañjī	malaharī	bhallātī	lalitā	rāmakriyā	guṇḍakriyā	dhanyāsī	deśākṣī
	megharañjī	vyālāvalī	hindolī/ āndholī	toḍī	varālī	gurjarī	karṇāṭagaula	gaula
RS	devakriyā	bilāhurī	āndhalī	deśī	rāmakriyā	guṇḍakriyā	kalyāṇī	ghaṇṭārava

	megharañjī	malaharī	bhallātī	mukhārī	varālī	ghurjarī	āhirī	kāmbhoja
	kurañjī	bāṇḍī	māhurī	lalitā	gaulī	pālikā	sāveri	śaṅkarā bharaṇā
RTC	dēvakriyā	balāhuri	bilahari	dēśākṣi	ghanavarāli	dhanyāsi	-	-
	kuriñji	bauli	dēvagāndhāri	dōmṭ	maṅgala kaiśiki	mālavaśri	-	-
	mēgharañji	malahari	sāvēri	lalita	śuddharāma kriya	mukhāri	-	-
SCand	dēvakriyā	bilahari	āndhāli	dēśi	rāmakriya	guṇḍakriyā	kalyāṇi	ghaṇṭāravam
	mēgharañji	malahari	pallāti	mukhāri	varāli	gurjari	āhiri	kāmbōji
	kurañji	pāḍi	jujuhuli	lalita	gaula	bauli	sāvēri	śaṅkarā bharaṇam
SM	devakriyā	velāvalī	kāmbhojī	deśī	parāṭ	guṇḍakriyā	narayaṇī	sāraṅgaṇṭā
	paurālī	malaharī	bhallātī	manoharī	drāvaḍī	ghurjarī	gāndhārī	nāṭ
	bahulī	kurañjikā	tuṇḍī	hamsī	gauḍī	rañjī	aharī	kāmbhārī
STR	devakriyā	velāvatī	āndolī	lalitā	rāmakriyā	gurjarī	dhanyāsī	deśākṣī
	kurañjī	malaharī	bhallārī	deśakārī	varālī	guṇḍakriyā	chāyā	rītigaula megharañjinī
	baulī	ā(sā?)hurī	tuṇḍī	kaiśikī	nārāyaṇa	karṇākāmbhārīa	gaulikā	purvagaula

Bibliography

Technical Works

Abhinavabharatasārasaṅgraha of Mummaḍi Cikkabhūpāla, ed. R Satyanarayana, Sri Varalakshmi Academies of Fine Arts, Mysore, 1960.

Aumāpatam of Umāpati, ed. Vasudeva Sastri, Government Oriental Manuscripts Library, Madras, 1957

Bṛhaddeśī of Mataṅga, ed. K Sambasiva Sastri, Trivandrum Sanskrit Series, Trivandrum, 1928.

Bharatasāttiram, published by Tanjore Cooperative Press Karunthittaikudi, 1952.

Bharatakalpalatāmañjarī, ed. B Ankaji Sastri and P Subba Rao, Bangalore, 1887.

Bharatasēnāpatiyam - mūlamum uraiyum - kurippuraiyuḍan, ed. S Kalyanasundaraiyar - II edition, U V Svaminathayyar Library, Madras, 1958.

Caturḍaṇḍīprakāśikā of Veṅkaṭmakhi, ed. S Subrahmanya Sastri, T V Subba Rao, T L Venkataramayyar, Madras Music Academy, Madras, 1934.

Dattilaṃ of Dattila, ed. K Sambasiva Sastri, Sri Setu Prasadamala Series xiv, Tiruvanantapuram, 1930.

Dattilaṃ of Dattila, (with translation) ed. Mukund Lath, Indira Gandhi National Centre For the Arts, New Delhi & Motilal Banarasidass, New Delhi, 1988.

Le Gītālaṅkāra of Bharata, ed. Ed. Alain Danielou, Bhatt N R, Institut Francais D'INDOLOGIE Pondicherry, 1959.

Mānasollāsa (Abhilaṣitārtha cintāmaṇi) of Someśvara, ed. S K Srigondhekar, Oriental Institute, Baroda, 1961.

Mahābharatacūḍāmaṇi (saṅgītādi rāgamelalakṣaṇam), ed. Mudikondan Venkataramayyar, & Visvanatha Ayyar, U V Svaminathayyar Library, Madras, 1955.

Mahābharatacūḍāmaṇi ennum bhāva rāgatāla-cingārādi abhinayadarppaṇa vilāsam, ed. R Visvanathan, Chapters-1-3, Madras Government Oriental Series, No. CXIV, U V Svaminathayyar Library, Chennai-20, 1955.

Nāṭyaśāstra of Bharata, Abhinavabhāratī of Abhinavagupta vol.I (Chapters: 1-7), ed. M Ramakrishna Kavi and Revised By K.S.Ramaswami Sastri, 1956, vol.II (Ch.8-18) ed. M Ramakrishna Kavi, 1934, vol.III (Ch.19-27) ed. M Ramakrishna Kavi, 1954, vol.IV (Ch.28-37) ed. M Ramakrishna Kavi And J S Pade, 1964. Oriental Institute, Baroda.

Nartananirṇaya of Puṇḍarīka Vṭṭhala, ed. with Translation by R Sathyanarayana, Indira Gandhi National Centre for the Arts & Motilal Banarasidas, Delhi, vol-1:1994, vol-2:1996, vol-3:1998.

Rāgalakṣaṇa - ANONYMOUS, ed. D K Joshi, Poona, 1914.

Rāgasāgara (MANUSCRIPT), Photocopy of the Manuscript, R7977, Government Oriental Manuscripts Library, Chennai.

Rāgatālacintāmaṇi of Polūri Govindakavi, ed. T V Subba Rao, Government Oriental Manuscripts Library, Madras, 1952.

Rāgavibodha of Somanātha, ed. S Subrahmanya Sastri, Adyar, 1945.

Rasikajanamanollāsini sārasaṅgraha-bharataśāstra of Veṅkaṭa sundarasāni, Published by B Veṅkaṭarāmayya, CTA Press, Mysore, 1908.

Saṅgītacandrikai of Māṇikka Mudaliyār, published by Chandrika Printers, Madras, 1902.

Saṅgītacūḍāmaṇi of Jagadekamalla, ed. D K Velankar, Oriental Institute, Baroda, 1958.

Saṅgītamakaranda of Nārada, ed. M R Telang, Gaekwad Oriental Series-XVI, Baroda, 1920.

Saṅgītapārijāta of Ahobala, Published by R S Gondhalekar, Pune, 1898.

Saṅgītaratnākara - ANONYMOUS, ed. Mariappa Bhatt, pulished by the Government Oriental Manuscripts Library, Madras, 1950.

Saṅgītaratnākara of Śārṅgadeva with the Commentaries Kalanidhi of

Kallinatha and Sangitasudhakara of Simhabhupala, vol.1 - ed. Pt. S Subrahmanya Sastri, 1992, vol.2- ed. Pt. S Subrahmanya Sastri , Revised By V Krishnamacarya, 1959. vol.3 -ed. Pt. S Subrahmanya Sastri, Revised By S Sarada, 1986, vol.4- ed. Pt. S Subrahmanya Sastri, 1953, Pub. By the Adyar Library and Research Centre, Madras.

Saṅgītaratnākara of Śārṅgadeva (TEXT and ENGLISH TRANSLATION), vol-1 by R K Shringy, Premlata Sharma, Motilal Banarasidass Publishers Private Limited, Varanasi, 1978, vol-2: by R K Shringy, Premlata Sharma, Munshiram Manoharlal Publishers Pvt. Ltd., New Delhi, 1989.

Saṅgītasamayasāra of Pārśvadeva ed. T. Ganapati Sastri, Published in the Trivandrum Sanskrit Series No. 87, 1925.

Saṅgītasārasaṅgrahamu of Tiruveṅkaṭakavi, ed. V Raghavan, published by the Music Academy Madras, 1940.

Saṅgītasarvārthasārasaṅgrahamu of Vīṇā Rāmānuja, published by Sri Cidananda Press, Madras, 1917.

Saṅgītasūryodaya of Lakṣmīnārāyaṇa, ed. Srikamataprasad Tripathi, Indira Kala Sangit Visva Vidyalaya, Khairagarh, Madhya Pradesh, 1986.

Saṅgrahacūḍāmaṇi of Govinda, ed. S Subrahmanya Sastri, Adyar Library, Madras, 1938.

Śivatattvaratnākara of Basavarāja of Keladi, ed. Narayanasvami S Sastri, Oriental Research Institute, University of Mysore, Mysore, 1964.

Svaramelakalānidhi of Rāmāmātya, ed. M.S.Ramaswami Ayyar, Annamalai University, Chidambaram, 1932.

Books & Articles in Journals

Bhatta Panduranga C, Contribution of Karnataka to Sanskrit, Institute of Asian Studies, Chennai, 1998.

Brhaspati Acharya, Sunita Kumari, Sangitacintamani, Sangeet Karyalay, Hathras, 1966.

Banerji, Suresh Chandra, Companion to Indian Music and Dance A, Sri Sathguru Publications, Delhi, 1990.

Danielou Alain, Northern Indian Music, vol.1, Visva Bharati, Calcutta, 1949.

Desai, Chaitanya P, Sangita Vishayaka Samskrta Grantha, Suvichar Prakashan Mandal, Nagpur and Pune, 1979.

Kavi Ramakrishna M, Bharatakosa, Sri Venkatesvara Oriental Series No: 30, Tirumala Tirupati Devasthanams, Tirupati, 1951.

Khatre S M, Gode P K (appendix-ii), Introduction To Indian Textual Criticism, Deccan College Post-Graduate And Research Institute, Poona, 1954.

Krishnamachariar M, History of Classical Sanskrit Literature, III edition, Motilal Banarsidass, 1974.

Mahalingam T V, Administration and Social Life Under Vijayanagar, Part-II Social Life, Madras University Historical Series-No.15, II edition, 1975.

Premalatha V, "Talakalabdhi of Acyutaraya: Discovery of a new work on Tala", Journal of the Madras Music Academy, Chennai, vol - LXXX, 2009.

Raghavan V, "Some More Names In Early Sangita Literature", Journal of the Music Academy, Madras, 1932.

Raghavan V, "Later Sangita Literature", Journal of the Music Academy, Madras, 1933.

Raghavan V, "The So Called Svararnava" Journal of the Music Academy, Madras, 1953.

Rajagopala Iyer P K, "Samskrta and Sangita", Journal of the Music Academy, Madras, 1982.

Ramachandran N S, Ragas of Karnataka Music, The University of Madras, Madras, 1938.

Ramanathan N, "Commentaries in the Sanskrit Textual Tradition in Music", Journal of the Sangeet Natak Academy, nos. 129-130, 1998.

Sambamurthi P, "The Walajapet Manuscripts", Journal of the Music Academy, Madras, 1943.

Sambamurthi P, Great Composers- Book II (Tyagaraja), II edition, The Indian Music Publishing House, Madras-1, 1970.

Sathyanarayana R , Abhinavabharatasārasaṅgraha of Mummaḍi Cikkabhūpāla, Sri Varalakshmi Academies Of Fine Arts, Mysore, 1960.

Sathyanarayana R, Bharatanatya- a critical study, Sri Varalakshmi Academies of Fine arts, Mysore, 1969.

Sathyanarayana R, Studies in Indian Dance, Sri Varalakshmi Academy of

Fine Arts, Mysore, 1970.

Sathyanarayana R, "Raga-Iconification in Indian Music", Vivekananda Kendra Patrika, volume-13, number-2, August, 1984.

Sathyanarayana R, Nartananirnaya, Critical Edition and Translation, published by the Indira Gandhi National Centre for the Arts, New Delhi & Motilal Banarasidas, Delhi, vol-1:1994, vol-2:1996, vol-3:1998

Seetha S, Rāgalakṣaṇamu of Śāha Mahāraja, Brhaddvani, Madras, 1990.

Sharma B N K, History of Dvaita School of Vedanta and its Literature A, vol-2, Booksellers' Publishing Co., Mumbai-4, 1961.

Vasudeva Sastri K, "Music And Dance Manuscripts At TMSSML", Journal of the Music Academy, Madras, 1948.

Vedavalli M B, Mysore as a seat of Music, CBH Publications, Trivandrum, 1992.

Calendars:

Pañcāṅgaṃ - (Hindu Calendar- from the year 1650.)

Indian Ephemeris, ed. Samikkanu Pillai.

Index

अ

अग्रं च तत्तवाटि ३,८२

अग्रेत्याङ्गुलि सर्वांगे ३,५२

अङ्गुलाग्रं च मूलं च ३,९३

अङ्गुष्ठं च कनिष्टं च ३,८५

अङ्गुष्ठाङ्गुल मानेन ३,७२

अङ्गुष्ठाग्रं च मूलं च ३,८४

अतिसूक्ष्मच सूक्ष्मच २,४१

अथर्वणस्त्रितीया स्यात् ३,३४

अधाद्युपक्रमेणैव रागं २,१०२

अन्ते च कांस्यवलयं ३,४१

अन्ये दक्षिणतर्जन्यां ३,१०७

अपाब्दमनामिक्यं ३,८१

अपस्वरेण दुष्टं च २,७५

अपूर्णचैव पूर्णच २,१००

अर्थहीनमपार्थं च २,७७

अर्धचन्द्रकरौ धृत्वा ३,६०

अलाबु कोटरं कृत्वा ३,३९

अीतिस्सप्ततिष्षष्टिच २,१५

अश्वमेध फलंचैव ३,१०९

अष्टभाषापदैर्युक्तं २,१८१

अष्टावधान विख्यात १,५

अष्टौ ऋतुचतुचैव २,३५

अष्टौ ऋतुचतुश्रोत्राः २,३६

अष्टौ रसचतुर्बाहु २,३४

अष्टौ रागास्त्रयस्सङ्ख्या २,१०८

अज्ञात विषयास्वादो २,१०

आहरि शङ्कराभूषा २,१५७

आ

आकाशसम्भवो नादः २,६

आत्ममध्य गतः प्राणः २,८१

आदौ भूमिस्थिते वस्त्रे ३,५४

आदौ मध्ये तथा चाग्रे ३,९८

आद्यन्तौ षड्जमाश्रित्य २,५४

आद्या चोत्तरमन्द्रा स्याद्र २,५१

आरोहिण्यवरोयुह्युक्तं २,७६

आलन्बनप्रचुर कोमल देशनाद्यं ३,९

आलिप्तिर्द्विविधा ज्ञेया २,९८

आहतोऽनाहतचैव २,५

आहरी पूर्णरागस्स्यात् २,१२६

उ

उच्चोच्चतरतायुक्ताः २,४९

उच्यते मुखवीणायाः ३,३१

उत्तरोत्तरतारास्तु २,४६

उत्तरोत्तरतारास्तु ३,६

उपाङ्गलक्षणं सम्यक् ३,६८

उभयोरग्रयोचैव ३,७३

ऋ

ऋग्यजुस्सामवेदेभ्यो १,१५
ऋग्वेद भैरविभूप २,१५१
एकलक्षणमन्यस्य १,८
एकलो यमलो बृन्दो २,१६३
एकस्वरविहीनच २,१०५
एकाङ्गुल प्रमाणेन ३,१५
एकैकाङ्गुल तस्याधः ३,२७
एते भरतकर्तारः १,४
एवं निरीक्ष्याथ समस्त २,१६२
एवं प्रधानरागास्स्युः २,१३१
एवं भेदानि षट्षष्टि ३,७
एवं स्वरान् समाकृष्य २,८

औ

औडवस्स्यात् घूर्ज्जरागा २,१२२
औडवो घुर्जरी प्रोक्तो २,११५

क

कच्छपि कुब्जिका चित्रा ३,३
कम्बली श्रिविका सर्ली २,७९
करालं कथितं सद्भिः २,१६९
करुणवीरश्रृङ्गार २,१४५
करुणाचायता मध्या २,९१
कर्पूररोचनंगन्धं २,१३८
कांस्यरूपिणी नाभिच ३,११
काकक्रूररवः काकी २,१७०
काम्बोदी पञ्चधा प्रोक्ता २,१३२
किन्नरो यक्षकिंपुर्ष २,१५२
कीर्ति प्रागल्भ्यसौभाग्य १,१६
कुङ्कुमागरुकस्तूरि २,२३
कुम्भकर्णस्य बोधार्थं ३,९४
कुम्भौ देवौ रविशशि ३,१०२
कुर्यान् मधुमयस्सर्वे ३,४२
कृष्णसर्पोऽपि तन्नादं २,१२
क्रमात् ग्रामत्रये देवाः २,८५
क्रमात् सप्तस्वराणां च २,१६०
क्रमात् सरिगमादीनां २,५९
क्रमादनुष्टुप् गायत्री २,३०
क्रमादेवं स्वराणां च २,१०६

ख

खड्गकुन्तगधाचक्रं २,२६

ग

गदाखड्गौ शाङ्र्ग कुन्तौ २,१४०
गन्धर्वी किन्नरीयक्षी २,२९
गान्धर्वं त्रिविधं १,९
गान्धारग्राम माचष्ट २,८४
गान्धारादिस्तथा वर्ज्यो २,१२३
गायको तुम्बुरे सम्यक् ३,२५
गुरुवारं सौम्यवारं २,१४७
ग्रन्थेस्तु विश्वकर्मस्यात् ३,७८
ग्राम स्वरसमूहः स्यात् २,५६

घ्र

घ्राणिनी पवनिङ्नीट मन्दा २,८०

च

चतुरङ्गुलं कृत्वाथ ३,४०
चतुरङ्गुल भूमध्ये ३,८०
चतुर्भिः पञ्चभिः षड्ि २,१८२
चतुर्वसुदशश्रोत्रं २,१५०
चतुर्विधं स्वरं वादी २,९३
चतुचतुचतुचैव २,५०
चतुस्त्री द्विमुखञ्चैव २,३३
चर्माणीजा च मृदङ्गाद्या ३,२
चूतखर्जूरकदळी २,२८
चूर्णिकावाक्यलोकैच २,१८९

छ

छागवत्वहनी कुर्वन् २,१७१

ज

जम्बुचन्दनवृक्षे चक्षेण ३,७१

जम्बूशाककुशक्रौञ्च २,१७
जम्बूशाककुशक्रौञ्च २,१४४
जलोदकौत्तराभाद्र २,१४६
जहार नारदादीनां १,१८
जातीचम्पकपुन्नाग २,२४
जीवाळ विष्णुवंशेशः ३,४३
ढ
ढक्का खादिरकाष्ठेन ३,९०
त
तण्डुना स्वगणाग्रण्य १,१२
तद्वाद्यं सर्पनामञ्च ३,४४
तद्वेको यवमात्रस्य ३,१०५
तन्नादं सप्तधा कृत्वा २,७
तर्जनी मध्यमाग्राभ्यां ३,६६
तस्योपरिस्तालपत्रं ३,५१
ताभिस्तु शिक्षिता नार्यः १,१४
तालं सूचितहस्तं तु ३,८७
तुम्बकि तुम्बुकाकारो २,१७२
तोडी सम्पूर्णरागस्स्यात् २,१२०
तोंग्गातधिंग्गणचैवा ३,८३
द
दण्डिका खादिरे जाता ३,१०
दत्तिलस्य मतेख्यातं ३,१९
दध्यन्नं पायसं भक्ष्यं २,२२
दक्षिणा तन्त्रिका ज्ञेया ३,१४
दीप्ताऽऽयता च करुणा २,८
दीप्ताऽऽयता मृदुर्मध्य २,८९
दीप्ताऽऽयते मध्यमे ते २,९०
दुःखातिशोकनिर्वेद १,१७
दुष्टं लोकेन शास्त्रेण २,७४
देवक्रिया मेघरञ्जी २,१०९
देवता ढक्कवाद्यस्य ३,९२
देवते कर्णिका द्वन्द्वे ३,७७
देववंशास्तु सगमाः २,१३
देवस्वराधिपो विष्णुः ३,५३
देशकारी षाडवस्स्यात् २,११९
देशाक्षरी च गान्धारी २,१५५
देशिकारी च सम्पूर्णो २,११८
द्राक्षकण्टकखर्जूर २,१४३
द्वादशाङ्गुलमस्यैवं ३,३२
द्वादशाङ्गुलमाकारं ३,२६
द्विचतुष्पञ्च सङ्ख्या च २,१४९
द्वितालं प्रथमं कुंभं ३,२२
द्वौ द्वौ राक्षसदेवानां ३,९६

धनुषीमीनकन्या च २,१४८
धन्याशी चैव काम्बोदी २,११२
धर्मार्थकाममोक्षाणामि २,९६
ध्रुवादि सप्ततालैच २,१८७
ध्वनिभेदाः क्रमादेवं २,५५

नकारं नादमित्याहुः ३,४५
नकारं प्राणविज्ञेयं २,३
नखवायुज चर्मानिज ३,१
नन्दा विशाला सुमुखी २,५३
नन्दिकेशं हृदिं ध्यात्वा ३,८९
नमचन्द्राय विविधे ३,६७
नमोस्तु पाञ्चजन्याय ३,५९
नमोस्तु पार्वतीनाथ ३,६३
नाटवेदं ददौ पूर्वं १,१०
नाटं नृत्तं तथा नृत्यं १,११
नादोपासनया देवाः २,४
नाभिकाथर्वणी धस्ता २,७८
नाभेरधस्तात् कर्तव्यं ३,१३
नाभ्यां हृदि च कण्ठे च २,४२
नारायणी निषादादि २,१२९

नित्यानन्दकरं शान्तं १,१
नीलाम्बरी षाडवस्स्यात् २,११६
नीचोच्चध्रुतमध्यादौ २,७२
नृणामुरसिमन्द्रस्तु २,४५
नृत्तं वाद्यं तथा गीतं २,२

पडमञ्जर रागस्स्यात् २,१२१
पदे करुण पूर्वं स्यात् २,१८६
पद्माभः पिञ्जरः स्वर्णवर्णः २,१६
पार्वतीत्वनुशासस्मात् १,१३
पुनस्तन्मार्गगमनं २,१०३
पुरा मुरासुरं हत्वा ३,६९
पूर्वतन्त्रिपतिः शंभुः ३,१६
पूर्वाह्णकाले मध्याह्ने २,६०
प्रकृति प्रत्ययैचोक्तं २,६९
प्रथमश्रवणाच्छब्दः २,६१
प्रबन्धानि षडङ्गानि २,१८३
प्रसारी गीयते तज्ज्ञैः २,१७३
प्रोक्तो राजास्वरारोहो २,९५

बङ्गालो षाडवो रागो २,१२७
ब्राह्मणौ तु समौ ज्ञेयौ २,१४
ब्रूमस्तुर्या तृतीयाऽऽदि २,८७

भवन्त्यङ्ग वदाङ्गानि २,१८४
भानुन्नमामि भगवन्तमनन्त भावं ३,३६
भीतो भयान्वितो गाता २,१६८
भूपालः षाड्वो रागो २,१२८
भूपालच मुखारी च २,१५६
भेरि वाद्य।।। ३,९७
भैरवचापि भूपालो २,१०७

मकारं बीजं इत्युक्तं ३,७५
मधुरं धुर्यलावण्य २,७३
मध्यमादौ स्वरादुक्तं २,६७
मध्ये ह्रस्वं प्रकुर्वीत ३,९१
मन्द्रादिषूक्ताश्रुतय २,४७
मल्लिका जाति वकुल २,१४१
महती वैष्णवी ब्राह्मी ३,४
मिश्रकोऽनवधानच २,१६६
मुक्ताफलो नीलवज्र २,२५
मुखवीणा परेप्राज्ञा ३,३५
मुखसङ्ख्या नासिकां २,३७
मुखारिका रेवगुप्ति २,१५९
मुरलीमूल पीडन्ते ३,५५
मूलनादेस्थितो विष्णुः ३,२८
मृदङ्गं त्रिविधं रूपं ३,७६
मेघरञ्जी मध्यमादि २,११७
मोदकं भक्ष्य शुद्धान्नं २,१३६

यथा शास्त्रप्रसारेण ३,११०
यद्वा धस्त्रिश्रुतिः षड्जे मध्यमे २,८३

रम्येण रेचकेनैव ३,६५
रन्ध्राधः च निषादस्यात् ३,३३
रागालिप्ति तन्ननादि २,९९
रामक्रिया वराली च २,१११

ललिता षाडवो रागः २,१२५
लक्ष्यस्वरूपं प्राकट १,७
लोकेषु बहवस्सन्ति १,६
लोहेन कुम्भौ द्वौ कुर्यः ३,१००

वंशजातिवयोवर्ण २,१६१
वज्रमुक्ताफलो नील २,१३९
वनेचरस्तृणाहारचित्रं २,११
वर्तुलं कांस्य ।।।। ३,१०४
वलयाकृततन्मूले ३,६२

वसन्तः षाडवो रागः २,१२४
वह्निर्ब्रह्मा शारदा च २,२०
वह्निर्वेदः शशाङ्कंच २,१८
वाणीं नमामि वरदां ३,२०
वादको दक्षिणाङ्गुष्ठ ३,४७
वादीस्वरच राजास्यात् २,९४
वामहस्तेन दारिद्रं ३,८८
वायुपूरित नादेन ३,४८
विप्रा भैरवभूपाल २,१३३
विश्वकर्मविनिर्माणं ३,७४
विश्वकर्मविनिर्माणां ३,२१
विश्वामित्रवसिष्टच २,१५३
विरस्सो नीरसो वर्ज्य २,१७४
वीणायां च नृणामिव ३,५
वीणावाद्यं शारीर ३,८
व्यक्तं पूर्णं प्रसन्नं च २,६८
व्यवहारे त्वसौ त्रेधा २,४३
शङ्कराभरणो रागः २,१३०
शङ्खञ्च वर्त्तुलंचैव ३,५८
शततारास्चित्रवसु २,३२
शब्दतालविहीनस्या ३,८६
शिवस्य पञ्चवक्त्रेभ्यः ३,३८
शिवस्य पञ्चवक्त्रेभ्यः ३,४६
शिार्वेत्ति पार्वेत्ति २,९
शुद्धछायालगौ रागौ २,१७६
शुद्धमित्रच सङ्कीर्णाः २,१०१
शंभुर्गौरी तथा ब्रह्मा १,२
शंभुर्विष्णुच शारदा २,१३५
श्रीमत्कञ्च सोद्फ—तं ३,७०
श्रीरागपत्न्यो हिन्दोली २,११०
श्रुत्युक्तपदाशब्दानि २,१८८
श्रुत्युत्पत्तिः स्वराणां च २,९२
श्वेतचित्रो रक्तनीलौ २,१३७
श्वेतः पीतो रक्तः नीलः २,२१
श्वेतौ भैरवभूपालौ २,१३४

षड्जग्रामः पञ्चमेच २,८२
षड्जमध्यमगान्धार २,५८
षड्जस्वरादि भूलोके २,४०
षड्जादिस्वरसम्मिश्रं २,९७
षाडवो देवगान्धारी २,११४
षाडवौडवसम्पूर्ण २,१०४
षाडवौडवसम्पूर्ण २,११३
षाडवौडवसम्पूर्ण २,१७९

सङ्गीतशास्त्रं २,१
सति वीरेऽद्भुते रौद्रे २,१९
सन्दष्टदशना गेयः २,१६७
सन्दष्टोद्घुष्ट सीत्कारो २,१६४
सप्ततन्त्रि समायुक्तं ३,२४
सप्ततन्त्र्यच तद्वेष्टा ३,२३
सप्तरन्ध्र समायुक्तं ३,२९
सप्तरन्ध्र समायुक्तं ३,५६
सप्तस्वरास्त्रयोग्रामाः २,५७
समाक्षरैर्लयस्थाने २,७१
सम्यक् ाारीरकृतञ्च २,७०
सरस्वती नाभेर्देवी ३,१७
सरी मन्द्रौ गमौ मध्यौ २,४४
सर्वदेवमय भूतं ३,१८
सर्वे रागाः प्रगायन्ते २,१५८
साम्बकस्तुम्बकी वक्री २,१६५
सूक्ष्मस्स्वरोहि सूक्ष्मत्वा २,६२
सोमनाथमते ख्यातं ३,६४
सोमनाथमते प्रोक्तं २,१८०
सोमनाथमते प्रोक्तं ३,३०
सोमनाथमते प्रोक्तं ३,५७
सोमनाथमते प्रोक्तं ३,१०३
सौवीरी हरिणाश्वा च २,५२
स्थानभ्रष्टः स यः प्राप्तं २,१७५
स्थायादिष्ववधानेन २,१७७

स्थायिस्वरोऽथ सञ्चारी २,६३
स्थूलसूक्ष्मस्थूलदीर्घं २,३१
स्थूलौ भैरवभूपालौ २,१५४
स्वरं स्वरं स्वरं स्वरान्तरं २,१८५
स्वराः मन्द्रादिषु स्थाने २,६५
स्वराणां लक्षणं सम्यक् २,३८
स्वस्वस्थानविपर्यासात् २,३९
हनुमान् विघ्नराजच १,३
हंसच सिंहभेरूण्ड २,२७
हंसो बर्हिशारिका च २,१४२
हृद्याभिजानुदेशे वा ३,७९
हृद्यूर्ध्वं नाडीसंलग्ना २,४८